Flaubert

Flaubert

A BIOGRAPHY

FREDERICK BROWN

WILLIAM HEINEMANN : LONDON

Published in the United Kingdom by William Heinemann, 2006

1 3 5 7 9 10 8 6 4 2

First published in the United States in 2006 by Little, Brown and Company,
part of the Time Warner Book Group, New York

William Heinemann
The Random House Group Limited
20 Vauxhall Bridge Road, London, SW1V 2SA

Random House Australia (Pty) Limited
20 Alfred Street, Milsons Point, Sydney
New South Wales 2061, Australia

Random House New Zealand Limited
18 Poland Road, Glenfield
Auckland 10, New Zealand

Random House (Pty) Limited
Isle of Houghton, Corner of Boundary Road & Carse O'Gowrie,
Houghton 2198, South Africa

The Random House Group Limited Reg. No. 954009

www.randomhouse.co.uk

A CIP catalogue record for this book
is available from the British Library

Papers used by Random House are natural, recyclable products made from
wood grown in sustainable forests. The manufacturing processes conform to
the environmental regulations of the country of origin

ISBN 9780434007691 (from January 2007)
ISBN 0434007692

Printed and bound in Great Britain by
Mackays of Chatham plc, Chatham, Kent

For Ruth

For Roger Shattuck

Contents

Flaubert

Prologue: Rouen

∿

Springtime gives me wild urges to leave for China or the Indies;
Normandy with its greenery sets my teeth on edge, like a plate of
uncooked sorrel.

(Flaubert to the Goncourt brothers, April 15, 1863)

FOR FLAUBERT, life began in Normandy and ended there. It was the province that furnished his imagination, as Touraine furnished Balzac's and Provence Zola's in the succession of great nineteenth-century French novelists. It was the landscape of his youth and of all his seasons. It was the taste in his mouth and the verdant prison where he dreamed of deserts.

In the early nineteenth century, Rouen still looked enough like the Norman capital in which Joan of Arc had suffered martyrdom four hundred years earlier to lure tourists fascinated by things medieval. Couched between the Seine winding north toward its mouth and the steep green and white spurs of an immense chalk plateau called the Pays des Caux, which, at its northernmost edge, beetled over the English Channel, it was largely a right bank settlement. Vestiges of the bastion that had resisted Henry V of England were torn down after 1810, but the streets continued to evoke the fortified city, like a parolee warped by long confinement. They twisted uphill in a maze of tall, decrepit houses, many with oak struts angling across stuccoed brick facades, or with balconies protruding toward the gables opposite. Even when the sun shone, which it seldom did over this maritime province, its light hardly reached street level. People and vehicles crowded through passages only five yards wide, and a large proportion of the ninety thousand inhabitants (Rouen being France's fifth-most-populous city) went about their business in a damp, crepuscular world. Water flowed everywhere, down gutters made by the cambered roadways and from thirty-five fountains, which served for drinking and laundering. Equally ubiquitous, as Arthur Young noted during the 1780s in *Travels in France,* was the stench of many more than thirty-five neglected latrines. Those who could afford it, he wrote, fled to country houses, though country houses offered no relief unless they were situated at least two kilometers outside town, beyond Rouen's malodorous penumbra.

Of the literary and artistic pilgrims who described their sojourns in the city, few ever seemed to breathe foul air, or else the spectacle of ecclesiastical grandeur inured them to ugliness. Their senses were all reserved for Gothic, and most particularly for Notre-Dame de Rouen, the thirteenth-century cathedral whose west facade, abounding in statues, latticework, and pinnacles of every description, would later, on an anomalously sunny day, inspire Claude Monet to brilliant effect. Surmounted by dissimilar towers — the Tour de Beurre and the Tour Saint-Romanus — this magnificent pile dwarfed the half-timbered dwellings round about and presided over Rouen's main commercial thoroughfare, the rue de la Grosse Horloge, with a display of hagiographical scenes, which included the Martyrdom of John the Baptist and the Feast of Herod. Notre-Dame had some impressive companions, however. Nearby stood a building of flamboyant style, Saint-Maclou, whose porch fanned out in five large panels adorned with medallions thought to be the work of the sixteenth-century sculptor Jean Goujon. And some distance uphill, beyond a bone yard for plague victims, towered the great nave of Saint-Ouen, an abbey church that rivaled Notre-Dame in size and beauty, and quite surpassed it in the exuberance of its flying buttresses. There were other houses of prayer besides, one for every parish. Indeed, Rouen's skyline seen from the heights of Mont Sainte-Catherine to the east, where artists usually sought a good vantage point, bristled with steeples. And from all of these, bells announced the Angelus morning, noon, and night. It was, by various accounts, an emphatically sounding city. When Victor Hugo, who called it "the Athens of the Gothic genre," wrote to his wife in 1835, "I have seen Rouen. Tell Boulanger that I have *seen* Rouen; he will understand everything contained in that word," the poet laureate of belfries had had carillons to sharpen his visual pleasure.

Many were similarly transfixed, especially foreigners visiting France after the Napoleonic Wars (who could not presume that a pregnant past participle would adequately communicate their wonder to folks back home). Young Henry Wadsworth Longfellow, without a proper guidebook during his first grand tour, "stumbled" upon the cathedral and was as amazed, he wrote, as if it had suddenly mushroomed from the earth. "It completely overwhelmed my imagination and I stood for a long time motionless, gazing entranced upon this stupendous edifice. I had before seen no specimen of Gothic architecture and the massive towers before me, these lofty windows of stained glass and rude statues, all produced upon my untraveled mind an impression of awful sublimity." Emma Willard echoed him almost exactly in her journal. Notre-Dame left her awestruck, her soul invaded by a feeling of sublimity "almost too intense for a mortal being." James Fenimore Cooper, who had preceded both of them, declared that it would be worth crossing the Atlantic just to see the monument.

Then, a few decades later, John Ruskin arrived with Effie in tow, and medieval Rouen may never have welcomed a more passionate devotee. The city was a center of his "life's thought." Where others saw streets lacking sidewalks and pedestrians jostled by donkeys laden with cabbages, the supreme esthete found "a labyrinth of delight." It was, he exclaimed, "quite Paradise," with its gray towers "misty in their magnificence of height, letting the sky like blue enamel through the foiled spaces of their open work." His sketchbooks always near to hand, he stood spellbound at street corners where corbels supported painted icons, or before church walls and gates "wardered by saintly groups of solemn statuary, clasped about by wandering stems of sculptured leafage, and crowned by fretted niche and fairy pediment — meshed like gossamer with inextricable tracery."

But this paradise, which rested upon the complete denial of a mercantile world, had already been lost. Outside its revered boundaries, unacknowledged, stood the city that John Murray in his popular handbook called the "Manchester of France," that is, the Rouen of ships discharging bales of cotton (much of it imported from America) and loading finished goods, of spinning factories and dye works, of textile marts and sturdy cloth with brilliantly colored stripes or checkered squares (*rouenneries*), of suburban smokestacks, of hovels for rural immigrants and mansions for spawning millionaires. When Young surveyed it during the ancien régime, Normandy between Rouen and Le Havre was already a landscape more of manufacture than of agriculture.

Among Rouen's industries, cotton, which came to dwarf every other, figured as the parvenu prince. Until the 1700s it had played a modest role in everyday life, with rope makers using it for cordage and chandlers for wicks. Some sixty years after Lewes Roberts declared in *The Treasure of Traffic* (1641) that Manchester merchants regularly commuted to London with "fustians, vermillions, dimities and other such stuffs" woven from Levantine cotton, only one Rouen entrepreneur had produced the "miracle cloth," or a mongrel version of it containing silk as weft. But all that changed dramatically in the wake of Louis XIV's death. An economy laid low by dynastic war and religious persecution bustled again. The prodigal habits of regency France worked to the advantage of thrifty Normans, and before the eighteenth century had run even half its course Rouen enjoyed full employment. A report issued in 1724 affirmed that 25,430 inhabitants —

better than one of three Rouennais — lived off cotton, spinning or weaving it. Thousands more, in villages throughout the Caux plateau, had looms to work the material furnished by Rouen middlemen, who often maintained workshops of their own. Venturesome artisans bought fiber directly from shipowners or yarn from factories, thus became *fabricants,* prospered, and left the old quarter for the northwest suburb of Saint-Gervais to build houses in which, typically, the family lived beneath a drying loft and above a store thronged with porters. Many more stayed behind, of course. In 1730 the municipality counted 2,544 looms operating in town.

The great leap of textile manufacture from piecework done in cottages to factory labor took place after midcentury and was made possible in large part by English technology acquired on the sly. The contribution of John Holker is an important case in point. This Scot who proclaimed his allegiance to the pretender Charles Edward Stuart too boisterously was imprisoned at the age of seventeen while serving an apprenticeship in Manchester. He escaped, reached France, joined the king's army, and distinguished himself. Apparently his grudge against England did not abate with the passage of time, for fifteen years later, in or around 1750, three Rouen merchants set on producing cotton velour persuaded him to revisit Manchester incognito and steal the secrets of its fabrication. So successful was his operation that by 1752 a velours factory had risen on the left bank, opposite Notre-Dame cathedral. Holker's stake in the enterprise earned him not only riches but the prolix title of "Inspecteur des manufactures travaillant avec des machines de l'étranger," a euphemism for director of industrial espionage. Soon more modern factories were built utilizing Arkwright's jenny, and in due course Crompton's mule jenny appeared at a plant at Déville, outside Rouen. Another village near Rouen, Darnétal, became famous for the much admired *rouge d'Andrinople,* or Turkey red, produced by Turkish dyers who had settled there in 1776 with the encouragement of Louis XVI.

Lean times followed on the heels of this midcentury boom. When France and England signed a free-trade agreement in 1786, Rouen suffered for it, especially artisanal weavers who could not produce anything like the inexpensive stuff imported from Lancashire. And the failed harvests of 1788–89 dealt another blow to the cotton industry in reducing demand for manufactured goods. There was general despair, which voiced itself best in *La mort du tiers-état,* a screed inveighing against various sources of misery — the justice system, or Parlement; the price of bread; English machinery — and demanding, among much else, that the treaty with England be redrawn. Unheeded, such outcries led to a kind of Luddite frenzy. Two days before the storming of the Bastille, unemployed and underfed Rouennais in their thousands ran amuck, attacking mills, raiding grain stores, threatening aristocratic parishes, sacking the Saint-Ouen abbey, and damaging factories.

Order was restored by bourgeois notables who had meanwhile wrested control over the economic and administrative life of Rouen from royal authorities. With stockpiled bales and a market for cloth still available in the West Indies, looms continued to operate, and when stocks dwindled, the Jacobin dictatorship of 1793–94, which supervised provincial governments, provided a sufficiency of grain and employment in arms factories. But this salutary improvisation was short-lived. During the anarchy that reigned after Robespierre's fall, Paris diverted foodstuffs from Normandy to sustain its own population. By then, few neutral ships were challenging the English embargo, plants had closed for lack of raw material, and Rouen became a city of paupers. Some fifty thousand people having been reduced to indigence, famine — the worst famine of the eighteenth century — gripped the old quarter, the working-class faubourgs, the Cauchois countryside. Between 1793 and 1797, it took an enormous toll of life. Rouen's main hospital, the Hôtel-Dieu, came to resemble the charnel house at Saint-Maclou, teeming with skeletons it couldn't feed.

Even after Rouennais crept from the grave in 1797, there would be no secure foothold as long as their livelihood depended upon the vicissitudes of Napoleon Bonaparte's convulsive regime. At first, prosperity seemed to beckon. A good harvest filled granaries and, with Mediterranean cotton available once again, industry resumed production, behind the shield of a law interdicting English merchandise. The Grand Army's stupendous requirements generated more orders from the Quartermaster Corps than Alsace and Normandy together could fill. Civilian demand for printed calico, or *indienne* — bolts of which abounded at the vast Halle aux Toiles, a textile market fair held every Friday near Notre-Dame cathedral in Rouen — did not slacken. But imperial expansion also created formidable obstacles. Napoleon's attempt to humble England by denying her merchant ships access to European ports ended up shackling the jailer. Protected from outside the mainland, French industry was subverted from inside the emperor's own dominion by countries annexed to France with which it could not always compete on equal terms — for example Holland, a producer of cheap cotton goods. Far more harmful were England's reprisals. Policing European waters, His Majesty's Argus-eyed fleet compelled all neutral ships to undergo inspection at an English port or risk attack. After 1808, the docks at Le Havre and Rouen handled increasingly meager cargos, as almost no produce from the Antilles made it through. Neither had government-sponsored experiments to grow cotton on plantations in the south of France — the Midi — yielded anything of consequence.

Isolated from the latest technology, Normandy in 1815, when Napoleon finally departed, was a backward child of the industrial age. Not for another five years did the restored Bourbons dare to fend off newly available English goods with protective tariffs, and only then did the economy flourish. As one contemporary put it, factories "rose from the earth like morels" all around Rouen, where streams running off the Caux plateau provided an abundant source of hydraulic power and the native population furnished well-trained hands. The Bourbon Restoration and Louis-Philippe's first decade were halcyon days for entrepreneurs. By 1840 a multitude of small-ish mills housing almost two million mechanized spindles produced suffi-cient thread with Louisiana cotton to keep a multitude of other factories weaving cloth enough for half the nation.

In 1788 Arthur Young had observed that unlike such ports as Le Havre, Bordeaux, and Nantes, whose merchants made fortunes in ten or fifteen years and built affluent quarters, Rouen did not generate enough quick wealth to inspire comparable efforts. Even in Young's time, however, inti-mations of a new city could be divined some distance outside the mossy ramparts, looking westward, where the Hôtel-Dieu stood virtually alone. Hospital administrators had moved it in 1758 from its site near the cathe-dral to a large structure built one hundred years earlier for plague victims and abandoned once the epidemic had passed. The municipality favored their decision. Not only did it make the hospital easier of access, with a wide street that extended through a city gate into the old quarter, but it vi-sualized this avenue, named the rue de Crosne, as the east-west axis of a fu-ture upper-class suburb. Before long, wide, rectilinear streets crisscrossing in a checkerboard pattern that embodied the distaste of enlightened men for the higgledy-piggledy of intramural Rouen were laid over the fields, like a vast picnic cloth. Those who could afford it, being cautious Normans, did not, on the whole, rush to establish residence there. Until the turn of the century the area remained rather bare, and the Hôtel-Dieu loomed over a derelict grid traversed by invalids and hospital staff. Eventually, however, af-fluence brought the virtual neighborhood to life. When Rouen's medieval wall came down, old money and new alike ventured west, with plans for the limestone houses of classical inspiration that soon rose throughout the Faubourg Cauchoise. Anything but stone was unthinkable; to escape a city of wood one built a suburb of stone, and quarried the Caux plateau for inner-city reconstruction as well. Handsome, uniform buildings six stories high eventually came to line the quays where shanties had once stood, hiding old Rouen from river traffic like a Potemkin facade.

But as late as 1806, Rouen still had the shanties, along with an undulat-ing bridge supported by ten old wooden pontoon boats; the city wall; and its sparsely populated outskirts. In that year, when news was still fresh of Napoleon's great victory over the Prussian army at Jena, a young physician named Achille-Cléophas Flaubert arrived on the diligence from Paris to begin a lectureship in anatomy at the Hôtel-Dieu.

I

The Surgeon at the Hôtel-Dieu

ACHILLE-CLÉOPHAS Flaubert hailed from a corner of Champagne bordering on the Île-de-France where Flauberts, or "Floberts," as civil records often identify them, inhabited at least sixty villages. The epicenter of this swarm was Bagneux, a riverine hamlet situated between Troyes and Nogent-sur-Seine, one hundred kilometers southeast of Paris. Had he concerned himself with genealogy, Achille-Cléophas could have traced his line back to seventeenth-century syndics who represented the community before royal deputies. But he undoubtedly knew little of any past more remote than his paternal grandfather, Constant-Jean-Baptiste, a *maréchal-expert* by trade — that is, a farrier, or combination blacksmith-veterinarian — and the father of three sons destined also to earn their livelihoods treating sick animals.

In his sons, Constant had not fathered pious apprentices, as he would surely have done several decades earlier. All three belonged to a generation that profited from the influence of the Enlightenment on rural mores. After 1750, animal husbandry was increasingly coupled with farming in a political economics that held land to be the fount of national wealth; government ministers who invoked this creed, men known as physiocrats, envisioned science as agriculture's handmaiden. Science became urgently relevant during the second half of the century, when cattle plague, or rinderpest, swept across France like mad cow disease. By 1766 two veterinary programs had been established, one at Alfort, near Paris, for training a professional cadre whose expertise would benefit domestic animals. The aim was to supplant the guild of *maréchaux-experts,* which considered the horse alone truly worth a farrier's ministrations and schooled apprentices in that feudal bias, but also to rescue beasts of the field from folk doctors — so-called empirics — applying remedies of every grotesque description. The new curriculum was based upon the same precepts that had begun to transform the study of human medicine. At the recently chartered Collège de chirurgie (formerly the Collège de Saint-Côme) in Paris — where an amphitheater, from which barber wig makers were banned, often overflowed with students who found the operations performed by surgeons of note more captivating than the lectures on Galen recited at the Medical Faculty — observation was the watchword. So too was it at Alfort. To learn about sick bodies, one looked inside them, and at the veterinary school, anatomy lessons counted for a great deal. To be sure, Galen's or any other systematic theory of disease would have ill served country boys whose peasant clientele, if they succeeded in acquiring one, regarded with great suspicion all medicine except familiar local nostrums. Indeed, Alfort's first director kept instruction basic, lest excessively sophisticated alumni flee the hinterland from which they had already been uprooted and yield to the temptation of practicing human medicine, or surgery, in Paris. Even so, a ladder had been planted in rural France for boys impelled, like Stendhal's Julien Sorel, by dreams of elevation. Science, however modest his provision of it, set the state-educated veterinarian's son — the *artiste-vétérinaire* — apart from his farrier father, rather as Julien's small Latin distinguished him from his illiterate siblings. And that intellectual distance, despite efforts to thwart its consequences, fostered social mobility.

More common than the arrivistes who clambered up to Paris were the graduates suspended in midair, who found themselves, on returning home from Alfort, shunned as alien by entrenched craft guilds and superstitious peasants. But more common still, perhaps, were *artistes-vétérinaires* who, successful or not in their practice, helped hoist the next generation out of country wallows. Such was the case with Constant-Jean-Baptiste's middle son, Nicolas. Known in the provincial administration (which hired him to treat horses at a state-owned stud farm) for his exorbitant fees as much as for his undoubted competence, and perhaps even for his 726-page herbal describing plants ordinarily used in animal medicine, Nicolas spent some considerable portion of his income on tuition at the Collège de Sens in Burgundy, where his own son, Achille-Cléophas, studied academic subjects between 1795, when he was eleven, and 1800. This commitment may seem especially remarkable in light of the fact that Nicolas had languished in a

Paris jail throughout 1794 after the Revolutionary Tribunal convicted him of making "counter-revolutionary pronouncements."* It was undoubtedly some time before he reestablished himself at Nogent-sur-Seine. The stigma of political incorrectness hung over him. And it didn't help to have a mildly deranged sister-in-law, nicknamed "la mère Théos," who preached against the godless republic on village squares and stood proxy for banished priests in conducting Sunday church service, singing the Latin hymns and baptizing newborns until threatened with long imprisonment or worse.

By July 1800, when Achille-Cléophas left the Collège de Sens at age fifteen, Nicolas had petitioned the communal subprefect for financial assistance on behalf of his son. Only the commonweal could justify any such request, and so he declared that he, virtuous father that he was, had impoverished himself to make the boy a "useful" citizen. Well-grounded in mathematics, as well as in those other "primary" sciences that "form the basis of a solid education," Achille-Cléophas would soldier through life with a burden of gratuitous knowledge unless the state paid his way at Alfort or Polytechnique. It would be an "act of justice," wrote Nicolas. The subprefect concurred and urged Paris to let Achille-Cléophas compete, after his sixteenth birthday, for entrance to Polytechnique (the prestigious school of military engineering) or to admit him at Alfort as a scholarship nominee from the Aube region.

How Achille-Cléophas came to reject these alternatives and at whose expense he entered medical school are unanswered questions. Although the Revolutionary government had decreed in 1794 that every district should select an *élève de la patrie* for the reorganized medical school, our one archival source indicates only that the young man was admitted on scholarship to Alfort. It is possible that a second scholarship was awarded or that Nicolas Flaubert, with his heart set on having a son study medicine in Paris, acknowledged Achille-Cléophas's own strong inclination and somehow raised enough to pay tuition. What one knows for certain is that the young man began his career at a seminal moment in the history of French medicine. Amid the rubble left by revolutionaries bent on smashing institutional structures that safeguarded privilege and consecrated traditional authority, adventurous minds found room to maneuver. The empirical method flourished, students sought instruction at Paris's Hôtel-Dieu on the Île de la Cité, and in this movement toward hospital medicine, surgeons held the torch for physicians. They who once trailed behind academic luminaries contemptu-

---

*In 1863 Flaubert would say that his paternal grandfather was arrested during the Terror at an inn where he was seen to shed tears over the execution of Louis XVI and saved from the guillotine by seven-year-old Achille-Cléophas, whose mother had had him memorize a pathetic plea for clemency and recite it before the Revolutionary Tribunal in Paris.

ous of their intimacy with the human body now constituted a brilliant, scientific vanguard.

The reversal had occurred slowly. Although France had produced the great surgeon Ambroise Paré in Rabelais's time, it took most of the eighteenth century and a battalion of philosophes challenging well-entrenched pieties to clear the ground for clinical medicine. Set against it were not only the church but a high culture whose apologists felt impelled to frame the physical or sensual world in rationalist hypotheses. Behind its ogives on the rue de la Bûcherie, the Medical Faculty, where lectures were given in Latin and readily understood by youths, mostly wellborn, who had earned a master of arts degree, restricted its teaching to humane letters, to natural philosophy, and to medical theory derived from classical texts. Never dissecting a dead person or laying hands on a sick one, future physicians became thoroughly conversant with Hippocrates and Galen but remained largely ignorant of humanity in the flesh. Proud to be called *antiquarum tenax,* this establishment, which scoffed, for example, at William Harvey's discovery that blood circulates, regarded surgery as a subordinate discipline, a manual or "mechanical" trade, fit for the dexterous and inarticulate. Here, as in the culture at large, much was predicated upon the superiority of head over hand. When Louis XIV's premier physician, Guy-Crescent Fagon, survived a lithotomy in 1701, receiving advice on a postoperative regimen from the surgeon, whom he dismissed with "I needed your hand, but I do not need your head," proved more painful than having stones removed from his bladder. In this curt rejoinder, he formulated the prejudice of almost all of his colleagues. Threatened as they increasingly were, they sought shelter from modern times in the distinction conferred upon humanists by their knowledge of the language that gave one access to medical scripture. However skillful the artisan, without Latin he spoke without intellectual authority. So it was that the faculty, unable in 1724 to veto royal patents endowing public courses for five eminent surgeons at the amphitheater of Saint-Côme, persuaded the crown to have those five appointed as "demonstrators" rather than "professors." It thus maintained the settled order of things by ensuring, titularly, that ignoramuses whose text was the body should not profess but, like children or nominal mutes, "demonstrate," show, point. An event even more portentous occurred twenty years later, when Louis XV's chancellor, concurring with petitioners from Saint-Côme who argued that "knowledge of the Latin tongue and the study of Philosophy" would greatly improve them — that a thorough command of logic, rhetoric, and grammar would broaden their professional horizon — declared the master of arts degree to be a requirement for the surgical mastership. With its very identity at stake, the faculty proclaimed from its bully pulpit the existence of an inherent difference between physician and surgeon. Did *surgeon* not derive from the Greek word meaning "manual operation"? asked a professor at the medical school. Literary culture, which had previously been seen as the surgeon's deficiency, was henceforth pictured as an encumbrance certain to dull the cunning of his hand. The hand that cut would now scribble, the mouth that demonstrated would now orate. "The [surgeon] demonstrators will have the title of professors," an alarmed opponent of reform exclaimed in 1743. "No longer will they demonstrate anatomy and operations by word of mouth, they will read from books; they will give lessons and not examples; they will play the part of orators to be listened to, instead of offering a model to be imitated." When one eminent physician argued that the hospital should serve as the surgeon's library and cadavers as his books, he wasn't voicing enthusiasm for dissection or the clinical method. He was simply putting a subordinate in his place. And, inversely, when the Revolutionary government proposed that the patent laws of 1791 (levying a tax on businesses) should include medicine, the umbrageous faculty declared itself, in what would prove to be its dying breath, a priestly caste, a transcendent corporation whose stock-in-trade was its aptitude for hermeneutics. "Nothing can legally verify the practice of a profession which is purely intellectual, and which is performed exclusively by verbal means, without the intermediary of any material object."

How far the values informing the conflict between surgeon and physician reached into cultural life beyond medicine may best be seen in the realm of theater. Here a battle raged throughout the eighteenth century between the King's Players and actors who earned their livelihood on the popular or fairground stage. Chartered in 1680 by Louis XIV, the Comédie-Française had been given, as its birthright, hegemony over Parisian theater. To "render more perfect the performance of plays," in language closely monitored for barbarisms, was its mission. It alone could utter French; the spoken word was banned from every other stage, and transgressions by the *profanum vulgus* would not go unpunished. At the Saint-Germain fair, police regularly dismantled jerry-built playhouses in which ingenious devices were used to circumvent the taboo against speech. A theater full of antic mischief, with personae descended straight from commedia dell'arte, marshaled its zanies against the classical company (whose members, nicknamed "Romans" in fairground parlance, dared never run onstage, much less tumble). In language necessarily gestural, Harlequin's slapstick matched the surgeon's scalpel, emblemizing a primitive world, at once older and childish, outside the precincts of culture. While officialdom beat a retreat under Louis XV, it did so in the same tactical spirit as the Medical Faculty declaring that erudition would cramp a surgeon's style. In time the censor came to allow speech on fairground stages, provided only that it be distasteful; judgments delivered thereafter show greater tolerance of smut than of literate badinage. Perverse as this may seem, it was consonant with a desire to keep high essentially distinct from low, to safeguard the one by preserving the other. Let Shakespeare marry eloquence and scatology, intellectual delight and visual excitement. In France, order hinged on their separation. "The crude multitude can derive no pleasure from a serious, solemn, truly tragic discourse and . . . this many-headed monster can know at most only the ornaments of theater," affirmed a noted esthetician.

Among academic physicians, the clearest expression of their disdain for knowledge gathered by the senses, and particularly by visual observation, lay in medical nomenclature. Whereas physicians practiced internal medicine, surgery was deemed "external," meaning that only men versed in theoretical systems of pathology could locate the true seat of disease and comprehend the fundamental workings of human life. He who concerned himself with first causes sought them not in open bodies but in humoral imbalances or the derangement of vital forces. Examining guts did not reveal the secret of anything. Dissection yielded only semblances, pictures, and making pictures was bound up with, once again, the idea of the surgeon as illiterate.

When medicine at last began to tilt decisively away from ancestor worship, visual analysis gained ground. Anatomical atlases gradually supplanted classical texts. The profession conferred honor, or even quasi-mystical prestige of a Romantic kind, on the diagnostic eye, and the ability to picture what had hitherto gone unseen figures as an obsessive trope in fiction celebrating great clinicians. Thus, auscultation, if it did everything the stethoscope's inventor claimed for it, would fulfill the ambition of philosophers to "place a window in the breast," wrote one commentator. Another declared that the hospital was as much a school to the physician as the picture gallery was to the painter. In eulogizing his teacher Pierre-Joseph Desault, chief surgeon at the Paris Hôtel-Dieu until 1795, who outraged the Augustinian sisters employed there by lecturing on operations in progress to a consistently packed amphitheater, Xavier Bichat, the father of histology, asserted that "what surgeons paint is a picture, not bookish abstractions." They attain their goal when "the opaque integuments that envelope us are no longer to their skilled eyes anything but a transparent veil revealing the organism as a whole and showing the relationship of its parts." And finally, there was the report on plans for a new medical school submitted to the Revolutionary legislature in 1794 by Dr Antoine Fourcroy, a disciple of Lavoisier. Fourcroy decried the Faculté de Médecine, which had been shut down (along with every other royal academy) several years earlier. "The old method did not give a complete course and was limited to words," he explained.

Once the lesson was finished, its contents vanished from the students' memory. In the École de Santé, manipulation will be united with theoretical precepts. The students do chemical exercises, dissections, operations, and bandaging. *Little reading, much seeing, and much doing will be the foundation of the new teaching which your committee suggests* [italics mine]. Practicing the art, observing at the bedside, all that was missing will now be the principle part of instruction.

As branches of the same science, medicine and surgery would be taught together, for in his view theory without practice conduced to "delirious fantasizing," while practice without theory led to "blind routine."

Not until 1803, when Napoleon took matters in hand, did this agenda become fully institutionalized. Although litters of unlicked army surgeons tumbled out of the École de Santé straight into beleaguered regiments, no competitive examinations had been given and no diploma awarded since 1790. Any quack who paid the patent fee could legally set up shop. Even so, scientific-minded youths came from far and wide to study at city hospitals with physicians who were making Paris the capital of Western medicine. Foremost among the latter stood Jean Corvisart, Napoleon's doctor and a masterful diagnostician, whose gift for predicting internal lesions by percussing, palping, and auscultating earned him enormous prestige. René Laënnec, who invented the stethoscope, learned medicine at Corvisart's knee. Elsewhere, brilliant disciples followed Desault on his rounds through the Hôtel-Dieu and subsequently did great credit to the school of pathological anatomy. There was the aforementioned Xavier Bichat, a tireless dissector of cadavers much preoccupied with disease at the suborganic level, who died young in 1802, one year after publishing his magnum opus, *L'Anatomie générale*. And there was Guillaume Dupuytren, the best-known surgeon of his day, who became a legendary figure thanks not only to his innovative procedures, his deftness, his pedagogical gift, and his autocratic manner but also to the jealous thrusts he delivered in unconditional warfare with rivals for stardom. No one formulated better than Dupuytren the new imperatives that governed medicine. "Seizing the facts gathered by pathological anatomy, medicine must illuminate them and, by linking them to their causes and effects, give them a productive role," he wrote at age twenty-six in the magisterial style he had already made his own. "But this partnership must beget a new science. The phenomena of life conform to laws even in the changes they undergo; there must emerge from the observation of these laws a pathological physiology advancing hand in hand with pathological anatomy and thus transcending the prejudice that has too long divorced physiology from medicine."

Under the tutelage of Dupuytren, who must have seemed to him more than seven years his senior, Achille-Cléophas Flaubert soon demonstrated uncommon ability. After one year of medical school, when students competed for admission to the École pratique, an intensive program taught by an elite staff, he passed the examination with flying colors and was repeatedly ranked first in his class. The school twice awarded him its anatomy prize, over classmates destined to make great names for themselves — François Magendie, among others. A state grant covered tuition, and an assistantship in Baron Thénard's chemical laboratory defrayed other expenses, but Achille-Cléophas scrimped until, after another severe triage, he entered the Hôtel-Dieu in 1804 as one of its first interns. There, for the many menial tasks they performed, the chosen few were given bed, board, lamp oil, and firewood. How often interns could consult Dupuytren, who had recently been appointed the Hôtel-Dieu's second-level surgeon (*chirurgien de seconde classe*), is open to conjecture. Hobbled by the department head, Philippe Pelletan, a distinguished veteran clearly ill at ease with this arrogant young master, Dupuytren kept himself busy at least three hours a day with private courses given at an amphitheater or dissection room in the Latin Quarter.

The year 1806 proved to be momentous in Achille-Cléophas's life. It started badly. Although he may have been a man of sturdy constitution, and taller than most at five feet nine inches, the obstinate spirit that often drove him beyond exhaustion undermined his health. Spitting blood, he contracted "pulmonary phthisis," or tuberculosis. As it happened, this calamity spared him from further misfortune. He eventually recovered — indeed, soon enough to cast doubt on his confreres' diagnosis — but not before the army found him unfit for military service. Instead of joining the 160,000 Frenchmen who set out for Prussia on October 8, and then amputating limbs at Jena or Auerstedt, he sealed his exemption with an indemnity of sixty-five francs.

No sooner had one twist of fate freed him to pursue a career than another provided him with employment. When a young intern hired as a lecturer in anatomy at Rouen's Hôtel-Dieu unexpectedly recused himself, the hospital's chief surgeon, Jean-Baptiste Laumonier, asked his brother-in-law, Michel Thouret, director of the medical school in Paris, to recommend a worthy replacement. Flaubert's name was put forth, with praise from Dupuytren, who, after enumerating his stellar accomplishments, described him as a friend. "Such, sir, is the assistant I am sending you," he wrote. "I will add, much less to give you a high opinion of him than to secure him a benevolent reception, that he has for several years been one of my special students and friends. For everything you do to further his instruction and career, and to afford him the material ease that a young man as well-bred as he needs, I would be infinitely grateful." A eulogy published forty years later, after Achille-Cléophas's death, would plant the idea that Dupuytren, fearful of nurturing a usurper, exiled him to Rouen. But this oft-repeated story, which apparently rests upon the conviction that no first-rate talent could thrive in a provincial milieu or happily resign himself to life outside Paris, is questionable. Even if the compliments Dupuytren paid Flaubert were disingenuous, he was still far from being the potentate who held sway over medical France with favors for the weak and letters of banishment for the strong. Furthermore, a year or two in Rouen worked greatly to the advantage of appointees. As Laumonier's surrogates, they enjoyed precocious authority at a major hospital. And under his supervision, they learned how little they had known about human anatomy. Laumonier, who spent several weeks each year teaching in Paris, was a gifted surgeon (even more widely admired perhaps for his wax models, which could have passed muster at the annual Salon had they been sculpted in marble, than for his surgical prowess).

The administrative commission of the Hôtel-Dieu in Rouen sought immediate authorization from the prefect to appoint Achille-Cléophas, whose name was recorded by a clerk unfamiliar with Cléophas, father of James the little, as Achille-Cléopâtre. No one on the prefect's staff questioned the new anatomist's ostensible hermaphroditism.

Four years passed before Achille-Cléophas obtained his doctorate with a thesis rich in aphoristic prescriptions for pre- and postoperative care derived from the experience he had meanwhile gained at patients' bedsides. Greatly impressed by the young man, Laumonier set him loose to do whatever he could, exploiting his boundless energy, good nature, and obvious talent. For the students enrolled in what had been a rump medical program, Achille-Cléophas organized courses on childbirth, bandaging, physiology, operative medicine, external pathology, surgical procedure, as well as anatomy. With twenty or so gathered around him, he spent hours each week dissecting cadavers, which were not hard to come by in a city whose immigrant peasant population suffered grievously during the economic crises that marked Napoleon's regime. He spent hours more escorting Laumonier on his rounds through the wards, which rivaled those of the Hôtel-Dieu in Paris for maladies associated with squalor and poverty.

The Laumoniers occupied a wing of the hospital built in the eighteenth century to accommodate a famous predecessor, the surgeon Claude-Nicolas Lecat, and it was there, soon after he arrived in Rouen, that Achille-Cléophas met Anne Justine Caroline Fleuriot, nine years younger than he, whom he would marry five years later.

UNLIKE ACHILLE'S family, Caroline Fleuriot's was rooted in Normandy. Her paternal great-grandfather, Yves Fleuriot, a prosperous linen merchant whose wife descended from a family ennobled in 1657, accumulated enough property to live comfortably on income from it, and gave enough away to qualify for burial in a village church near Caen, on the "gospel side" of the nave. Some of this fortune, though apparently none of the entrepreneurial spirit behind it, remained two generations later when Caroline's father, Jean-Baptiste Fleuriot, entered the world. Raised in bourgeois circumstances, he earned a modest livelihood practicing medicine in Pont l'Évêque as a country doctor of the subordinate kind called an *officier de santé,* or health officer. We know from their compatriot Charlotte Corday that his marriage to Anne Charlotte Cambremer on November 6, 1792, made tongues wag, for the parties, who incurred the displeasure of the vehemently anticlerical Revolutionary government by taking their vows in church with great Catholic pomp, were considered a social mismatch. Anne Charlotte's family had aristocratic pretensions. Her maternal uncle, Charles Fouet, a king's counselor ambitious of membership in the *noblesse de robe,* sported the name Fouet de Crémanville. And her father, Nicolas Cambremer, another prominent lawyer, whose claim to the nobiliary particle may have been even more tenuous, styled himself Cambremer de Croixmare, devised a coat of arms, and inhabited a seventeenth-century mansion, the Hôtel Montpensier. What no one doubted was that the Cambremers and Fouets, both favored by the crown with lucrative appointments, formed a quasi-incestuous bond in Nicolas's generation. In 1760, Nicolas Cambremer married his widowed niece, Anne Françoise Fouet, the daughter of his sister Anne Angélique by Charles Fouet, father of Charles Fouet de Crémanville and himself the king's counselor in the jurisdiction of Pont l'Évêque. From this union came Anne Caroline Cambremer's mother, Anne Charlotte. Born in 1762, Anne Charlotte did not marry until age thirty, a spinsterish age, owing perhaps to the dearth of eligible males in Pont l'Évêque, or of suitors bold enough to apply for her hand. The Hôtel Montpensier may have been seen as a perilous labyrinth, with Nicolas the Minotaur devouring intruders. Certainly locals knew Anne Charlotte's father to be a high-handed, surly man despised by those who farmed his land outside the village of Torquesne and by domestics who served him at home. On one occasion, two laborers attacked him in the fields and beat him bloody. Several years after his marriage, the king's counselor found himself shamed in a paternity suit brought by a former servant whom he had flagrantly abused. Perhaps because time had mellowed him, he gave the decidedly unaristocratic Jean-Baptiste Fleuriot his blessings.

Anne Charlotte's marriage took place in November 1792. Ten months later she died of puerperal fever, the scourge that killed more women in childbirth than all other infections combined. Her husband was left to raise their daughter, Caroline, alone under Nicolas Cambremer's roof, with the octogenarian for company. They made a sad little group in a dwelling

whose noble proportions called unwanted attention to them, most unwanted in 1793 when old scores were being settled by patriotic vigilantes.
Terror, which the Revolutionary government employed as an official instrument for rooting out "foreign agents," cast its shadow on the mansion
and deepened the gloom of a grief-stricken household. Growing up motherless in large, drafty, wood-paneled rooms that two centuries of damp
Norman weather had turned green with mold and stripped of gilt hardly
fostered girlish exuberance. To be sure, the Terror would end after Ther-
midor, but not so Caroline's tribulations. In 1796 the child lost her grandfather, and on a January day in 1803, Jean-Baptiste, at age thirty-nine,
followed his wife to the grave, making Caroline an orphan before her tenth
birthday.

Nicolas Cambremer's first cousin, a solicitor from Pont l'Évêque named
Guillaume Thouret (whose sons made their mark in the world, one as director of the Paris Medical School, another — guillotined during the Terror — as president of the National Constituent Assembly), became
Caroline's de facto guardian. He placed her in a very proper boarding
school in Honfleur run by two dames who had formerly been mistresses at
Saint-Cyr, the institution that Madame de Maintenon, Louis XIV's devout
companion, had founded for poor girls of good family. There she acquired
a lifelong friend in Mlle Marie Victoire Thurin, the future mother of Laure
and Alfred Le Poittevin, with whom Caroline's own children would form
lasting bonds. But death, that of her schoolmistresses, soon evicted her from
yet another home. Leaving Honfleur behind, she moved to Rouen at the
behest of her cousin and godmother, Marie Thouret, daughter of Guillaume, who had married Jean-Baptiste Laumonier some years earlier.

How her adolescence was spent can only be imagined. Having offered
her safe haven at the Hôtel-Dieu (renamed Hospice d'Humanité during the
Revolution), her guardians also agreed that she should receive further instruction, although, surrounded as she now found herself by people inclined to read Voltaire's philosophical fables rather than Bishop Bossuet's
sermons, Catholicism played a diminished role in her life. For entertainment, apart from the high jinks of the Saint-Romain fair, which lasted most
of every autumn, Rouennais went to the Théâtre des Arts, and it seems
quite likely that the Laumoniers occasionally attended plays, concerts, and
the opera with their ward, who would not have gone unnoticed. One friend
remembered that her dusky good looks gave her the air of a Gypsy.

She was apparently spotted very early along by Achille-Cléophas
Flaubert, himself an attractive man, dark and almond-eyed, with brows
sweeping out like wings and a long, thin nose making an imperious statement in the ovals of a full-cheeked face. Caroline knew him as her guardian
Laumonier's protégé and must have been told, when courtship became pos-

sible, that her surrogate parents favored his suit. The age difference of nine years was no impediment. Nor did the disparity of social background speak against them, given his excellent prospects and her orphanhood. But it behooved her kin to approve the marriage officially and scrutinize articles of a contract. Thus, a family council convened in January 1812, including surgeons, lawyers, landowners, and a member of the electoral college of Calvados. Caroline's dowry, which a husband could manage but not inherit under the *régime dotale* to which the future spouses pledged themselves, comprised a trousseau worth six thousand francs, bedroom furniture worth another two thousand, and a farm situated between Pont l'Évêque and Trouville. Achille in turn brought chattels estimated to be worth seven thousand francs, a not inconsiderable estate considering that few workers outside Paris earned as much as eight hundred francs a year. By an arrangement commonplace in Normandy, the contract provided for joint ownership of everything acquired during the marriage. When one spouse died, the survivor would inherit outright half the spouse's holdings and enjoy the usufruct of the rest.

Their marriage took place at City Hall on February 10, 1812, in a civil ceremony witnessed by Laumonier, the pharmacist of the Hôtel-Dieu, a banker friend, and several others, but not by Nicolas Flaubert, who, with only two more years to live, may have been ailing. The couple set up house on the rue du Petit Salut, a quiet street near the cathedral.

To most young people assessing their chances in February 1812, the future could not have looked bleaker. Bad harvests combined with massive unemployment among textile workers wrought havoc throughout Normandy. The famished queued up at street corners for Rumford soup, which was often all that saved them from starvation. In some of the larger cities rioters took to pillaging. "On approaching Lisieux," wrote the commissioner of police for Caen, "one sees ghastly pale faces and wasted bodies; miserable people are everywhere, sitting on the side of the roads, awaiting evidence of the travelers' sympathy. Milk, cooked herbs, cheese and coarse bran are the food of the peasant who cannot even afford oat bread." Meanwhile, sons and husbands in their thousands were called up to replenish the Grand Army as Napoleon played out his dream of world conquest with preparations for invading Russia. Between 1798 and 1807, 985,000 men had been drafted, or a thirty-sixth part of the entire population. That fraction now increased dramatically, and so did resistance to conscription. Young men poured acid on their teeth to make them rot, or kept self-inflicted sores open with water and arsenic. They would sooner suffer a hernia or broken leg or even suppurating genitals than risk evisceration by a Cossack. Only hospitals like the Hôtel-Dieu, where Dr Flaubert witnessed many such gruesome casualties, drove a thriving trade.

But for Caroline, the first years of her marriage were, she later claimed, the happiest of her life. On the eve of their first anniversary, she bore Achille-Cléophas a son, whom they named Achille. This event gratified her in more than the usual sense, no doubt. Surviving childbirth once again, this time as mother, not infant, or rather, as mother and infant together, helped right the original wrong. She who had cost her mother her life and robbed her father of sons made amends by presenting her husband with a male heir. Guilt, the expectation of failure, and the specter of abandonment had always been her baneful companions. Now, having created her own family, she was, for the moment, immune to their influence. Motherhood reprieved her from orphanhood.

Furthermore, family finances improved substantially when Dr Flaubert replaced Laumonier as chief surgeon at the Hôtel-Dieu in a succession that had seemed preordained until events of the day came to trouble it. Disabled by strokes, Laumonier was obliged to retire early in 1815, during the brief "First Restoration," which saw Louis XVIII occupy the French throne between Napoleon's exile to Elba and his return for the so-called Hundred Days. With wounded soldiers diverted from Paris's overcrowded hospitals spilling into the Hôtel-Dieu, administrators wanted Flaubert appointed chief surgeon right away but were frustrated by the prefect, a Bonapartist answerable to new masters who wished to impose a monarchist surgeon of no particular distinction. The prefecture resumed its loyalty after Napoleon's triumphant march across France, Flaubert gained the upper hand again, and the relevant ministry, which had had mountains of nominations to examine, approved his on the day before Waterloo. In a speech proclaiming him chief surgeon, the president of the administrative commission of Rouen hospitals lauded anatomical investigations "wherein the cold remains of men deprived of life are interrogated in order to extract the secret of keeping the living alive" but warned against students insufficiently imbued with respect for the bodies they dissected.

Achille-Cléophas lost no time staking out his domain. With a large bourgeois clientele, he joined the ranks of the affluent, but his main task, which by all accounts he performed devotedly, was to care for the indigent who came from Rouen, its faubourgs, and the villages beyond. As expansive as Caroline was reserved, he flourished in the wards, leading his entourage of students from sickbed to sickbed almost every day, comforting patients and lecturing on their pathology. It was thought that his flair for learned, subtle extemporization went hand in hand with a distaste for the solitary labor of writing, and in fact he never wrote much, except in the pages of his clinical diary. It was also true that as surgeon, teacher, and administrator, he wore enough hats to keep three men well employed.

In 1818 the Flauberts rented a larger apartment conveniently situated on the rue de Crosne and were about to install themselves when Laumonier, who had retained the chief surgeon's quarters after his retirement, died. The hospital became their home, and there they would live for many years, in a somber, graystone pavilion three stories high, which one entered through double doors at 17, rue de Lecat. It had a small courtyard hidden from the street by a trellised wall. To one side stood a shed for the Hôtel-Dieu's horse-drawn ambulance; on the other side, beyond the trellis and its leafy vines, was the building itself, with tall windows on the ground floor admitting what little light visited this enclosure into a kitchen, the doctor's office, and the tiered recesses of a dissection theater. Eating and sleeping above carved-up bodies appears not to have troubled family life. On the second floor were the Flauberts' bedroom, a billiard room, and a large dining room that adjoined the wards. Little Achille surveyed the hospital grounds from the third floor, where low-beamed rooms made up the children's dormitory.

One may speak of children in the plural, for in fact Achille did not often have the third floor all to himself. Next door were transients destined to become wee ghosts, who lived only long enough to knit with the family and, in dying, to rend its fabric. During a nightmarish interval of six years, Caroline lost two sons and a daughter. The girl, named Caroline, was born in February 1816 and died in October of the following year. Thirteen months after this loss she bore a son, Émile Cléophas, who lived eight months, until June 1819, when she was already pregnant with another boy, born in November. Jules Alfred showed greater promise of surviving childhood. He was still alive two years later and presumably old enough to resent the attention lavished upon a newborn brother in December 1821. For more than half a year the Flauberts numbered five, but in September 1822, Jules joined Caroline and Émile in the family netherworld.

The child born on December 12 at four in the morning was named Gustave. On December 13 Achille-Cléophas and two other "informants," a surgical intern and a health officer, presented him to the deputy mayor for the birth certificate that established civil status. On January 13, a Sunday, he was taken around the corner and received by the church in a handsome, eighteenth-century edifice, the Église de la Madeleine, whose clerics had more experience administering extreme unction to inmates of the Hôtel-Dieu than baptizing infants. Present, as godparents, were Paul François Le Poittevin, a rich textile merchant, and Marie Eulalie Vieillot. Absent was the father, Achille-Cléophas, presumably for reasons other than a wish to uphold the reputation he had earned with Restoration authorities of being liberal in his political sympathies.

II

The Cynosure of All Eyes

ACHILLE-CLÉOPHAS Flaubert may not have suffered for his liberalism under the restored Bourbons as his father, Nicolas Flaubert, had done for his alleged royalism during the Terror, but he underwent close scrutiny when the Academy of Medicine proposed to make him a provincial associate. Recommending the surgeon in a letter to the director of police, Rouen's prefect treated Flaubert's liberal bias as the harelip in an otherwise fair countenance. "The political opinions of this physician are liberal," he wrote on April 3, 1824, "but he has not foisted them on anyone. Quite the opposite, his public addresses bespeak wisdom and moderation, and his conduct is such that even people who don't share his principles generally grant him their trust."

In the wake of revolution and empire, France's rulers only intermittently aspired to "wisdom" and "moderation," and 1824, which saw an extreme right-wing faction ascend the throne with Charles X, was not a banner year for mild virtues. The "ultras," or "priest party," most of whose members fled France during the Terror, returned from exile after Waterloo with every intention of avenging themselves on recent history. Pledged to the "eternal contract" between throne and altar, they made this their rallying cry in a struggle for the reconquest of society. Seigneurial estates and church lands sold by the Revolutionary government as state property could not always be gotten back, but minds were another matter, and minds were seized with an evangelizing fist. Clergymen would descend upon a town, preach hellfire sermons, hold mass Communion, erect gigantic crosses, and stage ceremonies of self-flagellation for outrages perpetrated during the Terror. The archbishop of Rouen, one of many mitered aristocrats, ordered parish priests to display lists of noncommunicants on church doors and keep a record of neighbors living in concubinage. The censor responsible for French theater allowed no mention onstage of eighteenth-century philosophes. Courses taught by the philosopher Victor Cousin and the historian Guizot were suppressed, and in 1822 Monsignor Fraysinnous, who presided over public education, dissolved the elite École Normale Supérieure, which was seen to be an agency of seditious thought. "He whose misfortune it is to live without religion and not to be devoted to the royal family should feel deficient in an essential characteristic of the worthy teacher," he declared. No longer was the school day in Napoleonic lycées cadenced by drumrolls; it began with the *Veni sancte spiritus* and ended with the *Sub tuum praesidium*. In most cases senior boys learned philosophy from ecclesiastics more inclined to read, if they had any inclination to read, the theocratic arguments of de Bonald and de Maistre than Aristotle or Descartes. Grief, mourning, and, above all, expiation spelled prosperity for the church. Seminaries whose enrollment had dwindled to almost nothing before 1815 now attracted young men in strength, some heeding a call while others — like Julien Sorel's fellow seminarians in *Le Rouge et le noir* — merely sought comfortable employment. Ordinations swelled during the 1820s along with the religious budget, and twenty-five thousand women flocked into convent life. How far this zeal animated the population at large, outside traditionally Catholic-royalist provinces, is open to question. It was said by one commentator that France bred more shepherds than sheep.

The grandiose coronation of Charles X in Rheims cathedral bolstered the ultras, who, several years earlier, had led five army corps against republican Spain to rescue Louis XVIII's Bourbon cousin, Ferdinand VII, from his prison in the Trocadèro fortress at Cadiz (and on their return introduced the fashion of cigar smoking). After 1824 they made their influence felt ubiquitously through an order called the Congregation of the Virgin (the "Congregation," for short), which strove to promote the "re-Christianization" of France. Its members sat high in councils of state. Its charitable societies visited the poor, the hospitalized, the jailed. Under its aegis a Société catholique des bons livres combated antireligious literature. It lobbied for measures to stiffen press censorship and disenfranchise liberal voters. And it almost certainly had a hand in drafting the infamous "law on sacrilege," which nudged France a little beyond the pious extravagances of czarist Russia. Passed in April 1825, this remarkable statute prescribed that the public profanation of consecrated wafers should be treated as parricide, with the culprit subject to having his right fist amputated before suffering execution. "The execution shall be preceded by the public penance of the condemned in front of the principal church of the place where the crime was committed, or of the place where Assizes are held." A liberal Orleanist, the duc de Broglie, would observe in his personal recollections that this language was not uttered in 1204 on the eve of the Crusade urged by Pope Innocent III against the Albigenses, or in 1572 before the Massacre of Saint Bartholomew's Day, but in the nineteenth century "in a country where freedom of worship is openly acknowledged."

Although it did not result in any deaths, or even in life sentences of hard labor for wanton damage to holy vessels, the law on sacrilege and other legislation produced an anticlerical backlash. By evicting Voltaire and Rousseau from their tombs in Paris's Panthéon, which became once again the church it had originally been, the monarchy helped enrich publishers who churned out the works of Enlightenment figures: between 1817 and 1824 Rousseau appeared in thirteen editions and Voltaire in twelve. *Tartuffe* was performed in theaters large and small and often furnished an occasion for the angry impeachment of local clergy, whose custodial duties included the denial of Christian burial ground to actors. Great caricaturists such as Grandville, who were soon to feast on the next king, Louis-Philippe, honed their teeth on Charles X. Any dissident would have known by heart the polemical lyrics of Béranger. He might also have read *Le Courrier Français* or *Le Constitutionnel,* where a regular column concerned itself with reports, apocryphal or otherwise, of clerical mischief, of Protestant children kidnapped and raised as Catholics, of autos-da-fé, of trumped-up miracles, of schoolmasters fired at the behest of curates, of lewd priests. The abbé de Rohan, on a "mission" to the Collège Henri IV in Paris, exhorted his young audience to abide by the faith that had propagated France's "heros and saints." Had he exhorted students at another distinguished high school, Louis-le-Grand, 115 of whom were expelled for rebelling against the largely Jesuit faculty, he might have had brickbats hurled at him. Indeed, brickbats hurled at Jesuits came from every direction, even from within the Gallican Church, which considered the order a Roman threat to its independence. "One would think that the genius of France had nothing else to do than breathe fire against the Jesuits," observed Stendhal, no priest lover himself. The complicity of throne and altar inspired not only caricatures of the king dressed as a Jesuit but also the rumor that Charles, who wore royal purple for mourning in a procession during the Jubilee of 1826, had been secretly mitered by Pius VII and conducted surreptitious Masses at the royal palace.

If, as is likely, Rouen's Hôtel-Dieu resembled other city hospitals, surgeons bent on advancing medical science would not have taken for granted perfect cooperation from the sisters who nursed there or expected allegiance to a common ideal or inspired faith in the efficacy of their practice. It was by no means obvious that the diligent autopsies conducted in the dissection room benefited medical science at all. Until anesthesia became widely available after 1846, operations caused horrible suffering, with few brilliant results (indeed, some of Flaubert's contemporaries, notably the illustrious surgeon Velpeau, disdained anesthesia, believing that painless surgery was fraudulent surgery). No matter that surgeons worked rapidly: the nimble hand that performed a lithotomy in mere minutes was often an unwashed hand that had just groped through the entrails of a corpse. Cured of stone or of polyps, the patient often succumbed to septicemia, and succumbed the more readily for entering the hospital worn out by a life of ceaseless, ill–paid labor. Anyone with resources had himself treated at home. The Hôtel-Dieu served the indigent, many of whom were chronically ill or moribund. But even if sepsis had been understood and prognoses had been rosier, physical well-being mattered less than spiritual salvation to nuns who did the scut work. In this respect, little had changed since the early 1790s, when Lazare Carnot pictured hospitals as subversive priestholes.

Forced to take a Revolutionary oath or face imprisonment, the nurses disappeared from hospital service and reappeared in numbers only during the Restoration. Drudging sixteen hours a day for a pittance, these *filles de la charité,* whose origins were generally no less humble than their charges', shunned everything modern. In the spirit of Pius VII, who would not allow gaslight and smallpox vaccine (among much else) on pontifical lands, they wanted patients to see in the Hôtel-Dieu a place of convalescence from their dissolute, unruly lives, and with some splendid exceptions, they functioned as a kind of moral constabulary. One Rouen worker, Charles Noiret, wrote memoirs that criticize this proselytizing at the Hôtel-Dieu. Why, he asked, did the hospital need a kitchen, a pharmacy, a medical staff, surgeons, and beds if its raison d'être was to prepare souls for paradise? The spectacle of a priest administering extreme unction terrified the entire ward. And better health was not promoted by the man who rang Mass every day at the crack of dawn. Frightened patients would wake up with a start, unless they had been kept awake since 3 a.m. by the racket of benches being moved around the room in which worship took place. "When at last the hour for mass arrives," he wrote, "the sick are invited to attend. Attendance is not, of course, obligatory, but the nuns make their lives so miserable that they end up getting out of bed to save, and waste, themselves."

Although Achille-Cléophas feuded bitterly with the chief of medicine, Eugène-Clément Hellis, a crabbed, devout bachelor whose main contribution to medical literature was an article on hiccups, even those who didn't march with him admired him for his stalwart commitment to principle, his discipline, his candor, his lack of pedantry. There were thunderous temper tantrums but also spontaneous gestures of affection, and a biting wit that sympathetic colleagues called Voltairean was tempered by a compassionate view of human frailty. The willful country boy had clearly acquired enough savoir faire to disarm his Catholic antagonists at the Hôtel-Dieu and establish himself as a notable in Rouen, where, on the whole, notables exemplified Voltaire's contention that commercial enterprise fostered liberal thought. It was he who first occupied the chair of clinical surgery in the École secondaire de médicine situated at the Hôtel-Dieu. This honor, conferred upon him in 1828, made him a doubly qualified member of Rouen's Académie des Sciences, Belles-Lettres et Arts, to which he had been elected in 1814. Numbering forty, as befit a society with classical pretensions, this eighteenth-century institution, which regrouped after the Revolution, brought together scholars, professors, lawyers, archivists, librarians, some ecclesiastical savants, and rich connoisseurs like Alfred Baudry and Eugène Dutuit, who sublimated their industrial wealth in art collecting. Dr Flaubert would surely have seen Baudry's Holbeins and Matsus. He may even have been the exception invited to gaze at the Rembrandts, Ruysdaels, and Durers squirreled away in a mansion on the quai du Havre, near the Rouen Stock Exchange, where three Dutuit siblings — Eugène, Auguste, and Héloise — lived under one roof, nursing a grudge against Rouen not unlike Dr. Barnes's against Philadelphia. The immense cotton fortune left by their father, Pierre Dutuit, who had risen from artisanal obscurity during the Empire, did not earn them the place they felt entitled to in haut-bourgeois society, and their impregnable treasure trove embodied their rancor. Eugène, a nonpracticing lawyer with political ambitions thwarted by the prefect, was less reclusive than his brother, after whom Balzac might have modeled at least two characters. As frugal as Balzac's Père Grandet and as unappeasably acquisitive as his Cousin Pons, he traveled long distances third-class to spend huge sums on art, some of which never emerged from the packing case.

The object of Dr Flaubert's material appetite was real estate rather than art. In this he conformed to the values not only of his Champenois family but of the nouveaux riches with whom he hobnobbed. Owning châteaus gave textile millionaires the prestige enjoyed by aristocrats rooted in Normandy since the Middle Ages, and living "nobly" expressed the ambition of many a *fabricant*. No less important for men who knew how easily they could lose what they had gained almost overnight in the swift currents of the age was the security bound up with landedness. "So long as you have only money, you will always be living on the brink of insolvency," a rich Le Havre merchant warned the brother he was strongly advising to buy farm- land in the Caux. Not until midcentury, during the Second Empire, when stock market investment increased by magnitudes, did well-heeled bour- geois begin to find their income from tenant farmers inadequate. A 5 per- cent return satisfied their conservative expectations, and furthermore land, under a regime that tied electoral privilege to property tax, qualified the substantial landlord for membership in the so-called *pays légal*. According to the electoral law of 1820, only those who paid three hundred francs a year could vote, which meant eighty-eight thousand people in a nation of thirty-two million. Even fewer — some sixteen thousand — paid the thou- sand francs that made one eligible to serve as a deputy in parliament.

By 1824 Achille-Cléophas Flaubert was old enough and propertied enough to run for office if his convictions had recklessly prompted him to imitate liberal legislators such as Lafayette and Benjamin Constant in op- posing the triumphant ultras, who, after the assassination that year of Louis XVIII's nephew, the duc de Berry, clamped down on a querulous, insubor- dinate nation. With relatives on the alert for rural property, Achille- Cléophas bought everything that came his way in the 1820s, combining adjacent parcels of woodland, fields under cultivation, and pasturage, or snapping up whole farmsteads. Located in Champagne as well as in Nor- mandy, this acreage included the Ferme de l'Isle and the Domaine de la Cour-Maraille, which straddled three parishes on the outskirts of Nogent- sur-Seine, and the Ferme de Gefosse in Pont l'Évêque, which had belonged to a Cambremer de Croixmare.

Much the costliest acquisition he made during these years was not income- bearing farmland, however, but an eighteenth-century country villa three or four kilometers outside Rouen. Situated on high ground above the main north-south road in Déville and below an extensive wood called the Bois l'Archevêque, it had once been the estate of an aristocratic family, with ap- ple orchards quilting the hillside. By 1821, when Dr Flaubert purchased it for fifty-two thousand francs, ownership had passed to two ladies and a M. Chouquet, whose spinning mill undoubtedly flanked the river Cailly nearby, where it met the Clères in what Rouennais had begun to call "la petite vallée de Manchester." The house was an elegant structure three sto- ries tall and taller in appearance for sitting on a raised terrace to which one ascended by a horseshoe staircase. Large, rectangular casement windows helped make it a bright, airy retreat from the cloistral environment of the hospital. Its one drawback was, it soon became clear, insufficient space. Gustave arrived some ten months after the Flauberts took possession of it, and little Jules Alfred was still alive. Then, in July 1824, Caroline gave birth to a daughter, whom she named Caroline in accordance with the old custom of each parent bestowing his or her name on a child. To accommodate his growing family, Achille-Cléophas, with resolute optimism, added lateral wings. And to proclaim himself master of his domain, he installed a bearded bust of Hippocrates on a corbel above the main entrance.

Although Flaubert, who dwelled on the past, could reel off vivid images of life at the Hôtel-Dieu and at Déville, his oldest memory, he later told a friend, featured a château with a round expanse of greensward in the Mauny forest, midway between Rouen and Jumièges. There were tall trees, a majordomo wearing black, a long corridor leading to his room, "on the left." The year must have been 1825, when an incident traumatic enough to have engraved this scene in his very young mind disrupted family routine. On June 11, in the evening, Achille-Cléophas leaped out of a runaway coach hurtling down a dangerous slope and suffered a compound fracture of the left leg, his tibia piercing the skin. Treated by a former student named Licquet, who constructed a proper splint under his direction, he had himself transported to the estate of the marquis d'Étampes, where Caroline Flaubert, surrounded by her children, attended him in what must have seemed like another hopeless vigil. Achille-Cléophas could not have felt sanguine as the leg swelled and festered, and rumors of his impending death, which had spread through town, were no doubt kept from him. In four issues over ten days, the *Journal de Rouen*, a liberal paper that normally scanted local news, carried prolix reports on the condition of Rouen's beloved "friend of humanity," comparing him to the great Ambroise Paré, who exhibited "admirable sang-froid" in a similar predicament. "Such is the public's concern for the person of M. Flaubert that every scrap of information is welcomed with a kind of avidity," it claimed. "M. Leudet, assistant surgeon at the Hôtel-Dieu, joined M. Licquet in efforts to lessen the patient's suffering and to participate in the honorable mission of restoring, as quickly as possible, by every available means, this worthy successor of Lecat and Laumonier." The chief surgeon would soon be striding through the wards again at 7 a.m., with an imperious limp, while Caroline — of whom a young acquaintance later observed that she seemed to exist between memories of a sorrowful past and expectations of future sorrow — went back to enduring her fretful intermission. Her grand and solemn appearance remarked upon by acquaintances was dearly bought with severe migraines.

Gustave imbibed her anxiety like mother's milk, but a place associated with the fear of loss may also have stored memories of a new and important arrival. In 1825, Caroline, desperate for help to manage her vulnerable brood, hired Caroline Hébert, a twenty-one-year-old immigrant girl from the village of Bourg-Beaudouin near the Longboel forest east of Rouen. It being common in nineteenth-century France to rename female domestics when they entered service, especially under circumstances that might otherwise cause confusion, Caroline Hébert became "Julie." Unlike her father, an alcoholic postilion, and most villagers, Julie could read and write and speak comprehensible French as well as one or another of the dialects — bocage, cauchois — that served better than hedgerows to fortify Normandy's backcountry against penetration by the outside world. In adolescence, during a year of confinement, she had devoured the popular fiction borne from village to village in the wagons of rural peddlers. She could also recall almost everything she had heard since childhood on winter evenings at the storytelling sessions called *veillées*, which brought together her entire clan. As it happened, Julie was an irrepressible raconteur, with countless brigands, witches, goblins, ghosts, saints, and devil-twitters in her repertoire of supernatural yarns. This would not, of course, have been the quality Caroline valued most, but it worked greatly to the advantage of her younger son, alleviating the gravitas that marked family life at the Hôtel-Dieu. Julie peopled Gustave's imagination in childhood, and half a century later, having outlived him, salvaged the childhood itself, or some remnant of it, in anecdotes told to his niece.

Pampered by Mme Flaubert, who for obvious reasons could never regard even a minor ailment as merely that, Gustave gave every indication of flouting her dire premonitions. The portrait of him done when he was twelve shows a beautiful blond boy framed by the upturned collar of a soft white shirt and the floppy ears of a dark cravat. With his vaguely supercilious air, he might have passed for one of those young English lords much admired in Restoration France. The forehead is wide, the nose less beaked than Achille's, the mouth, which was fated to disappear under drooping mustachios, set in a chubby pout. Altogether, Gustave resembled Caroline Flaubert, and his eyes were the feature that marked this resemblance most conspicuously. Immense and blue-green, they seemed to fill their sockets to the brim, like opals beaming from a shallow dish. Well above them arched his long, dark brows.

At that age he was a quiet child who, foreshadowing the reclusive writer addicted to clay pipes, spent hours lost in thought with a finger stuck in his mouth. He was also famously credulous, and family lore included the story of a pestered servant shooing him away by ordering him to "go see whether I'm in the back of the garden or maybe in the kitchen." These traits — his credulity and thoughtfulness — combined to make him an ideal listener. Avid for tales, he kept Julie company in the kitchen and the sewing room and, when she wasn't free, prevailed upon other domestics — there were several in the household — to entertain him. His second most dependable resource was an elderly gentleman, known only as le père Mignot, who lived opposite the Hôtel-Dieu. Having moved to Rouen after farming all his life in the Norman "Vexin" near Les Andelys and rearing four children with a wife whose dowry now made retirement possible, Mignot took a great liking to Dr Flaubert's little boy. Gustave found the welcome mat laid out at all times. No sooner had he signaled from the rue de Lecat than Mignot, on the lookout for his small friend, would invite him over for sessions of storytelling. There were endless tales, and Mignot, being a teacher by inclination, may sometimes have shaped them toward a moral precept. But the ones that made the deepest impression on Gustave all came from *Don Quixote*, which had just appeared in an abridgment with several dozen illustrations perfect for coloring. He could not hear them repeated often enough, and the old man, grateful no doubt to have had this ministry conferred upon him, gladly indulged him. "Unconsciously one carries in one's heart the dust of one's dead ancestors," Flaubert wrote many years later. "I could give a precise demonstration of this in my own case. The same goes for literature. I find all my roots in the book I knew by heart before learning how to read, *Don Quixote*." If the artful conflation of reality and fantasy endeared Cervantes to Flaubert at thirty, all the more reason for him to love *Don Quixote* in childhood, when conflating them was as natural as breathing. Then, too, his delight in the picaresque adventures of Sancho Panza and Don Quixote may have reflected some vague sense of embodying their *folie à deux*, of being himself both a clownish peasant bound in ironical subservience to a deluded squire, and the squire pledged to an unattainable Dulcinea.

So avid a listener was he that teaching him to read proved exceedingly difficult. Although Mme Flaubert had had great success with Achille, Gustave, who already regarded the brother who had preceded him by eight years as a wonder of precociousness, was, for all his alertness in other respects, still illiterate at age seven and, to make matters worse, outstripped by four-year-old Caroline. "What's the point of learning, since Papa Mignot reads?" he exclaimed during one tearful scene. Dark suspicions enveloped him until his eighth year, when suddenly the Rosetta stone of French letters revealed itself. Thereafter everything changed. Père Mignot's enraptured hostage became a rapt audience for the written word. Turning pages with one hand while twirling a lock of hair with the other, he would forget where he was and, as he later recalled, sometimes tumbled right out of his chair, in a bruising rehearsal of falls to come.

The Flaubert household library, which Achille-Cléophas had furnished with classics, including a complete Voltaire, was rich pasture for a bookish boy. But, however scornful Gustave may have been later on of Rouen's philistine bourgeoisie, there was also nourishment to be found in the city itself, where cultural life revolved around theater, and those who could afford it or endure the pit regularly gathered at the Théâtre des Arts on the right bank three blocks down the quai du Havre from the Bourse. There, in a hall with nineteen hundred seats, whose ceiling pictured Rouen's great native son Pierre Corneille being crowned by the Muses, two companies plus a full orchestra offered bountiful menus of instrumental music, opera, comedy, tragedy, drama, vaudeville. Even if it was no longer what it had once been (as directors complained), the appetite for spectacle rivaled that for food, and evenings at the groaning board, five a week from mid-May to mid-April, might last four or five hours. The program of January 15, 1830, celebrating Molière's birthday began with von Weber's overture to *Oberon* and continued with *Tartuffe*, the overture to *Charles de France*, and *Le Malade imaginaire*. During the 1833–34 season, two stars of the Paris stage, Mlles Déjazet and Dorval, were induced to perform seventeen dramatic roles in the month of August. Over a four-year period, 1832–36, Rouen's theater served up something more than 100 dramas and comedies, 22 operas, 140 vaudevilles, and recitals by such great virtuosi as Paganini. Year in and year out, the municipal council begrudged it additional subventions. Directors resigned (or in one case committed suicide), and deficits mounted. Still, the banquet continued.

Situated closer to the capital than any other major provincial stage, Rouen aped the fashions of Paris. Norman chauvinism did not exclude a desire to be *à la page*, and being that during the 1820s and 1830s required theatergoers to keep pace with Eugène Scribe, who, in three hundred so-called well-made plays, presented a smug worldview debunking every expression of human magnitude or sublimity: literary genius, Revolutionary idealism, political principle, Napoleonic greatness. But far more adventurous items also traveled down the Seine. An English company led by Harriet Smithson, Berlioz's future wife, arrived in August 1828 after dazzling the Parisian public with productions of *Othello* and *Hamlet*. They had "revealed Shakespeare to France," as one prominent critic put it. And the company elicited almost as much praise in stolid Normandy with *Romeo and Juliet*, *Hamlet*, Thomas Otway's *Venice Preserved*, and Nicolas Rowe's *Jane Shore*. The way north was thus paved for young Romantics, who repeatedly summoned Shakespeare to testify on their behalf against French classical conventions. Alexandre Dumas preceded Victor Hugo to Rouen, and in the early 1830s *Antony*, *Richard Darlington*, and that goriest of dramas, *La Tour de Nesle*, electrified the Théâtre des Arts. It is safe to assume, of course, that most Rouennais of a certain class and generation — especially the cotton merchants, who were known to conduct business between acts at the bar —

found all the Romanticism they wanted in Rossini's operas, which always packed the house.

Among contemporary works that left an impression on Gustave, none may have impressed more forcefully than *L'Auberge des Adrets*, a quirky piece famous for the part played in it by Frédérick Lemaître. In 1824, nine years before he brought it to Rouen, the little-known actor, who would soon be lording it over the Romantic stage, found himself cast as the stock villain, Robert Macaire, of a melodrama thick with all the clichés in vogue at theaters on Paris's boulevard du Temple, or "Boulevard of Crime." A mischievous impulse prompted Lemaître to burlesque the role. So, rather than skulk onstage with his arms raised to hide his face, as black-robed villains customarily did, he made an ostentatious entrance, flanked by his gaunt sidekick, Bertrand, and got up like a scarecrow in threadbare pants, scuffed ballroom slippers, a dirty white waistcoat, a green coat much the worse for wear, an eye patch, and a half-crushed felt hat raffishly tilted over one ear. Far from displaying a guilty conscience at the end and repenting when accused of murder by the young hero, he quipped: "What do you expect, my son? Nobody is perfect." *L'Auberge des Adrets* provoked gales of laughter, bringing its two authors a tearful success, though not the success or the tears on which they had banked. And it married its star to a role — Robert Macaire — that shadowed him even beyond the grave.

With Lemaître thenceforth continuing to ad-lib freely as Macaire, black humor acquired a face and a demeanor. Having come into existence as a character in quotation marks or a send-up of the moral scheme sustained by melodramatic formulas, he spoke to the alienation that beset common people, intellectuals, and aristocrats alike after four decades of tumult. Where villains and heroes upheld the Just Society from opposite ends, Macaire, who combined features of both, was a kind of con artist transcending ethical distinctions, an "outsider" beholden to no common ideal, a *homo duplex* killing gratuitously or assuming aliases for the fun of it. "The people," wrote Heinrich Heine, "have so lost faith in the high ideals of which our political and literary Tartuffes prate so much that they see in them nothing but empty phrases — *blague* as their saying goes. This disabused outlook is illustrated by Robert Macaire; it is likewise illustrated by the popular dances, which may be regarded as the spirit of Robert Macaire put into mime. Anyone acquainted with the latter will be able to form some idea of these indescribable gyrations, which are satires not only of sex and society but of everything that is good and beautiful, of all enthusiasm, patriotism, loyalty, faith, family feeling, heroism, and religion."* Heine's good

---

*Heine was referring principally to the cancan, which became a popular craze during the 1830s and was sometimes danced by high kickers wearing no underclothes.

friend George Sand agreed with him. The spirit of the age, she observed, was an admixture of fright and irony, of consternation and impudence.

Every revival of *L'Auberge des Adrets,* with which Lemaître made do until he wrote *Robert Macaire,* transforming it from a play into a vehicle for satirical extemporizations, had phenomenal success. That he could drum up business simply by announcing, as he did on one occasion: "Ladies and gentlemen, regrettably we cannot murder a gendarme this evening, since the actor who plays the part is indisposed. But tomorrow we shall kill two," evokes the desert of mutual hatred dividing haves and have-nots.

Although Gustave, who was later to call Macaire "the greatest symbol of the age" and "the epitome of our times," would not have witnessed any fracases at Lemaître's performances during October and November 1833, social strife certainly impinged upon theater in Rouen. Following the revolution of July 1830, patriotic vaudevilles mingled with scheduled offerings. The cast led the audience in spontaneous renditions of the "Marseillaise," and from the cheap seats came requests for "La Parisienne," a popular song whose refrain was: *Victoire! plus de tyrannie, le peuple a reconquis ses droits* (Victory! no more tyranny, the people have won back their rights). Bourgeois in the loges felt much put upon, but, under glowering eyes, they stood up respectfully. Some, indeed, who professed liberal ideas may even have joined their working-class neighbors in forcing open the doors of a church when retrograde clergy denied funeral rites to Mme Duversin, a veteran character actress.

As if clergy didn't have enough to decry, theater was by no means confined to this hectic arena. On the place du Vieux-Marché, where Joan of Arc had been burned, stood the Théâtre Français, a house closely associated with the Théâtre des Arts and almost as enterprising. Then there were transient stages. For many Rouennais young and old this meant the Saint-Romain fair, which opened in the fall and gave the city a month's worth of antic pleasure. Wild-animal trainers descended upon Rouen along with clowns and tumblers. And amid their tents rose small playhouses cobbled together overnight with planks and painted canvas. Here the fare consisted mainly of simple comedies and melodramas, but some harked back to earlier times, when touring companies presented the stock characters of commedia dell'arte or Christian fable. Albert Legrain, a blond, bushy-bearded man affectionately known as Père Legrain, delighted children year after year with the only play ever performed in his puppet theater: *La Tentation de Saint Antoine.* Behind six little footlights poor Anthony defended himself as best he could against an intensely seductive Proserpine while fiendish imps chanted in chorus:

Allons, prenons le patron,
Tirons-le par son cordon,
*Faisons-le danser en rond.**

Legrain invented a bedeviled companion for Anthony and, much to his audience's amazement, rescued the fellow from teeth and claws by transforming him into a candle.

The bouffant trousers and embroidered collarettes of jugglers at the Saint-Romain fair enthralled Gustave Flaubert. So did horses in beribboned harness and flunkies in red-striped livery who accompanied itinerant mountebanks. He loved, above all, the spectacle of women with gold spangles and pendant earrings and jouncy necklaces dancing on ropes looped across the night sky. Gustave, as he later recalled, was drawn like a magpie to the brilliant things that lit up his foggy mercantile town. By age eleven or twelve, he had become a zealous connoisseur of every Rouen theater, from fairground shacks to legitimate stages. And his connoisseurship reached beyond. During a brief sojourn in Paris in 1833, after visiting Nogent-sur-Seine for their annual family reunion, his parents took him to the Théâtre de la Porte Saint-Martin (which Frédérick Lemaître called home) for performances of two Romantic dramas, *La Chambre ardente* by Bayard and Mélesville and Hugo's *Marion de Lorme*.

Dr and Mme Flaubert, who obviously nurtured, or at least acquiesced in, Gustave's enthusiasm, needed no urging to let him cultivate it at home. As soon as he learned to read, the boy began to write, and what he preferred to write were plays. A New Year's greeting sent on January 1, 1831, gives the first hint of it. "Friend, I'll forward my political and liberal constitutional speeches," he promised Ernest Chevalier, a bosom friend from Les Andelys boarding at the Collège royal in Rouen but spending weekends on the rue de Lecat with his grandparents the Mignots. "I'll also send you my comedies. If you'd like to join together for writing, me I'd write comedies and you, you'll record your dreams, and since there's a lady who consults papa and always talks nonsense to us, I'll write it all down." Whether or not Ernest recorded his dreams, Gustave had every intention of establishing himself under his father's roof as the *magister ludi*. Next to the salon was a billiard room seldom used in a household with little time for indoor games. This became the children's theater, and the oblong billiard table made a stage large enough for the cast of Gustave's productions, which, beginning in great earnest soon after his tenth birthday, took place on Sundays.

---

*Let's go, let's grab the boss/Let's jerk him by his cord belt/Let's make him dance round and round.

Assisted by beautiful little Caroline, his frizzy-haired, dimple-cheeked factotum, who memorized parts, prepared the set, and devised costumes, with permission to rummage through her mother's wardrobe, Gustave scribbled away. On March 31, 1832, he could proudly announce that his repertoire numbered thirty plays, including one, *The Pinchpenny Lover,* whose protagonist loses his mistress to a friend after denying her gifts, and another — a "farce" — about preparations in Rouen for King Louis-Philippe's visit (which was in fact greatly agitating the city just then). Three weeks later he rejoiced at the prospect of Ernest Chevalier returning from Easter vacation to participate in a Sunday of theater as bounteous as the "exceptional performances" staged at the Théâtre des Arts. "Victory!" he repeated five times. There would be four works on the bill, with none of which, he thought, Ernest was yet familiar: a play by Scribe, another by Berquin, a brief *proverbe dramatique* by the eighteenth-century writer Carmontelle, and finally Molière's *Monsieur de Pourceaugnac* (misspelled *Poursognac*), a play notable, under the circumstances, for portraying doctors, in one hilarious scene, as venal poseurs addicted to scholastic gibberish and Galenic nostrums. "The bills, the theater, . . . the 1st, 2nd, and 3rd class tickets are all ready and we've arranged dress-circle seats," he explained. "There will also be roofs and decorations. We've got the backcloth. Ten or twelve people may come to see us. So screw up your courage and have no fear. Little Lerond will guard the door and his sister will have a role." Among other spectators at this gala occasion, he expected Ernest's uncle and mother, Mme Flaubert, two servants, and "possibly some schoolmates." The presence of certain habitués who go unmentioned may have been taken for granted, most obviously the Le Poittevins. Caroline and Gustave were bound by quasi-familial ties to the children of a rich textile manufacturer named Paul Le Poittevin. Five years older than Gustave, Alfred Le Poittevin, who wrote poetry, applauded the boy's literary exertions. And Laure, who would one day give birth to another writer of genius, often mounted a garden stool to take star turns on the billiard table.

Theater was not the only outlet for Gustave's creative exuberance. Once he began wielding an inked goose quill (metal pens would never suit him), he tried his hand at every genre. We know about the "liberal constitutional" speeches he drafted at age nine, presumably in denunciation of Louis-Philippe, whom Achille-Cléophas found obnoxious. He wrote poems, one about the death of Louis XVI and another called "A Mother." *Don Quixote,* on which he took careful notes during Père Mignot's tutorials, inspired the idea of composing "novels" peopled with Cervantes's characters: Cardenia, the seduced and abandoned Dorothea, the tormented triangle of Anselm, Camilla, and Lotharió. And the historian he might have become appeared precociously in a synopsis of Louis XIII's reign, dedicated to his mother.

Nothing of this survives except a brief essay praising Corneille, which so impressed Père Mignot's lawyer son, Amédée, that he had it printed as *Trois pages d'un cahier d'écolier* ("Three Pages from a Schoolboy's Notebook"). It opens with apologies for his hubris. "Oh! father of French Tragedy, to portray you would require a Horace, a Virgil, a Homer. To sing your praises I would need Apollo's lyre, and if I had, would it sing in my hands?" The poet whose genius "gave tongue to the Caesars" is a voice that still "echoes throughout Europe" and a light that shines "like the sun" all around the globe. "Oh Corneille," he apostrophizes,

> Oh my dear compatriot, how many masterpieces in your head! Now your house is occupied by a crude worker; your study, which resounded with sublime words, yes, words that should deservedly rise to heaven, now hears the dull blows of a hammer. Why were you born if not to humble everyone else? Who would dare measure himself against you? Children, mature men, graybeards all join in applauding you. Your works are everywhere seen as flawless. You were born to glorify the reign of Louis XIV and in so doing immortalize yourself. There is some debate as to who possesses greater merit, you or Racine, and I say proudly: who has greater merit, he who clears a path of thorns or he who afterward strews it with flowers? Well, it is you who cleared the thorns, that is, the problems of French versification. Corneille, you win the laurels. I hail you.

Following this high-flown exercise, like Sancho Panza tagging after Don Quixote, is a brief paragraph entitled "La belle explication de la fameuse constipation," in which Gustave, very much of two minds about sublimity and himself, directs his talent for rhetorical figures to the lower regions. With evident interest in those female parts from whence he came, he compares the costive "hole" (the *trou merdarum*) that can't produce turds to the sea that doesn't froth and the woman who bears no children. He had gone, he told Ernest Chevalier, from addressing posterity to addressing posteriors.

All the same, it seems that being a published author gave him less pleasure at age ten than his theatrical exploits. He reveled in the experience of holding an audience captive with dialogue he himself had composed for auxiliaries happy to recite it. Overshadowed in most ways by an older brother already bound for medical school, he made himself, on Sunday afternoons, the cynosure of all eyes. Approval is what he craved, and his brilliant mimicries served that end even better than his rhetorical tours de force. Gustave the spellbound listener had been reborn Gustave the spellbinder. "Had I been well directed, I could have become an excellent actor," he lamented to Chevalier some years later, when faced with the dreaded prospect of choosing a career. "I felt it in my bones." And at twenty-five, still brooding over the paradox that he would have been most genuinely himself in the realm of impersonation, he declared: "Whatever people say, there is a showman at the core of my nature. In childhood and youth, my love for the stage knew no bounds. I might have become a great actor had I been born poorer."

UNLIKE OTHER children of privilege, Gustave, born and bred in a city hospital, was exposed from the first to life's crueler dispensations. Years later he was to observe that his frequent flurries of buffoonery kept at bay the anguish lurking underneath, that despair was his normal state, and so it may have been in youth that theater offered sanctuary in the ambient world of decrepitude. The halt and the lame, the dying and the dead, did indeed surround him, and Gustave sometimes accompanied his father on country rounds. His room overlooked the hospital courtyard, where, weather permitting, white wimples moved among pale invalids. In the garden reserved for the chief surgeon, Dr Flaubert's two younger children, Gustave and Caroline, risked tongue-lashings by hanging on a trellis to peer, awestruck, through the windows of the anatomy theater at dissections in progress. The apartment itself was a porous vessel. When its eyes were shut its ears remained open and moans from the hospital ward came through a door into the family dining room. This may have been particularly troublesome on Gustave's gala Sunday in 1832, during a spring marked by the cholera pandemic that had raced from India to Europe, and across France from Marseille to Paris.

What undoubtedly troubled Dr Flaubert's fellow notables as much as the disease was the prospect of its unleashing in Rouen something like the violence that had engulfed Paris. When cholera attacked the capital, so many Parisians died so quickly that omnibus hearses were needed to transport them to potter's field, and in due course word spread through working-class districts that the alleged disease was one more lie invented by authorities bent on poisoning poor people en masse. Once this notion gained credence, mobs began to lynch unfortunates seen leaning over wells or idling outside wineshops, and "To the lamppost with poisoners!" became a commonly heard death sentence. "It is not the thought of civilized people, it is the cry of savages," Prime Minister Casimir Périer declared before cholera made him its wealthiest victim. Scorned as vagrants in a land of property, as drunks in a sober nation, and as trash in a realm of avid collectors, the *petit peuple,* the very people who embraced Robert Macaire, had some reason to fear the unthinkable. Having manned the barricades in 1830, they saw their victory stolen from them by constitutional Orleanists as callous as Bourbon Legitimists had been, and they vented their rage proportionately. Those suspected of poisoning were strung up on the rue Saint-Denis, in the

Halles, on the Pont d'Arcole, and elsewhere in Paris. A particularly gruesome incident occurred on the rue de Vaugirard, where two men found to
possess a white powder were butchered. The mob, including one old
woman who beat them about the head with wooden clogs, tore out their
hair, their noses, their lips, and paraded the bloody, naked torsos to a chorus of "Here you have cholera morbus!"

On April 7, before the epidemic had reached Rouen, the *Journal de
Rouen* deplored this hysteria in a front-page editorial. "Three days ago, rumors of poisoning added fuel to the all too justified anxiety inspired by the
presence of cholera in Paris. Terrified imaginations are quick to credit baseless rumor! In its ignorance, let us go further and say in its brutality, the
Parisian populace has committed acts so barbarous as to invite comparison
with those of the most primitive hordes." No sooner did cholera declare itself in Rouen than the rumor of poisoning made the rounds. On April 21,
a regular columnist at the *Journal* noted that the disease had spread with particular intensity in Saint-Sever, a poor district on the left bank, and attributed the outbreak to "emanations" from industrial bilge. Residents did not
agree. When a doctor identified the sewage ditch as a source of infection
and urged them to drain it, they asserted that there was no cholera, that
people had been poisoned. Witch hunts followed. Several suspected poisoners set upon by the mob narrowly escaped with their lives. In point of
fact, a city whose putrescent alleys were ideal breeding ground for opportunistic microbes of every kind might have been expected to suffer worse
than it did. Cholera killed twelve hundred a day in Paris while only seventy-
five had succumbed in Rouen two weeks after Dr Flaubert diagnosed the
first case. But everything was writ larger than life. With death at large,
Rouennais who could afford it stayed home. Except to see Meyerbeer's
opera *Robert le Diable,* for which patrons were evidently prepared to run
mortal risks, the public deserted the Théâtre des Arts, ignoring assurances
that it had been fumigated. And in any event statistics published daily in the
official bulletin did not command belief as readily as the numbers dictated
by fear. "I remember 1832 living in the midst of cholera," Flaubert wrote.
"A simple partition, which had a door in it, separated our dining room
from a sick ward where people were dropping like flies."

How family life and hospital life tangled at the core of Gustave's sensibility, where partitions didn't exist, may perhaps be inferred from dreams he
recorded in an early, autobiographical work. One such took place in a green
countryside strewn with wildflowers. Walking alongside him on a riverbank
was his mother, who, all of a sudden, fell and disappeared beneath foaming,
rippling water. Not until the stream had begun to flow calmly again past
bulrushes did he hear her cry out. "I lay flat on my stomach in the grass and

leaned forward to look. I couldn't see anything; the cries continued. An invincible force anchored me to the ground — and I heard her shout: 'I'm drowning! I'm drowning! Help me!' The water went on flowing, flowing clear, and that voice rising from the riverbed plunged me into a state of rage and despair."

Another nightmare conjured up his "father's house," with everything furnished as he knew it to be but bathed in somber hues. The time was night, the season winter. A snowy landscape illuminated his room. Lying awake in a crib, he suddenly saw the snow melt and the landscape turn red, as if on fire. From the staircase came the sound of footsteps, accompanied by a blast of fetid air. The door flew open, whereupon seven or eight unkempt men, all darkly bearded, trooped in and surrounded him. Between their chattering teeth shone steel blades. They parted the white bed curtain, leaving bloody fingerprints, and stared at him unblinkingly. He stared back in turn, paralyzed with fear at the sight of lidless, half-flayed faces from the raw sides of which blood oozed. After lifting his bedclothes, which were soaked in blood, they broke bread. Like flesh, it, too, seemed to hemorrhage, and they laughed "a death rattle."

Suffice it to say here that the brave face Flaubert showed later on in portraying himself (to his mistress) as tougher or more "virile" for having seen the ghastly things he saw at a tender age is unmasked by his nightmare. Not with impunity did he watch Dr Flaubert and students, scalpel in hand, huddle over cut-up bodies. The boy who may have dared to feast on forbidden images in the theater of life — his parents having sex? — might have expected to suffer condign punishment from a father who became Jack the Ripper behind closed doors. There is, indeed, much to suggest that one dream was a punitive sequel to the other, not least of all the fact that Gustave associated erotic pleasure with drowning or suckling. Years later, in the aftermath of a passionate moment, he likened the heart of his inamorata, a mother some years older than he, to "an inexhaustible spring" from which she made him gulp mouthfuls. "It inundates me. It penetrates me. I drown in it. Oh! how beautiful was your head. . . . All I could do was look at you."*

Time eventually told how Flaubert's literary brilliance invested the act of looking. Fraught with danger or imbued with desire, predatory or impotent, that act would draw lines never to be crossed in life and shape distinctive paths for his creative energy.

IN 1832, the year of pestilence and stagecraft, Gustave underwent an important rite of passage. Having taught him at home until ten, an arrange-

*Or again: "When I love, my feeling is a flood that engulfs everything round about."

ment not unusual among bourgeois families, the Flauberts bound him over to the Collège royal for regular schooling. He entered the beginning class for its last trimester in May, rather like Charles Bovary's being thrust among children who had been together since October. Records indicate that during the following school year he became a boarder, in the next higher form.*

*In French schools, the lower the grade, or form, the higher the number. One entered in the eighth form and advanced to the first, which spanned two years, called "Rhetoric" and "Philosophy."

III

School Days

THE COLLÈGE royal, Gustave's first school, had occupied the hilly upper reaches of the right bank since 1593, tolling class hours from a baroque campanile over its monumental entrance. Founded by the Society of Jesus, it had remained a Jesuit institution until 1762, when parties antagonistic to the order persuaded Louis XV to banish it from France. During that span, the school had implanted itself in the life of the Norman capital. Where Flaubert undertook to learn Greek and Latin, generations before him had studied with well-trained classicists. In the derelict chapel where he claimed to see owls and jackdaws roosting, one of the great orators of the Counter-Reformation, Louis Bourdaloue, who later preached at Versailles, had delivered Sabbath sermons for which *tout Rouen* flocked together. Not by chance did the city emerge in the seventeenth century particularly hospitable to dramatic art: staging plays — mostly in Latin — was what Jesuits did with boys under their tutelage, and many of Rouen's elite, including Pierre Corneille, first developed a love of theater at school. Nor was it surprising that another famous graduate should have been the explorer René Cavelier de La Salle: geography figured prominently in the pedagogical agenda of a brotherhood that viewed the Seine at Rouen as a link not so much with Paris as with the oceans being crossed by propagators of the faith. Alumni who didn't explore the world or evangelize it joined forces in a Congrégation des Messieurs to raise money for missions and other pious works.

Like so many French institutions, this one had its name changed by every successive political regime. Two well-feathered angels holding a black marble escutcheon over the entrance stoically witnessed the vicissitudes of history as the Collegium regium Rothomagense became an École centrale during the Revolution, then a Lycée impériale under Napoleon, and finally a restored Collège royal after Waterloo. In the wake of the Revolution of 1830, measures were taken to separate it from throne and altar. A cross surmounting the belfry came down, along with other emblems of its sectarian past. The fortnightly award bestowed upon highest-ranked scholars was now a copper rooster rather than a silver fleur-de-lis. Graduates of the École Normale Supérieure replaced Jesuits for teaching philosophy to senior students. The handsome crossbreed of a Gothic-classical chapel fell into disrepair.

Still, boys who entered the main courtyard, or *cour d'honneur,* all filed past a large clock of Jesuit vintage, around whose rim was painted the inscription: *Hic labor, hic erequies musarum pendent ab horis,* "Here, work and the repose of the Muses depend upon the hours." No normal ten-year-old could have welcomed this admonition, but to a spirit as intolerant of external constraints as Gustave, who often lost all track of time in trances of reading and daydreaming, it sounded like *Lascia esperanza.* The ruthless clock would reign supreme, drawing and quartering the day, and watchmen monitored its poor subjects at work and at play, in the dormitory and refectory. Chief among them was the *proviseur,* or principal. Below him stood the *censeur,* a far more palpable presence to the six hundred collegians whom he evaluated at regular intervals. Responsible for the moral and material welfare of the community, the assistant principal concerned himself with its risings and retirings, with the food it ate, the clothes it wore, the images it might have smuggled in, the books it read in class or undercover. Ideally, nothing that bore on proper conduct eluded him. His Argus eyes were the custodians known as *maîtres d'étude,* who proctored study hall, snuffed out oil lamps at bedtime, and lit them again at dawn, when the long school day began. That day might last fifteen hours. Once a week Gustave would join fellow boarders on an orderly walk down the narrow, sloping rue du Maulevrier toward the place Saint-Ouen and around the neighboring streets or uphill into the countryside around the Cimetière de la Jatte. Shepherded by their masters, they wore little round hats for the excursion, royal blue jackets with an insignia of two large branches inscribed on yellow metal buttons, and waistcoats cut from the same cloth.

As evocative of the ancien régime as its sententious clock were the school's curriculum and pedagogical method, which resembled the Jesuits' *ratio studiorum* closely enough to put a seventeenth-century cleric at ease. Despite the secularizing ethos of France after 1830, boys were given religious instruction throughout high school. In the eighth form they learned Old Testament history, and they proceeded upward, in seventh form, to the New Testament. Playing a more modest role than previously, the chaplain had them memorize the diocesan catechism, but as Communion drew near, children became his captive audience at Mass every Thursday morning for lectures on Christian principle, with no concessions made to the son of a Voltairean doctor. Thereafter Bible study was managed by lay faculty in Greek and Latin. Class might open with a prayer recited by the master and the recitation of two verses from the Acts of the Apostles and two others learned the day before. Being called upon to balance classical Rome against the church, boys would often commit to memory both a paragraph of Cicero and a passage from the funeral orations of Bossuet, Fléchier, or some other great seventeenth-century ecclesiastical rhetorician.

The fact that apostolic verse was presented to older collegians under the aegis of classical letters reflects not so much a staunchness in keeping faith with Christian doctrine as the quasi-religious prestige conferred upon Latinity. It must have been made clear to Gustave from the outset that all of his other subjects — Bible history, French grammar, geography, arithmetic, handwriting — trailed after Latin grammar as pages after a prince. In any event it became abundantly clear when he entered the sixth form at age eleven. Whole mornings would be devoted to texts such as *De viris illustribus urbis romae* (About Illustrious Men of the City of Rome). The classical program encompassed geography, in which Gustave came to familiarize himself with maps of the ancient world, and composition, for which prescribed themes were drawn from mythology. The only French author read was La Fontaine, who qualified for a passport by appearing in the company of the Roman fabulist Phaedrus.

Had his older friend Alfred Le Poittevin lifted Gustave above the transom of the sixth form, he would have seen a future crowded with Greek and Latin names: Cicero, Sallust, Cornelius Nepos, Quintilian, Horace, Lucian, Titus Livy, Virgil, Ovid, Tacitus, Plutarch. He would also have seen goose quills in the upper-division study hall working seven and one half hours a day at the mandarin tasks required of candidates for the baccalaureate degree. Young men composed speeches in Latin and Latin verse (with a dictionary to hand called the *Gradus ad Parnassum,* or the Step Toward Parnassus). They did translations from Latin into French (*version*) and from French into Latin (*thème*). During the 1830s, their load grew heavier with essays on ancient Rome, assigned by a scholar of great intellectual promise whose mentor at the École Normale Supérieure had been France's preeminent historian, Jules Michelet.

This hermetic discipline may seem to have been as alien to bourgeois France as Louis XIV's periwig, but in fact, the more mobile and acquisitive French society became, the stronger was the appeal of such disciplines both to its conservative elements and to new money hankering after an instant patina. Culture would no longer deserve its name when it concerned itself with the quotidian or the practical; it was *désintéressée* — selfless, or impersonal. It raised its proprietor above nature; it established an inner distance that guaranteed his virtue; it forged an essence impervious to motive; and it sanctified power. Where the uncouth were swayed by opportunism or greed or lust, men bred on the ancients would, ideally, speak from outside the moment, their education having situated them there. One historian of French pedagogy explains how this "classicization" worked:

> To write an oration was to put noble words in the mouths of great personages. Maximian writes to Diocletian imploring him not to renounce the Empire, François I to Charles V complaining of his incarceration, et cetera. The subject who spoke was always a great one: king or emperor, saint, savant, or poet. And what did one have these personages say? To be sure, nothing one might have happened to hear in everyday life but, rather, sturdy aphorisms. As in Corneille and Bossuet — who became classics for this very reason — one exhaled only great sentiments. "What pure and virtuous souls!" Villemain exclaims. These princes are oblivious to reasons of state, jealousy, deceit. . . . Honor, dignity, nobility, virtue, courage, sacrifice, repudiation of the world: on these heroic summits, generosity was the air one breathed.

Throughout the century, rhetoric crowned the academic curriculum. Schools accorded high honors to those who had written the most eloquent orations and done so in a dead language. Lest pupils discover examples of turpitude in, say, Ovid or Tacitus, pedagogues either expurgated the original or wrote for the ancients a literature that conformed to their own edifying mission (*De viris illustribus urbis romae* was one such forged antique). As it had under the ancien régime and during the French Revolution, when Jacobins invoked Greek and Roman worthies, Latin served to enthrone virtue in history and to reestablish, in secular terms, a dispensation from which mankind had fallen. It was the premise of rhetoric that a child who "put noble words in the mouths of great personages" year after year would, by virtue of this histrionic exercise, transcend himself, the better to exorcise childhood itself; antiquity represented an external model, but an external model that society's elect might be expected to internalize. "Real and serious to the core" is how one prime minister of the 1830s, François Guizot, eulogized another, Casimir Périer, as if making the case for his interment in the Panthéon. It was Guizot who declared on another occasion that men without Latin were "intellectual parvenus." Whatever the qualities of a successful industrialist or merchant, he remained of lower caste for lacking the objective musculature developed in rhetorical *progymnastica.* "Our bourgeoisie, even the most humble members of it, holds Latin and Greek dear," wrote a candidate for election to the High Council on Public Instruction two generations later. "They are the badge of a true higher school education. If [those schools] should ever abandon them, the bourgeoisie will repair to Church institutions. How can one make it understood to those who accept this mutilation of the curriculum that a house in which one learns only French does not differ significantly from primary school?" Latin separated not only the upper classes from the lower (annual tuition at the Collège royal was 750 francs, the entire annual income of a textile worker) but the men from the boys. Greek marked the distinction even more emphatically. An important body of opinion held, as Thomas Macaulay did in his *History of England,* that an age devoid of eminent statesmen who could read Sophocles and Plato with enjoyment was an age in decline.

No one addressed this issue more straightforwardly than an influential nineteenth-century bishop named Félix Dupanloup, in whose pronouncements Latin is the basis for creating superior minds and souls. "Children think, imagine, feel, write never more vigorously than in Latin, and, what is more, in Latin verse," he contended. Weaned from their mother tongue, "which they speak poorly," raw youths are led by a dead hand to the Elysian Fields, "where they meet none but men of genius and know only the language of Cicero, Vergil, Plato, Homer." Their linguistic expatriation, he wrote, redounded to the advantage of French itself, with the high-mindedness acquired during their sojourn in antiquity ennobling the vernacular. Dupanloup, who was fond of the metaphor contained in *culture,* signifying both intellectual culture and tillage, prescribed the study of classical languages as a devotional exercise or stoic discipline:

> The point of it all is to reach not the vain and banal word, but *the true word . . .* To do that, the primitive, natural, vulgar word must be broken and grafted; through art, through true art, through the true culture and the great education, it must be given a kind of new form, nobler and more elevated. Vergil's dictum must be applied to the soil of the mind. *Et qui proscisso quae suscitat aequore terga / Rursus in obliquum verso perrumpit aratro* [Much service, too, does he who turns his plough / And again breaks crosswise through the ridges he raised].

Like the prelate who consecrated a new church by spreading ashes on the floor and tracing the Greek and Latin alphabets in them, Dupanloup declared classical *lycées* and *collèges* to be schools of divine right. "The ruling classes will always be the ruling classes because they know Latin."

Until the last years of the Restoration, classical letters held almost absolute sway in Rouen, as they did in all forty-one royal collegiate schools; French figured hardly at all in the list of subjects for which prizes were awarded at August commencement each year. After 1830, the government, placating its liberal constituents, cautiously allowed the modern world to infiltrate the curriculum. As disconcerted as he must have been by the hurdy-gurdy that regularly cranked out the "Marseillaise" on the rue Maulevrier, Professor Magnier, an intransigent classicist whose mantra was *Le beau est la splendeur du vrai* ("The beautiful is the radiance of the true," from Plotinus), was undoubtedly far more annoyed by the ministerial decree reserving highest philosophical honors in senior year for a French essay rather than a Latin one. This move opened the door a crack, and other ostracized commoners slipped in. Young faculty felt freer to introduce French authors other than seventeenth-century ones alongside Latin and to teach French composition (*narration*), even before it became a sanctioned exercise in second form. History, which had been given short shrift by a regime bent on concealing Revolutionary France under a pall of white lilies, was restored its dignity. Mathematics and physics rose from the grave to which Restoration officials had consigned all science. And midway through high school, students began obligatorily to learn elements of a foreign language — English or German — in courses that met once a week.

Being quite minimal except for history, these additions did not amount to anything like true reform. Rouennais who took a utilitarian view of their children's prospects felt that the *toga virilis* draped over the curriculum before 1830 still enveloped it ten years later. Many rejected the Collège royal for private establishments offering an education better suited to the mercantile world. Others insisted that their state school negotiate with nineteenth-century realities. Typical of the latter was a letter signed by self-styled *pères de famille* eager to have Italian taught at the *collège*. "It is widely believed at present," they petitioned the minister of education, "that ancient languages should not constitute the be-all and end-all of a young person's scholarship and that the study of sciences and living languages is essential to any good education. However, what may be an elective feature of the curriculum elsewhere is a core component in industrial cities, where most graduates will embrace business careers. As for Italian, there are commercial and literary grounds for including a language both rich in classic texts and spoken in the workaday world. It goes without saying that royal collegiate schools would profit materially from a greater responsiveness to the intellectual needs of the populations in the midst of which they are situated." The hopes kindled by officialdom's apparent concession were at least half-extinguished in August 1840, when the government ruled that the tried-and-true methods used in Greek and Latin courses should be applied to those in English, German, and Italian. Thus, most young men groomed by book and quill to be future notables remained monolingual, unlike young women, who, like Caroline Flaubert, often received instruction from foreign governesses. For the latter, speaking one or another of the modern languages was a suitable accomplishment.

Had disgruntled *pères de famille* concerned themselves as much with the physical conditions of life for boarders as with the curriculum, they would have had abundant material for another grievance. Gone were the drumrolls defining class hours, the swords and the drills that identified Napoleonic lycées as nurseries of a military state; nevertheless, students under Louis-Philippe continued to endure the hardships of soldiers in bivouac. Cooped up all day long, except for a "recreation" hour, which was usually spent making friends and enemies, they were never free to run wild. Not until All Saints' Day, November 1, did rooms get heated, and even then the administration scrimped on firewood. To stay awake in study hall during the winter meant fighting off the cold, which inevitably won out. Although Gustave, when he grew taller than most boys his age, would have had them believe that he descended from Viking rovers, his imagination came to embrace a sunlit Levant girdled by a limpid sea. Washing did not figure prominently in the daily routine of boarders, and those with sensitive noses suffered even more from foul odors than from chilblain. Nothing much had changed since Balzac's school days at the Collège Vendôme, where every room stank of what in *Louis Lambert* he calls "intramural humus." There was a fountain in the courtyard for splashing one's face, near an enclosed urinal, but the student body was bathed once a trimester on average, and in the best circumstances had its feet cleaned every fortnight, without benefit of soap or strigils. Grit accumulated underfoot as charwomen tried vainly to sweep floors clean. Food smuggled out of the dining hall eventually betrayed its presence in secret niches all over the dormitory.

Adolescents living as inmates deprived of sensual pleasure (for which they compensated with much masturbating and cigarette smoking in the urinal) made the collegiate school a tinderbox that wanted only one more deprivation or a political spark from the world outside to explode. In 1819, when resurgent liberals and ultraroyalists faced each other at daggers drawn, civil war broke out in three elite Paris lycées. In 1831, shortly before Gustave entered the Collège royal, students who had barricaded themselves in dormitories to challenge the expulsion of forty-seven classmates were flushed out with water hoses. Such full-blown mutinies (which in Rouen may have begun as a protest against the military exercises reinstituted briefly after the July Revolution) occurred, of course, far less often than individual delinquencies. But, whatever form it took, insubordination did not go unpunished. The school had a detention cell in which it locked up anyone guilty of major mischief. For lesser offenses the professor assigned the scapegrace a *pensum,* or task, and made him spend free time copying and recopying Latin aphorisms.

Later on, Flaubert, when he wasn't execrating the collegiate school or recalling it nostalgically, was able to understand boarding school as the first episode in a chronicle of internments. From that later perspective he would also have seen that the camaraderie he shared with Ernest Chevalier foreshadowed the succession of fraternal bonds to which he clung over the years like a castaway grasping a lifeline. The letters the two boys exchanged during holidays show Gustave reaching out for love and solace and companionship. "We are united by fraternal love, so to speak," he declared in 1832, at age ten, assuring Ernest that this wasn't just rodomontade. "Yes, I who have strong feelings, I would walk a thousand leagues if necessary to rejoin the best of my friends, for nothing is as sweet as friendship. Oh, sweet friendship! How would we survive without it?" In a letter sent from Nogent the following year and signed "Yours unto death," he informed Ernest that an apprentice to his Uncle Parain, the goldsmith, had made him a seal linking their two names. Never had Werther bereft of Charlotte or Adolphe of Ellénore felt emptier than Gustave in Ernest's absence, and Dr Flaubert, a normally indulgent father, more than once had to refuse him permission to visit Les Andelys. If it were up to him alone, Gustave wrote in September 1833, he would instantly reserve a seat in the stagecoach, but the idea had been vetoed (on other occasions the Flauberts visited the Chevaliers all together, and Gustave was to spend several Easter holidays with Ernest). "Man proposes and God disposes, as M. Delamier says toward the end of the last scene of the play *Le romantisme empêche tout.*" Already an inspired correspondent, Gustave kept account of letters sent and received, scolding the beloved friend who did not always return his coin in equal measure. "Here I've written you two letters and you've answered with only one, and not a big one at that." His hunger for confidences taxed a postal service that delivered mail several times a day, including Sunday.

Not surprisingly, the prepubescent chums engaged in irreverent toilet humor. What remains of Gustave's early correspondence (almost all of Chevalier's letters have disappeared) suggests that there was much giggling over the posterior, its functions and embarrassments. It tickled him to learn, for example, that the student of a well-known regional painter named Eustache-Hyacinthe Langlois (himself a former apprentice of Jacques-

Louis David) had almost met with disaster in his teacher's privy. "As soon as he placed his cheeks on the seat, it cracked, and if he hadn't held tight he would have fallen into Père Langlois's excrement." That this young man went by the sobriquet "Jesus" made his near mishap all the more amusing. Scatological associations were, indeed, often visited upon Christ.

The irreverence they cultivated even more exuberantly showed in a precocious disdain for social ritual and convention, for clichés and received ideas. His New Year's Day message to Ernest in 1832 was that he, too, found New Year's Day "stupid." Standing as godfather for a second cousin in Nogent did not do him credit until he half denied the honor of it with affirmations to Ernest that he had recited an Ave and a Pater almost inaudibly and, all in all, bungled his "poor" goddaughter's baptism. But above all, being unconventional required privileged bourgeois such as he to malign their royal benefactor, and Gustave, who may have repeated what Dr Flaubert or family friends said at home, joined the chorus of derision that made itself faintly heard when the king paid Rouen an official visit on September 9, 1833. In preparations for this signal event, city officials spared no expense. There were parades and fireworks. There was a command performance of Auber and Scribe's comic opera *Fra Diavolo* at the Théâtre des Arts, where new candelabras illuminated obscure corners of the huge hall. Spectators at a subscription ball queued half a mile uphill, as far as brothels on the rue de la Cicogne, for the pleasure of seeing M. Ernest Delamarre, a rich merchant, dance with the princess Clementine, and Nemours, the king's son, squire Mlle Josephine Teste. There were other festivities, all but one of which Gustave eschewed. "Louis-Philippe and family are now in the city of Corneille's birth," he sneered to Ernest. "How stupid people are, how dim-witted. . . . Imagine scurrying around for a king, voting thirty thousand francs for celebrations, importing musicians from Paris for thirty-five hundred francs, going to such trouble for what? for a king! Standing 5½ hours on line for what? for a king! Ah, how dumb can people be!!! I myself saw nothing, neither the military review, nor the king's arrival, nor the princesses, nor the princes. I did poke my nose out for the fireworks, only because I was being nagged to do it."

In the fullness of time he would gladly bestir himself for an emperor whose title to imperial grandeur was rather more questionable than Louis-Philippe's to kingship. Even so, he never relinquished visions of the subversive few, of himself and a soul mate united against the philistine world, marking letters with a common seal and signing works with a common quill. Gustave proposed that he and Ernest form an "association" to write one thing and another, whether comedies, stories, or dreams. The two were, as he saw it at age twelve, "children of literature," born on a green felt stage for some exceptional fate. Because they interrupted this companionship, school holidays, fervently anticipated though they may have been, brought a feeling of loss. And the thoughts that escorted Ernest around the collegiate school continued to seek him out from wherever the Flauberts took Gustave during the summer break: Déville, Nogent, Fontainebleau, Paris, Versailles, the Channel coast. Thrilled by a bloody melodrama at the Porte Saint-Martin theater, he could hardly wait for a reunion at the Hôtel-Dieu or the *collège* to describe all seven murders in it. Fishing with his father at a pond on Flaubert property outside Nogent, he greatly enjoyed himself, "as you would have done," he wrote, "had you been there." Collecting seashells at Trouville in August 1834, where stormy seas and the mist-shrouded sky made an awesome spectacle, he saved choice ones for his "friend of friends," whom he always had in mind. "Return, return, life of my life, soul of my soul, for I would like to compose again with friend Ernest . . . Vacation would be twice as good, and don't imagine that I'm exaggerating when I say that I'd find life insipid if you didn't come. That's the absolute truth."

The absolute truth lay somewhere between "twice as good" and "insipid." At Déville, walking the country lanes with a Newfoundland named Néo and playing with his beloved sister, he didn't languish. Nor did he feel desolate at Trouville, which was to figure as importantly in his youth as Cabourg would in Marcel Proust's. This hamlet fifteen kilometers down the Côte de Grâce from Honfleur is first mentioned in the 1834 letter to Ernest, years before it became a fashionable resort for well-heeled bourgeois lured by, among other things, Charles Mozin's lovely images of it at the annual Salon, and years before ocean bathing became an imaginable pleasure. The Flauberts traveled in several heavily freighted carriages via Pont l'Évêque, a short distance inland, where they visited relatives and inspected their farms. Following the river Touques north to its confluence with the sea, they left their vehicles just outside Trouville, a fishing village perched on the flank of a cliff that sloped steeply down to the tidal stream. A towpath and narrow quay ran alongside it as far as a knob-nosed promontory jutting into the Channel. To the east, where villas and hotels would one day stand side by side opposite a boardwalk, was pristine beach stretching several kilometers toward another bluff called les Roches Noires. Westward beyond the Touques, which people could ford on horseback at low tide if they had business in a tiny village called Dosville or owned one of the ten farms situated thereabout, lay swampy meadows good mainly for pasturing livestock. Under Napoleon III, Dosville would metamorphose into Deauville.

Not until the late 1840s, when steam-driven ferries with names like *La Reine des Plages, L'Hirondelle,* and *La Gazelle* began to ply between Le Havre and Trouville, did vacationers visit for a weekend or a day. Summer folk came to visit and stayed at the few hostelries available. An inexpensive boardinghouse run by a woman known as la mère Ozerais was the favorite domicile of painters who followed in Charles Mozin's footsteps. Others, including the Flauberts, rented rooms from Louis-Victor David and his wife, la mère David, at the Auberge de l'Agneau d'Or on the quay. Known for her cuisine, which recommended her mightily to a schoolboy sick of institutional food, la mère David cut as quaint a figure in her lace coif as her husband did in his tasseled wool bonnet. While she attended to guests, Louis-Victor played Maître Jacques, improving their livelihood by whatever means in a community that could hardly imagine prosperous times ahead. When he had done serving as tallier of the fishing fleet's daily catch, he became the town clerk recording births and deaths. Under Napoleon, landowners cognizant of his service in the Grand Army appointed him *garde-champêtre,* or rural constable, and five years later agreed to have him sacked for neglect of duty. This disappointment was apparently not held against Louis-Victor, for the affable man who greeted Dr Flaubert and family in 1834 did so not only as Trouville's principal innkeeper but as the village's deputy mayor.

Having taken lessons at M. Fessart's swimming school in Rouen, Gustave flourished in Trouville. Undaunted by a drowning that occurred during his first days there, he seemed to have found his true element and swam with strength and stamina. Physical exertion on land repelled him — it always would. But in the sea this slightly knock-kneed boy who chafed at rules and limits moved like a rapturous young Triton. Mornings were spent on the sandy beach, weather permitting. In the afternoon, the family, accompanied by Caroline's English governess, often took donkey rides up above the Roches Noires, across hills and dells, where immense, shimmering expanses of the Channel flashed into view through brambles lining the road. Other playgrounds were the dunes at Dosville beyond the Touques, which rose between a large, oval marsh that oddly prefigured the racetrack destined to make Deauville world famous and a beach that abounded in little creatures washing up from the deep. On excessively hot days the family kept to its rooms. "The dazzling brightness from without rammed bars of light through the blinds," he remembered. "No noise in the village. No one on the street below. This enveloping silence magnified the stillness of things. Somewhere in the distance, hammers could be heard banging plugs into hulls, and a sultry breeze wafted toward us the scent of tar." But when the fishermen returned toward evening, everyone made for the jetties to watch boats approaching Trouville with headsails billowing. The catch came ashore in hampers and filled pushcarts lined up at dockside.

When summer drew to a close in 1834, Gustave wended his way home again, wondering how the vacation that had been anticipated so eagerly two months earlier amid the bravos, the blaring brass, the elegant toilettes and valedictions of commencement day, had slipped away. Still, there were pleasant prospects to buoy him. He would, of course, retrieve his dear friend Ernest Chevalier, and he would study on a more sophisticated level at the collegiate school, with new teachers thought to be capable of recognizing intellectual talent and cultivating it.

IV

Stories and Histories

FOREMOST AMONG Gustave's new teachers was his professor of history, Adolphe Chéruel, a native Rouennais only twelve years older than he. Described by one school inspector as "lively, clear, precise," he exhibited those qualities in his entire person. With long dark hair and a prognathous jaw, the lanky Chéruel commanded more respect than he may have found useful in trying to make laconic Norman boys think aloud. He himself spoke very well indeed, lecturing without benefit of notes, moving nimbly from the probative detail to the larger picture, and placing great emphasis on the geographical context of events. Like his teacher Michelet — a brilliant writer whose genius for setting scenes chimed with the literary romantics' enthusiasm for local color — Chéruel adduced original documents wherever possible. His later works would include an edition of Mazarin's correspondence, a compendium of Norman chronicles dating back to 473, various monographs on Louis XIV's administration that drew heavily on manuscript material in the Imperial Library, and, above all, a *Dictionnaire historique des institutions, moeurs et coutumes de la France*. It was noted that he had a researcher's telltale pallor, but the tenacious archivist could shake off library dust, take wing, and deploy his immense erudition over a broader landscape. Almost all of this scholarly writing was done after Gustave's graduation from the Collège royal and after Chéruel himself left to assume a chair in Paris at the École Normale. During the 1840s he restricted his scholarship to medieval Rouen. The works with which he gained wider recognition were, if not equal to Michelet's *Histoire de France* in girth, still of encyclopedic proportions.

That anyone could view human affairs so comprehensively dazzled Gustave, and this example planted or nurtured the seed of what later blossomed into Faustian ambitions. Taken up with medieval France when European poets were kindling enthusiasm for everything medieval, Chéruel turned increasingly toward the classical period to study monarchical institutions, which Michelet, who indulged his own proletarian sympathies, did not treat evenhandedly. At the collegiate school, Chéruel surveyed all of Western civilization and, moreover, offered seniors a course in the philosophy of history that acquainted them with names such as Herder and Vico. The idea that societies were to be studied as evolving organisms governed by tradition, myth, language, and circumstance, that every age had a unique character manifest in all of its cultural expressions, formed the basis of Chéruel's pedagogy. What a student inferred from Plutarch would not have earned high marks from Chéruel, who marshaled all of his knowledge against the notion that history resided chiefly in the lives of great men or in the will and purpose of God.

Chéruel was young enough to recognize that even a boy smitten by the past, who would twice carry off prizes in history, might not always find the balanced disquisitions of even the most colorful historian as seductive as the tumult of historical potboilers. And he was literary enough to recognize that the fancy-free novelist with whom he couldn't compete turned rich soil for the historian's future gain. To be sure, Gustave loved Chéruel's lectures on the Burgundian court and at Chéruel's suggestion delved into Barante's voluminous *Histoire des ducs de Bourgogne*. He devoured the works of Michelet: *Histoire romaine*, the first volumes of his *Histoire de France*. The collegiate school did assign historical texts that straddled disciplines other than history (Latin with Titus Livy, among others, French with Voltaire and La Bruyère). But like many febrile adolescents, Gustave stole time from schoolwork for a dissident syllabus crammed with Alexandre Dumas (*Catherine Howard, La Tour de Nesle, Don Juan de Marana, Isabel de Bavière*), Victor Hugo (*Marie Tudor, Notre-Dame de Paris, Angelo*), and Walter Scott (*Quentin Durward, Anne de Geierstein*). Before long, halfway through his thirteenth year, Gustave — unlike most adolescents — decided to pay some bloody tribute of his own to the Moloch of the age. Between September 1835 and September 1836 he wrote five stories in the Romantic idiom of medieval and Renaissance court intrigue, all dramatizing brutalities unchecked by conscience and needing few scenes to produce half a dozen corpses.

The body count almost matches the tally of family romances. A flagrant case in point is a story called "La Peste à Florence," which calls to mind Alfred de Musset's celebrated play *Lorenzaccio* (published two years earlier) and reflects contemporary fascination with the hugger-mugger of patrician clans murdering one another in sixteenth-century Italy. Cosme de Médicis, the grand duke who rules Tuscany, has two sons — one, François, greatly favored over the other, Garcia. Even as the plague breaks out in Florence, the desire to kill François overwhelms Garcia. On learning that the pope has appointed François a cardinal, he arranges to confront his brother in the forest during a hunt organized by Cosme and slays him. "Ah, you tremble" are his parting words. "Tremble then and suffer as I have trembled and suffered. You and your vaunted wisdom, you had no idea how nearly a man resembles a demon when injustice has turned him into a wild beast. Ah, I suffer just seeing you alive." Brought to account, Garcia suffers François's fate at the hands of his avenging father, who impales him beside François's cadaver in a room "dank and sepulchral like a dissection theater."

Gustave had another go at the theme of sibling rivalry in an unfinished story entitled "Un secret de Philippe le Prudent." Here the feud, which involves sixteenth-century Spanish Habsburgs, pits Charles V's legitimate son, Philippe, against his bastard, Don Juan of Austria. Crowned emperor when Charles renounced worldly affairs, Philippe rules the more uneasily for having a half brother who, misbegotten though he is, possesses all those qualities of body and mind that he himself lacks. Key words of the Romantic lexicon link Don Juan, imbued with "energy," "strength," and "passion," to François, and a runty Philippe, limp and bloodless, to Garcia. Philippe, whose zealous prosecution of heresy through the grand inquisitor masks his craven purposes, will not feel imperial or even real until all of his male kin lie dead around him. Distressed to learn that Juan has escaped from prison, he is equally threatened by the specter of his self-imprisoned father, who commands more respect in sackcloth than he does in ermine. "Philippe feared the renown of this man, it weighed upon him, he cursed it, for whenever he entertained an ambitious dream, the face of Charles Quint would straightway appear before him as if to snatch his portion of immortality. The night after losing a battle, he seemed to hear a hollow, frightful voice saying to him: 'Philippe! Mind my crown and scepter! You are dulling their luster.' If he won a battle, the voice would return to utter only a single word: 'Pavia.'"* Meanwhile, under surveillance in the royal palace and bound to appear before the Inquisition is Philippe's son Don Carlos, another Romantic personage, distinguished by a Byronic limp and by passions

---

*Pavia was the site of Charles's victory over François I. Philippe's victories are trivial in comparison.

that fray his soul "like a sharp sword wearing out its scabbard." Philippe, who has made his son's inamorata his own bride, watches him intently through a peephole, fearful of all that is hidden from view.

To write these stories and others, Gustave, without scrupling much about historical accuracy, used an omnium-gatherum of sources: P. F. Tissot's *Leçons et modèles de littérature française,* the aforementioned works on his extracurricular syllabus, and P. L. Guinguenc's *Histoire littéraire d'Italie,* which was widely known. But none served him better than his own psyche and experience. The love he professed for father did not brim over onto brother, least of all during the mid-1830s, when Achille, a medical student in Paris, lived at home and received anatomy lessons from Achille-Cléophas. Nor did it spare him the anguish born of Oedipal conflict; on the contrary. As swords abound in Gustave's stories, so scalpels abounded at home. Entertaining murderous fantasies, touching himself surreptitiously, spying on his parents making love (which the story inverts, with father spying on son), playing for attention at the expense of rivals who cut up bodies every day, might have dreadful consequences. Baby Gustave surrounded by half-flayed faces with knives between their teeth told him so, in his recurrent dream. Still, he could not easily forbear. Perceived slights *en famille* felt like mortal wounds, and his wrath, which in any event made everyone take notice of him, was proportionate to the danger. It drowned out the voices that belittled him from within. "In every man's life there are pains and sorrows so keen, mortifications so poignant, that for the pleasure of insulting his tormentor he will abandon and contemptuously discard his masculine dignity like a theater mask" is how "La Peste à Florence" concludes.

Would Gustave, with this remarkable conclusion, have universalized the blackness in his heart and avenged himself on his own credulity? In losing his aplomb, the gullible boy unmasked "every man," and in so doing he proposed to reveal history itself as a masquerade of rogues tricked out in suits of virtue, of worthy heirs dressed in rags, of valets more princely than their masters but condemned by an accident of birth to wear livery. Gustave the author provided Gustave the student with therapeutic recreation. These stories of Romantic inspiration may indeed be said to have subverted the classical program laid upon him at school: far from impersonating great men in noble speeches, they uttered the unspeakable behind closed doors. One exception — and it stands as a rhetorical tour de force that boys years older than he might gladly have plagiarized — is the letter Charles V (now known as "Father Arsène") in "Un secret de Philippe le Prudent" writes, from a monastery, to his dear son Don Juan. It reads in part:

Here is a letter. It will perhaps be my last, and you will understand the reason when I acquaint you with my state of mind. Oh, if you knew in what straits your father, Charles Quint, finds himself, you would scoff at human nature and say pityingly: "Yes, he did well to remove a heavy crown from his wobbly head, to hand over the scepter with his shaky hands, above all to exchange his royal mantle for the shroud of a walking corpse." For a walking corpse is what I am in this monk's habit, I who count the hours as they pass, and pass too slowly, alas, to appease my weariness of soul . . . Ah! when evening falls and I, all alone, give free rein to my thoughts and memories, I often contemplate the heavy sword over my bed and think: "You, loyal companion of my victories and conquests, that smashed so many crowns, crushed so many thrones. Ah, if, perchance, posterity should cast an envious eye on you with the warrior in mind who whetted your blade on human skulls, say to them: No, don't deceive yourself! He knew no happiness! His happiness was the forced mirth of a professional jester, of the man who plays a part." Happiness? It's like one of those long-forgotten childhood dreams that come alive on a starry night when I sit gazing at the countryside through the bars of my cell . . . I am on my throne again, amid my courtiers, or on my black steed, at the battle of Pavia, and I remember what I saw, what I did, what I said in days of power and pride. Then I lower my gaze upon myself, I study hands furrowed with scars, . . . I finger my white beard and say: "There is Charles Quint, king of Spain, emperor of Austria, terror of François I . . . There he is, an obscure monk buried in a convent!" And I am seized with the desire to cast away this sorry existence, to mount my throne and horse, command my troops, wield my sword once more. I move toward it but totter, my hands go limp, my head slumps to my chest and I fall back on my bed, sadder and more desperate than ever. Only one memory cheers me and it is of you, dear Don Juan. Yes, when I think of you my heart sings, my soul blooms; should a light breeze ruffle my black garments at night, I say: "Oh! if only this same breeze were catching the feather in my Don Juan's cap!" Whereupon I suck it up lovingly and greedily . . . My thoughts go to that handsome dark head so full of fire and energy, that rosy countenance, those large blue eyes which epitomize life itself for me . . . For I love you, Juano, as much as the heart of a man blighted by royalty can still feel tenderness and love. If the legitimate son were that of the beloved woman, you would now be king of Spain.

There might not have been another adolescent at the collegiate school gifted enough to bring off this fantasy of a powerful father (identified with the blade he apostrophizes) retiring from active life of his own accord, taking monastic vows, honoring them regretfully, and bestowing upon his love child as upon his own impotent self a crown no longer his for the giving. That the story has no denouement is itself eloquent. It leaves Don Juan in limbo, a son but illegitimate, authorized by his father to rule but unable to wear his crown, and thus foreshadowing Jules in the original *Éducation sentimentale,* of whom Flaubert was to write: "Of his own free will, and like a king abdicating the day he's crowned, he had forever renounced possession of everything earned and bought in the world, pleasures, honors, money, the delights of love and the triumphs of ambition." How many Flaubertian heroes, beginning with Charles V's absent heir in "Un secret de Philippe le Prudent" and continuing with Frédéric Moreau frightened away from Zoraide Turc's brothel in *L'Éducation sentimentale* (definitive version), would turn out to be paradigms of the monarch who exits not after a glorious reign but the day or the hour before he assumes power.

Judging by an essay he wrote in March 1837, "L'influence des arabes d'Espagne sur la civilisation française du moyen âge," and the detailed outline of another composition on Emperor Henry IV's clash with Pope Gregory VII, one can easily imagine that Gustave might, like the great medievalist Fustel de Coulanges, have become a historian under Adolphe Chéruel's tutelage, if he hadn't gone after a career in theater. As the sway of historical fiction diminished, that of historical scholarship greatly increased. "Now that I'm no longer writing, that I've made myself an historian (so-called), that I read books, that I affect serious attitudes and in the midst of all that maintain enough sangfroid and aplomb to look at myself in the mirror with a straight face, I welcome the pretext of a letter to let myself go, to postpone my note taking," he confided to Ernest Chevalier in June 1837. A diligent note taker all of his life, Gustave tested his seriousness of purpose against some muscular figures. To be sure, he read lots of Walter Scott for a play entitled *Loys XI*. But he immersed himself in Michelet's *Histoire de France*, *Histoire romaine*, and *Mémoires de Luther*, in Abel Villemain's *Cours de littérature du moyen âge*, in Sismondi's *De la littérature du Midi en Europe*, and in Gibbon's *Decline and Fall of the Roman Empire*.

Not that he ceased to write stories, only that after 1836 he refrained from drawing upon history to people them. His fantasy was given freer rein, and, indeed, the "child of literature," as he described himself, made much of freedom. He had spoken for it as shrilly as the most rabid republican when in 1835 Louis-Philippe's government muzzled theater and the press. "I note with indignation that dramatic censorship is going to be reinforced and freedom of the press abolished," he wrote to Ernest. "Yes, this law will pass, because the representatives of the people are nothing but a bunch of vile toadies with eyes for the main chance [and] a spine for stooping . . . But come the third revolution, . . . royal heads will roll, rivers of blood will flow. The man of letters is being denied his conscience, his artistic conscience . . . Farewell, and let us always apply ourselves to art, which transcends people, crowns, and kings." Unmentioned in any letter is the act of terror that provoked these so-called September laws. On July 28, during a military parade through Paris, bullets from two dozen muskets fastened to a frame, positioned at apartment windows, and primed to go off all at once raked the royal entourage as it made its way down the boulevard du Temple (where Flaubert would one day reside), missing Louis-Philippe but killing some forty escorts. The vicious, often brilliant cartoons published by *La Caricature* and *Le Charivari* and articles in the republican press, which gave the king no quarter, were thought to have incited the botched regicide. Now they could no longer appear with impunity, although of course the laws against them did nothing more than blow away the foam of a boiling sea.

Gustave's pugnacious tirade reflects the confidence instilled in him by a master with whom he studied for two years, in the fifth and fourth forms. Henry Gourgaud-Dugazon, who hailed from the Caux region, joined the faculty in 1834 and had Gustave on his first roster. Significantly older than Chéruel, he cut a more paternal figure. "Zealous," "devoted," and "good at inspiring a love of work" is how school inspectors portrayed him at first. The prizes won in the Concours général, or national competitive examinations, by students he prepared corroborate this evaluation. But certain other traits, stigmatized as defects of character, which were soon to weigh heavily against him, may have been what Gustave found most appealing about Gourgaud. After several years it was noted that he lacked "aplomb," and this word, or words to the same effect, recurred in every subsequent judgment. One inspector faulted him for losing control of his class, then trying to regain it with onerous tasks. A move to Versailles in 1838, where Gourgaud taught until retirement, did not improve his reputation or advance his career. Negative touches now became broad strokes, picturing him as a learned man whose timidity made him the natural prey of boisterous adolescents. "Unfortunately he has always wanted firmness and initiative, and now wants them more emphatically than ever," concluded the official who at length urged him to quit. "Students acquire or maintain habits of dissipation, of irreverence toward the master, and their work suffers for it. Although they recognize his erudition and devotion, parents complain."

To Gourgaud, Dr and Mme Flaubert should have had nothing to express but gratitude for befriending their son in a harsh environment, for taking his ambitions seriously, detecting his gift straightaway, and nurturing it. The nurturing was done with composition topics called *narrations,* which normally got assigned to second-formers as preparation for Rhetoric, the penultimate year of high school. A typical exercise of this kind set forth a story line or "argument" and developed it in a narrative, on which the student, using figurative language wherever appropriate, modeled his own version. Another type might require him to portray a famous personage. In 1835–36 Gustave wrote six such exercises altogether for Gourgaud, moving so stylishly from one assignment to the next that his teacher must have felt like Cambuscan turning a pin in the ear of his brazen horse. Gustave's thick little notebook contains a caricature portrait of Lord Byron (galloping full tilt with a cigarette in his mouth), a humorous anecdote about Frederick the Great, a story inspired by Dumas's *Tour de Nesle,* another about the romantic exploits of a Corsican condottiere named San Pietro Ornano, a variation on Prosper Mérimée's *Matteo Falcone* (recently published), and a Gothic tale entitled "Le Moine des Chartreux" (The Carthusian Monk), based on one in a textbook called *Nouvelles narrations françaises* by A. Filon. In this last composition Gustave made the most of material peculiarly suited to his fantasy life. As Filon's "argument" goes, a Carthusian at the funeral of his prior notes that the corpse wears a gold ring on its finger, and resolves to steal it, which he does after entering the crypt in the dead of night. No sooner has he turned away, however, than he finds himself grabbed from behind, as if by the violated hand. Unaware that his wide sleeve has caught under a nail, he instantly dies of fright. And how was Gustave to make this tale his own? By making his own protagonist, Bernardo, a prisoner of his religious vocation who longs for worldly pleasures he will never enjoy, doomed to seek gratification in images and fetishes, one of which is the gold ring. All the monks know that the prior had taken vows in the aftermath of a passionate love affair, had salvaged only this ring from the wreckage, and wore it as if one part of him would never divorce memories of amorous youth. Driven not by money lust but by the obsessive desire to possess his superior's youthful passion, to live it vicariously, to inhabit a nuptial chamber rather than a cell, and to furnish his pretense with this golden talisman, Bernardo clearly springs from the same family as Charles Quint, who, wedded to a mainly emblematic sword, cherished the illusion of conquest through his proxy. Also related is Emma Bovary, embroidering the marquis d'Andervilliers' silver cigar case with erotic fantasies. From Bernardo's cell window can be seen a chateau, which substitutes for heaven:

> Oh! In there are men full of life, bounding over the dance floor in a jerky, delirious waltz! There are women spinning around and around, swept along in the arms of their partners; there are servants in gold livery, horses whose trappings cost someone as many hours of toil as my internment has cost me hours of anguish; there are resplendent chandeliers, diamonds sparkling in the mirrors.

Fright was not drama enough to satisfy Gustave. He has Bernardo fall backward, smash his skull against the coffin's lid, and bleed all over it. Visiting the crypt several years later, the monks discover a nameless skeleton pinned to their prior's coffin, with, on one of its digits, the ring that betrayed a dream of freedom and manhood.

The conjunction of *eros* and *thanatos* informing these earliest works was the keynote for much of what followed, and in Gustave's early teens, 1836–37, a dozen or more tales designated by literary historians as "philosophical" and "fantastical" flowed from him with a facility that would have confounded the older Flaubert. In December 1836, for example, three days after his fifteenth birthday, he produced a story entitled "Rage et impuissance" (subtitled "Conte malsain pour les nerfs sensibles et les âmes dévotes"), about a man buried alive. Here again, Gustave cut ready-made material to the measure of his own fantasy life. Visitations from beyond, preternatural colloquies, turning tables, galvanic resuscitations, animal magnetism, were all grist for a romantic generation that wanted material evidence of life after death or of some transcendent order of being. Under the July monarchy, with the cholera epidemic still a fresh memory, newspapers often reported stories from England or Germany of people buried alive while in a state of trance mimicking death and awakening in their tombs or during the funeral service. These would not have gone undiscussed at the Hôtel-Dieu.

The protagonist of Gustave's story is, indeed, a German, and a doctor. The name of his town, Mussen, may have been intended to suggest that he lived duty bound in the homeland of categorical imperatives, though his own name, Ohmlin, a play on *homme*, affirms his universality. Exhausted after an arduous day of rounds in harsh winter weather, Ohmlin takes opium tablets and lapses into a comalike sleep from which he cannot be roused by his servant or by colleagues assembled for the purpose of deciding whether he is still alive. The majority judge him to be dead, and a grief-stricken cortege buries him under snow-covered ground, despite his dog's protests. In the grave and having ostensibly shuffled off this mortal coil, Ohmlin, not yet awake, dreams of voluptuous women, of blue skies and sun, of incense and pomegranates in a city studded with golden minarets.

> The Orient with its fairies, its caravans crossing the sand. The Orient with its seraglios . . . [Ohmlin] saw the white wings of angels singing verses of the Koran into the ears of the Prophet, the pure, roseate lips of women, large black eyes with love for him alone . . . He dreamed of love in a tomb. But the dream evaporated and the tomb remained.

Freed from the shackles of dailiness, Ohmlin, like Bernardo, embraces a vision of ecstatic fulfillment for which there is otherwise no room in the prison house of life. What promised to save them damns them instead, and the golden pleasure dome shines ironically over their skeletal remains. But unlike Bernardo, Ohmlin, lying fully conscious underground, has time to vituperate against the God who won't resurrect him. "Do you think I'll pray to you in my last hour? . . . Should I bless the hand that strikes me, should I embrace the executioner? Oh, reassemble yourself in human form and visit me in my tomb that I may transport you toward the eternity that will devour you, too, one day." In a mock epilogue entitled "Moral (cynical) to indicate appropriate conduct at the hour of death," Gustave enlisted the authority of two writers who had meanwhile become his constant companions: Montaigne and Rabelais. How might they have expressed their view of prospects for life after death? he asked. Each in his own way, he answered: Montaigne with *Que sais-je?* (What do I know?) and Rabelais with *peut-être* (perhaps).

Rage and Impotence might serve as an apposite title for the collected stories, through which Gustave's characters parade like lifers in solitary confinement regretting the virility they lost or the women they could never possess. Another example is "Bibliomanie," which has something about it of Balzac's *Recherche de l'absolu* and Scott's *The Antiquarian,* but whose principal source was that of so much Romantic fiction: the *Gazette des Tribunaux,* or *Court Gazette.* Greatly impressed by the trial of a Catalonian book dealer convicted of murdering both a competitor, who had outbid him for some rare item, and clients, whom he robbed of valuable books they had just bought from him, Gustave turned it to his own account in Giacomo, a young man of sepulchral appearance who has become a monkish book dealer after being a bibliomanic monk. Except at auctions, Giacomo disdains the marketplace. In love with incunabula as objects to be admired for their material beauty — their gilt, their odor, their gothic embellishments — he cannot acquire enough "sacred" books. Lusting after each new prize, he lusts the more insatiably because he is in fact illiterate and lives amid his collection like the eunuch in a harem. This hermetic world collapses when another collector, his rich archrival, buys the only extant copy of the first book ever published in Spain, a Bible. "[Baptisto], whose fame he hated with an artist's hatred . . . had become a burden," writes Gustave, ingenuously depicting once again an Oedipal war waged at unequal odds. "He was always the one who carried manuscripts away from public auction; he outbid and obtained. Oh, how often did the poor monk, in his dreams of wealth and ambition, see Baptisto's long hand reach across the crowd, as on auction days, to make off with some treasure . . . he had long coveted!" The plot thickens as soon as Baptisto triumphs. His shop burns down with him inside, whereupon Giacomo, who didn't set the fire, nonetheless gains his vengeance by salvaging the prize of prizes. It won't be his to keep, however. Disaster befalls Barcelona in a crime wave that litters the streets with corpses, and the city, seeking its nemesis as Thebes sought a scapegoat for its plague, indicts Giacomo, who is found to possess the rare book. "People didn't know on whom to blame the horrible scourge; for misfortune must be ascribed to the stranger, but good luck to oneself." A clever defense lawyer, in discovering abroad a second copy of the Bible, subverts the case against him, but as it turns out, Giacomo would sooner die than forfeit the idea of possessing the first, the one-and-only, the rarest. He proclaims himself guilty of every crime alleged, securing his own extinction, and at the end rips apart the second copy with this parting shot: "You lied, Monsieur l'avocat. Didn't I tell you it was the only copy in Spain?"

"Bibliomanie" was Gustave's first published work, appearing in the pink pages of a short-lived review called *Le Colibri*, "The Humming Bird." A lateral step took his imagination from the book lover unable to read to a sensitive brute unable to speak in a story with the Latin title "Quidquid volueris," "Whatever you want." Here the protagonist, Djalioh, is the fruit of an experiment performed by a French aristocrat in Brazil, Paul de Monville, who for his callous amusement has mated a black woman to an orangutan. When de Monville repatriates himself to wed his beautiful, rich cousin Adèle de Lansac, he brings the ape-man with him. Djalioh excites great curiosity as he moves among titled ladies and gentlemen, mutely observing them and suffering their glances in turn. Humiliation has worn him out at seventeen. A creature of sensibility, unlike his jaded master, he is, however, without the means to order his thoughts, to make himself understood, to open his heart, to transcend his freakishness. When he does reach for an instrument of expression, seizing a violin at the Monvilles' wedding ball and playing it as a child might, cacophonously, he isolates himself further. "The bow leaped off the strings like an elastic ball," wrote Gustave, who had encountered an ape playing a violin in Balzac's *Physiologie du mariage*.

> The music was herky-jerky, high-pitched and shrill. One felt oppressed by it, as if the notes were of lead and weighed upon one's breast. Then there were bold arpeggios, octaves ascending like a Gothic spire, notes that bunched together, and scattered . . . And all these sounds [were] without measure, without rhythm, without melody, vague, fleeting thoughts that followed one another like a reel of demons, or dreams that eddy around in a ceaseless whirl . . . Sometimes he would stop, alarmed by the noise. He would smile stupidly and resume with more love the course of his reverie.

Denied all that he desires — the elegance of good breeding, the gift of speech, the grace of swans, the love of beautiful women, and, above all, Adèle de Monville, who in due course becomes a mother — Djalioh finally explodes. With his human impulses stifled, he yields to his bestial self, raping Adèle, killing her, dashing out her child's brains and then his own. Nor is this innocent granted recognition of his humanity beyond the grave. Humiliated in life, he is gawked at posthumously as a skeleton behind the glass of a zoological exhibit. Meanwhile Paul de Monville loses no time marrying another fortune. And, lest we wonder where Gustave's sympathies lie, in a brief epilogue some well-fed shopkeeper clucks over the affair. " 'It's horrible,' exclaimed a family of grocers assembled patriarchically around an enormous leg of lamb whose aroma made their nostrils twitch. 'How could anyone go kill *that poor little woman*,' said the grocer, an eminently virtuous man, awarded the cross of honor for good conduct in the National Guard and a subscriber to the *Constitutionnel*.'"*

Embedded more or less overtly in the name Djalioh are some of Gustave's sources. Djali, Esmeralda's goat in *Notre-Dame de Paris*, was one. The name also evokes Nadjah, the woman killed and raped by an orangutan in a story called *Le brick du Gange* (The Brig of the Ganges), published several years earlier, from which Gustave borrowed tidbits for his murder scene. And if, as is likely, he frequented Paul Lalanne's Saint-Sever circus, which opened in 1834 across the Seine from the Hôtel-Dieu and drew large crowds, he would have seen a mime play featuring "Jocko, the Brazilian monkey." In fact, since the recent introduction of primates to Europe — the Jardin des Plantes in Paris acquired its first orangutan in May 1836 — the origins of man had become an increasingly heated subject of discussion.

But Gustave was concerned not so much with anthropoid apes and man's origins as he was with novel figurations of the Romantic outsider marooned in a society that makes no room for inwardness, whose watchwords are money, class, power, utility. Djalioh's closest kin are not creatures taken from the forest but sensitive souls who might wish to seek asylum in it. He belongs to the family of Werther, Quasimodo, Chateaubriand's René, Musset's Octave (*La Confession d'un enfant du siècle* was published in 1836). "[Djalioh's] heart was vast and immense — but vast like the sea, immense and empty like his solitude . . . His heart was less tautly strung and more sonorous than that of others. Pain threw him into convulsive spasms, pleasure into sensual transports." Easily discernible as well are intimations of Gustave's future protagonists. In Djalioh's simian presence at the nuptial festivities arranged by Mme de Lansac, one can glimpse Charles Bovary embarrassing Emma at the marquis d'Andervilliers' château. And even Frédéric Moreau of *L'Éducation sentimentale* flits across this stage, for when Paul's asinine chums question him during the wedding ball about Djalioh's sexual appetite, he answers, "Once I took him to a brothel and he fled, carrying a rose and a mirror."

What remains to be said is that this sport of nature served as a receptacle into which Gustave poured his feelings about himself, and, beyond the recurrence of themes from "Quidquid volueris" in other stories, one particular episode drawn to the life leaves little doubt of it. In late September 1836 the Flauberts were invited by the marquis de Pomereu to spend sev-

*A progovernment paper under Louis-Philippe.

eral days over Michaelmas at the Château du Héron, near Rouen.* That brief sojourn became a fixed star in Gustave's imaginative firmament. The memory of it accompanied him everywhere, surfacing in odd places at odd moments and most oddly during his journey up the Nile in 1850, after a strenuous night with the courtesan Kuchiuk-Hanem. His postcoital pleasure was to go kill turtledoves on a shoot across the cotton fields. "I trudged along laboriously and thought of similar mornings, among others at the marquis de Pomereu's Château du Héron, after a ball," he wrote to a friend in Rouen. "I hadn't gone to bed and in the morning I went rowing on the pond, all alone, in my school uniform. The swans were watching me and leaves were falling into the water." Gustave had conjured up the Château du Héron much earlier, in "Quidquid volueris," where the unhappily chaste Djalioh takes his morning boat ride after a night of yearning for his inventor's new bride. "Poor, desperate and bereft, he laughed wildly when he thought about the ball, its flowers, those women, Adèle and her bare breasts and shoulder, her white hand . . . He saw Paul's smile, his wife's kisses. He saw the two interlaced on a silky couch." Contemplating swans gliding past him, Djalioh, the half-simian adolescent entranced by their graceful progress, glorifies creatures of the air. "When he approached people, they fled. He lived scorned among men. Why had he not been born a swan, a bird, something light that sings and is loved?" Gustave's sadistic impulse may have been deflected from women to birds; Djalioh's rage discharges itself in the rape, which occurs beside a loudly chirping aviary.

AT HOME, the only blood people shed flowed in surgery, and Gustave usually managed to conceal his heaviness of spirit behind a jovial demeanor. Life proceeded without recorded calamity, and the Flaubert household, for all that has been written about Caroline's remoteness, was a sociable place. After his wife, Eulalie Flaubert Parain, died in 1836, François Parain often came up from Nogent, making himself much loved by everyone and especially by Gustave, who craved and received the unqualified support an affectionate uncle could give. Among medical colleagues of Achille-Cléophas's, the closest family friend may have been Dr Jules Cloquet, who had studied anatomy with him at the Hôtel-Dieu before doing ward work at the Val de Grâce military hospital and establishing himself in Paris. Both Flaubert boys were to know him not only as a houseguest but as a traveling companion — Achille in 1835, when Cloquet escorted him around Scotland, and Gustave five years later (as we shall see) on a looping tour of the Pyrenees, the Midi, and Corsica. Another medical colleague and family

---

*There is some question as to whether the year of the invitation was 1836 or 1837. In any event it later inspired Emma Bovary's magical elevation at the Château de la Vaubyessard.

friend was Félix-Archimède Pouchet, who had also studied with Achille-Cléophas and who in turn taught Gustave natural history at the collegiate school, this presumably being an extension of his duties as director of Rouen's Museum of Natural History. A staunch Freemason descended from Cauchois Protestants, Pouchet, who helped Achille-Cléophas found the Rouen medical school, gained considerable notoriety under the Second Empire by his polemics against Pasteur's germ theory, which he held to be a manifestation of Catholic obscurantism consonant with Pius IX's *Syllabus of Errors.* He himself argued for spontaneous generation, securing an undesirable niche in the history of science.

Literature was not well represented at the Hôtel-Dieu, except by its writer-in-residence, but Dr Flaubert, a member of the Académie de Rouen, was disposed to welcome artists and musicians who had made their mark in the city or become Mlle Caroline's teachers. Hyacinthe Langlois, before he died in 1837, had ingratiated himself sufficiently with Gustave to be dubbed Père Langlois, a peer of his neighbor Père Mignot, and the father of another well-respected painter, Polyclès Langlois. Polish exiles present in Rouen after 1830 included Antoni Orlowski, a great favorite of the Flaubert household, who distinguished himself in the musical life of the city — directing the Philharmonic Orchestra, giving violin and piano recitals at the Théâtre de Rouen and piano lessons to rich young ladies like Caroline Flaubert. Orlowski profited even more from his friendship with Chopin. In an effort to supplement his income, he arranged a benefit concert for himself and induced Chopin to perform. On March 11, 1838 — a golden Sunday in the life of Orlowski — the Flauberts undoubtedly sat among the five hundred Rouennais who were "stunned, moved, and intoxicated," as one reviewer put it, by a sublime order of music making. As for Gustave, what may have mattered more to him than the musical offerings was the demonstrative, very un-Norman fellowship he enjoyed among the several dozen compatriots in Orlowski's crowd. Apparently neither Flaubert parent had qualms about letting their young teenager accompany his older brother to Easter Sunday celebrations of Polishness, where stuffing oneself with sausage, smoking, getting drunk, and, as Gustave put it, "vomiting five or six times," were de rigueur.

Still, the Flauberts' friends and acquaintances belonged predominantly to Rouen's rich, inbred bourgeoisie. Pouchet, the son of a mill owner (whose nephew, Pierre Pouchet, another mill owner, fathered André Gide's mother), need not have worked for a living. Achille-Cléophas and Caroline knew Frédéric Louis Baudry, the liberal publisher of Rouen's principal newspaper, the *Journal de Rouen,* through his two boys, Frédéric and Alfred, schoolmates of Gustave's, who were destined now and again to play a significant role in his life. Many such lines formed a network all over affluent Rouen.

But without question the most important line connected the Flauberts to the Le Poittevins, a family living on the rue de la Grosse Horloge,* in the center of town. Mme Victoire Le Poittevin had known Mme Caroline Flaubert since childhood. As best friends at the boarding school run by two maiden ladies in Honfleur, they grew up together and remained close. Both married in 1812, and both raised three children, whose own lives became intertwined. Paul Le Poittevin was as much a self-made man of the Napoleonic era as Achille-Cléophas Flaubert. Given to an uncle in the priesthood for upbringing after he lost his father at two, then cast adrift at twelve, in 1790, when the Revolutionary government exiled the priest for refusing to take a civil oath, he had become foreman of a dye works in Rouen by thirty and a manufacturer by forty. Victoire's dowry, which derived from a modest fortune made in the shipyards of Fécamp, where she also inherited real estate, helped build more factories. Sixteen years younger than her husband and cultivated enough to be considered something of a bluestocking in her circle, Victoire applauded louder than anyone at Gustave's theatricals, louder certainly than Mme Flaubert. She and the serious, discreet Caroline were perfect opposites. Where Caroline spent half her life in a black lace bonnet as if perpetually mourning her dead babies, Victoire, a good-natured woman, wore bright-colored dresses, yellow crepe de chine shawls, and hats with flowers in them. Caroline measured her words; Victoire, who wrote poetry, measured her alexandrines. As Mme Flaubert's granddaughter remembered Victoire:

> She was a very literary woman. She wrote poetry and listened to herself reciting it. The slightest phrases fell from her lips like something precious; with a rather slow manner, a sense of the ridiculous, she often made amusing remarks, and then she would herself laugh until she cried, shaking her head, and her two anglaises [ringlets] would tap her cheeks.

Victoire transmitted her love of literature not only to her two older children, Alfred (whose godfather was Dr Flaubert) and Laure, but to the following generation as well in the person of Laure's son, Guy de Maupassant. Born only three months before Gustave, Laure became another sister to him. Tall and slim, with large blue eyes, wavy auburn hair, and a theatrical streak that might have resulted in her, too, embracing a stage career had circumstances permitted it, she had brains to match her looks. Like Gustave, Laure read Shakespeare, and like young Caroline, who adored her, she spoke English well. Her Italian was equally fluent, thanks to a tutor she shared with Caroline. What set her apart from other accomplished young

*The rue de la Grosse Horloge was also known as the Grand'Rue at that time.

women of her class, however, was her knowledge of Latin and Greek. For this proficiency they may have been indebted to something that such classical autodidacts as Mary Wortley Montagu and George Eliot did not enjoy — the instruction and encouragement of an older brother.

All the children looked up to Alfred, who was five years Gustave's senior. In 1862, long after the young man with a patrician air about him had died, Gustave, whose adolescent image of Alfred never aged, wrote to Laure: "I know now what are generally called 'the most intelligent men of our time.' I measure them against him and I find them mediocre in comparison." Byron crossed with Epictetus might approximate the Alfred Le Poittevin idolized by his young friend. To be sure, Alfred was intellectually gifted. At the Collège royal he completed Rhetoric second in his class, with his name repeatedly cited for Latin and history prizes on commencement day. The letters he and Laure exchanged in Italian suggest that languages came easily to him. And his verse, which appeared in *Le Colibri* (where he doubtless helped Gustave publish "Bibliomanie"), would have received high marks for its academic suavity. Gustave had never encountered such breadth of literary culture. Nor had he ever met anyone who undertook to make sense of life by reading Spinoza, Hegel, and Kant on his own. Conversation with Alfred was the magic carpet that transported him beyond his ken. "Never have I made such voyages," he reminisced.

> We would travel far without leaving the corner of our fireplace, and high though the ceiling of my room was low. There were afternoons forever lodged in my head, conversations six hours long, walks through the hills round about, and troubles weighing us down, troubles, troubles! I remember it all in bright red, blazing behind me like a fire.

Among other things, one boy's need for an older brother in whom to confide and the other's for a brilliant protégé in whom to see himself aggrandized made them compatible spirits, despite the age difference. Gustave wandered in and out of Alfred's house, where the company might include Ernest Chevalier or Frédéric Baudry. They sometimes slipped away to canoe miles up the Seine as far as Oissel, or loitered on the avenue of poplars along the river, near M. Fessart's swimming school. "I have never known anyone with a mind as transcendental [as his]." Hardly a week passed between 1834 and 1838 in which they did not spend some time together, except during summer holidays, which the Le Poittevins spent in Fécamp, on the Channel. Gustave sometimes visited him and Laure there and remembered reading Hugo's early collection of poems, *Les Feuilles d'automne*, with them.

Although they did not beget a singular work or an illustrious career, the qualities of mind and character that gave Alfred his allure embodied a style as telling of that era in France as black humor, acid-etched caricature, and white-gloved nihilism. Tender at heart, he was yet inclined to train upon the world an ironical eye from which no one could feel altogether safe. Chivalrous in the ordinary conduct of life, he was nonetheless an enthusiastic reader of Sade's *Justine*. Born with every advantage, he professed to believe in no future for himself and, indeed, suffered from a feeling of out-of-jointness that went by the name of *ennui*. Feeling was itself burdensome to Alfred. And it may have burdened the would-be poet even more than it did the friend: to Gustave, who wore his heart on his sleeve in early autobiographical works, he preached the very ideal of impersonality that came to be identified as Flaubertian. When Gustave, vexed by a woman writer's exclamatory prose some years later, urged her again and again to "hide your life" (*cache ta vie*), one surmises that his counsel echoed Le Poittevin's. Here was the "transcendental" mind, self-enveloped and charismatic, of whom Gustave dreamed while reading Balzac's *Louis Lambert*. And if he had read Baudelaire's brilliant essay on dandyism in *Le Peintre de la vie moderne,* that, too, might have filled his dreams with Alfred. "[Dandyism] is a kind of cult of the self that can survive the quest for happiness in relationships with others, with a woman, for example; that can even survive everything that is called illusions," Baudelaire wrote.

It is the pleasure of astonishing and the haughty satisfaction of never being astonished. A dandy may be blasé and even wracked with pain; but in the latter case, he will smile like the Spartan lad having his guts gnawed by a fox. So one can see that in some respects dandyism borders on spiritualism and stoicism.

Beset with ennui and depressed by philistine expectations, Alfred spent three years, between graduation from high school in 1835 and admission to law school in 1838, doing little else but reading and, less often, writing. An untitled poem apparently written during this period describes a man who remembers how he went astray, like Dante, in midjourney. Others fought their way clear of the dark wood, but not he:

> Mais, vers aucun désir ne me sentant porté,
> Dans inaction je suis toujours resté,
> J'aimais à regarder, dans leur cours éphémère,
> Mes jeunes compagnons poursuivre leur chimère,
> Et, laissant hésiter mon esprit indécis,
> A l'angle du chemin je suis encore assis.*

*Spurred by no desire, I couldn't take a step. I liked to observe my young companions chase will-o'-the-wisps. And, favoring my indecisive spirit, I remained seated here at the crossroads.

Salvation for the haut bourgeois imbued with "pious love of past things," as he put it in another poem, lay in the "Orient" so dear to many alienated nineteenth-century souls. He embraced this chimera as others sought refuge, like Baudelaire, in a fantasy of "*luxe, calme et volupté*" and others still in the sands of Arabia's Empty Quarter, where only camels made tracks.

If salvation lay in flight to some primitive place outside Europe (east or west: Chateaubriand's René lives among the Natchez Indians), momentary relief from adult convention was to be found in broad farce, and Alfred, together with Gustave, regressed hilariously by improvising a kind of proto-Ubu they called "le Garçon," or Descambeaux. One or the other might have claimed paternity, but Descambeaux, "the Kid," soon became a collective creation, open to everyone in their circle, including Laure Le Poittevin, who remembered him as a true son of Gargantua.* "I collaborated (very modestly to be sure) in my comrades' improvisation and added a few episodes which were warmly welcomed. The Garçon had two boon companions, the 'Nègre' (blackamoor) and the 'Troupier' (trooper), and what extraordinary adventures!" Multiple parents made a multiple personality, but the Kid was born to be stuffed with incongruous odds and ends. What sounded like Pantagruel one day might sound more like Caligula the next, or Sade, or an acephalic haberdasher promulgating the kind of bromides Gustave later assembled in a *Dictionnaire des idées reçues*.

Certain circumstances inevitably stimulated the troll. Gustave and Alfred could not pass the Rouen cathedral, for example, without the one declaring: "It's beautiful, this Gothic architecture; it uplifts the soul," and the other laughing in response, stridently enough to stop passersby dead in their tracks: "Yes, it's beautiful. So is Saint-Barthélemy. So are the Edict of Nantes and the dragonnades. They're all beautiful, all of them!"† Which was the Kid, the earnest purveyor of trite sentiments, or the maniac bent on shocking bourgeois? The Kid had room for both and also lent himself, without women present, to scatological foolery, as when he played the role of a hotel keeper at whose establishment, the Hôtel des Farces, guests convene to celebrate a Fête de la merde during the "sewage" season (*vidange*, "sewage," evoking the annual grape harvest, or *vendange*). When a grue-

---

*The Kid doesn't altogether fit the Garçon, who is many things and of no specific age, but will have to do for a creature conceived as irreverent, obstreperous, and permanently ineducable.

†This is a nonsensical enumeration. On Saint Bartholomew's Day in 1572, Catholics massacred French Protestants. The Edict of Nantes, promulgated in 1598, accorded the Huguenots freedom of conscience and worship. The dragonnade was a practice, prevalent even before the Edict of Nantes was revoked by Louis XIV, of forcibly billetting the rowdiest troops, dragoons, in Protestant homes.

some crime made news, the Garçon as defense attorney delivered long, ribald pleas to a billiard room full of jurors. The room would also have been full for funeral orations in honor of some perfectly healthy but thoroughly despised townsperson. The Garçon, alias Descambeaux, was the comfort-loving, paunchy, smug petit bourgeois with cant for baggage, but he was also an irreverent agent of demolition. He was preachy yet underhanded, pious and wildly iconoclastic. He clucked at unconventional behavior but died with Flaubert's epitaph: *Ci-gît un homme adonné à tous les vices* (Here lies a man given to all vices). He might have let a priest pray over him or hurled obscenities with his dying breath, but either way he gained a certain immortality as the totem of this clique, and the shibboleth that would always, later in life, instantly throw open the doors to childhood. When Gustave embarked upon a long trip, his sister expressed the hope that "the Kid's robust constitution" would not fail him en route and that "the Kid's fastidious preparations" would serve him well. In 1847, when Ernest Chevalier donned his judicial robes in Corsica, a letter from the Garçon in Rouen forcibly reminding him of "the unyok'd humor of their idleness" may have unnerved the young magistrate: "I would like to visit your courtroom one fine morning, if only to smash and break everything, belch behind the door, overturn the inkwells and crap in front of the bust of His Majesty," wrote Gustave. "In short, to make the Garçon's grand entrance."

The Garçon, in whose skin Gustave attained the acme of his theatrical career, remained with him forever after, laughing his stage laugh, pouncing on evidence of notables enjoying in secret what they excoriated in public, and delivering outrageous harangues, or *gueuleries*. He was not only the doorkeeper to childhood; he embodied its very spirit in memories of safe transgression that put a dunce cap on every iota of sensible advice. In June 1843, Gustave, a woebegone law student, wrote to his sister: "I have in my ears your sweet, sonorous laughter, that laughter for which I would make myself a complete buffoon, empty my bag of jests, swallow my last drop of saliva." Alone in his room he would sometimes make faces in his mirror or shriek like the Garçon, "as if you were there to see and admire me, for I sorely miss my public."

As astute as she was, Caroline surely knew that the *farceur* had a thin skin to protect inside his carapace of mockery, that the actor who never felt more alive than when holding an audience rooted never felt more imperiled than in the magnetic field of a beautiful woman. If his capacity for erotic worship hadn't declared itself before 1836, it spoke loudly during the summer of that year.

V

First Love

THE YEAR 1836 was notable for decapitations in Paris. The first celebrated head to fall belonged to a criminal named Lacenaire, who, having robbed and killed an old lady, astonished witnesses at his trial with arguments eloquently justifying his right to commit murder. Connoisseurs of Robert Macaire and the Marquis de Sade, jejune aristocrats, society women intrigued by a thug as rhetorically polished as he was unconscionable and whose blue frock coat might have been tailored for a dandy, all embraced him, in a spirit not essentially different from that of rich snobs a generation or two later titillating themselves at low dives in the crime-ridden neighborhoods called "Apache territory." There were requests to meet Lacenaire, to paint his portrait, to sculpt his bust, to publish his memoirs (which did in fact appear in print). When he mounted the scaffold before the Saint-Jacques customs gate on a cold winter day, the carriage crowd flocked there, only to depart after the execution disappointed that their pet psychopath had lost his scornful composure in the presence of death. According to the *Gazette Médicale,* phrenologists who examined Lacenaire's severed head were puzzled by the remarkable prominence of the bumps measuring his capacity for goodness and "theosophy."

During the following months four would-be regicides mounted the same scaffold at the southern edge of town. First to die, in February, were three conspirators responsible for the bloodbath on the boulevard du Temple in 1835. As their audience was likely to include members of the radical republican Société des droits de l'homme, which had already provoked riots and insurrections against the regime, six thousand troops were present to maintain order. Many of the same troops reassembled for the same purpose in July, when a tumbrel transported Jacques Alibaud up the avenue de l'Observatoire and along the interior boulevard to the Saint-Jacques gatehouse. A twenty-six-year-old ex-sergeant from Nîmes who displayed something of Lacenaire's hauteur and sartorial elegance, Alibaud had fired at Louis-Philippe with a rifle concealed inside a walking stick as the king's carriage emerged from the Louvre. Had plans for the execution not been kept secret, many more Parisians might have trudged across the city in the predawn hours and seen him perform his last act with the panache that had been expected of Lacenaire. Once a guard removed the black gauze enveloping his head and the bailiff of the Court of Peers read the judgment against him, he declared in a loud, resonant voice: "I am dying for freedom, for the common man, and for the extinction of monarchy." It is said that his valediction, which caused great dismay in the royal household, affected even the unflappable Louis-Philippe.

These brutal ceremonies made the point that a bourgeois king, however genial in private life, would defend himself ruthlessly. Still, the enemy was a hydra, growing two heads where one had been lopped off, and in the mid-1830s many of them seemed to wear Napoleonic cocked hats. Or rather, they wore cocked hats and red bonnets almost indiscriminately, for when Napoleon became an iconic figure during the Restoration, he was glorified as many things: the lawgiver who restored order, the hero who kept the Revolutionary flame lit, the general who conquered most of Europe. An American physician visiting Paris in 1816, Franklin Didier, noted that the name Napoleon had been banished from public discourse. One heard scarcely any more of him than if he never existed, he wrote. "In fact, many of the people do not know where he is. When I say this, I allude to the political articles in the journals and the conversations in the coffee-houses, clubs, etc., for in private assemblies [his name] is often pronounced with veneration." Charles X carried censorship further than his brother Louis XVIII in forbidding street singers, of whom there were many, to extol the emperor. But Napoleon's star shone all the more brightly. Collections of patriotic lyrics made the poet Béranger a best-selling author, and most working-class French knew by heart "Waterloo," "Les Deux Grenadiers," and "Le Vieux Drapeau." Medals were struck, busts were sculpted, folksy Épinal images circulated via country peddlers. A prefect reported from Bordeaux shortly before the 1830 revolution that "effigies of the usurper" abounded, and where effigies could not be displayed, symbols might pass. Some loyalists took to sporting neckties printed with the Napoleonic eagle or the bicorne.

The Bonaparte clan did not reenter France with other political exiles when Charles X fell from power. Louis-Philippe was only slightly less disinclined than his Bourbon cousin to offer them purchase in French territory, even after Napoleon's son, the duc de Reichstadt, died in 1832 at age twenty-one. He equivocated over a petition demanding that France reclaim Napoleon's remains from England, until advisers, who warned him that the remains were more dangerous than the relatives, won the day. An attempt to pacify Bonapartists led the government to commission a new statue of Napoleon for the Vendôme column, which had stood headless since 1815. But Louis-Philippe's generally pacifist agenda secured no peace at home. On the contrary, the disenfranchised underclass shut out of the *pays légal* (the two hundred thousand Frenchmen qualified to vote after 1830) yearned for a *pays militant* in which the people, under arms, would march as one against a common foe. Torches from France had lit fires all over Europe, and the cry went up to help rebels in Belgium, Poland, and Italy rid themselves of a king, a czar, and a pope. Those torches ignited another insurrection in Paris itself during the great cholera epidemic. Its occasion was the funeral of Jean-Maximilien Lamarque, a republican legislator widely admired for having fought victorious battles as a general in the Revolutionary army and in Napoleon's campaigns. With Lafayette and another Napoleonic general named Clauzel holding the pall, Lamarque's coffin was followed across Paris from the place Vendôme to the Pont d'Austerlitz by National Guardsmen, workers' guilds, members of secret societies, foreign delegations, and a crowd numbering one hundred thousand, many of whom brandished sticks garlanded in foliage like maenads waving thyrsi. Delirious with fear of cholera as much as with political passion, the funeral cortege became an insurrectionary mob, now singing the "Marseillaise," now chanting "liberty or death." It overran much of eastern Paris before the militia, in several bloody clashes, beat back the armed crowds.

His assertion of authority earned Louis-Philippe a reprieve from Napoleon's specter, except on the popular stage, where certain actors enjoyed full-time employment playing the little corporal. Under a regime made for entrepreneurs, business thrived. Astolphe de Custine, the perspicacious author of *La Russie en 1839,* was moved to reflect that "mercenary glory, which promises so much and settles for so little, is only a shadow of the real thing: true glory accompanies high renown, while this counterfeit defers the reign of genius by usurping its charge and its place." Custine may have had in mind Louis-Philippe (often called "the usurper" by Legitimists) or merely writers such as Eugène Sue, who grew rich and famous with fiction published serially in newspapers that now found it possible, through modern technology, to treble or quadruple circulation. Candidates for papier-mâché laurels and tin crowns were not lacking. But the "glory" that deflated chauvinists found most obnoxious was epitomized in the term *utilité publique.* To foster enterprises deemed publicly useful, people could be forced from their homes and off their land. Like an irresistible vanguard, this bureaucratic formula cleared the ground for an occupying army of miners, canal diggers, road builders, factory owners, railway pioneers. Where Napoleon's troops conquered Europe, Louis-Philippe's bourgeois mastered the homeland. Industrialization began to transfigure France during these peaceful years, even if it caused no romantic hearts to beat more quickly.

Even so, the specter wouldn't disappear for good, and in 1836 events revivified it. The annual Salon, which opened in March, was an exaltation of Napoleonic warfare. Three big paintings by Horace Vernet depicted the battles at Jena, Friedland, and Wagram. Others by Bellangé showed the crossing of the Mincio and the battle of Landsberg, and in yet another, by Charlet, a column of soldiers wounded in Russia shuffled past Napoleon's lugubrious eye. All this heralded a momentous occasion for imperial hoopla. On July 28, the sixth anniversary of the July Revolution, a veil fell from the newly completed Arc de Triomphe, which had been three decades in the making. Almost twice as high as the Arch of Constantine, the edifice commemorated Napoleon's great battles, the generals who won them (including Lamarque), the army corps that fought them. Aging veterans of the Grand Army stood beside militia. Louis-Philippe's ministers presided over the inaugural ceremony. But not Louis-Philippe himself. It was said that word of an assassination plot persuaded him not to carry out his plan to review the troops. It was also said that he meant by his absence to mollify European powers furious with France for recording in stone the history of their recent subjugation. It may have been thought, furthermore, that he did not relish the prospect of losing even more dimension under this monument to the epic warlord.

On October 25, when the obelisk of Luxor was raised on the place de la Concorde, half a decade after Muhammad Ali Pasha had made a gift of it to the new regime, Louis-Philippe proudly witnessed the feat from a balcony of the Naval Ministry. But Napoleon took credit even for this; to many Parisians the obelisk spoke of a phallic young general crushing the Mamelukes in Egypt rather than a famously pear-shaped king carrying a rolled umbrella, and certainly the pasha knew full well that he would never have gained control over Egypt twenty-five years earlier without an army trained by Napoleon's officers and engineers.

The last of the Napoleonic epiphanies to plague Louis-Philippe in 1836 came in the form of news from Alsace that the emperor's peripatetic nephew, Louis-Napoleon Bonaparte — the same who later inspired Karl Marx's observation about history repeating itself, the first time as tragedy, the second time as farce — had unsuccessfully attempted a coup de main. Louis-Napoleon had been banished from France after Waterloo, along with his mother, who was Napoleon I's stepdaughter and sister-in-law (having been born Hortense de Beauharnais and having married Louis Bonaparte, king of Holland). He grew up near Konstanz beside the Badensee, where Hortense had him educated in a spirit that accommodated both imperial ambitions and socialist fantasies. These were legitimated during a reunion with his estranged father in Florence; reinforced eight years later, when he joined revolutionaries fighting to liberate the territory of Romagna from papal rule; and given free rein after the death of Napoleon's son in 1832. That year he privately published a pamphlet, entitled *Rêveries politiques,* which was smuggled to the noted republican journalist Armand Carrel. In due course an emissary of Louis-Napoleon asked Carrel if his opposition paper, *Le National,* would welcome a Bonapartist government ratified by plebiscite.

Louis' overture fell on deaf ears, but the plot went forward anyway. Garrisoned in Strasbourg was the Fourth Artillery Regiment, to which Napoleon Bonaparte had originally been attached. With help from a beautiful seductress, Louis and fellow conspirators won over its commander, a disgruntled colonel named Vaudrey. On October 30 the diminutive nephew donned the red and blue uniform of an artillery colonel, added a general's hat for good measure, and rehearsed his official proclamation: "I am resolved to conquer or to die for the cause of the French people . . . It was in your regiment that my uncle, the Emperor Napoleon, served as captain: it was with you that he won renown at the siege of Toulon; and it was your brave regiment which opened the gates of Grenoble to him on his return from the Isle of Elba. Soldiers! A new destiny awaits you. It is for you to begin a great enterprise; you will be the first to have the honor of saluting the eagle of Austerlitz and Wagram!" The allegiance of the fourth regiment was purchased with liberal bribes, and at dawn, behind Vaudrey, it marched through narrow streets into the courtyard of the infantry barracks. There, amid great confusion, a captain apparently thought that the little man claiming to be Napoleon's nephew and holding high an imperial eagle was suffering from delusions of grandeur, and placed him under arrest. Louis-Philippe prudently decided against imprisonment for the captives, lest it transform a pest into a martyr. He prescribed exile instead, and within days Louis-Napoleon found himself hustled aboard the *Andromède,* which would take four months to deliver him to Norfolk, Virginia, by way of Rio de Janeiro.

WHEN THE Flauberts left home to enjoy their annual holiday in August 1836, they were no doubt happy to postpone all thoughts of political unrest, surgery, and the syllabus of third-year Greek. Little did Gustave suspect how fateful this month would be for him. Trouville had become increasingly fashionable; in addition to painters spreading the word that the town offered beautiful vistas and its inhabitants cheap hospitality, there was the voluble Alexandre Dumas, who had summered there, touting its custom all over Paris. Two of his friends, Élisa and Maurice Schlesinger, decided to heed his enthusiastic advertisements and during the summer of 1836 rented a seaside cottage. On fourteen-year-old Gustave, whom they befriended, this unusual couple made an impression that would eventually bear fruit in a masterpiece of nineteenth-century fiction, his *Éducation sentimentale* (the second version).

Long before *L'Éducation* came the lesser fruit of *Mémoires d'un fou,* an autobiographical monologue in which particulars of Gustave's friendship with the Schlesingers (Élisa's name changed to Maria) weave through his dense reflections on love and life. While strolling one morning along the beach toward the Roches Noires, where bathers liked to congregate, Gustave noticed water lapping at a woman's black-striped red shawl and moved it a safe distance from the surf. His unexpected reward came during lunch in the dining room of the Auberge de l'Agneau d'Or. A young woman seated nearby with her graying husband introduced herself as the bather whose garment he had rescued, to thank him for a gallant gesture. The glance that accompanied this bouquet left him completely flustered. What he saw in his smitten state was a beauty eclipsing everything around her. Tall and full bosomed, with an aquiline nose, amber skin, and an abundance of dark hair, the twenty-six-year-old Élisa, who had given birth to a daughter four months earlier, looked more Mediterranean than Norman. Gustave found it all instantly flawless, including the fine bluish down that shaded her upper lip and gave her face a strong, almost masculine, cast. "She might have been faulted for being plump or careless of her person after the fashion of artists, and in general women found her common," he wrote. Her neglect made Mme Schlesinger the more desirable to Gustave, whose predilection would always be for ladies well upholstered and dark, like Mme Flaubert. And the tresses falling over her shoulders bespoke a freedom of spirit unimaginable in heads festooned, like topiary gardens, with ringlets and tubular curls. If there was anything left to bewitch, after her eyes fixed him, her voice performed the sorcery. She spoke slowly, with a soft, musical cadence.

Thenceforth Gustave's movements were governed by hers as he contrived obsessively to cross her path or sit near her at the beach. The myth of

Aphrodite rising naked from the foam of the sea, riding on a scallop shell, and landing at Cythera unfolded before his eyes whenever Élisa stepped ashore dripping wet, in a costume that must have seemed like none at all to a boy brought up with the elaborate accoutrements of bourgeois women. His heart raced, his faced flushed, his tongue cleaved to his palate, and on one occasion, seeing her suckle her infant daughter, he felt desire well up in him. From what distance could he observe "azure veins" beneath the dusky skin of her breast?

> Up to then I had never laid eyes on a naked woman [madwomen excepted, as we shall see]. Oh, the ecstasy in which the sight of that breast plunged me! How I devoured it with my eyes, how I would have liked to touch it! It seemed to me that if I had placed my lips on it, I would have bitten it with rage. And my heart melted just thinking about the fire this kiss would light in me.

Defeated by the thought of addressing the divinity, he might have remained forever outside her magic circle if not for her pudgy consort, Maurice Schlesinger, a convivial man and, by all accounts, a bon vivant who arrived in Trouville with cases of Rhine wine to keep his company well watered. Gustave's mere fourteen years did not prevent his joining that company, which attracted painters, writers, and musicians from round about. On the contrary, it may have endeared him to Schlesinger, and there is no indication that Dr and Mme Flaubert perceived any danger in such bohemian associations, or any that wouldn't cease to exist once Gustave found himself again under the family roof. He was at liberty to moon over Élisa in smoke-filled rooms, where words and "grog" flowed freely. While sister Caroline took drawing lessons at one atelier or another, Gustave might have been riding horseback with Maurice on the beach. Did Schlesinger also see him as a physical adornment to his circle? The tall, slender boy seemingly unaware of his good looks, who often wore a red flannel shirt, rough blue cloth trousers, and a blue scarf bound around his waist, was a sight for painterly eyes, and a good equestrian. First among all the animals he had ever wanted to be, he later wrote, came the horse.

Quite possibly no one in Trouville knew that the Schlesingers were in fact an unmarried couple, and much about the beginnings of their conjugal life still remains obscure. Élisa was a Norman girl from the town of Vernon, born in 1810 to Auguste Charles Foucault, who had fought under Napoleon at Austerlitz and Jena before retiring with the rank of captain. He sent her to the local convent school, where nuns taught her domestic arts and instructed her in the rudiments of music. At nineteen she married — under duress perhaps — a lieutenant garrisoned at Vernon, Émile Jacques

Judée, who was fourteen years her senior. Much has been written about what happened next, but for reasons that cannot be perfectly elucidated, her life went awry. In the most recent version of events, *Flaubert et le secret de Madame Schlesinger,* which derives from family lore, Élisa was raped on her wedding night by her impotent husband's fellow officers and immediately fled to Paris. There she found refuge with a married sister, Lia, who protected her against repercussions of the scandal. A year later, 1830, Judée left Vernon for Algeria. He had only recently returned from the colonial war when Gustave met Élisa. During much of that interval, she continued to live with her sister on the rue Montmartre, earning a livelihood making lace, in which she acquired exceptional skill, while taking voice lessons. It may have been through Lia, herself a trained singer, that Élisa met the music publisher Maurice Schlesinger, whose business was situated quite near their flat. However the meeting came about, she would soon have discovered that this vibrant Prussian Jew half a head shorter than she and twelve years older, with a notoriously roving eye, presided over one of Paris's cultural hubs at 89, rue de Richelieu. In Élisa, Maurice found a beautiful, intelligent woman. Did he also find her six months pregnant by a certain Count von F——, as the family contends? If so, he agreed to bestow his name upon the child. They set up house together, and in April 1836 Élisa gave birth to Marie Schlesinger. The couple's union would be consecrated in 1840, a year after news reached them that Judée had died. Caring no more about religious persuasion than about the forenames he changed or the passports he carried, Maurice converted to Catholicism at Élisa's behest, for the church wedding.

Maurice had been given the name Mora Abraham at his birth, in Berlin, where his father, Abraham Moses, or Adolf Martin, owned a bookstore patronized by the large community of expatriate Huguenots. Mora became Moritz and proved himself a worthy son of Adolf, who in 1811 established a music and book publishing company that began to prosper when contracts were signed with Spontini, Carl Maria von Weber, and Cherubini. After Waterloo, Schlesinger's Musikhändlung became the foremost enterprise of its kind in Berlin, thanks in no small measure to the successful negotiations of Moritz. No sooner had he joined the firm — a classically educated young man by then, and an ex-hussar — than Adolf enlisted him in a campaign to capture Beethoven. Moritz accomplished this mission, and his account of the way he did it during a meeting near Vienna at Modling, where Beethoven spent the summer, offers a vivid picture of both men. As he descended from his coach, he was greeted by the sight of Beethoven stalking out of the inn in high dudgeon. This did not augur well, but Beethoven consented to see him and explained that the innkeeper had had no veal to satisfy his sudden craving for a chop. "I comforted him," Schlesinger wrote,

> and we talked of other things. I stayed about two hours. I was afraid of boring him or disturbing him, but every time I tried to leave he detained me. As soon as I got back to Vienna I asked the innkeeper's son whether he had any veal in store. He did and I had him send it to Beethoven on the coach I kept at my disposal. The next morning I had not yet risen when Beethoven rushed in, kissed me, hugged me, and said I was the best man he had ever met. Nothing had ever made him happier than the longed-for veal.

In return for the chop, Moritz received various compositions to glorify the firm's eclectic list, including songs and piano sonatas 30 to 32, with a promise of more. He seems to have been equally good at charming Prince Frederick (among other members of the royal court), who wrote martial music. Schlesinger's complete collection of Prussian military marches was a lucrative item.

Just as Mayer Rothschild's sons went abroad to create satrapies of his financial empire, Moritz, a fluent French speaker, established himself in Paris in the 1820s. After several years of employment at a firm specializing in the importation and exportation of books, he applied for a license to trade books in his own right but was rebuffed by the Bourbon monarchy, which had somehow gotten wind of his politically liberal sympathies. It expressed no objection, on the other hand, to his setting up as a music publisher, and Schlesinger, who had all the instincts of a great impresario, did not remain unnoticed for long. Serious musicians came to recognize his colophon on piano reductions of Mozart operas as well as Beethoven's complete piano scores. In due course it also affixed itself to works of Meyerbeer, Liszt, Mendelssohn, Chopin, César Franck, Halévy, and Berlioz, although Maurice's profligate life could not have been supported without the income generated by fluffier merchandise — the "airs favoris" and "bagatelles" endemic to middle-class salons. What set him apart from other influential publishers, however, and ultimately made him *primus inter pares* on the Continent, was the *Gazette Musicale*. Founded in 1834 as a vehicle for promoting his list, this journal became something much more than that. Not only did it keep the public abreast of musical events all over Europe, with reports from correspondents in every capital, but it also opened its pages to writers and composers wanting a forum for some idea or grievance. Berlioz aired his pet peeve, the presumptuous humbug of musically illiterate music critics. Liszt denounced anachronistic taboos that inhibited the performance of sacred music in concert halls. Richard Wagner, whom Schlesinger employed at various tasks when he was living impecuniously in Paris, extolled the special virtues of Germany's musical personality. Balzac, George Sand, Alexandre Dumas, all wrote for the *Gazette*. And all paths intersected at 89, rue de Richelieu, which on most afternoons resembled a lively salon rather than a place of business.

The mind of a lovelorn adolescent could not hope to wrap itself around this capacious personage, who wagered on Trouville's future that summer by acquiring an inn near the harbor with every intention of building a large hotel there (he would in fact build one, named the Bellevue). Unless one did drudgework for him, like Wagner arranging operatic excerpts as fourteen suites for the cornet, it was hard to belittle or dislike him. Around Schlesinger, time seldom hung heavy. Whether aware or not of Gustave's enchantment with his wife, he did not mind being called "Père Maurice," and he invited the boy to festivities that brought him and Élisa together. Particularly memorable was a moonlit excursion on the river Touques during which a close friend of Schlesinger's, the Polish violinist Heinrich Panofka, played themes from Handel's *Saul*. In his account of the evening, Gustave omitted everyone but himself and Élisa, the sound of whose voice lulled him like the rocking boat. "She was near me, I felt the curve of her shoulder and the brush of her dress," he wrote. "I was besotted with love, I heard the oars dip rhythmically, the waves lap against the skiff, I felt touched by all that, and I listened to Maria's sweet, vibrant voice."

But this cradling adoration left him desolate and bitter, as the outsider condemned to feign intimacy by walking Élisa's dog or standing under her lighted window after dark. At night, when images of the conjugal bed kept him awake, Trouville became a lonely shore. Père Maurice's *droit de mariage* was Gustave's destitution. "To him belonged this woman entire — her head, her breasts, her body, her soul, her smiles, her arms embracing him, her words of endearment. His portion was everything, mine nothing."

Gustave's picture of himself commemorating the events of the summer during his coach ride home to Rouen anticipates the sad scene of Charles Bovary under the arbor wondering whether life with Emma hadn't after all been a rutilant dream couched inside his dun-colored life. "Farewell for good! she left like the clouds of dust flying up behind her." But he would see Élisa again, often; and before that, in 1838, he would revisit his awakening with *Mémoires d'un fou*.

There were many Rouen bourgeois on the edge of Dr Flaubert's social circle who found his younger son bizarre and who, when *Madame Bovary* appeared twenty years later, would not have been surprised to learn that at sixteen he had written an episodic meditation called *Memoirs of a Madman*. One such acquaintance was Dr Eugène Hellis, chief of medicine at the Hôtel-Dieu and a Catholic given to crossing swords with his Voltairean colleague. Hellis dismissed Gustave as "a wild and wooly head if ever I met one," a strange creature insensible to the essential fitness of things.

For an adolescent gnawed by self-doubt, *fou* was not idle talk. The fear of going mad haunted Gustave long before something very like madness came in a bolt from the blue. No doubt Mme Caroline Flaubert's incapacitating migraines worried him. And his anxiety may have been exacerbated by images formed at age seven, when François Parain, believing that a notoriously callous diversion of early-nineteenth-century Rouennais would make great entertainment for his nephew, showed him ragged, raving inmates on display in an insane asylum beyond the Saint-Ouen abbey. Rather than blame his cherished uncle, Gustave preferred to maintain that the spectacle had toughened him for life.* But this contention, a version of which may be found in the tribute Émile Zola paid to bullies who tormented him at his school in Aix-en-Provence, was largely braggadocio served up as antibourgeois fare. On a deeper level he shared Dr Flaubert's belief that no one enjoyed immunity from mental derangement and that madness might be caught from the mad, as cholera from the plague stricken, if one failed to keep one's distance. "My father always used to say that he would never have practiced in a mental hospital, for if one dedicates oneself to treating madness, one will surely contract it." Would keeping his distance from madness, however, have required an act of exorcism? Gustave was more than half convinced that "crazies and cretins" tagged after him, as he later told a correspondent, like dogs sniffing one of their own kind.

Wild and wooly, if not deranged, is how he presents himself in *Mémoires d'un fou,* at the same time implicitly priding himself, with the pride of the young Romantic, on a waywardness that to Dr Hellis would have signaled serious defects of mind and character. Life governed by the clock was, he declared, a tyranny promoting the death of the soul. "I've never liked schedules, set times, a tick-tock existence, in which thought stops with the ringing of the school bell, and everything is wound up beforehand, for centuries and generations." Not for dreamers like him was a "regularity" that abetted the hectic designs of his contemporaries. While the greatest number breathed happily in a society glorifying "materialism and common sense," to him they were as suffocating as a cloud of lampblack to a bird on the wing. He went off by himself and there read — "devoured" — *Childe Harold* and *Cain, Werther* and *Faust, Hamlet* and *Romeo and Juliet.*

Wandering off by himself did indeed reflect his aversion to all the beaten paths and straight lines, even the long corridors at the collegiate school, associated with success in life. Like the school clock that cut short the aleatory

---

* "Ce sont de bonnes impressions à avoir jeunes; elles virilisent" (They are good impressions to have when one is young; they make you virile).

course of his daydreams, the strict sequence of bourgeois expectations — gainful employment, marriage, parenthood — left Gustave feeling unfit for any future that might command respect in society's eyes. He spent prep time scrutinizing the floor of the study hall or a spider spinning its web on the proctor's desk leg. And when the mask of cynicism fell, he saw himself as a wastrel incapable of getting facts straight or showing himself disposed to learn a profession, "who would be useless in this world where everyone must partake of the banquet, and, in short, always remain good for nothing — or at best make a passable buffoon, an exhibitor of trained animals, a producer of books." Not unlike Djalioh fiddling up a storm outside the realm of harmonic composition is the *fou*, the "mad" memoirist unconstrained by "classic lessons," whose thoughts lead him at breakneck speed across torrents, up mountains, through space, on flights that end in scenes of carnage or orgy.

The only straight line for which Gustave seemed to display enthusiasm was one that traced the progress of a civilization wearing itself out as it scraped its bourgeois way toward oblivion. *Wear, worn, nothingness, emptiness, sepulchre,* are words that brought color to his prose. Unstrung by the prospect of someday entering society and "bruised" by contact with the *profanum vulgus,* he found a tonic for neurasthenia in visions of the final holocaust. "So when will this society debauched in mind, body, and soul finally meet its end?" he asks.

There will be rejoicing on earth when the mendacious and hypocritical vampire called society expires. Stripped of mantles, scepters, and diamonds, royalty will flee their crumbling palaces in the general exodus from fallen cities, to rejoin wild mares and she-wolves. After wearing out his feet on city pavements . . . man will die on forest floors. Fires will rage . . . and nature will henceforth yield only bitter fruit and thorny roses. Races will be snuffed out in the cradle like wind-battered shrubs that perish before flowering. Everything must end, and the earth must wear out for being trampled upon; the immense firmament must eventually tire of this human mote disturbing the majesty of nothingness with its hues and cries. Gold must wear thin passing from hand to hand and soiling them all. This vapor of blood must cool, palaces must crumble beneath the weight of treasures stored in them . . . Then a great guffaw of despair will be heard, when men behold the void.

As the throne goes, so goes the altar, and Gustave pictured bare, ruined choirs beside the rubble of palaces. In its dying days Rome glimpsed a crucifix "luminous with eternity," he wrote, but after eighteen hundred years, the cross had become petrified wood. On what could nineteenth-century man hang his dream of transcendence?

For this darkly eloquent collegian, the end of time was more agreeable to contemplate than the doomsday of graduation. Would a professional role result in lifelong self-estrangement? True selfhood required a vacant expanse over which his imagination could play as it wished, heedless of paternal signposts, ritual paths, curricula vitae, proprietary claims, alien judgments. Feeling connected only when bereft or marooned, the boy brimming with emptiness voiced his paradoxes in an epilogue to his account of his infatuation. In it he declares that Maria could not have known of his love because he hadn't loved her. "In everything I've told you [the reader], I lied." The lie became truth only two years later, when he revisited Trouville. Alone on the shore, in the woods and fields, he created Maria for himself, walking beside him, talking to him, looking at him. "I'd lie down and watch the wind brush the grass and the surf pound the sand and I'd think of her and reconstruct in my heart every scene in which she acted or spoke. These memories were a passion." Like a paleontologist excited by fossil remains rather than by creatures in the flesh, Gustave loved to embrace absences. With no external body confining his imagination and no historical circumstance thwarting his will, he made Maria into a Galatea. Though he couldn't possess the woman, he had something possessable in an image of his own devising and, as he says, preferred it that way. Never mind Lord Byron. Reading *Les Confessions,* he acquainted himself with a truly kindred spirit in Jean-Jacques Rousseau, or in the Jean-Jacques who left Mme de Warens's bed for a cottage behind her house, the better to fantasize about her from afar. This penchant for remote intimacy stayed with Gustave. He would always feel most himself in the fastness of indefinitely unconsummated love, of longing, of bereavement.

To be sure, there would soon be consummations, but not of love, nor at Trouville. In a geographical arrangement that reflected his psychological state as well as the etiquette of upper-class youths, the country was a proper venue for romances and the city a place for neutral sex. Gustave had other amorous brushes during summer holidays at the shore; at Rouen, several years later, with coaxing from Alfred Le Poittevin (his exemplar in all things venereal), he became a habitué of brothels on the rue du Plâtre and the rue de Cigogne. One can safely assume, if Rouennais conformed to the bourgeois rule, that more than one classmate of Gustave's at the collegiate school had been initiated by a family chambermaid (the *Manuel des pieuses domestiques* sternly warned against this danger). On Mme Flaubert's watch, however, no such initiation appears to have taken place at the Hôtel-Dieu.

By midadolescence Gustave had fallen quite completely under the influence of Alfred Le Poittevin. Emulating Alfred's style, which combined antic mischief and deep pessimism, gross buffoonery and a penchant for metaphysics, contempt for the civilities of polite society and total immersion in literary culture, Gustave couldn't skip through the gutter as nimbly as his friend or move with his ease from rhetorical tours de force to obscene banter. What seemed unforced in Alfred came off in Gustave as the swaggering of a brilliant brat whose voice had recently dropped an octave. Typical were comments he made in a letter written on September 23, 1837, after visiting le Paraclet — the monastery Pierre Abélard built near Nogent-sur-Seine and bestowed upon Héloise. Far be it for him to join lachrymose contemporaries who wanted the martyred couple reburied side by side at Père-Lachaise cemetery. "Master Abailard [*sic*]," he told Ernest, was a "lout" and an "imbecile" greatly to be scorned for sacrificing "a testicle" in the service of love. Adolphe Chéruel didn't fare much better than poor Abélard when Gustave learned that his history professor had married the widow of a colleague. Chéruel plugged Mme Bach's hole, as he told Ernest, lest the lady "die of solitary onanism"(a practice indulged in by Gustave himself and universally reputed to have dire consequences). Nothing made his irreverent heart leap higher than a well-founded rumor that the assistant principal charged with monitoring student morals at the *collège* had been surprised in a whorehouse. This was red meat for the predatory Garçon. "It does me good all over — chest, stomach, heart, entrails, diaphragm, etc.," he crowed to Ernest. "When I picture [him] caught in the act of ponderously thrusting his member, I can't help shouting, drinking, . . . giving full throat to the Garçon's cackle. I pound the table, tear my hair out, roll on the floor. What a great story!"

Mémoires d'un fou, begun soon afterward, suggests in its reflections on morality how quickly this jovial figure could lose countenance, how little it took for a Garçon full of Rabelaisian spunk to become a forlorn child of the century. Loss of faith in God had led him to doubt the existence of virtue, "a fragile idea that each century has erected on an ever more precarious scaffolding of laws," Gustave would write, and again, more somberly: "Around man all is shadow, all is emptiness. He would like some fixed point as he drifts in this immensity of vagueness. Trying to stop, he clings to one thing and another but sees everything slip out of his grasp — nation, liberty, belief, God, virtue." Another collection of *pensées* dating to these years and dedicated to Le Poittevin put it bluntly that in Gustave's middle-class universe the muses of theater held sway, that the respectable man's home was a facade and the brothel his real interior, that the nuptial couch was a prop for adulterous affairs, that "life is a mask, death the truth."

For fixed points and moral bearings, Alfred Le Poittevin couldn't help; quite the opposite. While on his own Gustave was discovering Montaigne and Rabelais, whom he described in a brief essay as the embodiment of "genuine, strong, brutal laughter, the laughter that breaks and smashes [icons]," he was familiarizing himself through Alfred with a literature sub-versive of the moral imperatives and rational ideals by which bourgeois so-ciety set store. The accomplished Latinist who would soon make a suave young lawyer and might eventually have made a cynical magistrate had he lived long enough (Frédéric Baudry thought so) introduced Gustave to By-ron, to Gautier, to Goethe's *Faust,* and most enduringly, as we shall see, to the works of the Marquis de Sade. Under Alfred's auspices, Gustave became a published author for the second time in *Le Colibri,* again at age sixteen, with a brilliantly mordant piece entitled "Une leçon d'histoire naturelle: Genre commis," which catches the scoffing spirit of Thursday evening confabulations at Alfred's on the rue de la Grosse Horloge. To ridicule the grocer, the clerk, or the bookkeeper was fashionably avant-garde. It was even more fashionable to invoke the great naturalists of the day by present-ing one's caricature as an exercise in zoological taxonomy. Brains have been racked, he begins, over the proper classification of an animal that combines features of the bradypodida, or sloth, the howler monkey, and the jackal. "His otter-skin cap as well as the long hairs of his brown frock coat indicate an aquatic life, while his wool vest, several inches thick, offers proof posi-tive that this creature originates in Northern climes; his hooked nails might suggest a carnivore, if he had any teeth. At length the Academy of Sciences officially dubbed him a biped, recognizing too late that he moves with the aid of an ebony cane."

Although briefer and more caustic than Balzac's *physiologies* and the study of social types that inspired *Les Français peints par eux-mêmes: Encyclopédie morale du XIXe siècle* (to which Balzac contributed during the 1840s), Gus-tave's sketches leave no doubt that he, like his Romantic elders, had devel-oped a keen ear and eye for mores susceptible of enshrinement in generic portraits. At work, he wrote, the clerk perches on his high stool with a pen stuck over his left ear and writes slowly, savoring the odor of ink on a large sheet of paper spread before him. "He sings what he writes between closed teeth and makes ceaseless music with his nose, but, when pressed, he has no peer for spitting out commas, periods, dashes, final flourishes . . . Office talk revolves around the winter thaw, slugs, the repaving of the port, the iron bridge, gaslights." For live entertainment, this voracious consumer of Paul de Kock's mildly pornographic novels goes to the theater every Sun-day, sitting in an upper gallery or in the pit. "He hisses the curtain raiser and applauds the vaudeville. When he's young, he plays a game of dominos dur-ing the intermission. Sometimes he loses, whereupon he goes home, breaks two plates, no longer calls his wife 'my spouse,' forgets Fido, wolfs the re-mains of yesterday's boiled beef, furiously salts the string beans, and falls asleep on dreams of audits, thaws, repavings, subtraction." Notwithstanding

his prurient turn of mind, he is, in middle age, the model citizen —
"peaceful and virtuous." He faithfully does municipal guard duty, retires at
9 p.m., and never leaves the house without his umbrella. The *Constitutionnel* beside his morning café au lait betrays a man of liberal sympathies. "He
is a warm partisan of the 1830 Charter and the July liberties. He respects
the laws of his country, shouts *Vive le Roi!* at fireworks displays and polishes
his National Guard breastplate every Saturday evening. The Bookkeeper is
an enthusiastic member of the National Guard. No sooner does he hear the
drumroll than he races to the parade ground, all flushed and tightly buttoned, humming: 'Ah, what pleasure it is to be a soldier.' "

It would have been easy for most readers to detect Gustave's enormous
admiration for La Bruyère and Montesquieu, but it would have required
prescience to see in his nameless bookkeeper the paradigm of literary clerks
yet unborn. "Yesterday I visited with Degouve-Denuncques [publisher of
Le Colibri]; my 'Commis' will appear next Thursday and on Wednesday
we'll correct the proofs together," he informed Ernest on March 24, 1837,
and thus proudly gave Rouen a character destined to enjoy posterity in
Flaubertian characters — in Homais, in Bouvard, in Pécuchet — like a ball
paying out yarn for the spinner throughout his lifetime.

That pride was no doubt shared by Achille-Cléophas, for whom Gustave
professed his love in a diary. How he felt about his son's lurid readings and
precocious cynicism isn't known. It may well be that he gave them little
thought. Much preoccupied with professional duties, the doctor devoted
leisure time to the management and acquisition of property as he greatly
enlarged the family estate. The Ferme de Gefosse in Pont l'Évêque and several parcels adjacent to Caroline Flaubert's farm in Touques were acquired
in the 1820s. In 1833 Achille paid the considerable sum of seventy thousand francs for twenty-three acres of income-bearing pasturage near Bet-
teville, some miles downriver from Rouen and quite near the ruins of the
eleventh-century Benedictine abbey of Saint-Wandrille. Three years later,
an even larger sum, ninety thousand francs, purchased the Ferme du
Côteau in Deauville, some sixty-five acres including farmhouses, land under cultivation, orchards, and meadow situated on a gentle slope that rose
to its highest point at Mont Canisy. During summer holidays Gustave
would often cross the Touques from Trouville to visit this farmstead and
chat up the tenants. So insignificant was Deauville village that he spoke of
his own future domain as "our farm, which is called Deauville."

Mme Flaubert's view of Gustave's literary predilections also went unrecorded. What she found even more noxious than Sade, perhaps — assuming she knew anything of *Justine* or *Philosophie dans le boudoir* — was the
pipe that became an inevitable accessory to Gustave's intellectual life. Tobacco smoke no doubt aggravated her headaches, yet nothing was done

about it. Its prohibition might have seemed excessively harsh in an age of epidemic puffing, when young men did not feel quite complete unless equipped with cigars or, as Daumier drawings show us, long-stemmed clay *brûle-gueules*. After making a smoker of George Sand, Jules Sandeau turned against tobacco, declaring that the weed was destined to spell

> the ruination of well-born young men. The immorality prevalent in gaming rooms and brothels will pale beside that of the perverse cigar . . . It will do us more harm than German literature, than the loves of Werther, the hollow dreams of *René* and the *Tales* of Hoffmann . . . The cigar, which has infiltrated the world of elegant salons, has made its presence felt above all in artistic circles . . . [It] is the insignia of the man of letters and of the artist.

Had Mme Flaubert read this to her son, it wouldn't have mattered, or the quote might have elicited a perverse counterquote. Letters written to Ernest during these school years make it quite clear that the future Flaubert, whose workday never began until he had sharpened his quills and smoked the first of some thirty bowls, was already thoroughly addicted in adolescence.* In August 1838, before joining Alfred at the Le Poittevins' summer house in Fécamp, he gave more thought to his provision of tobacco than to his wardrobe. "I've spent two days making my tobacco preparations for the journey. Just now I've spent another two hours wrapping a half-dozen pipes (no. 17). In addition, for the road, I'll bring two boxes of amadou [tinder], a half-dozen cigars, a wad of Maryland, etc., etc. I'm taking Rabelais, Corneille, and Shakespeare." Beginning with the school year 1838–39, during which he lived at home, Gustave made a habit of entering a café near the Collège royal every morning and stoking up. It consoled him in advance for the austerity and privations to be endured all day long on a wooden bench and nerved him much as it would later, at his writing desk. "Ah! What vices I'd have if I didn't write," he would exclaim to his future mistress (who wanted him more vicious). "The pipe and the pen are the two safeguards of my morality."

The feeling of being abandoned or lost, which crept over him whenever friends failed to answer his letters promptly, intensified after the summer of 1838. First, Alfred Le Poittevin departed Rouen to begin law studies, very much *à contre coeur*, at the University of Paris. Then it was Ernest Chevalier, who hadn't yet received a baccalaureate degree, leaving to complete work for it at a Parisian pension and enter law school in his turn. Over were the companionable walks they regularly took through the countryside outside

---

*Hospital records indicate that Dr Achille-Cléophas Flaubert occasionally prescribed tobacco for patients, violating hospital rules, from which one may infer that he was an indulgent parent in the matter of pipe-smoking.

Rouen. Gustave associated with classmates, with Orlowski, with junior faculty at the *collège* (two of whom — Horbach and Podesta, teachers of German and Italian — gave international scope to the Garçon in horseplay at the Flauberts' country house). But none could yet replace Alfred and Ernest. Had he only enjoyed the "unlimited power" he found so alluring in Sade's works, he might have used it not to practice sexual fantasies on women (or not right away) but to stop the passage of time. Time emptied him. It brought change. It made him feel laggard. It swept him inexorably toward the great Niagara of adult commitments. Left behind on the quay after bidding farewell to boon companions who had embarked upon professional life, he was further oppressed by the successful course brother Achille was shaping with evident self-satisfaction. In May 1839 the two Carolines, mother and daughter, joined Achille in Paris to offer him moral support during the public defense of his doctoral thesis (on strangulated hernias, published that year as *Quelques considérations sur le moment de l'opération de la hernie étranglée*). Present as well were Achille's fiancée, Julie Lormier, and his future in-laws, well-fixed Norman wool merchants. They saw the great tragedienne Rachel perform at the Comédie-Française and admired the waterworks at Versailles, where heat-prostrated crowds packed the galleries, and finally bought sister Caroline a new piano, honoring Gustave's request for one with a big sound. But they made it their main business to assemble Julie's trousseau. Gustave cast a jaundiced eye on these prenuptial rituals. "[My brother] is going to settle down," he informed Ernest spitefully, as befit a young man who had declared that if he ever set foot on the world stage it would be in the role of a "demoralizer" telling "horrible" truths. "Henceforth he will resemble those polyps clinging to rocks. Everyday life will revolve around the red cunt of his beloved; it will shine on the happy man as the sun shines on dung." Nothing, not even news that yet another insurrection by extreme left-wing republicans had raised barricades in lower Montmartre and swept tourists off the streets, seemed to distract him for long from thoughts of Achille's sex life under the new dispensation. "Tomorrow they marry," he wrote on May 31. "It's between June 1 and 2 that the fucking will begin and the soft creaking of bedboards in the dark of night will signal matrimonial bliss." When the newlyweds took their obligatory honeymoon in Italy several months later, Gustave surmised that Achille would return lighter by several ounces of semen.

The thought of exercising a profession was an abyss over which his soul hovered like a convict standing knock-kneed on the scaffold. True, it did not ruin him for school, where Chéruel awarded him second prize overall in history, and the redoubtable Louis Magnier, whom one inspector described as a "frank and loyal" professor of rhetoric hostile to the "delin-quencies" of Romantic literature, ranked him high in French composition. He twice took first prize in natural history. He worked diligently at classi-cal languages, as he always would. Nevertheless, the future preyed upon his mind. If need be, he would study law, he told Chevalier in February 1839, but with no intention of practicing it except to defend a murderer such as Lacenaire or another heinous cause. By July, when his senior year loomed larger, he had grown more despondent. To Ernest he declared angrily that he would take his place in society, he would become whatever convention dictated, a "cog like everybody else," a "blockhead" indistinguishable from others, a lawyer, a doctor, a subprefect, a notary, a run-of-the-mill judge — "because one must be some such thing and there is no middle ground." His mind was made up. "I'll go study law, which, instead of opening all doors, leads nowhere. I'll spend three years in Paris contracting venereal diseases. And then? All I want is to live out all my days in an old ruined castle near the sea." Praise from Ernest, who found his omnivorous intellect daunting, fell on deaf ears. He regarded himself as a prize imbecile. Even his writing bored him. Nothing was left, he complained, of the vanity or talent that had made him so productive.

There were nondeclamatory moments when Gustave, taking stock of his life, admitted that nothing in it justified his "endless jeremiads," that some-one so well surrounded by affectionate family and friends had only himself to blame for the thorns in his path. This realization didn't cheer him up. Feeling out of place and out of time, he comforted himself as best he could with palliatives available to a young man whose allowance may have equaled the ordinary worker's wages. To believe one of his jeremiads, he smoked until his throat gave out, he drank brandy whenever the opportunity pre-sented itself, he ate gluttonously, he visited a brothel on the rue du Plâtre. Bored is what he claimed to have been by that visit, but ennui or *embêtement* expressed an attitude — a kind of jaded *nil admirari* — fashionable among rebellious young literati. For sure, his sexual initiation was not accomplished between yawns. The event, which apparently took place several months be-fore Achille's marriage, inspired a tribute to prostitution that complied with another imperative of young rebels: *épatez les bourgeois* — shock the bour-geois. Trollops were preferable, in his considered opinion, to troublesome shopgirls wanting the kind of passionate relationship routinely served up at vaudeville houses. "Absolutely not, I'll take the ignoble in its unadulterated form any day," he assured Ernest, who did not share this view. "It's just an-other pose and one to which I respond more readily than to any other. What I crave is a woman beautiful and ardent and whorish through and through."

By praising the very women whom his contemporary Alexandre Dumas' famous son Alexandre (known as Dumas fils) would soon be denouncing as mortal enemies of bourgeois society, Gustave masked his fearfulness with contrarian bluster, and in *Smar,* an overwrought, tangled dramatic fiction written during the first months of 1839, he continued to play devil's advocate, subverting the bourgeoisie on a cosmic scale. No one knows how he arrived at this title — the exotic, oriental syllable may simply have sounded right — but it is clear that his "mystery," as he described the work, owes much to Goethe's *Faust,* Byron's *Cain,* and Edgar Quinet's *Ahasvérus.* Satan in the guise of a Greek doctor descends upon a pious hermit named Smar, who quickly yields to his hitherto unavowed appetite for knowledge of worlds beyond his Levantine retreat. Off they go on a flight through space, with Satan warbling: "Are you not the king of this creation? The eternity around you was created for your soul," and Smar exclaiming: "Oh! How wide my heart is! I feel superior to this wretched world lost in the vast distances beneath my feet." With the happy proportions of his former life skewed by exposure to the infinite, Smar, a vagabond who unlearns Candide's lesson (*Il faut cultiver notre jardin*), now beholds the garden he once cultivated as a prison house. Boundaries that defined him on earth fall away in his state of cosmic egocentricity. "All this seems to have been made for me," he exults. But Satan the deceiver undeceives Smar, reminding him of his mortality. Born under a death sentence, he is not free. And the expanding void he cannot encompass attests to the absence of a transcendent being in whose moral custodianship men stubbornly believe. "Yes, nothingness far surpasses the human mind and all of creation . . . Truth is a shadow that slips away as man reaches out to grasp it," says Satan. Incommensurate with everything, too bloated for the home from which he exiled himself and too human for the empyrean to which he aspires, Smar dissolves in perplexity: "I know nothing, anguish gnaws me . . . Why these worlds? Why anything? Why am I here?" Then, longing for a view of life down below, the orphaned soul encounters Satan's confederate, a villainous Sancho Panza named Yuk, who shows him the human comedy as it unfolds from one depraved scene to another. Virtue has no home in this godforsaken world, where the seven deadly sins are bourgeois aldermen, where husbands wear horns and priests join their concubines after Mass, where nobility has evacuated palaces and spirit has fled the church. "How beautiful [the church] must have been on winter days with its multitude of candles, its congregation singing and walking in the aisles, . . . when everything — vault, graveyard, stained glass, stone — was imbued with gladness." Now the saints are gray and weather worn, the rose window is discolored, the belfry silent. Presiding over this decadent spectacle is Yuk (Robert Macaire's posterity, and another avatar of the Garçon), of whom Gustave writes that he kicked over "a crown, a belief, an ingenuous soul, a virtue, a conviction" whenever he extended his foot. As "god of the grotesque," whose cruel laughter resounds throughout, he is, says Gustave, the divinity best qualified to explain human affairs.

That *Smar* would win neither the Montyon prize, conferred each year by the Académie française on a morally improving work, nor acceptance from mothers protective of their daughters' virtue gave Gustave great satisfaction. To "outrage public morals" — the charge Second Empire justice leveled against *Madame Bovary* twenty years later — was to enjoy the potency of the terrorist, and Gustave, bourgeois though he may have been in other respects, found nothing more exhilarating than beginning- or end-of-the-world scenarios, visions of Nero burning Rome, of Erostratus destroying Ephesus, of Caligula's incest, of Petronian revels for a moribund empire, of all taboos imaginable flouted on Walpurgisnacht. In *Smar,* the misfit who couldn't screw his mind to the prescribed agenda of his class imagined an empty universe bereft of purpose, with no port or promised land for a futile species condemned to wander through it ad infinitum as nomads and tumblers.

During his last year at the collegiate school, Gustave sustained himself with Tacitus's *Annals,* the *Epistolae morales* of Seneca, and, above all, the essays of Montaigne, whom he had come to consider a kindred soul, if not an ideal father. Utterly confounded by numbers, he implored Ernest to send him his notes on algebra, geometry, and physics. He declared himself illiterate in Greek after four years of it. Philosophy, which was learned from a manual based upon the ragout of sensationalism, idealism, skepticism, and mysticism called eclecticism (as professed by Victor Cousin, minister of public instruction, who became France's all-powerful arbiter in educational and philosophical matters), made it even more difficult to rise every morning, but here at least he achieved distinction. "I am first in philosophy. M. Mallet has paid homage to my aptitude for moral ideas. How absurd, me the laureate in philosophy, ethics, reasoning, good principles!" he declared to Ernest (setting aside the fact that he read far more Seneca and Montaigne than school required of him). What no philosophy could resolve was the paradox of wanting his baccalaureate degree instantly — if Ernest were a god capable of conjuring away the months yet to be endured before commencement, he would build him, he wrote, a "golden temple" — while dreading the sequel to it.

This grim paradox nearly waylaid him en route to graduation. Early in December, a substitute teacher imposed a *pensum* upon senior students guilty of premeditated mayhem. His report describes them bellowing as they entered the classroom and ignoring his pleas for silence. When he finally began the lesson, three students interrupted him, Gustave being one. Punishments meted out to them had little effect on the others:

> There was a shuffling of feet and low murmuring. Absorbed as I was in a difficult explication I couldn't identify the culprits, which compelled me, regretfully, to inflict the same punishment on all alike. This I did only after three warnings and with the understanding that the punishment would be repealed if the guilty parties came forward.

Thirty students declared their intention not to do the *pensum* (copying one thousand lines of verse) in a collective letter, whereupon Jean Paillat, an inflexible grammarian who had only recently been named assistant principal, selected three signatories for expulsion. At this point Gustave, along with some others of those spared, addressed a protest to Paillat's superior. Expulsion, they wrote, meant professional doom for the three. "It would have been advisable before taking so decisive, so grave a measure to weigh on an impartial balance the fairness or injustice of a chore assigned arbitrarily." Had Paillat pondered the matter further, they went on to say, he would no doubt have shown more lenience, but in any event the selection of exemplary victims made no sense. "We who signed the original letter and do not recant what we declared then are ready now to lay before you, sir, the reasons that explain our present action. Should you still rule against us, we the undersigned demand that we all do the task or all suffer expulsion, whichever you choose." They concluded by stating that since this appeal had been given much serious thought, they expected to be treated as mature seniors rather than impulsive sixth-formers. Twelve classmates joined Gustave in this declaration, including Émile Hamard and Louis Bouilhet, who would play important roles in his life. All to no avail. The principal did not heed them. Instead he imitated his assistant, to whom he wrote a note singling out three signatories for expulsion: "By refusing the *pensum,* students Flaubert, Piedelièvre and Dumont have automatically shut themselves out of the school. Thus, there will be no need to inform the parents of their absence."

The sentence proved less draconian than his terse note might suggest. Or else pressure to commute it was brought upon Principal Dainez by Dr Flaubert's influential friends. In either event, it could not have disappointed Gustave, unless he secretly hoped for outright expulsion as a radical solution to his quandary. Banished from the collegiate school, he would still be allowed to take baccalaureate examinations and, if successful, receive the degree. Thenceforth, with his father encouraging him, he exercised far more self-discipline than ever before, though not in the matter of pipe smoking. We know from a letter to Chevalier that he routinely got up at 3 a.m., retired at 8:30 p.m., and studied for hours on end. Quantities of Greek had to be memorized, including two books of the *Iliad,* which he read with difficulty. Cicero led a crowd of Latin authors on his syllabus. He labored through the sixty-two lessons of Professor Mallet's *Manuel de philosophie.* Chevalier's borrowed notes helped with physics, but nothing short of divine intervention, he felt, would help him succeed in mathematics. "It's a terrible ordeal for someone like myself who is made to read the Marquis de Sade rather than all this nonsense!" What hindered him in general was the emotional strabismus of a young man who looked forward desperately to liberation from his academic straitjacket while gazing backward with heartache to comradeships blasted by the diaspora of graduation. "Those delicious mornings when we'd smoke and chat in Rouen, in Déville, will always be alive for me," he wrote to Ernest. "They're as fresh as yesterday, I can still hear our words beneath the leafy boughs where we lay on the ground, with smoke rising from our pipes and sweat beading on our brows . . . Or else we're at the fireplace, you three feet to the left near the door, with tongs in hand, tracing a circle of white ash on the lintel."

Gustave struggled through to graduation day. Commencement exercises, at which his name was not cited for any prizes or honorable mentions, took place on August 17, 1840, in the school chapel. Because of inclement weather, fewer spectators than usual showed up. Worse still, administrative and military bigwigs who would normally have graced the podium were away attending King Louis-Philippe at the Orléans country estate in Eu. But, as always, the National Guard provided musical relief, and for once it was joined by a student ensemble whose more or less coherent performance moved the *Journal de Rouen* to note approvingly that school officials did not let "more serious branches of study" crowd out "the lively arts."

After a faculty member demonstrated his rhetorical prowess in a speech lauding the regime for reconciling freedom and authority, Principal Dainez followed with an equally orotund speech insinuating that national perils might require of graduates a willingness to sacrifice themselves. The allusion, as everyone in his audience knew, was to the perennial "Eastern question." One year earlier, when young Abdul Mejid I succeeded his father as sultan in Constantinople, few people thought he would occupy the throne for long, with Muhammad Ali, the mutinous governor of Egypt, routing Turkish armies throughout the Near East. Fearful that Russia might exploit his predicament to invoke the terms of a previous treaty and send warships down the Dardanelles, the European powers scheduled a conference in London. With clever diplomatic maneuvering, Czar Nicholas wedged himself between England, which had intermittently propped up the Ottoman Empire, and France, which was Muhammad Ali's constant ally. The London conference brought together Austria, Prussia, England, and Russia in a reunion of nations victorious at Waterloo. Having been denied any say in the political arrangements that were to govern the eastern Mediterranean until the Crimean War of 1854–56, France regarded her exclusion as a casus belli. On the eve of Napoleon's return from Saint Helena for reburial in the Hôtel des Invalides, chauvinist feeling ran high. Young recruits were called to arms, and Principal Dainez beat his own little drum. Mothers who had shed tears when their sons left home for school could now appreciate the manly product of enlightened discipline, he told Gustave's class. "Finding you [their sons] as good as ever, but more submissive, more lovable perhaps and no less loving, more worthy of them in a word, they will easily recognize that this discipline, which isn't as harsh as may appear, . . . is the stoutest pillar of our social order, and the surest guarantor of our pledges to duty." If need be, such well-trained civilians would make exuberant soldiers. "Should the country, having to defend its national honor, or rebuff absurd pretentions, call upon your patriotism one day, you will, walking in the footsteps of your elders, remind France's enemies that the throne and the institutions it protects cannot perish so long as they are supported by the affection and courage of a free people." The *Journal de Rouen* observed that his noble sentiments clearly resonated through the student body.

In Gustave they echoed through an empty chamber. The devilish mimic waited thirteen or fourteen years before ridiculing Dainez and his kind in *Madame Bovary* with the subprefectural official's speech at the Yonville agricultural fair. Meanwhile he restrained himself, wore his ceremonial wreath of moist oak leaves, found solace in the admiration of his intimate circle, and turned his thoughts to the voyage his parents had promised him as a reward for staying the course.

A voyage to where? We know now that his initial itinerary would have seen him travel through Spain as an apprentice in historical scholarship, for Adolphe Chéruel inquired of Michelet on his protégé's behalf whether the great teacher might wish to give him a research assignment lasting four or five months. The friend (as he described Gustave), although not very well educated, "like every other young man just out of secondary school," and certainly not burdened by the weight of knowledge he claimed for himself, was nevertheless full of ardor and intelligence. "He would love to be assigned work in an interesting country, such as Spain. Should his project materialize, he would visit you with a letter of introduction from me and accept any tasks you might want him to perform in Spain." When nothing came of it, another itinerary was drawn, this one leading farther afield, from the Pyrenees through the Midi to Marseille and across the sea to Corsica.

VI

~~~~~

The Grand Tour

ANOTHER EVENT to which conversation drifted in August 1840 was Louis-Napoleon Bonaparte's second, loopy invasion of France. After making his way back across the Atlantic, he settled in London, found a guardian angel in Lady Blessington (who introduced him to political eminences such as Disraeli), and surrounded himself with cronies loyal to his ruling obsession. Dreams of imperial glory flared anew in March of that year, when the Chamber of Deputies voted funds to bring Napoleon's bones home from Saint Helena. The moment seemed auspicious to rally disillusioned citizens against their drab, peaceable sovereign. This time Boulogne was chosen as a beachhead. Louis arrived there in the early hours of August 6 on a paddle steamer normally chartered for pleasure cruises. Fifty-six armed men in counterfeit uniforms disembarked under the mournful eye of a tame vulture acquired at Gravesend to impersonate the Napoleonic eagle and, led by a conspirator quartered in the local garrison, marched past the sentry guarding regimental barracks. An outraged colonel, whose absence had been counted on, foiled Louis' pathetic reenactment of the return of Napoleon from Elba. Resistance was offered. Shots rang out, and Louis himself wounded a soldier before fleeing with his motley crew. Another skirmish occurred near the ship, where two of the pursued were shot dead. Louis presented himself at his subsequent trial as a staunch champion of popular sovereignty. The Court of Peers agreed on a term of life imprisonment in the fortress prison of Ham, in Picardy.

The escapade might have died like spindrift on the Normandy shore if not for the parlous state of Anglo-French relations and the prospect of a Napoleonic apotheosis in December, when elaborate funeral ceremonies were scheduled to take place.* It added fuel to a fire of chauvinism raging so intensely among people from every walk that Louis-Philippe felt obliged to strike martial poses unbecoming to a paterfamilias of sixty-seven. Five hundred thousand men were mobilized in August and September, including eighteen new regiments of horse and foot soldiers. Ground was broken for a ring of connected forts around Paris. French and English warships squared off in the Bosporus, while Sir Charles Napier bombarded Beirut, which had been captured by France's protégé Muhammad Ali. As shrewd observers like James de Rothschild predicted, Louis-Philippe eventually backed down, abandoning Muhammad Ali to his fate, but the national uproar augured ill when Gustave set forth on August 22. His ever-fretful mother took comfort in the knowledge that three sober adults would be accompanying him: Dr Jules Cloquet, Achille's professor of surgery at the Paris Medical School, who had toured Scotland with him five years earlier; Cloquet's maiden sister Lise; and an Italian priest named Stefani.

In Paris, where Gustave, now sporting a blond mustache, received congratulations from his former teacher Gourgaud-Dugazon and unburdened himself of his worries about law school, the party boarded a diligence for the run to Bordeaux. This four-hundred-mile journey on wooden wheels in summer heat required exceptional fortitude. Enjoying the most favorable conditions, the travelers occupied the "interior" or middle compartment, which seated six, with privacy afforded by head-high leather partitions. Even so, the space was not designed to accommodate a strapping youth, least of all at night, when he tried to stretch his legs. If sleep came, it would have been interrupted every few hours by the hubbub of relays and postilions who had finished their shift jostling him for a tip. Worse still was the tacit ban against tobacco. Although he didn't note it, Gustave undoubtedly cast an envious eye at the *rotonde,* or sealed rear compartment, where poor passengers — workers, soldiers on leave, wet nurses suckling their charges — usually sat close together in a fog of pipe smoke. What he did record in his diary, after warning himself to keep his prose simple and direct, were images of the French countryside colored with literary associations. Between Blois and Tours, where the Loire narrowed to a ribbon of

---

*In the working class, Napoleon was as generally adulated as Louis-Philippe was despised. When the funeral cortege bearing Napoleon's ashes passed through Rouen on December 10, many thousands gathered and watched in a reverent hush.

water flowing over a shallow sandy bed and woods retreated from the banks and horses towed becalmed sailboats, Gustave decided that the riverine landscape had been made for Charles d'Orléans's decorous ballads. "It's neither large, nor beautiful, nor very green," he wrote, anticipating Taine's thoughts on the relevance of a specific milieu to a particular sensibility, "but it is, as it were, a Charles d'Orléans poem, one of those refrains whose ingenuousness emits a tender feeling so calm and feeble it has hardly any pulse." Picturing a lustier sixteenth-century native of the region, François Rabelais, served as an antidote to boredom, and the Garçon, alias Gargantua, might have improvised ribald commentary in mock archaic French had there been any chance of thus amusing the spinster, the priest, and the learned doctor. When they wheeled through Blois, Gustave, true to his weakness for depraved rulers, complained about being unable to visit the castle in which Henri III, who helped his mother, Catherine de Médicis, plot the Saint Bartholomew's Day Massacre, frolicked with pretty boys.

Warm breezes reached the young man south of Poitiers in a land of red berets and red-tiled roofs and revived him like a fragrant nosegay. The group spent several busy days at Bordeaux before setting out for the Pyrenees. Mindful of Dr Flaubert's precept that travel must broaden, Gustave visited museums, libraries, a natural history collection, a porcelain factory, churches. His aversion to the straight line set him against a city laid out rectilinearly, without anything "incisive" to recommend it, and bounded by a river as phlegmatic as itself. Swimming in the yellow, silty Garonne made his flesh creep. But there were excitements of a different kind. The crypt of the Saint-Michel basilica, which contained mummified corpses exhumed from the neighboring graveyard, had become an attraction for Romantics infatuated with the macabre (Théophile Gautier among others, who described it in his *Voyage en Espagne*), and Gustave attempted to follow their lead. "I can testify that [they] all have skin as drum-tight, leathery, brown and reverberant as ass hides," he wrote. "Not to have had any eerie ideas while standing amid these venerable mummies made me despair; I'm not sensitive enough to have experienced any horror either. In fact, I found their various grimaces diverting." What did send shivers up his spine was the 1588 edition of Montaigne's essays, a copy of which, with Montaigne's own marginal notes and amendments, had been preserved at the municipal library. Like the "bibliomane" of his story, he touched it, he said, in the spirit of true believers touching holy relics.

After a bibulous ramble through the Médoc vineyards and gourmet meals served by friends of Dr Cloquet's, whose far-flung circle included General Carbonel, commandant of the Gironde military district, they departed for Basque country, crossing the great pine forests of Languedoc en route to Bayonne, where Gustave finally found a river he liked in the Adour. At Biarritz, which was, like Deauville, a poor village destined to strike it rich under Napoleon III, the beach lured him away from his straitlaced company with fantasies of meeting another Élisa. Fifteen years later he might have found a voluptuous upper-class nymph there, but on August 30, 1840, his daydreams were interrupted by cries for help to save two drowning men. "I heard loud lamentations and a large woman all in black whom I took to be their mother ran toward me," he remembered. This matron, blessing and exhorting him in turn, helped him unbutton his boots. "I plunged in straightaway but with the same sangfroid I have on a normal swim, and indeed so imperturbably that while breasting the waves I quite forgot I was performing a mission of mercy." Unfazed by the emergency at sea as he had been unruffled by mummies in Bordeaux, did he fear that his equanimity bespoke a dearth of imagination, a lack of heart, or fraudulence? "The only thing that bothered me were my pants and socks, which I hadn't removed and were hampering my movements. I needed fifty or so strokes to reach an unconscious man being towed to shore by two others, laboriously." Neither victim could be saved, and Gustave (who dressed at this juncture of his grand tour in white gloves, a satin cravat, and a waistcoat with a lorgnon looped around the topmost button) mourned his ruined trousers.

A day spent on Spanish soil across the Bidassoa river frontier, when Don Quixote seemed to walk beside him and a sun more radiant than France's shone bewitchingly on barefoot peasant girls and every deep impulse told the dapper Norman that his true vocation was to be a mule driver, was not Spain enough for him. But one day of it was all he got. Inland from Bayonne loomed the forested slopes and snow-capped peaks of the Atlantic Pyrenees, to which Dr Cloquet's protégés now addressed themselves. Before long they were a mile high, looking at cliffs on either side of valleys carved by swift torrents called *gaves*. Up the Gave de Pau they made their way past Lourdes — still so obscure it gets mentioned only parenthetically — on a road winding along the mountainside toward Cauterets like a thin white tapeworm. On foot and horseback they reached the eleventh-century priory of Saint-Savin, perched above four converging valleys, whose community of Benedictine monks sang canticles at cloud level. One last push took them across murrain to the beautiful green expanse of the Lac de Gaube and the Pique Longue soaring behind it. There Gustave, who once again felt inadequate to an occasion for emotional release or imaginative freedom, inveighed against the others, as if their presence — or their collective stomach — interposed itself between his mind and its impressions. "Certainly being alone and staying after dark to see moonlight reflected in its green water, with the silhouette of snowy peaks . . . one could more easily grasp its beauty and grandeur; but no, one goes there as one goes everywhere, on a junket, which means that one can't dream or allow

oneself to indulge immodestly in flights of fancy. One arrives at noon, famished, and gorges on excellent salmon trout; the imagination is thus swindled of all its 'vaporosity' and prevented from rising aloft, to hover with
eagles." Not until he hiked through a narrow, boulder-strewn defile and,
where it opened out funnel-like, beheld a gigantic amphitheater of cliffs
called the Cirque de Gavarnie, from which glacial runoff cascaded into
scrubby wilderness, did Gustave embrace the mountainous world. "To the
left lay Roland's gap and the marble quarry," he wrote of the Cirque de
Gavarnie, in pages quite the equal of Hugo's well-anthologized journal.
"And the ground, which looked level from afar, slopes so steeply that one
ends up clambering on hands and knees to reach the foot of the waterfall;
earth crumbles underfoot, stones roll downhill into the torrent, the waterfall booms and drenches you with its mist . . . Gray, snow-edged masses of
the Marboré mountains stood out against a blue sky, and overhead floated
some small clouds, outlined in gold by the sun. It is a ravishing spectacle."

Of the almost daily letters Gustave exchanged with a family always clam-
oring for news, few have survived, but those few bear partial witness to the
tone and drift of conversation in a very private household. Persuading herself that her son's robust appearance did not conceal a frail ghost was difficult for Mme Flaubert, who, when she felt well enough to write at all,
fretted hypochondriacally about herself as well as Gustave. Could he reassure her posthaste that the long voyage south had not left him exhausted
and ill? God forbid that he should have any accidents on the road. As for
herself, migraines pursued her wherever she went, in Nogent-sur-Seine after a jolting ride from Rouen, and back in Rouen after a fortnight of worrying about dear Gustave, whose absence was unendurable. Until he
returned (when exactly did he plan to? she wondered), only letters could
dull her pain. "Letters! Letters! I await them most impatiently, and they will
be my greatest source of happiness during your absence," she wrote on August 24, and two weeks later, "Never, my good Gustave, will I complain of
having too many letters from you. Write as many as you like, they will always be received with great pleasure." Achille-Cléophas was another avid
reader, but where mother exhorted, father prescribed. "May your spirits
stay high and your heart good, as we know it to be," he urged, in a passable
imitation of Polonius. "Profit from your voyage and remember your friend
Montaigne, who recommends that one travel in order chiefly to bring back
the customs and humors of nations, and to 'rub and polish our brain against
that of others.' Look, observe, and take notes. Don't be a grocer on holiday
or a commercial traveler on his rounds. Always remember that you are the
youngest of the party and must be the most lighthearted, the first to have
his bags packed [Gustave being notoriously unmatutinal and dilatory]." The
doctor concluded his prescription with "Your father and friend, Flaubert."

Letters from sister Caroline, whom he nicknamed "joli Rat," "raton," and "Carolo," and who called him "Boun," "Gus," "Gust," and "mon gros farceur," were pure pleasure, with nothing in them to inspire guilt or anxiety. Adoring and playful, she had always been an excellent audience for the Garçon, whose nonsense delighted her. His burlesque of lectures on chemistry and physics (Charles Bovary's garbled understanding of the anatomy of clubfoot had a long history) was sorely missed, she complained, the evening a pedantic physician named Parfait Grout made these subjects his dinner conversation. "We speak of you a thousand times a day and agree, while singing your praises, that your antics are sometimes excessive. I say 'we' because I began the sentence in the first person plural, but I myself never tire of them and assure you that on your return I'll be laughing myself silly as usual at everything you say." Brother and sister confided in each other. If Caroline needed consolation or entertainment or advice, she had only to call and Gustave would appear straightaway. When her beloved Newfoundland and her nanny goat ceased to figure as adequate objects for affectionate outpouring, he may have been the first to know about her romantic interest in his classmate, friend, and fellow petitioner Émile Hamard, who apparently dropped by the Hôtel-Dieu to inquire after him during his voyage. But the confidants were also master and pupil. Gustave took pleasure in lording it over Caroline during regular lessons and derived special satisfaction from teaching her subjects that were thought to be the rightful and exclusive province of young men, notably history. In her eyes he was an intellectual eminence rather than Achille's kid brother, a mentor far more important than any at the private school she attended. "I have begun the first volume of M. Thiers [his ten-volume *Histoire du Consulat et de l'Empire*]," she wrote on September 7. "I intended to take notes, but notes on ten volumes would be a bit much, so I'm just reading it and hope you won't scold me for my lack of courage. If you're stern, I'll dissolve in tears and you will be doubly obligated to console me." A fortnight later she reported that she had soldiered through four volumes without skipping any descriptions of battles or passages of economic analysis. Such perseverance on the part of the sixteen-year-old was given due credit. How willingly Gustave praised skills to the refinement of which he couldn't contribute and for which he himself had no aptitude — dancing, playing the piano, drawing — was another matter. Asking her, for example, about her sessions in Charles Mozin's studio at Trouville, he wondered patronizingly whether the painter recognized her "*petit talent d'artiste.*"

After Bagnères-de-Luchon, which straddled the mountain road running between towns famous since Roman antiquity for their mineral springs, Gustave went downhill, emotionally as well as geographically. In a letter to Caroline dated September 28, he recited place-names that marked his voyage from the Pyrenees across southern France by way of explaining the fatigue to which he and his companions had finally succumbed. But his diary describes a more deliberate, even tedious progress through Languedoc. So sated was he with Romanesque architecture that the great church of Saint-Sernin in Toulouse, beautiful as he knew it to be, left him glassy-eyed. On a barge towed some one hundred miles down the Canal du Midi past Carcassonne toward Narbonne, he gazed upon the immense expanse of vineyards like a castaway squinting at the horizon and brooded once again about squandered opportunities for spiritual elevation and sensual enlargement. "Our vessel glides between rows of trees whose rounded heads are mirrored in the water, the water makes a pretense of murmuring to the prow, we halt at canal locks from time to time, the crank grinds, and the towline stretches. There are people who find this magnificent and swoon over the picturesqueness of it all; it bores me, just as descriptive poetry does . . . For that matter southern churches are all alike! — the exterior Romanesque, the portal usually Renaissance, the interior whitewashed." By then he felt that his assiduous companions, one of whom — Father Stefani — kept munching figs, and all of whom pledged absolute fealty to their guidebooks, had cheated him of adventure, and he consoled himself with *Candide,* a favorite novel. Not until they reached Nîmes, at the eastern edge of Languedoc, where his Latin culture sprang to life in the city's great Augustan ruins, did Gustave smile again. A welcome relief from the bland good humor encountered en route was the animation of street scenes he could imagine onstage in a comedy by Plautus.

The animation of Nîmes was a mere fife to the brass band of street life in Marseille, where Gustave and company recuperated at a hotel near the Old Port, on the rue de la Darse. This Babel of a neighborhood swarmed with sailors from every quarter and doxies for every taste. During the two days he spent there, Gustave joined the polyglot crowd in open-air cabarets, when he wasn't strolling on the Cannebière, swimming, or being the acquisitive tourist at a souklike market that put him in mind of Smyrna and caravans and seraglios — above all seraglios. Overwhelmed by so much promiscuity, he left Marseille with Turkish pipes, sandals, a rattan cane, and other paraphernalia required to make his forthcoming tour of Corsica more comfortable, or expeditionary. Pistols might have completed the picture.

As there had never been any question of Father Stefani's and Lise Cloquet's visiting an island still infested with banditti who did not necessarily see fit to honor women and clerics, Gustave and Dr Cloquet had only each other for companionship on a paddle steamer that weighed anchor at Toulon in the early hours of October 4. The passage took a full day and night through rough seas and proved to be exceptionally unromantic. Pitching to and fro under a constant spray from its wheel, the boat shivered with every stroke of the piston. Flat on his back, Gustave saw much more of a pewter basin filled with vomit than of the Mediterranean and would certainly have moaned amen to an observation made some twenty-five years later by Edward Lear during a similar crossing: "He is fortunate who, after ten hours of sea passage can reckon up no worse memories than those of a passive condition of suffering — of that dislocation of mind and body, or inability to think straightforward, so to speak, when the outer man is twisted, and rolled, and jerked." Adding insult to injury was the apparent immunity of three priests at table chomping away like famished otters. Not until he regained his land legs in Ajaccio did fixed objects stay still.

Though beautifully situated on a promontory with a castle at one end, Ajaccio cut a poor figure to eyes that had just feasted on the color and movement of Marseille. All along its principal street were tall, bulky houses as like one another as dominos. Hunched between the sea and the rugged escarpments of Mount Aragnasco, it had seemingly never been visited by an impulse to rouge its facades, to embellish windows with balconies and pediments, to rejoice in spires or describe the arches of a galleria. Gray venetian blinds suited Corsicans better than the bright green ones prevalent on the Italian coast, and in clothes this dourness of temperament countenanced nothing gayer than dark brown. The tourist who was enough of a naturalist to know that the island's indigenous species included the *Helix tristis*, or melancholy snail, might now have understood why, if he hadn't already taken Prosper Mérimée's word for it that in Corsica everything was grave. Everything except the red trousers of French soldiers.

Jourdan du Var, a genial and allegedly corrupt prefect (who resigned under a cloud five years later), housed his intrepid compatriots at his official residence until October 7, when the two departed on horseback for Vico. With Gustave half hoping to be waylaid harmlessly by banditti, they soon entered a world that surpassed their visions of primeval beauty. Almond trees were no longer in full bloom, but fig trees were still in leaf, and the mountain road crossed fields overgrown with low-slung mastic trees, cacti, golden-yellow broom, myrtle, and arbutus. Higher up it led through groves of wild olive, cork, and ilex, whose bright green foliage, in the midst of which immense oaks poked their gray arms, carpeted the hillside. Higher still, above the crowns of yellow beech, it wound along granite cliffs facing west toward the Gulf of Sagone, and then down, forcing riders to dismount, into the salty aroma of a seaside town. Here, under a brilliant sun, Gustave felt for once rapturously at peace with himself. "One is penetrated by the sun's rays, the pure air, suave and untranslatable thoughts," he noted in his diary. "Everything in you throbs with joy and beats its wings with the elements . . . The essence of animate nature seems to have infiltrated you, you smile at breezes wafting through the treetops, the murmur of waves lapping the beach. Something large and tender hovers in the light and then becomes impalpable radiance, like the dewy morning vapors rising toward the sky."

Careful plans were laid with a guide and three *voltigeurs*, or riflemen, hired as armed escorts. Gustave's excursion to Vico had prepared him for the rough journey across an island of remote towns nestling in valleys separated by deeply notched mountain ranges. Beyond Bocagnano the party followed a forest path that led east through cushion-topped pines growing eighty feet tall. With the white silhouette of Mount Renoso on one side and a ridge of stupendous precipices called Kyrie and Christe Eleison straight ahead, they trekked on foot and horseback until dark and halted at the terraced village of Ghisoni. Here Gustave spent a sleepless night swatting at fleas in a ramshackle farmhouse occupied by swine as well as peasants, but also gazing entranced at the moonlit countryside. News of a distinguished French physician's visit had preceded Dr Cloquet, who awoke to the sight of sick Ghisonians queuing up for free consultations. Once advice had been dispensed, the five began their arduous ascent of Christe Eleison, up a wooded slope, then above the tree line, and eventually out onto a high plateau called the Prato. "We could see one mountain range after another undulating toward the sea, each colored with the various hues of underbrush, chestnuts, pines, cork oak and heath," Gustave wrote. "The panorama stretched thirty leagues to the horizon and encompassed the Tyrrhenian sea, the isle of Elba, . . . a corner of Sardinia. At our feet lay the Aleria plain immense and white like an Oriental vista." It was twelve hours more, and a descent as perilous as the climb, before they reached Isolaccio, where hospitality was offered by the son of Captain Laurelli, their chief escort. After feasting on goat meat and sleeping on clean pallets, they bade farewell to all the riflemen save Laurelli some miles up the coast, near the Fium'Orbo district, whose crudely armed, ungovernable inhabitants had repulsed five thousand well-equipped French troops during the Restoration. Some miles farther north they turned inland and made for Corte.

Among Corsican towns, none was more picturesque than the island's ancient capital, midway between Ajaccio and Bastia, where Gustave and Cloquet arrived on October 14 after ten hours on horseback. Built on a jagged butte at the confluence of two rivers that flowed down gorges from nearby Mounts Artica and Rotondo, Corte was ideal for Romantic landscape painters as well as military garrisons. Only one rock face sloped gently enough for habitation, and tall houses covered it, receding upward like the blocks of a pyramid to a fortress perched on high. Tourists visiting the citadel walked through Corsica's tormented history, a recent chapter of which involved her futile struggle for independence during the 1760s, when the rebellion against Genoa was directed from within this bastion

(Genoa ceded the island in 1768, but to France). Did Gustave and Cloquet bother to tour it? We know only that here they parted ways with Captain Laurelli, who lived in Corte, and prepared to complete their tour under different escort.* Although Gustave, than whom no one found separation more painful, lamented the captain's departure, he had, he claimed, come to accept transient friendship as a sadly sweet concomitant of long journeys. "It's difficult to tear yourself away from that which pleases, but as habit gains the upper hand, one no longer wishes to cast backward glances, one thinks always of the morrow, never of the previous day. One's mind, like one's legs, grows accustomed to carrying one forward, and the world gallops past in a ceaseless panorama. Valleys deep in shadow, heaths thick with myrtle, . . . enormous forests of scraggy pine, confidences en route, long chats with friends made yesterday." Not once had the passing scene stopped long, or Captain Laurelli's *voltigeurs* strayed far enough, for banditti to leap from the maquis and offer Gustave a heroic moment. As consolation, he and Cloquet visited prisons in Ajaccio and Bastia, on some philanthropic pretext, to see truly feral Corsicans, like wildlife lovers on safari who, encountering no beasts in the bush, end up at an African zoo.

Disaster nearly struck on their last lap, when the guide, who wasn't quite sober, led them astray in a dark wood somewhere between Corte and Piedicroce. At length they found their bearings again, and the incident brought Gustave and Jules Cloquet closer together, Cloquet having shown himself by then to be a good-natured, even playful companion. At Bastia, where they set sail on the eighteenth, the two rested briefly in a city Europeanized by its proximity to Livorno, with cafés, baths, carriages, and other amenities of which Gustave, for all his dithyrambs about natural man (untroubled by law or law school), gladly availed himself.

Adventure of a different kind awaited him when he least expected it, on the mainland, soon after they disembarked in a mistral churning up Toulon's harbor. Sexual fantasies had been his most irksome companion since August. They were finally given their due, not at any of the brothels that abounded in Marseille, but by a dark-haired woman named Eulalie Foucaud, who, with her mother, ran the Hôtel de Richelieu on the rue de la Darse, to which both men returned after their first stay three weeks earlier. Had Eulalie been looking forward to Gustave's return from Corsica? Certainly the seduction, as the Goncourts related it twenty years later (with Flaubert's embellishments or perhaps their own), would seem to have been initiated by her. "He checked into a small hotel," they noted,

---

*Had they come several decades earlier, they, like James Boswell and most visitors of repute, would have stayed at the Franciscan monastery. By 1840 it lay in ruins.

where three French ladies back from Lima had brought home some sixteenth-century ebony furniture with mother-of-pearl inlay over which people oohed and aahed. Wearing loose silk peignoirs, they were accompanied by a nigger-boy got up in nankin and babouches. For this young Norman provincial . . . it was all deliciously exotic. Once, after he had returned from an afternoon swim, [the younger woman], a voluptuous creature in her thirties, lured him into her room. He gave her a long, soulful kiss. That evening she visited him and started right away sucking him. There were magnificent orgasms, then tears, then letters, then nothing.

Of Eulalie's civil status we know for certain only that she had a young daughter, came from a family of substantial merchants, and owned property in French Guyana. Of her heart much more is known, as she spilled it in letters to the handsome young man, who left for Paris the day after their lovemaking. This single conjunction turned her head. Gustave, she declared, was the breath that inflated her soul, the fire that awakened her flesh. Passionate letters followed him to Rouen via Paris, where Émile Hamard served as go-between. Until he came along, Eulalie assured him, she had been no more alive than an automaton. "You've become for me the breath of creation, and henceforth I shall not have strength enough to live without this love on which my happiness entirely depends." Gustave did not respond right away. When at last he did (in a lost letter), her pitch rose even higher. If he should visit her again in Marseille, thus answering her prayers, she could die without regrets. In the meantime he was to remember that wherever he went, her thoughts accompanied him; that however he felt, her feelings complied with his. "Henceforth my soul is so married to yours that they are but one, for better and for worse," she wrote in February 1841. "To have possessed you and now to be deprived of you is absolute hell . . . Oh my beloved Gustave! How I pity you if you are suffering as much as I, a poor woman exiled on this earth, indifferent to everything. I thought my heart was inured to all sensations, all desires, but you kindled a consuming fire in me, Gustave. Our hearts speak to each other. I have embarked upon a new existence, only to long and to suffer."

Ten months after their night together, the fire still smoldered. Having to visit "America" (presumably Guyana, for undivulged reasons), Eulalie predicted that her sojourn there would be brief, but the prospect of oceanic separation made her fret more explicitly about their difference in age. Her hair would not turn white during the interval, she assured him, and her kisses, at their reunion, would be just as "delirious." Was he too young to appreciate that love, like wine, improved with age, that the older vintages had richer body? Could he ignore her erotic savoir faire or the greater capacity for feeling that her years had given her? "At my age, Gustave, one is better able to love, to feel, than at yours," she wrote, half reproachfully, in August 1841. "The passions are more fiery, more alive! Unless you burn the candle at both ends and wear yourself out in orgies and libertinage, you will acknowledge in ten years the truth of what I say, however peculiar it may seem now. That's when you will be able to love truly and realize that the beloved woman embodies all the joys, all the sensual delights a man may dream of." The nineteen-year-old revolving dismal thoughts about the in-evitability of law school was urged by the thirty-five-year-old woman with whom he spent one night to throw it all over for love and was told, as in a chivalrous fairy tale, that after an apprenticeship of ten years he might hope to become her abject slave. "To love, Gustave, is to devote oneself [to the woman], to make her the sole and sacred object of one's thoughts and de-sires, to have no will, no joy, no pleasures but hers. It is to feel oneself ca-pable of performing the greatest and noblest deeds on her behalf, to feel one's heart quiver with happiness at her approach, to feel intoxicated by the sight of her, to yearn for her when she is absent, to see her everywhere day and night." Even then he would not love as ardently as his correspondent, she proclaimed. To experience what she did required a "soul of fire" and a temperament so prolific of tears and regrets that she couldn't, after all, wish it on him.

There is reason to surmise that Gustave felt many things: impressed with himself for inspiring such arias, relieved at escaping the bondage to which Adolphe falls victim in Benjamin Constant's great novel, fearful of Eulalie's coming north, bereft of a sexual partner unlike any other he had had, and responsible for her pain. Typically, he would announce his conquest by making light of it. How could he love a woman who spelled *automate* "*otto-mate*"?* He had merely feigned love in love letters to "la mère Foucaud," he claimed later, when a jealous mistress threw Eulalie's name in his face. But their one night affected him no less than it had her, and Gustave's imagina-tion was the equal of Eulalie's in its aptitude for feeding gluttonously on a crumb. She would not be forgotten. She may indeed have bequeathed something of her essence to Emma Bovary. In subsequent years, as we shall see, Gustave repeatedly visited the rue de la Darse, by then one of his pri-vate graveyards, to mourn Eulalie, whom he never saw again.

BEFORE LEAVING Marseille, Gustave walked along the waterfront, lis-tened one last time to the siren call of the Mediterranean, and promised himself to explore it from end to end. Life would remain half-lived until he

---

*Tellingly, Gustave made a similar mistake in misspelling the name of an acquaintance. In-stead of "Daupias" he would write "D'Oppia."

had seen oleanders flowering on the banks of the Guadalquivir in Andalu-
sia, the Alhambra, Toledo, Seville, Naples, Venice, and had sailed east for
the Golden Horn, where his imagination was a frequent sojourner. Place-
names ancient and modern swirled in a phantasmagoria of caravans, mosques
with porphyry columns, Alexander's encampments, she-camels, glinting
scimitars. It crossed his mind that a Norman as aberrant as he — who went
dreamy at the mere mention of Nineveh and Persepolis, who felt most at
home reclining on thick rugs and habitually fancied himself lording it over
obsequious slaves rather than functioning among equals pledged to the rule
of law — might have been Oriental in a former life, or mysteriously conceived elsewhere, like some exotic shrub born of a seed blown far from its
native soil.

The coach ride north was long and rueful. Clocks were heard to tick
again after two months of silence. Gustave, whose appetite seldom failed
him, consoled himself as best he could with the prospect of enjoying wild
duck and iced champagne, of seeing wheat fields ripen in springtime, of
rowing on the Seine at sunset. Alas, the late-autumn fog that shrouded
Rouen, making him wonder whether wheat would ever ripen again or rays
of the setting sun ever slant through poplars along the river, soon defeated
his effort to maintain an optimistic frame of mind. The sun, he railed, was
no more visible overhead than "diamonds up a pig's ass." And darkness fostered illness, it seemed. Mme Flaubert's migraines continued to paralyze
her, though never enough to interfere with the ritual of Sundays at Déville,
which Gustave and Caroline found increasingly tiresome. A chronic infection of the throat and pain in the lower back possibly signaling a renal disorder caused great concern for his sister, who was denied an active social life
and subjected to dietary superstitions that made her health more delicate
than it need have been. Achille-Cléophas, the indefatigable caretaker, also
required care when an infirmity diagnosed as rheumatism kept him bedridden in December and early January of 1841. One month later, almost
halfway through his last year of law school, Alfred Le Poittevin returned
from Paris with a stubborn respiratory infection that mimicked the symptoms of tuberculosis. Gustave put himself in harm's way by visiting him
nearly every day for five weeks.

It has been inferred from two details in Gustave's letters to Ernest Chevalier that he himself was unwell and that poor health might explain the year-
long deferment of law school after graduation. On April 6, 1841, he
announced that he would meet Ernest at Les Andelys for an Easter reunion
well supplied with pipes and cigars and tobacco, only to write two days later
that he no longer smoked, having given up all of his "bad habits." In July,
when there was some question of Ernest's returning the visit, Gustave
warned him, with the scatological bluster to which he often had recourse

as a palliative in worrisome matters, that his physical appearance might shock. "My brother was kicked by a horse . . . and has been bedridden for five weeks while the membrane enveloping the knee joint heals. As for me, I have become colossal, monumental, I am an ox, a sphinx, a bull-of-the-bog, an elephant, a whale, whatever is most enormous, thickest and heaviest, spiritually as well as physically." If his shoes had laces, his paunch would prevent him from tying them. All he did, he said, was huff and puff and sweat and slobber. "I am a chyle factory, a machine for producing blood that beats and lashes my face, for making shit that reeks and browns my ass."

No doubt gluttony and heavy smoking compromised his health. But it is less likely that the ill effects of overindulgence kept Gustave at home than that a depressive state bound up with the professional course charted for him by others led him to seek comfort in food and tobacco. His year off may have been part of a bargain Achille-Cléophas had struck with him even before he graduated from the collegiate school.

If so, it merely postponed the ineluctable necessity of laying his head under the blade of bourgeois expectations. With no practical alternative to law school, Gustave was free to spend days on end as a hostage pondering his fate and fantasizing about deliverance in the form of a rich American uncle. When Ernest asked what he hoped to become, he answered "nothing" and quoted, as he would often again, the Epicurean commandment: "Hide your life."* Since fate decreed that he must make something of himself, he would make of himself the least thing possible. "The mangiest ass still has a few hairs on its hide, the emptiest cask still holds two or three drops of wine, and next year I, my dear friend, shall study the noble metier in which you will soon be licensed," he wrote. What more radical expression of defiance could there be than acquiring an even higher degree of law than was needed to practice it, the better to spurn the law altogether? "I shall do law and even add a fourth year to prank myself with the title of doctor. I may then go off to become a Turk in Turkey, or a muleteer in Spain, or a camel driver in Egypt. I've always had a predilection for that kind of life."

How else Gustave occupied himself during this vexed sabbatical may be gathered from the references to classical authors that lace his correspondence. At the beginning of it he assigned himself a mighty syllabus, which served various purposes. There was pride to be salvaged for not having distinguished himself sufficiently at the Collège royal. There was mastery to be

---

*The maxim is quoted by one of Flaubert's favorite writers, Chateaubriand, toward the end of *Mémoires d'outre-tombe,* in a famous passage describing the last days of the Bourbon monarchy. During the revolution of July 1830 the author rushes to the Luxembourg palace at night only to discover that his fellow peers, who convened there, had fled. As he walks through the deserted gardens, he remembers Epicurus's maxim. Chateaubriand's memoirs, though completed in 1841, were not published until 1848–49.

won of foreign languages and a thirst for knowledge of worlds, especially vanished worlds, that fired his imagination. There was also the desire to prolong school days, to enjoy asylum in an academic program that rested upon Greek and Latin as a temple upon its central pillars. Thus, with notepaper and dictionaries near to hand, he read Horace, Tacitus, Thucydides, Xenophon, and, most persistently (like Goethe's Werther), Homer. On New Year's Day 1842, Gustave, who cultivated a local reputation for bearishness, closeted himself with the *Iliad* and the *Odyssey* after rising at 4 a.m. to begin puffing away — his abstinence from tobacco had been of brief duration — and creating the miasma that favored intellectual labor. "I still work at Greek and Latin and perhaps always will," he reported to Gourgaud-Dugazon. "I love the scent of those beautiful languages." Even so, depression had its way. Foul odors emitted by the future seeped through chinks in the ivory tower and distracted him from classical antiquity. When it came to grading himself on his postgraduate work, he was harsher than Professor Magnier had even been. "What am I doing? What will I ever do?" he wondered in private notes. "What is my future? Little do I care. I should have liked to work this year, but I don't have the heart for it, and am deeply disappointed. I could have learned Latin and Greek, English too. A thousand things tore the book from my hands, and I lapsed into daydreams longer than the lingering twilight."

What he certainly had to show for that year, on the other hand, was some considerable portion of his first long work, a novel begun soon after his return from Corsica and entitled *Novembre*. By January 1842 it was far enough along for him to announce its imminent completion (though in fact he wouldn't finish it until October of that year) to Gourgaud-Dugazon and describe it apprehensively as a "sentimental ratatouille" quite devoid of action. Analyzing the work, he said, would be a pointless redundancy, since its very fabric was analysis. "It may be beautiful for all I know, but I'm afraid it rings false and comes across as pretentious and stilted."

When he reread the unpublished manuscript later on, Flaubert, who neither disowned his firstborn nor ever ceased to scold it for its awkwardness, had very little difficulty recognizing himself in the brilliant effusions pitching between mania and depression. Stilted would hardly describe *Novembre,* but it is indeed devoid of action. Part 1 of the tripartite scheme is a meditation that loiters through the head of a troubled schoolboy. The eighteen-year-old narrator recalls himself as a fifteen-year-old with no emotional attachments binding him to a commonly shared life. His is the freedom of the prisoner locked outside, of the vagabond. He is a voyeur in love with love but afraid of women, starved for companionship but convinced that every heart is impenetrable, longing for a transcendent principle but praying in disaffected temples. "I saw nothing to cling to, neither society nor solitude, nor poetry, nor science, nor impiety, nor religion. I wandered amid all that like a soul rebuffed equally by paradise and hell." Only heaven or hell, salvation or damnation, seems a proper sequel to undergraduate life — not learning a profession, marrying, fathering, living life in the finite middle ground of ordinary human pursuits. Tormented by scenes of rich people gaily assembled in brightly lit rooms, he makes his pain serve his pride and takes loneliness as a sign of election. Or else, experiencing the opposite, he stands in a rapturous trance at the center of creation. One such experience — which Gustave describes with vivid pictures in mind of the Mediterranean viewed from above Vico but also of a midsummer walk through the countryside between Pont l'Évêque and Trouville — concludes part 1. "I found myself on a plateau, in a field of mowed hay," he writes.

> The sea lay spread out before me, very blue. Sunlight glinted off it like luminous pearls, and fiery rays striped the water. Between the azure sky and the darker sea gleamed the horizon. It blazed, in fact. The vault rose just above my head and dipped down yonder behind the waves, forming something like the closed circle of an invisible infinite. Flat on the ground, I lost myself in contemplation of its beauty . . . [Later] I ran downhill to the seashore, . . . inhaling the fresh breeze . . . I felt my heart swell, the spirit of God filled me. With something worshipful stirring deep inside, I would have liked to resolve myself into sunlight or become blueness in the blue immensity . . . Wild joy took hold of me.

When the narrative emerges from a state that Freud was to call "oceanic" in *Civilization and Its Discontents,* melancholy follows hard upon it. Reentering the world of dailiness brings acute suffering. "Just as I had experienced inconceivable happiness, so now I lapsed into nameless discouragement."

These diffuse feelings crystallize around a woman whose appearance in part 2 is the climax toward which everything tends, the initiatory moment that confers dramatic sense upon the narrator's life. Structured time now manifests itself and the prologue of yearning becomes, in one day, an epilogue of regrets. One day is all he spends with "Marie," a prostitute clearly modeled after Eulalie, who utterly captivates him. Unlike Maria in *Mémoires d'un fou,* Marie speaks at length and as eloquently as he himself does, recounting a past that rivals Messalina's for nymphomania and Saint Theresa's for erotospiritual self-abnegation. Her life began, she says, on a farm, where shepherding lambs and preparing Communion were her chief employments. The end of innocence came in a city to which the family moved after her father died. Destitute as they were, she could not afford at sixteen to spurn the proposals of a rich graybeard wanting a concubine. Thus she acquired wealth, but she also felt the need for an amorous absolute proportionate to her sacrifice, and this she has sought in a life of promiscuity. The two books always at her bedside, *Paul et Virginie* and *Les Crimes des reines*, display her divided nature. Ever the virgin born to couple providentially with a male alter ego, she also rejoices like a crowned head in the power of her sexual charisma, queening it over enthralled spectators from her loge at the theater. "I would run my eyes over the public triumphantly and provocatively, a thousand heads would follow the movement of my eyebrows, I dominated everything by the insolence of my beauty."

The narrator can readily identify with Marie's dream of domination. In the first part he confesses that he would like to have been an emperor for his slaves and a beautiful woman for hers. "I should like to have been . . . able to admire myself, to disrobe, to let my hair fall to my heels and see my reflection in streams." One is put in mind of Gustave's night with Eulalie, during which he describes himself as having been "taken" by her. Gender switches would come to literary fruition in *Madame Bovary*, where the beautiful heroine envies men their freedom, takes masculine initiatives in sex, and feels bitterly disappointed on learning that she has borne a girl child.

When, at length, Marie's libertinage leaves her wasted in spirit, she is visited by a quasi-religious impulse. The courtesan becomes a kind of temple whore and commits herself to the brothel like a repentant sinner retiring to a nunnery. There, as a blank page for men's fantasies, she serves all comers yet remains impenetrable. Foreshadowing Emma, who will wear Communion white on her deathbed, and a middle-aged Flaubert, who would declare in an oft-quoted flash of wit that every woman he ever slept with was a mattress for some ideal absentee, making him a perpetual virgin, Marie is the immaculate whore.* "Unknown to each other, she in her prostitution and I in my chastity had followed the same path, ending up at the same abyss," concludes the narrator. "While I sought a mistress, she had sought a lover, she in the world, I in my heart, both unavailingly."

After the climactic night he departs, with memories of passionate lovemaking, of a voluptuous Marie spread-eagled over him and deliriously proposing that they flee to a land of orange trees and perpetual sunlight. But far safer than the woman who offers herself is the image of her he comes to mourn. Never is she more indispensable than in her absence. The narrator will never see her again, though not for lack of trying: Marie and the brothel mysteriously vanish, as if they had never been quite real. A sequence of empty days is all her self-exiled lover foresees. "How empty is the

---

*Flaubert produces a variation of this image in *Novembre*, where the narrator declares that those around him know as little of his inner life as the bed on which he sleeps knows of his dreams.

world for the man who walks in it alone!" he exclaims. "What was I going to do? How was I to spend time? At what would I employ my mind?" How he spends his time thereafter is recounted by a friend, who completes this story in part 3 with arch reflections criticizing the hyperbolic style of the manuscript bequeathed to him (parts 1 and 2). Dead set against marriage, and wrong for all bourgeois careers, but without artistic gifts to match his love of art, the protagonist despairs. The oceanic raptures that once made him feel indissolubly bound to the world are supplanted by the conviction that he has absolutely no place in it. Attending law school is a ritual gesture that only aggravates his taedium vitae. "I was born with the desire to die," he had observed at the beginning of his memoir, and at the end death creeps insensibly into the scene of utter self-neglect that is his Parisian garret. "He died, but slowly, little by little, by dint of thought alone, without any organ's being diseased, as one dies of sadness."

In the family of literary adolescents to which he belongs — Werther, Chateaubriand's René, Prévost's Chevalier des Grieux, Constant's Adolphe, Musset's Octave, Sainte-Beuve's Amaury — the narrator may even be the most feckless of all. Adolphe and the chevalier, for example, fall as he does under a woman's sway just when they are called upon to establish themselves in masculine company. But the fact that both are motherless boys who would sooner wander the earth at the end of apron strings than rise to the ambition of their fathers gives their anomie a biographical dimension his lacks entirely: nothing is ever said of parents in *Novembre*.* And whereas they live with women, however briefly, in relationships that wax or wane, that embroil others, that derive psychological bulk from rebellious flight, from blame and deceit, from the need to rescue a distraught woman, to be loved, Gustave's narrator stands alone, except for one pivotal day on which he loses all consciousness of self. What he seeks is not companionship but salvation, not something that unfolds but the perfect union or utopian moment that would repeal personal history. Oppressed by time, which wears (the verb *user* occurs obsessively), he can't look forward to growing and maturing, only to melting ecstatically or dying. "As spring approached, . . . I was overwhelmed by desire to melt completely into love, to become absorbed in some large, soft feeling," he says, and again, "Oh! if only I could double myself, love this other being, and melt together with it." Telling stories thus becomes irrelevant. As nothing develops for the hero, there is no story to tell. There is only emptiness or plenitude, sameness or an epiphany, being a self-conscious *homo duplex* or an unconscious babe, enduring "the

---

*The title calls to mind the beginning of one of Werther's bleaker letters to Wilhelm: "As Nature declines toward autumn, autumn is in me and around me. My leaves are turning yellow and already the leaves of the trees nearby have fallen."

eternal monotony of hours that glide by and days that return" or suspending time in a sudden, momentary transport.

What else bears home the hero's sense of rapturous self-loss is a visual play that will recur throughout Flaubert's oeuvre, especially in *Madame Bovary.* The theory of animal magnetism propounded by Mesmer — of a magnetic fluid that powerful personalities project visually — had numerous adherents (Balzac among them), and Gustave turned to it in a description of Marie enthralling the narrator. "Her pupil seemed to dilate. Out of it came a fluid I felt coursing through my heart. Its emanations fascinated me like the flight of a sea hawk circling overhead. I was rooted to her by this magic." When they embrace, he "drinks" his first kiss of love and again deliquesces into her eye. "Her eyes gleamed, enflamed me. Her glance was more enveloping than her arms. I lost myself in her eye." Just so will Charles Bovary lose himself in Emma's.

Gustave, who seldom resisted the temptation to read his work aloud (during the voyage through southern France, he entertained the Cloquets with his travel notes), made no exception of *Novembre.* Caroline heard all 150 pages when he finished, the Goncourts heard excerpts twenty years later, and others listened in between. Gustave did not lose his fondness for a work that never really lost its pertinence. To be sure, he would read it in a voice of histrionic self-mockery, distancing himself from it much the way he distanced himself from clichés by italicizing them. He read it nonetheless. And though he declared that this "fragment" closed out his youth, he spoke more truthfully on one occasion, long after he had gone largely bald, when he said that *Novembre* not only commemorated the boy with a blond mane but contained enough unavowable things to explain the person he still was. The Goncourts, who seldom paid compliments freely, thought that it was a work of astonishing power for a twenty-year-old, with descriptive passages equal to the best in *Madame Bovary.*

Since November marked the beginning of the school year, it always dampened Gustave's spirits. It drowned them in 1841. Never had the month come more unbidden than on the verge of his twentieth birthday, when he visited Paris for two days to register at the École de Droit, the Law School. Attending an opera with Émile Hamard cheered him somewhat. And he had every intention of studying on his own, under the parental roof, during his freshman year (a not uncommon arrangement when end-of-term examinations were the only ones given). But the first fateful, shuffling step toward professional life had been taken. Even if he should pick an unlucky number in the draft of March 1842 — and army life would have been only a marginally more obnoxious prospect than law school — he knew that Dr Flaubert would buy him a substitute for military service.

VII

A Fortunate Fall

ALTHOUGH LAW school was the course usually prescribed for upper-class boys with literary aspirations, it should not be inferred from Daumier's derisive caricatures that law was necessarily the profession of last resort. In a society whose aristocratic predecessor had created a species of nobility called *noblesse de robe* (a reference to judicial robes), lawyering still enjoyed high status. Fortunes made by fathers in hospitals or factories were given a patina of couthness by sons sitting on the bench of assizes court or appointed king's counsel. Like Paul Le Poittevin and Achille-Cléophas, many well-heeled fathers were willing to pay the six or seven thousand francs that a law-school education cost in Paris over three years, if only to better their sons' odds of attracting a large dowry. The brilliant young advocate or precocious judge was less likely than the enterprising young industrialist or the surgeon to hear his titled mother-in-law-to-be resignedly quote Mme de Sévigné's offensive aphorism: "From time to time even the best soil may need some manure."* In the political and cultural establishments, graduates

---

*As for Jean-Paul Sartre's contention in *L'Idiot de la famille* that Gustave's assignment to law school was a reflection of his inferior status in a medical family, it should be emphasized that surgeons with social ambitions generally welcomed the prospect of a son choosing the law.

of the École de Droit were well represented. They came to outnumber every other constituency in Rouen's Académie des Sciences, Belles-Lettres et Arts, for example. And on the national stage they held sway over the Chamber of Deputies.

In post-Revolutionary France, a lawyer benefited from the prestige society accorded to men who demonstrated great powers of suasion in trial court and in legislative debate. The sacred mantle worn by great preachers of the ancien régime — the Bossuets, the Bourdaloues, the Massillons, whose eloquence flowed from scriptural authority — had devolved upon orators whose authority was the overflowing heart, the conscience imbued with love of country, the charismatic presence. Not that eloquence had fled the church altogether, or that great preachers had lost an audience. When the greatest of them, Father Henri Lacordaire (trained as a lawyer) discoursed at Notre-Dame on the moral and social excellences of the Christian faith, as many as six thousand people thronged the cathedral to hear his brilliant homilies. A numerous public, young and old, drawn from the salons and the schools, believers and freethinkers, flocked around him, according to François Guizot. Many, he wrote, were quite transported by the "Conférences de Notre-Dame."* Though Guizot worshipped at a Protestant temple and couldn't subscribe to Lacordaire's democratic ideals, he honored the rhetorical prowess of a priest who did not so much develop thoughts as "paint" them. But this was the era in which Alexis de Tocqueville declared that nothing seemed more admirable or more powerful to him than a great orator debating great questions of state in a democratic assembly, and eloquence had indeed moved its principal seats in Paris from the pulpit to the Palais de Justice and the Palais Bourbon, where lawyer-deputies of note, along with the poet-deputies Victor Hugo and Alphonse de Lamartine, faced off before large, appreciative audiences. People even

---

The hierarchy of the times may be judged by the memoirs of an American, John Sanderson, who spent some time in Paris during the late 1830s: "The students of medicine are mostly poor and laborious, and being obliged to follow their filthy occupation of dissecting, are negligent of dress and manners. The disciples of the law are more of the rich classes, have idle time, keep better company, and have an air *plus distingué*. The doctors of law in all countries take rank above medicine. The question of precedence, I recollect, was determined by the Duke of Mantua's fool, who observed that 'the rogue always walks ahead of the executioner.'" Still, it is noteworthy that when Flaubert was fifteen, school authorities marked him down for a career in medicine.

*One who did not yield was a visitor from Philadelphia who wrote: "He was too eloquent! Oratory in this country, at least in the Pulpit, has her trumpet always at full blast, and announces the smallest little news with the emphasis of a miracle. Her method is to run up to the top of the voice and then pour out her whole spirit, as your Methodist on Guinea Hill, until human nature is exhausted, and then to take a drink and begin again. I will set you a French sermon, if you please, to the gamut, and you may play it on the piano."

took pleasure in reading about orating, to judge from the success of Antoine Berryer's *Leçons et modèles d'éloquence judiciaire* and especially Louis de Cormenin's *Livre des orateurs,* which proposed to analyze the oratorical style of different political regimes. With this book Cormenin, an eminent jurist, became a best-selling author. It found its way into the Flaubert family library.

For those involved in shaping the future at Paris's École de Droit, life was contentious in a less theatrical way. One faction, which founded the review *Thémis,* sought to expand the scope of legal studies with courses that reflected the intense ferment occurring in such cognate realms as history, philosophy, and political science. It seemed vitally important that France's embryonic leaders be humanists acquainted with legal theory and capable of evaluating French law contextually, now from a broad historical perspective, now by its responsiveness to economic and social realities of the day. Inspired by the Committee of Political and Moral Sciences, which Guizot and de Tocqueville, among others, had set up to amass documents constituting a library for scholars concerned with the sources of jurisprudence, philosophy, and civil institutions, the *Thémis* group envisaged law school as an intellectually ambitious enterprise suited to the modern state. In this, however, they were outnumbered at the École de Droit. Most of their colleagues took a dim view of thought that ran free between law and politics, politics and philosophy. Pledged to the interests of the ruling class, they functioned as custodians of a quasi-sacred text called the Civil Code and understood legal studies to be a matter of pious exegesis. Students who had roving minds did not thrive under them.

Clearly, the democratization of public life demanded an enlargement of the curriculum. In 1834 Guizot decreed that it should include lectures on constitutional law. Five years later, reformers forced through a course (albeit elective) on the philosophy of law, declaring that the study of the first principles of law consisted in an examination of different philosophical systems, this being the source for an adequate comprehension of the original spirit of the law, its origins, its raison d'être. But until 1848 such victories for reform were few and hard-won. Conservative faculty heedless of the need for creative legal minds to staff a world of increasingly complex relations between the private and public domains fended off all challenges to privilege. So long as they had their way, a student spent the bulk of his time poring over the *Corpus Juris Civilis,* the body of Roman law on which France's legal system had been modeled. Success at the École de Droit was all too often measured by one's ability to quote chapter and verse of the *Institutes* (part 1 of the *Corpus,* a general survey of Roman law) and the *Pandects* (part 2, containing not only the law in concrete form but selections from thirty-nine noted classical jurists).

Hidebound though it was, secondary-school graduates flocked to Paris's École de Droit, which had double the enrollment of eight provincial law schools combined, and Gustave was one of almost two thousand freshmen matriculating in November 1841. Those who might have pursued military careers under Napoleon, when the prospects of advancement for bright, energetic youngsters were very good, now chose law, or had it thrust upon them by parents mindful of one noted jurist's prediction that in litigious times lawyers would constitute the aristocracy of the century. Had Stendhal pictured a Julien Sorel twenty-five years after Waterloo, under Louis-Philippe, rather than eleven years afterward, under Charles X, *black* might have signified trial robes to him rather than clerical garb.

What soon resulted was a professional glut. For every aspirant destined to achieve success pleading at the bar, sitting on the bench, orating on the rostrum, counseling industry or enforcing government, many more fell by the wayside. One particularly baleful observation came from E. de Labédollière, a lawyer and journalist, who refuted the commonly accepted notion that law-school diplomas unlocked all doors. How did graduates fare once they had soldiered into the larger world, thousands strong? Had they all found honorable and lucrative employment? Alas, no, he concluded in an essay written for *Les Français peints par eux-mêmes* and published in 1840. "The majority never step foot in the Palais de Justice. Some become notaries, solicitors or bailiffs; the rest fan out into various professions. The commercial agent negotiating the purchase and sale of remaindered inventory holds a law degree. This 'romantic lead' in a ragtag theater company shambling through the provinces holds a law degree. This scribe who turns compliments in prose and verse for scullery maids holds a law degree. This playwright who concocts spectaculars for Madame Saqui's theater took the lawyer's oath." Army ranks and bureaucracies and shops and street stalls all swarmed with former students vegetating in their jobs and wanting back the three years lost "allegedly learning the laws, of which they remain perfectly ignorant." The idea propagated by bourgeois ideologues (preeminently Guizot) that men who occupied the uppermost story of the social edifice after 1830 owed their success and authority to a rational "capacity" missing in the common run of men would have struck Labédollière as highly dubious. Influence often counted for more than capacity in the making of a career, and the Flauberts were nothing if not well connected.

Unfortunately, Gustave viewed connections likely to help him establish himself in the profession the way a disconsolate bear might view zookeepers doubling the bars of its cage. On the eve of 1842 he looked back nostalgically to New Year's Eves past, when he and his houseguest, Ernest Chevalier, stayed up late talking by the faint light of embers in their long-stemmed, white porcelain pipes. Some three weeks later he hadn't yet opened his law books and announced plans to preserve their virginity until as little time before the July exam as needed to make a credible pretense of having learned the *Institutes*. Should he fail, he told Chevalier, he would dismiss his examiners with the customary slurs. Should he pass, the "bour-geois" would consider him a surefire bet to confer distinction on the Rouen bar by defending the erection of property walls and people who shake their carpets out the window, assassinate the king, or hack up their parents and hide the pieces in gunny sacks, "all things the French are in-clined to do." His old teacher Gourgaud-Dugazon, who had lent him a sympathetic ear the previous September, heard some of the same things couched in more ingenuously desperate language. His predicament was "critical" and required Gourgaud-Dugazon's "competence" and "friend-ship." At the crossroads where he now stood, life and death hinged on his choice of direction. Taking the wrong path, he wrote, would be tragic, for the obstinate, stoical person Gourgaud-Dugazon knew him to be was like an inanimate object governed by inertial force: once launched this way or that, he could not change course. "If it comes to that I will earn a law de-gree, [but] I must admit that when people say: 'This bloke will plead effec-tively,' because I have wide shoulders and a vibrant voice, I chafe inwardly and don't feel cut out for this material, trivial life." With every passing day, he continued, his admiration of beloved poets, in whom he found things that had previously escaped him, grew stronger. There were three stories he planned to write, each illustrating a different genre. Gourgaud-Dugazon would help him decide whether they embodied definitive proof of talent. "I'll invest them with as much style, passion, intelligence as I can, and then we'll see."

Gustave did not spend the entire spring of 1842 on the horns of this dilemma. In February, for example, he dressed up in a black suit, silk stock-ings, and pumps for a masked ball and persuaded two seasoned courtesans — women kept by the Rouen aristocracy, he proudly informed Chevalier — to dine with him and Orlowski. Whatever the erotic denouement of the evening may have been, Gustave valued the women as sources to be ex-ploited for the portrait of Marie in *Novembre*. Why should he not consider people around him so much material for books? was his thought. The world, he told Chevalier in formulating a brief Ur creed of literary realism, is an instrument from which the true artist draws sounds that transport people or send shivers up their spine. "Society high and low must be stud-ied. The truth lies in both. Let us understand everything and blame noth-ing. That's how to know a great deal and to be calm, and being calm is not negligible, it's almost being happy."

But gaining distance from his anxious self and from a hazardous world — the remoteness that would give him room for calm, if not happiness, as well as a basis for literary creation — finally eluded him. The best he could do was keep most people away by smoking his pipe, which he did incessantly, and inveigh against almost everything, which he did just as often. These scatological rants, or *gueulades,* were thunderbolts in a lowering sky. They released anger over his inability either to write or to study, and often smote poor Ernest Chevalier, Gustave's principal correspondent, whose diligence exasperated him. The single-minded law student was urged to enter cafés and leave without paying, to play practical jokes at night, to crush top hats, to bugger the dog, to belch in people's faces, to thank Providence for having been born in happy times. "Railroads furrow the countryside," the Kid declaimed, "there are clouds of bituminous smoke and pitch raining down, asphalt sidewalks and wooden pavements, penitentiaries for young felons and savings banks for thrifty domestics to open accounts in with money stolen from their masters." While Ernest, a future magistrate, crammed day and night, Gustave asserted that he would die laughing at the spectacle of one man judging another if he weren't compelled to memorize the absurdities rationalizing such judgments. Nothing, he said, seemed more stupid than the practice of law, except the study of it. "I work with extreme distaste, and am drained of heart and spirit for anything else."

If one may believe his constant lament, the Justinian and Napoleonic Codes wouldn't sink in. It took him months to negotiate one and a half books of the *Institutes.* By late May he was raging over it and declaring that civil penalties should be assessed against people who used words like *usucapion, agnats,* and *cognats.* Late-afternoon swims off the Île du Petit-Guay followed by a glass of rum with Fessart the swimming instructor helped him persevere when the weather turned warm. In June he digested as best he could a hundred articles of French law, but the likelihood of saying something intelligible about any one of them at the August examinations seemed small. "I know almost nothing, or, more accurately, nothing whatever," he told Chevalier on the twenty-fifth.

Still, there were motions to go through. Early in July he took his place at the École de Droit in lecture courses for which he had registered two and a half months earlier, during a fortnight spent in Paris. Ernest Chevalier had just finished law school, and Gustave moved into his room at 35, rue de l'Odéon, a short walk from the École de Droit, which occupied a cramped corner opposite the Panthéon. This convenience, acquired at the expense of Ernest's company, made his studious regimen — what he called "my ferocious life" — only slightly less onerous. Separated from Alfred Le Poittevin, who was already practicing law in Rouen, and from his family, who left for Trouville soon after he left for Paris, Gustave felt unutterably forlorn, despite efforts by everyone, including Dr Flaubert, to maintain a steady flow of letters. His father administered equal doses of small talk and exhortation. "Your mother insisted on writing to you, but I opposed her doing so to spare her from aggravating a headache which, happily, is not her usual migraine," he wrote on July 3:

> She already imagines you afflicted with pleurisy [*pleurésie*], peripneumonia [*péripneumonie*] and every other illness ending in *ie* because you drank two pitchers of iced water on your arrival. Her advice is that you shouldn't drink so much of it so cold. I hope your spirits are high and that you've turned your thoughts away from Trouville to law school. Before long you'll be rejoining your family, friends, and our excellent mayor M. Coyère who, for the good of the region, would like to see the Touques river "canalated" [meaning canalized]. Your sister took a little walk and donkey ride, then bathed in the sea, which gave her much pleasure without tiring her out. Miss Jane [her English tutor] and I didn't fare so well; I have a headache and she has painful finger joints from having clung so tightly to my person in the surf. We hope that you'll apply yourself like a reasonable lad and return hale and hearty with good grades.

Gustave applied himself, but in a spirit of martyrdom. Irregularly attending the courses of Oudot, Ducoudray, and Duranton — three famously parochial minds who made common cause against any speculation liable to subvert the powers that were — he was offended as much by lecturers' jargon and appearance as by their subject. The lowing of cattle had more literary resonance than the lessons of these sclerotic gentlemen, he assured sister Caroline. Did they not threaten to drown out his inner voice with gibberish, to destroy the aptitude for expressive language in which his manhood was entirely vested (he spoke of "moral castration")? How was he to learn yet stop his ears? Satisfy his father's expectations and keep this Trojan horse at bay? "Barbarous books" were all he read now, and, lost in a "maze of bad prose," he couldn't restore himself at night, for the law, invading his dreams, fouled even that sanctuary. Worst of all — indeed, a sure sign of alienation — was the fact that he didn't think about the Kid for days at a stretch or entertain himself with bellowing harangues.* As usual, Chevalier, who may have needed some encouragement himself, was the ear into which he poured repeated avowals that the mania of the age for social advancement or power

---

*On at least one occasion, however, he bellowed quite successfully in public. It was a dinner party given by a banker named Tardif, whom he knew through his parents. When the consul general of Portugal and his wife — "rabid Louis-Philippards," as he described them — began to praise the king, Gustave seized this opportunity to denounce Louis-Philippe for having disfigured a work by Gros at Versailles. Since the picture had not been large enough for a particular wall panel, its frame was removed and several square feet of painted canvas added. Gustave's discontent with the "bourgeois monarchy" was raised to a boil by the immense amount of official homage to the dauphin, who had recently died in a carriage accident.

had not affected him. "Do I desire to become strong, to be a great man, known throughout a district, a department, three provinces, to be a scrawny fellow with stomach problems? Do I entertain ambitions, like the boot-blacks, coachmen, and valets who want to become booters, grooms, and masters? Do I have my heart set on serving as a deputy or cabinet minister? It all seems very sad to me."

Although distracted by an oversexed neighbor fornicating loudly and nightly, Gustave absorbed enough of what he read to conclude, after wit-nessing a public examination, that he might pass his own in August. Un-doubtedly Cloquet and Gourgaud-Dugazon, both of whom he visited, gave him moral support. Dr Flaubert assured him that fear of examinations was quite normal, that a little brass and bluff would help him through. Prospects dimmed, however, when Professor Oudet, known to Gustave's correspondents as "the cretin," announced that no candidate could take the exam without a "certificate of regular attendance" and that proof of regu-lar attendance resided in a complete set of notes for his course. Gustave ap-parently tried to obtain someone else's. Unable to perpetrate this fraud anyhow, he deferred his exam until December and joined the family in Trouville earlier than planned, with well-rehearsed arguments of self-justification to mollify his disappointed father.

Six or more weeks of restorative ocean air made up for a torrid summer in Paris, where he had vainly sought relief at crowded, fetid swim clubs on the Seine. Beginning in mid- or late August, he spent his days bathing, sun-ning himself on a sandy beach (the expanse of which was marred, in his view, by flags honoring the late duc d'Orléans), eating, smoking, walking his large Newfoundland, Néo, practicing his small English on Caroline's tu-tor, Miss Jane, regaling Caroline herself (still bruised from having fallen off a donkey), sketching (preferably tumbledown shanties), watching the clouds scud, savoring Ronsard's poetry, and reading other literature strictly unre-lated to law. He also saw much of family and friends. Dr Achille the younger, wife Julie, and daughter Juliette were there. So were Gustave's traveling companions of 1840. His much-loved uncle François Parain spent two weeks in Trouville and went home when his daughter and son-in-law, Olympe and Louis Bonenfant, arrived from Nogent-sur-Seine. The Rouen crowd included Antoni Orlowski, whom Gustave dubbed Avare (Miser) Orlowski — perhaps for having made himself the beneficiary of a benefit concert or, perversely, for being so generous to Polish exiles even more im-pecunious than he — and a cotton manufacturer named Stroehlin with whose wife Mme Flaubert had become good friends. Gustave taught Mme Stroehlin, as best he could, how to swim.

The Le Poittevins, who summered every year at Fécamp some distance up the coast, did not visit. Nor did the Schlesingers appear, Maurice having packed his wife off to Germany and departed for the Levant in the company of Heinrich Panofka.

Gustave found that he missed being under Élisa's spell, but the disappointment at not seeing her opulent person on the beach may have been tempered by a flirtation with two young Englishwomen named Gertrude and Harriet Collier. Expatriate since 1823, the Collier family had lost large sums in a bank failure and, like so many indebted English of the period, fled to France, where life was cheaper. With what remained of his inheritance, Captain Henry Collier, a naval officer, settled his large family in a house on the Champs-Élysées. Ostentatiously monolingual and pleased to browbeat Frenchmen, who during the Restoration made much of everything from victorious Albion, he came to rely on his older daughter, Gertrude, as an interpreter. At Trouville, which owed its appeal to being a wild, unfrequented place with no bands, crowds, or esplanade, they were as conspicuous a clan as the Flauberts. Memoirs written years later explain how these families met. Intrigued by Charles Mozin's chalet perched on the Roches Noires, Gertrude, then twenty-two, recruited a cousin to accompany her on an impromptu visit to the artist (her younger sister, Harriet, had chronically poor health and was often confined to bed or a chaise longue). "We boldly scrambled up the rocky eminence in the hot sun and found ourselves at a wide open door leading into a beautifully proportioned lofty room running the whole length of the house with a window at each end," she remembered. There they encountered Caroline Flaubert.

> The walls were of stained wood hung with various skins and covered with all kinds of indescribable odds and ends . . . But more beautiful than the dark blue sea we saw from the chalet windows or anything in that room was a young girl drawing at one of the tables. She was simply dressed in some cool muslin — looked up at us for a moment and then continued her drawing with proud indifference.

Destined, as Mrs. Gertrude Tennant, to entertain the likes of Gladstone, Tennyson, Ruskin, and Huxley at her London town house, this sociable young woman soon vanquished Caroline's aloofness, then set her cap at Caroline's supercilious brother. Strolling on the beach in his luxuriant crown of blond hair and red flannel shirt, a six-foot-tall, well-proportioned Gustave impressed not only Gertrude and Harriet, who were instantly smitten, but Captain Collier, who paid him the backhanded compliment, "What a superb young fellow that is, what a pity he is a Frenchman." (He would undoubtedly have applauded the observation William Thackeray made after a tour of France that "nature, though she has rather stinted the bodies and limbs of the French nation, has been very liberal to them of hair.")

Gertrude was as ill equipped to conceive that Gustave's haughtiness disguised shyness as to imagine this "Adonis" in Paris enjoying fellatio with a whore named Léonie. When in time he thawed enough to banter, he gave the girls something of what he got from their chauvinistic father. English habits interested him, but they were grist for the Kid's mill. He ridiculed their observance of the Sabbath. He claimed to find the notion of duty, which they held sacred, preposterously quaint. *Épicier* was a catchword for middle-class philistinism, and Gustave's droll caricatures did not spare John Bull.* While Gertrude the half-fledged Victorian matron lectured him on fixity of purpose, he in turn parried with the assertion that he wanted only to look at the blue sky, green waves, and yellow sand. "My coquetry," she wrote, "was only a sort of ambition. Truly I ignored that I loved him, that I secretly and inwardly agreed with all his wild aspirations."

Gustave, Caroline, and the Colliers became fast friends after a near catastrophe. One evening, in a second-floor bedroom of the Collier cottage, a muslin curtain caught fire blowing into a candle. The alarm had no sooner been raised than Gustave, who saw flames from his own room, arrived to carry Harriet downstairs. The incident affected her badly, and it was decided at summer's end that she should spend several weeks convalescing in Rouen under Dr Flaubert's supervision lest her health prove unequal to the rigors of a long, uninterrupted coach ride home. During the Colliers' brief sojourn there, frequent rendezvous took place among all concerned. And with the resumption of law-school classes in November, Gustave found himself enthusiastically invited for dinner at their residence on the Champs-Élysées.

DINNER WITH the Colliers (sometimes preceded by an afternoon of reading Chateaubriand or Hugo to the eternally chlorotic, lovelorn Harriet) would be one of the few pleasurable intermissions in his tortured perusal of the Civil Code, and the Champs-Élysées a welcome change of scene from the Latin Quarter. His new address was 19, rue de l'Est, a street bordering the Jardin du Luxembourg, which later, during Haussmann's reconstruction of Paris, became the boulevard Saint-Michel at its southernmost extent, near the Observatory. Three hundred francs a year, or twice

---

*Balzac, who wrote an essay in defense of the grocer, noted that *épicier* had become a thoroughly pejorative term. "From the heights of their false grandeur, of their implacable intelligence or their artistically groomed beards, a few people have made of the grocer's name a word, an opinion, a thing, a system, an encyclopedic, European-wide stock character. It is time to rout these Diocletians of the grocery store. What does one blame in the grocer? Is it his more or less brownish-red, greenish- or chocolate-colored trousers? His blue socks and clogs, his cap of mock otter skin . . . ? But dare you punish in him, base society without an aristocracy, . . . the estimable symbol of work?"

what poor students generally paid for cold, diminutive hotel rooms, purchased him comfort, light, and a view of the Luxembourg garden nursery. Faced with the daunting task of furnishing his room, he found an eager auxiliary in Émile Hamard, who appears to have been as unfazed by the practicalities of life as Gustave was nonplussed. With Hamard's help, he acquired a bed three feet by six, three chairs, fireplace hardware, and other paraphernalia described in letters to his insatiably curious sister.

On a long walk from the rue de l'Est to the Champs-Élysées, Gustave would have traversed neighborhoods that would disappear or undergo radical change after 1851, under Napoleon III. Rue de la Harpe, the main north–south artery of the Latin Quarter, which followed the original Roman road, was a narrow, clogged thoroughfare. Amid pedestrians who risked life and limb if they weren't vigilant, hackney carriages heading toward the Palais de Justice and Notre-Dame in one direction and the Sorbonne in the other jostled stagecoaches bound for Brittany and the Loire valley. At several bridges vehicular traffic still encountered toll barriers, though not at the Pont Saint-Michel, where Gustave could stop and observe barges being drawn by horse from towpaths on either side of the river. Stopping on the Île de la Cité after dark was, however, unwise, for the dimly lit, stinking alleyways that coiled around Notre-Dame sheltered Paris's thuggish *bas-fonds.* Juxtapositions of majesty and squalor were a Parisian commonplace before Baron Haussmann tidied up the capital. Gustave would have seen another example from the rue de Rivoli on the Right Bank, where bright gaslight had begun to replace oil lamps. Napoleon I did not demolish every hovel in creating the rue de Rivoli. Many survived on ancient streets that formed a ghetto between two palaces, the Louvre and the Tuileries. These houses, which Balzac described in *La Cousine Bette,* were perpetually enveloped in shadow, as the courtyards of the surrounding royal residences had been banked well above ground level. "The shadows, the silence, the frigid air, the cavernous depth of the streets, conspired to make them crypts of a sort, living tombs." So it undoubtedly was at night. By day this quarter teemed with antiquarians, philatelists, peddlers of bric-a-brac and curiosities, and art dealers, who, when they found no room on the street, set up shop on the place du Carrousel.

Balzac might have applied equally morbid imagery to the place de la Concorde, which until 1834 looked like an arena punished by neglect for hosting so many decapitations, above all that of Louis XVI, during the Revolution — and indeed, farmers claimed that oxen pulling their wagons across Paris to the wholesale market at night shied away from it, as if the paving stones retained a scent of slaughter. Overgrown with rank vegetation and scored with muddy ditches, it became the elegant hub one sees today under Louis-Philippe, who vetoed his Bourbon predecessor's plan to install an expiatory chapel as its centerpiece. The Luxor obelisk rescued it from the internecine warfare of French history.

Beyond the place de la Concorde Gustave could look forward to a last lap up the Champs-Élysées as far as the Rond-Point, where Captain Henry Collier lived in greater comfort than his creditors may have known much about. After 1828, when France officially ceded the Champs-Élysées to Paris, this impressively landscaped avenue, which had jutted out from the city, with very few buildings lining it, toward a derelict Arc de Triomphe, dressed up for urban life. Mansions were built, and several hotels. In 1841 two *cafés-concert* opened right next to each other, the Alcazar d'Été and the Café des Ambassadeurs. In the same year there appeared on the north side a circus of monumental proportions, the Cirque d'Été. Hittorf, who built it, was also responsible for a huge rotunda near the present site of the Grand Palais featuring panoramas of Napoleonic victories. Panoramas, as Balzac mockingly noted in *Père Goriot,* were all the rage, though Gustave may never have seen one.

What he must have seen on walks through the city was abundant evidence of a phenomenon destined to affect his own life quite directly, to transform Paris, and to create a whole new economy: the railroad. In 1835 an audacious financier named Isaac Péreire obtained permission to construct a line from Paris to the suburban town of Saint-Germain-en-Laye, hoping that this pilot project would convert the many doubters in public office. By 1837 the project had been completed. Two years later trains were serving Versailles from terminuses on either side of the Seine. But several factors, not only conservative antagonism, hindered more ambitious efforts. While England and Belgium and America were connecting everything in sight with iron track, France merely talked about doing it. The *Journal des Débats* urged national railroad construction on legislators as a peacetime analogue of Napoleonic campaigns, that is, as a project grand enough to supplant class conflict with patriotic cohesion. "Given the present state of minds, it is urgently important to harness public opinion to a great thought . . . The genius of peace may overcome the genius of war only if it can deploy something that will stir and dazzle."

When at length this view prevailed and the question of government ownership versus private enterprise had been thrashed out, bad luck threatened to halt further progress. On May 8, 1842, a train crowded with Parisians returning from their Sunday excursion to Versailles derailed at full speed. Trapped inside locked carriages, more than fifty people burned to death and dozens suffered grievous injuries. Public outrage matched capitalist trepidation. A mob threatened to destroy the newly constructed

Montparnasse station, and financiers such as Rothschild reconsidered their investment in the six lines proposed for development. But, unexpectedly, the event steeled France's resolve to make up for lost time. With the passage of enabling legislation, work began on track that would link Paris, Rouen, and Orléans. During Gustave's first year at law school, modernity established bastions in the form of two railroad stations: one near the Seine — the Gare d'Austerlitz — and the other much farther west on the Right Bank, the Gare Saint-Lazare, which would witness his comings and goings from that time forward. After May 1843 he could travel the eighty-four miles home in four hours, on trains that made six daily runs between Paris and Rouen. By 1860 the express run took two hours and forty minutes.

Meanwhile his movements were largely confined to the Latin Quarter, where, as one contemporary put it, law students were "unrivaled sultans" providing landlords, restaurateurs, *cafetières,* and tobacconists with regular incomes. Had Gustave cut a typical figure, he would have sported the red beret and belt that identified a law student to generally ill-disposed gendarmes. He would have worn his hair and beard long and shaved the latter off on the eve of examinations. He would have accentuated his rebellious air by sporting a pipe bowl carved into the image of Saint-Just or Robert Macaire and puffing conspicuously as he swaggered through the Jardin du Luxembourg. He would have cruised the allées of the garden for a grisette or nanny hospitable to his advances. He would have procured a hookah and struck Oriental poses on a divan covered in Utrecht red velvet. He would have eaten at greasy spoons, unless the shopgirl with whom he had found favor could cook.

Gustave did indeed wear his hair long, and almost obsessively well combed, but he did not otherwise conform to type during his first months at the École de Droit. "Here's what my life is like," he wrote to Caroline on November 16. "I rise at 8 o'clock; I go to my course; I return and have a frugal lunch; I work until five in the evening, at which time I have dinner. I'm back in my room by six; I do whatever I please until midnight or 1 a.m. Once a week at most I cross the Seine to see our friends [the Colliers]." Years later, in the privacy of his study, he might lounge à la Turque in white and red striped culottes, but at law school he usually wore a black suit, a white tie, white gloves, and highly polished boots (the grime of the city wasn't allowed to follow him indoors), until teasing by friends convinced him that he looked too much like the best man at a wedding. For sustenance he took meals in a local restaurant at monthly rates, wolfing them down and speaking to no one except the owner, who, impressed by his physical stature, Gustave claimed, showed him great consideration. The main problem with eating was chewing. His teeth tormented him so, he informed his father (similarly afflicted), that if the pain did not subside he would have three or four of them pulled by his dentist, who occasionally joined him for dinner.

To Caroline, whom Dr Flaubert moved downstairs lest her bedroom be harboring the mysterious cause of her poor health, Gustave wrote that pain from rotten teeth was far more endurable than the Civil Code, that studying law would soon make him a babbling idiot, that his only diversion on the eve of his twenty-first birthday was polishing boots and rearranging them in the closet. "Think of it, since I left you I haven't read a single line of French, not six paltry verses, not one decent sentence. The *Institutes* are in Latin, and the Civil Code is written in something even less French than that. The gentlemen who drafted it sacrificed very little to the Graces. They've concocted a document as dry, as tough, as foul and flatly bourgeois as the lecture-hall benches on which one develops piles while listening to juridical explications." It seemed grossly unfair, he continued, that he should poison his mind with revenues and easements while she practiced Chopin scherzos and mixed colors on her palette. Not for the last time did he quote, or misquote, the passage from "De l'expérience" in which Montaigne declares jurisprudence, especially French law, to be as unnecessarily opaque as anything else of human invention.

Achille-Cléophas spent several days and nights on the rue de l'Est, mainly to shore up his son's ego. By December 21, one week before the exam, a pugnacious Gustave, who desperately looked forward to celebrating New Year's Eve at home, assured Caroline in the manic voice of Descambeaux that he would pass with flying colors and give anyone who thought otherwise "what for." Sleep-deprived, almost gaunt, and meeker than the Kid, but unrepentantly bearded, he submitted himself on judgment day to three robed, toqued examiners and satisfied them with recitations of the Civil Code, even if the colors they awarded him were not flying. A black ball signified failure, a white one indicated success, and a red one tepid approval. Gustave received three red balls.

At this he heaved a sigh of relief all the way to Rouen, where much was made of him and his achievement by the entire family, including Uncle Parain and Caroline's English tutor, Jane ("Missy") Fargues. Although life in the capital may have been somber, it had enriched his comic repertoire. Throughout a cold, gray January, he avenged himself on Paris with imitations funny enough to distract Mme Flaubert from her migraines, Dr Flaubert from his lithotomies, Caroline from her lower-back pain, and Uncle Parain from his dominos. In return for the antics that put some fizz in a subdued household, Gustave wanted the security of knowing that he had his place there, that he could in fact count on three women to dote on him.

There was ineffable comfort in hearing the patter of familiar voices outside his room and in giving Carolo bear hugs as often as he pleased. Back in Paris he would write to her, "I'm alone now, thinking about all of you and wondering what you're up to. You're all gathered around the fireplace, where I alone am not. You're playing dominos, shouting, laughing, everybody is together except me, sitting here like an idiot with my elbows on the table wondering what to do." Affectionate kin and the kindred spirit he had always found in Alfred Le Poittevin lightened the burden of thoughts about his future that ordinarily weighed upon him. To be sure, Alfred's debut at the Rouen bar, which had been marked by two favorable verdicts, might have left Gustave feeling even more aberrant, but Alfred never let on that his initial success was a source of pride or that he now entertained ambitions of making his mark in the law. While Gustave complained that the École de Droit would yet reduce him to imbecility, Alfred voiced fears that his professional activity in a vulgar world (*vulgar* being a word he often used) would rob him of the leisure, if not the will, to cultivate his mind. With these two reunited, January proved to be a famous month for talking poetry and Spinoza and resuscitating the Garçon.

After January Gustave felt bluer than ever, with nothing good to say for Paris and nothing bad to remember about Rouen. But Rouen was not the convivial place he imagined in his absence. Nor was Paris the dismal, Rhadamanthine netherworld he habitually pictured to correspondents. Caroline reported that the household, especially Uncle Parain, had worn a long face since his departure, that laughter left the Hôtel-Dieu when he returned to Paris. Although champagne flowed during a meal celebrating their parents' thirty-first anniversary, it didn't pour as freely as it might have done had he been there, and for Mme Flaubert the event resulted in confinement with a particularly atrocious migraine. Card games proceeded, but solemnly. Friends of Caroline's parents, the Maupassants, were invited to dinner, but the Maupassants would reciprocate several days later and the prospect of having to endure twice-told witticisms at successive soirees depressed her. It were better, she advised, that he dance the cancan or see *Phèdre* with his friend Hamard than miss Rouen.

Gustave's genius for idealizing places from which he felt exiled or excluded made it difficult to take good advice. In Paris he yearned for Rouen, and on the Left Bank he gazed enviously, not unlike Balzac's provincial heroes, at toffs gallivanting on the Right. "Over there they go to the Opéra every night, to the Italiens, to soirees," he lamented to Ernest. "They smile with pretty women who would have their concierges turn us away if we should venture to show up at their doors in our soiled overcoats and dark three-year-old suits." One's Sunday best on the Left Bank was weekday attire on the Right. Students on the Left Bank mooned over shopgirls with chapped hands, or when they could afford it found satisfaction at brothels, while the gilded youth slept with marquises. On the Left Bank one walked, on the Right one rode, in one's own carriage.

In fact, his own life did not really exemplify student deprivation. If walking across town was onerous, he hired a cabriolet (quite unaffordable for the average student). Running up tailors' bills out of all proportion to his allowance, Gustave frequently called upon Dr Flaubert to pay them, and when the likelihood of another lecture from father filled him with dismay, he used Caroline as an emissary.* He would sooner have gone naked than leave his flat in a soiled overcoat. Nor did he ever want for invitations to socialize on both banks. Jules Cloquet and the Colliers may have been his most zealous hosts, but there were others, notably the Schlesingers, with whom he dined every Wednesday for several months and occasionally on weekends at their country house in Vernon. He sometimes crossed the Seine to mingle with other visitors at Maurice's business establishment, seldom knowing beforehand whom he would encounter in a scene that changed with the concert season, the random appearance of contributors to the *Gazette Musicale,* the latest enthusiasms and estrangements of his temperamental friend. Fifteen months earlier, Richard Wagner, who met Liszt through Schlesinger, might have been present, though impossible to engage in conversation unless one spoke German. Musical virtuosi flocked like pigeons around 89, rue de Richelieu, eager for crumbs of publicity that the impresario deigned to throw their way. "I had ample opportunity to see with my own eyes illustrious artists prostrate themselves at his feet," wrote Heinrich Heine, Paris correspondent of the *Augsburg Gazette.* "Still visible on the laurel crowns of virtuosi to whom the capitals of Europe pay homage was the dust of Maurice Schlesinger's boots." When Gustave first appeared, Heine had recently been banished from the premises after committing what he himself called a "juvenile blunder." Still, the law student stood to meet Liszt, Alexandre Dumas, or Hector Berlioz. As for Élisa, one would have thought that any day he saw her was a memorable one, but Élisa in the flesh already interfered with the image Gustave meant to preserve of his Trouville divinity.† Some four years later he confessed that revisiting her helped

---

*Achille-Cléophas began one letter with: "I thank you for thinking of me from time to time, especially when your purse is not yet empty." On another occasion he bailed him out and wrote: "Go pay your tailor, about whom you are always speaking to me, and for whom I am so often sending you money."

†There were many ways in which he idealized, or fetishized, absences. The wooden form of a woman's high-heeled shoes in a shoemaker's display case always aroused him. Walking in the morning on sidewalks where prostitutes had patrolled the night before made his legs tingle.

him understand aristocratic émigrés who, upon seeing their châteaus again after years of exile, wondered how they could ever have lived in them (to be sure, the confession was perhaps skewed by the fact that its jealous recipient, Louise Colet, needed constant reassurance).

Outside the lecture hall he saw very little of classmates at law school, the exceptions being fellow Rouennais. There was Émile Hamard. There was also Ernest Le Marié, a brilliant, waggish boy who might have participated in Descambeaux's foolery had he not transferred from the Collège royal to the Collège Charlemagne in Paris. Le Marié shared quarters near the Île de la Cité slum with an aspiring writer named Maxime Du Camp. Gustave appeared unannounced at their doorstep one day in March 1843, his hat raffishly tilted over one ear. He lost no time striking up a friendship that was to survive periods of estrangement and last all his life.

Born two months after Gustave, Maxime Du Camp was, like the florid Norman who stood as tall as he, the son of a distinguished surgeon. Unlike Gustave, he had never known his father. Dr Théodore-Joseph Du Camp died at twenty-nine of tuberculosis, leaving his year-old boy, an only child, to be reared by a teenage widow. That the rearing took place in a Mansart town house on the place Vendôme attests to the wealth of Maxime's parents. He had a cosseted childhood, with weekends spent at a villa not far from Paris and summers at a château on the wooded estate of his maternal grandmother, born Marie-Antoinette de Frémusson. Until his ninth year, when it was decided that boarding school would provide the masculine rigor missing in family life, he enjoyed the constant companionship of a boy his own age named Louis de Cormenin, who later became Gustave's friend as well.* Separation seemed unimaginable. It frightened him, and would have under any circumstances, but the Collège Louis-le-Grand, where, unbeknownst to Maxime, Charles Baudelaire was a fellow sufferer, made it unendurable. Or rather, he endured by rebelling against a discipline even crueler than that which Gustave experienced at the Collège royal. Maxime never reconciled himself to this regime. His years at Louis-le-Grand included whole days spent in solitary confinement copying thousands of lines of Latin verse, and the wonder is that he should ever have learned to read Latin with pleasure. Romantic literature was another matter. Smuggled past the Cerberus responsible for sniffing out dangerous works, Hugo's *Feuilles d'automne* also helped him endure. He wrote poetry after the fashion of Musset and identified with Alfred de Vigny's Chatterton.

By fourteen, Maxime had been expelled from Louis-le-Grand and made himself known as a miscreant at the Collège Saint-Louis, another Latin Quarter institution. Two years later, everything crashed around him when

---

*He was the son of the author of the aforementioned *Livre des orateurs*.

his beloved mother, Alexandrine Du Camp, suddenly died. Grandparents gave him a safe home, but compassion for the orphaned boy lay beyond the emotional reach of schoolmasters. No one seemed to understand that unruliness might express anger or that anger might feed on grief. Predictably, a second expulsion followed. He then entered a private school whose chief virtue was its slovenliness. Forced to educate himself in the absence of strong authority and external discipline, Maxime mustered the will to do so, toughing it out with help from Louis de Cormenin. He performed brilliantly on the baccalaureate examination in August 1841. No sooner was his family done celebrating this success than he fluttered the dovecote by announcing that he intended to become not a diplomat or a lawyer but a man of letters. Had the sheaf of poems he sent to Victor Hugo for comment not elicited hyperbolic praise? (Hugo received such sheaves every week and always gave hyperbolic praise.) Had he and Cormenin not embarked upon the writing of a novel together? In any event, his fortune made him far more independent than Gustave, if subject still to the admonitions and legal restraints of his guardian.

Where Achille-Cléophas offered Gustave a grand tour after graduation, the fatherless Maxime proceeded to lead the indolent life of a Right Bank swell as soon as he had his diploma in hand, running with a fast crowd whose extravagance might well have seemed infinitely desirable from Gustave's toilsome perspective. The constant pursuit of pleasure took him to Paris's forested outskirts for stag hunts, to the racetrack, to gaming parlors, to Café Tortoni, where Gustave sometimes went to observe the beau monde, and backstage at various theaters for assignations with young actresses. When a family council put his fortune under lock and key, he had recourse to usurers who accepted IOUs due on his twenty-first birthday. By then Maxime was no longer squandering. After six months of self-imposed sequestration in his grandmother's medieval château, he emerged from the retreat a new man pledged to serious goals. Or so he insisted. The new man needed a new ambiance and found it halfway across the Seine on the quai Napoleon, looking toward the Right Bank, where he and his high school chum lived in a clutter of books, watercolors, and sheet music. The ex-wastrel introduced to Gustave had become an energetic dilettante whose savoir faire impressed the awkward provincial. Maxime looked every inch Jockey Club material. Long-legged, thin, and dark, more at home in irony than in farce, he had finely chiseled features, a sharp eye, and a Vandyke well-suited to the superior smile habitually playing at the corners of his mouth. In March 1843 he might have smiled more broadly than usual, as a substitute to do his military service had just been bought for twenty-six hundred francs and a gold watch. That problem never arose with Gustave, who, as previously noted, had drawn a lucky number one year earlier.

The two were opposites attracted to each other. As their friendship developed, Maxime's name began cropping up in Gustave's correspondence. On March 11 he wrote to Caroline that he was hard-pressed to compose his letter because "my friend Du Camp is here in my room and insisting on dictating something — periods, commas and all. I must strain to follow the thread of my ideas, which, given that I haven't any, leads nowhere." Maxime noticed no such dearth of ideas in conversation that sometimes lasted all night and, he remembered many years later, ranged from the putative existence of God to buffoonery at little theaters on the boulevard du Temple. Louis de Cormenin, now a student at the École Normale, often joined them. When Alfred Le Poittevin, whom Maxime described as "sinuous like a woman," visited Paris, all four would dine at Chez Dangeaux on the rue de l'Ancienne Comédie, near the Odéon. These were memorable occasions. With at least three exhibitionists present, the evening frequently became a contest of wit and erudition. At other times, Le Poittevin's habit of pronouncing Macairian enormities as if he were commenting on the weather tilted reason off the table. Gustave exercised his talent for parroting people and delivered an especially appreciated imitation of the celebrated actress Marie Dorval, whom he had seen in Dumas' *Antony*. But more often than not an eavesdropper would have heard talk about literature and philosophy, as conversation ran harum-scarum from basements to steeples. Maxime wrote in his *Souvenirs littéraires,* "I remember one colloquy that began with us guffawing over a farce at the Palais-Royal, continued with the analysis of a work on esthetics by Gioberti, and ended with an exposé of Herder's *Idées hébraiques.*"

Even if Gustave hadn't told him so, Maxime might have independently concluded that Gustave was a would-be actor. Maxime knew how much time the handsome young man whose broad shoulders belied his delicately strung nerves spent in front of a mirror rehearsing various characters. After evenings at the theater, Gustave's elastic personality might slip into the skin of a role that captivated him for one reason or another, and questions of identity bound up with the fear of losing himself to passion or with the pressing need for an audience were obviously much on his mind. But only when the young writer read aloud *Novembre,* which he had brought down from Rouen, did Maxime know anything about his unpublished oeuvre. The reading took place in circumstances that intimates would come to experience as an initiatory ordeal of friendship with Gustave. The latter invited Maxime upstairs, sat him down on one of his three chairs, and held forth until dawn. Almost half a century after the event, Maxime claimed that he listened spellbound all night long, with the growing conviction that a great writer had been born.

Meanwhile Gustave skipped lectures at law school, read whatever he pleased, dreamed of Levantine pleasures, wrote whenever he could, drank carafes of coffee, and forced himself, in a mechanical parody of studiousness, to copy verbatim disquisitions on mortgages and marriage contracts. A second major examination loomed, and thinking about it rattled his brain, he told Chevalier, like a hammer pounding an anvil. The simile may have alluded to physical symptoms as real as the paroxysms of rage he described in a letter to Caroline several months later, when he began cramming around the clock. "From now until August I will be in a state of permanent fury. I am sometimes seized by twitches and flail about with my books and notes as if I had Saint Vitus' dance . . . or were falling with the falling sickness." Was anger — the anger he vented in Descambeaux's foul-mouthed tirades and nightlong recitations of Petronius's *Satyricon* — a defense against depression? If so, it didn't always work. Several times a week he would sleep uninterruptedly for sixteen hours. Getting out of bed was an Oblomovian struggle.

Two weeks in Normandy over Easter steadied his nerves, or at least gave him the opportunity to replace one object of loathing, legal prose, with another — railroad worship. The rail line from Paris having finally reached Rouen, Rouennais could talk about nothing else, and the official inauguration eclipsed all other news. It took place on May 3 with much fanfare, as thousands of National Guardsmen assembled on the Champ-de-Mars to march across town through neighborhoods draped in tricolor bunting. Tricolor adorned the hats and lapels of workers and students parading among the troops in guild formation. At a half-finished terminus on the outskirts, this cortege prepared to greet a trainload of visitors from Paris, among them two of Louis-Philippe's sons, the ducs de Nemours and de Montpensier. Spectators stood for hours, spread out over fields, while dignitaries ate copiously at a banquet offered by the railroad company, and priests (whose presence offended liberal spectators) blessed the tracks. One journalist wondered whether the good-natured mingling of bourgeois and "proletarians" in the festive crowd might not prefigure a new social harmony abetted by rapid transit. Another, referring to the already operational Paris-Orléans line, waxed even more eloquent. "Here are two great lines promoting circulation in the purlieus of the capital," he wrote in the *Journal de Rouen*.

Yesterday Orléans and today Rouen have seen the distance that separated them from Paris vanish. A curious parallel comes to mind on the occasion of these inaugural ceremonies taking place successively in two cities where the memory of Joan of Arc lives on: Orléans was the scene of the heroine's triumph and Rouen of her martyrdom. The solemnity with which Rouen resolved to inaugurate the railroad does honor to the intelligence of our industrious town. We would have liked Orléans to seize the advantage of priority with more éclat. The face of the world may well be changed by these avenues of rapid communication; one must therefore recognize how fortunate one has been to enjoy priority over other sites in the accomplishment of a great and noble conquest.

The clichés spouted at the mere mention of railroads infuriated Gustave, who nevertheless started traveling by rail as early as June 1843. He expected to develop jaundice, he said, if he heard another "grocer" sing its praises. This biliousness (which did not dampen his sister's enthusiasm) may also have been induced by news that track work soon to begin between Rouen and Le Havre via Déville would make the Flaubert villa uninhabitable. Invoking a law that conferred expropriative power on enterprises deemed to have "public utility," the railroad acquired several acres from Achille-Cléophas. Since trains would be passing just beyond the garden wall, Achille-Cléophas decided that everything should be sold. The prospect of abandoning a house filled with memories greatly upset Gustave, who always experienced change as loss. In no other respect was he more the Romantic than in his emotional commitment to ruins, to absence, to haunted houses, to places from which life had fled.

A letter dated July 1843 from Dr Flaubert scolding his gullible son for having allowed himself, like some "provincial simpleton," to be swindled by a confidence man or a whore (we don't know which or how) and concealing the misadventure from a father in whom he should trust could only have made Gustave more fearful of behaving like a simpleton at his public examination. An effort to puff himself up did nothing to convince him that he wasn't ill prepared, but neither would he countenance any attempts by his mother to sway examiners through an influental woman friend. ("Such shenanigans are not my style," he told Caroline, perhaps fearful more of success than of failure.) The reckoning occurred on August 24. Maxime Du Camp, who accompanied him to the École de Droit and helped him don his academic gown, presently witnessed a humiliating spectacle that resulted in two black balls and two red. Did Gustave ask himself why he had brought this failure upon himself? To do so would have been entirely out of character. Rather, it provided him with an opportunity to test his belief that exorcism helped more than insight, that the repeated shouting of *Merde!* was (as he later said) a balm for life's miseries. In a letter to Chevalier written ten days later, he fulminated against all of bourgeois society and cursed his own existence. Would that heaven wreaked destruction upon his birthplace, upon the walls that sheltered him, the bourgeois who knew him as a child, the pavements on which he began to "toughen his heels," he exclaimed. Nothing could please him more than seeing Attila, a "likable humanitarian," return at the head of four hundred thousand horsemen and "immolate France the Beautiful, land of under-the-shoe trouser straps and suspenders, beginning simultaneously with Paris and Rouen."

In a coach ride that put him in uncomfortable proximity to his father for many hours, the Flauberts traveled *en famille* to Nogent-sur-Seine immediately after the debacle. Gustave stayed there several weeks with François Parain's son-in-law Louis Bonenfant, who practiced law. A brief sojourn at the Le Poittevins in Fécamp toward the end of September, when Alfred was suffering from gonorrhea as well as tuberculosis, undoubtedly helped both men banish their woes with Garçon humor. It was to be their last reunion in Fécamp.

Otherwise Gustave may not have seen the seashore that summer. By November of 1843 he was back in Paris preparing his second go at the failed exam, or poring sightlessly over law books (and eschewing brothels, if one may credit later correspondence with Louise Colet, which states that a period of sexual abstinence began at around this time, or perhaps somewhat earlier). His social life was mainly a gastronomic round of familiar dinner tables. He continued to visit the Colliers and occasionally joined them at the opera, in the box of a wealthy friend, the comte de Rambuteau, which was theirs for the asking. Dr Cloquet had grown exceedingly fond of him. So, it appears, had Élisa Schlesinger, who insisted that he dine with them at their country house on New Year's Day. He encountered Gertrude Collier at the home of the sculptor James Pradier on the quai Voltaire, quite near Delacroix's former atelier. Invited by Louise Pradier, born Louise d'Arcet, whose parents had known the Flauberts since their early married years, Gustave paid his first recorded visit in November, when brother Achille was staying with him, and it proved to be memorable not only as the first of many consequential soirees but as the occasion of his meeting Victor Hugo. "You're waiting for details about V. Hugo," he wrote to Caroline.

> What can I tell you? He's an ordinary-looking man with a rather ugly face and a common exterior. He has magnificent teeth, a superb forehead, no eyelashes or eyebrows. He doesn't talk much, gives the impression of watching himself lest he let the cat out of the bag. He's very polite and a little stiff. I very much like the sound of his voice. I took pleasure in contemplating him from close up. I looked at him with astonishment, like a jewel box with millions of royal diamonds in it, and thought about everything that had come out of that man seated next to me on a little chair. My eyes were glued to his right hand, which had written so many beautiful things. Here was the man who had always made my heart beat faster than any other writer, and whom I perhaps loved better

than anyone I didn't know personally. The conversation was about torture, vengeance, thieves, etc. It was I and the great man who chatted the most; I can't remember whether what I said was intelligent or rubbish. But I said a lot.

Obviously much concerned with the impression he was making, he did not observe the lecherous Hugo ogling Louise and the beautiful Louise enticing Hugo. Had Louise, who was seven years older than Gustave, given him encouragement, as she would do in time, he might not have noticed that either, despite a recent letter from Alfred Le Poittevin telling him that he had much to gain by cultivating the Pradiers, "a mistress perhaps," and useful friends at the very least. Gustave, Achille, and Gertrude Collier may have been the only guests unaware that Pradier's patience with his compulsively promiscuous spouse had run out. "Theirs is a house I like very much," he wrote to Caroline. "One doesn't feel constrained there, and it's completely my style."

Gustave decided that he had best postpone his examination until January or February 1844 and celebrate the New Year with his family rather than with the Schlesingers. Having been invited to a ball by a Rouen social matron named Mme Gétillat — the very woman who, if encouraged, would have pulled strings at the law school — he instructed Caroline in no uncertain terms to decline it on his behalf. He didn't dance or play games, and he had already refrained as much as he could bear to from inveighing against Louis-Philippe before smug, beribboned Louis-Philippards. His plan was to spend the fortnight in Rouen curled up like a bear in its winter den, "far from all bourgeois." The only thing that could entice him out-of-doors was an inspection of the Flaubert property at Deauville, where, after much intramural debate over the most advantageous site, Achille-Cléophas had made arrangements to build a cottage overlooking the ocean.

Few days in Flaubert's life would prove more fateful than January 1, 1844, the day he and his brother visited Deauville. What happened near Pont l'Évêque on their way back expunged their memories of the visit itself. They were riding south at night, through farmland pitch-black except for a lantern outside a country inn and untraveled except for a cart coming up behind them when suddenly Gustave, who held the reins of their two-seat cabriolet, fell unconscious. All he could remember afterward was the sensation of having been swept off in a "torrent of flames." Ten minutes passed before he regained consciousness. Uncertain, during the comatose interval, whether his brother was dead or alive, Achille transported him to the inn. There, assuming that Gustave had suffered an apoplectic stroke and relying, as his father did, on the humoral theory that apoplexy derived from a plethoric condition, he bled him profusely.

Not until Maxime Du Camp dared pronounce the word *epilepsy* in *Sou-*

venirs littéraires, published two years after Flaubert's death, did the public know what intimates had long whispered among themselves. Questions will always remain unanswered, but eminent neurologists who have studied the matter closely, above all Henri Gastaut, agree that a lesion in the right temporal lobe or in the occipital cortex (which would account for the visual hallucinations) sparked short circuits elsewhere, leading to a generalized or grand mal seizure characterized by spasms, aphasia, loss of consciousness, and an aftermath of great fatigue. The fears that Achille's report excited at the Hôtel-Dieu when the two finally, somehow, made it home, can be imagined, yet Gustave left Rouen for Paris several days later, doubtless over Mme Flaubert's protests, having meanwhile experienced no recurrence. More blood had been drawn by Dr Flaubert, who, trying to raise a vein with hot water, scalded his son's right hand. It left a permanent scar.

Why did Achille-Cléophas, a prudent man, not insist that Gustave convalesce at greater length from an obviously grave episode? If the doctor, who had spent time enough in the hospitals of Paris and Rouen to witness many epileptic seizures, thought his son had suffered one, it may be that denial gained the upper hand of prudence, for there was good reason to deny a disease so untreatable or treated so brutally, and so freighted with pseudo-scientific myth. As one nineteenth-century physician wrote: "There is scarcely a substance in the world capable of passing through the gullet of a man that has not at one time or another enjoyed the reputation of being anti-epileptic." Before Charles Locock discovered a truly efficacious medicine in potassium bromide thirteen years after Gustave fell ill, the patient might have been prescribed wild valerian, peony root, mistletoe, digitalis, quinine, white dittany, rue, narcissus, opium, asafetida, garlic, camphor, cantharides, copper, zinc, lead, antimony, mercury, iron, silver, carbonic acid, or phosphorus: every specific had its champion, among city doctors as well as rural empirics. Bloodletting was commonly practiced, nerves were cauterized or cut, blisters were raised with vesicants, and cathartics administered. In extreme cases, physicians, including the famous neurologist Brown-Séquard, might recommend castration.

The epileptic was no longer seen as a vessel for prophecy or as a soul possessed. Orphaned of God and Satan, he could not escape the imputation that he suffered at his own self-abusing hand. While medical science had discredited demons, Enlightenment physicians demonized masturbation, and Dr Samuel Tissot was only the most prominent among them to see the specter of onanism behind most nervous afflictions. In flouting nature, the onanist ran a greater risk than the debauchee of going mad, Tissot declared in his classic treatise on masturbation. "Too great a quantity of semen being lost in the natural course produces dire effects; but they are still more dreadful when the same quantity has been dissipated in an unnatural manner. The accidents that happen to such as waste themselves in a natural way are very terrible, those which are occasioned by masturbation are still more so." Such terrible accidents befall the onanist, he went on to say, because he subjects himself to want without being in want, and accedes to the importunities of "habit" and "imagination" rather than of glands. How pervasive this argument had become may be inferred from Flaubert's own later reflections on the malady he could never bring himself to call by name. Describing its effects some ten years after its onset, he wrote: "Madness and lust are two realms I've explored so deliberately, through which I've charted so willful a course, that I'll never be (I hope) a lunatic or a Sade. But I've paid a price for it. My nervous malady is the scum of these little intellectual pranks. Each attack has been a kind of hemorrhage of innervation." The myriad images that flashed through his head like fireworks were, he said, a "seminal discharge" of the brain's "pictorial faculty."

But in an age increasingly preoccupied with issues of heredity, tainted or otherwise, innumerable theories and statistical studies were available to parents who might have been disposed to hold themselves inherently responsible for a child's illness. Guilt was laid at their doorstep by alienists finding the source of epilepsy in those afflicted with migraines, with tuberculosis, with syphilis, even with an excessively vivid imagination. The mere sight of an epileptic fit or of some other spectacular disorder might cause a pregnant woman to reproduce it in her fetus, declared the venerable Dutch physician Hermann Boerhaave (a notion propagated as "impregnation" by Jules Michelet in *La Femme,* according to which powerful images can be imprinted upon the somatic material of women). Although Mme Flaubert never recorded her thoughts on the subject — it seems likely, given her draconian conscience, that she somehow incriminated herself — Dr Flaubert firmly believed in the imaginative or visual contagion of epilepsy. Years earlier, he had urged Gustave, for that reason, not to imitate an epileptic beggar seen near the hospital.*

If Achille-Cléophas entertained any suspicions that Gustave's seizure had been in part a hysterical flight from judgment day at the École de Droit, he might have felt that rallying him would do more good than indulging him. When, almost three weeks afterward, Caroline voiced the family's anxiety about his health and readiness to send someone down to Paris at a moment's notice, her letter contained the ambiguous postscript: "Papa read your letter and said nothing to me about your [burned] arm, but here is my prescription: rest and lard." Had he not said anything to her about his son's

---

*It is quite possible that the beggar was himself an actor. Beggars simulating epilepsy, known as the "Cranke," who became stock characters in European cities during the sixteenth and seventeenth centuries, had not completely disappeared from the scene.

head? Or did he assume that a favorable verdict by the law-school jury would set everything right? In any event, "Hide your life" might have served, even more thenceforth than in the past, as a family motto.

It never came to verdicts. Sometime in late January Gustave visited Rouen for a brief respite. During that visit he had another seizure, which was called a "congestion of the brain" or an "apoplectic fit in miniature" (Gustave's words). This time Dr Flaubert, who may have witnessed it, took the matter quite seriously and prescribed an array of gruesome therapies, plus regular doses first of valerian and then of quinine. "I almost came before Pluto, Rhadamanthus and Minos," Gustave informed Ernest, referring as cheerfully as he could to the three judges of the underworld. "I'm still in bed with a seton in my neck, which is a high collar even more rigid than that of an officer in the National Guard, with many pills, infusions, and above all that specter worse than all the illnesses in the world called Diet." It followed from a diagnosis of cerebral congestion that the body should be bled, purged, and drained, which meant that leeches were regularly placed behind his ears, syringes thrust up his rectum, and setons applied to the nape of his neck. Most medieval was the last, a collar with a cord threaded through two incisions to keep them open and thus allow impure humors or *materia peccans* to escape. Performing his daily toilette, as he described it in colorful language, required feats of contortion. Still, he would have writhed gladly if rewarded with a daily smoke. Neither the seton nor the mercury rubs nor the "buggery" nor even the orange blossom water with which he washed down his insipid victuals exasperated him more than forced abstinence from tobacco. "You will understand how profound my sadness must be and how difficult it is to live when I tell you that the pipe — yes the pipe, yes you have read me correctly — that old pipe *is strictly forbidden!!!* I who loved it so much, who loved it alone! with a cold grog in summer and coffee in winter," he wrote to Ernest. All this renunciation did not spare him further seizures. He had many during the first part of 1844, and between seizures he experienced gut-wrenching fear. His whole person — knees, shoulders, stomach — would tremble at the least provocation like an aeolian harp vibrating under the slightest breeze. Life had come to feel extraordinarily precarious. Not a day passed, he said, that his field of vision wasn't littered with figments resembling clumps of hair or illuminated by Bengal lights. Years later, to the philosopher Hippolyte Taine, Flaubert gave his most precise account of grand mal aura. "First there is an indeterminate anguish," he wrote in 1866,

> a vague malaise, a painful sensation of waiting, as before poetic inspiration, when one feels that "something is going to come" (a state comparable only to that of the fornicator feeling his sperm well up just before discharge. Do I make

myself clear?). Then suddenly, like a thunderclap, the invasion, or rather, the instantaneous eruption of memory, for in my case the hallucination is, strictly speaking, nothing but that. It is an illness of memory, a slackening of what holds it in. One feels images escaping like torrents of blood. One feels that everything in one's head is bursting all at once like the thousand pieces of a fireworks display, and one doesn't have time to look at the internal images furiously rushing past. In certain circumstances, it begins with a single image that grows larger, develops, and in the end covers objective reality, like, for example, an errant spark becoming a conflagration. In the latter case, one can turn one's mind to other thoughts, and this gets confused with what we call "black butterflies," that is, little satin discs that some people see floating in the air when the sky is grayish and their eyes are tired.

An American neurologist, John M. C. Brust, has described this phenomenon as something wholly internal and representing an exhibition of the mnemonic process or the very act of remembering as much as the summoning of specific memories. At any rate, terror was the overwhelming sensation; he felt that his personality, torn from his body, had rushed out the door and left it open for death to enter.

In April, Gustave, still tied to his subcutaneous leash, which luckily caused no systemic infection, spent several days in Paris settling business and clearing out his room on the rue de l'Est before recuperating with the family at the small seaside village of Tréport, near Dieppe. Everyone felt ill. Caroline (ever the voracious reader, and deeply absorbed in Schiller) had her chronic sore throat. Mme Flaubert suffered from her migraines and, as usual, dulled the pain with laudanum, which sometimes showed in purple smears on her forehead. A bowl of leeches would also have been at her side. Dr Flaubert's teeth tormented him. The world being fraught with danger, Gustave hesitated to mount a horse, to brave the surf, to climb the steep cliffs that dominated Tréport, or to do any of the other things he would have done exuberantly a year earlier. But his malady had nonetheless served him well, he felt, in saving him from law school. "My illness will have had the inestimable advantage of convincing people to let me occupy myself as I please," he wrote several months later to Emmanuel Vasse de Saint-Ouen, a former schoolmate. "There's nothing in the world I myself prefer to a good well-heated room, with books one loves and all the leisure one desires."

Just as Marcel Proust would escape from health, on the pretext of seeking it at Dr Sollier's sanatorium, in order to closet himself with *À la recherche du temps perdu,* so it was for Gustave that sickness offered the possibility of a life in art.

VIII

Deaths in the Family

GUSTAVE'S SEIZURES may have convinced Achille-Cléophas, if he needed convincing, to acquire another country retreat for his chronically ailing family. As it turned out, this did not involve a prolonged search. On May 21, 1844, barely six weeks after selling the property at Déville to a local manufacturer, he became the landlord of a much larger residence on the right bank of the Seine, three miles downriver from the Hôtel-Dieu, in the tiny hamlet of Croisset. It had been put up for sale by the estate of Charles-Antoine Piquerel when Piquerel died in December 1843, leaving more than a million francs to his heirs and a debt of 255 francs to his physician, Dr Flaubert. The civil tribunal of Rouen accepted Achille-Cléophas's bid of 90,500 francs.

A white, gabled, oblong structure three stories high (including a furnished garret) with tall windows in the style of Empire and Restoration villas, the house was a conspicuous landmark to boat traffic. It stood only yards away from a towpath, nestled between the Seine, which mirrored it, and the broad, grassy flank of a hill that reported the tollings of a parish church hidden from view. Its long garden path led to a square pavilion built in the previous century, when, before its renovation, this estate had served as supplemental quarters for a Benedictine abbey. Opposite on the left was a farm of six or seven acres attached to the *maison de maître* and a small apple orchard behind it. Passersby could see very little of the terraced garden, hedged with yews, unless they dared to peek through the wrought-iron entrance gate. A wall nearly six feet high afforded privacy. Above the river, near a little dock where Gustave would moor his dinghy, half a dozen tall poplars stood side by side like grenadiers at attention.

Amid the turmoil of carpentry, servants — in particular Julie and Achille-Cléophas's valet, Narcisse Barette — were kept busy moving furniture brought from Déville as well as wardrobes, a piano, pots, and overflow from the family's impressive library. There was ample space for all of this, although Achille-Cléophas insisted on adding a billiard room. The Flauberts had at their disposal not one but two dining rooms, a vast kitchen, and huts for laundry and bathing. The salon, whose gilt-trimmed wood panels and enormous mirrors may have struck them as excessively ornate, featured a white marble fireplace with replicas of Egyptian mummy cases. White stucco figures modeled after Bouchardon's sculptures of the Four Seasons graced the door lintels. One flight up, a long corridor provided access to three bedrooms and a *cabinet de toilette*. Gustave took possession of a large room at the pavilion end, from which he could survey the river through a large tulip tree in one direction and tall, pruned lindens lining the garden path in the other. Like every room, it had a fireplace. Fall and winter brought harsher weather to Croisset than to Rouen. Damp rose directly from the Seine. And where Rouen lay beneath the protective hump of Sainte-Catherine, north winds blew unimpeded through riverside villages.

This room became Gustave's study. By November 1844 he had thoroughly imbued it with tobacco smoke. The seton, which made even a bookish life arduous (especially one that involved the constant leafing of ponderous classical dictionaries) came off at last, but Gustave's nerves continued to misfire, and the benighted regimen prescribed by Dr Flaubert did not otherwise change. As if Greek were not difficult enough for him, he slogged through Homer, Herodotus, and Plutarch with fat leeches behind his ears, like an Amazonian explorer wading through infested mangrove swamps. Among Latin historians most often mentioned in correspondence, Tacitus was the one his enduring fascination with the morbid extravagances of Nero always led him back to. He read omnivorously, all the more so now for knowing that any departure from home invited the possibility of falling unconscious in public. "My bedside authors are Montaigne, Rabelais, Regnier, La Bruyère and Le Sage," he wrote to Louis de Cormenin in June 1844 (the usual recipient of his letters, Maxime Du Camp, was abroad on his first grand tour of the Levant). "I have read *Candide* twenty times over, I've translated it into English . . . In time, when I feel better, I'll resume

Homer and Shakespeare. Homer and Shakespeare, they say it all! Other poets, even the greatest, seem dwarfish in comparison."

The letters Gustave wrote to Ernest Chevalier and Alfred Le Poittevin in the aftermath of his first seizures show a young man upon whom the shadow had fallen trying hard to make something redemptive come of it. Now that he "consented" to be irremediably sick and to abdicate "practical life," he told Alfred, he felt rather at peace with himself. Was this illness a providential circumstance or a sign of election setting him apart, where he had always located himself anyway? Were the terrible ordeals it visited on him an initiatory discipline by which he might gain access to his own world, to the true life, to the inner sanctum of Art? Like a revenant, he beheld once-familiar things from a great psychological remove. The symbols and liturgy at a baptism, for example, suddenly seemed as cryptic as if they belonged to a pharaonic rite. Simple, unvarnished statements had the ring of Delphic conundrums. "The most banal remark leaves me openmouthed with admiration. There are gestures, timbres I marvel over, and nonsense that makes me swoon. Have you sometimes listened attentively to a foreign tongue you don't comprehend? That's how matters stand with me." This assertion of innocence may have been hyperbolic, but Alfred Le Poittevin, for one, knew that there could be no doubt of Gustave's desire to inhabit a flawless, unselfconscious mind from which all judgments, wills, purposes, and meanings other than his own had been expunged. "Hide your life" was not his only obsessive command. "Break with the external world," he advised Alfred, in a harangue anticipating the memorable declaration of a later period that his ideal work would be a book about nothing, a book devoid of external ties "upheld by its own internal force of style, as the earth turns with nothing holding it aloft."

The perfect self-possession he sought through art entailed a vow of chastity as well as poverty, or so it seemed, for in proposing to fortify himself against life, he could not imagine having a woman share his dispassionate aerie without being evicted from it himself. Loss of control might have dire consequences. To the belief that carnal knowledge neutered when it didn't kill, his eyesight testified most eloquently. The terror and fascination exercised upon him by women — Medusas who held him fixed in their gaze, leaving him paralyzed, dumbstruck, blinded, or bent under a magnetic "weight" — recall the aura of epileptic seizures, which he often described as filling his eyes with flame before bringing him to his knees and rendering him speechless. One pathology heightened another. But in voyeuristic ceremonies of the kind he experienced or pictured fictionally, his own eyes supervised an emotional distance that gave him power as the unseen seer. "Fornication no longer teaches me anything; my desire is too universal, too permanent and too intense for me to have any desires," he wrote to Alfred on May 13, 1845, when his profound reluctance to risk humiliation, along with the dampening of libido that often attends temporal lobe epilepsy, cost Rouen's brothels a familiar patron. "I don't use women. I do what the poet in your novel does, I consume them by sight." Curiosity no longer impelled him to discover "the unknown" inside a woman's corolla of petticoats, to grope for flesh amid ruching and flounces and horsehair bustles. So peculiarly extraneous had women become that he hadn't had sex in two years. Like someone "on whom love had been lavished," he wanted no more of it. Or, he wondered, was he himself the prodigal party? "Masturbation is the cause of it, moral masturbation I mean. Everything comes from me and circles back to me. I can't produce those magnificent secretions that have been too long boiling inside ever to spill out." Besieged meanwhile by news of friends flocking to the altar, Gustave raised his defenses ever higher. He was what he was — a paradox who would not have wanted to seal himself off had he not been so porous. "Normal, regular, sustained intercourse would take me too much out of myself, would discompose me. I would find myself plunged again into active life, physical truth, into the common way of things, and whenever I've attempted that it's harmed me." Erotic fantasies were one thing, but resolving to consummate them quite another, he told Alfred, in whom he saw a fraternal outsider. "You and I are made to feel, to narrate, and not to possess."

His alleged detachment did not prevent him from lashing out bitterly at those who without apparent anguish pledged themselves to the world of convention. "It's raining marriages, it's hailing nuptials, it's a downpour of rectitude," he exclaimed. The vision of his former schoolmate Alfred Baudry on a priapic honeymoon in the Pyrenees called his mind away from Quintus Curtius's *History of Alexander* and an eruption of painful boils. "How his cock is excited by the prospect of mountains! He compares waterfalls to his ejaculations, truffles to his bride's mound."* Of Podesta, the professor of Italian at the collegiate school, he surmised that his bride might have a whorish penchant for sex in carriages. And eleven months before marrying the cousin to whom he was engaged, a former classmate named Alexandre Bourlet de la Vallée was already the object of Flaubertian taunts. "How about his constancy! One day he will be found in his bed dead of erection, stiff and straight like a frozen rabbit." Ernest Chevalier, still further removed from marriage in this conjugal declension, had not even acquired a fiancée when Gustave began throwing barbs his way. "It will happen to you one of

*Baudry married the daughter of the attorney who was later to mount a successful defense of *Madame Bovary* against government prosecution.

these days," he wrote in June 1845. "I'm anxious to see you provided with a little Victor or Adolphe or Arthur, to be nicknamed Totor, Dodofe, or Tutur, dressed in an artilleryman's uniform and asked to recite fables." But Ernest already qualified for ridicule by marrying the law. A frail young man who had spent time in the care of a physician at Les Andelys after earning the doctoral degree, he embarked upon his career with an appointment to Calvi in Corsica as public prosecutor. "There you are now, a staid, established, pious man invested with honorable functions and responsible for defending public morals," Gustave joshed. "Look at yourself in the mirror right now and tell me you're not greatly tempted to laugh out loud. So much the worse for you if you aren't. It would prove that you're already so mired in your metier as to have become witless." He enjoined him to prosecute malefactors as best he could without losing his sense of philosophical irony. "For love of me, don't take yourself seriously."

Only Alfred Le Poittevin, to whom he spoke in the language of Montaigne cherishing his dear friend La Boëtie or with bawdy salutations in the spirit of the Garçon, was exempt from rancor. After an auspicious internship at the Rouen bar, Alfred had apparently fallen into a despondent state and postponed, if not yet sworn off, the well-decorated future envisaged for him. Spending as much time in Paris as in Rouen, he wrote poems about doubt and disillusionment. His verse dwelt on his reluctance to go one way or another, to choose between a profession for which he felt no enthusiasm and a contemplative life for which he had insufficient discipline. Typical of his moroseness are these lines from "To Goethe":

> Dès que je me connus, je me sentis mobile,
> A toute impression cédant comme l'argile,
> Et dans ma vanité, toujours humilié
> D'une agitation qui faisait pitié*

The first line parodically echoes Racine's Hippolyte recalling, in *Phèdre,* the pride he had felt upon discovering his father's heroic past, being eager to perform comparable feats, and declaring: "Je me suis applaudis quand je me suis connu." With Le Poittevin, self-recognition is greeted not by the self-congratulation of an ambitious aristocrat proclaiming his inborn mettle but by the self-contempt of a feckless bourgeois regretting his malleable nature. Still, Alfred would more readily have claimed descent from an oyster than honor anything of the entrepreneur in himself. His writing is fraught with images of lassitude, inaction, paralysis, impasse, ennui; but ennui bespoke a

---

*When I discovered who I was, I found myself to be changeable, Yielding like clay to every impression, And in my pitiful vanity constantly galled by imagined slights.

state of heavenless transcendence or of godforsaken elevation that passed for nobility among Baudelaire's contemporaries.

What may have mattered more is that all this higgledy-piggledy led Alfred to Spinoza, whose works he studied carefully and urged upon Gustave. The word *external,* as both men used it in correspondence, alluded to *The Ethics.* Powerfully cogent to Alfred, it seems, was Spinoza's distinction between "active" feelings and "passive" feelings and the argument derived from it that an active man, whose experience is the outgrowth of his own nature, walks free, while the passive man goes where emotion tugs, like an infant on a lead. Moral progress, in this view, means ascent from bondage to selfhood, from alienation to identity, and intellectual progress follows suit. At a primitive stage, man is the creature of opinion, under the sway of things outside himself. Only when reason grows strong enough to fend off external allurements can he find his center and, in occupying it, understand how passions distort. Thus will he gain distance from resentments, regrets, and disappointments; achieve serenity; and should he ascend still higher, see an eternal order reflected in every iota of creation. There externality itself disappears, as mind, borne aloft by "intuitive knowledge," identifies its thoughts with cosmic thoughts and its interests with cosmic interests. Beginning his journey outside himself, in the dark lowland, man will complete it at this impersonal summit. As for Alfred Le Poittevin, what he took from *The Ethics* forms the conclusion to his *Promenade de Bélial,* a Spinozan tour of contemporary mores guided by the devil. "Even in its higher stage, Mind must recapitulate the three phases with which you are now familiar," he wrote. "Gripped by the wonders that nature lavishes upon it, it will at first become its slave again, then repudiate it to gain its freedom, and at last, returning to nature, rule over it. The infinite aspirations one feels confusedly gestating inside oneself all have corresponding realities, when they mature."

Unfortunately his body betrayed him. Sapped by a weak heart, and at one point burning with gonorrhea, he found alcohol more helpful than Spinoza in his attempt to escape from the slough of despond. Gustave, a disgruntled teetotaler for the time being, cautioned him against it and protested his love every chance he got, lest the lifeline that bound them go slack. Each felt vague, incomplete, and aimless when apart from the other, he declared. Alfred, whom he greeted as a "dear and great man," was *dimidium animae meae,* or half of his soul. "After our last separation I again experienced heartache, which, though it astonished me less than it once did, still left me grief-stricken," he wrote from Nogent-sur-Seine on April 2, 1845. "Three months have passed since we were together, alone — alone in ourselves and alone together. Is there anything comparable to the curious conversations that take place at a corner of the sooty fireplace where you come and sit, my dear poet? Rummage through your life and you will admit, as I do, that we have stored no better memories — none more intimate, more profound, more tender even in their loftiness." Coimprovising the puerile antics of the Kid had already gone some way toward placing them on level ground, despite their age difference, but now Gustave felt free to rally his perplexed elder with an air of moral authority. The Spinoza preached by Alfred came back at him from Gustave in prescriptions that mimicked Dr Flaubert's tough love. "Find out what your nature is and act in accordance with it," Gustave insisted. "'Sibi constat [*sic*],' wrote Horace, and he had it absolutely right."* Alfred was advised to follow his surly example. "*Break with the exterior,* . . . drive out everything, everything except your intelligence." Unlike happiness, the absence of unhappiness might be an attainable goal, but only inside the castle keep of Art, behind a lowered portcullis. When Alfred, trying to convince himself at age twenty-eight that he might have produced good work had he found some way of becoming an artist, declared that what he lacked was willpower, Gustave pestered him to roll up his sleeves, to "chisel away," and train his lungs to breathe in an anaerobic bourgeois climate. "That way they will expand all the more joyfully when you stand on high and suck in great gusts." He claimed not to agree entirely with Buffon's maxim that genius is having enough patience to stay the course ("Le génie est une longue patience") but produced a variation on the theme, "C'est dans une lente souffrance que le génie s'élève" (Slow suffering is what nurtures genius). Salvation for him lay in daily toil.

Willpower and stamina were not Gustave's deficiencies. Although Maxime Du Camp contended many years later that epilepsy had transformed a fluent writer into a famously deliberate one, his illness did not hinder Gustave from resuming work four months after the first seizure on a book he had begun in February 1843, when at law school, and that he finished in January 1845. Destined to metamorphose completely over the next twenty-five years, this novel, which attempted a great deal more than *Novembre,* kept its original title throughout: *L'Éducation sentimentale.* The first version would be published posthumously, as an appendix to the 1909–12 edition of the complete works.

L'Éducation sentimentale concerns itself with the divergent paths taken by bosom friends, Henry and Jules, who must separate when Henry leaves for Paris and law school. Three long letters from Jules give him a mere toehold in what is mainly, except toward the end, an account of Henry's vicissitudes. Like so many nineteenth-century fictional adolescents from provincial France whose purpose in moving to Paris gets mislaid five minutes after

---

* *"Sibi constet,"* meaning "May he remain in agreement with himself."

they pass through the city gates, Henry becomes a naturalized citizen of Babylon, where anything that doesn't offer immediate gratification counts for little or nothing. Gratification lies near at hand, in the genteel student boardinghouse to which his nouveau riche parents have sent him. Run by a corpulent master excessively fond of his knitted skullcap and tartan bathrobe, the pension smells more of perfume emanating from the master's beautiful, dark-haired wife, Émilie Renaud, than of midnight oil. Gustave portrays this character at some length. Trapped in a loveless, childless marriage, she presides over the establishment as a figure of frustration, stifling her maternal longings and romantic fantasies until Henry, ripe for adventure, enters her life. Clandestinity, shyness, pangs of conscience, seductive strategies, the Oedipal challenge, exacerbate a passion that obscures everything else. Indifferent to past and future, the delinquent law student has found his Lotte, his Mme de Warens, his Ellénore, his Sophie de Rênal. For Henry, whom Émilie calls *mon enfant,* the world is henceforth defined by the compass of her eyes: to be is to live within it, and to die is to fall outside. "She had long, upturned lashes, black pupils streaked with yellow filaments like gold glittering against an ebony ground," Gustave observes early along. "The skin all around her eyes was of a reddish hue that gave them their weary, amorous expression. I love the thirty-year-old woman's large eyes, almond-shaped, hooded eyes with dark, emphatic brows, tawny skin shaded by the lower lid, languid, Andalusian looks, maternal and lecherous." Later Henry will confide to Jules: "Yesterday she visited me in my room. All day she had glanced at me strangely and I couldn't tear my eyes away from that look; it surrounded me like a hoop circumscribing my life." When Émilie, throwing off all pretense of conjugal fidelity, surrenders herself, lovemaking is described by Henry as a visual event. "The whole earth disappeared, I saw only her pupil, which opened wider and wider." So will it be for Charles Bovary lying in bed with Emma the morning after their nuptial night.

The outcome of this ecstatic consummation is restiveness. No sooner have they created a world entire unto itself than Henry begins to feel imprisoned by the attentions of a possessive mother and Émilie to fear being abandoned. Life continues, but as trysts become routine, the sense that each has somehow lost his self to the other displaces the completeness they briefly knew. Expelled from paradise, they look outside themselves, in the world, for a center. "The monotony of their existence, the very regularity of their happiness, irritated them, made them long for a vast, less cramped happiness. They situated it elsewhere, in a new country, far from the old, and separated from their entire past by the depth of the seas." But there will be no new dispensation. Gustave launches them across the Atlantic to America, land of rich uncles and assumed identities, where their money soon runs out, aggravating the emotional predicament they brought with them. Worse than material destitution is the psychological wear that makes Henry feel more and more unreal. Down-at-heel in New York, his inner being indentured to Émilie, who hovers over him solicitously, he becomes the ghost of himself. And where love has fled, lewd fantasies take hold. "Monstrous desires invaded his soul, new appetites, forms from another world. He would have liked eyes to burn him like live embers, arms to smother him with superhuman embraces, thighs to entwine themselves around him like a serpent, marble teeth to bite his heart . . . He sought relief in a carnal frenzy." After eighteen months abroad, the expatriates come home. Without apparent resistance, Henry is pried loose from Émilie and placed with an uncle in Aix-en-Provence to continue the study of law. She unhappily resumes married life while he insouciantly cuckolds other husbands. Three years later Henry enters the social arena as a suave nonentity, with an eye for the main chance, and a chameleon-like talent for matching his principles to his environment. "He is a man in all his inconsequence and the Frenchman in all his grace," Gustave concludes. Of course, when Henry marries, he marries rich.

In the meantime, Jules, who will justify Gustave's own ideal itinerary, avoids social intercourse. Employed as a clerk, he lives disconsolately among bourgeois, unloved for his literary talent until the director of an itinerant theater company proposes to stage a play he has written (in the Romantic mode). Salvation beckons, and, indeed, Jules exhibits symptoms of religious rapture. Like a true believer seized by the Spirit on entering consecrated space, he is entranced by actors weaving spells behind the proscenium arch. In a philistine world, only theater offers hospitality to his imaginative life.* "He was a gullible, trusting child," writes Gustave, himself a credulous man never happier than in playhouses, who would one day create a character famous for believing her stuffed parrot to be the Holy Ghost. "Nervous and feminine by nature, with an easily broken heart, . . . he would rejoice or droop for no apparent reason and need very little to set him daydreaming. Trifles sparked great hatreds and certain words enraged him. He ardently desired baubles . . . and adored all manner of foolishness. An innate expansiveness heightened the intensity of his joys or sorrows." This spiritual island turns out to be his Cythera as well. The magic that has rescued him, this mere clerk, from oblivion informs the whole theater company and first of all its principal actress, Lucinde, with whom Jules falls in love, to the dis-

---

*After visiting La Scala in Milan in 1845, Gustave would write: "A theater is as sacred a place as a church. I enter it with religious emotion because there, too, human thought, sated with itself, seeks to leave the real; there, too, one comes to weep, to laugh or to admire, which about describes the compass of the soul."

. may of his parents. Lucinde intimates that his love will not go unrequited, which intimation is sufficient collateral for the one hundred francs she borrows from him. Jules' eyes open only when the company disappears overnight without having performed his play. Illusions collapse like a struck stage set. To Henry, he writes despairingly: "I no longer have hope, projects, strength, will; I move and live like a loose wheel that won't stop rolling until it falls, like a leaf that will flutter so long as there is air to pillow it . . . a machine for shedding tears and brewing sorrow."

Gustave's scheme requires of Jules an inward spiraling to balance Henry's centrifugal career. One wears thinner, the other bulks larger. One revolves with the world, the other turns around his own axis. Not that Jules can resist straightaway the impulse to idealize what he is not, to covet what isn't his, to romanticize what is no more, to imagine life fuller elsewhere. While nature, in growing wildflowers even over the dead of blood-soaked battlefields, forgets every insult, the mind inescapably contemplates itself, like a king tied to the throne he might wish to abdicate. So Jules grieves and doubts and envies. But he will (several pages later) rise above the slough of human embarrassments to become an observer of men, just as he will satisfy his lust for riches and power by acquiring a wealth of knowledge. *"L'ensemble"* is his watchword: the "whole" surveyed from an impersonal vantage point. "He who would heal men's wounds accustoms himself to their odor," writes Gustave.

> He whose domain is the human heart must wear a suit of armor to live serenely amid the fires it lights, to be invulnerable at the battle he views; whoever participates in an action doesn't see the whole of it, the player doesn't feel the poetry of the game, nor the rake the grandeur of debauchery, nor the lover the lyricism of love . . . If every passion, every commanding idea in life were a circle, one could not measure its circumference or extent from within, only from outside.

Having stepped outside the circle, Jules retires as a character to serve in his fictional afterlife as a mouthpiece for Gustave's dispute with exclusionary norms, with moral absolutes that enforce a parochial view of human nature. Trespassing on orthodoxies like a migratory animal ignoring national boundaries, he travels through history and, in the spirit of Hugo's preface to *Cromwell,* levels every signpost en route, every partition, every banner flown by academic landlords. "Theories, dissertations, claims made on behalf of good taste, declamations against barbarism, systems scaffolded on some idea of the Beautiful, apologia for the ancients, slurs pronounced in defense of pure language, twaddle about the sublime all helped him appreciate the risible vanity of different schools and eras."

Six petites vues de Rouen,

Dessinées d'après nature et Lithographiées par Émile Deroy.

An early-nineteenth-century view of Rouen, showing the rue Damiette running uphill to the magnificent abbey church of Saint-Ouen. (Bibliothèque Municipale de Rouen)

Gustave's mother as a young woman, possibly young enough to have been the ward of Dr. Laumonier. (Bibliothèque Nationale de France)

Caroline Flaubert, Gustave's mother, in 1831. At age thirty-eight she glumly displays the fashions of the period: balloon sleeves that made her look much wider than she was, and artificial hair in an unadorned version of the "Apollo knot." (Bibliothèque Nationale de France)

Dr. Achille-Cléophas Flaubert, Gustave's father, chief surgeon of the Hôtel-Dieu. Painting by J. Court. (Musée Flaubert et histoire de la médicine. Photograph by C.H.U. Rouen)

Gustave's birthplace, a room in the Flauberts' apartment at the Hôtel-Dieu.
(Bibliothèque Municipale de Rouen. Photograph by Thierry Ascensio-Parvy)

Dr. Achille Flaubert,
Gustave's older brother.
Portrait by Hippolyte
Bellangé. The doctor's face
unnerved Gustave's young
niece. (Musée Flaubert.
Photograph by C.H.U.
Rouen)

Caroline Flaubert, Gustave's sister. No other image of her survives. The bust is by James Pradier, who also sculpted Gustave's father. (Musée Flaubert. Photograph by C.H.U. Rouen)

Gustave in 1830, age nine, by Eustache-Hyacinthe Langlois. (Bibliothèque Nationale de France)

Gustave in 1833, age twelve, by a relatively unknown painter. (Bibliothèque Municipale de Rouen. Photograph by Thierry Ascencio-Parvy)

The Flauberts' wing of the Hôtel-Dieu, to the right, viewed from the place de la Madeleine.

The walled garden of the Flauberts' hospital quarters.

A letter from Gustave to his beloved childhood friend Ernest Chevalier. It is dated 1831, the year he began his formal studies at the collegiate school. (Musée Flaubert. Photograph by C.H.U. Rouen)

Entrance of the school Gustave attended from the age of ten, known then as the Collège royal and since renamed the Lycée Corneille. (Milbank Memorial Library, Teachers College, Columbia University)

Alfred Le Poittevin, near the end of his life. He was Gustave's boyhood idol, always portrayed as his *maître à penser*. Le Poittevin's nephew was Guy de Maupassant.

Élisa Schlesinger, Gustave's first love and the model for Marie Arnoux in *L' Éducation sentimentale,* with her daughter, Marie. Painting by Achille Devéria. (Bibliothèque Nationale de France)

View from across the Seine of the Flaubert house at Croisset, three miles down-river from Rouen. (Bibliothèque Municipale de Rouen)

If one supposes that Gustave's allegiance to "impersonality" was bound up not only with Dr Flaubert's clinical method but with his struggle against the explosion of personality in clonic seizures or the fantasy of controlling his flawed self from outside it, one may equally suppose that his distaste for the moral and esthetic taxonomies that went unquestioned by most people had some connection to the stigma of epilepsy.* "Fair and foul are near of kin," Yeats's Crazy Jane informs the bishop, and so says Gustave in his tacit indictment of a world that calls everything singular outlandish. "What seemed at first glance to be jarring and confused in history gradually disappeared," he writes, "and [Jules] began to see that the monstrous and the bizarre also had their laws, like the graceful and the severe. Science recognizes no freak, it ostracizes no creature, and it studies with equal love the boa constrictor's vertebrae, the miasmata of volcanos, the larynx of nightingales, the corolla of roses." Ugliness exists only in the eye of the beholder, and the swoonings caused by beautiful objects merely argue infirmity of mind. "Nature cannot make such distinctions. Everything in it is order and harmony: wheat fields are beautiful, but equally beautiful are storms, barren rocks. Spiders have their beauty; crocodiles, apes, owls, hippopotomi, vultures have theirs. Crouching in their den, wallowing in their filth, howling over their prey, they spring from the same womb . . . and return to the same dust — all rays of one circle that converge at its center."†

In the realm of humankind as well, partitions separating high and low are dismantled. Without regard for the blood or knowledge of Latin on which one class predicated its superiority over another, Jules finds evidence of skulduggery in the Panthéon and of virtue in the prison house. Further subverting received ideas, he detects humor in tragedy, depth in masks, man in woman. Everywhere he looks, contradiction breeds. Nero, just before his suicide, sobs over the loss of an amulet given him by Agrippina. The ho-

---

*Years later, in a divagation on the need to distance oneself from one's emotions in the creative process, Flaubert wrote to Louise Colet: "If my brain had been more solid, doing law and being bored would not have made me sick. I would have derived some advantage from it instead of illness. Instead of remaining in my skull, grief flowed into my limbs and convulsed them. It was a *deviation*. There are many children who get sick from music. They are greatly talented, they can remember scores note for note after only one hearing, they are quite carried away when playing the piano; their pulse races, they grow thin and pale . . . These are not the Mozarts of the future. The *vocation* has been displaced."

†Flaubert will again elaborate this idea in his account of a journey through Brittany, *Par les champs et par les grèves,* after observing mutant specimens in a museum of natural history: "If what are called freaks of nature share anatomical features . . . and physiological laws, . . . why would all that not also have its particular beauty, its ideal? Did the ancients not think so? And is their mythology anything but a monstrous and fantastical universe replete with forms impossible for our nature, yet so harmonious and congruous among themselves as to be beautiful?"

mosexual Henri III sends letters written in his blood to a young woman. One brave general, Turenne, jumps at shadows, and another, De Saxe, recoils from cats. That these were capable of being tweaked by demons sets matters right for Jules. It makes his own frailty more respectable, writes Gustave. It restores his place among men.

Shredded pieties whet Jules' appetite for as much knowledge as the banquet table can support. Being mindful of Spinoza's proposition that a free man is one who confronts things as they necessarily are in the only possible world and strives to understand their manifold interconnectedness, he displays the *generositas* of an intellectual aristocrat, unwarped by prejudice or petty calculation. While Henry pants after his fugitive self on two continents, Jules, occupying his own dispassionate center, swallows the world whole. "Poetry at its greatest, intelligence at its broadest, nature in all its facets, passion with all its cries, the human heart and its abysses combined in one enormous synthesis every bit of which he respected out of love for the whole, not wishing to deny human eyes a single tear or to remove a single leaf from the forest. He saw how everything that eliminates curtails, how everything that selects forgets, how everything that prunes destroys, how epic poems were less poetic than history." The all-inclusive plenitude of history gives the measure of what art must aspire to. Nothing of reality should fall outside its domain, Gustave declares through Jules, who reveres Homer and Shakespeare as the supreme omnivores.

Given the philosophical counterpoint of *L'Éducation sentimentale,* it may be that Gustave intended the anecdotal story to support the disquisition on Jules' thought, like a platform built for a lecturer. Curt abridgments and self-indulgent longueurs suggest that proportions were skewed by months of sick leave. The novel is far from seamless. Authorial interventions of the kind one might expect, in theater, from a nervous young director constantly halting rehearsals trouble its narrative flow. But Flaubert the master can readily be seen throughout this apprentice work. The lyrical brilliance of his plea for a literature humane enough to recognize the dark, irrational face of mankind supports Paul Le Poittevin's contention that he would have made a formidable courtroom presence. There are minor characters that illustrate a gift for parodic portraiture worthy of La Bruyère. There is a droll confrontation between Monsieur Renaud and Henry's parents in which Gustave mimics the forsaken parties with an ear wonderfully attuned to sanctimonious prattle. Above all, there is the sense (even if Jules comes to scorn the quotidian) of a story unfolding scene by scene and within a historical context. Allusions to works published during the 1840s, external events, datable entertainments, fashionable clothes and decor all create a Louis-Philippean ambiance. And the psychological refinement evident in the depiction of Émilie and Henry is itself temporal: as painters may convey with color the impression of things receding in space, so here emotions developing in time are what make time pass.

They didn't make time pass quickly enough for Achille-Cléophas when Gustave read him the novel, or so wrote Maxime Du Camp, who claimed, in memoirs written thirty-seven years after the event, that the doctor nodded off, and on waking denigrated the literary vocation with jovial nonchalance. Writing, he is quoted as saying, might be better than haunting cafés and gambling dens, but its chief virtue is its inoffensiveness. "Why need one write? A pen, ink, and some paper, nothing more . . . Literature, poetry, what purpose do they serve? No one has ever known." In Du Camp's anecdote, Gustave riposted by asking what purpose the spleen served. "You have no idea, doctor, do you? Nor do I, though we know it is indispensable to the human body, as poetry is to the human soul!" Whereupon the doctor shrugged his shoulders.

Among much else, the large collection of literary and historical works lining many walls of the Flaubert residences casts doubt on this story, which has misrepresented Gustave's father for generations. One may suppose that the anecdote was embellished, if not fabricated, to suit Maxime's ambivalent feelings toward Gustave himself; that a description of Jules and Henry as incompatible sensibilities touring Italy together in *L'Éducation* presciently describes — at Henry/Maxime's expense — the voyage he and Gustave later took through the Levant. Maxime's narrative may also have voiced his ambivalence toward art, for he had never shared Gustave's exalted view of it and by 1882 had more or less turned his back upon literature to write a monumental survey of Paris's social and administrative institutions. At that later time he would quite possibly have identified as much with the half-apocryphal Dr Flaubert as with Gustave.

What does seem plausible in the story are Achille-Cléophas's untimely nap and Gustave's umbrage. While the doctor would in all likelihood have denied that he thought literature a genteel diversion of little consequence, his taste undoubtedly ran to taut, apothegmatic prose rather than lyrical embellishments and psychological analysis, to Voltaire rather than Goethe or Hugo or Musset. It is quite possible that after a long day in the hospital, he could barely follow his son through the penetralia of two difficult adolescents. Wasn't Gustave later to say that he had been born speaking an idiom all his own, that no one really understood him, and that the doctor, among others, shed tears of incomprehension? Wanting redemption for having twice disappointed his father, he may have bristled at failing him yet again.[*]

---

[*]After Dr Flaubert's death, Gustave would write to Ernest Chevalier: "You knew and loved the good, intelligent man we lost, the sweet and high-minded soul who has departed."

From companions he solicited the unstinting praise denied him at home. Maxime wrote that Alfred Le Poittevin and he helped by applauding his work. "He often read us *L'Éducation sentimentale,* as if to recruit witnesses against paternal injustice." As previously noted, reading works in progress became a lifelong ritual of friendship with Gustave (who also recited sentences while composing them). This would always bolster him. And because he found it indispensable, nothing bothered him less than the contradiction between these performances in which he held forth as playwright, director, and cast all together and the principle he was later to enunciate that a writer should be in his work as God in his creation, everywhere felt and nowhere seen.

After several years, when Gustave gained distance from his lopsided child, he stopped requiring that friends compliment him and in fact judged the work rather harshly himself. A letter written to Louise Colet on January 16, 1852, speaks of his two literary selves: one a romantic transported by the soaring of eagles, lofty ideas, "rants," and "all the timbres of a sentence"; the other a stickler for pertinent detail whose ambition was to make the things he depicted materially palpable to a reader. "Unbeknownst to me, *L'Éducation sentimentale* was an attempt to fuse these two tendencies of mind . . . I failed. I could tinker with it and perhaps will, but whatever alterations I make, it will still be defective. It lacks too many things. I'd have to recast the whole . . . and, most daunting of all, include a chapter that shows how, inevitably, the same tree trunk had to fork, why this personage or that one turned out as he did." His recasting of the novel during the 1860s would leave nothing intact but its title.

IN 1845 — when Victor Hugo was made a peer and Ingres a commander in the Legion of Honor, when Rouen was abuzz with news of electric telegraphy connecting it to Paris, and the failed potato crop, which preceded a calamitous wheat harvest, gave Louis-Philippe's tight-fisted, uneasily prudent government ample notice that uprisings would occur unless it addressed the problem of widespread pauperism — the Flaubert family could think about little else but twenty-one-year-old Caroline. On March 3, 1845, Gustave's sister married his friend and former classmate Émile Hamard.

Hamard, who signed the fateful school protest of December 1839 and, like Gustave, published satirical pieces in *Le Colibri,* came from a family of substantial means. His father, Charles-Pierre, had left the Hamard stock farm to settle in Rouen, where he did well in marrying Désirée Dupont, the daughter of a merchant well known as president of the Chamber of Commerce and of a lady born Mlle Du Creux, whose forebears included jurists ennobled in the seventeenth century. Charles-Pierre died young, but the fatherless Émile and his younger brother never suffered for it materially. They lived on an elegant outer boulevard, near the place Cauchoise.

There is reason to suppose that on school holidays Hamard, whose relatives moved in the same social world as the Flàuberts, sometimes paid Gustave visits at the Hôtel-Dieu. We know that he kept Caroline company during Gustave's postgraduate voyage, when, reassuring her jealous brother that no one could replace him, she wrote: "I'm quite convinced that the melancholy H. will not have all your verve and that you will think of me from time to time." His melancholy may have been a welcome change from the coarse jocularity of the Kid. By late 1841 Caroline was calling Hamard "my delicate friend" and inquiring after him. He and Gustave saw each other regularly in Paris, suffering through the same law-school lectures, attending the theater, dining with mutual acquaintances. Even so, time spent together never resulted in a close friendship; Gustave, who loved affectionate nicknames, invented none we know of for Hamard. Caroline, meanwhile, grew much fonder of him. It distressed her that "*ce pauvre* Hamard" might bypass Déville en route to his younger brother's funeral at Pissy-Poville in May 1843, and it pleased her inordinately that the *"gentiluomo galantissimo,"* as she now dubbed him, came visiting. When he betrayed no sign of grief during their conversation, however, she wondered whether delicacy masked a hollow heart. Gustave, to whom she addressed her concern, set her mind at rest. "What you told me about Hamard made me feel better," she wrote. "I would rather he were sorrowful than insensitive." Several months later, shortly before their August examination, Gustave rekindled her sympathy with a description of the young man "rotting" on a pallet in the damp prison cell where he spent twenty-four hours for refusing to do National Guard duty. Diligent and rebellious, Hamard had brought his law books with him.

Caroline's doubts about Hamard's capacity to grieve, if any lingered, were dispelled in January 1844 when his mother, whom he loved deeply, took sick and died. Gustave, still shaken by his first epileptic seizure, comforted him as best he could but fled Paris for Rouen to escape scenes of wailing bereavement. "In less than two years he will have lost everything he loved, this poor Hamard — go see him, for he has often told me how much he likes you," Caroline had urged her brother on January 17. To a tender-hearted young woman, Hamard's orphanhood and knit brow may have been his most attractive features. Caroline found herself assiduously courted in the spring and summer of that year. By September, when graduation from law school required only that he defend his thesis, which he would successfully do in January, the time had come for a proposal. Hamard submitted one to Dr Flaubert through Gustave, who, preoccupied as he had been with illness and *L'Éducation sentimentale* (blotting out objectionable reality), was taken unawares. "You've heard about our big news," he wrote to Ernest Chevalier in November, the month of Caroline's engagement. "What can I say? Whatever you like. Comment as you please on this business. I summarized [my own opinion] in the one word I uttered when told of it: AH!" Ernest knew full well that Gustave's coyness did not imply approval, that the pregnant syllable contained a virtual diatribe against the sister planning to abandon him and the sly friend intent on stealing her. It felt like a betrayal, though he couldn't say so outright, except perhaps to Mme Flaubert, who shared his feeling. The generous reaction was Maxime Du Camp's rather than Gustave's. "If I had been your sister's father, I wouldn't have chosen another mate for my daughter: he is one of the best, most honorable men I know," Maxime wrote from Rome, on his way back to France after months in North Africa and Turkey.

> If those two aren't happy, I don't know where one would seek happiness. Your sister could have married someone who would have separated her from her family, you would have seen one another at rare intervals, you might have worried about her state of mind, while this way, with her married to your close friend, the bonds that tie you will be strengthened. Hamard hasn't written to me about it and the news took my breath away. I reread your letter twice before it sank in. When it did, I practically jumped for joy at the thought of their happiness.

But Maxime's rhetorical question, "Aren't we always inclined to embrace the affections of our dearest friends?" must have had Gustave wondering whether their friendship could withstand such bromides. For him Hamard's hateful affection meant loss.

Caroline coped well. The need to wrest herself free from a possessive family did not prevent her taking measures to assuage the pain of it. For help she called upon her uncle, who, along with brother Achille, would be a witness at her wedding. Her idea was that he spend several months in Croisset before the event and another month there during the Italian honeymoon, as the image of a forlorn household preyed upon her mind. Her poor mother, she wrote in September or October 1844, couldn't stop fretting about the voyage to Italy,

> because like all young newlyweds with some money in pocket we plan [such a voyage]. On our return we will spend four months in Croisset, whereupon we shall find a residence in Paris and settle down. You see, good and dear uncle, how much you will be needed during my absence; and we are always so eager to have you we don't know when best to beg you to come and stay. Here are my thoughts. Spend November, December, and January here. Return to Nogent in

February, then come back while I'm away traveling . . . What would become of mother in Croisset without you? I'm counting on you, uncle, and will depart easier of mind knowing that she has you for company.

To protect Hamard from the impression that he was the Flauberts' son-in-law on sufferance, Caroline recruited an amiable presence in Uncle François Parain and encouraged him to visit her fiancé at his flat on the rue de Tournon, near the Palais du Luxembourg.

Assembling a trousseau took almost one full week in Paris, after much preliminary correspondence. It proceeded garment by garment and day by day, from the wedding dress to the corset to shawls and lace, with Mme Flaubert at her daughter's side, bravely fighting off a migraine. These prenuptial exertions may have helped the women work up robust appetites, though even three hungry Normans couldn't finish the meal Hamard ordered at Véry, a gastronomic shrine in the Palais-Royal (later renamed le Grand Véfour). "Tell Gustave that yesterday, with him in mind, I had turtle soup at Véry," Caroline reported to her father. "In addition, the meal included three dozen green oysters, two filets financière, two soles in mayonnaise sauce, a hot pâté en croûte in madeira sauce, two bottles of Graves. It all cost twenty-six francs and Hamard, who was responsible for the double portions . . . and had been boasting about how cheaply he ate, was crestfallen." Perhaps the twenty-six francs, which represented about ten days' wages for the average worker, who could barely feed himself in years of inflated bread prices, still lay on Hamard's conscience three years later, when he embraced the revolution.*

No bourgeois marriage could go forward before a notary had drawn up a contract whose precise stipulations regulated the couple's economic future, and so everyone concerned gathered at Maître Boulen's office on March 1, 1845, to agree that Caroline's dowry of 105,000 francs should remain inalienably hers under the *régime dotal,* this being an advance against her eventual inheritance. Dr Flaubert would keep the principal in trust, relinquish it only on condition that Hamard use it to buy property for Caroline, and transmit interest in quarterly payments to be collected by Caroline or Hamard at the parental home. Hamard's contribution, apart from several small annuities and 90,000 francs, was real estate. He had inherited three cottages, four income-bearing farms at Cambremer in the Calvados and at Pissy-Poville downriver from Rouen, and, as bare ownership with-

---

*There was literary solace to be found in Balzac's *Illusions perdues,* where the vain young hero, Lucien de Rubempré, arriving in Paris from his native Angoulême determined to do the fashionable thing, dines at Véry on Ostend oysters, a fish, a pheasant, macaroni, and fruit, and washes it down with bordeaux, all for fifty francs. Either Balzac greatly exaggerated or the Rouennais got off cheap.

out usufruct, an apartment building in Rouen itself. The couple were well provided for. They would be still better off when Hamard began to practice law as chief clerk of the Cour des Comptes, or Commercial Court, in Paris.

Little is known about the wedding, but a great deal more about the honeymoon, for reasons that forced Hamard to postpone the pleasure of complete privacy with his tall, blond, blue-eyed bride. Whether they liked it or not, the newlyweds would be escorted as far as Genoa by Caroline's family (all except brother Achille, who minded the store), thence travel to Naples while Gustave and his parents toured southern France. This was not necessarily seen as a peculiar arrangement, for journeying five together in an age of arduous travel offered distinct advantages. It has always been said, furthermore, that Dr and Mme Flaubert were concerned about Caroline's health, although, if that were so, one may wonder why they considered going separate ways after Genoa. It was just as likely that a mother tormented all her life by childhood memories of separation could not yet accept the prospect of her daughter's independent life. At any rate, Gustave minutely chronicled the journey in letters to Chevalier and Le Poittevin and, above all, in the notes he kept.

To begin with, there were brief sojourns in Paris and Nogent-sur-Seine where François Parain gave Hamard his avuncular blessings. Another family reunion then took place in Dijon. At Chalons's river pier the post chaise was wheeled onto a steamboat, which transported Dr Flaubert's group seventy-five miles down the Saône to Lyons, progressing rather too slowly for Gustave, who sequestered himself inside the parked carriage with Horace's poetry. Under a gray, wet sky, Lyons looked its dismal worst. In telegraphic prose he spilled out assorted impressions — of the famous Catholic-royalist philosopher Bonald, a gaunt figure standing on his terrace; of two magnificent Rubenses at the city's Musée des Beaux-Arts; of the Rhône roiling southward at its confluence with the Saône. He could hardly wait to resume his journey aboard a vessel bound for Avignon, which sailed between dark red mountain ranges and after several days deposited passengers beneath the machicolated walls of the papal palace. Gustave, whose mood was strongly influenced by light, felt his spirits rise as soon as he entered the pastel city bathed in brilliant Vauclusian sunshine. "It's the Midi, people out-of-doors, whitish hues, warm air gusting down munificently graceful streets. Faded frescoes in an old cloister, a round church — mills abound." A diligent tourist, he saw all the consecrated sights, with special attention of course to the papal palace — where his guide, a frenetic old lady in a white bonnet and black wig, took pleasure descanting upon bloody relics of the Inquisition — and wandered away from his family whenever possible. Getting lost was almost as enjoyable as getting directions at a brothel. "The place was squat and white, three or four [prostitutes] in front, one wearing pink, a negress. Beds in the back [half a dozen, placed end to end], something cool and alluring — I seem to remember that there were blue flowers on the windowsill."

Several days later, on a quiet sunny morning in Arles, early enough for residents to be seen dumping night soil in the great Roman theater across the street, Gustave stopped at another brothel. This time the object of his search was not directions but some trace of the adolescent who had been there in 1840. From Avignon to Nîmes to Arles to Marseille to Toulon he kept retracing his younger self, nostalgically, like a man bereft of the future. In Nîmes memories gathered around the Coliseum, or a wild fig tree that had grown up right beside it through one of the upper-story apertures made for poles that supported the great canopy stretched over first-century audiences. In Marseille he visited the rue de la Darse and contemplated the now derelict hotel where "an excellent lady with big tits," as he put it to Alfred, had offered him such "pleasurable quarter hours." In Toulon, from whose port he and Jules Cloquet had shipped out, every stone spoke to him of that first voyage, so poignantly that images one day old merged with others stored for five years and all became equidistant: "After a while light and shadows mingle, everything acquires the same tint, as in old paintings. Drab days take on the coloration of gay ones, happy days steep in the melancholy of others. Which is why one likes to return to one's past: it is sad, yet charming."

The group was worn out by hectic sightseeing even before they reached Italy, and Mme Flaubert's migraines may have been the least of their ailments. Troubled by an ophthalmic disorder that began to afflict him almost as soon as he left Rouen, Dr Flaubert squinted his way across France, worrying all the while about patients placed in Achille's care. Caroline's chronic back (or kidney) problem eventually dissuaded the newlyweds from venturing beyond Genoa. And Gustave, who had come along for recreation, had two full-blown seizures, one of which occurred in the presence of a chambermaid at an inn on the Corniche. It seemed unlikely now that he would heal quickly, if at all, he told Ernest Chevalier. His favorite placebo, he added, was the word *shit*. It worked best when repeated over and over again.

Not being alone with his thoughts or master of his itinerary bothered a dispirited Gustave almost as much as losing control of his brain. A letter to Alfred sent from Marseille inveighs against his companions for vetoing his proposal to visit the fortified medieval city of Aigues-Mortes, the pilgrimage site of Sainte-Baume, and the field near Aix on which Caius Marius repulsed the Teutones in 102 BC. This would be his second grocer's tour of the Mediterranean, he complained, with an envious thought no doubt of

Maxime Du Camp traveling abroad by himself and sending back colorful accounts of his adventures in Constantinople. "By all that you hold sacred, if you hold anything sacred, by the true and the great, oh dear and tender Alfred, I beg you in heaven's name and my own, travel with no one! No one!" What the others insisted on seeing also irritated him. In Toulon, the infamous prison offered visitors entertainment on otherwise tedious Sundays. White-gloved men and women, he noted indignantly, were to be seen there holding up their lorgnons and inspecting (from afar) convicts on filthy plank beds, not unlike the proper ladies in Zola's *Thérèse Raquin* looking over the rotten cadavers of drowned men and women laid out on slabs at the Paris morgue. He felt a greater affinity to the criminal mind than the bourgeois. "One feels enraged with the stupid race of public prosecutors, with their smugness, with gentlemen imprisoning men who acted according to their position and their nature. One is tempted to break their chains and loose them upon the world."

But worst of all was a thought hectoring him throughout this voyage (as it had during the former one) that he couldn't really take in the marvels he beheld, that the presence of others interposed itself between things and his image of them. *Seul* often recurs in notes about some particularly vivid or memorable experience, as if the best moments were those stolen from company. He breathed freer when a sudden change of plans that called for them to tour Campania all together came to nothing. "The exquisite sensations aroused in me by Naples would have been sullied one way or another," he told Alfred (warning him not to repeat the confidence).

> When I go there I want to enter the marrow of antiquity, I want to be free —
> completely my own man — alone or with you, not with others. I want to be
> able to sleep under the stars, to go out not knowing when I shall return. Only
> then will my thought heat up and flow unobstructed. The color of things will
> soak my eyes. I will be absorbed in them. Traveling must be serious work. Oth-
> erwise it makes for bitterness and stupidity, unless one tipples all day long. If you
> knew how much [my companions] unwittingly quash in me, how much they
> rend from me, how much I lose, it would anger you.

Half a century later, when tourists began swarming over Europe with cameras at the ready, Gustave (who almost never allowed himself to be photographed or caricatured,* any more than he allowed publishers to produce illustrated editions of his work) might have appreciated the double enten-

---

*During the Second Empire, permission to publish a caricature was required of the subject, and when the famous caricaturist Gill asked Flaubert for it in 1869, Flaubert rebuffed him, declaring, "I reserve my face for myself."

dre embedded in the word *cliché,* which means "snapshot" as well as "commonplace phrase." For him, there was no middle ground. If, as a Spinozan paragon, one didn't absorb the world entire, then one harvested only the husk of things, and travel gave this truth more immediacy. Could he ever escape self-consciousness in a rapturous union, or transcend the mere accumulation of images in a sightless embrace? The burden he placed on his sensibility conduced to disappointment, though less so at night, when people fell silent and the darkened world yielded itself to him. "The night! I inhaled it like a perfume," he wrote of a moonlit walk through the deserted streets of Fréjus. "At night the soul spreads its wings and soars in peace. I love the night. My whole being swells in it, like a tautly strung violin whose pegs are loosened." His habits would always be nocturnal. Daytime noises easily distracted him.

Unlike Nathaniel Hawthorne, for whom in 1859 "it was really like passing from death into life, to find ourselves in busy, cheerful, effervescing France after living for so long between asleep and awake in sluggish Italy," Gustave came alive on the Italian side. Not until he left France, the land of invidious comparisons, where at every turn — but especially at the Eulalie-less Hôtel de Richelieu — he kept deliberately bumping into a younger, greener, preepileptic self, did his eyes truly open. Genoa in particular enthralled him with its labyrinth of steep alleys and convoluted streets suddenly opening out to views of the Mediterranean. His passion for mineral splendor was nourished by this city in which majolica tiles clad the tallest spire and black-and-white marble striped the facades of medieval churches, in which one ascended marble staircases, while marble Tritons disported themselves around marble basins. During a brief excursion on horseback into the Ligurian hill country, he contemplated Genoa's magnificent clutter of domes and campaniles. Down below, as much time as his itinerary allowed was spent looking at old masters in the Renaissance palazzi that flanked the Strada Nuova. Replete with detailed descriptions — most notably of Breughel the Younger's *Temptation of Saint Anthony* at the Palazzo Balbi, which fired his imagination — Gustave's notes display a keen and retentive visual memory. But Italian women also caught his eye. During an outdoor concert on the Acquasola esplanade he was smitten by a lady in mourning, whose white, black-bordered veil did not conceal her pallor, aristocratic nose, and large blue eyes. "Something cheerful about her face (though this must not be her usual expression) and elegant — her eyelids fluttered. I think she's the most beautiful woman I've seen — I drank her in as one slakes one's thirst with long draughts of an exquisite wine; she must have been beautiful, for I blushed in astonishment at first sight, and was afraid of falling in love." When his resurgent libido drew him back to the Acquasola several days later, he found another desirable woman in her place, this one wearing a white hat and rather less sublime: "Jutting mouth and chin, bluish lips, sharp nose, an unbutton-your-pants look, a tired, languid bearing but behind it an intimation of screams and bites." Then there was the mistress who supervised poor girls at a convent-cum-workhouse called the Fieschine Conservatory, famous throughout Europe for its artificial flowers. "Small, very plump, dressed in black, delicate hands, pleasant odor, her skin white and clean — chestnut hair parted on the left side, a wide brow, two wrinkles on her neck — white teeth and outlined lips; mixture of goodness and soft sensuality," he wrote, in a telegraphic style that skips confusingly from painted or sculpted images to live people. "What a shame I didn't utter a word! On the other hand, I looked and looked and looked at her." Outspoken in his predilection for older women, especially those with ample bosoms, he declared her to be well worth fantasizing about and maintained that forty-year-olds had not been given their due in literature. All of which augured some Eulalie-like climax. Regrettably, it never happened. On the morning of his departure from Genoa, he rose at dawn, walked down to the harbor, rented a boat, and rowed it beyond the breakwater in choppy seas, "to see one last time," he told Le Poittevin, "the blue waves I love so much." Afterward sadness muffled him for days.

A week or two later, during a tour of the Villa Sommariva at Lake Como, Gustave unleashed his pent-up desires on the beautiful nude with outstretched arms in Canova's *Amor and Psyche,* surreptitiously planting kisses all over her body (the ardent connoisseur wrote, by way of self-justification, that it was beauty itself whose armpit he had kissed).* Otherwise he continued to look and look as the exhausted party circled back toward France via Milan, the Lago Maggiore, the Simplon Pass, Lausanne, and Geneva. A bespectacled ecclesiastic guided him through the dank Ambrosiana Library where Petrarch's edition of Virgil, Lucretia Borgia's letters, and Breughel the Younger's *Water* and *Fire,* among much else he saw there, had somehow managed not to molder. He walked on the stage of La Scala, examined its traps, entered loges, and reverently saluted audiences past. At Monza, another opportunity for museological groping presented itself in the church's treasury of medieval relics, and Gustave seized it to groom himself with the gold and ivory comb of a sixth-century Lombard queen named Theodelinda. "[I thought about] the unknown hair it once held together on a royal nape. Her head must have been proud, haughty — a large, stout woman, belonging to the race of Fredegonde and Brunhilde; a hybrid beauty . . . Roman bronze overlaid with Teutonic color."

His most memorable communion awaited him at the fortress of Chillon

---

*He may not have known that he was making love to Adamo Tadolini's copy of Canova's masterpiece. The original was closer to home, if less accessible, at the Louvre.

on Lake Geneva, which had become a pilgrimage site not only for Swiss patriots remembering François de Bonivard, the sixteenth-century rebel imprisoned there, but of Romantics who knew Byron's poem "The Prisoner of Chillon" by heart. Byron had etched his name on a pillar in the dungeon. Blackened to set it apart from those of other visitors (among them George Sand, Victor Hugo, Alexandre Dumas), it had become an iconic signature, and, indeed, Gustave, who would translate "The Prisoner of Chillon" in the 1850s with a young Englishwoman, Juliet Herbert, felt his pulse quicken at the sight of it. "[It] filled me with an exquisite joy," he wrote to Alfred. "I reflected upon Byron more than upon the prisoner; tyranny and slavery didn't even cross my mind. All the while I imagined that pale man arriving one day, walking back and forth, inscribing his name, and departing. One must be very bold or very dumb to imitate him . . . Victor Hugo and George Sand did so, . . . which pained me. I assumed they had better taste." Byron was to be coupled with another idol several days later when, forty miles west, Gustave attended a band concert on the little island opposite Geneva named for Jean-Jacques Rousseau. "The program lasted quite some time. I kept delaying my return from symphony to symphony. I finally left. At either end of the Lake of Geneva there are two geniuses who cast shadows higher than the Alps." With cigar smoke wreathing around his head, Gustave found those great Romantic vagabonds acquiring his and Le Poittevin's features in a vision of transcendent congeniality. From Geneva he wrote a letter that described them as fellow travelers alone of their kind and locked together like twin stars isolated in the firmament. "Providence has us think and feel harmoniously." The unthinkableness of marriage, bourgeois or otherwise, was one thing they had in common.

GUSTAVE AND Alfred spent an evening talking and strolling on the boulevards of Paris sometime after June 8, during the Flauberts' three-day layover in the capital. But Gustave would see very little of his friend that summer. Having apparently taken a sabbatical from the law, Alfred was leading a restless life. He might have set out for Turkey had health permitted. Instead he toured the Normandy coast and stayed for weeks at a stylish hotel on the rue de Castiglione in Paris, and when late August came, migrated, as he did every year, to the family's summer house up the coast from Étretat, in Fécamp. Except for a burlesque tale called "La Botte merveilleuse," possibly inspired by E. T. A. Hoffmann or by Diderot's *Les Bijoux indiscrets,* very little came of literary ambitions that would neither die nor bear serious fruit. Ennui fatally seeped into every corner of his consciousness. "I used to believe that happiness didn't exist, but now I believe in it because I've met men who have told me in all seriousness that they were happy," he confided to Gustave, who in turn felt that the expectation of happiness caused untold misery, that the word itself was better left unspoken. "Having nerves is a nuisance, and that's the cause of all one's trouble . . . the mind." Alcohol and women for hire were solace. He drank himself sick and spent freely on prostitutes, taking no precautions against syphilis.*

To Gustave, who brooded over the paradox of being so well-knit yet so impressionable, having nerves was worse than a nuisance, but he continued to bless the virtue of his frailty. Nerves had won him "freedom" and "leisure," misfortune had made him a home greatly to his liking, professional invalidism had bounded his horizon, and the deathlike trance had focused his energies. Croisset was his den and the bear was his totem. He would have liked to hang a picture of one over his mantelpiece but procured a white bearskin instead, which covered the floor of his study. He had weaned himself from so many things that he now felt "rich in the bosom of absolute privation." If privation was defined only by the measure of intimacy with women — not by the allowance from one's father, one's mother's indulgence, the service of domestics, local transportation in a private carriage, a larder filled by one's tenant farmer, a wardrobe replenished at fashionable Parisian clothiers, books that accumulated faster than shelves could be built for them — then privation was indeed absolute. And for the moment this suited him. A regular, laborious, monkish existence, sheltered from emotional turmoil, is what he hoped the future held in store. Letters informed friends that his ways had been set, that he was as immutable as an old boot worn wherever leather could wear but still highly polished.

The challenge of classical languages still held him in thrall, and hours were spent each day deciphering Herodotus, whom he was determined to read fluently by year's end. Afternoons were generally reserved for Shakespeare and Roman historians, though masters of every kind passed across his desk, including Confucius. When he didn't have company, he would often lucubrate until early morning at his desk or on a green leather sofa, with his windows open to the tulip tree, the towpath, and the Seine beyond, glistening on moonlit nights. Aside from the notes he habitually took, very little writing got done. For his illness, against which two commonly prescribed specifics, valerian and orange blossom water, had been ineffective,

---

*Thus, this letter dated December 20, 1845: "Having collected a streetwalker, I unhesitatingly followed her home, where I stayed for two hours. I made her strip and promised her five francs if she swallowed my ejaculate: one must encourage natural aptitudes. While her tongue excited this old Priapus, her finger plowed my ass. I sighed for seven or eight minutes, legs spread like Dorothée's in de Sade (vol. 3), or rather like a shameless whore's, and I ended up swooning as I came. All this is literal. I didn't stop there . . . It goes without saying that I laid her. Despite my fear of the pox I entered without a condom and kept my tool in the fire for a quarter hour, then withdrew it. Such was my prodigality that I gave the wench twenty-five francs and one to the pander. When I got home, I rubbed my skin with saturn water, astonished by my imprudence."

Gustave was now given Peruvian bark and massive doses of sulfate of quinine.*

That summer, friends and family trooped through the house. Maurice Schlesinger, who appeared unannounced without Élisa, met Gustave for lunch at a restaurant in Rouen called Jay's (where the Flauberts, presumably loyal patrons, had had a pudding named after them) and got his traveling companion, Heinrich Panofka, to offer the residents of Croisset an impromptu violin recital. In August Gustave welcomed his former history professor Adolphe Chéruel, now an academic luminary teaching at the École Normale Supérieure, on whose head official laurels had been laid; notwithstanding Chéruel's description of him as "an odd bird" (*drôle de corps*), they had become and would remain cordial friends. Uncle Parain came up from Nogent. Brother Achille, his wife, Julie, and daughter, Juliette, were weekly dinner guests. As for sister Caroline, having survived her honeymoon ordeal and accomplished the labor of furnishing a flat on the rue de Tournon in Paris, she convalesced at Croisset during the late summer. Alfred and Gustave saw each other briefly when the former betook himself to Fécamp from Paris via Rouen.

A conspicuous absentee until late July was Maxime Du Camp, who had completed his Mediterranean circuit shortly before the wedding party left Paris. Through Caroline he set dates for a visit to Croisset and kept canceling them. Mystified by his dilatoriness, Gustave knew nothing of the personal circumstances that explain it. Maxime had returned from North Africa with typhoid. His grandmother nursed him for weeks in her flat near the Madeleine. Although upright enough to pursue a new mistress, he hadn't yet regained his emotional balance and, half-exsanguinated by leeches, wobbled between abstractedness and insolence. His insolence provoked several duels. His abstractedness made him something of a nightwalker, knocking about Montmartre in a narcotic haze. Opium pills did indeed contribute to these perambulations, as well as to the quasi-delirious state he would enter at the sound of music. In mid- or late July he finally set out for Croisset, where Gustave, still polishing *L'Éducation sentimentale,* eagerly awaited him. They enjoyed three weeks together. "I spent part of the sum-

---

*Some idea of medical knowledge in the field may be gained from remarks about valerian in a treatise on epilepsy by a respected neurologist of the day, Louis Delasiauve. "In truth, and perhaps as a result of differences in the mode of preparation or administration, valerian has not retained its former prestige . . . Indispensable to its application are a number of conditions. The plants must be of good quality. The variety harvested in elevated regions has more strength, a more penetrating aroma, and intoxicates when inhaled at length. It must not smell of musk, this odor having been communicated to it by the urine of cats, which have exhibited a great appetite for it and seek out places where it is drying out. It is sometimes harvested and sold together with crowfoot, a worrisome detail inasmuch as the latter root has venomous properties that may induce grave disorders in the digestive tract."

mer at Croisset, on the banks of the Seine, opposite one of the most beautiful countrysides to be seen anywhere in Normandy," Maxime reminisced. His host would row him around the islands or fit his dinghy with a mast and confidently sail him up and down the Seine. "Sometimes we would go to the end of the garden and settle ourselves in a little pavilion overlooking the towpath." In that pavilion, which is all that remains of the Flaubert estate today, less its red plush ebony furniture, Gustave read his novel aloud with great attention to emphasis and rhythm, smoked innumerable pipes, and joined Maxime in dreaming up wonderful voyages, the implausibility of which did not much matter. Alfred Le Poittevin was also present.

Until her arrival in August or early September, Caroline had been an even more conspicuous absentee. It saddened Gustave that she was no longer available to be strangled in a parody of Dumas' *La Tour de Nesle,* to roll on his bed like Néo, and generally to play the enthusiastic straight woman to his jackanapes. That her vacant room did not leave him feeling even emptier than it did surprised him. It testified, as he put it self-mockingly, to his big heart, or to his fondness for "this good Émile." But other heartfelt lines betrayed quite different sentiments. His mouth sometimes wanted the sensation of kissing her cheeks, which he compared to seashells in their freshness and firmness. "I could say to you what a seventeenth-century writer said of something or other: 'a spectacle made expressly for the pleasure of one's eyes.'" Did she remember his history lessons? His coming home from school at four o'clock? Her standing in a green velvet hat waiting to be fetched by him at her pension? Their outing with Ernest Chevalier at the Saint-Wandrille abbey? "All of that comes to mind when I think of you, poor child* . . . I hear your voice and I see your eyes smile. If you love me it's only right that you should, for I in turn have loved you well."

Far from liking Émile Hamard, Mme Flaubert refused to forgive the man who had absconded with her daughter. When, after the marriage, it was borne in on her that the couple would leave Rouen definitively, she was irate. Caroline found herself convicted of betrayal during a confrontation in Paris and begged for understanding. "As for our flat, my good mother, you knew that we would take one, since, even before my marriage, we often discussed the matter; you gave me advice about the household, and, if you recall, I told you that my greatest pleasure would be to receive you, that I would do everything to make you feel at home." Promising that she would fly up to Rouen on a moment's notice if needed for any reason did not placate madame. "So you no longer regard your daughter as a good daughter. After all kinds of reproaches, you hardly kissed me when you left me yes-

---

Pauvre (poor) was an expression of tenderness rather than pity, favored by his mother. Flaubert used it all of his life in that spirit, as an endearment.

terday. I never would have believed that you could be so displeased with me, and Papa as well, . . . he whom I love so much and who usually smooths your feathers when I ruffle them. Tell me what he thinks of me and whether he truly feels that I behaved badly. Answer right away, for you can't imagine how tormented I am."

Caroline became pregnant during the honeymoon, and endless reassurances that her health was tolerably good fell on deaf ears. Mme Flaubert clung to the belief that death would snatch her from under Hamard's limp wing. "As I promised, my good mother, I will tell you the truth," Caroline insisted in one of several surviving letters.

> For the last couple of days my throat and lower back have bothered me. It's a very minor version of what I had fifteen months ago, so don't fret and please believe me when I say that there's nothing more to it than that. Besides, the pains are fainter today and I'm hopeful that tomorrow I'll be able to get up . . . Nothing could have occasioned this attack, for since your departure I've left the flat only twice, once to see Cher ami [Dr Cloquet] and once for dinner with M. de Tardif. After Sunday, feeling very tired, I stayed at home, read, and embroidered. The day before yesterday I took to my bed with a sore throat and dieted on redcurrant syrup and herbal broth. Émile wanted to summon M. Cloquet, but I know perfectly well what is required, and M. Cloquet would no doubt prescribe a lot of concoctions and poultices I don't want. I prefer to treat myself, remembering the way papa cared for me in these circumstances.

Giving her all she could drink to slake an unquenchable thirst, Émile Hamard waited on her devotedly.

> I couldn't ask more of him, though I often have you in mind. You should not bear him any ill will, as you do. He is very sensitive to it and would take greater pleasure in visiting the house if your welcome were warmer. It seems to me that he's done nothing to displease you except take your daughter, and any son-in-law would have done the same. If only you two were united and confiding, how happy it would make me. I had hoped for that outcome and, despite my own unconciliatory character, I shall do and say whatever I can to bring it about.

In a postscript she repeated once again that her indisposition was mild and, by way of mollifying Mme Flaubert, who must have blanched when Hamard asked her to regard him as one of her children, signed the letter "Tenderly, your daughter and friend C. Flaubert."

In June, Achille-Cléophas, never one to suffer fools or holidays gladly, resumed his onerous schedule at the Hôtel-Dieu with a sigh of relief. Known as *le père des pauvres* (who dispensed medicine more freely than the hospital's

frugal administration thought proper), he was doing more and more char-
ity work and that summer volunteered his services to victims of a tornado
that had leveled three factories in Monville, a town near Rouen where he
owned property. So indefatigable was he under normal circumstances that
complaints of fatigue throughout the fall caused great consternation. In
November, when his health declined markedly, an examination revealed an
abscess deep in the thigh, requiring surgery. Cloquet came up from Paris,
but Achille-Cléophas chose his namesake to operate. It failed, as many such
procedures performed by unclean hands did. Nursed around the clock, Dr
Flaubert lingered for ten weeks, vomiting copiously while young Achille
kept assuring the family that he was on the mend, and died of septicemia
on January 15, 1846, at age sixty-one.

Rouen mourned his loss. A detachment of foot soldiers rendered him
the military honors due a member of the Legion of Honor. Townspeople,
many of whom had been patients, gathered in the courtyard of the funeral
home and on streets outside. On January 17 shops closed. Dock workers
who had requested the privilege carried his coffin to the Madeleine, where
all six of his children had been baptized. The church was draped in black.
After four colleagues, a doctor, and a medical student delivered eulogies,
Gustave, Achille, and Émile Hamard led the funeral procession through
crowds of Rouennais to a cemetery situated uphill, quite some distance
away, beyond the collegiate school and the peripheral boulevard. "Seldom
has our city witnessed a solemn ceremony of such magnitude," reported the
Journal de Rouen. "Never has a whole city grieved more unanimously for a
man of sterling character, of science, and of talent. All social classes came
in numbers." Speaking for Rouen's Medical Society, Dr Parfait Grout declared that Flaubert, "one of the deans of our profession," had recently accepted an invitation to sit on its board. "The authority of his opinions, his
knowledge of the scope and limits of the medical art, would have helped
us enormously in our work. As remarkable an adviser as he was a doer, he
would have presided over us with that voice which has commanded our respect and charmed us since our student days." The eulogy became a plug
for Achille the younger, against whom rivals of Achille-Cléophas in the
hospital administration had begun to conspire. "And you, my dear Achille,"
Grout went on, "his older son, his assistant, our colleague, and our friend,
continue to replace your worthy father in and for everything, and to bring
him alive before our eyes; our vows and wishes will accompany you as you
pursue a brilliant career sustained by your zeal, your love of science and humanity, your proven talent, and the lessons of your venerable father."

Mme Flaubert was prostrate with grief, and Gustave actively engaged in
soliciting contributions for a statue of his father when, on January 21, Caroline gave birth to another Caroline. Three days later, puerperal fever, her

maternal grandmother's killer, declared itself. Shaking with chills and palpitations, she grew progressively weaker as the streptococcal infection, which
a woman who had kidney trouble would have found especially difficult to
fight off, spread through her body. Doctors were helpless. In desperation the
family resorted to a camphor cure touted by the celebrated chemist François
Raspail; Uncle Parain, with Maxime Du Camp's help, somehow tracked
him down in Paris (Raspail, wanted for revolutionary activities, was hiding
from the police). All to no avail. On March 15, Gustave described a household in which his infant niece couldn't stop screaming, his mother couldn't
stop sobbing, his delirious sister couldn't remember anything clearly, his
bearded brother stood dumbstruck. "As for myself, my eyes are as dry as
marble," he wrote to Maxime. "It's odd, but as expansive, fluid, abundant
and overflowing as I feel where fictional sorrows are concerned, to that
same extent do the real ones sit in my heart bitter and flinty; the minute
they enter it, they harden." Misfortune was hungry, he said, and would not
depart until it had had its fill of them. "I'm going to see once again the
black sheets and I shall hear the ignoble noise of undertakers in hobnailed
shoes stomping down the staircase."

Caroline died on March 22. Two days later, after mourners at the Cimetière
Monumental had waited until diggers enlarged a pit too narrow for the coffin, she was buried in her wedding dress with bouquets of roses, violets, and
immortelles. Hamard knelt at the grave sobbing and blowing kisses. Gustave, who would later claim that he attended the funerals of his father and
sister in his imagination before they took place in the world, couldn't cry.
He threw his hat down and let loose a rueful shout at no one in particular.
One family friend reported, whether from hearsay or direct observation is
not known, that it was his nervous malady.

The previous night he had sat beside her for hours, reading Montaigne's
essays. "Straight as can be, she lay in her bed, in that room where you've
heard her play music," he told Maxime. "Wearing a white veil that descended to her feet, she seemed much taller and more beautiful in death
than in life. When morning came and she was put in her coffin, I gave her
a long kiss of farewell." The undertaker's assistants prepared a death mask
for James Pradier, who eventually sculpted her bust as well as Dr Flaubert's.
Gustave would keep that effigy in his room, along with a parti-colored
shawl given to her by Harriet Collier, a lock of her hair, and the writing
desk at which she had taken notes during history lessons from her brother.

Darkness enveloped Croisset. Gustave, whom we shall now call Flaubert,
though everyone in Rouen assumed that Achille rather than he would glorify the patronymic, returned from the funeral to cold rooms on a gray day,
with wind whistling through leafless branches and the Seine in full spate.
He felt stupefied, and his nerves were shot, even if they had not, to his sur-

prise, given him fits. "Will I never resume my tranquil life of art and leisurely meditation!" he exclaimed in a letter to Maxime. "What a vain thing is the human will. I scoff at its pitiful pretension when I think that I've wanted to master Greek for six years, and circumstances have been such that I haven't even learned to conjugate verbs."

It would be December and the eve of his twenty-fifth birthday before he thawed enough to admit how desperately he missed the family he had once found oppressive.

IX

Louis, Louise, and Max

CAROLINE'S DEATH may have passed almost unnoticed in Rouen, where conversation revolved around a sensational trial that began two days after the funeral and drew crowds to the great hall of the Palais de Justice. Brought up from Paris under guard was Jean-Baptiste Rosemond de Beaupin de Beauvallon, a large, bewhiskered man of twenty-five who had killed the publisher Alexandre Dujarier in an allegedly rigged duel. Dujarier's name was associated with Émile de Girardin's on the masthead of *La Presse,* a young newspaper that had transformed French journalism since 1836, selling as it did at half the price of its rivals, containing far more information than opinion, and featuring serial novels, or *romans-feuilletons,* on the front page. Many subscribers discovered Balzac through *La Presse,* which serialized *Le Curé de village* and *Honorine,* among much else. Although Balzac wasn't in Rouen on March 26, another writer whom Dujarier had befriended, Alexandre Dumas, did bear witness against Beauvallon and arrived at the Palais de Justice in an open carriage like the prince of letters he rightly considered himself to be.

Dumas's appearance created a stir, but the Rouennais, the stenographic reporters, and the curious Parisians in attendance were more intrigued by the testimony of Lola Montez. After striking sparks throughout Germany and Russia, the beautiful Irishwoman who reinvented herself as a Spanish dancer had come to France in 1844. Letters of recommendation from her former lover Franz Liszt led to a brief engagement at the Paris Opéra, remembered most vividly by young men into whose midst she had flung a garter. While critics panned her pseudo-Iberian gyrations, the lions of Parisian society ardently sought her favors. Dujarier won the prize, set her up in an elegant apartment next to his, helped her recover from her fiasco with an engagement at the Théâtre de la Porte Saint-Martin, where she performed a number called "La Dansomanie," and prevailed upon Théophile Gautier to write a laudatory review declaring that in her cachuchas Lola brought to the stage "an unbridled audacity, a mad ardor and a wild verve" no lover of classical *ronds de jambes* could tolerate. Everything bid fair until Dujarier insulted the umbrageous Beauvallon over a game of lansquenet at the Trois Frères Provençaux and, though unfamiliar with arms (Lola, on the contrary, was a crack shot), accepted Beauvallon's challenge. When his mistress learned of it, he had already fallen in the Bois de Boulogne with a bullet in his head. Balzac and Dumas served as pallbearers. They joined other friends walking behind the hearse as it proceeded from the Church of Notre-Dame de Lorette to the Montmartre cemetery.

Compelled to efface herself at the funeral, Lola Montez took center stage one year later at the trial. Costumes were her forte, and she dressed for the part of bereaved widow in a black silk dress, a black veil, black gloves, and a black floor-length cashmere shawl. Lest anyone doubt that Dujarier had concealed his intentions, Lola plucked from her bosom the note he wrote on that cold March morning before riding to the Bois. "I am leaving to fight with pistols," it read. "This explains why I wanted to sleep alone and also why I didn't come to see you this morning. I need all my composure and I must avoid the emotions that seeing you would have stirred. At ten, it will all be over, and I'll rush to embrace you, unless . . . A thousand tendernesses, my dear Lola." Tears streamed down her face when she recalled in heavily accented French how her lover's bloody corpse had tumbled out of a coach into her arms. All this to no avail. Deliberating within earshot of a raucous mob outside the Palais de Justice, the jury exonerated Beauvallon (duels were illegal but duelists seldom convicted). By then, Lola had returned to Paris. Seven months later, she would establish herself in Munich with a handsome stipend from her new lover, King Ludwig I of Bavaria, over whom she held absolute sway.

Even if Flaubert had wanted to witness for himself these judicial proceedings, he could not have left a grief-stricken household to satisfy his curiosity. In any event, his mind dwelt elsewhere, on the practical sequelae of his family tragedies.

To begin with, there was a struggle at the Hôtel-Dieu to decide whether or not Achille Flaubert would replace his father as chief surgeon. Achille-Cléophas had no sooner died than a former student and longtime assistant, Émile Leudet, who had been challenging his authority since 1834, insisted that the title and its prerogatives should, by reason of seniority, devolve upon him. This claim challenged a tradition that had its roots in the craftsmen days of surgical practice, when apprentice sons normally succeeded their master fathers. Several eminent nineteenth-century surgeons, notably François Broussais at the Val de Grâce, warmed a seat for their children, and such were the younger Achille Flaubert's expectations at the Hôtel-Dieu. "His father had won the scepter of surgeon of Normandy," one contemporary observed. "He himself was already chief surgeon in his mother's womb and heir presumptive to the monopoly created before his birth." Not that Achille lacked impressive skills. His hands were dexterous and quick. Furthermore, he cut a magisterial figure, being tall and angular, with dark, glowing eyes set in a finely chiseled face, the lower part of which disappeared at an early age beneath a luxuriant beard. But if signs of it were not already clear, time would tell how far filial piety exceeded scientific inquiry in shaping his career. Holding himself aloof from professional societies, he made do with the baggage of opinions, theses, and doctrines taught by Achille-Cléophas. *Pater dixit* was his rule, and paternal wisdom, often articulated in his father's salty language, almost always set him against innovation. When, for example, other surgeons adopted ether, Achille hesitated at first, defending the view that pain was a necessary declaration of nature. Like Achille-Cléophas, he contributed almost nothing to medical literature, as if it would have been beneath him, or hubristic, to do so. Jealous of his name and reputation, he wanted them propagated by elegant ligatures and extracted stones, not by his pen. His confreres could detect nothing in him of Gustave Flaubert's histrionics. Uncomfortable on the dais in professorial robes and bonnet, he was happiest peering through a speculum, or at home, behind closed doors, smoking a pipe. Some thought that his hidebound skepticism clothed a brittle ego. Others described him as "atonic" and "morose." All might have agreed that the heir had not inherited the combative spirit of a self-made man.

It was for his younger brother to fight Leudet, and Flaubert, the bourgeois "bourgeoisophobe" (his term), took up arms with gusto, deriving a kind of virile satisfaction, as he always would, from the effective deployment of family power and influence. Pulling strings made him cocky. In late January he informed Ernest Chevalier that the hospital administration, despite the immense services rendered by his father, had wanted to "boot out" Achille. "Sir Leudet was behind it. But I gained the upper hand. I've been to Paris twice (I return a third time tomorrow) and have acted to such good effect that, the way matters now stand, we feel quite certain he will succeed his father in and for everything." Matters stood differently one month later, when Maxime Du Camp spoke of a "setback" and surmised that the relevant government agency, heedless of appeals from Jules Cloquet and James Pradier, *inter alios,* dismissed the whole affair as a provincial spat not worth its intervention. But Flaubert's feverish networking, along with partisan maneuvers in Rouen, led to an acceptable compromise. Thenceforth the Hôtel-Dieu would have two chief surgeons and the medical school two professors of surgery. After further negotiation, administrators awarded Achille the hospital apartment, which had been his home since 1818. To survivors desperately wanting continuity, this privilege meant everything.

Another, more vital, link to the past was little Caroline Hamard, custody of whom became a sad, ugly, and in some respects mystifying issue. Mme Flaubert resolved that the son-in-law who had confiscated her daughter should not have her daughter's daughter as well. Flaubert knew it and expected trouble. An amicable arrangement was no longer possible, he confided to Maxime soon after his sister's funeral. "It will have to be settled in court. Should we act expeditiously, it will still take three months." In fact, the family did sort matters out among themselves, or so it seemed. By an arrangement in which Hamard acquiesced, Caroline remained under her grandmother's care, with a paternal granduncle, Achille Dupont, serving as surrogate guardian. Hamard quit his clerkship, left Paris, and found quarters in Croisset very near the Flauberts. When Mme Flaubert rented a Rouen town house at 25, rue de Crosne for use during winter months, which were cold enough to freeze the Seine, Hamard opened a law office on the street floor, trying to establish himself in private practice. He commuted into Rouen every day and saw his child regularly.

The practice did not flourish. As bored by law as Flaubert, Hamard might have made a go of it had Caroline been at his side, but the deaths of his mother and wife removed any incentive to overcome his antipathy. Nor did anything on which his ego might feed come from the hostile Mme Flaubert and a self-absorbed brother-in-law. Depressed, he gradually wandered off the beaten path into a maze of literary and scholarly ambitions, and Flaubert blamed himself for encouraging this waywardness by example. The same imitative spirit or need for comradeship that had prompted Hamard to sign Flaubert's school petition seven years earlier was still at work, he thought. "When I confided to you that I believe I've had a baleful influence on him, I didn't mean that I've inoculated him with my intellectual vaccine, only that in keeping me company his mind has been poisoned by the notion that he can live a life like mine, solitary and meditative," is how he explained the predicament to a friend. "It makes him vain, and vanity in turn makes him obdurate. There's nothing for it but to let time, that grindstone, do its grinding. Meanwhile, he's wearing himself out, he's dying of sloth, of melancholy, and of bottled-up projects." One year after Caroline's death, in despair over his shattered existence, he thought that a foreign setting might help him reassemble himself differently and, through his former professor Adolphe Chéruel, with whom he had kept in touch, solicited letters of reference from Jules Michelet, hoping to do research for an English historian. He also considered studying paleography at the École des Chartes. These ideas led nowhere, and neither did the daily ride to his nominal office in Rouen. Little Caroline, who seemed destined for an early grave, couldn't stiffen her father's resolve. Faring poorly during the first months of life, she was a puling embodiment of all he had lost. "My mother and I," wrote Flaubert, "are very worried about my brother-in-law. Grief has left the poor fellow so broken in spirit that we believe *he's going mad. His head just won't hold out. This is bound to end badly.*" As prospects of attracting a clientele dimmed, Hamard began to spend more time in Paris, writing poetry, ingratiating himself with an eminent, famously dyspeptic literary critic named Gustave Planche, and flirting with radical politics in dubious bistros. Mme Flaubert might have wished on more than one occasion that he would disappear from her life altogether, although this was not yet to be the case. Meanwhile, she was a mother again at forty-nine, rocking, cooing, fretting, and doing everything for the newly delivered Caroline that she once did for the freshly buried one, except suckling her.

Torn between a desire to flee and the need to anchor himself, Flaubert assured Maxime on April 7, the day after Caroline's baptism, that if his mother died he would instantly settle in Rome, Syracuse, or Naples, but declared a month later that, like Frollo suspended over the abyss in *Notre-Dame de Paris,* he was clinging to what he still had: friends and work and his corner study at Croisset. Every day his study became his Syracuse or Rome as he immersed himself for eight or ten hours in classical literature and ancient history, reading, among other things, Michelet's *Histoire romaine.* So entranced was he with everything of antiquity that metempsychosis (on which he had undoubtedly heard Alfred Le Poittevin expatiate) began to make great sense. "There's no doubt I lived in Rome under Caesar or Nero," he told Maxime. "Have you ever dreamed about a triumphal evening when the legions were returning, when incense was perfuming the air around the victorious general's chariot and captive kings were walking behind. And then, that magnificent old amphitheater! That's where one must live, you see. There's where one has air to breathe, poetic air, lungfuls." The *Journal de Rouen* reported two more attempts on Louis-Philippe's life and bread riots in the Saint Antoine district of Paris. According to George Sand, social reformers, herself included, enjoyed unprecedented freedom to moot their criticism of the regime. Flaubert hardly paid attention. His mind was elsewhere, in Rome, or with Nicias's troops in Epipolae during the disastrous siege of Syracuse in 413–411 BC. Only one person, a Parisian upholsterer whom he had commissioned to refurnish his study, could lure him from Croisset; like the robe he wore when he wrote, the décor of his literary labors was a matter of some importance.

Flaubert and his mother did not suffer in isolation. Achille's family — "les Achille" as Flaubert called them — ritually showed up for dinner on Sundays, though often late enough to exasperate the household. François Parain, a benign presence, accomplished his seasonal migration from Nogent-sur-Seine, preceding Olympe and Louis Bonenfant. Maxime visited Croisset in May. At Mme Flaubert's request he returned for three weeks in mid-August, when they were often joined by Louis Bouilhet, a classmate of Flaubert's at the collegiate school (and signatory of his famous petition) whom he had come to know as a friend since February. The threesome of Louis, Gustave, and Max made brief excursions to La Bouille at the first great loop of the Seine, and farther down the seaward-flowing river to the great Benedictine ruins at Jumièges and Saint-Wandrille. Sedentary fun for these literary young men was translating Aristophanes's *Lysistrata* and Plautus's *Rudens*. There were all-nighters devoted to the composition of a verse play parodying bombastic eighteenth-century tragedy, in correct alexandrines and with every noun obligatorily replaced by a periphrase. They came up with ornate metaphors to prove that anything could be said in high-flown language, wrote Maxime. Or they did the opposite. "We'd go over the edge pushing the comic into outright obscenity . . . That was an excess not always easy to skirt with Flaubert, who, like Béranger, believed that where words were concerned, one couldn't be too gross." Bouilhet shared with Flaubert and Le Poittevin, cocreators of the Kid, a sense of humor that enthusiastically placed erudition at the service of the scatological. They all loved to ennoble the gutter and desecrate the temple.* By the same token, all had seen bodies cut up. Flaubert's brother allowed Maxime to witness amputations.

It seems that Bouilhet occupied a vacated space in Flaubert's life, that this new friendship was the measure of his growing estrangement from Alfred Le Poittevin. In a letter written toward the end of March 1845, Alfred de-

---

*There is, for example, this excerpt from Le Poittevin's letter to Flaubert in Paris, dated March 18, 1843: "What are you doing with your carcass down there? Have you seen Elodie again, and in that lascivious slut's bush sniffed the vapors of her clitoris? A happy man you are. You make me think of Polycrates, so favored by fortune that he threw his ring into the Ionian sea, as if to appease it. And similarly you plunge your precious phallus into the cunt of Parisian whores, as if wanting to contract the pox. But in vain. As the fish returned his ring to Polycrates, so the most soiled cunts restore your treasure intact . . . Ha! Ha! Ha! What a comparison. What periods! What a model of eloquence. Read that to the Garçon's two servants, the Trooper and the Blackamoor, and proclaim me *Virum dicendi peritum* ['A man adept at talking,' taken from Cato the Elder]."

scribed his life as anarchical, his health as poor, his outlook bleak, his spirit stifled. Misunderstood, as he saw it, by those who professed love for him, he may have been under considerable pressure to get married and resume the career that had begun auspiciously. Several months later, when Flaubert was in Italy, he took a brief trip along the Channel coast, visiting Boulogne, Honfleur, and Le Havre, where a moonlit night stirred memories of summertime. "I dreamed of love there when I was very young, love I'd refuse today, wherever it came from, whatever it might be." Time had not blunted the keen edge of his sexual appetite, but no longer could he kiss without feeling outside the gesture, at an ironical distance from his lips, like that Greek, he wrote, who couldn't smile again after entering Trophonius's cave. Alfred's plan was to make a virtue of his predicament, to embrace irony rather than throttle it and revisit the landscape of his adolescent infatuations with a whore chosen at random. Instead he did the unthinkable. Suddenly he decided to marry, and early in 1846 he plighted his troth with Louise de Maupassant, the daughter of his parents' friends. (At the same time, his sister Laure plighted hers with Louise's brother Gustave.)

Flaubert, who sometimes greeted bosom friends — there would always be one such Castor to his Pollux — with a Latin phrase, *solus ad solum,** summarizing his belief that brotherhood was necessarily born of alienation or of mutual singularity, was flabbergasted by this event. He felt betrayed and made no effort to conceal his feelings from Alfred. On May 31, five weeks before the wedding, he unburdened himself in a letter remarkable as much for its unwillingness to hear Alfred out as for its sententiousness. "I fear that you are deluding yourself, seriously deluding yourself, which happens whenever one undertakes some action in the world," he pontificated, declaring that although his advice had not been solicited, the powers of foresight with which he was unhappily endowed compelled him to set his misguided friend straight.

> Are you quite sure . . . that you won't end up a bourgeois? I've always imagined us united in my dreams of art. That is what's making me suffer. It's too late! If it must be so, let it be! You will always find me here, but it remains to be seen whether I will find *you* again. No, don't protest! Time and the drift of things are stronger than we are. I'd need a whole volume to explain the least jot or tittle on this page. No one wants your happiness more than I, and no one has graver doubts that it lies at hand, if only because your seeking it is itself an abnormal act. Do you love her? All well and good. If not, try to.
>
> Will there still be, between us, that arcane store of ideas and feelings inaccessible to the rest of the world? Who can say? No one.

---

*"From one solitary soul to another."

Marriage was the issue, not the fact that Alfred had abandoned their iconoclastic perch for a colorless young woman, somewhat less wealthy than he but with clear title to the nobiliary preposition in the middle of her name.* So long as his idol remained unmarried, he could bear being treated dismissively by bourgeois who scorned bachelorhood. "Another one lost to me," Flaubert sadly informed Chevalier. Although they continued to exchange affectionate greetings, anger seethed beneath the surface. And circumstances did not favor reconciliation. Having unsuccessfully sought government employment as a deputy public prosecutor within the jurisdiction of Rouen, Alfred moved to Paris. After several months, during which no professional opportunity materialized, the couple joined Louise's parents at the Maupassant home in La Neuville-Chant-d'Oisel, a village near Rouen, where Alfred, slowly dying by then, retired from active life.

IN JUNE and July 1846 Flaubert visited Paris at least twice, each time on a specific errand but undoubtedly grateful for any pretext to escape the gloom hanging over Croisset, to see different faces and brood with Maxime Du Camp over Alfred's defection. The studio of James Pradier, whom he knew through the sculptor's estranged wife, Louise, was one of his destinations.† Pradier had been chosen by a commission in Rouen to sculpt Achille-Cléophas's bust, and Flaubert, through whose good offices this arrangement had been brokered, found himself obliged to mediate between an impatient artist and impossibly dilatory bureaucrats. The recognition it earned him from someone powerful who stood *in loco patris* was bracing for the twenty-five-year-old. Pradier, a Swiss transplanted from Geneva (where Flaubert had recently smoked cigars under his statue of Jean-Jacques Rousseau on the Île Rousseau), enjoyed great renown, with marble figures advertising him all over the capital — in the Tuileries and the Madeleine, on the Champs-Élysées, at the place de la Concorde, the Invalides, the Palais du Luxembourg, the Palais Bourbon. His languorous nudes, which provoked from one rival, Auguste Préault, the crack, "Every morning Pradier leaves for Athens, but never gets past the rue Notre-Dame-de-Lorette" (a street favored by prostitutes near the rue Bréda where Pradier had an atelier), were as ubiquitous as his civic statuary. And Parisians unfamiliar with the art couldn't miss

*After Alfred's death, a close friend of his, Boivin-Champeaux, told Flaubert that several days before his marriage, Alfred had thought of breaking it off and proposed that Boivin and he take a quick trip to parts unknown.

†Louise Pradier, née d'Arcet, was the older sister of Flaubert's high school classmate Charles d'Arcet. Their father, a distinguished chemist, had been appointed director of the mint and lived in the handsome eighteenth-century Hôtel des Monnaies on the quai de Conti, quite near Pradier's apartment at 1, quai Voltaire. Flaubert visited both during his law-school years, and later.

the artist as he swanned around town in gaudy costumes often featuring a wide-brimmed Tyrolean hat, a black velvet jacket, gold-embroidered leotards, a short coat lined with blue silk draped over one shoulder, a white jabot. From his sartorial panache one might not have inferred a sensibility enamored of classical Greece. Both the dandy and the prodigiously laborious Hellenist appealed to Flaubert. "He is an excellent man and a great artist, yes, a great artist, a true Greek and of all the moderns the most ancient," he enthused. "A man who concerns himself with nothing, neither politics nor socialism nor Fourier nor Jesuits nor the educational system, and, like a good worker with sleeves turned up, toils from dawn to dusk, wanting only to do his task well, out of love of art. Love of art is what it's all about." Equally appealing was Pradier the host, who worked best when surrounded by models, rough-hewers, and visitors to his principal atelier in the Palais abbatial behind the church of Saint-Germain des Prés. One didn't need an invitation. People came and went and hobnobbed volubly while he chiseled away in his white smock, talking all the while. Many significant convergences occurred at this informal salon. One took place in June 1846, when Flaubert met the strikingly attractive Louise Colet.

Eleven years older than Flaubert and therefore exactly the same age as Élisa Schlesinger, Louise had, eleven years earlier, married Hippolyte Colet, a minor composer who proved far more resolute in lobbying for a professorship on the faculty of the Paris Conservatory than in holding his wife to her vows. Born Louise Révoil, she hailed from Aix-en-Provence, where the family tree had branched high into the judicial aristocracy, the *noblesse de robe.* Her maternal grandfather had turned coat during the Revolution, serving in the legislature that condemned Louis XVI, but, unlike his friend and compatriot Mirabeau, survived to bankrupt his family as a prodigal, unemployed champion of republican causes. The country estate near Saint-Rémy on which Louise spent much of her youth had been saved from ruin by her father, Antoine Révoil, a bourgeois functionary sworn to king and altar. She thus grew up amid oxymoronic loyalties. Her early years, as she described them, were lonely. Like Julien Sorel knocked off the rafter on which he sat reading Las Cazes's *Mémorial de Sainte-Hélène,* she endured the taunts of older siblings who scorned her literary enthusiasms and armed herself against sarcasm with the belief that some exceptional fate had been assigned to her. "Alone in the desert, bound over to my mute sorrow, I would have perished had God not made me a poet," she wrote.* After 1830, politics exacerbated these family antagonisms. Among the Révoils, where identifying with one's aristocratic forebears meant reviling kingship,

---

*"Seule, au désert, livrée à ma douleur muette, / Oh! j'aurais succombé . . . mais Dieu me fit poète!"

Louise and her mother upheld the liberal view while her brothers and sisters (the father died in 1828) spoke for royalty. Arguments flared over every issue of church and state. The name George Sand, which had become synonymous with free love when *Indiana* and *Valentine* appeared, was a match to tinder.

If God made Mlle Révoil a poet, Julie Candeille gave her an audience. How Louise met this remarkable woman, who had retired to Nîmes (a short distance from Servanes and Avignon) with her third husband, Henri Périé, after occupying a secure niche in the cultural life of Paris for forty years, is not exactly known. A dancer, a successful playwright, a tragedian at the Comédie-Française, a singer, a composer, a poet and novelist, a virtuoso pianist and harpist, Julie was compelled to deny the rumor that she had also been a Jacobin sympathizer cast in the role of Reason at the Fête de la Liberté during the Terror. This statuesque, abundantly energetic figure lost no time organizing a salon when Périé took up his duties as a curator of Roman antiquities. The intelligentsia and artistic elite of Nîmes would assemble every week at her home for musical soirees. She became a superior specimen of what Balzac called "the departmental Muse." Young poets eager to be heard found themselves welcomed, and especially welcome was Louise Révoil, in whom Julie Candeille may have admired something of her own younger self. Certainly the beautiful, tall, full-bosomed young woman with dark blue eyes and silky, light brown hair, who poured herself into shapely alexandrines, seemed an ideal protégée. Louise's feelings for Julie went beyond mere admiration. To an ambitious provincial, the versatile alumna of major stages embodied everything she wished for herself, all the images of glory and artistic distinction conjured up by the word *Paris.* Memoirists, even friendly ones, agree that the spoiler of Julie's many gifts was a bluestocking haughtiness. But it spoiled nothing for Louise, who, on the contrary, modeled herself after the *précieuse.* And she was not unique. Along with George Sand, Julie Candeille spoke to many women of deliverance from pinched, parochial existences in the hinterland. "When, after the Revolution of 1830, George Sand's star shone over Berry," wrote Balzac, "many towns were rather disposed to honor the most meager feminine talents. Thus did one see many Tenth Muses in France, young girls or young women led astray from peaceful lives by a mirage of glory." A sister-in-law was later to observe that Louise "incorrigibly nurses illusions about herself, as about everything."

Louise acquired her passport to Paris at Julie's salon in the person of Hippolyte Colet. Being dowerless and approaching twenty-five (the age of "braiding Saint Catherine's tresses," when women were said to enter old maidenhood), she decided that the violin teacher, who had his sights set on Paris, would make a plausible mate. He became even more attractive after her mother and Julie Candeille died two months apart early in 1834. The marriage took place near Servanes, unattended by members of Louise's family. No doubt this insult made it easier to leave Provence without a backward glance, which the couple did straightaway, Colet having meanwhile obtained an assistantship at the Conservatory. A small, dark, poorly heated flat five flights up in the crowded neighborhood of Saint-Denis was all they could afford, but the promised land under any conditions suited her better than exile. Buoyed by the conviction that her poems, collectively titled *Fleurs du Midi,* would win her fame and fortune, she set about circulating them.

Hippolyte may already have guessed that Louise would not hesitate to flaunt her natural endowments for literary advantage. As soon as she had done surveying Paris, she made the rounds of magazines, scraped acquaintance with editors, and immediately placed several poems at *L'Artiste* (a journal in which, some twelve years later, Baudelaire would review *Madame Bovary*). More difficult to elicit was the unqualified praise of an influential sponsor. Chateaubriand, upon whom she called after sending him a poetic compliment, did not show her anything of the benign gentleman reputed to dispense hyperboles on request. And when she approached Charles Sainte-Beuve with an earnest plea for frank criticism of a poem, he had the audacity to take her at her word. Some years later he would say what he had always felt about her, that in her poetry there was a simulacrum of excellence, a false air of beauty. "Her verse has a rather lovely front, but is it bosom or busk? It's like the woman herself. 'Do you find her beautiful?' I was asked one day. 'Yes,' I answered, 'she *seems* beautiful.'" Her tireless demonstration of a poetic persona, the facile suavity of her verse, tended to offend or charm. She liked being called "the Muse," and she would be called just that, not necessarily with tongue in cheek, by male acquaintances.

Undaunted, she pushed the manuscript of *Fleurs du Midi* across many cluttered desks before one publisher bought it. It appeared in February 1836, whereupon Louise, a born publicist, flooded Paris with complimentary copies, petitioning editors and prospective reviewers for as much notice as they could spare. Few spared her any. The volume was buried, but not so Louise's amour propre. She emerged from the funeral playing a role in which she had schooled herself since childhood, that of martyr. How could *Fleurs du Midi* expect long life in the philistine world of 1836? It had been consigned to oblivion by profiteers flogging the cheap merchandise of *romans-feuilletons,* by a crowd concerned only with bread and circuses. "The violent games that the Roman populace once required of its master are now required of *romans-feuilletons* by the Parisian populace," she later wrote. "Contemporary literature has not lifted the people to its level but has abased itself to the people's. Creating shock, surprise, fright with exorbitant scenes has become the preoccupation of this breathless batallion of serial hacks." Her slim tome, her shapely figure, her vulnerable air, and her intoxication with stardom all endeared her to the famous poet-songwriter Pierre Béranger, who may in turn have won her the sympathy of Louis-Philippe's daughter Marie d'Orléans. It was through Marie d'Orléans that Louise came to receive a state pension, which the Colets hardly deserved but desperately needed. While clawing his way up the academic ladder against opposition from the Conservatory's director, Cherubini, Hippolyte earned the wages of a modest functionary.

Béranger may also have encouraged Louise to compete when the French Academy announced a prize for the best celebratory poem about the opening of Versailles as a national museum. He may even have had a hand in guaranteeing her success, although others contend that of the sixty dithyrambs submitted, hers, which included deep curtsies to the Orléans family, was the least mediocre. In any event, she collected four thousand francs, stirred controversy, and, above all, secured an introduction to the academic potentate Victor Cousin.

Cousin would become minister of public instruction in 1840. Before his elevation, however, he became Louise Colet's lover. This was an astonishing conquest, for the literary parvenu could hardly have hitched her ambitions to a better vehicle than the man considered by many to be France's dominant intellectual personality. Expounding a spiritualist creed called eclecticism, which stitched together elements of Kant, Schelling, Hegel, and others and would greatly influence the New England transcendentalists, Cousin held forth at the Sorbonne with an eloquence that obscured his crooked seams. "He was looked upon as a very open-minded man, assimilating promptly the substance of other thinkers, sufficiently well-versed in antiquity and literature, highly ingenious, ardent, eloquent, indisputably the first of Frenchmen," wrote one close observer. "The crowds that assembled in the great amphitheater of the Sorbonne and overflowed into the courtyard would greet his appearance with frantic outbursts of applause . . . It was a thrilling sight." By 1840, when Louise may have been regularly attending these lectures (the substance of which became official doctrine in high school curricula; Cousin truly "ran" philosophy between 1830 and 1848), the lovers had dubbed each other "le Philosophe" and "Penserosa." *Penserosa* was the title of her latest volume of poetry.

In 1840 Louise gave birth to a daughter, Henriette. It was almost certain that Cousin had fathered the child, but appearances still counted for something, and during her pregnancy, when a scandalmonger of the day named Alphonse Karr blew the gaff, Louise — doing what Hippolyte didn't dare do — avenged herself in a manner calculated to bring her more notoriety than her collected works. Armed with a kitchen knife (a more elegant weapon would have been "theatrical" is how she explained herself, asserting that her "acute pain" required her to seize whatever lay nearest to hand), she encountered him in front of his apartment building and inflicted a flesh wound so slight that Karr lost little of his blood and nothing of his composure. "I certainly would have been gravely injured if my attacker had knifed me with a direct horizontal thrust instead of lifting her arm high over her head in a tragedian's gesture, surely in anticipation of some forthcoming lithograph of the incident," he later remarked. Her tormentor conceded that the courage she displayed, in broad daylight, alone, and nine months pregnant, showed real character, while her lover honored her in Latin with the epigram: *Maxime sum mulier: sed vicut vir ago* (I am a quintessential woman, but I know how to act like a man). It was noted that her hoarse voice and mannish walk told against her feminine features.

Wanting to succeed on her own while the mistress of an intellectual celebrity eighteen years her elder, whose most irresistible feature may have been his long arm, was rather like the familiar dilemma of a woman wanting to be swept off her feet by a man she can dominate, and the conflict provoked lovers' quarrels no less bitter than the conjugal ones. Peace required mutual beguilement, which is to say that Cousin could pull strings for her when she published her books provided he didn't tell her, while she feigned ignorance of his puppetry. Motherhood does not appear to have distracted her from her literary labors. *Penserosa* appeared early in 1840, and later that year, when Napoleon's remains arrived amid preparations for war, Louise hastened to write a long ode rallying the flustered nation:

> *Soyez unis dans le danger*
> *N'ayez qu'un amour, la patrie!*
> *Et qu'une haine: l'Etranger!**

Mindful of her obstreperous grandfather, of the citizen army's victories at Valmy and Jamappes, of Julie Candeille allegedly posing at the Fête de la Liberté, she turned to the eighteenth-century Revolution for subject matter: first with a one-act prose play on Mirabeau, then with dramatic poems on two female martyrs, Charlotte Corday (who wielded a knife against the demagogue Marat more effectively than Louise had done against Alphonse Karr) and Mme Roland. Meanwhile, financial problems hounded her. Hippolyte Colet's salary might have sufficed had his wife been thrifty or venal, but Louise was neither. A martyr to her prodigality and her pride, she paid

---

*Let us be united in danger, Let us have but one love, the fatherland! And but one hatred: the Foreigner!

for them by churning out remunerative prose in the form of an impressionistic travel book on Provence and two volumes' worth of stories about brutalized, exploited women — *Coeurs brisés* (Broken Hearts). Another poetry contest sponsored by the French Academy, this one to celebrate the Molière monument unveiled in January 1844 near the Comédie-Française, garnered her another prize, two thousand francs, which tided the family over approaching reefs. Béranger, who coached her in the composition of the poem, also promoted her cause.*

Energy, the trait most glorified by European romantics, was what Juliette Récamier claimed to admire in Louise when the two were introduced during this period. For Louise, the esteem of Mme Récamier and the consequent admission to her salon brought social and literary prestige beyond anything the French Academy could vouchsafe her. At the Abbaye-aux-Bois, a convent on the rue de Sèvres to which ruined ladies of distinction retired without taking orders, the great beauty once exiled by Napoleon for her liberal sympathies had held court since 1814. It was there that Delacroix, Hugo, Balzac, Lamartine, Sainte-Beuve, Benjamin Constant, Musset, and Stendhal had mingled with political eminences. There ambassadorial posts were won or lost in the 1840s, and Juliette's platonic cavalier, Chateaubriand, a recipient of several such posts, appeared every afternoon at three to read her passages from his enormous work in progress, *Mémoires d'outre-tombe.*

Still, Louise's initiation did not dull the pain of life. In 1843, another child, a son fathered by Cousin or Colet, died after several weeks. Hippolyte contracted tuberculosis; having to nurse the husband she had long since ceased to love or like further embittered her. Her relationship with Cousin also wore thin, though even at the worst he never ceased to provide an allowance for her child and discreetly to help publish her work. Temper tantrums that flashed like bolts from the blue confirmed the impression that Louise had absolutely no aptitude for contentment. "Oh sad personality!" Cousin exclaimed. "She is her own enemy and flees happiness for not knowing how to give it." A woman friend against whom she turned for no reason except perhaps favors received wrote that she was a poor creature crying over the debris she herself had strewn.

One refuge from her troubles was Pradier's atelier on the rue Bréda near her flat on the rue Fontaine-Saint-Georges. With his keen eye for feminine beauty, Pradier appreciated Louise and sculpted her twice, first in 1837 as Sappho pensively reclining against a tree trunk by a stream, then, nine years later, as herself. The notorious philanderer he was may have wished to add

---

*She ably promoted her own cause in her own parlor, which filled every Thursday with academic luminaries (those known for their liberal views) introduced by Cousin.

her to a list of model-concubines that included Hugo's beloved Juliette Drouet, but in this case he would settle for the part of intercessor when, several weeks after meeting at his principal studio in the Palais abbatial, Louise and Flaubert became lovers.

That event took place during the anniversary of "les Trois Glorieuses," the "three glorious days" (as July 27–29 was known) marking Louis-Philippe's accession to power in 1830. Celebrations began with two shots fired at the king from below a palace balcony on which he presented himself for a public concert in the Tuileries. Paris hardly paid attention to yet another failed assassination attempt, and Flaubert least of all, who had been transfixed at the abbatial studio by Louise in a blue dress, her long curls of hair, or *papillotes,* brushing against her bare shoulders. When night fell the *papillotes* were fanned out over a pillow in a hotel room on the rue de l'Est, but the twenty-ninth ended as ingloriously for the writer as it had for the king, with Louise comforting a young man unable to have sex. "I'm a poor excuse for a lover, aren't I!" wrote Flaubert, who could not easily forgive himself this spell of impotence. "Do you know that what happened had never happened to me before? (I was dog tired and as taut as a cello string.) Had I been a man proud of his person, I would have been terribly upset. I was indeed upset, but on your account." While another woman might have made "odious suppositions" — about herself or him, doubting her allure or his virility — she did neither. "I was grateful to you for a spontaneous intelligence that saw nothing drastically amiss when I felt bewildered by what I took to be an unheard-of monstrosity." Since no such disaster had ever befallen him in the company of trollops, she could assure herself that it signified love and respect rather than the opposite.

At any rate he made amends the next evening, or the evening after that, in a hansom cab, during one of two excursions they took through the Bois de Boulogne.* Were he rich enough, he wrote, he would buy the coach and store it in his shed as a relic of the tender moment they experienced together. Louise's eyes mesmerized him, he wrote. "The gentle lilt of the springs and our glances, more intertwined than our hands. I saw your eyes shine in the night. My heart melted . . . It was sheer ecstasy feeling your pupil riveted on mine and slowly drinking in its effluence." Louise wished that his passion came free and clear, but from the outset it was cumbered with presentiments of doom, as in another image harking back to another carriage, another night ride, and his first epileptic seizure. "What irresistible

*Another prefiguration of Emma Bovary's escapades. Exactly when the affair began is not clear, but it probably didn't take place on the thirtieth, during the fireworks display, when Louise's daughter, Henriette, was with them in the cab, sleeping. Less significant than the precise date of consummation is the likelihood that Louise may have seemed less daunting, because more sluttish, in a cab than in bed.

force pushed me toward you?" he asked. "For a split second I stood at the edge and saw the dizzying abyss, then pitched forward." Louise had fallen as well, less ambivalently. Flaubert makes it clear by his denials that she discerned the greatness in him. Nothing remains of the letters that interpret these events from her perspective, however. Almost all were destroyed.

By November they would have written the first volume of what became an epistolary love affair. No sooner did Flaubert arrive in Rouen than he obeyed Louise's injunction to send her a letter a day. Since his own stationery still displayed the black border of mourning, he used ordinary paper, wanting "nothing sad," he explained, to pass between them. "I should like to bring you only joy and surround you with a calm felicity and repay you some small measure of all you have lavished upon me." Just as he often complained, in travel notes, that his response to external beauty was inadequate, so now, while writing "What a memory! and what desire! . . . We were alone, happy . . . ," he voiced the fear of sounding "cold, dry, and egotistical," of being impotent or anyway unequal to the passions heaving inside him. "It seems to me I'm not writing well, that you're going to read this coldly, that I'm not saying anything of what I mean to express." Later he waxed lyrical in describing how the thought of her sang to him, how it danced before his eyes like a "joyous fire" imparting warmth and color. He visualized the "provocative" movement of her mouth as she spoke, her "pink, moist mouth" summoning him to kiss her, "sucking" him toward her.

More often than not, Flaubert's desire struggled to make itself heard above a howling of anxieties. The muse who admired his language and erudition was also the antimuse who would paralyze him by insisting that he publish. The demonstrative beauty who had set him above Victor Cousin was the mother whose preference for him might cost him his virility. The emancipator who had pried him open was the femme fatale who would evict him from his inner life. After five days in Croisset he wrote: "You have made a wide breach in my existence. I had surrounded myself with a stoic wall; just one of your glances blew it away like a cannonball. Yes, it often seems to me that I can hear behind me your dress rustling on the carpet." Declaring that men too fondly caressed as children die young, he would die unto himself, he feared, if, with all her caressing, he came to find her indispensable. "[The prospect] makes my head spin. Your image pulls me, gives me vertigo. What will become of me? Never mind, let's love each other, let's love each other." A constant theme, from the moment he got home, was his paralysis. Nearly every letter told Louise that the letters to her were crowding out some other project or that the image of her lodged in his brain had, Medusa-like, stilled his pen. Quills got sharpened ritually, but to no effect. His study had become a room for pacing and lying on the green leather couch. "You can see that I no longer have heart or will for anything," he lamented on August 11. "I'm a tender, flaccid creature existing at your beck and call. My life is a dreamworld lived in the folds of your dress, at the end of your soft curls. I have a lock of your hair right beside me. How wonderful it smells! If only you knew how often I think about your voice, the scent of your shoulders! Lord, I intended to work, not to converse with you. I couldn't, I had to surrender." A fortnight later, after enduring relentless petitions for a meeting in Paris and tirades against his excessive theatricality or penchant for self-analysis, he repeated his lament, without the sensual envoi. "I'm not doing anything, I'm not reading anything, I no longer write, except to you. Where is the poor and simple life of toil I used to lead? I say 'used to' because it's already long past."

What usually accompanied these indictments of the antimuse were protestations of unworthiness. The more Louise gloried in the amplitude of her love, the more Flaubert denounced himself for the insufficiency of his. While she, who dismissed her husband with a casual sweep of her lovely arm, kept wanting to enfold him, he constantly interposed Mme Flaubert, declaring again and again that he was not an unattached man free to satisfy his desires but a hostage to his mother's grief. Could he simply leave everything behind and live elsewhere? he asked her in response to her taunting observation that he comported himself like a young woman under strict surveillance. "It's impossible. Were I entirely free I'd go to Paris; yes, with you there I wouldn't have the strength to exile myself from France, a project cherished since youth, which I shall accomplish one day. For I want to live in a country where no one loves me or knows me, where my name doesn't pluck heart strings, where my death, my absence won't cost anyone a tear." As he put it on another occasion, his life was lashed to the tyrannically protective Mme Flaubert, who, having no raison d'être except her younger son, obsessively imagined him taken from her by her nemesis. Gone were the pleasures of maneuvering a sailboat in a stiff wind: he had consigned his gear to the attic. He didn't even dare ring for wood or candles or tobacco: his mother, convinced that he had had a seizure, would rush up the staircase, preceding the servant. If only Louise could have witnessed the deep depression into which Pradier's bust of Caroline had cast Mme Flaubert, she would better understand his predicament, he thought. Meanwhile, no one understood. A teary face bid him farewell when he left Paris, and another one greeted him when he arrived in Rouen. "The two women I hold dearest have run a bit with two reins through my heart. They tug me alternately by love and sorrow." A bit or a seton?

Needing emotional distance, the young man who made so much of impersonality felt easier in Croisset conjuring an erotic image of Louise from his drawerful of fetishes than he did in Paris dealing with an uncontrollable woman. Besides the lock of hair there were a scent bag, a handkerchief, a portrait, her letters (he would sniff their musky odor), and bloodstained slippers, which aroused him more intensely than anything else.* A second, larger portrait sat against a pillow on the chintz sofa salvaged from his student flat, between two windows, where he could imagine her sitting in person someday. "I'll leave it there like that," he wrote on August 14, 1846, the day Maxime Du Camp delivered it. "No one will touch it. My mother saw it, your face pleased her, she found you pretty, with — in her words — a lively, open, good-natured air. I told her that I and others were visiting you when you received proofs of the freshly printed engraving and that you gave them to us as gifts." Louise may already have begun to wonder whether she would ever sit on the chintz sofa between two windows or meet her august rival (from whom the relationship was hidden with fibs and deceptive postal arrangements), whether objects imbued with such life for Flaubert did not in fact consecrate her absence. Certainly the fuss he made several weeks later over a new armchair awakened dire suspicions. "With this letter I christen the armchair on which I am destined, if I live, to spend long years," he wrote. "What will I write in it? God only knows. Will it be good or bad, tender or erotic, sad or gay? A little of all that, probably, and nothing exclusively one or the other. In any event, may this inauguration bless all my future work." If his celebration of an object that embodied from the outset his preference for epistolary relations offended her, so did his obtuse response to her indignation. "How can you possibly reproach even my innocent affection for an armchair!!! If I spoke about my boots, I believe you'd be jealous of them." Only years later would he admit that he had furnished the study with a feminine eye to every detail, as his spiritual well-being depended on his alienably personal appointments.

Nowhere are his cruel naïveté and the impulse to push off when clasped tight as flagrant as in a letter that might have deterred a woman less infatuated than Louise with martyrdom or modest enough to realize that Flaubert's iron rule allowed of no exceptions. "I want to gorge you with all the felicities of flesh, to make you weary of them, to make you die of them. I want you to remember those transports in your old age and to feel your desiccated bones quiver with joy at the thought," he wrote. Flaubert loved Ronsard's ode "À sa maîtresse," but what he gave his own mistress was a perversion of *carpe diem:* the transports of pleasure he hopes to share with

---

*Though highly eroticized for Flaubert, as for many men of the age, a woman's shod foot was not entirely fetishized in the classical sense in which erotic interest is completely displaced from the genitals. Here the two are conflated in an image of slippers stained with menstrual blood.

her count only as the stuff of memories cherished in lonely old age. He imagines Louise and himself seizing the day only to leave her empty-handed, like a sated lover sneaking off in the dead of night, or an actor striking the set after his star turn. Applause for a performance that would finally obliterate the fiasco of his first night and eclipse Victor Cousin meant more than the pleasure itself. Flaubert knew, moreover, how distressed Louise was by harbingers of middle age. Every Saturday a coiffeur, with whom she had daily appointments to restore the proper curl and fall of her *papillotes,* plucked out her white hairs.*

Brief meetings took place at wide intervals, the first in Paris toward the end of August, a second assignation three weeks later in Mantes, a village on the Seine beyond Les Andelys, where his visit to Ernest Chevalier, home from Corsica during the summer recess, provided an alibi for Mme Flaubert's consumption. One night was enough to inspire weeks of tortured reminiscence. Guilt curdled desire. The image of Louise arched over him with teeth chattering in passionate intercourse mingled with that of tears streaming down her face when they parted at the train station. Always inadequate after the fact, he hardly knew whether their lovemaking had been a climax or an ordeal. "You found me strong and inflamed," he wrote on returning from Mantes. "Well, it seems to me now that I was cold, that I could have showered you with more ardent kisses. At the first opportunity I will efface the memory of that night, just as that night effaced the memory of its predecessor. You no longer doubt me, isn't that right, dear Louise? You are quite certain that I love you, that I will continue to love you for a long time. And I swear no oaths, I promise you nothing, I keep my freedom as you do yours." He couldn't forget her eyes shining as she lay on top of him, her lovelocks dangling from under her nightcap, and the soft warmth of her body. "Do you remember my rapture?" he asked. Did he remember her pain? she may have wondered. The separations tore her apart; but a constantly fraught relationship, a love affair maintained at high emotional pitch, satisfied her perhaps as much as the opportunity to straddle her young man. Judging by her verses,

> *Contre une heure d'amour, de pure volupté*
> *J'échangerais ma vie et mon éternité,*[†]

---

*When Louise Colet decided to keep a diary in 1845, her first entry was a physical self-portrait, which reads, in part, as follows: "My figure is no longer svelte, but it is still elegant and shapely. My bosom, neck, shoulders, arms, are very beautiful. People still admire the way my neck merges with my face. The drawback is that the face, as a result, may appear too round. I correct this flaw with my coiffure."

[†]For an hour of love, of pure sensual pleasure / I would trade my life and my eternity.

one might say that she lived for such romantic interludes, that they helped her through the *banal quotidien* like arias in a dry recitativo. Flaubert prescribed resignation to a "paler, duller" existence organized around work, and with doctorly gravitas warned her that her "convulsive state of soul" would have fatal consequences. "May my image warm you instead of burning you." All to no avail.

Since Flaubert often stated his resolve neither to marry nor to sire children out of wedlock, Louise expected him to rant or faint upon learning midway through September that she might be pregnant. In fact, he reacted with equanimity and advised her not to travel some distance from Paris for an abortion, as she proposed to do, until a physician, preferably one who didn't know her, had confirmed her worst fears or until she had taken medicine that would induce menstrual flow (called *les Anglais* in this correspondence) if pregnancy was not the cause of its arrest. "An emotional crisis may suffice to delay it," he reassured her. "Traveling abroad for a solution to a nonexistent problem would be folly. I believe this is wise counsel and I beg you to follow it. Also, burn this letter." Two or three days later she apparently announced, with sarcasm, that the abortion had taken place. If a child had come, he answered, he would not have been the woebegone figure she imagined. "I wail a lot before events, very little during. I'm afraid of danger so long as it doesn't exist. Once it presents itself, I accept it unthinkingly." As a child he had been afraid of shadows and ghosts, not of horses or thunder, and so he remained. Still, things had turned out for the best. "One less wretched soul on earth," he exclaimed in the prelude to a nihilistic *gueulade*. "One less candidate for ennui, for vice or crime, certainly for misfortune. So much the better if I have no posterity! My obscure name will be extinguished with me and the world will continue on its way just as if I had left an illustrious one. The idea of absolute nothingness pleases me . . . [Anyway], think what a nuisance it would have been for you, what a thorn in your pillow." The irate denunciation of a society much concerned with lineage (and likely to regard his older brother as the truer issue of their illustrious father) mollified him; after delivering his tirade he fell to his knees in adulation of suffering Louise:

I came, you accepted me in the sublime naïveté of your guileless love. Then, without my demanding it, you sacrificed your body, your soul, your feminine modesty, the love of superior men who surrounded you, and, egotistically determined to enjoy myself no matter what, I repaid you by inflicting upon you a punishment all the more terrible for costing you so dearly. And you were resigned to it in advance, poor angel! You were still content, though you rue it now. Oh! how I embrace you. I am moved, I am sobbing. Yes, let me kiss you over that poor heart beating for me! Oh! How good you are! Devoted! Were

you born ugly, your soul would still shine in your eyes and render you charming with a charm that touches . . . You're right to say that I've never been loved
as you love me. Nor will I ever be. It happens only once in a lifetime.

Back on his feet, he urged her to work hard, to girdle her sentimental em-
bonpoint in "sober, severe" prose, and to offer him a "big, beautiful
work" — presumably in lieu of a big, beautiful baby. Taking daily baths
(most unusual for the day) would also do her good, as it did him.

Throughout the fall, eight or ten clandestine letters flew both ways between Paris and Croisset each week, carrying messages of love on wings of
reproach. Why did he devote so much precious space to Shakespeare? she
complained. What should he talk about if not the things he held dearest? he
answered. Her constant plea was that he come to Paris or invite her to
Croisset, and his usual response was that circumstances prevented it. She
taxed him with having more imagination than heart, with being bizarrely
whimsical, with enjoying the company of family and friends while she
lived a forlorn existence. He insisted upon being recognized as the undis-
puted lord of loneliness, and alluded to what may have been petit mal
seizures, or "absences," experienced in her presence.* "It is I who am
alone, who have always been. Didn't you notice two or three absences in
Mantes . . . when you cried out: 'What a weird character you have! What
are you dreaming about?' I don't know what about, but the state you have
rarely seen is my usual one. I am with no one, nowhere, not in my country
and perhaps not of the world. People surround me in vain, since there is no
me to surround. Death didn't alter my spiritual condition when it snatched
away my kin; it perfected it. Previously I was alone inside myself, and now
I am alone outside as well." Had she been excessively indulgent, Louise
might have ascribed certain hurtful blunders to this disconnect rather than
to a mean streak in him. When he found out, for example, that a cousin of
hers was bound for Guyana, he wrote Eulalie Foucaud a flirtatious letter
and sent it to Louise with the request that her cousin deliver it as soon as he
arrived at Cayenne. Worse yet, he invited her to read it. "She's an old acquaintance, don't be jealous of her, you may read the letter provided you
don't tear it up," he instructed. "I wouldn't tell you all this if I regarded you
as an ordinary sort of woman. But what may indeed displease you is the fact
that I treat you like a man rather than a woman." He begged her to rely
more on her mind than on her temperament in her relations with him.

Absences was introduced as the term for passing mental confusions with no definite physical
symptoms by a French neurologist, L. F. Calmeil, in 1824 (and renamed "dreamy states" by
the great English neurologist John Hughlings Jackson). Louise did not witness a full-blown
seizure until August 1851. She recorded the event in a journal but never otherwise wrote
about it.

"Later your heart will be grateful to your head for this impartiality. I always thought I'd find in you less of feminine personality, a more universal conception of life." While Louise wanted uxoriousness in her epistolary lover, Flaubert wanted, or claimed to want, a man's mind in a woman's body. What he got was indignation. "So you found my letter [to Eulalie Foucaud] a little too affectionate?" he asked disingenuously, having evoked, with some nostalgia it seems, Eulalie's large breasts. "I wouldn't have suspected that. I thought on the contrary that it verged at times on insolence and that its general tone was somewhat high-handed." It wasn't true, he asserted, that he had ever loved Eulalie. Only that, like an actor compelled by his role, he could persuade himself of anything with pen in hand. "I took my subject seriously, but *only in the course of writing.* Many things that leave me cold when I see them or when others speak of them, excite, irritate, wound me if I myself do the speaking, or especially the writing. It goes to show that I'm a born showman." The letter to Eulalie was a rehearsal for Rodolphe's to Emma Bovary, with Louise in the audience entertaining doubts about the sincerity of his letters to her.

Every thrust by Louise was deflected with a simile. When she winced at some rude remark, he protested that he had hurt her unintentionally, like a tomcat bloodying the female it caresses. When she questioned his remoteness, he stated that he had not been made for love or happiness, that, like a hungry beggar at a restaurant's cellar grate feeding on aromas from the kitchen below, he had never tasted either. His cunctations drove her mad. Winter arrived, then the New Year, and the torrent of letters slackened. With her delivering the same brief ever more acrimoniously, and with him barking the same arguments in self-defense, their correspondence became, as Flaubert put it, "epileptic." The mediation of Maxime Du Camp, in whom he urged Louise to confide, hoping no doubt that the presence of a tactful envoy would calm her, only made matters worse. She imagined her confidences betrayed.

Flaubert may already have given some thought to constructing a drama around the figure of Saint Anthony. Prominent in his study was Callot's engraving based on Breughel's *Temptation.* But he didn't write, or wrote very little, and references to the blank page run through his abundant correspondence with Louise like a lugubrious obligato. Had the refinement of his intelligence and taste stunted his vitality? Had his zeal for perfection subverted his ability to appreciate anything that fell short of it? Would it finally paralyze him altogether? The fear of impotence migrated from his bed to his desk. "For me a subject to be treated is like a woman with whom one is in love," he confided in October, declaring that he would begin work again in the spring. "When she yields, you tremble with fear, it's a voluptuous fright. One dares not touch one's desire." Seldom did Louise see him so naked. He usually clothed himself in pathos or humility and claimed that his ambition had been buried alongside his father and sister, or that his time was better spent reading the masters than trying to be one. The year 1847 opened with a salvo from Louise condemning his "intellectual orgies" and Flaubert pleading chastity. "I no longer write, what's the point?" he sighed. "Everything beautiful has been said and well said. Rather than construct a work, it might be wiser to discover new ones under the old. It seems to me that the less I produce, the more I enjoy contemplating the masters, which is what I do, since spending my time agreeably is all I desire." Theocritus and Lucretius were his masters of the moment. "What artists, those ancients! And what languages those languages! None spoken since is their equal." Louise, who had wanted Latin lessons from him and been rebuffed, undoubtedly felt that his reverence for the esoteric world to which he denied her access was, in part, a kind of contemptuous posturing.

By mid-February 1847, when Flaubert arranged to see Pradier's bust of his father and pay the d'Arcets a condolence call (their son, Louise Pradier's brother, having been killed by an exploding gas lamp), relations had deteriorated so far that Louise learned of his planned visit to Paris from Maxime Du Camp. A meeting, certainly not fortuitous, took place at the Palais abbatial. Afterward they clinched their estrangement with a bitter quarrel in which she aired her grievances against him, all except the suspicion, reserved for a letter, that he had become Louise Pradier's latest lover.* Flaubert took refuge from the storm at Maxime's apartment, where, in the evening, a violent seizure disabled him. Two weeks later he collected his thoughts in a churlish letter to Louise, saying, at length, that neither was to blame for their basic incompatibility. How could someone like himself, "three-quarters of whose day" was ordinarily spent admiring Nero or Heliogabalus, have cheered the "small moral devotions" and "domestic or democratic virtues" she claimed to uphold? "Entirely partial as I am to the pure line, the prominent curve, the loud color, the ringing note," he wrote, "I always found in you a tone dripping with sentiment that watered down everything and spoiled your thought." If only she had been satisfied to love intermittently, it might have worked, but

---

*In August 1847 Pradier, in the middle of a conversation with Maxime Du Camp, suddenly asked him: "What [sic] is Flaubert screwing when he comes to Paris?" Although taken unawares, Du Camp claims not to have lost his head: "I answered with a slight indication of scorn for you: 'Well, what can I say, he's screwing some bitch of a kept woman known as Madame Valory. I'm very annoyed to see him mingling with a crowd like that.' I pulled it off very well." This is the best evidence that his fling with Louise Pradier began now rather than in the 1850s. Pradier had surprised Louise in flagrante delicto (her lovers were legion) in December 1845, repudiated the staggering debts she had incurred, and expelled her from the flat.

you wanted to draw blood from a stone, you chipped it and bloodied your fingers. You wanted to make a paralytic walk; he fell on you with all his weight and is now more paralyzed than ever.

⁓

DURING MAXIME Du Camp's sojourn at Croisset in August 1846, he and Flaubert had discussed the idea of a summer-long journey, on foot whenever possible, down the Loire valley and around the Breton peninsula. It wasn't the Levant, but Brittany, a province in which many villagers spoke only their native Celtic language, wasn't quite France either. Nor was it beyond the geographical limit of Mme Flaubert's ability to tolerate separation. As Maxime, who had thoroughly won her over, seemed a responsible companion, she blessed the scheme, with the proviso that she, traveling by coach, meet them once or twice at designated towns. By late April 1847 the two were ready to depart. Notes would be taken en route for a collaborative work. Flaubert had already researched the history of Brittany in Rouen's municipal library, while, in Paris's Bibliothèque Royale, Maxime taught himself Breton geography and mores and as much as he could absorb of Celtic monuments. The clothes-conscious pair had given serious thought to their matching outfits, which included calfskin haversacks weighing thirty pounds full, white leather boots with crocodile teeth for cleats, gray felt hats, leather gaiters, thick staffs used in the horse trade, linen vests, billowing linen pants, Tyrolean pipes, knives, canteens, and suits for town wear. On the morning of May 1 they walked in full fig from Maxime's flat along the quays to the Gare d'Orléans and boarded a train bound for the Loire valley. Cannon were heralding Louis-Philippe's name day — the last of his reign — but Flaubert heard a booming summons to forget women's tears on wild craggy shores and on moors carpeted with golden furze, among Celtic megaliths and the bare ruined choirs left by revolutionary brigades.

The "fatality" of his own nature couldn't be shuffled off at will. Soon after reaching the Loire region he suffered another grand mal seizure, not between cities, fortunately, but in Tours, where Maxime, with great presence of mind, contacted Pierre Bretonneau, an eminent physician (known today as the discoverer of diphtheria and the first man to formulate a germ theory of disease), who administered massive doses of quinine. No further episodes occurred during their three months on the road.

By coach and cart, by steamboat and on foot, they moved westward toward the Atlantic coast, visiting Renaissance châteaus positioned along the Loire like half-forgotten dowagers once celebrated for their beauty. The railroad was soon to give Blois, Chambord, and Amboise a whole new generation of courtiers equipped with Baedekers, but in 1847 royalist pilgrims honoring the exiled Bourbon pretender, Charles X's grandson, the comte de Chambord, would still have been more numerous than middle-class tourists. One gathers that Maxime and Flaubert, who knew from their research what was of historical or artistic note at every site, often wandered through the great houses almost alone. At Chambord, whose rotten floorboards made any inspection perilous, what they had for company was a she-ass suckling her young. At Blois, where consoles had been stripped of the bawdy statues they once supported, the concierge's wife hung her wash on the castle esplanade. Chenonceaux may have been more visited than others for its lovely span over the river Cher, but Flaubert reported no inane conversation distracting him as he gazed upon Diane de Poitier's bed with the same mischievous ardor that impelled him to kiss Canova's Psyche.

Instead of sharing Diane's bed, he slept on a pallet in a Trappist monastery near Meilleraye, ate sorrel and porridge, and heard *Salve Regina* sung at vespers. The two wayfarers had left matters of room, board, and transportation largely to chance. They would spend one night in a departmental prison house after chatting up the warden, and the next in a city hotel. When darkness or weariness overtook them, they settled for stables, cabarets, farmhouses, rooms under the eves of country inns normally occupied by unwashed ostlers. On one occasion their host was the local customs officer, on another a loquacious survivor of Trafalgar and Napoleon's Russian campaign.

The adventure began in earnest once they reached the Loire estuary at Nantes, skirted the salt pans north of Saint-Nazaire, came around through Guérande, and entered Lower Brittany, where their appearance puzzled natives more likely to believe in elves than in sightseers. Several more days of travel by one means or another, during which they dined repeatedly on the Breton staples Flaubert ended up calling "our inevitable omelette and ineluctable veal," brought them to Vannes on the Morbihan gulf, an inland saltwater sea with pine-covered islands. This they crisscrossed by chartered boat, dutifully inspecting the extraordinary burial chamber of dolmens with swirls like fingerprints excavated fifteen years earlier on the Île de Gavrinis and the confusion of menhirs and tumuli on the Locmariaguer peninsula before visiting Brittany's Stonehenge at Carnac, where vertical slabs formed a rough crescent in ten rows. How did they view the megaliths? With a yawn, according to both, though the self-styled "Celtophobes" later had peasants do some digging for them in hopes of finding artifacts or, better yet, prehistoric skulls. They would sooner have made the trip to see Breton headgear than Breton stones (and in particular a wicker hat so capacious that Flaubert thought it best described as a planisphere). What did interest them about the stones was the lush growth of speculation mantling this mysterious debris. They amused themselves with impish conspectuses of several recent theories. "This trivia constitutes so-called *Celtic archeology,* a science in whose charms we simply must initiate the reader," wrote Flaubert, already anticipating his *Bouvard et Pécuchet.*

> One stone placed on others is called a dolmen, whether it be horizontal or vertical. A collection of upright stones topped by consecutive slabs, thus forming a series of dolmens, is a fairy grotto, a fairy rock, a fairy table, a devil's table, or a palace of giants, for, like bourgeois hosts who serve the same wine under different labels, Celtomanes . . . have adorned identical things with diverse names. When these stones are arrayed in an ellipse, with no hat on their ears, one must say: "There is a cromlech." When one descries a stone laid horizontally on two verticals, one is looking at a *lichaven* or *trilith* . . . Sometimes two enormous blocks support each other, appearing to have only a single point of contact, and one reads that "they are so balanced that a gust of wind is sometimes enough to make the upper one sway." I don't deny this assertion, although the allegedly impressionable blocks never budged when we gave them some swift kicks.

If invited to offer his own opinion he would have staunchly stood his ground and, girded against the shocked reaction of learned commentators, declared that "the stones at Carnac are very big stones indeed."

Nature was quite another matter: the words he withheld from stones embodying a cryptic message were splurged on plain rocks available to his thoughts and feelings. These he found all along the jagged coast but especially at Belle-Île, eight miles off the Quiberon peninsula. Lured by quartzite cliffs rising sheer out of the Atlantic and sparkling with sunlight, he and Maxime made for them as soon as they landed at Le Palais beneath the star-shaped citadel built by Vauban. A path ran around the island's edge. They followed it over moors and descended to the sea, where landslides had created a manageable ravine. On they walked for hours, heedless of time and tide, along sand beaches and over rocks colored mother-of-pearl. Even more rapturously than during his happiest moments in Corsica, Flaubert yielded to the world round about him. "The shape of seaweed, the softness of grains of sand, the hardness of the rock clicking under our shoes, the height of the cliffs, the fringe of the waves, the indentation of the coast, the voice of the horizon, the sea breeze caressing us like invisible lips: . . . our spirit tossed about in the profusion of these splendors, we fed our eyes on them, our nostrils flared, our ears pricked," he wrote.

> Something vital drawn magnetically from the elements by our amorous gaze reached us and merged with us . . . We became nature, we felt its envelopment, and our joy was immeasurable. We should have liked to lose ourselves in it, to have been ravished . . . Just as in transports of love one wishes one had more hands for groping, more lips for kissing, more eyes for beholding, more soul for

loving, so we, covering nature in a delirious fling, regretted that our eyes couldn't penetrate the bosom of rocks or reach the bottom of seas or rise to the farthest expanse of heaven to see how rocks begin, how waves are made and stars are lit.

To Belle-Île he was the lover Louise had yearned for. Drenched from walking fourteen hours in the sea mist and with toes poking out of torn boots, they reached the island's walled town just before its gates closed, fell sound asleep, and, still intoxicated by the memory of abounding joy, rose at dawn to set sail for the mainland.

The farther north they went, sauntering this way and that between impenetrable hedgerows and past Celtic crosses erected at crossroads or traveling in open country, the more it seemed as if they had entered a time warp. Small towns had no sidewalks or gaslight, and in villages few people spoke French. During Mass at an eleventh-century church crowded with parishioners from Quimperlé, he decided that everything about them — their dress, their faith, their work, their anatomy — declared that they had not lost their identity to the contradictions besetting modern man. The men were "beautiful" because they exhibited in the wrinkles of their timeless faces, in the pleats of their traditional *bragou-brass* trousers, and in hands dyed with the gray of plow handles the insignia of their race. "Perhaps that's why they seem so full, why each seems to carry within himself more things than are ordinarily found in a man." *Complete* and *full* — recurrent words — proclaim his longing for a kind of organic selfhood.

Not that this primitivist idealizing (which had an analogue in his idealization of "blooded" aristocrats) ever blinded him for long to the somber realities of a wretched, priest-ridden hinterland, and when it did, beggars from whom he couldn't shake loose set him straight. Only penance and toil and deprivation came naturally to the Breton. Village festivals were a wooden mimicry of men and women at play. "[People] don't dance, they turn," he wrote of a celebration in the Finistère. "They don't sing, they whistle." While bagpipers sitting on a wall bleated shrilly, two lines arrayed toe to heel in the courtyard below slowly coiled around and around each other, keeping no perceptible rhythm. The contrast with gold-spangled Italian saltimbanques who materialized out of the blue several weeks later at a procession in Guingamp could not have been starker.

Nature in Brittany more than made up for its inhabitants' solemn demeanor. It almost swallowed them up one day when they wandered into a bog concealed beneath fields of gladioli. From a grassy hilltop called the Menez-Hom, it presented a patchwork quilt spread out as far as the Atlantic. Westward lay wild promontories along whose treacherous cliffs Flaubert and Maxime clambered, sometimes on all fours, to see waves crashing five hundred feet below or, at the Pointe du Raz, rocks jutting out of the ocean like the backbone of a submerged sea monster. Inland they roamed through gorse and woods. "We'd follow beaten paths and always stumble upon some clearing in the middle of the forest," wrote Maxime. "Like truant schoolboys, we crossed streams reciting verse as we went. There was no one else around. We wandered free, necks bare and hair tousled."

The long homeward voyage, after a survey of Brest's shipyards and brothels, took them to Roscoff, Saint-Malo, and Mont Saint-Michel on the Channel coast, with a pilgrimage to Combourg, where they reverently toured the castle in which Chateaubriand had grown up, visiting every hallowed nook and cranny to which they were granted access. Flaubert's paraphernalia included that bible of Romantic youth, *René,* and at sunset the two read it aloud beside a lake described by Chateaubriand in *Mémoires d'outre-tombe.* Flaubert tried to imagine his idol as a child watching rain stream down the mullioned windows of his turret room and suffering the "bitter loneliness" of adolescence. No matter that one cannot tell how great works gestate, he wrote, "one still thrills to see where they were conceived, as if those places harbored something of the unknown ideal yet to be born but already animate." With Chateaubriand — who straddled disparate centuries, who belonged to both and to neither, whose being and art were knit of contradiction — he identified passionately. "At the twilight of one society and the dawn of another, it was for him to embody the movement from one to the other, to resume within himself memories and hopes. He was the embalmer of Catholicism and the herald of liberty. Steeped in old traditions and illusions, he was constitutional in politics but revolutionary in literature. Religious by instinct and education, he vented his despair and trumpeted his pride before all the others, Byron included."

Combourg's four gloomy turrets cast a shadow over the last lap of the expedition. And Chateaubriand still haunted Flaubert six weeks later when he and Maxime reunited at Croisset to write a book about their adventure, with each contributing alternate chapters. Out of him spilled anecdotes, brilliantly sketched portraits, landscapes, reflections on history and esthetics, all tied together in elegant, richly figured language that marked his true coming of age as a prose artist. "The difficulty of this book," he wrote several years later, when it was obvious that it would be published posthumously, if ever, "resided in the transitions, and in the whole to be forged from a multitude of different things." Another difficulty may have resided in questions posed by the voyage, or by travel itself, about enigmatic traces, the evanescence of memory, and the transitoriness of life. A recurrent image in what they entitled *Par les champs et par les grèves* (By Fields and Shores) is that of wagon tracks leading nowhere.

No sooner did Flaubert reestablish himself at Croisset than he suffered another epileptic seizure, the first since Tours. He blamed it on the frustrations that attended his effort to find in language an adequate receptacle for his thought. Writing, of which he had done very little during the previous two years, made him irritable. The mot juste was an elusive quarry, and at every turn his doubts beat him back. "Happy are they who don't doubt themselves and whose pens fly across the page," he wrote. "I myself hesitate, I falter, I become angry and fearful, my drive diminishes as my taste improves, and I brood more over an ill-suited word than I rejoice over a well-proportioned paragraph." A lackluster adjective or a crowd of relative pronouns mortified him (in letters he would dissociate himself from his imperfection by underlining the offending words, like a schoolmaster). "The more I study style," he confided to Louise Colet, "the more ignorant I perceive myself to be."

From Brittany Flaubert had written to Louise, perhaps wanting to assure himself, by rekindling her hopes, that he was still worth dreaming about. Louise answered him, even though she had meanwhile found solace in the arms of a young Polish refugee named Franc. And so they picked up where they had left off. Long letters were exchanged very like the ones they had exchanged months earlier. Their old quarrel flared anew. It continued through the fall, alternating between recriminatory *vous*s and supplicatory *tu*s. All this unnerved Flaubert. Seizures (of which there were at least three major ones in 1847), carbuncles, toothaches, earaches, and whatever other extenuating circumstance he could adduce to postpone a rendezvous availed him nothing. Nor did his pleas of poverty earn him Louise's lenience. She firmly believed that Maxime Du Camp, who abandoned his role as go-between in sheer exhaustion, after receiving three hundred letters from Louise (by his count), had influenced Flaubert against her. Flaubert declared himself to be his own man, endowed with free will, and, alas, "radically" incapable of making any woman happy. They simply couldn't get along, he sighed, "like two people who had married late in life." His affectionate, conciliatory New Year's greeting would prove to be a kind of valediction. Several months later, he learned that Louise was pregnant by her Polish lover.

Disheartening, too, was the moribund state of Alfred Le Poittevin, whom Flaubert and Maxime visited at La Neuville-Chant-d'Oisel, near Julie Hébert's village of Bourg-Beaudouin, on September 18, 1847. With thinning hair, shortness of breath, a grayness of complexion, and hands that had barely enough strength left in them to finish *Bélial,* Alfred looked far older than thirty-one. The three strolled down a tree-shaded lane chatting desultorily. When Alfred's father-in-law joined them, the subject turned to politics and to a movement operating nationwide through so-called banquets, by means of which reformers circumvented a law against political rallies. To the dying man everything seemed mortal. Louis-Philippe was doomed, he asserted. The new parliamentary majority, standing on feet of clay, would fall, and government bonds would crash.

Alfred, who spent his last weeks studying Spinoza, died on April 3, 1848. Accompanied by his mother, Flaubert, who hardly spoke during the coach ride, traveled fifteen miles to Neuville and remained there three days, having brought books for the vigil to be held over Alfred's corpse. The first night (after an insufferable dinner at which various Maupassant kinfolk puzzled over Alfred's affection for Spinoza and concluded that the poor man had been a victim of "erroneous systems") he read Creuzer's *Les Religions de l'antiquité* until 1:30 a.m. "I smoked, I read, the night seemed long to me — and yet my mind was working so intensely that I was afraid of losing that state." He slept very little and early the next morning returned to the mortuary chamber, where a maidservant sat beside the coffin, darning black stockings. Later he fell asleep in the fields, behind a sheaf of broom. The second night his companion was Victor Hugo's *Feuilles d'automne,* a copy of which he had found on Alfred's bookshelf. From time to time, he would lift the veil to contemplate his friend's face, Flaubert told Maxime.

> I myself was muffled in a coat belonging to my father, which he wore only once, the day Caroline got married. At first light the attendant and I set to work. I lifted him, turned him over, and wrapped him. The impression of his cold, stiff limbs remained with me all day long, in my fingertips. He was horribly putrefied, the sheets were soiled right through. We used two shrouds, which made him look like an Egyptian mummy, and I experienced a kind of upwelling of joy and freedom for him. There was a white fog outside. As it lifted the woods appeared. The two torches shone in this nascent whiteness, two or three birds sang, and I recited to myself this line from his *Bélial*: "The joyous bird will go and greet the sun dawning through the pines," or rather I heard his voice reciting it and throughout the day I was deliciously obsessed with it.

On a wet morning, pallbearers carried the heavy coffin to the cemetery, where Flaubert, along with Louis Bouilhet, who had come later than he, heard Alfred eulogized windily. "I couldn't prevent myself from drawing close to the edge of the pit and remaining there," he wrote. "I felt a dry-eyed bitterness. I couldn't cry. I had sobs in my belly. How the clods of earth kept hitting the coffin lid! It sounded like a hundred thousand shovelfuls. The thought occurred to me that I may have looked as if I were striking a pose (I was cold, I had buttoned my overcoat partway and set the candle on the ground against one of the poles used to lower the coffin) and so I drew back." Several hours later, he mounted his buggy, lit a cigar, and, with Bouilhet beside him, made for home in great haste, shouting at the horses as he had shouted at no one in particular when Caroline was lowered into the earth. A wry, poignant letter informed Ernest Chevalier of these sad events. "You who knew us in our youth know how I loved him and what pain this loss must have cost me," he wrote. "Existence is a shoddy business. I seriously doubt that the republic will invent a remedy for it."

By then, Alfred's prophecies had been borne out. Paris had risen, the rest of the country had followed suit, and a republic had replaced the constitutional monarchy. Louis-Philippe, whom the mayor of Trouville hid for several days, had taken ship from Le Havre disguised as Mr. William Smith and settled with his family in a mansion placed at their disposal by Queen Victoria. Sparks from France were setting fires all across Europe.

X

1848

THAT MME Flaubert, who paid the bills, had ample reason to despair of her ungainfully employed son's ever learning the value of a franc may be inferred from comments he made to Alfred Le Poittevin about James Pradier's estranged wife, Louise. Appalled by the draconian treatment that adulteresses such as she received from courts meting out Napoleonic justice, he comforted her (not without ulterior motives) during a visit in April 1845. Gone were her young children, whom she was forbidden to see, much less raise. Gone too were the gilt ceilings and purple silk of her enormous salons at 1, quai Voltaire. In her furnished flat, wrote Flaubert, she lived impecuniously, "dans la misère," scraping by on six thousand francs a year.

Two decades later, when the franc purchased much less, an income of six thousand francs, which happened to be Gustave's allowance, was what young Émile Zola reckoned he would need to support his mother, his future wife, and himself comfortably, employing a full-time maid. The Flauberts' beloved retainer, Julie, earned three hundred francs, if her wages conformed to the average annual salary of domestics in Rouen before 1848. Country-school teachers earned not much more. Throughout France unskilled laborers worked twelve-hour days for two francs. In *La Cousine Bette*, Balzac noted that the government paid dockers at the Toulon naval yard one and a half francs, which forced them to subsist as best they could on bread and courage.

A working man might begin the day with bread dipped in a chicory brew sweetened by molasses. He commonly lunched at his workplace on potatoes, cabbage, turnips, or carrots, ate bread in midafternoon, and had more bread with café au lait for dinner. The lard that moistened his potato mash was the closest he usually came to tasting meat. Bread kept him alive. When harvests were bountiful and jobs available, adults consumed a kilogram of rye a day. When crops failed and factories closed, they starved.

In 1845–46 the cereal crops failed and the potato blight ravaging Ireland visited France. Huge sums were spent to import wheat from Russia, which resulted in a serious loss of reserve. With families spending disproportionately on food, industry saw the market for finished goods dwindle. To survive, overstocked businesses laid off workers, who then relied on the dole or went begging. Beggars crowded French cities, and nowhere more conspicuously than in Rouen, where many cotton mills had fallen silent. To be sure, 1847 brought better harvests, but everything else lagged behind. By then, moreover, economic distress had exacerbated dissatisfaction with a regime that stood on spindly legs, like the king's ample torso. It had a narrow electoral base and resisted efforts to enfranchise members of the liberal professions who owned little or no property. Even so, the legislature after 1846 included distinguished deputies cognizant of the need for political and social reform. Indeed, *reform* became their watchword. It was often spoken in parliamentary debate, it gave its name to a newspaper whose influence far surpassed its circulation, and it rallied progressive bourgeois to "banquets" by means of which a law forbidding the unauthorized public assembly of more than twenty persons was circumvented.

These banquets, where a spartan meal set the stage for political harangues masquerading as toasts, concentrated the diffuse energies hostile to Louis-Philippe's politics. The first took place on July 9, 1847, at the Château Rouge, a popular open-air dance hall near Paris's northern customs barrier. Twelve hundred people attended, including eighty-six deputies, one of whom apologized profusely for his previous benightedness and pledged his allegiance to "reform." Everyone sang the "Marseillaise," moderates and radicals alike, in a rousing show of unity. Before long, provincial cities followed this example. At a banquet in Dijon, the socialist Louis Blanc, whose book *L'Organisation du travail* propagated the formula "From each according to his abilities, to each according to his needs," declared that the slightest breeze would suffice to shake rotten fruit loose from the tree of state. In Macon, Alphonse de Lamartine, Romantic poet-turned-statesman, made more ornate prophecies under a sky lit by flashes of lightning. A particularly energetic apostle of reform, Odilon Barrot, who traveled from banquet to banquet, fetched up on Christmas Day with other reformist luminaries at Rouen, where hundreds gathered in a huge suburban hall hung with tricolor flags. Pacing back and forth like an evangelical thumper, Barrot received frequent applause, though at least three dyspeptic banqueters — Louis Bouilhet, Maxime Du Camp, and Gustave Flaubert — sat on their hands. It annoyed Flaubert mightily that purveyors of political cant should be greeted with more ballyhoo than gifted poets. "What taste! What cuisine! What wines! And what speeches!" he exclaimed to Louise Colet, knowing that these sentiments might be taken as an attack upon her own liberal bias. "Nothing could make me more scornful of success, considering the price at which it is purchased. I sat unmoved, nauseated by the patriotic fervor they whipped up with mealy platitudes such as 'the abyss toward which we are running,' the 'honor of our flag,' the 'shadow cast by our standards,' the 'fraternity of peoples.' Never will there be a quarter as many ovations for the most beautiful works of the masters. Never will the hero of Musset's 'La Coupe et les Lèvres' cause as much adulatory breath to be expelled as one heard all over the place when Barrot and Crémieux stood onstage, the one bellowing his personal virtue, the other lamenting our national insolvency." After nine hours in a cold hall at a table laden with cold turkey, where his shoulder was slapped by a locksmith whenever the orators made a salient point, he went home to thaw. "What a sad opinion one forms of men, what bitterness grips one's heart when one sees such delirious asininity on display." Settled in the belief that no principle could remain uncontaminated by the bluster in which politicians couched it, he may have been deaf to momentous issues. It was hardly imaginable at the time that three months later, during the chaotic aftermath of Louis-Philippe's fall, he would toy with the idea of applying for a diplomatic post in Rome, Athens, or Constantinople.

Another banquet, one that would have assembled several thousand people at a hall on the Champs-Élysées had it ever taken place, set in motion a chain of events leading to the king's abdication. Barrot and fellow leaders of the loyal opposition planned for it to occur on February 22, 1848, in conjunction with a protest march of workers and students organized by men whose opposition was decidedly less than loyal. The government prevailed upon Barrot to cancel the banquet, but the march went ahead as scheduled, on a cold, drizzly morning. Singing the "Marseillaise," thousands congregated at the place de la Madeleine, gathered strength from loiterers, and surged toward the place de la Concorde, where detachments of military police blocked their route to the National Assembly. Those who made it across the Seine were repulsed by dragoons. Most dispersed or retreated to the Ministry of Foreign Affairs on boulevard des Capucines, chanting "À bas Guizot" (as foreign minister and prime minister, Guizot was doubly the object of protestors' anger). Shops remained open, though not gunsmiths', several of which were broken into with omnibus shafts and looted. In these events the National Guard — the citizen army that had empowered Louis-Philippe eighteen years earlier — played no part. Well aware of its sympathy for reform and fearing mass defections, the interior minister kept it muzzled.*

After nightfall, when Maxime Du Camp strolled through his neighborhood, a bright glow was visible in the west. There, on the Champs-Élysées, he encountered bonfires built with wicker chairs lining the promenade. "Ah! That's how the July Revolution began," his concierge later exclaimed.

The concierge was more prescient that the reformers, whom Du Camp likened to the sorcerer's apprentice. Having mobilized support for a more liberal monarchy, they couldn't limit it to the accomplishment of their moderate agenda, as events were soon to show. On the twenty-third, in the working-class district around the rue du Faubourg Saint-Denis, Maxime watched as hungry, chilled soldiers who had imprisoned some rabble-rousers let them walk free in exchange for bread and wine from an amiable crowd. Later, at the place des Victoires, he saw even more clearly which way the wind was blowing when the commander of a National Guard unit charged with protecting the Bank of France stuck his peaked cap on his bayonet, raised it high, shouted, "Vive la réforme!" and marched his men to the outer boulevard. This would not be an isolated case. Dismayed by the prospect of general mayhem, officials had belatedly summoned the National Guard, only to be reminded why they had previously temporized. Insubordination was rife. Guards ignored the call or mustered in battalions more often seen to shield demonstrators from army regulars than to hold back the unruly. The fact that so many in his Praetorian guard had turned against him finally persuaded Louis-Philippe to sacrifice his prime minister. Guizot was replaced on February 23, and news of their victory quickly spread among insurgent reformers. When Flaubert and Louis Bouilhet arrived at the Saint-Lazare station in midafternoon of that day to witness the riots ("from an artist's perspective," they told Du Camp), they must have felt like Fabrice del Dongo in La Chartreuse de Parme catching up with the Grande Armée at Waterloo after traveling across France to claim a share of Napoleonic glory. Patrolled by dragoons, the streets of Paris seemed if anything more quiet than usual, except for companies of National Guard hailing the king. It was, they soon discovered, a lull before the storm.

*Since 1816, taxpaying Frenchmen between the ages of twenty and sixty had belonged to the National Guard. Although membership had become a patent of bourgeois respectability, barely one-third of the sixty thousand who served in Paris paid enough taxes to enjoy electoral privilege, and this had been an increasingly vexed issue since 1832 and 1834, when the National Guard put down republican insurrections.

On their way to les Trois Frères Provençaux for a copious dinner, they saw neighbors hanging paper lanterns from their windows as celebrants below shouted: "Illuminez! Illuminez!" Later, on their way back to Du Camp's flat opposite the Madeleine church, they hurried past a column of unarmed National Guard marching behind a large, hirsute man in a felt hat and blue tunic. "His long brown beard came down to his chest," wrote Du Camp. "I observed him carefully, thinking that I recognized him from artists' studios, where he often posed as Christ. He seemed a real firebrand. Fatigue and probably alcohol as well gave him a rasping voice. He held a torch and waved it back and forth." Access to the boulevard des Capucines, which the three friends would normally have taken, was barred by soldiers of the Fourteenth Regiment and dragoons. When at last they reached Du Camp's building, a loud burst nearby stopped them dead in their tracks. To Flaubert, who proposed that they go investigate, it sounded like the crackle of musketry. Du Camp, who thought it far more likely that petards were being hoisted by boisterous kids, did not fancy another crowd scene. And so they went upstairs to hear Bouilhet read portions of his long poem *Melaenis.*

Flaubert had guessed right, as they learned in due course. Numerous demonstrators, including militant republicans and working-class Parisians fed up with half measures — for whom the red flag under which many had marched from the Saint Antoine district to lower Montmartre made a more inclusive statement than the tricolor — had gathered in front of the offices of the left-wing paper *Le National* at around 10 p.m. on February 23. There, its principal editor, Armand Marrast, preached tenacity, insisting that citizens demonstrate until the regime had instituted parliamentary and electoral reform. No sooner had this febrile audience begun to move toward the place de la Madeleine, with shouts of "À bas Philippe! Vive la République!" drowning out "Vive la réforme!" than it joined another crowd fresh from compelling employees to illuminate the Ministry of Justice on the rue de la Paix. Together they encountered the troops Du Camp and Flaubert had glimpsed earlier, who had meanwhile formed a defensive square on the boulevard des Capucines in front of the Ministry of Foreign Affairs. What happened next no one can elucidate. A shot was fired, perhaps by an agent provocateur determined to aggravate the situation, or by a soldier seeing a protestor thrust his torch at the commanding officer. In any event, the Fourteenth Regiment spontaneously fired a volley into the dense crowd, with devastating results. Sixteen corpses bled pools of blood on the boulevard, and at least twice that many men and women lay wounded. While terrified soldiers sought refuge inside the ministry, a tumbrel was found. And while tocsins sounded all over Paris, the dead were carted through the Saint Antoine district, accompanied by witnesses to the massacre shouting "Vengeance! Vengeance! They're slaughtering the people!" Their final destination was the place de la Bastille; the bodies were deposited at the foot of the July Column and eventually buried underneath it.

Parisians needed no further admonition to cut down trees for barricades, which rose overnight throughout the eastern half of the city, some only blocks from the Tuileries. All night long, within the palace, Marshal Bugeaud, who had crushed a republican insurrection in 1834 as Paris's commandant, and Adolphe Thiers, who had helped Bugeaud crush that insurrection as prime minister, were equally busy cobbling together a new cabinet, which would have included Alexis de Tocqueville and Victor Cousin. At daybreak, the insurgents joined the battle in earnest. Before long they had beaten back on every front an army directed to fight mercilessly one moment and to make conciliatory gestures the next. At noon, all that stood between them and the Tuileries was a warren of alleys around a large rock-work fountain called the Château d'Eau. Thiers and Bugeaud proposed that the king flee to Saint-Cloud while he could, then attack Paris with sixty thousand troops (a strategy Thiers would employ twenty-three years later against the Commune), but Louis-Philippe, who since awakening had seemed weirdly unperturbed, rejected the idea. What did jolt him was the greeting of "Vive la réforme!" rather than "Vive le Roi!" from National Guardsmen attached to the Tuileries. After reviewing them he retreated to his study in a state of shock and let generals, ministers, sons, and wife tug him every which way. Convinced that sops he had thrown out during the previous twenty-four hours would soon placate his subjects despite the continued clamor for reform, the king kept reality at bay until the publisher Émile de Girardin, whose paper, *La Presse,* was friendly to the regime, declared that he must abdicate or like Louis XVI become the casualty of a republic. Girardin thus joined the ranks of journalists who played central roles in the revolution. Louis-Philippe immediately wrote a letter abdicating in favor of his grandson. As it happened, immediately was too late to save the throne, and almost too late to save his skin. With the royal stables under siege near the Château d'Eau, the royal family escaped the Tuileries in three one-horse carriages. Attempting to apprise the mob of Louis-Philippe's abdication, an elderly marshal on a white horse preceded by a trumpeter went unheard.

Early in the morning of the twenty-fourth, Flaubert and Bouilhet had hurried from their hotel on the rue du Helder to 30, place de la Madeleine several blocks away, fetched Maxime Du Camp, and proceeded to chase down events, beginning at Tortoni's café, where stockbrokers were trading information about the massacre on the boulevard des Capucines. Uncertain of their next move, they received marching orders from a column of riflemen shouting, "To the Tuileries!" The noise of battle grew louder as they approached the place du Palais-Royal, and Du Camp briefly lost sight of

Flaubert on the mobbed rue Saint-Honoré. Bouilhet disappeared altogether. Pandemonium reigned. Flaubert and Du Camp found each other
near where a disheveled, half-naked woman with a butcher's knife was urging an armed band to join those insurgents who had begun moving against
soldiers positioned near the Château d'Eau in a last-ditch defense of the
Tuileries. This regiment, again the ill-starred Fourteenth, stood no chance.
Once it had been overpowered, the palace gates swung open, although
most people hung back, as if doubting whether one could yet walk through
them safely. Informed by a National Guard officer that the king's corps
d'elite had disarmed, Du Camp and Flaubert were among the first to enter.

At first they encountered almost as many marooned members of the
royal household staff as combatants. The latter behaved like respectful
tourists. To be sure, one of them could not resist the temptation to ape royal
salutations from a gilded armchair in the throne room, while others held
what they called a reform banquet at a dining room table laid with royal silver. But bayonets were sheathed lest they inadvertently smash crystal chan-
deliers or tear brocade hangings. All this changed in short order. "We saw
the first mob rush in from the place du Palais-Royal," wrote Du Camp. "An
enormous din of loud voices and rattling weapons rose up to us on the second floor. We ran to the head of the central staircase and faced a multitude
howling 'death' and 'victory.' It was a stampede such that the banisters almost gave way. When they reached the landing, they rushed through apartments. We heard several blasts: guns were being fired at mirrors. The genius
of destruction . . . had made its grand entrance." Under these circumstances, the better part of valor compelled Du Camp and Flaubert — two
very conspicuous bourgeois — to utter prudent, democratic oaths.*

The genius of destruction had also entered the Palais-Royal, the Orléans's
ducal home, where Du Camp and Flaubert loitered after leaving the Tuileries. Into five bonfires lit around the garden, revolutionaries heaved whatever they had ransacked upstairs: furniture, mirrors, porcelain. Du Camp
tried to salvage a silver cup embellished with antique gold medallions but
threw it back at gunpoint. He then implored a student of the École Polytechnique, whose dapper uniform reassured him, to intervene. "I explained
that there were valuable paintings in the palace, signed by illustrious names,
and we couldn't let them go up in smoke . . . Lifting his arms dejectedly, he
said: 'What would you have me do?'" As far as Du Camp could tell, every-

---

*In his memoirs Alexis de Tocqueville states that in the days immediately following the rev-
olution, he observed a general inclination to trim sails to the prevailing wind. "Great landlords delighted to recall that they had always been hostile to the middle class and
well-disposed to the humble; priests again found the dogma of equality in the Gospel and
assured us that they had always seen it there; even the middle classes discovered a certain
pride in recalling that their fathers had been workers."

thing had been fed to the flames except wine looted from the cellar. This was consumed by the insurgents themselves, more than one of whom staggered around the garden menacingly.

Flaubert's peregrinations were not over when he regained Du Camp's flat (and found a bone-weary Bouilhet, who had been pressed into service building barricades), for Louis de Cormenin dropped by with news that a republic was to be declared later in the evening at City Hall, the Hôtel de Ville. They all knew about the abdication, but only later would they find out how the monarchy had breathed its last during a session of the rump Chamber of Deputies. Hurried from the Tuileries across the Seine to the Legislature even as insurgents were entering the palace gates, Louis-Philippe's daughter-in-law, the duchesse d'Orléans, and her small son, the king's designated successor, had attended a furious debate between dynasts intent on having her appointed regent and republicans arguing for the establishment of a provisional government. Frayed tempers had managed to respect parliamentary etiquette until a mob swept into the Chamber, led by a uniformed rogue who mounted the tribune, brandished his saber, and proclaimed: "There is no longer authority here except that of the National Guard, represented by me, and that of the people, represented by forty thousand armed men surrounding this place." Mayhem ensued, with rough hands jostling deputies still present, but somehow order was sufficiently restored to give the verbose Lamartine his say. What he finally said, after a long exordium, was that only a provisional government could separate the combatants and that at the earliest opportunity a democratic congress should determine France's political future. Halfway through his speech, another mob — this one armed with pikes and cutlasses — burst into the Chamber shouting, "Down with the Chamber! Out with the corrupt!" Ledru-Rollin, a republican deputy whom insurgents recognized as one of their own, requested a voice vote for each name on a list of prospective ministers drawn up by the two opposition papers, Le National and La Réforme. Whose voices belonged to legislators and whose to people from the street may not have concerned him excessively. By then, most conservative legislators had taken seats on the uppermost tiers, like flood victims seeking higher ground, and the would-be regent had fled with her virtual king. The list was ratified and power conferred upon an executive authorized to convene at City Hall.

In thin drizzle and fog, the Hôtel de Ville, to which members of the new cabinet now directed their steps, presented an apocalyptic scene. Horse carcasses and broken weapons littered its esplanade. Terrified by the crowds, the celebratory musket fire, the petards, the wavering torchlight, cavalry horses left to fend for themselves ran wild. Fleeing troops had abandoned four well-primed cannons. Notre-Dame's great tenor bell tolled away.

Flaubert later wrote of Frédéric Moreau in *L'Éducation sentimentale* that "the magnetism of zealous crowds pulled him in," that he "took deep, exhilarating breaths of air acrid with gunpowder." But for Alexis de Tocqueville, who had had enough of disorder after enduring a tumultuous afternoon at the Chamber, and for Lord Normanby, the English ambassador, who could not believe, as he noted in his diary, that "a great nation like this can really submit permanently to the dictation of a few low demagogues, none of them, except Lamartine, of any personal following, but hoisted into power by base desertion of duty on the part of all the armed forces, and at the pleasure of the very scum of the earth," the Hôtel de Ville was a scene to be avoided. While Lamartine and his confreres deliberated in the council room, workers, students, and functionaries milled about in the corridors outside. At every turn another orator speaking for himself alone or representing one of the clubs that multiplied during this period expounded a formula for political salvation to whoever would listen. (One of the more radical clubs, Blanqui's Club républicain central, included among its members Maurice Schlesinger, who may have become persona non grata in France after Louis-Napoleon's coup d'état.) Turned away from destructive ends, the energy of the mob begot harangues, and one such harangue reached the executive committee when Louis Blanc, an indomitable socialist, interrupted its deliberations to plead for a republic. Over this fundamental issue the committee split into two factions, those who wanted a republic to be declared unconditionally and those who shied away from announcing a definitive form of government. With great resourcefulness, Lamartine drafted a proclamation that began as follows:

> A retrograde and oligarchical government has just been overthrown by the heroic people of Paris. This government has fled, leaving behind it a bloody imprint that will forever prevent it from returning. The people have bled as they did in July [1830], but this time their generous blood will not be betrayed. They have won a national, popular government that reflects the rights, the progress and the will of this great citizenry.

Calling upon each citizen to consider himself a magistrate responsible for civil order, he declared that the provisional government wanted a republic, subject to its choice being endorsed by the nation in a referendum to be held expeditiously. Even before the proclamation arrived from the printer's, workers hoisted a large white canvas with "The republic one and indivisible is proclaimed in France" written in black chalk. When, late at night, the printed document became available at last, hundreds of copies were released like doves from the windows of City Hall.

On February 25, a Sunday, Flaubert, whose absence from home under these circumstances must have given Mme Flaubert one of her severe migraines, entered a city that did indeed honor the government's call for order. There was, to be sure, widespread destruction. Wooden coach shelters lay smoldering in roadways — those that had not been torn down for barricades, along with trees, lampposts, and railings. Looters broke into armorers' shops. A poster signed by printers and associates of the workers' newspaper *L'Atelier* appeared on walls enjoining "brothers" not to wreck mechanical presses but, rather, to blame "selfish, short-sighted government" for their misfortunes. Worse instances of Luddism occurred elsewhere, in Rouen for example, where gangs raging against the technology introduced by English engineers sacked the railroad station and burned a railroad bridge called the Pont aux Anglais. But in Paris, witnesses remarked upon the prevalent calm. What impressed Alexis de Tocqueville even more than this civility was the fact that working-class civilians maintained it in the absence of soldiers and gendarmes. "The people alone bore arms, guarded public buildings, watched, commanded, and punished," he wrote.

> It was an extraordinary and a frightening thing to see the whole of this huge city, full of so many riches, or rather the whole of this great nation, in the sole hands of those who owned nothing; for, thanks to centralization, whoever reigns in Paris controls France. Consequently the terror felt by all the other classes was extreme; I do not think that it had ever been so intense at any other moment of the revolution, and the only comparison would be with the feelings of the civilized cities of the Roman world when they suddenly found themselves in the power of Vandals or Goths.

As far as he could tell, a "morality of disorder" tolerating other mischief but not theft held sway, so that affluent Parisians prepared for the worst had mostly been spared. And because both adversaries were stunned — monarchists by their defeat, insurgents by their lightning-quick success — there had been no time, de Tocqueville went on to observe, for passions to boil over. All the same, many bourgeois wore thick shoes, carried umbrellas, and tried to look as much like their own concierges as they could.

A ritual of reconciliation that became quasi-official in France, but especially in Paris, was the planting of *arbres de la liberté*. Throughout March and April young poplar trees appeared at intersections, in squares, at markets, at the Opéra, in the courtyards of official buildings. People would gather, the mayor of the arrondissement (or deputy mayor in the case of Victor Hugo) would effervesce, Revolutionary hymns would be sung, salvos fired, branches garlanded, and in conclusion, a local priest fetched to water the sapling with his aspergillum. On March 4, at a funeral procession held for all who had died during the three February days — soldiers and insurgents alike — Parisians marched en masse in a fraternity of mourning that touched even those ill disposed to the newborn republic. With flags, hats, and hand-kerchiefs being waved and perfect strangers addressing one another famil-iarly as *tu* (which appalled Balzac), everything had a festive air. Flaubert wondered, doubtfully, whether the new regime would prove friendlier to art than the old.

By April 20, during the Fête de la Fraternité, when army regulars and National Guardsmen trooped up the Champs-Élysées to pledge allegiance to the republic at the Arc de Triomphe, fraternity had already become a misnomer. The antagonisms masked after February 25 wore through their false face in the run-up to elections for a Constituent Assembly. Despite its ideological factiousness, the provisional government agreed on significant measures: it undertook to guarantee employment for every citizen and es-tablished workshops, or *ateliers nationaux;* it created a commission to address workers' problems; it decreed universal male suffrage; it abolished slavery throughout the French colonies. Still, radical leaders such as Auguste Blan-qui, who presided over the most vociferous of the several hundred clubs at which people discussed politics, brewed hostility toward an executive more concerned with maintaining order and safeguarding property than rearing an egalitarian society. Fearful that elections would produce a conservative result unless time were sufficient to wean the common man away from those on whose wisdom he had traditionally relied — employers, notables, local clergy — the radical left petitioned for a postponement. "Enlighten-ment must reach even the tiniest hamlets. The workers must lift up their heads, which have been bowed by servitude, and recover from the state of prostration and stupor maintained by oppressive interests." The left re-quested a year; it was given a few weeks. But even that nominal concession angered bourgeois, who rued the course events had taken and would have spurned banquets if only the previous year could be lived over again. Talk of legitimizing divorce, of "reorganizing" property, of nationalizing indus-try, of bringing down hierarchical pillars, of purging this and that, of boot-ing the regular army out of Paris: all of these alarmed them, especially after March 17, when one hundred thousand workers marched in protest from the place de la Concorde to the Hôtel de Ville. "The population of kings in overalls grows larger day by day," an Austrian diplomat noted in his diary. "They strut about the streets, sometimes alone, sometimes in great masses, to take part in all manner of demonstrations which are, of course, always directed against law and order . . . Everything must be razed to the ground, nothing must remain standing. That's what they want, these thousands upon thousands of tyrants who reign over us." Middle-class Parisians, some of whom had neglected National Guard duty in the past, hastened to sign up for it. Maxime Du Camp was one such ardent volunteer. He endured long watches, patrols, nights spent in a station house, and, eventually, pitched battles.

An equally heavy atmosphere enveloped Rouen, where the republic was proclaimed at the Hôtel de Ville on March 1. National Guardsmen regularly tilted with protesting workers convinced that they were once again, as in 1830, about to be cheated of their revolution. Toward the end of March, a crowd invaded the central prison and the Palais de Justice, where rioters were being held or judged. Several days later mill workers, who like many unemployed had expected instantaneous prosperity under the republic, died in skirmishes with police. This was a prelude to the bloodier confrontation that took place after the elections of April 23, when news of a conservative victory spread through Rouen's poor neighborhoods. An angry mob laid siege to City Hall and then, repelled by mounted police, fled into the nearby narrow streets, throwing up barricades. Flaubert had already left his house on the rue de Crosne, but the sound of muffled cannon fire would have reached him at Croisset. It took the army only a day to quell the revolt, and, being of a mind to avenge its February defeat, it did so implacably. Thirty-four people died, but many more were wounded. Two months later, the same would occur in Paris, with far greater bloodshed. Flaubert never mentioned these events in the meager correspondence surviving from early 1848. One assumes that he ignored them as best he could, though even had he wished to follow Du Camp's example, there would have been no question of an epileptic doing National Guard duty.

Alfred Le Poittevin's death preyed upon his mind, and in the writing of a book about Saint Anthony, to which he had devoted himself for a year or more, nothing came easy. "I'm gnawed by anger, impatience, impotence," he wrote to Du Camp in a woeful state of mind. "Yesterday, père Parain found me *changed*. And today I kept pissing all afternoon . . . There are moments when my head bursts with the bloody pains I'm taking over this. Out of sheer frustration I jerked off yesterday, feeling the same bleakness that drove me to masturbate at school, when I sat in detention. The ejaculate soiled my pants, which made me laugh, and I washed it off. Ah! I'm quite sure Monsieur Scribe never stooped so low!" Louise Pradier, whom he apparently saw on unrecorded trips to Paris and whose prodigal favors he shared with, among others, an anonymous Englishman shocked by her predilection for oral sex, may have supplanted Louise Colet in his onanistic fantasies.

Only days before the June insurrection that tore Paris apart, trouble visited Flaubert in the person of his brother-in-law. Since Caroline's death, Émile Hamard had fared poorly. He had made only half-hearted attempts to establish a law practice in Rouen. The existence of little Caroline consoled him, but not enough to ward off his demons, and the in-laws next door didn't emit much warmth. He was mortally aimless, according to Flaubert. In April 1847 Hamard had crossed the Channel, with or without the recommendation Chéruel had solicited from Michelet on his behalf. After five months, about which nothing of his movements has been traced, he left England to take up residence in Paris. The revolution was a providential event for men at loose ends who couldn't find purchase in settled society, and the woebegone drifter became a militant republican. Frequenting what the Flauberts considered "suspect milieus," by which they presumably meant radical clubs, he hoped, in vain, to reinvent himself as a deputy. Worse yet, he helped finance the cause with his inheritance, squandering thirty thousand francs on it (Flaubert reported) and trading away family jewels. The little one knows suggests that depression had shifted to mania, or perhaps grief to anger. Certainly the Hamard who descended upon Rouen was a man determined to reclaim his two-year-old daughter.

How this drama unfolded can be roughly pieced together from Flaubert's letters. Having learned of Hamard's intention to seize Caroline, Flaubert and his mother somehow deceived him into thinking that they had departed for Nogent-sur-Seine. There Hamard went and knocked at the door of François Parain's son-in-law, Louis Bonenfant, who treated him courteously. The ruse gave them a head start. During Hamard's absence on this fool's errand, they fled with Caroline to Forges-les-Eaux between Rouen and Dieppe, where friends offered asylum. Meanwhile, an Hamard uncle as convinced as they that his nephew was not of sound mind took measures to have him committed. "If you knew the effect all of this has had on me," Flaubert complained in a letter to Bonenfant, "you'd wonder whether they might not end up having to lock me up next to Hamard." When threatened with incarceration, Hamard hired a lawyer and sued Caroline Flaubert for custody of the child. By the terms of an emergency ruling to which all parties acceded, it was decided that Mme Flaubert should keep little Caroline until the case against Hamard's sanity could be adjudicated or at least until January of the following year, with Hamard enjoying visitation rights in the interim. Of these he availed himself "day and night," to everyone's despair. The case against Hamard would never go forward, but neither would Hamard's suit for custody. He surrendered to a very resolute grandmother, left town, and thereafter showed up irregularly at Croisset or in Rouen at the house ensconced within a walled garden near the Hôtel-Dieu that Mme Flaubert rented after returning from Forges-les-Eaux. The fear that he might at any time demand his due as legal guardian cast a shadow on the household. "When I grew up enough to feel shame and vexation," his daughter later wrote, "he filled me with both as he contradicted by his manners and words all the bourgeois values of order and regularity bred into me." He was not debauched or dishonest, she insisted, but "unhinged by typhoid fever, sorrow, and inactivity." She shed no tears when news of his death reached her many years later, in 1877.

The thought undoubtedly crossed Mme Flaubert's mind that if her wretched son-in-law had not chosen the end of June to have a litigious tantrum, he might have perished at the barricades, for during their domestic brawl in Rouen, civil war had again erupted in Paris, and the reprise claimed many more lives than had been lost four months earlier. What set it off was a decree expelling unmarried workers from the *ateliers nationaux,* the national workshops established after February. Other decrees had already served to reduce benefits available through these workshops, which a newly elected, conservative government regarded not only as an intolerable burden on taxpayers but also as dens of socialist sedition. The measure convinced Parisian workers that an institution epitomizing their victory was soon to be abolished.

They mobilized throughout slum districts in an apparently spontaneous insurrection that began on June 22, 1848, when a crowd at the Hôtel de Ville denounced the government's plan to offer idle Parisian workers employment draining swamps far from Paris, in Sologne. By midevening eight or ten thousand people had crossed the river and started up the rue Saint-Jacques. "Along their route shopkeepers closed early and frightened faces appeared at windows," wrote Maxime Du Camp, who witnessed this demonstration. "Unarmed, they marched in cadence and chanted lugubriously, 'Bread or lead! Bread or lead!' It was sinister and really striking." Urchins with candles preceded them to the place du Panthéon, where they spread out around speakers standing on a makeshift podium. At the edge of this huge circle police informants heard talk of further demonstrations. Overnight, cobblestones were dug up to build foundations for more than two hundred barricades, some fifteen feet high.

In the government's call to arms, drums and bugles made a hellish racket and National Guardsmen, distressed by the anarchy they had abetted by their defections four months earlier, during the first uprising, responded zealously. As de Tocqueville saw it, Paris resembled those besieged cities of antiquity whose inhabitants performed heroic deeds in the knowledge that defeat would mean enslavement. But he also noted a bloodlust peculiar to internecine warfare.

In conversations [on the city streets], I noticed how very quickly, even in this civilized century of ours, the most pacific people will attune themselves to the spirit of civil war, and how in those unhappy times a taste for violence and a contempt for human life suddenly spread. The men I was talking to were sober, peaceful artisans whose gentle mores . . . were even further from cruelty than from heroism. But they were dreaming of nothing but destruction and massacre. They complained that they were not allowed to use bombs or to sap and mine the streets held by the insurgents, and they did not want to give quarter to anyone anymore.

From far and wide, traveling aboard history's first troop trains, came volunteer militia eager to tame the capital that had so often imposed its will on provincial France. They joined army regulars in a fierce campaign brilliantly improvised under General Louis Eugène Cavaignac, the war minister, whose republicanism did not prevent his taking full advantage of dictatorial powers vested in him by the Constituent Assembly. Blood flowed freely on both sides of the barricades. Insurgent snipers fighting "without a battle cry, leaders, or flag," as de Tocqueville put it, kept their powerful enemy at bay for two days but eventually yielded to artillery barrages, which pulverized everything. In the final tally of dead were five generals and Monsignor Affre, archbishop of Paris, who is said to have been clutching an olive branch. Insurgents died in their thousands. Thousands more were transported to Algeria.

A bullet through the leg cut short Maxime Du Camp's military service. He was wounded fighting at barricades adjacent to Paris's northern customs barrier and described the moment with the clinical punctilio of a doctor's son. "I sat down, I examined my wound. The shot had traversed my leg at a downward angle. The tibia had been spared, thank God, but I knew beyond a doubt that the fibula was shattered, for I immediately extracted a long splinter of bone from the open wound." While reassuring Flaubert in a letter written barely twelve hours later that there would be no serious consequences, he privately wondered whether his dream of exploring the Orient could be accomplished on a peg leg. Flaubert visited the convalescent midway through July, when it seemed safe to leave his mother. By then the streets had been swept clean, the bodies had been buried, a commission of inquiry on the insurrection had been named, the machinery for condemning rebels to transportation had been set in motion. Parisians seeking relief from memories of the bloodbath flocked to a fair on the esplanade of the Invalides. And since Du Camp couldn't join them, Flaubert hired one of the attractions — a farmer with a five-legged sheep — to visit his apartment on the place de la Madeleine.

When bourgeois citizens laid down their muskets, many took up their pens to reflect upon June 1848 in the language of Armageddon. "French civilization survived one of the greatest perils ever to face it," wrote Du

Camp. The attorney general of Angers, in his report to the commission of inquiry, claimed that fellow Angevois, suspending their political differences, had gone "to the aid of society, whose very existence they thought threatened by a horde of barbarians subverting it from within." Since society, or civilization itself, was at stake, and workers played their part as the Hun, mercy would have been suicidal. "The struggle these last few days," a journalist declared in *Le National*, "has been clearly and forcefully delineated. Yes, on one side there stood order, liberty, civilization, the decent republic, France; and on the other, barbarians, desperados emerging from their lairs for massacre and looting, and odious partisans of those wild doctrines that the family is only a word and property naught but theft."

Flaubert, the affluent bourgeois sustained by unearned income from farmland, had no use for egalitarian doctrine. Declaring that only three or four hundred men a century had historical weight, he regarded utopian socialism as the worst despotism. Inherently unintelligent was the mass qua mass. But with his animus against the bourgeoisie, neither could he stomach the proprietary claim to civilization of gentlemen who traded in received ideas. Still less could he tolerate the call for "moral order" now heard wherever conservatives spoke and destined to echo down the century like a mantra. What these beneficiaries of social mobility urged on contentious workers was pious resignation, and in no city did they sermonize more harshly than in Rouen. Had Flaubert read a local paper called *La Liberté* on July 3, he would have seen it stated that religion alone could instill a "sense of hierarchy" in workers. Not knowing why he scrimped when rich men lacked nothing, the poor man was ripe for conversion to violence. "He blames our social system and sees some sort of justice in overthrowing it." Greed had made him a transgressor. No longer convinced that his portion had been divinely ordained, he wanted all the good things of life. "This becomes a consuming and intoxicating passion. It is no longer a question of a victory over some verbal quibble, or over the form of the government. What is at the root of these impious endeavors is the total reshaping of society. From political riots we have passed to social war." Even de Tocqueville, a civilized, subtle, and otherwise compassionate Norman, concurred to some degree with this view. The populace wanting a reprieve from "the necessities of their condition," he wrote, had been led down the primrose path by a mirage of well-being to which ideological mountebanks had made them feel entitled. It was, in his opinion, the mixture of greed and "false theories" that gave the insurrection its peculiar combustibility.

Flaubert wished a pox on both antagonists. Likewise, he found little to choose between the outside world, which he regarded as a landscape of desolation, and his family, which he called, among less pejorative names, a quagmire. Hamard's antics having flustered them, he and his mother clashed more heatedly than usual. After one outburst, Flaubert offered profuse apologies and swore never again to behave as he had. "You see that I'm not proud, that I recognize my faults," he wrote to her in Rouen from Croisset. "I am far from being a strong man, the problem lies with my blasted nerves, and then, too, one can't practice my metier without suffering consequences; one ends up with a flayed sensibility for putting a whip to it every day. Think about that and forgive me." There were no more entreaties from Louise Colet to make him appreciate internment and to balance the emotional weight of Mme Flaubert's crying over him at one end of the Paris-Rouen line, although the once-and-future lovers remained minimally in touch. Louise had taken a flat on the rue de Sèvres opposite Juliette Récamier, whose close confidante she had become. Old and blind, Juliette gave her a lock of Chateaubriand's hair when her eighty-year-old swain died. Louise in turn sent it to Flaubert, by way of acknowledging his reverence for the author of *René*, and of sweetening his memory of her. He sent it back.

Flaubert's own confidant was Louis Bouilhet, with whom he had bonded since 1846, and especially during the harrowing months of private and public upheaval. What do we know about this childhood acquaintance rediscovered several years after their graduation from the collegiate school? Unlike Flaubert and Maxime Du Camp, Bouilhet came from a family accustomed to straitened circumstances. His father, Jean-Nicolas, had served in the Napoleonic administration as director of field hospitals under Marshal Oudinot, a post that exposed him to constant danger and ultimately, during the disastrous midwinter retreat from Moscow, undermined his health. After 1815, Jean-Nicolas was appointed deputy manager of an aristocratic estate on the Caux plateau near Cany, where he met and married Clarisse Hourcastremé, who taught at a girls' boarding school founded by her father. Both spouses had strong literary leanings. Jean-Nicolas wrote songs, fables, a comedy, reams of poetry, and a memoir of his military campaigns. Clarisse was adept enough at versifying to compose official welcomes on those rare occasions when a celebrity visited Cany. Tutored at home, she had received excellent instruction from her father, Pierre Hourcastremé, whom Louis Bouilhet remembered as an octogenarian in culottes and a powdered wig. Through this grandfather Bouilhet felt singularly connected to the age of Enlightenment, when Pierre wrote philosophical essays, mathematical treatises, and ballads that earned high praise from no less a personage than Voltaire. Before 1789 the young polymath had corresponded with Condorcet and with the physiocratic economist Turgot.

A touching epigraph to Jean-Nicolas's memoirs makes it clear that they were intended for Louis. "I cherish the idea that one day my son will recount with pride the dangers his father endured," he wrote. "He will track me [across Europe] in reading the story of my misfortunes . . . and boast-fully insist upon the courage it took to swim the Berezina. A belated and feeble compensation the future promises me . . . when I no longer exist." Lest the timidity that had always bedeviled him afflict his son as well, he hoped with his memoirs to project an image of valor, but Jean-Nicolas died in 1832, two years before Pierre Hourcastremé, and the shaping of Bouil-het's character devolved largely upon Clarisse, who did not allow much room for self-assertiveness. Hostile to the ideas by which her father had set store, she toed a reactionary line in religion and politics. Home life was de-cidedly dour. If Bouilhet, unlike his two younger sisters, escaped the full ef-fect of Clarisse's priggish regime, he could thank his grandfather for it. Through connections, Pierre Hourcastremé had gotten him enrolled at a nearby boarding school, and when the headmaster, M. Jourdain, affiliated his establishment with the collegiate school and moved it to Rouen, Bouil-het became Flaubert's classmate. Despite a shy, gentle nature that might have consigned him to obscurity, Bouilhet made his presence felt by brilliant scholarship, especially in classical languages. No one equaled him for writ-ing Latin verse, and in Greek, which, as we know, Flaubert labored all his life to master, he was so fluent that Jourdain had him tutor the slower *pen-sionnaires*. In 1839, his penultimate year, the principal awarded Bouilhet the *prix d'excellence* for graduating first in his class. What, then, was everyone's astonishment, four months later, to find his name affixed to the letter of protest against unjust penalties that resulted in Flaubert's expulsion (but not his own)? Tall and handsome, resembling Flaubert far more closely than Achille did, he was the ideal scholarship boy — a classical whiz who duti-fully wrote long letters to his mother every Saturday.

He also wrote poetry, and poetry of a kind that bespoke the extracurric-ular influence of Victor Hugo and Alfred de Musset. "I don't know what the dreams of schoolboys are nowadays," Flaubert reminisced many years later, "but ours were splendid in their extravagance — the last exhalations of Romanticism, stifled in a provincial milieu . . . One was not merely troubadourish, insurrectionary and oriental; one was above all an artist. Af-ter homework had been completed, literature began, and one strained one's eyes reading novels in the dormitory." While Flaubert had little talent for versification, Bouilhet's mind was naturally tuned to measured cadences.

As his family wanted no starving Chatterton on their hands, they urged him to study medicine, and in October 1840 Bouilhet entered Rouen's medical school. For two years the compliant young man survived without much sleep, attending lectures, often doing night duty in the wards, and giving lessons in classical languages at a student boardinghouse. He then be-came one of four interns under Achille-Cléophas's supervision, an experi-ence that may have been for him what swimming the frigid Berezina to escape Cossack marauders had been for his father. How to reconcile the time-consuming assignments of a rigorous discipline with the private lessons on which he depended and with the leisure needed for poetry, conversation, or dalliance was his insoluble dilemma (Maxime Du Camp claimed that he composed verse in his head all the time, even when helping the senior surgeon perform arterial ligatures after an amputation). Still, he persevered and might have gone on to practice medicine if not for an incident very like the one that had resulted in Flaubert's expulsion from the collegiate school. In August 1843, interns, disgruntled at having to sleep in their hospital quarters when not on call, discreetly protested. The protest was ignored, whereupon all four, including Bouilhet, staged a strike. The Hôtel-Dieu dismissed them summarily. Three obtained internships at other hospitals, but Bouilhet, who may have been the least militant among them, was also the least anxious to overcome the consequences of his rebellion. After completing courses at the Hôtel-Dieu, he informed his aggrieved mother in March 1844 that he had failed examinations for the degree, and put medicine behind him. Poems he had composed during the previous three years, most of them written in stately cadences but with a sweet, elegiac voice sometimes coming through, were about love, glory, the poet flouted by the philistine. "In evil as in good, there is nothing great nowadays, nothing broad," he lamented in a notebook of philosophical reflections. "Morality is bigoted and crime is bourgeois! We are swollen with lymph."

Tutoring young men for the classical baccalaureate became Bouilhet's full-time occupation. Candidates were not hard to find. When Flaubert met up with him again, apparently soon after the death of Dr Flaubert, he was living in a cheap hotel called the Trois Maures. Tedious though it must have been, eight hours a day of tutorial work afforded him more leisure than his internship at the Hôtel-Dieu. An inveterate frequenter of cafés, he spent evenings enveloped in pipe smoke with friends (above all Charles LeBoeuf, the vicomte d'Osmoy, a younger man whose name may have inspired that of Flaubert's country doctor). He found time for at least one blighted love affair and the tortured wooing of a harlot named Rosette. Before long invitations to join Flaubert, or Flaubert and Maxime Du Camp, began arriving every week from Croisset, where his brilliance was warmly corroborated. "Bouilhet, who blushed when eyes rested on him and felt ill at ease in a salon, held firm beliefs and argued them with brio," wrote Du Camp. "He was droll, he had the deftness of a fencing master for irony, and he might have become a comic poet if his early education, the romantic craze, and a certain aspiration to grandeur hadn't hustled him into lyric poetry." As Du Camp tells it, the three concocted a burlesque tragedy called *Jenner,* *or The Discovery of Vaccine*, with Bouilhet setting their goofy plot in polished verse, to the particular delight of Flaubert, who soon bestowed upon him various nicknames (Bardache, Hyacinthe, l'Archevêque, Monseigneur), which were, as ever, tokens of affection.* Bouilhet's ability to spin off rhymed verse of any length astonished Flaubert, rather as perfect pitch might seem preternatural to someone incapable of carrying a tune. Bouilhet's facility in classical languages made no less profound an impression. Du Camp declared that he never met a more distinguished humanist. "There wasn't a Greek or Latin poet he didn't know; he read them regularly and wore his erudition lightly." His abortive career as a surgical intern also worked to his advantage. Knowing the Hôtel-Dieu from the inside gave him and Flaubert common ground. And disappointing Dr Flaubert fortified it. Bouilhet was his true brother, a foil to Achille, a soul mate, a fellow derelict in the world of bourgeois professions.

By autumn 1848, when Maxime Du Camp was tottering around North Africa, these two saw each other every Sunday and spent long afternoons ensconced in green armchairs. Grateful for an enthusiastic audience, Bouilhet often read his verse, meaning almost always the rhymed stanzas of a narrative poem set in ancient Rome that ultimately exceeded three thousand lines. Flaubert's *Tentation de Saint Antoine*, a work in progress since 1846, had begun to grow above the humus of scholarly tomes that carpeted his corner room at Croisset but remained its author's secret labor. For two years Flaubert had been reading the Church Fathers and the council decrees, beginning with the Nicene, compiled by Labbé and Cossart. He had immersed himself in scholasticism, the lives of the saints, and whatever he could find on early Christian heresies. Bouilhet warned him against displaying more erudition than befit his subject. "Be careful! Saint Anthony was a simple soul and you're going to make him a learned man." He didn't listen. Like Jules, the coprotagonist of *L'Éducation sentimentale* (first version), Flaubert found himself driven to satisfy other lusts — for riches and power — by amassing a wealth of knowledge. Synopses and digests wouldn't do. In this mystery play, as he conceived it to be, the phantasmagoric creeds marshaled past Anthony required enormous research. Only a learned man could transform the desert retreat of a simple man into a carnival ground for theological grotesques.

What Flaubert pictured was the fall from dogmatic security into vexed selfhood. Anthony buckles at the outset, when, during an introspective moment before evening prayer, he remembers how the experience of pariah

---

*Bardache was slang for catamite or male prostitute, apparently derived from the Arabic *bardaj*.

thoughts suddenly flooding his mind persuaded him to flee society years earlier. "I felt desperately unable to control my thought; it slipped the bonds with which I had it tied and escaped me," he says in a monologue that evokes Flaubert's description of epileptic seizures. "Like a rogue elephant, [my mind] would race beneath me with wild trumpetings. Sometimes I'd lean back in fright, or else boldly try to stop it. But its speed stunned me, and I'd get up broken, lost." Remembering one invasion lays him open to another, which now commences. Desire is first to breach the hermitage, and its embodiment is Mary, who, as Anthony kneels before an icon of Christ's Virgin Mother, suddenly seems a tart striking lubricious poses. Images of incest more oblique than this one will recur throughout the narrative. For Jesus the charismatic son, whom Anthony impersonates, women abandon their husbands. They are said (by an inner voice) to flock from everywhere, avidly in pursuit of a messianic fulfillment incommensurate with everyday life. Flaubert brings onstage, among others, the Queen of Sheba, laden with gifts as on her biblical procession to Jerusalem, who has rebuffed Solomon for Anthony — the bearded patriarch for the childlike monk. Anthony abominates his fantasies, but again hears a subversive voice. Speaking from inside Flaubert's hero, "Logic," flanked by the Seven Deadly Sins, argues that truly spiritual men must throw off all restraints. Ritual, law, and taboo are nothing but the institutional edifice of sclerotic priests. Only outside this prison house can the soul expand. "Let it throw open its dormer!" Logic exhorts. "May it gulp air from every wind, may it fly south, north, to dawns, to setting suns, for Samaria is no longer accursed and Babylonia itself has been dried of its tears."

But forbidden thoughts are not entertained with impunity. Penitence shadows lust all through the work, and references to blades, to the sharp edge of unconsummated desire and self-mutilation abound. During her striptease, Mary promises Anthony that she will hold him tight and "plunge" him into her eyes, "which glisten like the steel of swords." In a later scene, Anthony swoons with pleasure as he flagellates himself, and the devil presents three wantons, one of whom — a tall, svelte blonde named Adultery, whose black shawl spirals around her bare flesh like the coils of a Cretan snake goddess — asks:

> Have pensive adolescents related their dreams to you? The wife gets out of bed and gropes down the dark corridor barefoot. Her chemise, damp with perspiration, makes the night lamp flicker. She smiles as she shivers, and the finger she puts over her mouth indicates that she is afraid the child stirring in its crib will wake up.
>
> I delight in the play of hidden perfidies.

If the crib, nighttime, and the dark corridor were not obvious enough links to Flaubert's recurrent dream of himself as an infant surrounded by bloody, half-flayed faces with knives between their teeth, Adultery is seen carrying a mask in one hand and a dagger in the other. Daggers in the hand appear again during the procession of heresies, when a sect practicing self-castration chants: "Here [the knife] is what destroys concupiscence root and branch. Here [a crown of thorns] is what attacks pride at its seat. Thanks to the blade, temptation does not imperil us; beneath the crown of thorns, desire will find itself needled into submission." Often invoked by Flaubert in times of exasperation (though not in this work) was the great and prolific Alexandrian exegete Origen, who, according to Eusebius, castrated himself.

After colluding in the saint's ambivalent pleasures, Death and Desire are pried apart and, like Artemis and Aphrodite quarreling over Euripides' Hippolytus, made to compete for Anthony in an eloquent debate that signals the finale of *La Tentation*. Torn between his life force and a death wish, he favors each in turn. Death (La Mort) and Lust (La Luxure) are stubborn litigators, each unwilling to surrender the last word. When Death boasts of its invincibility, Lust, personified as a woman, evokes her pervasive influence in human affairs.

A magistrate caresses thoughts of adultery beneath his red gown; the scholar interrupts his meditation to find a whore; a fisherman tallying the haul swoons with pleasure as his dory pitches to and fro; a priest can hardly keep from trembling when he fills the Communion cup and hustles the penitent object of his lust into the cool sacristy; an Egyptian embalmer, latching the door to the lower chambers, flings himself on the corpse of a beautiful young noblewoman. You, Death, when at night you prowl through silent cities and look at bawdy houses, have you heard kissing lips or seen tangled limbs or sniffed damp sheets? Puffing under their nightcaps, spouses couple; the excited virgin wakes from her dream, the son of the house does a midnight flit, the stable boy mounts the chambermaid, the bitch in her doghouse answers the male barking at a street corner. Veiled matrons, old men on crutches, long-haired adolescents, princes in their palaces, wayfarers in the desert, slaves at the mill, courtesans in the theater — they're all mine, they live through me, they brood over me. From the inquisitiveness of childhood to the prurience of dotage, from the lover who has palpitations when his beloved brushes against him on a walk in the meadow to the man who needs dismemberments and whips for his pleasure, I possess beings, willy-nilly. Do they resist me? Do they avoid me? Who can conquer me? It is not always you.

And she lays hold of her coveted trophy. Whereupon Death pulls her back by her dress, tearing it from hip to heel, and, rattling his bones, says to Anthony: "Come here! I am repose, I am peace, oblivion, the absolute." Lust rejoins: "Come! I am truth, joy, eternal movement, life itself."

No sooner does Lust disrobe and throw her head back to shower Anthony with petals from her crown of roses than Death throws off his shroud. Bewilderment overcomes the Hamletian saint:

> But what if you were both lying? What, oh Death, if there were other ills beyond you? And what, oh Lust, if I were to find in your delights an even more somber void, an even more enveloping despair? On the faces of the dying I have seen something like a smile of immortality, and on the lips of the living so much sorrow that I know not which of you is the more sepulchral.

There follow fifty pages in which once-powerful pagan gods, with much lamentation, prove the devil's point that all divinities perish, and that there is no foundation for the normative or the orthodox. In the end, Anthony still clings to his own god, uttering desperate appeals to Jesus, which go unanswered. No one has the last word, even if the devil has the last laugh, and his derisive "Hah! Hah! Hah!" concludes *La Tentation*.

Triumphantly, Flaubert recorded the devil's guffaw on September 12, 1849. Several months earlier he had still been despairing over the work and no doubt wondering whether another seizure would leave him speechless once and for all. But aphasia was not his problem, as Maxime Du Camp and Louis Bouilhet could attest, much to their own despair, when Flaubert summoned them to Croisset for an exposé of the work he had kept under wraps since beginning it in May 1848. The reading took thirty-two hours (almost as long as it had taken the copyist to transcribe it), during which the auditors reserved comment, at Flaubert's behest. They listened eight hours a day for four days, from noon to four and from eight to midnight. Caroline Flaubert unsuccessfully tried to ferret out their thoughts. "[After the Sphinx, the Chimera, Montanus, Apollonius of Tyana, the Gnostics, the Manicheans], we concentrated harder yet on the Marcionites, the Carpocratians, the Paternians, the Nicolaitens, the gymnosophists, Pluto, Diana, Hercules, and even the god Crepitus," Du Camp recalled in his *Souvenirs*. "It was futile! We didn't understand, we couldn't guess where he wanted to take us, and in fact he led us nowhere." Du Camp never recognized the bones of Flaubert's essential argument, but after four days of captivity at Croisset, even a mind more intuitive than his and more hospitable to romantic expatiation might have been numbed by the swarming pageant of historical, mythological, and allegorical figures. Yearning for some — for any — dramatic convergence and rolling their eyes at the sadistic monologist, who would periodically exclaim, "Hold on, you'll see!" Du Camp and Bouilhet waited in vain. When their turn came, they avenged themselves

with criticisms not unlike those that would be leveled at *L'Éducation sentimentale* in its final version two decades later. "You proceed by expansion,"
Du Camp told a shaken Flaubert. "One subject sweeps you toward another,
and you end up forgetting your point of departure. A droplet becomes a
torrent, the torrent a river, the river a lake, the lake an ocean, the ocean a
tidal wave. You drown, you drown your characters, you drown the event,
you drown the reader, and your work is drowned." Flaubert presented a defense of self-quotation, rereading favorite passages and challenging his critics not to declare them beautiful but — as Du Camp remembers it —
finally conceded the point that many were otiose. Du Camp would later
take credit for advice that made Flaubert the disciplined author of *Madame
Bovary*. When Flaubert wondered how someone in whose nature it was to
exaggerate — to breed five-legged sheep, as it were — could change his literary habits, Du Camp allegedly said: "You must choose a subject in which
lyricism would be so unseemly as to compel you to abstain from it." Balzac
pointed the way, not Hugo. "Choose a down-to-earth subject, one of those
incidents in which bourgeois life abounds, something like *La Cousine Bette*
or *La Cousin Pons*, and force yourself to treat it . . . without those divaga-
tions that, albeit beautiful in themselves, hinder the development of your
scheme."

In Du Camp's account, Bouilhet, who overcame his shyness where literature was concerned, spoke even more bluntly. He thought that as a product of misguided industry, the manuscript was best burned. Flaubert
wouldn't burn it, being a hoarder rather than an arsonist, for all his paeans
to Nero, and Saint Anthony became another revenant in his life.

WITH DECEMBER 12, 1849, in the offing, Flaubert might have felt un-
speakably depressed had he not looked forward to the prospect of leaving his
fiasco behind him, departing France, and celebrating his twenty-eighth
birthday in Egypt. For this he could thank Du Camp, with whom he would
embark on a voyage destined to last many months and to lead them across
the Ottoman Empire, from Cairo to Damascus. Du Camp had been organizing it since his brief tour of Algeria and Morocco during the fall of 1848,
but Flaubert, a hostage to his unpredictable illness and to his mother's anxiety, did not figure in his plans until February 1849, when events took a surprising turn. The two were together in Rouen that month. Exasperated by
the prospect of an adventure he couldn't share, Flaubert voiced anger and
despair. A family dinner at the Hôtel-Dieu offered Du Camp the occasion
to broach the matter with Achille, who agreed that travel in sun-drenched
lands might be excellent therapy for his brother and urged this opinion on
Mme Flaubert. After Dr Jules Cloquet seconded him, she gave her grudging
approval, though the world must have seemed more dangerous than ever in

the midst of a cholera epidemic that claimed sixteen thousand Parisians between March and May 1849. "I need fresh air, in the fullest sense," Flaubert wrote to Ernest Chevalier on May 6. "My mother, seeing how indispensable it is to me, consented, and that's that. The thought of giving her cause for worry fills me with anguish, but I believe it's the lesser of two evils . . . Anyway, the matter is settled, and I've been long in settling it. The struggle with my passion for the open road has taken so much out of me that I've grown quite thin. Right now I'm beginning to make preparations."

Struggling not only with his "passion for the open road" but, according to Du Camp, with the fear that his resplendent visions of the Orient might shatter against reality, he overcame his ambivalence long enough to seek a factotum for the voyage. His uncle's gamekeeper in Nogent, Leclerc, who had impressed him by recently killing a wolf on Parain property, came to mind, and for fifteen hundred francs Leclerc did indeed make himself available.* His duties, wrote Flaubert, would include pitching tents, cleaning weapons, feeding horses, brushing boots, plucking game, cooking meals. Etiquette would require him to wear native dress, to abstain from alcohol, and to stay away from women whose sexual favors might bring down upon them all the wrath of a jealous Muslim. "Furthermore," he added, "he will ride horseback alongside us, he will be armed to the teeth and hunt game of every description: red pheasants, lions, crocodiles. On the road this will be his chief employment . . . In short, he will participate fully in our way of life." Maxime Du Camp, meanwhile, induced government officials of his acquaintance to provide credentials that would command respect at French consulates throughout the Levant. Flaubert's improbable mission was to keep his ears pricked at ports and caravanseries for information in which French chambers of commerce might be vitally interested.

By the first or second week of October, their equipment — saddles, camera tent, and vessels specially designed for the chemicals needed to produce calotypes — had been dispatched to Marseille in two crates weighing twelve hundred pounds. No expense was spared, and the voyage was to cost Mme Flaubert dearly.† She bade her son farewell at Nogent, where François Parain and the Bonenfants would help her bear the pain of separation, though not before insinuating that she planned to take her meals alone, as befit a *mater dolorosa*. The incessant barking of a neighborhood dog in Nogent that day seemed a bad omen. So did the company of four nuns and a priest, who boarded the Paris train with him. He debated with himself even then whether

---

*Flaubert's uncle had made him a present of the wolfskin. Ultimately, Du Camp's Corsican valet, Sassetti, was chosen over Leclerc.

†Some twenty-eight thousand francs. (What a customs officer, or some other minor government functionary, might expect to earn over thirteen or fourteen years.)

to leave for Egypt. Brother Achille could not offer their mother much comfort in his absence. Relations between Mme Flaubert and her older son were troubled. She never visited the Hôtel-Dieu, which harbored too many memories, and was thought to have held Achille responsible for botching Achille-Cléophas's operation. Nor did it help matters that she found her daughter-in-law, Julie, gross of body and mind.

Until his last day in Paris, Flaubert, stricken with guilt, sent his mother one letter after another, insisting that she summon him home from abroad if his absence proved unendurable, and protesting his love. The departure had been scheduled for October 29. There were last-minute social calls paid to Jules Cloquet, James Pradier, and Pradier's estranged wife. Hamard, during a brief encounter that confirmed Flaubert's view of him as unhinged and sottish, wondered why anyone should embark on a long voyage to the Levant when so much Molière was being performed in Paris. Flaubert attended a peformance of Meyerbeer's *Le Prophète,* which he found "magnificent." Maurice Schlesinger (now residing year-round in Élisa's hometown, Vernon) bade him farewell after a jovial reunion at the Opéra-Comique. With Bouilhet he viewed the Louvre's collection of Assyrian bas-reliefs and visited his favorite brothel near the Palais-Royal, la Mère Guérin's, for a final currying by French whores. On the evening of October 28, Flaubert, Du Camp, Louis de Cormenin, and Bouilhet dined at the Palais-Royal in a private room of the Trois Frères Provençaux, with Maxime's acquaintance Théophile Gautier, whom Flaubert was meeting for the first time. "Yesterday Gautier voiced an opinion, which has always been mine, that 'only bourgeois croak,' in other words, that 'when one has something in one's gut, one doesn't die before one has shat it out,'" he wrote as a kind of consoling valediction to his mother. What he had in his gut ensured that he would come back alive from the Orient.*

---

*This conflation of birth and defecation in an image reassuring his mother that he would not abandon her as her husband had but would come back to rescue her from grief, and promising her the gift of a future work, calls to mind what Freud had to say about gifts, incest, and rescue. In "A Special Kind of Object Choice Made by Men," for example: "The idea of 'rescue' actually has a significance and history of its own and is an independent derivative of the mother-complex, or, more correctly, of the parental complex. When a child hears that he owes his life to his parents, that his mother gave him life, the feelings of tenderness in him mingle with the longing to be big and independent himself, so that he forms the wish to repay the parents for this gift and requite it by one of a like value . . . He then weaves a phantasy of saving his father's life on some dangerous occasion by which he becomes quits with him, and this phantasy is commonly enough displaced on to the Emperor, the King, or any other great man . . . So far as it applies to the father, the attitude of defiance in the 'saving' phantasy far out-weighs the tender feeling in it, the latter being usually directed towards the mother. The mother gave the child his life and it is not easy to replace this unique gift with anything of equal value. By a slight change of meaning, which is easily effected in the unconscious . . . rescuing the mother acquires the significance of giving

The conventional itinerary of tourists traveling from Paris to Marseille had not changed since April 1845, when the Flauberts accompanied their daughter, Flaubert's sister Caroline, on her honeymoon, though more of it could now be negotiated by rail. On October 29, 1849, Maxime Du Camp and Flaubert boarded a diligence bound for Dijon and Chalon.

---

her a child or making one for her — one like himself, of course. The departure from the original meaning of the idea of 'saving life' is not too great, the change in sense is no arbitrary one. The mother gave him his own life and he gives her back another life, that of a child as like himself as possible."

XI

~~~~~~

Voyage en Orient: Egypt

QUITE APART from archeological revelations such as Paul-Émile Botta's account of the dig at Nineveh in a four-volume work that excited great interest when it appeared between 1846 and 1850, voyages through the Near East had yielded an abundance of travel literature by midcentury. The book that most often compelled young literati to undertake what became a rite of passage and that defined the itinerary known as *le voyage en Orient* was François-René de Chateaubriand's *Itinéraire de Paris à Jérusalem*. Published in 1811, five years after his perilous loop around the rim of the Ottoman Empire by land and sea, it was the work of a classically educated Catholic pilgrim rather than a casual adventurer. Enraptured by antiquity, Chateaubriand glossed over the present as he moved from ruin to ruin, drinking at the founts of his cultural being. The word *souvenir* recurs again and again, as if his destination were the memory pregnant enough to reprieve him from temporality itself — the still point in a hugely turbulent life. "Why is it," he asked, a century before Proust, "that the memories one prefers to all others are those nearest one's cradle?" Mindful of the illustrious Spartans celebrated by Plutarch, he walked along the river Eurotas in a trance of moral elevation. Approaching Athens on the Sacred Way, he felt as rapturous as Gibbon had in Rome when touring the debris of the Forum "with a lofty step." Glimpsing Mount Carmel from aboard a ship crowded with Orthodox Greeks who all suddenly fell silent, he knelt in awe of the "land of prodigies," where human history had taken a messianic turn. "I was about to set foot on those shores which had been visited by Godefroy de Bouillon, Raimond de Saint-Gilles, Tancred the Brave, Richard Lion-Heart, Saint Louis . . . How would I, an obscure pilgrim, tread soil consecrated by so many famous predecessors?" The aliens in this transcendent Orient were the impious and uncouth who inhabited it. An Ottoman governor sitting cross-legged on a carpet spread before the Temple of Athena with his back to Phidias's masterpiece and looking vacantly out upon the Saronic Gulf focused Chateaubriand's contempt. En route from Rosetta to Cairo he noted that the ancient Greek historian Diodorus Siculus, could he revisit Egypt, would be astonished to find loutish riffraff in the valley once farmed by a people of legendary wisdom and industry. In their stark gratuitousness, the Pyramids stood as reproaches from beyond to a world that valued utility above moral grandeur. So said the Breton aristocrat.

When another aristocrat, Alphonse de Lamartine, headed east twenty-six years later, *Itinéraire* was his vade mecum, and echoes of it are to be heard throughout the book he published in 1835, *Voyage en Orient*. Chateaubriand, crossing the Peloponnese, had bedded down one night under a laurel tree, wrapped himself in his coat, and fallen asleep with eyes fixed on the constellation of Leda's Swan directly overhead; and just so did Lamartine lie down one afternoon under a fig tree in Galilee, wrap himself in his coat, and gaze fixedly upon a pastoral scene unchanged since Abraham's day. To Chateaubriand, Mount Carmel had loomed on the horizon like a gigantic omphalos, true center at last. Lamartine, who had been similarly tossed about in the maelstrom of French politics, found on that summit bits and pieces of himself assembling into a coherent identity. In these epiphanies, the Oriental netherworld restored a lost fullness of being. Chateaubriand felt it on the road to Eleusis and Lamartine in the hill country north of Jerusalem. "All of those mountains have a name and a role in the first stories we ever heard on our mother's knee," wrote Lamartine. "I know that Judea is out there, with its prodigies and its ruins, that Jerusalem lies there just behind one of those mammiform hillocks, that I'm separated from it by a few hours of marching, that one of the most yearned-for destinations of my long voyage lies at hand. I exulted in this thought as man exults whenever he nears one of the goals . . . that some passion has assigned him."

Fulfillment of a sensual kind was another goal associated with the Orient, and young men bent upon finding themselves in the landscape of their cultural patrimony may have been just as determined to lose themselves on a foreign shore innocent of the mores girdling bourgeois Europe. To be sure, Paris and Rouen did not lack women who would expertly comply with the sexual fantasies of well-heeled patrons. But mythology demanded its due. The Platonic ideal of Roman antiquity to which Chateaubriand paid homage in his mystical assertion that "human nature preserves its superiority in Rome, though superior men may no longer reside there" had a carnal analogue in the vision that inspired Ingre's *Odalisque and Slave*, Delacroix's *Death of Sardanapalus*, and countless other images of Algerian dancers, harem bathers, Jewish femmes fatales, and dark Nubians. Travelers bound for holy sites might also without fear of contradiction hope to find a premoral world where the Oriental woman, vested with erotic prestige greater than any French courtesan's, figured as a primitive divinity (perhaps even Chateaubriand himself, for what is to be made of his bedtime enchantment with Leda's Swan?). "Mademoiselle Malagamba possesses the kind of beauty hardly ever seen outside the Orient: the form as perfect as in Greek statuary, the Southern soul naturally revealing itself in glances . . . and in a directness of expression that characterizes primitive peoples" was how Lamartine extolled a young Levantine woman. "When these traits unite in the visage of a blossoming adolescent, when a dreaminess and waywardness of thought suffuse the eyes with soft, liquid light . . . , when her suppleness expresses the voluptuous sensibility of a being born to love, . . . beauty is complete and the sight of it fully satisfies one's senses." It helped to contemplate all this in brilliant sunlight, which intensified the sensual pleasure of northern Europeans used to wet, overcast skies. So, for that matter, did primary colors. Under Louis-Philippe, black had established itself as the mark of respectability in male dress and an exsanguinated pallor as the complexion that best suited upper-class ladies, some of whom drank vinegar to bring it about. Enveloped in a tea cozy of petticoats, the woman who valued her social status would appear slightly *souffrante;* "rude health," like boldly dyed cloth, was seen as vulgar.

HIS MOTHER'S shriek at the moment of his departure was still ringing in Flaubert's ears when the train from Lyons reached Marseille on All Saints' Day, even if momentarily drowned out over the weekend by crooners at *cafés chantants* and the hubbub of dockside entertainment. Regrets pursued him onto the steamship, where Maxime Du Camp would remember him standing at the port rail gazing sadly shoreward. In Marseille he visited once again the boarded-up Hôtel de Richelieu to commemorate his night with Eulalie. Letters, the first of many, went off to Mme Flaubert (*pauvre chérie, pauvre vieille adorée,* were his usual endearments) asserting that fevers and brigands were no longer the scourges of Egypt. For this he invoked the authority of his new acquaintance Antoine Barthélemy Clot — or Clot-Bey — a French physician who had expatriated himself in 1825, organized military hospitals under Muhammad Ali, the all-powerful pasha of Egypt, and after the latter's death in August 1849 returned to France (laden with antiquities, which he eventually bestowed upon the state). Clot-Bey, he said, would reassure her in person, when he visited his friend Jules Cloquet during the winter, that a tour of Egypt was as safe as a jaunt through the Norman countryside.

First they had a sea to cross, and by the time their packet, *Le Nil* of les Messageries françaises, docked at Malta on November 7, Du Camp had no quarrel with the Murray guide's claim that for "living, civility, cleanliness, and a greater certainty of arriving at the promised time," English steamers outclassed French. *Le Nil*, in his description, was a large tub without equilibrium or power. He and Sassetti, the valet, lay seasick in their cabins throughout this leg of the journey. Flaubert, on the other hand, who vomited only once, as he proudly reported to his mother, struck romantic poses and charmed fellow passengers. "There are strolls on deck, dinners at the captain's table, watches on the bridge . . . where I pretend I'm Jean Bart, a cigar in my mouth and my cap tilted over one ear," he wrote, the reference being to a French naval hero of the seventeenth century. "I absorb nautical lessons, inform myself of maneuvers, etc. Evenings I contemplate the waves and I dream, enveloped in my pelisse like Childe Harold . . . I'm not sure what it is, but I'm adored on board. I show so greatly to advantage on the watery element that these gentlemen have taken to calling me papa Flaubert." After twenty-four hours in the Valetta harbor, *Le Nil* weighed anchor for Egypt under an ominous sky. A storm soon caught them. Fear gripped everyone, and with the ship creaking in heavy swells and its rudder slapping against the transom, the captain finally turned back. Flaubert availed himself of this contretemps to tour Malta before he and Du Camp reboarded *Le Nil* for a second attempt at crossing to Africa. Again the packet labored through heavy seas, with groans that terrified the French gilders, silverers, and wig makers being brought over by Muhammad Ali's feckless successor, Abbas Pasha. Flaubert, who roped himself to the stern rail, gloated. Far from begging absolution of the great, almighty Protector, after the manner of Panurge, his favorite coward, he wished he could clamber up the mast like a Viking. "I feel a mariner's instincts; saltwater foams in my heart." Still, landfall thrilled him as much as it did his faint-hearted companions when *Le Nil* approached Alexandria on November 15 after five days at sea. Perched in the rigging, he caught sight of the white dome of Muhammad Ali's seraglio from several miles out and, amid the importunities of porters, boatmen, donkey boys, and camel drivers, set foot on what felt like sacred soil. "An apprehensive and solemn impression when I felt my foot press against the soil of Egypt," he noted in a diary.

An interpreter, or dragoman, named Joseph Brichetti, who was to become their constant companion, met the three at dockside and shepherded them and their voluminous baggage through a Turkish slum to the European quarter, where foreigners generally set up at the Hôtel d'Orient. Dazzled by all they had seen on disembarking — camels, pelicans, beggars, bearded stevedores in ballooning breeches, merchants in brilliantly vivid turbans, women wearing veils pulled over one eye and supported from the forehead by a string of beads, black girls a mere glimpse of whom aroused the insatiably lustful Du Camp — they took their dinners at the table d'hôte but explored Arab neighborhoods at every opportunity. It was his good fortune, Flaubert informed his mother, to witness a torchlight procession noisily celebrating the circumcision of a sheik's son. During their brief sojourn he and Du Camp mingled with tourists at the catacombs, at the Saracenic round tower, at Pompey's Pillar (a third-century column honoring Diocletian), and at the two red granite obelisks nicknamed "Cleopatra's Needles" that had been transported from Heliopolis to command the harbor opposite Pharos island. Unlike other tourists, they came encumbered with heavy photographic apparatus, Du Camp's mission being to record for the Académie des Inscriptions as many as possible of the Egyptian antiquities surveyed by Champollion two decades earlier and Lepsius in the 1840s. French officials who retained sufficient influence under the new pasha had an armed bodyguard accompany Du Camp lest curious spectators interfere.

Their first sight of desert came after three days, during an excursion east along the Mediterranean coast to Rosetta. Between surf and dunes they rode horseback in donkey tracks, halting at Aboukir, where the wreckage of the Napoleonic fleet destroyed by Nelson in 1798 still lay strewn over the beach, and occasionally testing their rifles on unfortunate cormorants, much to the delight of urchins who scrambled after them. Seen against a crepuscular sky, the palm trees and white minarets of Rosetta made Flaubert, always sensitive to dying light, catch his breath. "There is crimson melting above us, then red clouds of a deeper hue shaped like gigantic fish bones (for one moment the whole sky reddened, while the sand turned dark as ink)," he wrote. "To our left, in the direction of Rosetta and the sea, swatches of delicate blue appear. Our mounted shadows jogging side by side are huge. They keep pace with us, like a vanguard of obelisks." Rosetta's gate swung open for two young "Francs" in Turkish dress important enough to be carrying a recommendation from Suleiman Pasha to the governor, Hussein Pasha.* As a putative *chargé de mission,* Flaubert felt obliged for the first and only serious time to visit a factory during the two days spent in Rosetta, but he did so with clenched teeth, industry being the very contradiction of what he sought in Egypt. Otherwise, his diary re-

---

Francs was the term for Europeans generally, used since the Crusades.

volves around his alimentary canal. Together with fleas and barking dogs, stomach trouble from overindulgence in sweet, flaky galettes kept him up at night, even if it did not compromise his appetite the next day, when the Turkish ritual of drinking strong coffee and smoking a pipe before lunch made him impatient to be fed. The main meal at Hussein's headquarters comprised thirty dishes (served by almost as many valets), only one of which he found delectable, the pastry. "I tasted Arab bread, uncooked dough in wide patties. I was careful not to betray my distaste." Turkish cuisine soon had a conspicuous effect on his anatomy. The young man who had departed Rouen slender returned well padded, more recognizably the Flaubert of surviving photographs. Just two weeks after his gastronomic disappointment, a tailor would be summoned in Cairo for urgent alterations. However, Maxime Du Camp, skin and bones to begin with, was no less gaunt at the end.

Outside Rosetta they beheld the Nile flowing to the sea between sandy hummocks and green rice paddies a thousand miles north of the Second Cataract in Upper Egypt, toward which their thoughts would turn before long. But the heart didn't leap. A one-masted vessel, alone on the great river, somehow saddened Flaubert, who saw "the true Orient" — or perhaps himself — in its slow, lulling progress. "One already has presentiments of a pitiless immensity in the midst of which one is quite lost." (He had used the same image to describe the provincial law student adrift in Paris.) Nearby they came across the white, cubelike tombstone of a holy man, a "santon," whose guardian insisted that they sample fruit from the Egyptian sycamore spreading overhead. Flaubert's colic erupted again.

In letters to a mother mortally worried about epilepsy, trachoma, bubonic plague, and cholera as well as the more benign afflictions, Flaubert, who would apparently suffer at least one seizure during the trip, feigned perfect health and assured her that Du Camp was scrutinizing him with excessive vigilance.*

Wrapped in flannel to insulate themselves against the chill, they retraced their steps along a shoreline pounded by rough surf and after eleven hours reached Alexandria, where logistical arrangements needed to be made for the next leg of their journey, a boat trip south across the delta to Cairo. Of-

---

*Diseases of the eye were especially feared. The Murray handbook includes this observation: "The streets of the bazaars are kept cool by watering, which, though it may contribute to that end, has a very prejudicial effect, the vapour constantly arising from the damp ground in a climate like Egypt tending greatly to cause or increase opthalmia; and to this may, in a great degree, be attributed the startling fact that one out of six among the inhabitants of Cairo is either blind or has some complaint in the eyes." In *Notes on a Journey from Cornhill to Grand Cairo*, William Thackeray noted: "Everybody has big rolling eyes here (unless, to be sure, they lose one of ophthalmia)."

ficials encountered the previous week at consular parties and in personal audiences proved helpful. The foreign minister under Abbas Pasha, an Egyptian of Armenian descent named Artin-Bey, gave them a firman, or letter, commanding the hospitality of governors all the way south. Useful advice came from a Frenchman in charge of Egyptian fortifications, General Gallis-Bey. Above all there was the aforementioned Suleiman Pasha, another general, who took it upon himself — charmed as he obviously was by his tall young compatriots — to have their half ton of baggage transported to his residence in Cairo. The name Suleiman Pasha had opened the gate to Rosetta and would presently open many doors. Proud of this sponsorship, Flaubert called him "the most powerful man in Egypt, the conqueror of Nezib, the terror of Constantinople."

Indeed, no one knew more about the Egypt they were about to explore (or for that matter the European balance of power as it played out in the Ottoman Empire) than this rough-hewn veteran of the Napoleonic Wars whose handlebar mustache resembled the horns of an African water buffalo. Born Joseph Sève at Lyons in 1788, he had entered the Sixth Regiment of Hussards in 1807 after service as a seventeen-year-old gunner on the *Bucentaure* at Trafalgar and had fought in battles all over Europe — at Borodino, Pordenone, Leipzig, Munich, Brienne, Waterloo — before retiring during the Restoration with a dozen scars from saber cuts to illustrate his citations for bravery. Civilian life did not suit him. The ex-lieutenant couldn't move from casque to cushion. Utterly devoid of ordinary social graces, he failed in business and fled to Egypt, a land seldom visited by peace. There, identifying himself as Colonel Sève, he impressed Muhammad Ali, the Ottoman sultan's contentious viceroy. Ali recognized a kindred soul. Both had risen from the ranks, and neither was troubled by considerations of humanity or principle or by love of Turks. An Albanian from Thrace, Ali had acquired prominence during the anarchy that beset Egypt after Napoleon's expulsion, when native beys or princes marshaled the formerly powerful warrior caste called Mamelukes against the sultan. As leader of a fierce Albanian contingent numerous enough to tilt the balance, he had sided now with one party, now with the other, and in 1805 found himself elected pasha (governor) by Cairo-based sheiks looking to install a firm, autocratic government. The sultan ratified this fait accompli, whereupon England, which hitched its interests to Mameluke rule, landed troops near Rosetta. An ambush by Muhammad Ali's army decimated them in the narrow streets Flaubert would traverse forty-two years later, and they beat a desperate retreat, leaving behind several hundred slain whose heads were planted on stakes along the main street of Cairo's European quarter. Beys and Mamelukes had already suffered a similar fate in Cairo itself; the pasha's guard slaughtered a regiment that had broken through the gates of the capital, decapitated them, stuffed their heads with straw, and sent this tribute to Constantinople. Survivors sought refuge in Nubia to the south, but flight did not avail them as Ali cast his net farther and farther afield. By 1820 he had conquered Nubia and in Arabia had driven the Wahabis from Jidda and Mecca. Certain that military success would pit him against his overlord in Constantinople, he determined to rebuild the Egyptian army along European lines. At this point Joseph Sève appeared opportunely and before long had founded an infantry school at Muhammad's behest, with himself the chief instructor. Once Sève converted to Islam, which he did in 1821, dignities rained upon him. First an aga, then a bey and a pasha, Suleiman (or Soliman), as he now styled himself, commanded troops at Acre, Jaffa, and Jerusalem when Muhammad and the sultan finally clashed. Promoted generalissimo, he fought at Nezib in Syria in 1839, routing the Turks in a battle that might have given Muhammad Ali the entire Ottoman Empire had European powers (excluding France) not intervened to confine his authority to Egypt and the Sudan. With enemies subdued inside and out, Muhammad reigned until his death in 1848, while Suleiman rested on his laurels in a palace on the Nile. There, heedless of the Muslim prohibition against alcohol, he welcomed eminences and eminences-to-be from France. Flaubert found him agreeably blunt. "He couldn't have been more cordial," he wrote. "He will give us orders for all the governors in Egypt; he has offered us his carriage . . . It was he who arranged the hire of horses for our Rosetta excursion . . . He has apparently taken a shine to us." His cordiality would become more opulent in Cairo, the next destination of the two men after eleven days in Alexandria.

On the trip to Cairo down the Mahmudija canal, Flaubert was diverted by fellow passengers: a Belgian diplomat, a bibulous Arab engineer, an Englishwoman who with her inane chatter and green eyeshade reminded him of a sick parrot. When he reached the Nile at Atfeh, however, he had eyes and ears only for the wide yellow river. Determined not to miss anything of his first night on it, he dressed warmly, set up a camp bed alongside Maxime's on deck, and fell asleep under a starry sky, thinking about Cleopatra. He awoke to a view of sycamores in green meadows and desert and pyramids. On November 26 they anchored at Bulak, Cairo's port, where the voyage ended in much the same pandemonium that had greeted them at Alexandria. Norman Macleod, Queen Victoria's chaplain, described it best on his return from the Holy Land. "In vehemence of gesticulation, in genuine power of lip and lung to fill the air with a roar of incomprehensible exclamations," he wrote, "nothing on earth, so long as the human body retains its present arrangement of muscles and nervous vitality, can surpass the Egyptians and their language." They took rooms at the Hôtel d'Orient but soon moved to a hotel run by countrymen named Bouvaret and

Brochier — the former a retired actor and an inspiration for the names of two Flaubert characters — who decorated their establishment with Gavarni lithographs torn out of *Charivari*. Here they would spend some weeks, not wanting to continue their journey until they had witnessed the spectacle of pilgrims returning from Mecca through Cairo's Victory Gate.

Besides Suleiman Pasha, other distinguished French expatriates stood ready to greet Du Camp and Flaubert in Cairo, many of them engineers pledged to the scientific-industrial utopia envisioned by Claude-Henri de Saint-Simon, whose foremost disciple, Prosper Enfantin, had visited Egypt fifteen years earlier at Muhammad Ali's invitation with an entourage of forty technocrats and visions of a trench across the isthmus of Suez. Among them was Louis-Maurice-Adolphe de Bellefonds, commonly known as Linant-Bey. Recommendations from Clot-Bey opened Linant's door on the rue Hab el Hadid to the two young voyagers, and inside they found a Breton engineer responsible for dams, irrigation systems, and the surveys on which Ferdinand de Lesseps would presently depend in launching the Suez Canal project. Another remarkable engineer was Charles Lambert-Bey, who had embraced Saint-Simonianism with the zeal of a catechumen after graduating from the École Polytechnique first in his class. The diversion dam several miles downstream from Cairo attested to his technical brilliance, but the intensity of his philosophical conversation would also be remembered by his friends. Maxime Du Camp later waxed hyperbolic over Lambert, "the most intelligent man" he had ever met. "Never have I encountered a more capacious brain, a more nourishing and indulgent spirit, greater comprehension of other people's feelings, a more constant aspiration toward the good," he wrote. "His language, which was highly figurative yet precise, elucidated the most obscure problems — by this I mean his spoken language, for he simply couldn't write; as soon as he tried to, his thoughts would cloud and his sentences tangle. The two or three virtually incomprehensible opuscules he published on metaphysical questions are reminiscent of the Apocalypse. For him, Saint-Simonianism was a religion, and Enfantin . . . the greatest apostle since Saint Paul." Ill disposed to the arguments of evangelical utilitarians, Flaubert nonetheless appreciated their company. Evenings with the French beys were welcome, if only for their expert advice on traveling in Upper Egypt. Nor did he disdain ceremonies that required formal dress at the consulate and at Abbas Pasha's palace. "Our time at present is nibbled away by visits to make and to receive," he informed his mother. So long as French newspapers could be acquired, they read them.

Every day, the three pyramids southwest of Cairo beckoned, and on December 7, Du Camp; Flaubert; their valet, Sassetti; and Joseph Brichetti set out with provisions sufficient for a week in the desert, hiring boatmen to ferry them and their horses south as far as Gizeh. There the foursome could plainly see the Pyramid of Cheops, situated 130 feet above the flood plain. It kept looming larger as they splashed toward it across streams and swamps, and finally Flaubert, unable to restrain himself, galloped ahead with shouts that excited the Arabs round about. Bathed in sunlight under a blue sky, the pyramids and the Sphinx overwhelmed him. "At first glance, these astonishing hulks don't appear all that immense, since there is no other structure nearby to provide a comparative measure," he wrote to his brother. "But the longer you remain beside them and especially as you begin climbing them, they grow prodigious and seem so likely to crush you that you hunch your shoulders. As for the view on high, . . . I don't think anyone, even Chateaubriand, can do it justice. You wrap yourself in your coat, since the cold air bites, and you shut your mouth; that's all." The "chaffering and bargaining" that spoiled Thackeray's visit to the Pyramids hardly fazed him.

He and Du Camp climbed Cheops, which covers eight acres and rises almost five hundred feet, before dawn, after a wakeful night of listening to Arabs sing around the campfire and hearing jackals howl. Totally exhausted by their laborious ascent — Flaubert described the pyramid blocks he scaled as being chest high — they rested at the summit until daybreak, when fog lifted from meadows striped with irrigation canals and Cairo's minarets came into view. Later they crawled up and down the steep, smooth passages to the pharaoh's empty burial chamber, greeting Englishmen crawling in the opposite direction. Death, as they discovered, was the landscape. What no Murray or Baedeker mentioned, besides the multitude of fleas, from which not even a sandstorm offered relief, were the human bones and bits of mummy cloth that littered the area. Femurs served as sticks. The great pyramid itself stood on a rocky platform with hollowed-out tombs (in which at least one contemporary, Eliot Warburton, who had improvidently come without a tent, spent his nights undaunted by the "charnel chill" and bat guana and scorpions). At Saqqara, where locals peddled yellowed human skulls, Flaubert would acquire a mummified ibis in its earthen pot.

While Du Camp performed the onerous photographic maneuvers that were eventually to yield a celebrated album of calotypes, Flaubert smoked his chibouk, gazed dreamily at the purple and pink of western sands, and rejoiced in a sensation that felt rather like breathing salt air at Trouville after a winter in Rouen. "I adore the desert," he exclaimed to his mother. "The air is dry, and as bracing as the sea breeze, a comparison that seems all the more apt when one tastes salt on one's tongue after licking one's mustache . . . We've spent the last six nights under a tent, living with Bedouins, . . . eating turtledoves [they had bagged], drinking buffalo milk . . . Our horses were specially shod for travel over sand: we've ridden them at full speed, we've absolutely devoured space in all-out charges." This expedition took them south as far as Saqqara, through the rubble of Egypt's ancient capital at Memphis (where they bivouacked under palms on ground covered with lilac bushes, near a fallen colossus), and past smallish pyramids built during the Old and Middle Kingdoms at the edge of the valley. For supplying all their needs, Joseph the dragoman, whom Flaubert described as a fifty-year-old Arabized Italian, proved indispensable. Usually phlegmatic, he sprang to life when haggling with merchants over mere piasters on behalf of the two Frenchmen. Excellent meals emerged from a primitive camp kitchen, all of the food to Flaubert's taste and most of it detrimental to his waistline. Joseph was practicality itself. He knew shortcuts, he fixed bridles, he spoke to camels, he made temple rubbings. Sassetti became the subaltern's subaltern.

Although Flaubert still abided by a dictum he came to consider entirely spurious, that Europeans commanded more respect in Western dress, he now often sported a red tarboosh on his shaven skull and in the desert wore a djellaba.* Thus was he attired as he rode back toward Cairo on December 12, his twenty-eighth birthday, up the west bank of the Nile, bent forward under a hot sun. Doubts weighing on him may have contributed to his poor posture. "When I think . . . about my future," he wrote to Mme Flaubert a few weeks later, "(this seldom happens, for I think about nothing at all, contrary to what one should be thinking — lofty thoughts — in the presence of ruins), when I ask myself: 'What shall I do upon my return? What shall I write? What shall I be worth at that point? Where should I live? What line should I follow?' etc., etc., I am filled with doubt and irresolution. All through life I have arranged not to look myself straight in the face, and I'll die an octogenarian without being any the wiser on that score or having produced a work that shows what stuff I'm made of. Is *Saint Antoine* good or bad? I often wonder. Who is mistaken, I or the others?" He recoiled from this self-examination and asserted that such questions didn't really fluster him, since he was living like a plant imbued with sunlight, air, and color. But in ways that may not always have been conscious, doubt — exacerbated by the daily companionship of the friend who had declared *La Tentation* to be a fiasco — nagged him throughout the voyage.

Cairo was a powerful distraction from his quandary. He loved picturesqueness, even when he found it in the maze of alleys that stank to a higher heaven than Rouen's infamous rue de l'Eau de Robec. Had he not already made the bear his personal totem, he might have chosen the camel.

*His head was shaven except for one lock of hair, which Muslims left for the convenience of the angel of resurrection, to pull them out of their graves.

He was enchanted by urban dromedaries queuing up like ruminant taxi-cabs; thrusting their cleft snouts into food stalls; grunting under bundles of faggots as wide as the narrow streets; or, in the case of a proud male from the royal stable with feathers on its head, strands of bells around its neck, and mirrors on its kneepads, transporting a gorgeous tent. Overhead, on the domes and green-tiled minarets that bristled across the skyline, storks fought vultures for the most advantageous roosts, while below merchants jostled one another for business in the multitude of covered bazaars, each dedi-cated to a particular class of commodities or affiliated with a particular eth-nic group. There were the Turkish, the Persian, the Frank bazaars. Walking down cluttered, shadowy corridors, Flaubert visited the bazaar of per-fumers, of jewelers, and of Arab slave traders, where he was invited to have a young Nubian woman disrobe for him. His dragoman, he wrote, could gladly spend half a day haggling over some trivial item. Children chanting rhythmically toted baskets of bricks and mortar for turbaned masons in blue chemises and worn red slippers. Cairenes shivered that winter, but on warm days water carriers tinkling brass saucers to announce their arrival circulated with jars of sherbet. Monkeys made irresistible beggars, and, indeed, beg-gars abounded, the most conspicuous being wild-eyed dervishes naked ex-cept for sheepskin rags tied around their loins. Escorted by a slave or a eunuch, harem wives rode around on donkeys, bundled in white linen that according to one observer gave them the appearance of bloodless banshees. Street life provided endless entertainment. Among the singular spectacles Du Camp and Flaubert witnessed during these months was a ceremony held every year to celebrate the miracle of a holy man who en route to Mecca had ridden horseback over glass jars without breaking any. For Dauseh, as the ceremony was called, Cairenes thronged the main square, milling around expectantly. Then palace eunuchs cleared a path in which dervishes proceeded to stretch out crosswise like tightly wedged cobble-stones. "The sharif in a green turban and green gloves, with a black beard, waited until the human roadbed had been made quite level before walking his Arabian horse over it," Flaubert noted in his diary. "By a rough count there were about three hundred on the ground. The horse bridled, stamp-ing its hind legs no doubt, and once it passed, the crowd swarmed behind it. We couldn't tell whether anyone was killed or wounded."* Beside him, pressed against a wall, stood some Walachian whores whom he and Du Camp had already met at a masked ball in the brothel district.

Even before he sighted Muhammad Ali's seraglio at Alexandria on No-vember 15, Flaubert may have decided that he had booked passage to the id of human continents, that Egypt must in every possible way comport with

---

*Any who died were deemed to have suffered for the evil in them.

Pliny's proverb *Semper aliquid novi Africam adferre*, "Something new is always coming out of Africa." It's as if he had dropped anchor in a dreamworld innocent of moral constraints upon the imagination and of the taxonomical partitions segregating high culture from low in Europe. There were primitive extravaganzas at every turn: obscene buffoons, conjunctions as hallucinatory as the Sphinx, scenes out of the Marquis de Sade. Camels hopped like turkeys and balanced like swans. Women veiled their faces but bared their breasts. Holy men enjoyed unrestricted sexual license. In bathhouses, heterosexual men acquiesced in the erotic manipulations of the masseur, or "al-Moukaissati." Feeling compelled to flout bourgeois taboo where promiscuity reigned supreme, Flaubert, the bourgeois *malgré lui,* had himself manipulated with as much repugnance as pleasure and ambivalently watched boys dancing for an audience of pederasts.* Nothing would have satisfied him more, he told Louis Bouilhet, than befriending a eunuch. To Bouilhet he related the following anecdotes:

> One day, to amuse the crowd, Muhammad Ali's jester seized a woman in a Cairo bazaar, laid her out at the doorsill of a shop, and raped her right there while the unruffled merchant went on smoking his pipe.
>
> On the road from Cairo to Choubra, some time ago, a weird young man had himself buggered in public by an ape . . .
>
> Recently a holy man, a marabout, died. He was an idiot and reputed to be a God-struck saint. All the Muslim women would regularly pay him visits and pollute him, so that he finally died of exhaustion. It was a perpetual debauch from morning till night . . .
>
> *Quid dicis* about the following incident. Some time ago, an ascetic priest was strolling through the streets of Cairo naked save for a skullcap and a codpiece. To pee he'd lift the latter and barren women wanting a child would hunch under the spout of urine and rub themselves with it.

As he had done in Bastia some years earlier, Flaubert visited a madhouse attached to the mosque of the sultan Kalaoon, indulging his lifelong fascination with lunatic performances (in this case, an old woman seductively baring her pendulous breasts, another woman banging a dance rhythm on

---

*Of the bathhouse experience he wrote: "Traveling for our instruction and charged with a government mission, we considered it our duty to yield to this mode of ejaculation." The pederastic dance took place "in a nasty little cabaret [where] three or four kids between twelve and sixteen wiggled around a violin and mandolin. Inept costumes, no verve, complete absence of art . . . As for pederasty, forget it . . . These little gentlemen are reserved for pashas. We couldn't possibly feel them up. Which I'm not in the least sorry about, because their dance disgusted me. In this, as in so many things of this world, one must content oneself with remaining at the threshold."

her pewter chamber pot, a black eunuch from the royal household kissing his visitors' hands and feet). There was much more to satisfy morbid curiosity at a hospital for syphilitic Mamelukes, where the worst-off displayed their cankered anuses at a doctor's command, and just outside the city near an ancient aqueduct, where Cairenes dumped dead camels, donkeys, and horses. Du Camp and Flaubert went there for target practice on kites and lammergeiers circling overhead but ended up shooting the wild dogs that made this gruesome suburb their home and roamed through Cairo in packs. "They sleep in holes dug in the sand," Flaubert noted. "Some have muzzles purple with dry, sun-caked blood . . . Striped hoopoes peck out earthworms from between the ribs of carrion — the flat, strong ribs of a camel look like palm branches bent and stripped of leaves . . . There is a stench of flesh rotting in the heat of a midday sun, the gnawing and belching of dogs." Sex could be had for a pittance with army whores who loitered under the arches of the aqueduct. Flaubert gave his three donkey drivers a piaster and a half each to pleasure themselves.

Flaubert's and Du Camp's curiosity was not all morbid or erotic. Through Lambert-Bey they made the acquaintance of a gentleman named Kalil Efendi, who had studied in Paris as Muhammad Ali's protégé but had fallen from grace on his return and embraced Protestantism in order to receive a small retainer from the British consulate. Kalil spent four hours a day with the two travelers at their hotel, discoursing on Muslim birth rites and funeral ceremonies, on circumcision and marriage, on pilgrimages and the afterlife. When they finally departed Cairo, his pupils would know as much about Islamic prescriptions as many cultivated Arabs and would possess copious notes dictated by their mentor. A visit to El Azhar, the tenth-century mosque that had become the chief theological seminary of the Islamic world, complemented this program, although Flaubert's favorite among religious institutions was undoubtedly the convent of dervishes, where an ecstatic monk rolling on the ground with a dagger in hand, to the booming accompaniment of darbukkah drums, gave him gooseflesh. Monkton Milnes's friend Eliot Warburton might well boast that "the firm, vehement will of the Norman must ever ultimately prevail over the wild enthusiasm and unconnected activity of the Oriental," but Flaubert the traveler, if not Flaubert the apostle of formal beauty and discipline in art, was one Norman happy to submit.

After seven weeks in Cairo, he eagerly anticipated his journey up the Nile. Du Camp, who had thus far had little success with paper normally employed for prints in the Talbot calotype process, learned about Blanquart-Evrard's innovations from an amateur photographer en route to India, the baron Alexis de Lagrange, and was now awaiting the delivery of material.

On January 18 the two Frenchmen hired Ibraham Farghali, a young *reis*, or boat captain, to transport them to upper Nubia on a cangia (also known as a dahabiah) by oar, sail, and tow rope if need be. Flaubert assured his mother, who saw him poised at the edge of an abyss, that his living conditions would be excellent. The boat was blue and its cabin divided into three compartments. "The first contains two small couches placed opposite each other. Then there is a room large enough for two movable plank beds, and beyond that are recessed areas with an English watercloset to one side, and a wardrobe to the other. Sassetti will sleep in the third room, which will also serve as storage space. As for our dragoman, he'll sleep on deck. Since we've known him, the man has never taken off his clothes." If all went well, he continued, they would spend three months on the Nile, pushing as far south as favorable winds allowed before turning around to sail slowly north with the current.

On February 5 Du Camp and Flaubert dined with Suleiman Pasha at his riverside villa. The next day, after billiards, they boarded the cangia in a freshening breeze. By nightfall they had lost sight of Cairo's citadel perched on a spur of the Mokattam hills.

THE FAVORABLE wind proved deceptive. It died before sunset, forcing the crew of twelve to tow their fifty-foot vessel several miles upriver and moor it at an island near Saqqara. With slack sails, they made slow progress that week, but worse befell them when the wind picked up again, for now it blew adversely, from the desert, and whipped sand through everything, obscuring the sun, spinning boats around, ruining stores of food. To reprovision themselves, the voyagers went ashore at the earliest opportunity with rifles and, as Flaubert proudly reported, brought back no fewer than fifty-four pigeons and turtledoves. "We're living on what we bag!" he exclaimed. "Imagine, me a hunter!" The monotonous diet was to be supplemented with oranges, dates, figs, and Joseph's dense pastry. Flaubert, who lamented the fact that he had already acquired an ignoble cushion of fat, gave his mother all details of his daily fare.

Monotonous in an equally pleasurable way was the landscape they were free to contemplate from beneath an awning on deck once good weather returned. Looking toward the Mokattam cliffs, which undulated at a distance of more than three miles, the eye crossed the wide riverbank, then an endless strip of vegetation, palms, and sand. To the west it encountered wild bean fields, date trees, avenues of thorny acacia, and tracts planted with millet and sugarcane before sighting the Libyan Desert. Identical mud-brick villages half-hidden in palm groves recurred hour after hour, from El Minya to Asyūt to Thebes. Between them rose skeletal columns, small, ransacked pyramids, and other debris of pharaonic antiquity. The Nile itself was more various. It abounded in huge, whiskered fish. Snakes twined along the banks, crocodiles began to appear beyond Manfalūṭ, and spits of sand for which the *reis,* squatting up front, kept careful watch, often quivered with wild fowl. Flaubert slept soundly, despite the strong coffee consumed and bowls of Latakia tobacco smoked all day long at regular intervals. Joseph Brichetti prepared meals over a brick-faced charcoal pit built near the bow. When the crew, who slept in apertures between deck planks, were not furling and unfurling lateen sails, they entertained one another with lewd capers. Their cotton breeches and long blue shirts hung loose enough for dances of the most unabashed obscenity, Flaubert gleefully informed his mother. A better linguist than the dragoman would have been needed to help him savor their ribald songs, but there were also musicians onboard, and the shrill, reedy notes of a Nile flute piercing the vastness of the African night needed no translation. Much time was spent with books. Du Camp immersed himself in the Bible while Flaubert, forever working at his Greek, read Homer's *Odyssey* or sat in a golden doze, with thoughts coming and going like motes in a sunbeam.

The plan to travel south as quickly as possible did not prevent them from exploring ruins, although they would do so in much greater earnest on the return voyage. Inspired by Herodotus, Pliny, and Strabo, who all mention a large, brackish lake west of Beni Suef, they marched across Faiyūm province through marshland, to Birket Quārūn, or Lake Moeris, "the lake of the horn," where mounds, crude brick pyramids, stone walls, and an underground funerary complex called "the Labyrinth" testified to the importance that the fertile oasis had enjoyed in 1800 BC, during the Middle Kingdom. Flaubert never got as far as the Labyrinth, but he made amends ten days later at Siut, or Asyūt, a port town famous for catacombs cut in the limestone of surrounding hills. High above the Nile, which wound its silvery way across the green savannah, he entered the Deir el-Gabrawi, a necropolis arranged in tiers to hold tombs at different elevations. A vaulted portal introduced lofty halls and small chambers with hieroglyphic inscriptions, wolf mummies, sculptures of men bringing offerings and women smelling the lotus flower.* The slope outside these catacombs, where individual graves had been scooped out of rock, looked like a gigantic rabbit warren. An English traveler described the scene as ghoulish: "I stood a long time among these solitary tombs, surrounded by fragments of the mummied dead . . . Man and child, they were three thousand years old, and scat-

---

*In antiquity, this settlement, whose inhabitants revered a wolf deity, was named Lycopolis by the Greeks.

tered in such variety and profusion, that one might fancy the hillside to be the workshop of Frankenstein 'in extensive business.'"

When their crew moored the cangia, Flaubert and Du Camp usually went ashore in search of live bodies rather than dead ones, and to judge by Flaubert's notes, no whorehouse between Cairo and Nubia was so low that they wouldn't stoop to enter it. On all fours they crawled into a thatched hut no more than chest high for sex with a *belle laide* whose furniture consisted of a straw mat and a dim lamp. (Foreigners being easy prey under such circumstances, a boatman stood guard outside to ward off thugs.) On hands and knees they crawled again at Siut, to lie in an even smaller, dimmer hut beside the Nile with a fifteen-year-old girl whom Flaubert found clever and winsome. "Feline gestures sorting through the piasters in the palm of my hand. She showed me her rings, her bracelet, her earrings." The farther south they traveled, the duskier their partners. Nothing would have amused the Garçon more than an English tourist's reflection that the malodorous castor oil with which scantily clad Nubian women protected themselves against the sun also afforded the traveler protection against "unconscious fascinations." The Frenchmen's libidos weren't so fastidious. Nor did a need for privacy inhibit them. They apparently had sexual intercourse in one another's company, and even with Joseph the interpreter present.

Erotic pleasure of a different order awaited them some thirty miles beyond Thebes. An *almah,* or courtesan and dancer, of great repute named Kuchiuk-Hanem made her home at Esna (Isna), to which many dancers formerly domiciled in a village outside Cairo had been banished by the mullahs. As soon as they stepped ashore, Kuchiuk-Hanem's confidante, accompanied by a pet sheep dappled with yellow henna, fetched the pair and led them to a spacious house of assignation. Kuchiuk-Hanem, who greeted them from the top of an outside staircase, instantly joined the elite roster of charismatic women who subjugated Flaubert at first glance. With the deep blue sky as a backdrop, she looked splendid in her striped pink silk trousers and gauzy purple blouse — a wide-shouldered, bosomy, coffee-colored Syrian with wiry black hair and kohl-lined eyes. "She wore a tarboosh surmounted by a convex gold disk in the middle of which was set an imitation emerald," wrote Flaubert, who registered every detail of her person, noting, for example, how the blue tassel of her hat "caressed" her shoulder and that one incisor needed dental care. "Her bracelet is made of two thin gold rods twisted around each other, her necklace consists of three strands of hollow gold beads. Her earrings are gold disks, convex, with gold beads around the rim. A line of blue writing is tattooed on her right arm." He especially admired her beautiful kneecaps.

In a letter to Bouilhet, Flaubert reckoned that during the next seventeen hours he had survived five rounds of copulation and three more of oral sex, with coffee breaks and longer intermissions for meals, a tour of the Ptolemaic temple dedicated appropriately to a ram-headed god, and dances performed by four *almah*s. Two rebec players bowed away stridently, and when Kuchiuk shed her clothes to dance, they covered their eyes, one with a black veil, the other with a flap of his turban. Flaubert describes the woman in one dance repeatedly thrusting out a hip to effect a seductive limp. Another dance featured a cup of coffee placed on the floor and Kuchiuk picking it up with her teeth after wiggling to her knees, playing castanets all the while. Yet another, the Wasp Dance, involved much leaping about. Overcome by exhaustion, they all finally surrendered to sleep. Du Camp, who had had a lesser share of Kuchiuk, slept on the divan upstairs. Flaubert lay beside her in her ground-floor bedroom. "I covered her with my fur pelisse and she fell asleep, holding hands with me," he confided to Bouilhet.

> I hardly slept a wink. I was plunged into a state of intense reverie, which is why I stayed. I gazed at this beautiful creature snoring as she slept with her head pressed against my arm, and . . . I thought about her, her dance, her voice singing songs I couldn't understand, about my brothel nights in Paris, a slew of old memories. At 3 a.m. I got up to piss in the street. Stars were shining in a very high, clear sky. She woke up, fetched a pot of coals, spent an hour next to it on her haunches warming herself, then went back to sleep. As for the orgasms, they were good. The third one was especially keen, and the last one soulful. We exchanged many tender words and toward the end hugged each other sadly and amorously.

At one point he nodded off, almost against his will, with one finger twisted around her necklace, as if to prevent her from deserting him while he slept, in a gesture that put him in mind of Judith and Holofernes. "How sweet it would be for one's pride," he noted in his journal, "if one could be certain, after one's departure, of leaving behind a memory — that she would remember you more vividly than the others, that you would remain in her heart." Taking her head along, in a sexual reversal of the biblical story, might have been tantamount to leaving a memory of himself behind. The head would have constituted another trophy demonstrating his manhood.*

Time to brood about losing and remembering was what there was most

---

*Of course, the image of Judith and Holofernes may also be construed as an occult reference to his fear of punishment (castration, syphilis), especially as Kuchiuk had encouraged him to sleep elsewhere for fear that his presence might attract the ruffians who ubiquitously preyed on foreigners. After gratifying himself without reserve, the interloper would have his head handed to him. These ruffians, called Arnaouts, of Balkan origin, were nominally soldiers in the service of the pasha but in fact a piratical tribe who robbed, raped, and killed with virtual impunity.

of beyond Esna, where the river began to narrow and the hills to enclose it — where trees grew taller, the population sparser, and Flaubert's beard fuller. Cangias with British tourists were seen returning from Wadi Halfa. Others ferried loads of elephant tusks and black slave women, some with suckling infants, whose boat the two Frenchmen were able to board for a closer look. Du Camp occupied himself with photography but lamented an absence of wildlife on which to gratify his penchant for random slaughter. The Coptic cenobites who a week earlier had leaped into the Nile from rocks below their monastery and, heedless of crocodiles, swum around the hull begging, "Carita! Per l'amor di Dio! Christiani! Elieeson!" would have been a welcome diversion. Saddened by the separation from Kuchiuk, Flaubert was more profoundly distressed by a letter received at Beni Suef from his mother, imploring him to think about his future. "You think up all kinds of ways of tormenting yourself, poor old dear," he wrote.

What do you mean when you assert that I must have a position, "a modest position," as you put it? . . . I challenge you to tell me what kind it would be, in what field of endeavor? Can you honestly say that there is any position for which I am qualified? You add: "one that wouldn't take up too much of your time and prevent you from doing other things." You delude yourself! It's what Bouilhet had in mind when he embarked on medical studies, and what I myself thought when I went for law and almost died of stifled rage in the process. When one does something one must do it wholeheartedly and well. A mongrel existence in which one sells tallow all day long and composes verse after dinner is made for the banal intelligence equally hopeless in harness or saddled, being unfit to pull a plow or leap over a ditch.

A position, he continued, made sense for the money with which it rewarded its holder or the honor it vouchsafed him, and neither applied to her idiosyncratic son. Whatever he could do would be viewed by the world as unprofitable, and honor concerned only his own eyes.

My vanity is such that I don't feel honored by anything: an office, however high it may be — and that's not what you're asking for anyway — will never afford me the satisfaction my self-esteem confers when I have put the finishing touch on something well done . . . Weigh all my arguments, don't cudgel your brains over an empty idea. Is there any position in which I would be closer to you? More yours? The main thing, at least in part, is making life as tolerable as possible, isn't it?

But questions as to whether he could justify himself on his own terms floated upriver with him like a dark cloud in the blue African sky. To

Bouilhet, who knew as well as Mme Flaubert how much Gustave needed a responsive audience, he confided that his intelligence had dimmed calamitously, that the poor reception his closest friends had given *Saint Antoine* was still hurting. What would he do when he came home? "Shall I publish? Shall I not publish? What will I write? Will I write at all?" Ideas that took shape one moment dissolved the next. He was briefly inspired by the story Herodotus tells in *Euterpe* of Pharaoh Menkaure violating his daughter, who then commits suicide, and burying her in a gilded coffin. Nothing came of it. It was best, Flaubert wrote, just to be an eye while traveling, whatever risks eyes ran in Egypt.

No doubt the need for an audience and a thinly veiled fear that his absence would cost him a place in the memories of delinquent correspondents unless he coaxed or shamed them — that there was not enough substance in him to prevent his falling out of the world — helped make Flaubert a brilliant, generous, prolific letter writer. In his symbiotic relationship with Mme Flaubert, separation portended death, his and hers alike, unless letters bridged the silence. Bound up with his concern for her welfare and the reassurances he continually sent her that no Homeric calamity had befallen her Odysseus was a need to imagine her poring over a map of Egypt and following him step by step. "Do you know that we are nearly fourteen hundred leagues apart?" he wrote on March 24. "How far that must appear to you, poor old thing, and how long that map of Egypt must seem! As for me, it takes me some time to calculate the distance, for I feel that you are near me, and that if I wished I could see you anytime." Describing his antics onboard the cangia and Du Camp's previously unsuspected talent for mimicry, he explained: "I include all this nonsense, dear mother, because it is *you*. I know that you take pleasure in every aspect of our domestic life. You can see how cheerfully we pass the time of day. Still, I'll be glad to reach Cairo and collect your letters." Nearness did not suffice. He wanted to dwell inside her, inalienably, just as others, even beyond the grave, lived inside him.* Alfred Le Poittevin, for example, was so much on his mind that he felt himself to be his dead friend's *porte-parole*. "At Thebes, [Alfred] was constantly with me," he told Mme Flaubert. "If the Saint-Simonian system [which embraced certain mystical beliefs] is true, he may have been traveling at my side. In that case, it wasn't I thinking about him,

---

*In December 1850, when news of Ernest Chevalier's marriage prompted Mme Flaubert to ask her younger son whether he had plans for getting married, Flaubert answered as follows. "No, no, when I think about your good face, so sad and so loving, about the pleasure I have living with you, so full of serenity and serious charm, I feel that I shall never love another woman as I love you. Come, fear not, you shall have no rival. The urges or the fantasies of a moment shall never take the place of what abides, well secured, within a triple sanctuary."

it was he thinking through me. And there are the others too. I can't admire anything in silence. I need shouts, gestures, expansion. I have to bawl, smash chairs, in a word, enlist others to amplify my pleasure."

It is certain that the distance Du Camp gained from Flaubert with his camera did more to make cohabitation agreeable for eighteen months than mandatory duets of enthusiasm. Photographing temples, tombs, and colossi postponed conflicts brewing under the surface. The photographer didn't require the dreamer's help; nor did the slightly myopic dreamer, who used a lorgnon to focus precisely but otherwise contented himself with impressionistic views, want silver nitrate or albumen on his hands. They often spent hours apart, and in 1853 when Du Camp produced his account of the voyage, he left Flaubert behind: written in the form of letters to Théophile Gautier, *Le Nil* makes no mention of a fellow traveler.

Nevertheless, Du Camp sailed alone only once, in March 1850, when their boat ascended the First Cataract over rapids as encumbered with wrecked hulls as Polyphemus's cave with the bones of human victims. From a prudent vantage point on the rocky heights, Flaubert watched one hundred Nubians pull a rope lashed to the mainmast and a white-bearded master shout cadences above the turbulent water like a demonic coxswain, while Du Camp braced himself in the cangia. They rejoined each other for the last stretch of their southern voyage, to Wadi Halfa, on a green river flowing between the rough, pockmarked cliffs of the Libyan range and magnificent groves of date palms, maples, and blackberry bushes. Scavengers crowded around a crocodile carcass. Lining the shore were the low mud huts of dark-skinned Arabs called Ababda, who wore little more than loincloths. High above them loomed dilapidated fortresses built by the Mamelukes. Near Wadi Halfa they hired donkeys to carry them three hours up a mountain at the threshold of Upper Nubia, from whose summit they commanded the western desert. Much closer was the unnavigable river cascading through a jumble of massive red granite rocks. At this Second Cataract, they ruefully turned around for the voyage back to Cairo.

Sails were reefed, stronger oarlocks fitted, and north they rowed, with Du Camp's unwieldy camera near to hand. Before they revisited the First Cataract, he had already photographed temples carved into a mountain at Abu Simbel during the reign of Ramses II and monuments on the sacred island of Philae. "We stop at every ruin," Flaubert wrote to his mother on April 22, 1850.

The cangia docks, we clamber off, there is always some temple poking out of the sand like a disgorged skeleton. Ibis- and crocodile-headed gods are painted on walls white with the droppings of birds of prey perched in stone niches. We thread our way around the columns, raising old dust with our palm staffs. Swatches of brilliant blue sky show through breaches in the ruins . . . A flock of black sheep often grazes nearby, its shepherd a naked boy nimble as a monkey, with cat eyes, ivory teeth, a silver ring in his right ear, and stripes cut into each cheek. At other times, poor Arab women dressed in rags and necklaces surround Joseph, who want to sell him chickens, or who harvest dung with their bare hands to fertilize their meager plots. One marvelous thing [in Egypt] is the light, which makes everything gleam. Walking through city streets, we are dazzled, as by whirling colors at an immense costume ball. In this transparent atmosphere the white, yellow, and sky blue of garments stand out with a rawness of tone that would make any painter swoon . . . I try to wrap my mind around it all. I would like to imagine something, but I don't know what.

The most glorious ruins, those of Thebes at Luxor and Karnac, where they arrived in late April on a moonlit night, held them fast until mid-May. The French engineers who had spent eighteen months harnessing the obelisk destined for a Parisian afterlife on the place de la Concorde had served compatriots well by building themselves a residence with bricks, broken shafts, stones (some of which bore hieroglyphic inscriptions), and other architectural debris. There Du Camp and Flaubert camped among sand-swept statues and columns, in a ghost town seemingly scaled to a race of Brobdingnagian giants. What fascinated them in Luxor quite as much as the sanctuary erected by Amenhotep III was the imbrication of pharaonic grandeur with Arab rusticity. The great colonnaded square had become a yard for strutting chickens. An outer wall painted with scenes from Egyptian mythology served as a buttress for the local mosque and another wall as backing for a granary. Mud-brick huts had sprung up around the temple pylons and the remaining red granite obelisk, pigeons roosted in sculpted lotus leaves and on colossi buried up to their chests in sand and rubbish.

With a hectic sense of mission that Flaubert usually found daunting, Du Camp photographed the monument from every angle and in due course lugged his heavy apparatus through fields of meadow grass and along a road lined with sphinxlike rams to the temple complex at Karnac, where columns seventy feet tall overshadowed those at Luxor. After several days the two left the French hut for a temple chamber just outside Karnac's central colonnade, or Hypostyle Hall, preferring total immersion in Egyptian antiquity to the relative comfort of a house or houseboat, though the move exposed them to stinging beetles, scorpions, and horned asps. At night they smoked narghiles amid images of Amon, Mut, and Khonsu and watched salamanders darting around a pond once used for ritual ablutions. "In whichever direction one turns to contemplate these vestiges of a civilization long gone, one is astonished and confounded by such marvels," wrote Du Camp in his memoirs. "Look west . . . and one sees Thutmose's promenade, obelisks that seem to have found a pedestal in the granite sanctuary, jumbles of stone blocks, the inner face of immense pylons, and beyond it all the Libyan mountains pocked with funerary grottos. Look east and one surveys overturned towers, skewed gates, the architraves of lateral naves, the capitals of the great colonnnade and reeds growing on open tracts. To the north rise the disjointed, tilting, proud columns . . . of the Hypostyle Hall surmounted by stone beams . . . Look south and admire propylea in the midst of graceful palms, the triumphal gate of Ptolemy Euergetes, the temple of Khonsu."

What appears to have impressed Flaubert most powerfully was the necropolis opposite Karnac known as the Valley of the Kings, where he and Du Camp pitched their tents during their last days at Thebes. Here royalty and priests had had themselves buried not in pyramids but in sepulchres with painted rooms and pumiced corridors, which ran deep into the mountainside. Descending stairs cut through the rock, the two men came upon a phantasmagoria of multiheaded serpents walking on human feet, of monkeys hauling ships, of green-faced kings sporting inhuman appendages, of hieroglyphic eulogies. "The paintings are as fresh as if they had not yet dried and might come off under one's thumb," wrote Flaubert, who toured the valley on horse, kicking the scree that littered this most barren of landscapes.

He and Du Camp departed Thebes on May 13, sad but exhilarated as well by the prospect of a side trip across the desert to Quseir on the Red Sea. Three days later, drivers were hired and provisions bought at Keneh (Quena today). Early in the morning of May 18 they mounted camels for the hundred-mile transit, which would pass through ancient Roman posts strung along the Russafa Road. Their heads swaddled in thick cotton kaffiyehs to defend against a sun so intense that the pommels of their saddles couldn't be grasped with bare hands, they were not long in discovering the wonders and pitfalls of desert life. The Nile had only just disappeared from view when a hot wind, or khamsin, suddenly gusted from the south, enveloping them in clouds of reddish sand. Rotting lamb and chicken became food for vultures, and stolen provisions made a jackal's feast. An exception to the rule of Arab hospitality was the village of La Dijta, in which Ababda goat herders refused them milk. Frightened by something or other, Joseph Brichetti's skittish camel loped off one night with loud, gurgling roars and might have inspired a general mutiny had the dragoman not retrieved it straightaway. Another camel stepped into the underground gallery of kangaroo rats, a common menace, and broke its leg. Wells contained brackish water. Swollen feet suffered inside weatherworn boots. But nothing compared to the desert night under a star-spangled sky. And the mountain range they crossed through gorges opening toward the sea presented a spectacle of mineral beauty even grander than the welter of syenite at Wadi Halfa. Cliffs that push up from the gray, pebbly desert shone pink, red, dark green, violet, and bronze as sunlight hit facets of porphyry and feldspar. They formed the lustrous rampart between Egypt and a wide, sandy littoral where Flaubert and Du Camp, after three days in the wilderness, excitedly scanned the Red Sea from their dromedary perches. "To the right thirty or so tents, widely spaced, make dark splotches on the reddish sand," wrote Du Camp. "To the left, several shanties lean against the last little hump of hill country. A Negress balancing an iron pot on her head walks near us, and every gesture causes her long, withered breasts to swing back and forth. Dogs, bearded vultures, crows, squabble over refuse. There are fishing smacks nearby, some beached, others tied to stakes with filaments of palm." A crenellated bastion announced Quseir, once the principal port for goods arriving from India. Though now moribund, it still rated a French consular agent, who made the travelers welcome. They remained only long enough to recuperate, fill their lungs with sea air, reprovision themselves, and observe pilgrims gathering for the voyage to Jidda. Flaubert bathed in the warm sea with voluptuous pleasure. It was, he wrote, like "lolling on a thousand tits."

Their trek back across the desert took four days, during two of which Flaubert infuriated Du Camp by commemorating the tangy refreshment of lemon ices at Tortoni's in long, sadistic rhapsodies after a mishap had emptied their goatskin water bottles and left everyone desperately parched. Not until they reached the well of Bir-Ambert, twelve miles from Keneh, could humans and animals slake their thirst, whereupon Flaubert offered apologies. He dismounted at Keneh in poor health, with a fever that was to persist on his voyage down the Nile. It taxed what little energy he still had for temple touring and grotto groveling but only slightly compromised his appetite for pleasure in the arms of local *almah*s.

Even so, at Dendera he deserted his sickbed on the boat to visit a temple sacred to Hathor, goddess of love and festivity, and came away from it with an opinion less settled than that of his contemporary Florence Nightingale, who three months earlier had declared it to be "a vulgar, upstart temple, covered with acres of bas-reliefs which one has no desire to examine: built without faith or purpose." On June 12, on the stretch between Asyūt and Manfalūṭ, he summoned the courage to crawl through passages sticky with pitch for a look at the heaped-up mummies in a subterranean charnel house at Simoun. This macabre expedition, from which Du Camp harvested various body parts — gilded feet, a pair of withered, blackened hands, a head with long hair — left Flaubert wheezing, and the oppressive heat of June made matters much worse. Progress was slow, as strong, hot squalls forced the cangia to tack and sometimes sail back upriver.

By June 23 a full moon was silhouetting Gizeh's pyramids against the western sky. After almost five months on the Nile in a nether realm of ruins and graves, Flaubert returned to what Miss Nightingale called "the world of civilized wants and customs." But he did so with more dread than relief, for that world pointed him toward his vexed future. A long letter to Bouilhet, sent several weeks earlier from Asyūt, dwells on imponderables. "Neither of us is either established or committed," he wrote, stating a self-evident truth after making sardonic, obviously defensive allusions to the recent marriage of Achille Flaubert's brother-in-law. "As for myself, it won't happen. I've given the matter much thought since we parted, poor old chum. Seated at the prow of my cangia while watching water flow by, I mull over my past life and recall many forgotten things." Was he about to turn a new page or, on the contrary, enter a period of complete decadence? he asked. "From the past I meander dreamily into the future, and there I see nothing, nothing whatever. I am without plans, ideas, projects, and what's worse, without ambition. The eternal refrain 'What's the use?' runs through my mind and stands as a brazen barrier on every avenue I propose to follow in the land of hypotheses. Travel doesn't make one cheerful." Wondering whether the spectacle of ephemeral majesty, which evoked his father's example, had crippled his ego, he felt deficient in the physical strength needed for all the tasks associated with publishing. "Isn't it best to work for oneself alone, to do as one wishes according to one's own ideas, to admire oneself, to give oneself pleasure? Furthermore, the public is so stupid. And who reads anyway? And what do people read? And whom do they admire?" The Flaubert who twenty-five years later would discourage Émile Zola from publishing novels with prefaces that argue a literary creed before the court of public opinion was now rehearsing his aristocratic pose. Greatly to be envied, he went on, were the self-possessed authors of a bewigged age who stood comfortably on high heels, above the *profanum vulgus*. In bourgeois France, where the ground trembled underfoot, one couldn't keep one's balance. "On what can we lean? . . . What we lack is not style or that flexibility of bowing and fingering called talent. We have a large orchestra, a rich palette, varied resources. In the matter of ruses and gimmicks, we are far more sophisticated than our predecessors. No, what we lack is the intrinsic principle, the soul of the thing, the very idea of the subject." Like the handsome bachelor unable to plight his troth, this virtuoso orphaned of a score spoke to Flaubert's persistent fear of impotence. "We take notes, we embark on voyages, . . . we become scholars, archeologists, historians, doctors, cobblers and people of taste. But what about heart and verve and sap? We're good at licking cunt. But humping? Ejaculating in order to make a child?" In due time he would, while domiciled beside another river, construct an imperishable monument, but for the moment, Croisset appeared on the distant horizon not as a setting in which to create but as a hermetic refuge. Seated at his round desk with views of the linden path and of the Seine, he would, he said, expunge all thoughts of French patriotism, French literary criticism, a public presence, the entire world. Du Camp, who was frankly ambitious, found such talk obnoxious.

They reached Cairo on June 25. The bustle of the city, an accumulation of letters from his mother and Bouilhet, and the imminent prospect of sailing to Beirut combined to raise Flaubert's spirits. Sinai had once figured in their itinerary, but the land passage out of Egypt would have been too slow and costly. For the same reasons they eliminated Persia, where in any event uprisings by fanatical followers of the mystical "Bab" made travel hazardous. The course they now improvised would take them to Syria, Palestine, Cyprus, Crete, and Rhodes. Their plan was to ride on horseback from Smyrna to Constantinople via Troy, and to tour Greece methodically on their way home.

Flaubert could not have contemplated the next leg of his arduous journey without some trepidation. Sailing back to Alexandria from Cairo on the Mahmudija Canal, he suffered an epileptic seizure.

XII

◦———◦

Voyage en Orient: After Egypt

FLAUBERT AND Du Camp's ship, the *Alexandra,* embarked early in the morning of July 18. It docked two days later in Beirut's fog-shrouded harbor and released them to Ottoman authorities, who, for fear of cholera, escorted all passengers to a beautifully situated but rudimentary quarantine station, where they spent six or seven days. They spent another week in Beirut mingling with French expatriates, the most congenial of whom was a painter employed as director of the postal service, Camille Rogier. Rogier fed them, provided them with female company, and helped them make material arrangements for the trek to Jerusalem. When they set forth on or around August 1, their company numbered eight men and ten beasts. Du Camp, Flaubert, Joseph, and Sassetti rode horseback, a fifth horse bore fodder, the chief muleteer settled for a donkey, and his three subordinates walked beside four heavily laden mules.

This quaint party headed down the coastal plain toward Sidon, a well-watered region of carob trees and rosebays growing in thick clumps. On their left the Jebel Liban range walled off the early-morning sun, except where it shone through several deep clefts. They themselves rose before dawn and journeyed until sunset, with one long pause for a midday meal. The route frequently took them to higher ground, along stony paths, across wadis, and over bridges that inspired little confidence. "Syria is a beautiful land, as full of wildly various scenery and colors as Egypt is calm, monotonous, unmerciful to the eye in its sameness," Flaubert wrote to his mother. They relied on chance for shelter, laying down their pallets in caravansaries, in monasteries, in cafés, or, when no man-made roof presented itself, under trees.

Flaubert's pulse didn't quicken until they ascended the chalk cliff called Elephant Rock and beheld Tyre at the end of its long, low isthmus, sitting like a huge white gull in the lap of the sea. No longer visible from this height were the grotty streets so prevalent below, the desolate town squares, the refuse on beaches, the severed forefingers and gouged-out eyes of men who mutilated themselves to escape military conscription. Several miles farther along they would view Palestine from even greater heights as they ascended Mount Carmel, which rose out of a promontory at Haifa. Surveying the plain of Jezreel, scripturally identified with the field of Armageddon, Flaubert thought of Chateaubriand and Jesus Christ, in that order. "On the slope leading to the monastery, enormous olive trees, hollow inside: here begins the Holy Land." Unmentioned in his journal are the oaks, pines, myrtles, and wildflowers clothing Mount Carmel. Nor does he note anywhere that this luxuriant nature had absorbed the blood of monks slaughtered after Napoleon's retreat in 1799. A monastery recently built over an older one destroyed in 1821 struck him as being unworthy of its biblical panorama.

The difficult, steep descent took place without incident. After halts along the Mediterranean at Dora and Caesarea, they turned inland, moving briskly from Jaffa to Gazerel-Karoum, where the Plain of Sharon wrinkled into hill country. Tormented by fleas and excited by what lay ahead, Flaubert had sleepless nights, and when Jerusalem appeared at last he spurred his horse forward, as if to reassure himself that the fortified city with walls so unexpectedly intact was not a mirage.

Once they had passed through the Jaffa Gate and found their hotel, Flaubert and Du Camp contacted the French consul, Paul-Émile Botta, who would feed them well during their two-week sojourn. In Botta they encountered not only a distinguished archeologist who had brought the Louvre many of its Assyrian treasures but a Catholic obscurantist enamored of Joseph de Maistre and of almost no one else, whose endless jeremiads against modernity passed for conversation. The adaptable Du Camp lent him a sympathetic ear, as he had done with Lambert-Bey. "His angular gestures, his outbursts, his sunken eyes and barely dilated pupils, his herky-jerky walk across the consulate salon, his fingers nervously telling beads, the spasms of rage provoked by materialist creeds, the apologies earnestly tendered when he thought that a sharp word had given offense — altogether they made for a strikingly original personality." Flaubert, who may have met his match in the sport of misanthropic ranting, thought this fellow alumnus of Rouen's collegiate school quite mad and liable to throw a fit if his interlocutors contradicted him. Botta was a man of ruins in a city of ruins, he wrote, adding that the excellent tobacco and refreshments dispensed at the consulate persuaded him to hold his tongue. Still, the two were of one mind in their aversion to the technocratic utopia envisioned by Auguste Comte, whose *Cours de philosophie positive* Botta disgustedly thrust upon Flaubert, who must have known that Botta had studied medicine with Achille-Cléophas.

After all his anticipation, Jerusalem — which had virtually shut down for Ramadan, though merchants peddling crucifixes and rosaries drove a thriving trade — seemed to Flaubert lifeless, or lively only in sectarian squabbles over holy sites. The glorious *ville sainte* was, in his jaundiced view, part tourist trap and part midden. Rereading Gospel accounts of the Passion didn't help. Dung underfoot, streets choked with rubbish (except in the Armenian quarter), the reeking offal of an outdoor slaughterhouse, and decrepit buildings kept his historical imagination earthbound. It took wing briefly at the Temple Wall as he watched Jews genuflect in prayer early one morning. Otherwise, sadness prevailed, and sadness kindled resentment of profiteering ecclesiastics whose stock-in-trade was Christian martyrology. Beset by images of tortured saints, he ended up sympathizing with their torturers. "After my first visit to the Church of the Holy Sepulchre I returned to the hostel weary, exasperated through and through," he wrote. "I opened my copy of the Gospel according to Matthew and read the Sermon on the Mount with a blooming heart . . . Everything has been done to make the holy sites ridiculous. It's a whorish scene, rife with hypocrisy, avarice, imposture, impudence . . . I was unmoved and I blame these knaves." When a priest gave him a rose and blessed it, he felt doubly impoverished for receiving the flower with nothing of the warmth that would have suffused a pious soul. "No, I wasn't there as Voltaire or Mephistopheles or Sade. I was, on the contrary, very open-minded. I went there in good faith and my imagination was not stirred. I saw Capucin monks drinking demitasses with janisaries, and Brothers of the Holy Land snacking in the Garden of Olives." Emma Bovary's religious fantasies would similarly find no purchase in the vulgar world.

Carnal fantasies were another matter, and the saga of fornication richly embroidered in Egypt grew longer in the Near East, where opportunities abounded. "I am becoming a pig," he modestly wrote to Bouilhet from Damascus. Thanks to his *arbiter elegantiae*, Camille Rogier, Beirut had been an especially opportune venue. One morning there had been spent with five women recruited by the painter, whose genitalia, Flaubert assured

Bouilhet, were commensurate with his sexual appetite. "I screwed three women and came four times — three times before lunch and once after dessert. I even proposed intercourse with the pander, but since I had rebuffed her earlier, she rebuffed me in turn . . . The young Du Camp came only once. His member was still sore with the remnant of a chancre given him by a Walachian whore. The Turkish women found me revoltingly cynical for washing my crotch in public." Presently he, too, found himself afflicted with chancres, which did not dissuade him, even before they healed properly, from visiting brothels in Constantinople and Athens.

On August 23 he and Du Camp left Jerusalem for Damascus, after an excursion to Jericho, where they had slept under a full moon on the lofty terrace of a Turkish castle, and to the Dead Sea, where the fortresslike cliffs of Pisgah riveted them. They journeyed north by way of Janin, Cana, and Nazareth, traversing the Plain of Jezreel with an armed escort to fend off Bedouin marauders, one or more of whom had already attacked their party near Mar-Saba. In pools built for Ibraham Pasha on the shore of the Sea of Galilee, Flaubert found relief from the stomach ailment that had plagued him intermittently since his arrival in Egypt. He was eager to visit Tiberias; he soon discovered that it swarmed with Hasidic Jews in side curls who, to his dismay, all wore fur-trimmed hats despite the warm, gusty weather. Leaving Tiberias on August 29 at 3 a.m., Flaubert, Du Camp, Joseph, Sassetti, and three armed Turks made their way out of Palestine down lava slopes, across the Jordan Valley, and up the Golan Heights to a basalt tableland, with Mount Hermon's nacreous peak closing up the northern horizon. They rode single file, mostly at night, when the plateau cooled off, and often in such darkness that Flaubert relied for direction on the white rump of Du Camp's horse. Overcome by fatigue, he nodded as he jogged, but to no ill effect. There were verdant patches in which the men rested under Oriental medlars. For Flaubert, who had finally stopped brooding over the unsuccess of *La Tentation*, Syria might have been Cervantes's Spain. It all had the fragrance of tales from *Don Quixote*.

More reminiscent of Moorish Spain was what he found in Damascus, a white minareted city whose narrow streets angled around mobbed and colorful bazaars. An English traveler called them "a theater exhibiting out-of-the-way life and at every yard revealing . . . strange oriental groups" without reporting behavior he may have found unspeakable. Flaubert, on the contrary, dwelt on everything likely to shock fellow bourgeois and, as in Egypt, morbid spectacles no less than sexual ones. His journal describes barren wives petitioning God for children by kissing a holy man's genitals at the marketplace, in plain view. It also contains the description of a leprosarium situated outside Damascus, near a swamp alive with scavenger birds. "We enter a kind of small farm or farmyard in which we see lepers, five or six male and three or four female," he wrote.

> They're getting some fresh air. There's a woman whose nose is completely eaten away, as if by the pox, and a few encrusted sores on her face; another has a red face, flaming red . . . They all whine, shout, moan. The two sexes are together, with no distinction except for degrees of suffering. When they received our alms, they raised their arms to heaven and repeated, "Allah!" and called his blessings down upon us. I especially remember the noseless woman, the whistling gibberish that came out of her larynx.

In a letter from Flaubert, Bouilhet was presented with the image of a lipless, purulent leper whose fingers could easily be mistaken for green tatters seated beside a fountain under beautiful shade trees. The Lazarist brother who gave them their guided tour told them that he had surprised two students sodomizing each other in his monastery and noted the commonplaceness of homosexuality. "Great excess of men, but no women; women aren't wanted."

Flaubert shared with more conventional tourists an acquisitive interest in the wares that spilled out of market stalls. He purchased silks and, like a self-indulgent schoolboy, gorged on sweetmeats. Every evening a blond-bearded merchant accompanied by an Abyssinian eunuch brought antique objects to his hotel. "At the moment, Maxime, in a sleeveless tunic, is haggling over a bronze bowl," he wrote to his mother on September 9. "God, how Joseph bawls! The merchant is a pretty young man dressed in an embroidered turban and sky blue robe." The hotel itself offered welcome relief from flee-ridden caravansaries. Red, green, blue, and black stripes ran across the whitewashed facades of a courtyard planted with oleanders. Flowering plants hung in swags from the balcony. A baby gazelle capered on the colored marble terrace where Flaubert, blond bearded himself, whose customary dress was now a long, flowing Nubian shirt, wrote his letters. They stayed ten days at the Hôtel de Palmyre, adding shawls, pots, and carpets to the eight dozen rosaries they had acquired in Jerusalem for older relatives and acquaintances.

A circuitous route back to Beirut led them north from Damascus over the Jebel-Esh Sharqui range and into the Bequaa Valley, their intermediate destination being Baalbek. Du Camp had no sooner photographed the Roman temples shattered by an earthquake in 1759 than difficulties arose. Joseph fell gravely ill. The companions decided to go separate ways so that their dragoman, escorted by Du Camp, could seek medical help in Beirut as quickly as possible. Flaubert and Sassetti would cross the Lebanon Mountains on their own and await Du Camp at Aden. The plan worked, though not before an acute illness struck Sassetti as well. By the seventeenth of September they had reached Beirut. There, mindful of Caroline Flaubert's anguish and running so short of funds that Maxime borrowed money from Camille Rogier to frank his letters, they revised their itinerary once again. Crete would be sacrificed. Later they would also rule out the trek across Anatolia via Troy and book passage on a boat that plied the Mediterranean between Smyrna and Constantinople.

In Beirut they spent four days packing, with intermittent frolics at Camille Rogier's home. Having fulfilled his photographic mission, Du Camp swapped the ponderous camera for a bolt of silk-and-gold cloth. On October 1 he and Flaubert boarded the *Stamboul*, an Austrian Lloyd packet sailing to Cyprus and Rhodes. Joseph was left behind and Sassetti shipped ahead.

Of life aboard the *Stamboul*, Flaubert remembered most vividly a harem occupying all the first-class portside cabins, and of Rhodes, a mere transit point for them, he remembered, after quarantine, three or four days on a belligerent mule in rugged countryside strenuously viewing the island's major churches, monuments, and fortifications. They had meanwhile hired a dragoman fluent in Turkish and Greek, named Stefany. It was mid-October when all three left Rhodes on a chartered skiff. Disencumbered of their baggage, which had been forwarded to Smyrna with Sassetti, they acquired mounts in Marmaris and headed north, riding up and down pine-clad hills along the Ionian coast, across the Menderis River, and, after eight days, on to the rolling plain of Ephesus. Wayworn and bothered by suppurating chancres, which he dressed every night, Flaubert felt nonetheless exhilarated. "Ah, how beautiful it is!" he wrote, noting that it was a compulsion of his, whenever he drew near a destined site or a last chapter, to rush forward. "Orientally and anciently splendid! Reminiscent of a lost sumptuousness, purple mantles embroidered with gold thread. Erostratus! What ecstasies he must have felt! The Diana of Ephesus! . . . On my left, rounded hills look like pear-shaped tits. Following the beaten path, we cross a patch of shrubs (*ligaria,* in Greek)." In fact, Ephesus, whose reputedly wanton burning by Erostratus Flaubert alludes to in *La Tentation*, was hardly more than a historical conceit. In 1850 tourists found only shards and debris. Not until the 1870s, when J. T. Wood excavated the Temple of Artemis, did its great bones begin to rise from the earth. But even if it had been otherwise, Du Camp and Flaubert couldn't tarry, for Constantinople lay ahead. In late October they arrived at Smyrna, passing a caravan of several thousand camels on the way, and there decided, with the cold, wet season upon them, to proceed by sea rather than land.

Camels were the best thing they saw that week. Incessant rain kept

Flaubert indoors, dyspeptically reading Eugène Sue's *Arthur*, and what he saw during occasional walks through Smyrna looked like a bleak provincial town in France. Worse yet, he found himself in the anomalous position of nursing his companions, who were all sicker than he. Du Camp lay bedridden with fever and, despite six weeks of abstinence, a fresh eruption of chancres. Stefany had fallen prey to food poisoning. Sassetti had contracted gonorrhea. "There's nothing like travel for one's health," he quipped. Twelve days passed before they felt well enough to board another Austrian vessel, the *Asia*, which sailed on November 8, stopped at Gallipoli, and entered the Golden Horn on November 13.

What Flaubert saw dazzled him. It might have done so in any circumstances, but the better part of a year spent on a cangia or on the backs of beasts in sparsely populated expanses had dulled his urban reflexes: in Constantinople he felt like a bumpkin unable to cope with the metropolis. To his mother he described an immense, heterogeneous world. "Imagine a city as big as Paris with a port wider than the Seine at Caudebec and more vessels docked there than in Le Havre and Marseille combined," he wrote. "Imagine forests inside the city, which are actually cemeteries. Certain neighborhoods call to mind Rouen's old streets, while others are sheep pasture. It rises like an amphitheater on a hillside, full of ruins, bazaars, markets, mosques, with three seas bathing it and snow-capped mountains towering behind." To Bouilhet he wrote that the omnium-gatherum of nationalities in Constantinople lent credence to Fourier's vision of the city as a future world capital, and confided a more personal view as well. In human terms, he confessed, its sheer size overwhelmed him. "The feeling you had when you first entered Paris of being crushed, that's what I'm feeling here, pervasively, as I rub shoulders with so many strangers — Persian, Indians, Americans, English — so many distinct individualities the sum total of which squashes one's own. And then, it's immense, one gets lost in the streets, one can't see the beginning or the end." Only when he cruised up the Bosporus in a slim caique or, like a sailor in a crow's nest, surveyed Constantinople from atop the great fourteenth-century round tower at Galata did he regain his composure. Consular officials treated him generously. Flaubert liked the unpretentious, back-slapping ambassador, General Jacques Aupick, who was to enter French literary history in his own right as Charles Baudelaire's despised stepfather.

Constantinople captivated him at times, though not the yawning nave of Hagia Sofia and still less the gilded apartments of the seraglio. Rather, he loved certain quiet intersections of nature and urban life peculiar to Oriental culture. There was the woodland cemetery of Stamboul where donkeys grazed and whores plied their trade and cypresses grew tall. Nothing seemed more unbourgeois than a population cohabiting with the dead.

"No wall, no moat, no separation or enclosure whatsoever. In the city and outside it you come upon [graveyards] all at once and everywhere, like death itself . . . You traverse them much the way you cross a bazaar. The tombs are all alike. Only their age distinguishes them one from another. As they age they sink and disappear, like one's memory of the occupants (a Chateaubriandism)." Descendants of Byzantine emperors lay among the indistinguishable, and he thought he may have trod upon a Comnenus or a Palaeologus when he rode horseback through the cemetery en route to another favorite site, the decrepit fortifications built by those same Byzantine emperors. "Three *enceintes* . . . Constantinople's walls are not sufficiently praised. They are stupendous! We go past the Golden Gate, immured, and the Seven Towers and arrive at the choppy sea." For Flaubert, in whom the piety of remembering and the fear of being forgotten matched his terror of eviction and his fantasies of hermetic security, the intramural burial ground and the thrice-encircling rampart had kindred meaning. They sheltered, defined, repulsed. They argued a paradox of inclusiveness beyond the grave but exclusiveness on this side of it — promising eternal *droit de cité* to one's own, and denying it forever to the stranger with designs upon one's identity.* Moreover, the city wall, like the cemetery, straddled history and nature. Vegetation clothed stones against which Avars, Saracens, Bulgarians, Crusaders, and Ottoman Turks had dashed in waves since the early Middle Ages. Overgrown with brambles, ivy, and shrubs, they exemplified what Flaubert liked to call "the prodigality of ruins."

Turkey never haunted him as Egypt did. The "pictured roof and marble floor" that furnish Byron's *Turkish Tales* had nothing of the magic he found in a crimson sunset over a baked landscape. Even so, he loved the place and deplored signs that Constantinople, in yet another invasion, was losing its Oriental character under Western influence. After performances by whirling dervishes, society flocked to the ballet. *Lucia di Lammermoor* played to a packed house. In affluent neighborhoods, patent leather boots and white gloves had become commonplace. Eunuchs at the seraglio sported vests with watch chains, and a dwarf outside the throne room wore trousers with gaiters and understraps. Flaubert predicted that in a hundred years the harem would have succumbed to the example of European women. "One of these days their counterparts here will begin to read novels. Then it will be curtains for Turkish tranquillity!" The Second Empire, during which French industry waxed imperial, was to bear him out. Plans were already

---

*We have seen another image of the triple wall in the previously quoted letter to his mother, in which he declared that he would not exchange the pleasure of living with her for marriage, that the artist is a sport of nature destined to observe life from outside it. Years later he would depict Carthage in *Salammbô* with a triple ring of fortifications.

afoot to finance an Ottoman railroad under the auspices of Péreire's Crédit mobilier, and the Orient Express made its appearance soon thereafter. "Now's the time to see the Orient," he told his mother, "because it's disappearing, it's getting civilized." A few decades later, as Orhan Pamuk tells us, prosperous Turks would be furnishing their salons not with ottomans and divans but with the unplayed grand pianos, stiff chairs, and curio cabinets that proclaimed their Westernization.

Flaubert had spent his twenty-eighth birthday riding back to Cairo from Memphis under a blazing sun. He spent his twenty-ninth galloping full tilt over trackless, snowy hills on the Asian side of the Bosporus with a Polish count named Kosielski, who like many of his compatriots had found refuge in the Ottoman Empire. Both men were sad, but for quite different reasons. To a nostalgic exile, the wintry landscape spoke of a homeland he might never see again. To the leisured vagabond it announced the final season of his reprieve from Rouen, from time, from social norms and expectations. Three days later Kosielski would help him aboard a steamer bound for Greece. On the eve of his departure he sent a long letter to Caroline Flaubert, who had received word of Ernest Chevalier's engagement and begun to worry ambivalently that her younger son might also — or never — acquire a wife. "Never, I hope," he asserted.

> Ceaselessly rubbing against the world for fourteen months has had the effect of pushing me deeper into my shell. Père Parain's contention that travel changes people doesn't apply to me. I shall return the same person who left, with fewer hairs on my head and many more landscapes inside it . . . When one has led, as I have done, a wholly internal life, full of effusive analyses and buttoned-up passion, when one has so often fired oneself up and calmed oneself down and devoted one's entire youth to maneuvering one's soul, like a rider spurring his horse to gallop, slowing it to a trot, making it leap over ditches or canter or amble, all this just for his amusement, well, if one hasn't broken one's neck in the process, chances are one won't. I, too [like Chevalier], am *established,* in the sense that I've found my place, my center of gravity.

His center of gravity was his study and literature, which he likened to a religious discipline entailing vows of celibacy. Alfred Le Poittevin's marriage had been the blunder of an apostate.

> When one wants to deal with the Good Lord's works, one must not, if only for hygienic reasons, allow oneself to play their dupe. One will picture love, women, wine and glory provided one does not become a drunk, a lover, a husband, a rollicking soldier boy . . . When embroiled in life, one can't see it clearly,

one is too pained or pleased by it. The artist is, as I see it, a monstrosity, something outside nature. All the woes Providence heaps on him derive from his stubborn denial of this axiom.

He himself was determined to live as he had previously lived, alone, with the bearskin that emblemized his ursine soul, and surrounded by "the crowd of great authors" who made up his society. "I don't give a damn about the world, about the future, about social faux-pas, about wagging tongues, about an establishment, even about literary renown, which used to keep me awake at night, dreaming. That's how I am; such is my character."

After a farewell dinner hosted by General Aupick at the embassy, Flaubert regretfully turned his back on all he hadn't seen or might never see again: Persia, Troy, veiled women, camels, Turks in cafés smoking chibouks and paring their toenails. Four days later he and Du Camp girded themselves for another tedious quarantine, this time at Piraeus, where they landed on December 19, dead broke but furnished with a letter from Aupick upon presentation of which the French consul would give them money sufficient to let them continue their tour. In quarantine, Du Camp availed himself of his enforced leisure to leaf through Thucydides, Diodorus, and Pausanias. Flaubert in turn read Herodotus and the first volume of Thirwall's *History of Greece*.

Regrets pursued him. They also preceded him, for while thinking about Greece several weeks earlier he had complained to Bouilhet of his abysmal ignorance and, as usual, grieved over all the hours spent in quest of an elusive fluency. "Ah! If at least I knew Greek!" But the exclamation marks punctuating his despair — a despair all the more ineradicable for inventing its own evidence — soon came to trumpet the Greekness he experienced on the Acropolis. He was, he told his mother on December 26, in an "Olympian" state, sucking up "brainfuls" of antiquity. "And the ruins! the ruins! What ruins! What men those Greeks! What artists! We're reading, we're taking notes . . . The Parthenon moved me as deeply as anything I've ever seen." English reserve wasn't Flaubert's style, and the ample gestures with which he undoubtedly conducted these transports must have called further attention to the conspicuous figure he cut in Athens. A tarboosh, which invited stares from patriotic Greeks, disguised his receding hairline. An unkempt beard hid his face. Visible lower down was the girth that Turkish cuisine had added to his tall frame. He towered over young Mediterraneans, whose dark good looks astonished him. They made him feel ponderous, and Caroline Flaubert was warned that her formerly handsome son would return from his odyssey a gross version of himself.

Du Camp and Flaubert had no sooner established residence at the Hôtel d'Angleterre than they equipped themselves for day trips to the great classical sites of Attica. Christmas was celebrated with a fifteen-mile jaunt over mountains beyond the Athenian plain to Eleusis. There they found what must have been Demeter's fountain and fluted marble drums lying higgledy-piggledy on the hillside. Nothing remained of the Telesterio and the temple of Artemis Propylae, both leveled by Alaric fifteen centuries earlier. But the glorious vantage point remained. From it they gazed upon the slate blue Bay of Eleusis and possibly made out the Salamis strait, where, as Herodotus recounts, small Greek vessels overwhelmed the Persian armada. Two days later they rode off to Marathon in bad weather, slogging through wet pine forests, past Mount Skarpa, and fetching up at the tumulus built for Athenian hoplites who had repulsed the army of Data and Ataphernes. Between excursions they were introduced to surviving heroes of a more recent war, notably Constantin Canaris, the man Victor Hugo honored in *Les Orientales* as "Canaris, demi-dieu de gloire rayonnant!" It was Canaris who had avenged the massacre of rebellious Greeks on Chios in March 1822 by maneuvering a fireboat through a Turkish squadron moored off the Ionian coast and ramming it into the pasha's flagship, which sank with three thousand men aboard. "Every time I've found myself in the presence of men celebrated for some heroic act, I've been disappointed," Du Camp wrote in his *Souvenirs littéraires*. "With Canaris, even making allowances for age and wear, I couldn't persuade myself that this uncouth peasant had been the torchbearer immortalized by great deeds . . . I thought that the laced shoes, blue stockings, thick woolen twill frock coat and black silk hat were a disguise . . . I would have preferred him in greaves, a gold-braided jacket, a blue-tasseled fez." More compatible was the aging General Morandi, formerly an itinerant freedom fighter, who liked to reminisce about his comrade in the war of independence, Lord Byron.

On January 4, 1851, the two men set out for Thermopylae with a Greek dragoman, a cook, an armed escort, and muleteers. Their excursion lasted ten days and took them across the plains of Eleusis and Plataea, over the Cithaeron range and Mount Helicon, to Delphi. Du Camp writes that en route they embellished a landscape shorn of the past with classical recitations inspired by place-names as familiar to them as those of the Île-de-France. What Flaubert remembered, on the other hand, were hours of wordless jogging interrupted by parodies of old men asking foolish questions about the voyage. Either way, during the journey back from Boeotia they managed to go astray in rugged country west of Thebes. Rain fell day after day, flooding the plain. Dressed in goatskins like a pair of bedraggled Robinson Crusoes, they forged ahead and had gained the northern slope of Cithaeron when a blizzard descended on them. Their mud-caked boots froze. It was not a moment to commemorate Pausanius's victory over the Persian general Mardonius just below that snowy expanse. In the wind-whipped drifts, they couldn't locate the mountain pass or discern any sign of human habitation. A muscular, well-padded Flaubert fared better than the gaunt Du Camp, but flesh and bone might have perished together if not for a dog barking directions to a village, where they found shelter in a stable that served as the local inn. "Whenever someone arrived," wrote Flaubert, "a cry of 'Khandi! Nadji!' was heard, the door would open, a man and his steamy horse would enter, the horse would settle at the feeding trough and the man at the fireplace . . . I thought of the age of Saturn as Hesiod describes it! This is how people traveled for centuries." The next day, warmed by quantities of raki, they moved downhill from deep snow to olive groves, with Flaubert riding an ill-shod stallion whose irritability tested his superior horsemanship.

They returned on January 13 and left Athens eleven days later to tour the Peloponnese, which was still so seldom visited that even in Sparta crowds were apt to gather around a foreigner. Indeed, the road west of Mégara by which one entered the peninsula would have discouraged timid souls. Hugging the side of a cliff, it allowed no margin for false moves; only one inattentive step to the left meant certain death in the Saronic Gulf. Flaubert traveled it with sufficient aplomb to admire the mottled red of rocks beetling overhead and pools of bottle green drifting offshore. When, lower down, the road acquired shoulders and ran through a confusion of bushy pines and dwarf oaks, he felt moved by something transcendently serene in the landscape. He would have knelt down, he wrote, had he known a language and formula for prayer.

Prayerfulness didn't always win out over bone weariness during the next fortnight, as he and Du Camp rode with yet another retinue past the four promontories that jut toward Crete like splayed claws — from Corinth to Argos, Sparta, Messene, Megalopolis, and finally Patras. This wilderness of ridges and ravines offered travelers almost no level ground. A basin was only a brief dip in mountains around it, the most formidable of which, the snow-capped Taygetus range, extended the Arcadian uplands south, rising like a wall between those ancient rivals, Sparta and Messenia. Up and down they went, and across torrents that might have separated them from their baggage if not for resourceful improvisations, drying out in khans more flea ridden than the caravansaries of Syria. Where Chateaubriand communed with Lacedemonian heroes at the river Eurotas, Flaubert sniffed Messene's unwashed descendants at the foot of Mount Ithome. "Dinner at the village of Meligala. Women pass, loaded down with wood. They are so filthy that as one approaches them one smells the stable, the manure pile, the wild, and something sour and damp." But a gladness animated him throughout, tinged though it was with the queasy knowledge that early in February, when they planned to leave for Brindisi, parenthetical brackets would close around his life of adventure. Walking through rust-colored gorges, dense with wild pear trees, lentisks, and blond-wigged oaks in velvet sleeves of moss, he felt what he had felt in Corsica. Beside the Temple of Apollo Epicurius, halfway up a mountain overlooking the fertile plain that spread between Taygetus and Ithome, the Messenian Gulf, and the Ionian Sea, he rose above his anguished thoughts about the book for which he hadn't yet found a subject (though not above the temptation to embezzle marble fragments). Freedom was the thing, and a final farewell to it was played on bagpipes by two itinerant musicians near Gastouni. Why, he asked himself, did such people exercise such attraction upon him? "The contemplation of these vagabond existences, apparently regarded almost everywhere as accursed, . . . tugs at me. Perhaps I wandered that way in a former life. Oh Bohemia! Bohemia! You are the land of my kindred souls!"

At the end, Du Camp and Flaubert made a dash for Patras lest they miss the boat, covering fifty-five miles in one day on pitifully worn-out horses. Patras had almost nothing of ancient culture or modern commodiousness to recommend it, he told his mother: No important ruins, no Turkish baths. "As far as the real voyage goes, it's all over."

THE "Voyage en Orient" may indeed have been over, but not quite yet the grand tour, which resumed in earnest on February 27, when their diligence entered Naples through the Capuan Gate after a jarring ride cross-country from Bari. They registered at the Hôtel d'Athènes, consulted their banker, and betook themselves to the Chiaia for a stroll along the bay. In due course there were matinees at the Teatro San Carlo, followed by six hours a day of reimmersion in European art at the Borbonico Museum.* It had been almost two years since Flaubert visited a picture gallery, and his diary shows a conscientious eye observing in great detail not only the Roman antiquities but Correggios, Rosas, Durers, da Vincis, and Caravaggios from the Farnese collection. "It's truly inexhaustible," he told his mother in one of the last of the sixty or so letters (all numbered) with which he had kept her informed and entertained since his departure in 1849. Du Camp and he also made up for the sexual abstinence they had practiced during their weeks in the Peloponnese, welcoming the solicitations of Neapolitan pimps, who abounded. "Here in soft Parthenope I have a perpetual hard-on," he reported to his lecherous friend in Beirut, Camille Rogier. "I'm screwing like an unbridled jackass. The merest grazing against my trousers makes me stiff." His preference, he continued, was for the "mature ladies, stout women" whom he found at an establishment that specialized in "ma-

---

*The Borbonico contained antiquities of the present-day National Archeological Museum plus paintings later transferred to the Capodimonte.

ternal pleasures." Stout is how he now appeared to himself, the more so since shaving himself clean; exposed were jowls and a double chin.

His tarboosh, which drew as many stares from Neapolitans as Rica's turban from eighteenth-century Parisians in *The Persian Letters*, went the way of his beard. He wore proper bourgeois attire in the city, but not outside it on excursions to Pompeii, Paestum, and Capri, or for a climb up Mount Vesuvius, where, despite a fever that sapped him of strength, he reached the crater's edge. Young Goethe had done it; so would he. Gadding about Naples, Du Camp and he took pleasure in Rossini at the concert hall, in the spectacle of horses adorned with peacock feathers and of lovers under the holm oaks of the Chiaia, in an opportunistic romance with the hotel-keeper's daughter (Du Camp) and a brief infatuation with a French vaude-ville actress (Flaubert). They took full advantage of a world governed by the natives' *savoir-vivre*. Any event was pretext sufficient to close up shop, Flaubert observed. "Things are closed because of Lent, because it's Sunday, because the queen is sick, because she isn't sick, because the prince of Salterno is dying; soon it will be because he died, for rumor has it that death may come any moment now." Unwary tourists had violets thrust upon them by flower girls who aggressively patrolled the bayside prome-nade. Elsewhere, trollops ran after coaches with gentlemen inside, hitching their skirts up to their armpits. Flaubert only wished that Bouilhet could see it for himself. In correspondence, which may have been subject to censor-ship, no mention is made of the police state maintained by King Ferdinand, who feared that the revolutionary movements of 1848 everywhere else in Europe might spread through southern Italy. Agents spied on tourists, and Flaubert could not visit sites such as Paestum unaccompanied. All this to no avail. The revolution would come nine years later with Garibaldi, whose army of Redshirts would include, among other foreign volunteers, Maxime Du Camp.

To Bouilhet Flaubert confessed that the completed "voyage en Orient" had not been Oriental enough. Just as in 1840 he vowed, on returning from Corsica, to circle the Mediterranean, so now he yearned to push beyond the Second Cataract and to trek east through Persia. Balanced against a need for perfect confinement was this Faustian urge to swallow the world whole. His fantasies, Bouilhet learned, were of Berbers, of elephant hunts, of Hindu dancing girls, of riotous color. In a letter to Ernest Chevalier con-gratulating him on his engagement, he wrote: "Well, yes, I have seen the Orient and I'm no further along for it. I want to go to India, to get lost in the American pampas, to visit the Sudan . . . Of all possible debauches, travel is unsurpassed by any I know. It's the one invented after all the others have ceased to excite."

On March 28 Flaubert and Du Camp departed for Rome, where they bade each other farewell. Litigation over the fortune his grandmother had left him urgently required Du Camp's presence at home. Flaubert, in turn, would enjoy, if not maternal pleasures of a venal kind, the company of his mother, who could no longer endure her son's absence and was even then sailing with her servant Eugénie from Marseille to Cività Vecchia. This reunion had been the subject of epistolary exchanges since the previous September or October. Flaubert encouraged it but hedged his invitation with caveats, the most important pertaining to five-year-old Caroline Hamard. If Mme Flaubert left the child behind, in the care of François Parain's daughter Olympe Bonenfant, might Hamard, who had been quiescent, seize the opportunity to claim custody — which was still an unresolved issue — on grounds of abandonment? Even if he behaved himself, would her worrying about little Caroline, nicknamed "Liline," not cast a shadow upon Rome and Venice? And did it not reflect misplaced priorities? "It would be sacrificing her to me, that is, placing me before her, and she needs you more than I do, this poor child of my beloved Caroline. So, mother dear, I don't want you to make the sacrifice, do you understand?" He suggested that she bring Liline along and get a note from Cloquet adducing some pediatric condition likely to improve in warm weather.

Mme Flaubert ignored his advice, with at least one of the consequences he foresaw. In Italy, she may not have fretted out loud, but boils — a lifelong affliction possibly triggered by nerves — erupted all over her body. She whose life had been a story of abandonment blamed herself for leaving the child. Furthermore, it disturbed her to find that her son's manners had become "brutish," an imputation to which the normally courteous Gustave pleaded innocent while acknowledging that at times his temper had very nearly flared. Quarrels were inevitable. As much as Flaubert loved Venice, where he and his mother continued the assiduous museum-going of their month in Rome and Florence, the great adventure was over. Venice was not a place to visit with one's mother. Croisset had descended upon him, and the leash from which he could not and would not free himself had been reattached.

Nonetheless, his mind had room for sentiments other than regret and nostalgia. In Rome he had written to Louis Bouilhet: "As far as my emotional state goes, it's odd: I feel *the need for a success*." Coming from a young man who usually pretended to lack ambition and even despise it as the poisoned fruit of enslavement to philistine authority, his confidence may have startled Bouilhet. A fire had been rekindled. It stayed lit all the way home. After a circuitous voyage, which took him and his mother through Cologne and Brussels, Flaubert reached Paris in the second week of June 1851.

XIII

⁓

The Perfect Hostages

HAD FLAUBERT been told during his travels abroad that Maurice Schlesinger was selling his house in Vernon after relinquishing his publishing firm and was leaving France with Élisa to settle in the fashionable spa of Baden-Baden, the news would have choked him up. He hadn't seen Élisa since 1846, but she nonetheless accompanied him through life as a vivid stowaway. Indeed, all the women he had ever loved at first sight, though there was no question of living with them, continued to inhabit his mind as he first knew them, always young and charismatic. He himself recognized that emotional fullness consisted for him in the experience of loss, the ache of absence, the hallowing of mementos. A shuttered hotel became the sepulchre of an erotic revelation commemorated whenever he visited Marseille. Blood-stained slippers stood for Louise Colet. During a morose reunion on his return trip down the Nile, he stared hard at Kuchiuk-Hanem in order to fix her image. And twenty years later, in 1871, he would be able to assure a white-haired Élisa Schlesinger that the sands of Trouville still preserved the imprint of her bare feet. More recently, during his tour of Italy with Mme Flaubert, Élisa had come alive again in an Italian woman encountered at San Paolo fuori le Mura in Rome. The epiphany took place on April 15 under the cupola, where he and his mother were admiring a mosaic of Christ among the evangelists. "Turning my head to the left, I saw a woman in a red corsage approaching slowly," he wrote.

> I grasped my lorgnon and stepped forward. Something was drawing me to her. She had a pale face with dark eyebrows and a wide red ribbon knotted around her chignon and falling to her shoulders. How very pale she was! She wore green doeskin gloves; her short, squarish figure twisted slightly with leaning on the arm of an elderly maidservant. Desire burst in my stomach like a sudden thunderclap, I wanted to spring on her, I was dazzled.

Red and black were emblematic of Élisa, and what made the unknown lady's red ribbon appear not just bright but "fulgurating" was undoubtedly Flaubert's memory of a red shawl with black stripes on white sand. The light in her dark, lustrous eyes reflected Élisa's "magnetic" glance. With Élisa she shared fine, bluish down at the corners of her lips. And her eyebrows, which he found especially beautiful, described a familiar arc.

Only Louise Colet insisted upon retaining a carnal presence in Flaubert's life. As we know from her personal memoranda, she had never given him up emotionally and inquired after him through mutual acquaintances. On July 29, 1849, she tearfully remembered the third anniversary of their first night together. More tears were shed two months later when it became obvious that there would be no farewells on the eve of his departure for Egypt. How could he leave, she cried, without a word about the disposition of her letters and souvenirs? "Oh! Dreary are these irreparably broken loves, which don't leave a trace! None in the man's heart I should say, for in mine the wounds stay open and bleed forever! What? Is it possible that when two beings have loved each other sincerely, have merged in each other, one of them can detach himself, forget everything — everything, my God, of those magical days?" Tears continued to flow, and often in the presence of a young sculptor named Hippolyte Ferrat, who while groping for her favors got damp from her grief. "How I'm suffering, my God!" Louise wrote in her diary, in December. "Despite myself I cried in front of Ferrat. I spoke of Gustave amid my tears, I am too unhappy. I'd like to die . . . Alone, alone, always." Earlier that year a son whose father was Franc, the Polish refugee, had died at six months of age, her second son lost in infancy.

Louise had suffered yet another blow in May 1849. Juliette Récamier, her neighbor, protectress, and close confidante, fell victim to the rampaging cholera epidemic (which also killed a famous actress of the Romantic stage, Marie Dorval). Louise's loss became doubly bitter in the aftermath, when she found herself subjected to imputations of betrayal and venality. Juliette had given her for safekeeping sixty love letters written during the last years of Napoleon's reign by her suitor Benjamin Constant. No sooner was Juliette dead and buried than Louise arranged to publish them, with a brief introduction, in Émile de Girardin's popular daily, *La Presse*. Being hard up, as usual, she needed the money.* But she hid her neediness in a cloak of virtue, declaring herself bound to make public the epistolary masterpiece of a writer whose genius had never been sufficiently honored. Publication began on July 3 with great hoopla, and readers flocked to their newspaper kiosks. Three weeks later, after court papers had been served on Girardin enjoining him to halt publication, those readers were queuing up at the Palais de Justice for a trial that pitted Louise against Juliette Récamier's legal heir, Amélie Lenormant, a deep-dyed royalist who apparently did not regard any family relationship with the eloquent liberal Constant as worthy of commemoration. It was alleged that Louise had acquired his letters with a bogus deed of donation signed unwittingly by Juliette. Mme Lenormant could not prove the allegation, and several notable witnesses attested to Louise's honesty. Defending her in court and out, Victor Cousin, for example, wrote: "Poor Madame Colet . . . is as incapable of fraud as I am of stealing your handkerchief. She has neither the qualities nor the faults needed for such deception. She has an excellent heart but a poor head." Flaubert, though greatly preoccupied with *Saint Antoine*, could not have failed to read Louise's introduction in *La Presse* and accounts of the trial. Nor would he have missed the verdict, which acquitted Louise of all charges while prohibiting further publication of Constant's letters.

Louise's loneliness was a crowded scene. By scrimping and borrowing she assembled the wherewithal to entertain guests at her Sunday salon, which attracted liberal politicians as well as literary lights. Émile de Girardin came regularly. So did two of George Sand's former lovers: Michel de Bourges, a radical deputy, and Eugène Pelletan, a journalist closely allied to Lamartine. On any given Sunday afternoon the guests might have included Théophile Gautier, Leconte de Lisle, Charles Baudelaire, Champfleury, Alexandre Dumas, and Hugo's two sons, Charles-Victor and François-Victor. In 1850 the habitué most likely to linger after others had left, unless duty called him, which it often did, was Désiré Bancel, a firebrand of the parliamentary left, twelve years younger than she, whose child she conceived and miscarried. When Bancel ran for cover from Louise's vituperations, his place in bed was taken by an even younger man, twenty-three-year-old Octave Lacroix, Sainte-Beuve's private secretary, who would later gain distinction as the publisher responsible for signing up Zola's *Rougon-Macquart*. By 1851 Louise had tired of his besotted avowals

---

*Although Flaubert would offer to help Colet out financially, she always felt that, as one who had never earned his livelihood, he was insufficiently sympathetic to her plight.

and taken up with a lawyer Flaubert's age, Auguste Vetter. "Do I love Auguste?" she mused one spring day. "It feels more like friendship than love. He has a noble character, but is more impressive than endearing . . . His proposal that we live together! Quite out of the question! My heart is too worn with the emotions that have crowded through it to entertain the idea."

Her heart remained young enough to quiver at the mention of Gustave's name, however. Had a mutual acquaintance said of Louise Colet's lovers what Flaubert reportedly said of his various bedmates — that they were mattresses for some dreamed-of absentee — he might not have been far wrong. Flaubert recognized no exceptions, while Louise intermittently made an exception of Flaubert. "Will Gustave come see me?" she wrote on May 25, 1851, a month after the death of her consumptive husband, whom she had nursed at the end.

Her question assumed that he had received a letter sent on May 14 in which she pleaded for the opportunity to achieve closure in one last encounter, wooing him with a confusion of romantic gush and maternal reproach. Even if someone as disloyal as he hardly deserved a secure place in her heart, she implied, he nevertheless enjoyed one. Not that passion warmed and brightened it any longer, only that it would have a question mark over it until its tenant showed himself to have been marked by her. "I would have you, and you alone, understand what feeling remains in my heart for you. What I hope to elicit from you, in turn, is one last proof of affection, or memory of affection. Oh! Never fear. My hopes and expectations are not compelling enough to lure me from the course of detachment I charted four years ago." Their last scene could be staged on short notice. He was not to answer her letter at length, she commanded, for a tender response would shake her resolve and a callous one aggravate her misery.

Flaubert may never have received this summons, or may have interpreted her proposal as an invitation to start the affair anew. Whichever the case, he did not answer it, and when, on June 16, Louise learned that the Flauberts were in Paris, she dispatched a message first to Gustave's usual hotel, where for once he was not residing, then to Maxime Du Camp, who kept the messenger at bay. Enraged, she wrote another letter on June 18 but didn't post it. A draft survives, which begins with the assertion that her script would never again insult his eyes. Since he couldn't show her the kindness or courtesy to which she was entitled and, indeed, found everything about her odious, she insisted that he return her letters. "I in turn shall . . . give *all* your letters and those of your friend [Maxime Du Camp] to whomever you send for them. When I was so sick eighteen months ago [after the miscarriage], I wrapped them up in case I should die. Oh! How sad all this is."

She had waited for years, she declared, and would have waited longer if he had made some token gesture of friendship. He was assured, in a characteristically mollifying envoi, that she bore him no ill will.

What happened next got Flaubert's attention. On June 26, a week before crossing the English Channel with an album of autograph correspondence from various luminaries for which she hoped to find a dealer in London, where the Great Exposition was attracting huge crowds and big money, Louise paid Flaubert an impromptu visit at Croisset. This took nerve, as she knew full well that to trespass upon Mme Flaubert's domain was to flout one of the iron prohibitions by which Flaubert compartmentalized his life. She dined in Rouen with her daughter, Henriette, installed the girl at her hotel, bought sweets for Liline, hired a boatman, alighted at Croisset, and entered the grounds through a door next to the main gate. In her hand was a note explaining that urgent matters dictated her sudden appearance and reassuring Flaubert that she had come not as a scold but as a repentant friend. Julie, or some other servant, delivered it. "I waited for her in the grassy courtyard of the farmhouse . . . beside the stables," she wrote in her journal. The servant told her that "Monsieur," who could not abandon his guests at table, would join her afterward in Rouen if she left her address. Distraught at not being allowed to cross the magic threshold, she contemplated the house on which her imagination had dwelt for years, like a fairy-tale drudge walled off from the prince in his castle. "I would have liked at least to tour this airy cottage in which he had spent almost all of his life; at the gate I turned around, I looked it over, its whiteness, its elegance, its open windows, the dining room with several people at dinner . . . It breathed contentment." A vexed Flaubert suddenly presented himself to tell her in person — using the formal *vous* and addressing her as "Madame" — that conversation under his mother's roof was impossible. Louise took up where she had left off more than three years earlier with masochistic remonstrances. "Do you believe that my visit would dishonor Madame your mother? I can't even see this child of your sister, whom I have spent so much time thinking about and for whom I brought a little gift!" Flaubert's altered appearance may have made her feel all the more an intruder. Wearing baggy Turkish pants, a smock of Indian inspiration, a yellow cravat with silver and gold thread, he looked noticeably older. Thin lines creased his forehead. His mustache had grown longer and droopy. His hair had thinned — had in fact fallen out in clumps. His face showed a redness that could be taken for roseola. We know he was drinking syrup of mercury and would do so again whenever chancres reappeared, fearing, with good reason, that he had contracted syphilis. It cost him some teeth, though not as many as his eternal pipe would.

Louise acceded to his ultimatum that they meet in Rouen or not at all.

Later that evening, her ex-lover, who in 1848 had concluded his valediction to her with the assurance that she could always count on him, heard her out and urged her, like an unsentimental bourgeois paterfamilias in Oriental drag, to secure herself materially and socially by marrying Henriette's putative father, Victor Cousin, stale though the prospect might be. Happiness for her, she replied in her most abject style, would be to live in Rouen or a neighboring village, to raise her daughter there, to work, to enjoy his affection, and to be always at his beck and call. The journal evokes a wrenching scene. "I kissed him passionately; he kissed me as well, but stiffly. I decided to walk him to the edge of town. Not wanting to leave a tedious impression of myself, I tried my best to be cheerful and talk about things that might please or interest him. We stopped three times and repeated 'We must part,' and each time I embraced him and said: 'Not until the next lamppost' . . . At last I hugged him tight, he returned my embrace and our parting words were 'au revoir.' I returned to the hotel; en route, the memory of being barred from Croisset, yes barred, came to mind like a slap in the face." To make sure that Flaubert would abide by his "au revoir," she entrusted him with two plays in manuscript.

A month later, when Louise was despairing over the unprofitable results of her trip to England, Flaubert, who would soon visit London himself, attempted to set matters straight. "You must have found me very cold the other day in Rouen," he wrote on July 26. "Yet I have tried to be as little so as possible. I was kind but not tender. That would have been disingenuous, an insult to the truth of your heart . . . I wish your disposition were such that we could see each other in a tranquil atmosphere. I love your company when it isn't all thunder and lightning. The storms that excite one in youth cause distress in later years." The metaphor prompted a comparison between women and horses. "It's like equitation. There was a time when I loved to gallop all out. Now I trot, with the reins lying slack." Echoing the homilies of their earlier correspondence, he urged her to seek solace in work. "There's nothing for peace of mind like single-minded labor. It's an opiate that numbs the soul." Meanwhile Louise chaffed him for hiding behind his mother's ample petticoats. Little did she know that his mother had been shocked by his ungallant behavior and called him to account for it.

André Gide once described himself as a naughty boy shackled to a Protestant pastor who bored him stiff. Flaubert was an equally uncomfortable couple, and he settled their inner arguments by indulging each disputant in turn. Lustful and guilty, he would have sex, then lecture his inamorata, or mount her in Paris, then retreat to the chaste realm of literary servitude in Croisset, enjoying the pleasure of vice and the honor of expiation. When exactly he resumed his tortured intimacy with Louise Colet isn't clear, for this particular anniversary wasn't celebrated. The second affair may have begun in August. By January 1852 the familiar *tu* had supplanted *vous* and reintroduced those querulous exchanges that had become as ritualized an element of their correspondence as the stichomythia of Greek drama. "Poor child! will you then never understand that things are as I declare them to be?" Flaubert railed. "You accuse me of being mean or at least egotistical, inconsiderate of others, loving only myself. But in that respect I am no worse than others, and I would even say less a sinner than most if praising oneself were allowed. You will, I'm sure, give me credit for being straightforward." Like everyone else, he declared, he could not act outside the boundaries of his nature. "You should not have fallen for a man like me, worn by the excesses of solitude, with nerves as delicately strung as a swooning woman's, harried by suppressed passions, full of doubt. I love you as best I can; badly, not enough, I know — my God do I know it! Whose fault is that?" Flaubert may have described their predicament best when he signed one letter "Your infirmity."* Each was a perfect hostage to the other's baffled dreams.

IN LONDON, the Flauberts, including Liline, were guests of Gustave's sister's former governess Miss Jane, whom they now knew as Mrs. Farmer, the mother of two small children residing with her husband, an iron and tin merchant, in Upper Holloway. During his brief London sojourn, which began on September 25, 1851, Flaubert did not see Gertrude Collier, who had married a rich attorney twenty-four years older than she named Charles Tennant and set up house at 62 Russell Square. On the other hand, he escorted Gertrude's sister, Harriet, still single, through Hyde Park one foggy Sunday afternoon, reminiscing all the while, as he was wont to do, about autumn afternoons of bygone days in Paris. There was a compulsory visit to the Crystal Palace, where, since May, six million people had milled across nineteen glass-enclosed acres of prodigious clutter, bright with yellows, reds, light blues, and the green of three elm trees. The tall, myopic Frenchman, sometimes seen carrying his five-year-old niece on his shoulder, applied his lorgnon to objects of interest and took precise notes, like a schoolboy on a class exercise. The Indian and Chinese pavilions yielded detail for future reference on musical instruments, women's attire, the palanquins and silver brocaded harness of elephants. "Is *all of China* not present in the woman's slipper lined in pink damask and with cats embroidered on its vamp?" Such description abounds, though apparently nothing under

---

*The expression may have been suggested to him by Maxime Du Camp, who, on October 1, 1851, wrote to Louise: "I look forward to keeping you company on Friday evening. We will chat about you and your infirmity."

that stupendous roof delighted him more than Tippoo's Tyger at the East India Company Museum on Leadenhall Street — a life-size wooden tiger with an organlike mechanism inside it simulating predatory roars and the screams of a doomed European pinned by four huge paws. Not far from Upper Holloway was the Highgate cemetery, which Flaubert, an aficionado of graveyards, found decidedly inferior to the one in Constantinople. Its neat, well-tended plots and vainglorious monuments repelled him. "These people seem to have died in white gloves," he wrote to Louise.

The Flauberts' main purpose in visiting England was to find a proper governess for Liline. After interviewing young teachers at a boarding school, they hired Isabel Hutton, a prim, dark-haired woman scarred by smallpox, who seemed equal to the task of disciplining an unruly five-year-old without friends her own age or a mother's warmth. Isabel would take up her duties in November, at Croisset, Mme Flaubert having moved out of the house on the rue de Crosne in Rouen, where she had previously spent the winter months. According to Flaubert, his mother seemed somewhat at loose ends. Ragged from sleeplessness and rheumatism, she was often peevish.

No sooner had Flaubert reestablished himself in his study and begun to face the Gorgon-headed future from which he had usually been able to avert his gaze in Egypt, Turkey, and Greece than France itself became a distraction. On October 29 Du Camp, who was as brimful of enterprise as Flaubert was beset with doubt, wrote him a long letter declaring, among much else, that the times did not favor art, that literature had surrendered much of its prestige to philosophy and politics. Events seemed to bear him out a month later, on December 2, when Louis-Napoleon, president of the republic, launched a coup d'état and dissolved the National Assembly. Prominent opponents were arrested. France's most famous writer, Victor Hugo, who served as a peer, might have been jailed along with them had he not eluded capture and found refuge on the Channel Islands, where he ultimately spent almost two decades in exile.

Louis-Napoleon's rise from megalomaniacal nuisance to prince-president was the stuff of Romantic drama, or, as Marx saw it, of farce. Having escaped the Ham prison fortress by a daring ruse and fled to England, he marked time there with an entourage of true believers. Only the true could believe that this cryptic little man dressed in a buttoned-up frock coat, strapped trousers, and tight shoes (and whose recommendation of a chiropodist named Eisenberg for the removal of painful corns appeared in a London *Times* advertisement) might one day wear the imperial crown. He made his first move on February 27, 1848, entering France incognito and registering at a Paris hotel. His identity was soon revealed, word spread, crowds gathered for a glimpse of him, and overnight, "as if by magic," wrote one observer, his portrait, entitled simply "Lui,"* went on sale in shopwindows and kiosks. Reluctant to detain him lest it thereby stir the live embers of Bonapartist sentiment, the provisional government requested that he leave France at once, and Louis-Napoleon, eager to store up goodwill, acquiesced. "The people . . . are intoxicated with victory and hope," he told a conspiratorial friend who had urged him to stay. "All these illusions must perish before a 'man of order' can make himself heard." They perished soon enough, during four June days at the barricades, when tens of thousands died in the rebellion against a conservative legislature largely unsympathetic to republican institutions and the plight of workers. With a propaganda campaign conducted by his agents, who pictured him as all things to all men — as the author of a book entitled *L'Extinction du pauperisme* but also as the very symbol of "order, glory, and patriotism" — he won a seat in the Assembly. Thereafter, everything worked to his advantage, despite the poor figure he cut on a public rostrum speaking in Swiss-accented French. The banishment of the Bonaparte family was repealed, the committee charged with drafting a new constitution recommended that the French president be elected not by the legislature but by universal suffrage, the Constituent Assembly adopted that proposal for fear of alienating the country at large, and forward on a rising tide of public opinion rode Napoleon's nephew, whom Hugo dubbed "Napoleon le Petit." Among his more enthusiastic supporters was Maxime Du Camp's close friend Louis de Cormenin, whose lawyer father, a staunch Bonapartist, had chaired the constitutional committee. In December, voters cast almost four times as many ballots for Louis-Napoleon as for Cavaignac, the general with blood on his hands from the June 1848 civil war.

Seasoned politicians were soon disabused of their assumption that the new president was a cypher whom they could easily manipulate. Once in office he exhibited his Napoleonic gene for administration, appointing loyal prefects who constituted an intelligence network, surrounding himself with henchmen in a kitchen cabinet that included his shrewd, ruthless half brother, the duc de Morny, and transforming the gendarmerie into a military force more reliable than the National Guard. Hand in hand with sabotage went panache; while the sapper busied himself underground, the showman seemed to transcend party politics. Contemptuous of right and left, he represented Catholic France when sending troops against Italian republicans who had driven the pope from Rome and spoke for republican France when directing Pius IX to endorse a general amnesty, a secularized

---

*This contained a pun and a widely known literary reference. The pun was on his given name and the allusion was to Hugo's glorification of Napoleon I in the poem "Lui" (Toujours lui! Lui partout! — ou brûlant ou glacée, / Son image sans cesse ébranle ma pensée).

administration, the Napoleonic Code, and a liberal government. On a triumphant tour of the prison fortress at Ham, he attended a Mass of thanksgiving in his honor, then liberated the Algerian chief of the Kabyles, Abd-al-Qadir, from the apartment in which he himself had been imprisoned for six years. His utopian dream of extinguishing pauperism was glibly reconciled with his advocacy of a residence requirement calculated to disenfranchise three million workers. "The great events of history are like 'la grande cuisine,'" he confided to the Austrian ambassador. "One must not look at it too closely, for the details are of no importance; it is the result that matters."

During Flaubert's voyage in the East, events at home had hastened the implementation of Louis-Napoleon's grand design. In March 1850, republicans soundly defeated government candidates to gain twenty seats in the Assembly, provoking a red scare and a widespread flight of capital. More ominous for Bonapartists was the refusal of a legislature still monarchical in the majority to amend a constitutional article that barred the president from serving two consecutive terms. Louis would obligatorily retire after May 1852 unless the republic fell, and plans for its execution, code-named Operation Rubicon, were therefore set in motion. This coup d'état was so widely anticipated that when George Sand, walking past the Élysée on December 2 at 1 a.m., saw a darkened palace, she remarked facetiously: "It won't be tomorrow, then." Her mistake should have been borne in on her later that morning by the tolling of bells and the beating of drums; however, arrangements had been made to slash the drumheads overnight and to post guards around belfries. Before dawn, gendarmes fanned out across the city with warrants of arrest for seventy-eight well-respected men — journalists, deputies, generals — whose words might have inspired resistance. The printing presses of opposition papers were closed. The Palais Bourbon, where the National Assembly met, was surrounded by Louis-Napoleon's faithful constabulary. Had National Guardsmen tried to arm themselves at posts around the capital, they would have found barrels of wet powder. It was midmorning when France's new savior, wearing a general's uniform, emerged from the Élysée with his uncle Jérôme and mounted his horse. A proclamation from the president of the republic to the people declaring that the present situation could not continue any longer had already been posted in every arrondissement. "Frenchmen!" it began. "With every passing day the dangers to the country mount. The Assembly, which should be the backbone of order, has become a center of conspiracy. Instead of passing laws in the public interest, it is forging weapons for civil war; it is encouraging all manner of wicked passions; it is destroying the peace of France. I have dissolved it, and I leave it to the public to judge between it and me." To the army, which couldn't have been more compliant, Louis-

Napoleon portrayed himself as the embodiment of national sovereignty. "Soldiers!" he exclaimed.

> Be proud of your mission, you will save the fatherland, for I am counting on you not to violate the law but to enforce the country's foremost law, its national sovereignty, whose legitimate representative I am. You have long been suffering, as I have, from the obstacles raised against all I have sought to do on your behalf and against your demonstrations of sympathy for me. These obstacles have been razed. The Assembly struck at the authority vested in me by the entire nation; it has ceased to exist.

Unable to celebrate the advent of a sham Napoleon, however congenial his social reveries, or to mourn the demise of a counterfeit Republic, George Sand, who felt very little that day, was not alone in her indifference. Barricades rose where they traditionally did, but few people manned them, and the bloodiest incident claimed the lives of more noncombatants than armed protestors. Twenty-six thousand Frenchmen identified by prefects as suspect were tried by "commissions," which sentenced a third of them to exile in Algeria or hard labor in the penal colony at Cayenne. Some were later amnestied. Others, like the hero of Zola's *Le Ventre de Paris*, returned clandestinely.

Having occupied a hotel room on the rue du Dauphin (now rue Saint-Roch) since shortly before December 2, Flaubert was well within earshot of the fusillade that left as many as two hundred people dead on the boulevard des Italiens, and he unburdened himself in a letter to Harriet Collier, who had previously opened herself to him. Alexander von Humboldt's *Tableaux de la nature* had set him fantasizing about yet another possible escape from his "frightful country," this time to South America. If only he could leave France and never hear of it again, he declared in a tirade that drowned out Harriet's plaintive song of unmarried futility. Ennui, which Baudelaire would famously picture as a sensitive monster smoking a Turkish waterpipe and yawning the world away, was for Flaubert the gargoyle leering over midcentury spirits. "The ennui that corrodes us here is a bitter fruit, a vinegary sop that makes one's jaws clench. We live with stifled rage and it will soon drive us all mad." Speaking as a man tormented by public events as well as private demons, he found that the former compounded the latter. It seemed to him that he and France had entered a somber decade arm in arm.

The lack of an itinerary after two years of "going places" — of progressing from one storied destination to another on a more or less preordained course — kept him awake nights, and anxiety became something more like panic in quarrels with the irrepressible Maxime Du Camp, who had begun unabashedly to shape a definite career for himself. Almost as soon as Du Camp reached Paris in May 1851, his old friend Louis de Cormenin proposed that they revive *La Revue de Paris*, a literary journal of note defunct since 1844. Arsène Houssaye, director of the Comédie-Française, with whom both Du Camp and Cormenin were on terms, had acquired the title, and another, more famous confrere, Théophile Gautier, would join them as senior man of letters. All four set to work with such enthusiasm that the inaugural issue, which carried a manifesto by Gautier declaring that the editors would not favor any one literary doctrine or school, appeared on October 1, only six weeks after the idea was first aired. "My heart is beating fast," Du Camp wrote to Flaubert on September 30. "Tomorrow or the following day I shall be known among literary folk as an idiot or a maverick: everybody is madly anticipating this review. I'm dog tired, having spent two of the past three nights and seven hours today at the printer's correcting Balzac. It's frightful." A week later he reported that the review had made a big splash. He was set to publish all three thousand lines of Louis Bouilhet's poem *Melaenis* and urged Flaubert to submit his own work or, better yet, to leave Rouen altogether for a more adventurous life in the capital.

Du Camp's feverish encouragement unnerved him. Every Sunday at Croisset his friend Louis Bouilhet convincingly argued the case against offering up passages of *Saint Antoine*, which he regarded as Flaubert at his philosophico-visionary worst, and every Monday morning Flaubert awoke in a muddle. His correspondence with Du Camp shows him strongly disinclined to publish, but writing letters may also have been a way of casting out demons. He hated himself equally for shying away from the literary rough-and-tumble and for heeding those who urged him forward. "If I should publish, it would be done stupidly, out of obedience . . . and without any initiative on my part," he declared to Maxime Du Camp on October 21. "I feel neither the need nor the desire . . . It disgusts me that the idea arises not from within me but from another, from others. Which may only prove that it's I who am in the wrong." The extrinsic rewards he might covet — money, social prestige, the love of women — were so many temptations to be resisted in the service of a spiritual discipline. Should art be practiced for anything but its own sake, it would lose its sacerdotal function and the artist his self-referential center. "Wouldn't I be a bloody cretin after four years?" he continued. "I'd have a goal other than art itself, but art alone has sufficed for me until now, and if I require something more, it will mean that I have become less than what I am . . . I fear that the demon of pride may be wagging my tongue, otherwise I would immediately say no, absolutely not. Like the slug afraid of soiling itself on the sand or of being crushed underfoot, I crawl back into my shell." A voice inside the shell de-

clared that flawed work was better hidden than put forward for recognition,
and that self-imposed abstinence in Croisset was greatly preferable to emas-
culation in Paris.

> Why haven't I had mistresses? Why have I preached chastity? Why have I re-
> mained in this provincial swamp? Do you think I don't get erections like anyone
> else? And that I wouldn't like to play the gallant down there? — Yes, that would
> amuse me rather. But seriously consider this noddle of mine and tell me if you
> think it's possible. I am no more fit to swan around Paris than to nimbly waltz
> around a ballroom. Few men have had fewer women than I (punishment for that
> "plastic beauty" so admired by Théo*), and if I remain unpublished it will be
> retribution for all the crowns I wreathed around my brow in greener days. One
> must obey one's nature, and I may be right in finding movement repugnant.

Describing himself as a mind pervaded by fog and a body caught in the toils
of inaction, he sounded like Gulliver in Lilliput to Du Camp, who would
later hold epilepsy responsible for tying him down. Certainly the seizures,
which were a constant threat, inclined him to solitude. It is possible, moreover, that his laboriousness was somehow bound up with the experience, in
aphasia, of being conscious but speechless, or, as he put it, balled up on
himself "like a hedgehog stuck by its own needles."† But epilepsy hadn't
dammed the flow of long, rich letters from Egypt or made him fearful of
galloping full tilt at Scutari or kept him away from Levantine women.
Abroad he often felt free. In France, where art was made, he had his face to
save or lose, and hostile judges searched him for the least weakness. "My
youth, of which you saw only the tail end, made me a kind of opium fiend,
stupefied for the rest of my days," he told Du Camp. "I hate life — there,
it's said — and whatever reminds me that I must suffer it. I'm fed up with
having to eat, to dress, to stand up . . . The clear, precise person you are has
always rebelled against these Norman vapors, which I couldn't find a graceful way of excusing and which prompted remarks that cut me to the quick;
I put them behind me, but they hurt."

A depressed, childlike Gustave crawling naked in the rubble of his pride
begged for guidance and was told to stand up straight by a manic Du Camp
who identified with Balzac's supreme arriviste, Edmond de Rastignac.
"You always push things to a crazy extreme and that's what you did when
you wrote, barely cracking a smile, that you're no waltzer," he chided. "My
God! No one said anything about waltzing! What you need above all is

*"Théo" is Théophile Gautier.

†The image evokes another in which he likens the writer groping for language to the ascetic tormented by his hair shirt.

what you lack radically, knowledge of life; your ignorance has already wronged you, and out there in the larger world it will put you at a disadvantage even against ungifted dolts." He continued with vows of friendship on the one hand and an asperity born of resentment on the other. Did Flaubert's dedication to art for art's sake not clearly imply contempt for Du Camp's careerist maneuvers?

> You say: do with me what you will, decide for me. That's not possible. I refuse. I don't take charge of souls. Even if it means being misunderstood and mistreated by you, I must leave you in your state of uncertainty . . . But whatever decision you make, . . . I am here and, trust me, I shall relieve you of the more onerous tasks. The day you want to publish, you will find your place ready and reserved, a privilege no one enjoys. Not for a second have I separated myself from you in thought.

He stopped just short of characterizing everything Flaubert had written thus far, including the fragments of *Saint Antoine*, as the doodlings of a brilliant wastrel. Endowed with a surname that commanded respect, free from material cares, and waited upon hand and foot, the heir was squandering his advantages. "What have you made out of them? Nothing, and you are thirty years old! If you don't get going in the next two years, I can't imagine how it will all end up." To his baffled friend, Du Camp preached the gospel of change and commotion, insisting once again that salvation for him lay in Paris. "Solitude profits only the *very strong* and even then only when they are strict with themselves about producing a work. Are we *very strong*? I don't believe so, and for us the teachings of other people are not superfluous. If you want to succeed, if you want to arrive, I'll go further and say, if you want to be *authentic*, leave your lair, where no one will seek you out, and enter the light of day." Flaubert was urged to cultivate makers and doers, to polish his rough surface in society without losing his idiosyncratic soul. Perfidious remarks were dropped behind his back. In conversation with Louise Colet, Du Camp expressed the view that Flaubert, whom he now found tiresome, lacked the stuff needed for a literary future.

Flaubert did not hobnob in drawing rooms or join Du Camp at the banquet table. He holed up in his study between the lane of lindens and the Seine, where, on September 19, a full month before petitioning Du Camp to help him salvage his life, he had recorded, with trepidation, the first lines of *Madame Bovary*. "This is my third try [after *L'Éducation* and *La Tentation*]," he wrote to Louise Colet. "It's high time I succeeded or jumped out the window."

XIV

⌁

Madame Bovary

THE MYTH propagated by Maxime Du Camp in his *Souvenirs littéraires* — that one day, on the Upper Nile, Flaubert began shouting, "I've found it! Eureka! Eureka! I'll call her Madame Bovary" — led many readers to suppose that the novel as well as the name of its heroine suddenly sprang from the deep. *Madame Bovary* did indeed spring from the deep, but by no means suddenly. The same wanton who tells the saint in *La Tentation de Saint Antoine* how much she relishes "the play of hidden perfidies" had been inspiring Flaubert since early adolescence, when he rough-hewed Emma in a story entitled "Passion and Virtue: A Philosophical Tale." Its characters include an unfaithful wife named Mazza Willer, the banker husband she cuckolds, and Ernest, a callous rogue who seduces and abandons her, all three modeled after people involved in a horrible drama of which the *Gazette des Tribunaux* gave a full account on October 4, 1837. In Gustave's telling, their story illustrates the ease with which desire transforms a conventional bourgeoise into a wild woman scornful of all moral strictures. "Limitless" is his word for the heaven and hell of solipsistic passion in which Mazza loses herself after escaping social confinement. Where desire holds sway it rules like a tyrant, jealous of allegiances to anything but itself, leaving no room in consciousness for past or future, for filial piety, conjugal obligation, or maternal love. "When her lover's arms no longer clasped her, she felt like her rumpled clothes, tired, downcast," wrote the fifteen-year-old smitten with Romantic monsters, "as if she had fallen from a great height . . . She wondered whether there wasn't sensual delight even keener than what she had experienced, consummations beyond pleasure. Her hunger for infinite love, for limitless passion, was insatiable." The fallen Mazza retains only enough virtue to find transgression intoxicating. So voracious are her needs that Ernest seeks refuge from her in America. Encumbered with a husband and two children, she poisons them. But when her lover, whom she has hopes of rejoining, informs her that he will soon marry a young American heiress, Mazza turns her rage against herself and swallows prussic acid. "Still, I feel I would like to live and make others suffer as I have suffered," says this Norman Medea before her parting deed. "Happiness is a dream, virtue a word, love a deception."

By 1840 Flaubert had read Balzac's *Physiologie du mariage*, a potpourri of aphorisms and reflections on marriage in which adulterous wives are portrayed as superior beings subjugated by Napoleonic law who recover extramaritally the adulthood they are made to forfeit at the altar. The book impressed him, but while Balzac took a compassionate view of such women (his own mother had been one), arguing that the peccant wife, though her misbehavior would wreak social chaos if left unpunished, is what men have made her, in young Flaubert compassion was eclipsed by an Oedipal fascination with women who stray. To the narrator of *Novembre*, the word *adultery* sings. "There is a sweetness about it, a magic scent; it is the subject of every story told, every book written for the delectation of young men, who find in it a poetry combining ecstasy and brimstone." The adulterous woman is "more woman" than her compliant sister, he declares.

Flaubert was therefore entirely disposed to listen when Bouilhet, who had savaged *La Tentation*, encouraged him after his grand tour to draw inspiration for a novel from the domestic tragedy of Eugène Delamare, a country doctor trained by Achille-Cléophas. In comments about the origins of *Madame Bovary*, Maxime Du Camp portrays Mme Delphine Delamare as a dowerless wife with just enough schooling to support her pretentions and a body whose sinuousness made men forgive her her freckled face, her washed-out blond hair and thick Norman accent. For her husband, who worshipped her, she had no use; to her lovers, of whom there were many, she appeared the eternal supplicant. Nymphomaniacal and wildly profligate, she was, wrote Du Camp, beyond redemption.

> With creditors hounding her, and beaten by her lovers, for whom she stole money from her husband, she poisoned herself in a fit of despair, leaving behind a small daughter whom [Delamare] decided to raise as best he could; but the

poor man was ruined. Unable to repay his wife's debts, treated like a pariah, utterly despondent, he prepared potassium cyanide for himself and went off to rejoin the woman whose loss he couldn't endure.

Since Delamare died late in 1849, there can be no truth to Du Camp's assertion that Bouilhet told Flaubert the story before his departure for Egypt. It is likely that he heard of it from his mother (who was acquainted with Delphine Delamare) when they spent weeks together traveling through Italy. Not until July 23, 1851, is it mentioned in correspondence. On that date Maxime Du Camp asked Flaubert about possible projects. "What are you doing? What have you decided? What are you working on? What are you writing? Have you chosen yet between Don Juan and the story of Mme Delamarre [*sic*], which I find most appealing?"

Pertinent though it is, scholars agree that, if anything, too much has been made of the Delamare scandal, and too much credence lent to Du Camp's embellished version. Didn't Flaubert have sufficient pollen for honey in his own garden? Enough of himself went into the composition of Emma to vindicate his alleged quip, "La Bovary, c'est moi," and available as models for one Bovarian feature or another were adulteresses of his acquaintance; Louise Colet comes to mind of course, but so more specifically does Louise Pradier. In March 1845, before the family's nuptial voyage with Caroline, Flaubert had visited Mme Pradier, a notoriously indiscreet woman, in hopes of collecting bedroom stories about her recent quarrel with her husband, who had caught her in flagrante delicto and begun divorce proceedings. "Ah, what a great study I made there! And what a face I put on!" he informed Alfred Le Poittevin. "I approved of her conduct, declared myself to be the champion of adultery, and may even have astonished her by my indulgence. What is certain is that she found my visit extremely flattering and invited me back to dine with her . . . All of this should be painted, chiseled, narrated in detail . . . How deplorable, the baseness of these people baying at the poor woman just because she spread her legs for a dick other than the one designated by His Honor the Mayor. Her children, everything, have been taken away from her." He might have leaned a little more sympathetically in the direction of James Pradier had he known about bailiffs appearing one day at the sculptor's residence and claiming all its contents to satisfy Louise's creditors. The extent of her indebtedness and promiscuity was impressed upon Flaubert only several years later, apparently during the late 1840s or early 1850s, by an anonymous manuscript discovered in 1947 among his notes for *Bouvard et Pécuchet*. Internal evidence suggests that the author was Louise Boyé, a devoted auxiliary whom Louise Pradier employed as an instrument in the prosecution of her complicated love life and in schemes to raise money for her escapades. Semiliterate but blessed with total recall, Mme Boyé told a tale from which Flaubert would later borrow significant details. How he acquired the manuscript entitled *Les Mémoires de Madame Ludovica* is open to conjecture, one possibility being that he actually commissioned it.*

By March 1852, when part 1 of *Madame Bovary* was half-finished, Flaubert had written to Louise Colet the first of more than 160 letters chronicling his progress or lack of it, his despair, his thoughts about style and the creative endeavor. Style was uppermost in his mind. Tied to a subject that did not comport with his taste for exuberant prose, he struggled for sobriety like a dipsomaniac married to a temperance worker. But under this regime of self-imposed prohibition, words eluded him, and expressing clearly what his mind saw obscurely was painful, he complained. "I have sketched, botched, slogged, groped. Perhaps I'm on the right track now. Oh, what a rascally thing is style. I don't believe you have any idea what kind of book this one is. I'm trying to be as buttoned-up in it as I was unbuttoned in the others and to follow a geometrically straight line. No lyricism, no reflections, the personality of the author absent. It won't be fun to read." Impersonality encompassed polar opposites. In Flaubert a dream of making the world materially present through language — of abolishing the space between words and what they represent — had to compete with his vision of formal perfection embodied in a work representing nothing external.†
Even as he was assembling a portrait of rural Normandy so meticulously furnished that it would not, he feared, entertain readers, he spoke of wanting to produce a book so hermetic that it would be altogether unreadable. Louise Colet might have agreed with Maxime Du Camp that her epistolary lover pushed everything to extremes. "What strikes me as beautiful," he wrote to her on January 16,

> what I would like to create is a book about nothing, a book without external attachments held aloft by the internal force of its style, as the earth stays aloft on its own, a book that would have almost no subject or at least in which the subject would, if possible, evaporate. The most beautiful works are those that have the least matter; the closer expression hugs thought, the more words cleave to it and disappear, the more beautiful it is. Therein lies the future of Art. As it grows, it grows more ethereal, from Egyptian pylons to Gothic lancet windows, from Hindu poems twenty thousand lines long to Byron's ejaculations.

*"Ludovica" is Latin for Louise.

†As for abolishing the distance between words and what they represent, let us recall what he wrote to Le Poittevin from Italy in 1845, that he wanted the color of things to soak his eyes, to be totally absorbed in them. The anxiety of travel was bound up with the sense of monuments and landscapes remaining outside him, or passing him by.

He considered it axiomatic that beauty and ugliness reside not in subjects but in style, style being all by itself "an absolute way of seeing things."

These thoughts would leach into the substance of Emma Bovary, who is seen almost immediately as an anxious soul longing for salvation outside the wet, rustic world through which men and horses slog and outside the wet female body in which she feels imprisoned. Outside all of that is her convent school, where the sounds, sights, and odors of the family farm yield to the perfumed envelopments of chapel service, the whisperings of confession, the vocabulary of celestial love, the prattle of an old aristocratic dame marooned in nineteenth-century France with eighteenth-century memories and contraband Walter Scott novels for the lending. "She wished she could have lived in some old manor house, like those chatelaines in low-waisted bodices under their trefoiled Gothic arches, spending their days, elbows on the parapet and chin in hand, peering across the fields for the white-plumed rider galloping toward her on his black steed. In those days she worshipped Mary Stuart and venerated other illustrious or ill-fated women. For her, Joan of Arc, Heloise, Agnes Sorel, La Belle Ferronnière, and Clémence Isaure blazed like comets against the vast dark backcloth of history." Already condemned to mimic transcendence, to wear the trappings of grace over an emptiness of belief, Emma leaves convent school, rejoins her family, and is presently rescued from the farm by a lovesick country doctor named Charles Bovary, who makes his rounds not galloping on a black steed but dozing on an old nag. The gluttonous wedding feast that inaugurates her marriage with barnyard humor, and the pregnancy announced at the end of part 1 like a death knell or a brutal non sequitur (given her aversion to sex with Charles), show her sinking into corporeality before her fall into infidelity. To be sure, she briefly plays the perfect spouse as she once played the perfect neophyte, but she tires of one as she tired of the other. All is theater. Only in dramatic epiphanies can she feel real, never in dailiness or routine. Too earthbound for flight, and too flighty for happiness on earth, she is an actress living life "as if."

Emma the actress finds a proper stage for her character early in the novel, at a ball in the château of a local blueblood, the marquis d'Andervilliers. Flaubert escorts her and Charles through the scene brilliantly, participating in her excitement while depicting events from an ironical remove. It begins with their arrival in a one-horse buggy at the mansion, which is a secular counterpart to Emma's convent chapel. She steps across the threshold into the space of elevation.

> Its floor was of marble and its ceiling very high; footsteps and voices echoed as in a church. At the far end rose a straight flight of stairs, and to the left a gallery facing the garden led to the billiard room, from which a clickety-clack of ivory

balls became audible as one drew near. There, on her way to the salon, Emma saw grave-faced men gathered around a table with their chins poised on high cravats; they all wore decorations and smiled silently when wielding their cue sticks. On the dark wainscot panels hung large gilded frames with names inscribed at the bottom in black letters. She read: "Jean-Antoine d'Andervilliers d'Yverbonville, Comte de la Vaubyessard and Baron de la Fresnaye, slain at the Battle of Coutras on 20 October 1587." And beneath another: "Jean-Antoine-Henry-Guy d'Andervilliers de la Vaubyessard, Admiral of the Fleet and Knight of the Order of St. Michael, wounded at the Battle of Hougue-Saint-Vaast, 29 May 1692, died at La Vaubyessard on 23 January 1693." She could barely make out those farther down the line, for the lamps were suspended low over the green felt of the billiard table. What light shone on the canvases splintered into fine lines along ridges of cracked varnish, randomly illuminating one feature or another: here a pale brow, there two eyes trained on the spectator, elsewhere wigs curling over the powder-flecked shoulder of a scarlet coat, or the buckle of a garter above a well-turned calf.

This billiard room enshrines Emma's idea of history as a series of momentous occasions starring romantic heroes, with dead time in between. That the portraits illustrating a martial tradition hang ignored in a game room full of beribboned guests who do battle at a billiard table is the ironic prelude to her escape from ordinariness, and irony informs every detail. Nobiliary particles — the profusion of "de"s — are all that link past to present. The great warriors of a heroic age died in battle; the feckless descendants, armed with cue sticks rather than swords or lances, wield them against ivory balls, their only field of honor being an expanse of green felt. Indeed, Flaubert's painted characters exhibit more élan than his live ones. While the latter, with heads "poised" on high cravats like another set of billiard balls, stand grave-faced around a table, the former move combatively as light "splinters" against the canvases, over a landscape of ridges, and body parts leap into view. Nothing indicates that Emma can tell the difference. Where all is theater, all ribbons denote privilege, all particles signify place.

Neither is she disillusioned at another table — a dinner table as heavily laden as the groaning board of her wedding feast — by the spectacle of an old duke with red-rimmed eyes got up in a bib to catch the sauce drooling from his pendulous lips. In much the same way that Proust's Marcel repairs his ideal image of the duchesse de Guermantes after seeing her in the flesh, blemishes and all, Emma smuggles the duc de Laverdière out of his senile incarnation. "Great and glorious before the days of Charlemagne, the Guermantes had the right of life and death over their vassals; the duchesse de Guermantes descends from Geneviève de Brabant" is Marcel's self-hypnotic litany, and Emma likewise reminds herself that Laverdière, who lived at court before the Revolution, was rumored to have been Marie-Antoinette's lover.

The climactic event is the ball itself, for which Emma, in the bedroom she and her husband have been assigned, primps "with the fastidiousness of an actress making her debut." Sharply rebuked when he plants a kiss on her bare shoulder and instructed to keep off the dance floor, the extraneous Charles can play no part in her performance, which will last all night long. Transported by music, by the glint of diamonds, the scent of jasmine, the froufrou of satin, the varnish of antiques, the porcelain white of complexions, she enters a second state culminating in vertigo as a titled partner waltzes her, spellbound, around the ballroom. Only once does anything of the real world impinge upon Emma's consciousness.

> From the ballroom, where the air was stuffy and the gaslight dimming, people began to flow toward the billiard room. A servant stood on a chair and broke two panes; at the sound of shattering glass she turned her head and saw peasants in the garden with their faces pressed against the window. Memories of Les Bertaux [the family farm] sprang to mind. She saw the muddy pond, her father in his smock under the apple trees and herself in the dairy skimming cream off the milk churns with her finger. But the fulguration of the present hour dispelled her past life, which had until then been clearly etched in her memory. She came close to doubting that she had ever lived it.

In breaking windowpanes, the servant breaks the mirror at which Emma had composed herself for the evening. What shatters is the illusion, the mask, the new being achievable only onstage, in a role. Once open to the outside world, the ballroom-cum-theater is opened to the gaping face of history — not the glorious history recounted by patrician portraits but that which betrays humble origins. Flaubert's concern with absolutes of interiority and exteriority as they bear upon fictional creation — upon language — thus came to inform a central scene of *Madame Bovary*, dramatizing his heroine's relentless attempts at self-creation. Windows almost invariably frame her futility. While mirrors befriend the imagination, windows show her what she is or isn't, and this adventure ends with Emma looking through one, in a guest room, after the ball. "The first light of dawn found her looking at the windows of the château and trying to place behind each one the people she had remarked that evening," writes Flaubert. "She would like to have known how they lived, to have penetrated their existences, mingled in them." The window emblemizes a distance from Being, from *la vraie vie*. When in due course the squire who makes her his mistress jilts her, she will read his letter of farewell at a window and stop just short of defenestrating herself.

~

ACCUSTOMED AS a child to hearing that her uncle was preoccupied with "La Bovary," Flaubert's niece Liline took the name to be a French word for "work." And that mysterious work was understood to dictate not only the permissible volume of household noise but, in general, the rituals of daily life at Croisset. Mme Flaubert might complain about it. She might even declare at times that the goose quill from which her son could not long be parted had sapped his humanity.* Still, she never failed to come and sit beside him, like a chamberlain at the prince's *petite levée,* when he summoned her, as he did every morning soon after waking up, by tapping the wall that separated their bedrooms.

Days were as unvaried as the notes of the cuckoo. Flaubert, a man of nocturnal habits, usually awoke at 10 a.m. and announced the event with his bell cord. Only then did people dare speak above a whisper. His valet, Narcisse, straightaway brought him water, filled his pipe, drew the curtains, and delivered the morning mail. Conversation with Mother, which took place in clouds of tobacco smoke particularly noxious to the migraine sufferer, preceded a very hot bath and a long, careful toilette involving the regular application of a tonic reputed to arrest hair loss. At 11 a.m. he entered the dining room, where Mme Flaubert; Liline; her English governess, Isabel Hutton; and very often Uncle Parain would have gathered. Unable to work well on a full stomach, he ate lightly, or what passed for such in the Flaubert household, meaning that his first meal consisted of eggs, vegetables, cheese or fruit, and a cup of cold chocolate. The family then lounged on the terrace, unless foul weather kept them indoors, or climbed a steep path through woods behind their espaliered kitchen garden to a glade dubbed La Mercure after the statue of Mercury that once stood there. Shaded by chestnut trees, near their hillside orchard, they would argue, joke, gossip, and watch vessels sail up and down the river. Another site of open-air refreshment was the eighteenth-century pavilion. After dinner, which generally lasted from seven to nine, dusk often found them there, looking out at moonlight flecking the water and fishermen casting their hoop nets for eel.

In June 1852, Flaubert told Louise Colet that he worked from 1 p.m. to 1 a.m. A year later, when he assumed partial responsibility for Liline's education and gave her an hour or more of his time each day, he may not have put pen to paper at his large round writing table until two o'clock or later. The tutorial was important, no less to Flaubert, who in that familiar role

---

*Flaubert's need to dissociate the enterprise of writing from what he regarded as mechanical tools was extreme. He hated not only metal nibs but also metal type and hated to visit printing plants.

could imagine himself bringing his sister back to life, than to the girl, who desperately needed his avuncular devotion. "I'd leap on the great white bearskin and cover its big head with kisses," she wrote in her *Souvenirs intimes*, fondly remembering the odor of tobacco and cologne that imbued his studio, the wreathed oak columns of his bookshelves, the writing table covered with a green cloth, the high-backed tapestry chair, the porcelain frog inkwell, the gilded Buddha, the marble bust of her mother on a pedestal between two riverside windows. "My uncle would meanwhile place one pipe on the mantelpiece, choose another, fill it, light it, sit . . . at the far end of the room, cross his legs, lean back, and file his nails." He fed her gobbets of Plutarch as she sat near him on a chaise longue, riveted to the story and the storyteller. "He thus taught me all of ancient history, relating facts to one another, sharing reflections within my reach but so well observed that more mature minds would have found nothing puerile in his teaching," she wrote. "I would sometimes stop him and ask, apropos of Cambyses, Alexander, or Alcibiades, whether they were good or not. The question disconcerted him. 'Good? . . . Well, they certainly weren't accommodating gentlemen. What difference does it make anyway?' But this answer never satisfied me and I thought that *'mon vieux,'* 'my old man,' as I called him, should know every last thing about the people he introduced to me."

A thick sheaf of detailed notes on ancient history, written in his small, neat hand, attests to the gravitas of Flaubert's pedagogical mission. But these notes were prepared for a Liline old enough to browse through the Flaubert library and take notes in her own right. For Liline the child he collected cards, spheres, and jigsaw puzzles and favored images over books. Geography lessons were held in the garden, where, equipped with a bucket of water and a shovel, he dug up soil to model islands, peninsulas, gulfs, promontories. When at length she seemed ready for serious reading, he insisted that she neither abandon a book once begun nor proceed by fits and starts. How could one understand the totality of a work, he told her, if one swallowed it piecemeal? She was therefore to read books as he read them: at one go. The received idea of nineteenth-century bourgeois that women did not naturally possess an *esprit de suite* — intellectual coherence and doggedness of mind — made this discipline all the more imperative.

A much less gratifying family ritual was the Sunday meal at Croisset with "les Achille" — brother; sister-in-law, Julie; and niece, Juliette. To intimate correspondents, an exclamation mark after the report that they were expected for dinner concisely signaled his displeasure, but he often went further and mocked them in ways that suggest a need to dissociate himself from kin bearing the stigma of philistinism. Did they serve in a way as useful scapegoats? "Live like a bourgeois but think like a demigod," he would later say, and assuredly "the Achilles" helped him feel comparatively divine. When at one point they showed greater warmth than usual, he attributed their flush to Mme Flaubert's having had the old billiard table repaired for them. Achille's wife and his mother-in-law, Marguerite Lormier, were favorite objects of ridicule. "Mother Lormier is said to be growing 'thick,' 'weary' — her expressions," he wrote to his Uncle Parain on New Year's Day 1853. "As if it were not bad enough to have been stupid all her life, she is now verging on imbecility. Even her children have started to worry, and it's high time they did! What perspicacity! . . . You will find me unchanged, *mon vieux; my hatred of the bourgeois* has not diminished, though it's now more a serene rage against my species." Occasionally he signed his letters "Bourgeoisophobus."*

Damning his species was one thing; being excluded by it was another. It angered him that his brother did not invite him to a soiree for local notables at the Hôtel-Dieu. He consoled himself with the reflection that these "fine folk," banal as they were, could not tolerate anyone out of the ordinary. "In every possible way I enjoy almost no consideration in my country and my family!" he boasted plaintively. Some years later it would give him great satisfaction, after five days of attendance at imperial festivities in the Palais de Compiègne, to imagine Rouen bourgeois being abashed by news of his hobnobbing with Napoleon III's court.

Flaubert nevertheless accepted invitations to dine with Achille (early dinners, as bedtime for the surgeon was 9 p.m.) and fought his brother's fights for him, welcoming the opportunity to prove himself more effective than he, more combative and virile. In 1846 he had marshaled influential acquaintances against those who opposed Achille's appointment to the Hôtel-Dieu. Now, in 1853, a waffling Achille, fearful of being bested by the landowner in negotiations for a farm near Trouville, had Gustave represent him. "I have downed many glasses of rum since yesterday!" Flaubert wrote to Bouilhet. "What a study they are, bourgeois! . . . What milktoast characters, fainthearted wills, anemic passions! How wavering, evasive, feeble is everything in those brains! Oh, practical men, men of action, sensible men, how clumsy I find you, how numb, how limited!" It pleased him to report that he was never flummoxed by the landowner and, at the end of

*Flaubert never lost his love of sobriquets. His niece Caroline was "Mon bibi" as well as "Caro," "Carolo," "Liline," and "Loulou." To her he was *"ton vieux ganachon"* (your old fogey) and, in later years, "Polycarpe" (Saint Polycarp being the first-century Greek bishop of Smyrna known for his fire-and-brimstone denunciation of early heresies). Bouilhet — "Archbishop" or "Monsignor" — was the primate of an ideal diocese in which Flaubert occupied the position of grand vicar. They called their friend d'Osmoy "the Idiot of Amsterdam," in perverse honor of his keen wit.

Flaubert may have known that Polycarp was for some reason a name commonly given to foundlings at the Hôtel-Dieu.

the day, summarized his discussions for Achille in what he called "a model of business prose."

On another level of feeling he may have sympathized with his brother's tetchy diffidence. Certainly he did not hestitate to applaud when one day Achille, after reading all three thousand lines of *Melaenis* in the *Revue de Paris*, heaped praise on Bouilhet. This sign of redemption compensated for much sibling disappointment. Discovering an esthetic sense where he had previously seen only conventional wisdom came as such a surprise that Flaubert swore, in a short-lived vow, never again to pass judgment on anyone. "Stupidity and Mind are not neatly divided. They're like Vice and Virtuc. Cunning indeed is he who can tease them apart."

All the same, he had no doubt that Bouilhet, the superior classics scholar, who came from Rouen almost every Sunday, had more than his share of mind. This is not to say that their conversation was always lofty, and least of all when it involved literary gossip or turned to women, as it often did. The two hid very little from each other. Flaubert kept Bouilhet abreast of events in his relationship with Louise Colet. Bouilhet, in turn, sighed for a married woman introduced to him by Louise during his residence in Paris, Edma Roger des Genettes (with whom Flaubert later formed a warm friendship), and described the events of his ultimately successful campaign to win her favors. Everyone knew everyone else, and everyone corresponded, like four hands engaged in cat's cradle, drawing strings between Rouen and Paris. This symmetrical entanglement reinforced Flaubert's belief that he and Bouilhet were two of a kind, clouded in their love affairs but radiant in their friendship. While love affairs unraveled, Sunday after Sunday this friendship became an increasingly seamless thing. Indeed, they ended up looking like fraternal twins, with congruent paunches, identical mustaches, and similarly bald pates. *Non amici, fratres, non sanguine, corde.*

High-minded they nonetheless were, for the most part. Common interests of every other kind hinged on a shared love of literature and the conviction that informed their literary affinities. Both men were passionate readers. In the early 1850s, when Flaubert began staying awake until 4 or 5 a.m., hours of the day and night were spent not at his desk with *Madame Bovary* but on his couch with Apuleius, Molière, Chateaubriand, Dante, Shakespeare, Sophocles, Boileau, Stendhal, Balzac, La Fontaine, Montaigne, Bossuet, Hugo, Horace, and Homer, to mention only authors cited in correspondence ("One must know the masters by heart, idolize them, strive to think like them," he advised Louise, "and then separate oneself from them forever").* Usually open at his bedside was Goethe's *Faust.*

---

*He warned his niece more than once that keeping bad literary company would inevitably show in one's own prose.

Bouilhet, who had comparable range, accompanied him on Sunday excursions into Rabelais, Cervantes, and sixteenth-century lyric poetry, which they took turns reciting. "What a poet! What a poet!" Flaubert wrote of Pierre de Ronsard. "What wings! He's greater than Virgil and, in lyric spurts, the equal of Goethe. This morning, at 1:30, I was reciting verse that gave me so much pleasure my nerves went haywire. It's as if someone were tickling the soles of my feet. We two are gaga, we foam and pity everyone on earth ignorant of Ronsard. Poor great man, if his shade can see us, how happy he must be!" These effusions *à deux* were a dominical binge after weekdays of stoical labor, a popping of the cork that released all the effervescence Flaubert had kept bottled up in the practice of his art.

To be sure, Bouilhet was as much a critical voice as a coreligionist, and his acumen profited not only *Madame Bovary*, which Flaubert read to him chapter by chapter, then part by part (150 pages at a stretch), but also the work of Louise Colet, who often sent them poems and plays for repair. Fluent in the best of circumstances, Louise may have been even more so in the worst, when debts, unhappiness, and grandiosity combined to spur her on. Every other year the French Academy offered a substantial purse for the best poem on a subject appropriate to its role as an institution that safeguarded France's cultural heritage while concerning itself with matters of moral improvement. In 1851–52 the assigned subject was Mettray, an agricultural colony near Tours founded in 1838 to rehabilitate wayward youths. In 1853–54 competitors were invited to celebrate the Acropolis, where a French archeologist named Boulé had recently conducted important digs. With help from her auxiliaries in Rouen and lobbying her suitors in the Academy (of whom there were at least two), she won both prizes. This launched her on a long didactic poem called *Le Poème de la femme*, which was to unfold in six parts illustrating the various forms of servitude endured by women in a patriarchal society: "The Peasant Woman," "The Servant," "The Nun," "The Bourgeoise," "The Princess," "The Woman Artist" (alternatively titled "The Superior Woman"). Flaubert brought to bear upon his editorial task the same conscientiousness that marked his writing. Alone, or with Bouilhet, he devoted whole afternoons to "La Colonie de Mettray" and "La Paysanne" and hours more to a correspondence that marched her through her work line by line, weeding out repetitions and assonances, decrying mixed metaphors, prosecuting banality, correcting her grammar, offering alternative lines of verse.* Vetting Louise might have given him

*A specimen of Flaubertian editing is this commentary on a line in "La Paysanne": "Et le soleil plombait ses cheveux blancs" (And the sun gave a leaden glaze to her white hair): "Bad; one uses 'plomber' metaphorically only in the preterit: lead colored, livid; if you're using it in this sense, the verb is neuter and there's an obvious grammatical error here, for neuter verbs do not take a direct object."

full-time employment had he not had *Madame Bovary* to write. "Be sparse" was his refrain, and he repeated it tirelessly, with a regretful thought, perhaps, to what he called the "wordless tendernesses" of Oriental women. At the end of a stringent letter twenty pages long dated November 28, 1852, he noted that his comments were all his own, since Bouilhet had not joined him that Sunday. "I've worked on them for six hours straight," he claimed.

> *Everything I haven't commented on seems to me good or excellent,* so don't be alarmed. The revisions you've made generally pass muster. Spend a week or more reflecting on the last part before changing anything . . . You have a lovely work and you must make it irreproachable. *Classical.* You can do it. All you need is patience, my impetuous one. The other week I spent four whole days writing a very beautiful page, I exhausted myself over it, and now I've scrapped it because it didn't fit in. One must always bear in mind the whole work . . . Tomorrow, before dining at my brother's place, I'll deliver your "Paysanne" to Bouilhet; I wager that he'll share my opinion of the ending. I'll tell him to write to you this week.

A fortnight later he implored her again to take time pruning her work. "Learn to be self-critical, my dear savage." When she protested that her friend Babinet, a distinguished astronomer, appreciated lines that he and Bouilhet had found maladroit, his temper flared. "Ah! Musette, musette,* how fickle you are. Make a habit of *meditating* before you write!" He felt certain that gold could be mined from her ore; otherwise he would have pronounced her work impeccable just to rid himself of it, "for it shows how you cling to your revoltingly slipshod ways." As for Babinet's opinions, he dismissed them outright, suggesting that it were better her friend study the night sky. "I repeat once again that [the two verbs to which I took exception] are stupid. Now keep them if that's what you want. Many people will be charmed by them." Bouilhet, who had pondered a poem for six years before composing it, was held up to her as an example of patience and probity. "In a month of relentless work, he has written only forty lines, but they are right as rain." He also quoted Horace's dictum that a work should not be shown the light of day until it had survived eight years of obscurity.

Couching his admonitions in language that implies a constant struggle between masculine and feminine, he urged upon her not only the muscular prose for which he professed exclusive admiration but the *retenue,* or restraint, bound up with aristocratic ideals of manhood. He would have had her be less a woman splurging herself in her need for constant approbation

---

*Flaubert is using as a term of endearment the poetic word for bagpipe (also meaning, by extension, a pastoral air to be accompanied by that instrument). Perhaps more to the point, it was for him a diminutive of *muse.*

and more a man depriving himself of cheap rewards in his allegiance to a noble cause. Such a man was Bouilhet. Another was Flaubert. The martyrdom he suffered at his desk gave the measure of his virility, just as the Virgilian pace of work on *Madame Bovary* argued his spiritual mission, and tormented progress reports (which also served to justify his protracted absences from Paris) recur throughout the correspondence. If she could imagine a pianist playing with lead balls on each digit, she could imagine him laboring at his desk. "Since we last saw each other six weeks ago I've written a grand total of twenty-five pages," he informed her on April 24, 1852. "I have done so much revising and recopying that I have fire in my eyes." Her black moods, he declared, paled next to his. "I sometimes wonder why my arms don't fall off my body from weariness and why my head doesn't dissolve into mush. I lead a harsh life devoid of all external joy, with nothing to support me but a kind of permanent rage." Midnight on the fifteenth of May found him in the middle of a page to which he had devoted the entire day, he told her. "I'm setting it aside to write this letter, and anyway it may occupy me until tomorrow evening, . . . for I am often hours chasing a word and I have more yet to track down." Mush, or *bouillie*, was a favorite expression. "If only you knew how much I cut out and what mush my manuscripts are! I have one hundred twenty acceptable pages, but have written at least five hundred." In January 1853 he announced that the novel had grown by only sixty-five pages during the previous five months. "I reread them the day before yesterday and was startled to see how much time I had spent to so little effect . . . Each paragraph is good in itself, and there are, I daresay, perfect pages. But for that very reason, *it doesn't work*. It's a series of well-turned paragraphs that don't flow into one another. I will have to unscrew them, loosen the joints, as one reefs the mainsail on a boat to catch more wind. I am exhausting myself in pursuit of an ideal that is perhaps absurd in itself. It may be that my subject does not comport with this style." This vain pursuit had begun in childhood, he wrote, when Julie the servant helped him write down the sentences he invented. "I have continually seen the goal recede before me, from year to year and progress to progress. How often have I fallen flat on my face just when I thought it lay within my reach. And yet I feel that I must not die before the style I have in my head has been able to sound somewhere, over the din of parrots and crickets."

ON JULY 18, 1852, Flaubert and Bouilhet traveled seven miles downriver to Grand-Couronne, where farm families were assembling for the regional fair called les Comices. Flaubert took abundant notes, but another seventeen months would pass before they bore fruit in the chapter that nudges Emma toward adultery. Unreconciled to village life in Yonville, the bore-

dom of which is not alleviated by motherhood, she has begun to embroi-
der wayward fantasies around a callow young bachelor, Léon, when a country squire named Rodolphe Boulanger appears. Her tentative flirtation with
the one has ripened her for a full-blown affair with the other, and Rodolphe,
experienced womanizer that he is, recognizes Emma as easy prey. He initiates the seduction at the village fair. Sauntering among animals brought in
from the farm to compete for ribbons and peasant women encumbered
with children and picnic baskets, he cuts an anomalous figure. "There was,
in his attire, that casual mingling of the plain and the recherché which ordinary people take to be evidence of an eccentric life, of inner tumult, of
enslavement to the tyrannies of art, of perfect contempt for social convention . . . Thus did his batiste shirt with pleated cuffs billow out of his gray
twill jacket whenever the wind gusted, and his broad striped trousers exposed ankle-length nankeen boots vamped with patent leather so shiny that
it mirrored the grass. He walked right through horse manure, one hand in
his coat pocket and his straw hat tilted at a raffish angle." Rodolphe flatters
the stylish young woman with the sartorial complaint that it is hardly worth
dressing up for yokels ignorant of fashion, and further awakens her sympathy with allusions to some mysterious sadness weighing upon his soul.
When a drumroll announces the arrival of a minor government official,
livestock and people fill the village square, where notables occupy a stage in
front of Yonville's Hôtel de Ville. Emma and Rodolphe are not among
them but inside the empty building, seated by themselves at a second-floor
window above the crowd. What follows is a scene in which the prefectural
councillor's peroration and the couple's dialogue weave together ironically.
It makes for brilliant counterpoint, as both councillor and seducer recite
canned ideas, each to a gullible audience. The councillor begins:

> Gentlemen, may I take the liberty first of all, with your permission, before ad-
> dressing the object of our gathering today — and you will all, I trust, share this
> sentiment — may I take the liberty, I say, of paying tribute to the higher admin-
> istrative echelons, to the government, to the monarch, gentlemen, to that sov-
> ereign, our beloved king, for whom everything that touches upon individual
> prosperity and the commonweal is of vital concern and who holds the reins so
> steadily and wisely as he guides the chariot of state through the constant perils
> of a stormy sea, maintaining respect for peace and war alike, for industry, com-
> merce, agriculture and the fine arts.

Whereupon Rodolphe tells a puzzled Emma that he should draw his chair
farther away from the window. "Why?" she asks, as the councillor's voice
rises several decibels:

Gone are the days, gentlemen, when civil strife spattered blood over our public squares, when the landlord, the merchant, even the worker never shut their eyes in peaceful slumber at night without a quaking thought to the prospect of being awoken by incendiary tocsins, when the most subversive slogans were flagrantly undermining the very pillars . . .

"Because my reputation is so bad," Rodolphe explains, secure in the knowledge that a hint of cloven hooves will thrill the young woman. "Oh! You wrong yourself, I'm sure," she protests, tacitly inviting him to reaffirm his moral pariahdom. He complies with "No, no, it's worse than bad, it's execrable, trust me." The orator and the rake wax more eloquent.

"But gentlemen," the councillor continued, "if I cast these somber images out of my memory and regard our glorious fatherland as it is today, what do I see? Blooming everywhere are commerce and the arts; everywhere new lines of communication, like so many arteries in the Body Politic, are fostering new contacts. Our great manufacturing centers have resumed activity; religion, firmly anchored in our midst, smiles upon us all. Our ports bustle, our confidence surges, and France breathes at last."

"Besides," Rodolphe added, "by its own lights, society may be right to shun me." "What do you mean?" she asked. "Come!" he said. "Don't you know that there are souls in ceaseless torment? They insist on dreaming as well as acting, they will settle for nothing less than the purest passions, the most rapturous pleasures — and risk madness in their headlong pursuit of whatever captures their fancy." She looked at him as one might gaze upon someone who has traveled through fabulous lands and said: "We poor women don't have recourse to such distractions!" "Sorry distractions they are, for they don't bring happiness." "But can happiness ever be found?" she asked. "Yes, one day you encounter it," he answered.

"And that is what you have realized," the councillor was saying. "You, husbandmen and tillers of the soil; you, peaceful pioneers of a civilizing enterprise! You, men of progress and morality! You have realized, I say, that political storms are truly more to be feared than atmospheric disturbances . . ."

"One day you encounter it," Rodolphe repeated, "one day, out of the clear blue, just when you were despairing. Suddenly you glimpse new horizons, as if a voice were shouting: 'There it is, yonder!' You feel the need to tell that person the secrets of your life, to yield your all to him! Explanations are superfluous, everything is guessed. You have seen each other in your dreams." (And he looked at her.) "At last it is there, the dreamed-of treasure, right in front of you, shining, sparkling. And yet doubts persist, you dare not believe it. You are dazzled, like someone emerging from darkness into blinding light." At this

Rodolphe pantomimed his sentence. He drew his hand across his face . . . and let it drop on Emma's.

Flaubert often cut his big scenes from the same cloth, and a common pattern matches this one to the aristocrats' ball, for here again is an illusory space of elevation, another stage on which Emma the actress disavows a past she would see if she dared look out the window. At Andervilliers' château her trance is broken, momentarily, when the shattered panes reveal an audience of all-too-familiar peasants. At Yonville's town hall, entranced by her artful squire, she stars in a parody of romantic drama, and she plays her part well, having rehearsed it since girlhood, but plays it to a barnyard parterre with its collective back turned (a paradox that will shape a later scene, in which Flaubert has Emma fornicate on a daylight coach ride through Rouen, publicly but unseen, as the shades are drawn). Moreover, both episodes conclude with falls. After the ball, Emma, cheated of redemption, measures time as an empty expanse separating her further and further from her magic moment; it had hollowed out her existence, writes Flaubert, "like the mountain storm that opens a huge crevasse overnight." After the fair, when she yields her all, time will be the emptiness between rapturous assignations. Either way, life for her is a pneumatic ordeal, a swelling or collapsing, a filling of the void or a becoming the void.

AT AGE thirty-three Franz Kafka resolved to stop making grandiose comparisons between himself and Flaubert, whose *L'Éducation sentimentale* (in its final version) was his constant companion for years. Unlike himself, he wrote, Flaubert did not calculate but acted, being "a man of decision" well seated in himself. Had he read his hero's correspondence, Kafka might have been cheered to discover territories of neurotic cousinage. The arrangements and deferrals that made each reunion with Louise Colet a signal event, though nothing quite as snarled as those that drove Kafka's lover Felice Bauer half-mad, were still convoluted enough to be called Kafkaesque. Their most memorable trysts took place not in Paris or Rouen but in Mantes-la-Jolie, a picturesque town on the Seine between the two cities and outside the ken of gossipmongers. On April 15, 1853, for example, Flaubert informed Louise, after pronouncing himself undone by the bourgeois vulgarities his subject compelled him to dramatize, that he could probably interrupt his work in three weeks. The anticipation of amorous embraces warmed him, he said, but everything hinged on how *Madame Bovary* had progressed, and the thought of all the blank pages yet to be filled dampened his ardor.

On April 26 he reported that he had adopted the modest goal of tying up loose ends before they met — completing five half-written pages, writing three new ones, finding four or five sentences that had eluded him for some time — since the section he had hoped to finish by then required another month's labor. On April 29 an infected tooth threatened this plan, but on May 3 he finally set a date, May 9, with all kinds of provisos — that his abscess would have drained, his swollen glands subsided, his temperature fallen, his cerebellum ceased to report shooting pains, his mouth be able to accept real food. "Dear friend," he wrote to Louise on May 7, "trains from Paris depart at 11:00, at noon, and at 4:25 and arrive in Mantes at 1:00, 1:50, and 6:15; departures from Rouen are at 10:35, 1:25, and 4:15. The most convenient one for me would be the 1:25 (express). But since it arrives in Mantes at 3:39, you would have to wait two hours (assuming you catch the noon train). We're better off with me leaving at 10:30 and you at exactly 11:00. You will then arrive at 1:00 on the dot, a quarter-hour before me. So, it's settled, take the 11:00 train and wait fifteen minutes. My teeth are better."

For Flaubert the sequel to these brief idylls, which were spent at a whitewashed inn near the large collegiate church that Corot later made famous, was most often sadness warring with guilt and anger. His letters echo Emma Bovary's nostalgic evocations of her soiree at Andervilliers' château. The same phrases recur. But again and again, directly or inferentially, Cupid's arrow delivered the ominous message that he could not easily reconcile a passionate relationship with work, that only two or three days away from Croisset in thrall to the softer side of his nature meant days more of relearning the austere discipline by which he otherwise set store. Twenty-four hours at Mantes, Flaubert wrote before one rendezvous, would allow more intimacy than five or six visits to Paris, without interrupting his "train of thought." When twenty-four hours stretched into forty-eight, the train derailed. "You won't soon forget our forty-eight hours at Mantes, my dear Louise," he wrote. "They were good hours. I've never loved you so much! . . . Your image has followed me all evening, like a hallucination. I got back to work only yesterday. Until then I could do little but think about those fugitive moments. *I must calm down.*" Custom did not make the intervals any easier to bridge. Nine months later, after their fourth rendezvous in Mantes, he ended a letter with yet another ambivalent protestation. "I hardly have the energy to write to you. Before resuming my work, I always experience, as I do now, a stupefying sadness. The memory of you makes my stupefaction complete. This too will pass; consoling knowledge." His assertion that memory, or an image, could "finish" him was not rhetorical. Like Kafka imploring Felice to write him only one letter a week and to time it for delivery on Sunday because her words made any concentrated effort impossible, Flaubert, when he wasn't touting his combativeness, pictured himself as a habitation defenseless against the force of "external objects." Since his memory for images was astonishingly retentive, mortal danger lay in those thrust upon him from without or in hallucinations independent of his will. The author who devoted himself stubbornly to a delirious anchorite was also the epileptic terrified of losing his mind and the lover fearful of being tyrannized by desire (all three combined to make up the man who, fighting shy of cameras, sat only once or twice, grudgingly and late in life, for a photographic portrait). It was to be expected, then, that he would feel incapable of serious work except in the intimately familiar surroundings at Croisset. He could relocate his person but not his thought, he told Louise whenever she urged him to take a flat in Paris. "Since [my thought] is never one with myself and not at all at my disposition, since I do its bidding rather than it mine, the least disturbance will scare it off: the buzz of a fly, the rattle of a cart, the crooked fold of a curtain. I could never, like Napoleon I, work in the thunder of cannonfire. The mere crackling of wood in my fireplace is enough to make me start . . . I know all too well I have described a spoiled child and a paltry man." Years earlier, when with the family in Italy, he wrote much the same thing to Alfred Le Poittevin, complaining about the ordeal of traveling in company and having the spell cast by a beautiful object or landscape destroyed by a fatuous comment.

Undaunted, Louise kept after Flaubert, creating turmoil even as she buoyed his ego through rough passages, including the grand mal seizure he had suffered in his Paris hotel room the previous year, during the summer of 1852. On that occasion he experienced the usual prodromes and warned her, before blacking out, not to summon help; he remained comatose for ten minutes, foaming at the mouth, gurgling, and clutching her arm in a viselike grip that left her bruised. The nightmarish episode strengthened her bond to him, she wrote.

Louise might have given up sooner than she did were it not for her mistaken belief that she still had sufficient allure to rescue him from maternal thralldom, or that his mother, if only she could meet and charm her, would promote their union, or that earnest repetition could make her plea audible to a deaf ear. Still, vanity and naïveté alone don't explain her persistence. There was, for one thing, enormous admiration. Long before Flaubert achieved fame with *Madame Bovary*, Louise, after reading the early manuscript of *L'Éducation sentimentale*, had come to regard him as a great writer — a "master," a "genius" — and his splendid letters, which almost always arrived twice a week, only confirmed her judgment. She might complain about his self-absorption, but so long as the distant Flaubert corresponded brilliantly, he seemed far more attractive than proximate candidates for her affection. "It's been a fortnight since Gustave left," she noted in her journal on September 4, 1852. "He was more loving, more tender than usual; it is he whom I esteem, he who attaches me, he to whom I feel most deeply, most compellingly attracted." And again, on April 7, 1853:

> How downcast I've been the last few days! It seems to me that I am already bearing the weight of old age and feeling it hollow out my bones. Nothing supports me. In his letters Gustave never speaks about anything but *Art* or himself. Not a word about my financial embarrassments. Ah, so what! Such as he is, he still sweetens my life. I haven't had any letters from him in a week, and they have never been more necessary to me.

To be sure, Flaubert played the role of mentor with gusto. He fancied himself behind a lectern at the Collège de France, like Adolphe Chéruel, preaching the gospel of impersonality in formulations such as "The only way to enjoy peace is to leap above humanity and have no truck with it except as an observing eye." Still, Louise's work benefited from his lessons on art and his schoolmasterish stringency. And although she felt that only an egotist of independent means could afford to eschew humanity and urge her to do likewise, she also benefited nominally from his inheritance. He lent her five hundred francs on one occasion, despite Mme Flaubert's frowns, and offered a gift in that same amount some months later, when a hoped-for prize was not awarded.

Furthermore, his letters were often amorous enough to justify her conjugal dreams. "Your love penetrates me like warm rain," he wrote in the month of May 1853, "and drenches my heart. Everything about you invites love: your body, your mind, your tenderness. You have a simple soul and a clever head . . . There is nothing but good in you, and all of you, like your bosom, is white and soft to the touch. The women I've known were not your equal." And again on August 21: "I love you as I have never loved. You are and will remain *alone* and incomparable . . . We are bound by a pact independent of us. Have I not done everything to leave you? Have you not done as much to settle your love elsewhere? We have nonetheless returned to each other." He held her at arm's length, but held her nonetheless. There were assurances that he would indeed take a flat in Paris once he finished *Madame Bovary* and, before that, come down from Rouen for a week every two months. He also insinuated that Mme Flaubert — from whom he shooed Louise away by portraying her as supercilious, if not downright inhospitable — might receive her after all. Madame, he wrote, had appreciated her poem "La Paysanne."

Flaubert may have been flattered that the woman who kept exhorting him to claim her had kindled a distant fire in Victor Hugo. Hugo, whom Louise had never met, backed her for a poetry prize when he still occupied his seat at the French Academy, and he continued his support after December 1851, to the extent that recommendations sent from his place of exile on the island of Guernsey could influence colleagues in Paris. She sent him poems, which he never failed to praise. He in turn used her as a mail drop for letters to correspondents under government surveillance and pamphlet-length diatribes against Napoleon III. He dedicated "Pasteurs et Troupeaux" to her. She delighted him with her own impeachment of the avaricious parvenus ruling a land now hostile to the life of the mind, whose citizenry had abandoned its temples and academies for the stock market. Complicit in this exchange, which could have earned Louise a jail sentence, was Flaubert, who saw to it that the correspondence followed a devious route, passing each way through two middlemen, himself in Croisset and Mrs. Jane Farmer in Upper Holloway. Eventually he, Hugo, and Louise formed an epistolary ménage à trois. Hugo wrote to Flaubert (via Mrs. Farmer) thanking him for his mediation. Flaubert, irritated though he was by Hugo's sentimental populism and unimpressed by his polemics, gave the great man his due. "You have been in my life a charming obsession, an enduring love, sir," he wrote on July 15, 1853. "I have read you during sinister vigils and at the seashore, on soft beaches, in broad summer sunlight. I took you with me through Palestine and I had you to console me in the Latin Quarter as well, ten years ago, when I was dying of boredom. Your poetry has permeated my being like a nurse's milk." He was rewarded with a photograph of Hugo, an invitation to help in broadcasting his tirades, and an imperative compliment. "I want correspondence, I demand correspondence. So much the worse for you, sir. It's your fault. Why have you written me such noble and witty letters? Blame yourself. Henceforth you must write to me." Flaubert's code name for Hugo was "the Crocodile." It was just as well that the gallant Crocodile couldn't swim home, he told Louise, feigning something like the jealous fire she would have liked to light under him.

Had there been jealousy to excite, she would have stood a better chance with her reports of assiduous courtship by a star of lesser magnitude in the Romantic firmament, Alfred de Musset. George Sand's quondam lover looked older than his years — he was Louise's age — after a life of self-squander and was destined to die in 1857. The fact that he had just been elected an "immortal" of the French Academy when Louise met him in 1852 gave him almost as much allure in her eyes as his former relationship with Sand. He read her work, commented upon it, and soon received invitations to the rue de Sèvres, where his habitually drunken state, or that combined with syphilitic asthenia, rendered him impotent. Louise told Flaubert not about Musset's presence in her bedroom but about his rage after one such fiasco during a ride across Paris. She threatened to leap out of the carriage unless he unhanded her and then made good her threat, falling on cobblestones at the place de la Concorde. "I bruised my knees, I thought I had injured myself more seriously, for I felt a kind of commotion in my gut. However, without so much as wincing I got up and hid behind a construction site." Flaubert denounced the atrocious manners of a celebrity with pretentions to gentlemanliness and, in several letters, thrashed Musset the poet. "Musset has never separated poetry from the sensations it completes. According to him music was made for serenades, painting for portraiture, and poetry for consolations of the heart. When one attempts thus to tuck the sun into one's breeches, one ends up burning one's breeches and pissing on the sun. That's what has happened to him . . . Poetry is not a weakness of mind, and these nervous susceptibilities are precisely that." Voyeuristically rather than jealously, he insisted that she keep him abreast of any subsequent contretemps in the relationship.

The relationship lasted another few months. Louise did not tell Flaubert that Musset had, with eloquent supplications, wheedled his way back into her boudoir. Neither would Flaubert tell Louise the following year that during a sojourn in Paris, he himself had taken his pleasure, probably not for the first time, with Louise Pradier.

HAVING A bear skin for a rug at Croisset, Flaubert pictured himself the ursine master of his realm, but as animals go, his profounder identification was with the horse. Horses figured in many of his cherished memories, as well as in a notably traumatic one. There had been the horse and carriage in which he accompanied his father on medical rounds. Riding up and down the beach at Trouville had helped him recuperate, every summer, from the sadness of confinement at the collegiate school. Obliged by his stylistic imperatives to write laboriously, he enjoyed, on horseback, the thrill of the gallop. Horses show up in tropes throughout his correspondence. All that concerned him, he wrote on a bad day, after declaring the publication of one's work to be a betrayal of one's art, was that his manuscripts should last as long as he. "It's a shame I'd need too big a tomb or I'd have them buried with me, as the barbarian king had himself buried with his horse." Taking aim at Louise Colet's protégé, Leconte de Lisle, he spoke of the poet's ink as being too pale and of his muse as anaerobic. "Thoroughbred horses and styles have veins bulging with blood, and you can see it pulse beneath the skin and beneath words, from ears to hooves. Life! Life! Getting it up, that's what it's all about." Louise undoubtedly wondered in any given week whether she had to do with the monkish servant of Art or its ithyphallic cavalier. When his pen wasn't an instrument of tortured abstinence, it was an emblem of equine virility. "Genius, like a powerful horse, pulls grudging humanity along the paths of original thought," he reminded her. "In vain does humanity tighten the reins and, in its stupidity, bloody the bit; its roan canters undeterred on brawny hocks, from one dizzying height to another." In the midst of Emma's seduction at the agricultural fair, he wrote to Louise one midnight that he was feeling what he used to feel after long days on horseback in the Orient. His whole head burned. "Today I rode my pen very hard."

It is to be expected then that the horse should make its presence felt in the most dramatic scenes of Emma's brief career. Rodolphe first mounts her on a wooded hilltop, while their horses browse nearby, and when she returns from her adulterous union, villagers note the stylish figure she cuts in a saddle, with one knee crooked over the neck of her capering mare. "She was charming, on horseback!" Her second adulterous affair begins in a hackney coach, which bewildered pedestrians study as it lumbers aimlessly around and around Rouen streets with shades lowered, like a fantasy of blind locomotion. To subsequent rendezvous she travels in a stagecoach drawn by a troika of horses whose galloping amplifies her heartbeat. The hooves of a three-horse team are heard again at the end, when Dr Larivière's post chaise arrives, rattling every window, to pronounce a death sentence on the moribund heroine. "It was Larivière. The descent of a God would not have caused greater commotion."

But in no other scene is the horse more pertinent than in that of the operation to which Emma, through her uxorious husband, subjects the club-footed stable boy Hippolyte, hoping that a medical tour de force will accomplish what romance had not and liberate her from her provincial prison. For good reason did Flaubert, who enjoyed the ironical interplay between Greek mythology and his Norman yokels, name Hippolyte after Theseus's son Hippolytus. In his own way the stable boy is, like the Greek prince, a chaste athlete brought low by a woman possessed. One is horse crazed, the other centaurlike. Hippolytus is a virtuous youth who inspires incestuous passion, Hippolyte a freak the virtue of whose deformity his neighbors and above all Emma are unable to see. "In order to know which of Hippolyte's tendons to cut, it behooved [Charles Bovary] to determine what kind of clubfoot he had," writes Flaubert.

His foot made almost a straight line with the leg, which didn't prevent it from turning inward, so that it was equinus with something of varus to it, or a slight varus markedly tending toward equinus. But on this equinus, well named because it was as wide as a horse's hoof, with rough skin, wiry tendons, huge toes, and nails as black as a horseshoe's, on this foot the taliped galloped like a stag all day long. He was usually to be seen at the marketplace hopping around the carts with his game leg thrust out first. It seemed, if anything, more vigorous than the other. One might have thought that long service had imbued it with moral qualities of patience and energy, and he preferred to rest his weight on it when given heavy work to do. Now, since it was an equinus, the Achilles tendon had to be cut and the anterior tibial muscle left for a second operation.

Everyone has a personal agenda vested in the success or failure of the operation. Homais the pharmacist wants his medical pretentions legitimized. The Yonvillois want their obscure hamlet put on the map. Afterward, when gangrene dooms Hippolyte, the local priest ascribes it to his sinfulness. Dr Canivet, a popinjay of a surgeon who with great solicitude makes sure that his horse has enough fodder before exuberantly amputating the young man's limb, sees in this calamity the evil hand of Parisian innovators eager to find remedies for the irremediable and addicted to such palliatives as chloroform. Emma sees in it a demonstration of Charles Bovary's ineptness, nothing more. That Hippolyte has had his virile member sawed off hardly concerns her. She proposes to make good his loss with the gift of a well-turned wooden leg.

Flaubert's principal medical source for *Madame Bovary*, Vincent Duval's *Traité pratique du pied-bot* (A Practical Treatise on the Clubfoot), reveals another level of irony in this astonishing chapter. We learn from Duval that Achille-Cléophas had once treated a female patient named Mlle Martin not by operating on her clubfoot but by keeping it in an iron splint for nine months, to no effect. Duval himself subsequently cured the young woman with an operation. Did Flaubert intend, convolutedly, to disparage his father? The argument can be made. While Dr Flaubert may have been a model for the great Larivière, who at the end descends from his carriage like "a God," he is also tarred by the unsuccess of poor Charles. That the hapless country doctor ventured where the eminent chief surgeon of the Hôtel-Dieu demurred matters less than their common failure; and the iron splint in which they both box the limbs of their unfortunate patients supports the association. It would appear, moreover, that Flaubert was taking a swipe as well at his brother, Achille, an introverted shadow of Achille-Cléophas, whom one contemporary, Louis Levasseur, portrayed as notoriously obscurantist. "His paternal heritage includes a whole inventory of opinions, theses, doctrines that are for him the law and the prophets, and he stubbornly marshals them against certain novelties." Hostile to the spirit of invention, Achille was, like Canivet, inclined to dismiss every new discovery as humbug. "There was a time when one thought he would cry *vade retro* to ether because it renders people insensible during bloody operations," wrote Levasseur. "He went about repeating the old, allegedly biblical, proposition, that pain is a concomitant of nature."

⁓

IN SEPTEMBER 1853, news of François Parain's death, though not unexpected (he had become quite senile), reached Croisset, casting a pall over things. The world, which wouldn't stand still for Flaubert, hurt him again in November 1853 by removing from Rouen his bosom friend Louis Bouilhet, who had helped him replenish on Sundays the store of self-confidence expended during the week. Having saved enough to quit the tutorial service he had organized four years earlier with three former schoolmates, Bouilhet decided to try his luck in the capital as a playwright. Flaubert was not the only party aggrieved by his departure. On the floor above Bouilhet at 131, rue de Beauvoisine lived Léonie Le Parfait, a farm-girl, and the seven-year-old son she had borne, several years before she met Bouilhet, to a Norman aristocrat named Chennevières-Pointel, who later presided over the Ministry of Fine Arts. Mother and child had become Bouilhet's common-law family.

No one proved more helpful at this juncture than Louise Colet. She found Bouilhet a flat on the rue de Grenelle in her own general neighbor-hood, presented the socially awkward provincial at her salon, promised to furnish him with tutees if need be, and persuaded theater friends to give him season passes. Gratitude for all he had done in the way of improving her verse surely counted, but Bouilhet understood full well that Flaubert's companionship was the real object of her benefactions: a contented Bouil-het was more likely than a disgruntled one to lure his friend from Rouen. In fact Bouilhet had the same goal as she, and he acted on his own behalf as well as on hers in making the case one Sunday at Croisset that Flaubert should join him. "I spoke eloquently, with emotion," he informed Louise, whom he called "my dear sister" or, like Flaubert, "dear Muse." Gustave was so shaken, he continued, that victory seemed assured. Two hours later, however, the "hedgehog" (his image) had curled into a protective ball. "Still, the situation isn't hopeless. We shall torment him, we shall wear him down. Just be sure to go about doing it with adroitness, with moderation."

Adroitness and moderation had never been Louise's strong suit. They were even less evident in 1853, when, at forty-three, she finally began to despair of having enough feminine allure to keep her young man. Letters from Trouville, where Flaubert spent August, evoked yet another world in which her presence would be intrusive. Flaubert denied that she was a mar-ginal figure for him. He insisted once again that he loved her as he had never loved a woman, that she was beyond compare, "[Our relationship is] something intricate and profound, something that has complete hold of me, that flatters all my appetites and caresses all my vanities." Unconvinced by his protestations, she wanted him to bring her out of the closet and in-troduce her to Mme Flaubert (who, he admitted, was complaining that ex-cessive solitude had made him sour). She pestered him, but he put her off with the customary invocations of his bondage to art and his slender con-nection to life.

You go at life tooth and nail; you're determined to get a resonant beat out of this poor drum, which keeps collapsing under your fist . . . Ah! Louise! Louise! Dear old friend (for it will soon be eight years that we've known each other), I stand accused. But have I ever lied? Where are the oaths I violated, and the lines you say I spoke and speak no more? . . . Don't you realize that I am no longer an adolescent and that I have always regretted it for your sake and for mine? How can you imagine that a man besotted with Art as I am, continually hungering for an ideal he can never attain, whose sensibility is sharper than a razor blade and who spends his life scraping it against flint to make sparks fly . . . , how can you imagine that such a man could ever love with a twenty-year-old heart? . . . You speak to me of your last days in bloom. The bloom has long since gone off mine, and I'm not sorry. It was all finished at eighteen. But people *like us* should use a different language to speak about themselves. We should not have blooming days or blasted ones.

Louise regularly poured out her frustration to Bouilhet, declaring, among much else, that for the sake of physical pleasure with a monstrous egotist she had compromised her daughter's future (meaning presumably that an inheritance from the girl's putative father, Victor Cousin, had been put at risk). As soon as she learned that Mme Flaubert had come to Paris in December, she importuned Bouilhet to tell the inaccessible mother that she, Louise, was in love with her son. "For the moment I am in a state of great exasperation," Bouilhet wrote to Flaubert. "I'm not sure whether I'll see the Muse again as in the past. She has been most obliging to me but her purpose was so obvious that I feel ashamed . . . Perhaps I'm taking too dim a view of the matter. Reply posthaste with advice."

Flaubert himself was bewildered. There were bad days when he thought of resting his head on Louise's bosom instead of "masturbating" it to "ejaculate" a few sentences. There were good ones when *Madame Bovary* had no rival. Affectionate letters followed close upon others that treated her work roughly, and his criticism was most implacable when tact might have been most appropriate. A fortnight after her tirade against the monstrous egotist, Louise sent Flaubert the second long installment of her *Poème de la femme*, "La Servante," in which she rounded upon a thinly disguised Musset. The tone of moral indignation exasperated Flaubert, who may have seen himself the likely victim of similar invective in the future. Ill intentioned, ill conceived, and badly written was how he judged it, warning that "La Servante" was bound to make her look ridiculous. Why she had shown Musset no mercy baffled him, but even if the vilification were proportionate to the crime, a writing desk was not to be confused with a pulpit. He found her sententiousness as insufferable as she had found his "sepulchral detachment."

Who appointed us moral overseers? . . . This poor fellow never sought to do you in. Why harm him more than he harmed you? Think of posterity and reflect upon the shabby figure cut by those who have insulted great men. Once he's dead, who will know that Musset drank himself sodden? Posterity is forgiving of misbehavior. It all but pardons Jean-Jacques Rousseau for having delivered his children up to a foundling hospital. And how does that concern us anyway? *By what right? This poem is foul play* and you have been made to pay for it, because the result is feeble . . . You wrote it from the skewed perspective of a personal passion, ignoring the fundamental conditions of every imaginative work.

Somewhere in the Gustave Flaubert whose sensibility perched at extremes of enchantment with both the material world and platonism, glorifying unruly, sociopathic, large-lunged genius or fussing over stylistic minutiae as obsessively as a Byzantine grammarian — somewhere in all that Louise looked, against all reason, for the makings of a husband.

It may be the case that by now, having reached an impasse, she resolved to move her immovable lover by cuckolding him and during the early months of 1854 set her cap at another graying Romantic elected to academic immortality, Alfred de Vigny. A liaison was hinted at in her everprolific correspondence with Flaubert. Matters only went from bad to worse. Flaubert, who smugly declared that he would feel jealous if he had not heard credible rumors that Vigny was past having sexual intercourse, thought she would be well served for academic prizes by this advocate whom he respected. He did state that his firm intention was to see her more often and, come October, to stay in a pied-à-terre for which he would search during the summer. With *Madame Bovary* two-thirds written, he anticipated a dramatic sprint through the last third to his heroine's death. But Louise couldn't quite believe any of it. Hopes kindled in one letter were extinguished in the next. "I tried to love you and do love you in a way that isn't the way of lovers," he wrote on April 12, after dismissing her protégé Leconte de Lisle as an anemic parlor poet eager to have women coo over him. "We would have thrown sex, decorum, jealousy, politeness at our feet and made of them a pedestal on which to stand high above ourselves. The great passions, by which I don't mean the turbulent ones but the broad and lofty, are those that nothing can vitiate."

Even more hurtful was a long letter denouncing the sentimental clichés in a poem she had written about her daughter. It may therefore have been inevitable, when he visited Paris, that tempers would flare. Flare they did, but without either party subsequently recounting in detail the scene that took place. Whatever he said on that day in May, she kicked his shins for it. Whatever she said convinced him never to see her again. And he never did.

Caroline Commanville, Flaubert's niece. (Bibliothèque Municipale de Rouen. Photograph by Thierry Ascencio-Parvy)

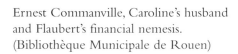

Ernest Commanville, Caroline's husband and Flaubert's financial nemesis. (Bibliothèque Municipale de Rouen)

The Princess Mathilde Bonaparte, Napoleon III's cousin, of whom Marshal Canrobert wrote, "On her admirably regular countenance she wears the mask of the Caesars." Portrait by Ernest Hébert, 1867. (Photo Modernage)

The salon of Mathilde Bonaparte, in her mansion on the rue de Courcelles, where Flaubert often attended Wednesday-evening soirees. Painting by Charles Giraud. (Réunion des Musées Nationaux. Photograph by Gérard Biot / Christian Jean)

Jeanne de Tourbey, one of the more cultivated courtesans prominent during the Second Empire. A good friend (possibly an intimate one) of Flaubert's and the mistress of Mathilde Bonaparte's brother "Plon-Plon," she later married the comte de Loynes and is thought to have served as a model for Marcel Proust's Odette de Crécy. Portrait by Eugène Armory-Duval. (Réunion des Musées Nationaux)

Edma Roger des Genettes, another of Flaubert's close woman friends and indispensable correspondents. (Bibliothèque Municipale de Rouen)

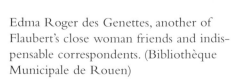

Aglaé (or Apollonie) Sabatier, known to the artists and writers who gathered around her during the 1860s as "la Présidente." She was Baudelaire's "white Venus." (Bibliothèque Nationale de France)

Jules Duplan, Flaubert's closest friend, after Louis Bouilhet, during the decade of the 1860s. (Bibliothèque Municipale de Rouen)

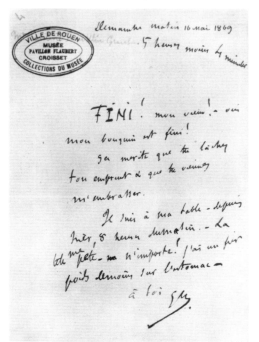

A note from Flaubert to his friend Jules Duplan announcing the completion of *L'Éducation sentimentale*. "FINISHED! old man!—Yes, my book is finished!" (Bibliotheque Municipale de Rouen)

Ivan Turgenev, photographed toward the end of his life by Nadar. (Bibliothèque Nationale de France)

George Sand, photographed by Nadar in 1864, two years before she and Flaubert established their friendship. (Bibliothèque Municipale de Rouen)

Edmond de Goncourt, the elder of two brothers who collaborated in the writing of many novels but are best known today for their journal, which chronicles the literary life in Paris during the second half of the nineteenth century. Photograph by Nadar. (Bibliothèque Nationale de France)

Emile Zola. A photograph taken in the mid–1870s, when the thirty-five-year-old author, whom one contemporary described as having a cannonball head, was five novels into his epic cycle *Les Rougon-Macquart*. (Bibliothèque Nationale de France)

Ernest Renan, whose *Life of Jesus,*
the first volume of a five-volume
History of the Origins of Christianity,
elicited a wrathful response from the
church and made him famous
throughout Europe. Flaubert
admired his prose and erudition and
enjoyed his company at the Magny
dinners. (Photograph by Melandri.
Metropolitan Museum of Art. The
Horace W. Goldsmith Foundation
Gift)

Flaubert's publisher, Georges
Charpentier. (Bibliothèque
Nationale de France)

Edmond Laporte, the manager of a textile factory near Rouen and an impeccable friend during Flaubert's declining years. His relationship with Flaubert was a casualty of Ernest Commanville's financial embarrassments. (Bibliothèque Municipale de Rouen)

Guy de Maupassant, the nephew of Alfred Le Poittevin, whom Flaubert took under his wing. An extraordinarily prolific writer and a powerful athlete, Maupassant is seen here in the early 1880s, several years before the onset of syphilitic dementia. (Bibliothèque Municipale de Rouen)

Léon Gambetta, the effective organizer of a provisional government after Napoleon III's abdication and prime minister under the Third Republic. In 1878, after dinner with Gambetta at the Chevaliers', Flaubert wrote: "At first I found him grotesque, then reasonable, then agreeable, and finally charming." (Bibliothèque Nationale de France)

Flaubert, portrait by Eugène Giraud.
(Bibliothèque Municipale de Rouen)

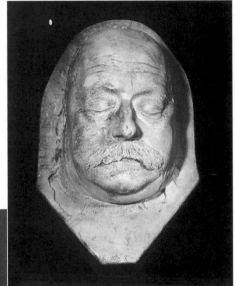

The death mask of Gustave
Flaubert. (PMVP / Photo Joffre)

The death mask of Flaubert's mother.
(Bibliothèque Municipale de Rouen)

Nor did he ever write, except to discourage her, in a note sent ten months after their clash, from calling at his flat in Paris. Addressed to "Madame," framed in the polite "vous," and signed "G. F.," it made its point bluntly. "I have learned that yesterday evening you went to the trouble of coming here three times. I was not at home. And lest such persistence on your part meet with affronts on mine, gentlemanly prudence compels me to warn you that I *shall never* be at home." By then he had, like Bouilhet, begun consorting with an actress, Béatrix Person.

The private conflict distracted them from bloody warfare in the world outside. Their correspondence suggests that neither paid much attention to news of Czar Nicholas's occupying Walachia with designs upon Constantinople, and French troops shipping out for the Black Sea in September 1854 to join English and Turk forces besieging a Russian fortress at Sebastopol, on the Crimean peninsula.

For Louise, as many loose threads were left hanging from this rift as from the previous one. Through Bouilhet, who answered her letters, she inquired after Flaubert, wanting to know in September 1854 if Flaubert had read her latest collection of poems, *Ce qu'on rêve en aimant*, and what he thought of them. At some point it became clear that she hoped for a reconciliation, but Bouilhet, who may have proposed to make love to her himself, would not play go-between.* "I thought, in good conscience, that relations between you two had broken off and your indignation did not seem to allow any possibility of getting together again," he wrote in his last letter to her. "What I beg you to believe, and I won't say it again, is this — that having done nothing to detach him from you, I shall do nothing to prevent him from returning, if he sees fit to do so. It isn't in my character to play the role of Molière's Monsieur Robert. One's fingers always get pinched between the tree and the bark, and I need mine to write."

Scorned, Louise set her own fingers to work writing autobiographical novels, beginning with *Une histoire de soldat*, in which Flaubert, alias "Léonce," comes off badly. This did not banish her demon, however. Fifteen years later, the image of a "brutal, dominating" Flaubert would torment her in a hallucination — described at length for readers of the Paris daily *Le Siècle*, which had hired her to cover the inauguration of the Suez Canal in November 1869. It occurred during a sleepless night on a cangia

---

*The main evidence of a brief affair, or sexual advance, is this ambiguous entry in Louise's diary: "Bouilhet just couldn't contain himself anymore; he needed a woman . . . If I had not loved Gustave, would I have started a liaison with him? None of this is clear in my mind." Flaubert might not have been averse to fobbing her off onto Bouilhet. But neither the tone of Bouilhet's letter nor the implication of Louise's entry suggests that they had been intimate.

sailing up the Nile. At Esna, Louise went ashore, as Flaubert had done, and scouted the brothel district in search of his unforgettable lover Kuchiuk-Hanem.

⁓

IN OCTOBER 1854, with the coast clear, Flaubert rented a flat on the rue de Londres, near the Gare Saint-Lazare, intending to spend at least part of the season in Paris. Bouilhet had warned Louise that his friend would reside there *en famille*, which was half-true. Mme Flaubert and Liline took separate quarters, but in the same neighborhood.

XV

~~~~~~~~

On Trial

MAXIME DU Camp concerned himself more than Flaubert with European politics, the "Eastern question," and the Crimean expedition, but he, too, was privately embattled, and the letter proclaiming his grand ambition three years earlier had been framed in the language of military maneuvers. "Since I've struck out on this path, since I *want* to reach my goal, I shall," he wrote to Flaubert in October 1851. "I'm off, bon voyage! I carry sidearms, I've studied my itinerary, and anyone who would dare stop me had better think twice about it." The *Revue de Paris* was a strategic emplacement in what he called his life-or-death struggle. "In the literary revival now brewing, I must be a captain and not a grunt . . . I have worked, I have had others work under my orders, and managed to blast open with one volley this citadel I've been slowly and quietly besieging since 1847."

Many contemporaries would have said that he achieved his goal after only three years. Despite early setbacks, the *Revue de Paris* went from strength to strength, with contributions by Gautier, Lamartine, de Vigny, Musset, and George Sand as well as representatives of a younger literary generation, notably Charles Baudelaire and the Goncourt brothers. Gautier and Louis Cormenin eventually resigned from the editorial board to accept remunerative positions elsewhere, and when Arsène Houssaye fell foul of

Du Camp in January 1853, he too resigned, making Du Camp sole proprietor of the title. Shortly before this event, 125 of Du Camp's photographs appeared in a volume entitled *Egypte, Nubie, Palestine et Syrie: Dessins photographiques recueillis pendant les années 1849, 1850, et 1851*, for which he also wrote the long introductory essay on ancient Egypt. It was a work of seminal importance, and it earned him membership in the Legion of Honor. *La Revue* then began to serialize his *Livre posthume: Mémoires d'un suicidé*, an autobiographical novel whose hero wakes up from the somnambulistic trance of a generation lured over the edge by Goethe's *Werther* and Chateaubriand's *René*. Enough readers shared Du Camp's animus against morose *enfants du siècle* to make the novel, when it appeared between covers, enormously successful.* He enlarged upon his credo in the preface to a volume of poetry, *Chants modernes*, in which academicians wed to classical models are ranked alongside Romantic woolgatherers as enemies of modernity. In 1855 he published *Le Nil*, a detailed, albeit well-scrubbed, account of the voyage through Egypt.

This hectic Parisian, who condemned the coup d'état but admired the ethos of a despotic regime run by technocratic ideologues building a modern capital, found his contradictions accommodated at the home of Valentine Delessert. Du Camp's passionate affair with this woman fifteen years older than he gave him purchase in very high society. Possessing great wealth and aristocratic lineage, Valentine, whose father had helped bring Louis-Philippe to power and whose husband, Gabriel, had served as Paris's prefect of police until 1848, presided over a glittering salon at which statesmen, writers, painters, and intellectuals mingled freely. Valentine chose lovers seriatim from each of these constituencies, Du Camp's predecessor having been Prosper Mérimée and Mérimée's an Orleanist minister named Charles de Remusat. Bonapartism was officially anathema here, but in fact the salon transcended party lines. Beginning in 1836, Valentine had cared for young Eugénie de Montijo, the daughter of a Spanish friend and Louis-Napoleon's future empress. Her husband, Gabriel, in turn, had tutored Louis-Napoleon's half brother, the duc de Morny, who after 1851 became France's all-powerful minister of the interior. Morny often visited the Delesserts at their home in Passy and on one such occasion was shown Du Camp's photographs. This resulted in an audience at the Elysée with Louis-Napoleon, who congratulated the intrepid photographer.

Du Camp's Sunday evenings belonged to Apollonie Sabatier, a free spirit his own age and of an entirely different social order, who held court near place Pigalle in the neighborhood known for its artists and kept women

---

*Between 1854 and 1866 it sold sixty thousand copies, a figure seldom approached by novels in nineteenth-century France.

called New Athens. Apollonie's parents were a seamstress and one of Louis XVIII's aristocratic prefects, but to all official intents and purposes she was the daughter of an illiterate, battle-scarred sergeant whom the miscreant nobleman had induced to claim paternity. Born Aglaé Savatier (the *v* later became a *b*), she radiated a charm and warmheartedness that opened doors for her at an early age. The mistress of a local boarding school in lower Montmartre, where she grew up, gave her lessons she could not otherwise have afforded. A neighbor who had retired from the Opéra-Comique trained her voice, which Baudelaire would later describe as "rich and sonorous." When her love of music drew her to piano, a composer named Armingaud taught her to play. Finally, however, it was more her beauty than her conviviality that fortune smiled upon. Tall and voluptuous, with a perfect complexion, wavy gold-brown hair, tendrilous hands, eyes of unusual brilliance, and a distinctly triumphant air, she had by midadolescence begun to stop men dead in their tracks. Two bedazzled art students painted a portrait of the fifteen-year-old Aglaé, who soon thereafter cast off her given name. It was as Apollonie, during a benefit concert in which she took part at her singing teacher's request, that she captured the attention of a Belgian named Alfred Mosselman.

Instantly smitten, the rich young industrialist, whose immense family fortune derived from banking and coal mines, wasted no time acquiring a mistress and setting her up in a pleasant flat on the rue Frochot, quite near James Pradier's studio. Overnight, Apollonie found herself surrounded by men of wealth or talent or both in the stylish bohemia that suited Mosselman. The seat of her new world was a seventeenth-century mansion at one end of the Île Saint-Louis, the Hôtel Pimodan, where Mosselman introduced her to, among other residents and habitués, Théophile Gautier, Auguste Préault, Baudelaire, Henri Monnier, and Ernest Meissonier. Here, during the 1840s, the sound of a harpsichord and of animated conversation often filled the *hôtel*'s ornate salons, along with moans emanating from a room in which *les hachichins,* or hashish eaters, spooned up their dearly bought provision of a narcotic jam called dawamesc.

By 1850 this sanctuary on the Seine had had its day, but the salon reassembled on the rue Frochot. At twenty-eight, Apollonie was more than ever an object of universal affection. Artist friends painted her and helped design the flowing white dresses she habitually wore. Gautier and Baudelaire — the former a bawdy confidant, the latter a shy worshipper — celebrated her in verse. Parisians had come to know her better than they realized at the Salon of 1845, where a marble nude in an attitude of erotic rapture, euphemistically called *Woman Bitten By a Viper*, scandalized the bourgeois public. Its sculptor, Auguste Clésinger, had copied a plaster cast of Apollonie's body commissioned by Mosselman two years earlier.

Soon after Du Camp returned from the Orient, Gautier led him to Apollonie, and Flaubert followed in turn. On Sunday evenings her company looked like an editorial meeting of the *Revue de Paris*. Almost everyone associated with the journal gathered around her dining room table, vented opinions, and ate, to the accompaniment of bullfinches and waxbills chirping until nightfall in a large aviary. Dark red cloth covered the walls. Among the canvases that hung everywhere was Meissonier's portrait of Apollonie dressed as a seventeenth-century noblewoman.

That Flaubert and Du Camp preserved any kind of bond would have seemed improbable, judging from the asperity of their correspondence between 1851 and 1854. On June 26, 1852, Flaubert, in response to a letter from Du Camp prodding him with "hurry up," "seize the day," "now's the time," and "establish yourself," shot back that he was as baffled by such exhortations as a red Indian. "To 'arrive'? But where? At the eminence of Messieurs Murger, Feuillet, Monselet, etc., etc., etc., Arsène Houssaye, Taxile Delord, Hippolyte Lucas and seventy-two others besides? No thank you," he wrote. "To be 'known' is not my main goal in life. Only arrant mediocrities ask for nothing more. And as far as that's concerned, does one ever know how much will be enough? Even the most egregious celebrity does not sate one's hunger for it, and one almost always dies wondering whether one's name rings any bells . . . I aim higher — to please myself. Success seems to me a result and not the goal." A second letter of remonstrance written that summer, when *Madame Bovary* showed real promise, came close to being a valediction. "Why do you keep harping on the same old thing and insisting that a man who presumes to consider himself healthy follow an invalid's regime? I find the pain you suffer on my behalf comical . . . We're no longer steering the same course in the same boat. May God therefore lead each of us to his chosen destination. As for myself, I'm seeking the high seas rather than safe harbor. If I sink, you're excused from mourning me." Every reference to Du Camp during these years was a slight. "Do you think I'd be worthy of appearing in the *brilliant circles* frequented by Du Camp?" His own friendships, he sighed, were thinning faster than his hair. "People are leaving me to pursue fortune or renown and, blushing at their wayward youth, abandon me with an egotism so blatant that I'd laugh if I didn't cry." He found *Le livre posthume* "pitiful," except for what had crept into it from Du Camp's reading of *Novembre*. It suggested "radical exhaustion." It was the work of a man "blowing his last note." The part of himself emotionally bound up with Du Camp had rotted away. "For him, for good old Maxime, I am altogether devoid of feeling. Gangrene has gradually mortified his place in my heart; there's nothing alive there."

Flaubert's rage sprang from what he perceived to be a betrayal of shared values and from Du Camp's boisterous *arrivisme*. But there were certainly aggravating factors at play. When he informed Louise on one occasion that recent strides he had made in Greek argued against the diminution of mental powers "diagnosed" by Du Camp (no Greek scholar himself, we are told), one infers that the latter, long before he described epilepsy as intellectually crippling in *Souvenirs littéraires*, had said something to awaken Flaubert's worst fears.* And "diagnose" suggests that Flaubert's sibling rivalry had devolved upon his friend. This connection becomes explicit in a letter that ridicules "men of action," or the superior manliness they arrogate to themselves, with society's blessings. It was he, he told Louise Colet, who had physically carried a weeping Du Camp away from the corpse of his grandmother. It was he who had arranged a duel for the blusterer. What could be more fatuous than vanity growing out of sterile turbulence? "Action has always revolted me," he wrote.

> It strikes me as belonging to the animal side of existence (who hasn't felt the fatigue of his body! How heavy flesh weighs!). But when I have had to, or chosen to, I have acted decisively, quickly, and well. When Du Camp needed help to get his ribbon in the Legion of Honor, I did in one morning what five or six men of action couldn't accomplish in six weeks. The same thing happened with my brother when I secured him his position at the hospital. From Paris, where I was living at the time, I trumped the entire medical school of Rouen and arranged *to have the king* write to the prefect, to force his hand.

Far from signifying a lack, Flaubert went on to say, the incapacity of thinking men for practical affairs, when their own advantage was at stake, indicated an "excess of capacity." Just so, the "drop of water" that amounts to nothing in a large vessel easily fills "small bottles."[†]

Once he established residence in Paris for the winter in 1855, Flaubert saw Maxime Du Camp more often than he had during the previous two or three years. The thaw in relations may not have been complete, but to some extent they enjoyed each other's company again. Flaubert rented a small flat on the rue de Londres, while Du Camp, whose grandmother had made him much richer, occupied a house several blocks away on the rue du Rocher, nearer the Parc Monceau, where he surrounded himself with the

---

*The *ramollissement de cervelle*, or "softening of the brain," allegedly diagnosed by Du Camp calls to mind the polar terms of mushiness and muscularity Flaubert often applied to prose writing. In whatever Du Camp said, he may have heard a threat of effeminization.

[†]To another female correspondent he would later write: "It is easier to become a millionaire and live in Venetian palaces full of masterworks than to write one good page and be satisfied with oneself."

emblems of his various personae: weapons, statues of Hindu gods, a plaster cast of the mass murderer Lacenaire's hand, a bronze bust of himself by Pradier. We don't know what Flaubert thought of this mise-en-scène, though we do know that he came to have his own at 42, boulevard du Temple, with gold crescents painted on blue doors in a red living room. On Sunday afternoons he occasionally joined a group at Du Camp's house for conversation before dinner on the rue Frochot. By the late 1850s his place at table was reserved, beside Du Camp's. More than one habitué remembered Apollonie Sabatier as a nurturer of friendship, and, indeed, grudges did not fare well in the warmth of an inner circle whose initiates gave one another nicknames celebrating their community. Mosselman was "Macarouille," Ernest Feydeau "Nabouchoudouroussour [*sic*]," Bouilhet "Monseigneur," Du Camp "le colonel Petermann," and Flaubert "Vaufrilard." Everyone called Apollonie "la Présidente."

Du Camp had always assumed that he would serialize *Madame Bovary* whenever Flaubert finished it. He never wavered in his resolve, even during the sorest period of their friendship, and Flaubert himself doubted only that *La Revue de Paris* would survive long enough to publish him. After 1854, with the end of the novel in sight and hours freed up that had once been reserved for letters to Louise Colet, work progressed apace. Diversions were few, the most spectacular being the Paris Exposition of 1855, which rivaled in scope the London Exposition of 1851.

Flaubert's last chapters round out a perfectly coherent vision. His heroine's suicide and the way she kills herself are of a piece with her desire for something transcendently fulfilling, which had shaped her character around a desperate emptiness. Poison suits Emma. Throughout the novel food tends to sicken her or, on the contrary, to lose all material relevance in her fantasy world. When guests at her wedding feast eat, she sees peasant mouths being stuffed, but when patricians at the Andervilliers château gather around a table with victuals piled high amid bouquets of flowers, cut crystal, and silver cloches, she sees a beautiful *tableau mort*. The woman who starves, hating her body, cannot nourish others, least of all the unwanted daughter farmed out to a wet nurse for suckling. Only once does she eat with appetite, and that is the meal she makes of death. "[She] seized the blue jar, tore out the cork, stuck her hand inside and, bringing out a fistful of arsenic, wolfed down the white powder." The anorexic gluttony of her last supper prepares one for the incorporeal lust of her farewell. "The priest got up with a crucifix in hand, whereupon she craned her neck as if to have her thirst quenched and spent all that was left of her strength in one last kiss, the most passionate she had ever given, planting her lips on the body of the Man-God."*

---

*Many years later, answering a questionnaire from Hippolyte Taine about the creative

After Emma's ultimate kiss comes Charles's blind grief, and therein lies the conceptual beauty of *Madame Bovary*. Forming a circle of incomprehension, it begins with Charles the dim-witted country boy mocked by younger classmates at a Rouen collegiate school and ends with Charles the mourner bereft of a wife he had never known, whose infidelities, once revealed to him, make her at once more inaccessible and more desirable. As Emma had always sought reality in romantic communion with paltry stand-ins for the Man-God, so had poor Charles always sought his own image in the opaque mirror of his idol's mind. Especially poignant is Flaubert's description of Charles as a young husband peering into Emma's eyes when she opens them in the morning.

> Mornings, lying face-to-face, he'd watch the sunlight play over the golden down on her cheeks, partly covered by the scallops of her nightcap. Seen from so close, her eyes loomed large, especially when she fluttered her lids upon awakening. Black in the shade and dark blue in broad daylight, it's as if their color were layered in depth, more opaque toward the back but brightening as it approached the enameled surface. His own eye got lost in these depths, where he saw himself from the shoulders up, a miniature bust with a silk scarf wrapped around his head and his nightshirt open.

The mineral cave of her inner being sightlessly reflects a tiny, insignificant votary. Idols don't see, they reflect, like the "inscrutable Sphinx" in Baudelaire's poem "La Beauté," who fascinates her "docile lovers" with "pure mirrors that make everything more beautiful." (In a letter to Baudelaire about *Les Fleurs du mal*, Flaubert singled out "La Beauté" for praise.) After Emma's death, Charles still loses himself in her eyes. The mirror remains, as Charles, trying to resuscitate Emma in his very person, strikes poses that might have won him her approval. "To please her, as if she were still alive, he embraced her predilections, her ideas. He bought patent leather boots, he took to wearing white cravats, he slicked his mustache with perfumed wax, he signed promissory notes, as she had done. She was corrupting him from beyond the grave." Finally each dies in character, she by her own hand, he passively, of a broken heart, hopelessly entranced by the woman who visited herself on him like a whirlwind, rendering him unfit for a life proportionate to his nature.

The serialized publication of *Madame Bovary* in *La Revue de Paris* under

---

process, Flaubert wrote: "Imaginary characters drive me mad, haunt me — or rather it is I who am in their skin. When I described Mme Bovary's poisoning, the taste of arsenic in my mouth was so strong . . . that I vomited my dinner."

a regime that did not gladly suffer floutings of artistic and moral convention was bound to exhaust the goodwill Maxime Du Camp and Flaubert had stored up since 1854. Although Flaubert always respected (sometimes with stubborn contestation, to be sure) the editorial advice of Louis Bouilhet, whom he called his artistic conscience, changes recommended by Du Camp and his new associates at the *Revue* — Léon Laurent-Pichat and Louis Ulbach — were another matter. *Madame Bovary* finally left Croisset in March 1856, and one month later, after a fair copy had been made in Rouen, traveled to Paris. Flaubert had Du Camp read it, conferred with him on April 27, and spent all of May revising the manuscript. He who had always expressed revulsion at the mingling of art and money was delighted to have signed a contract for two thousand francs. "Yesterday, at last, I dispatched *La Bovary* to Du Camp, about *thirty* pages slimmer, not counting many lines deleted here and there," he wrote to Bouilhet on June 1. "I suppressed three of Homais's windy harangues, a whole landscape, the conversations of bourgeois at the ball, an article by Homais, etc. etc. So you see, old man, how heroic I've been. Has the book improved for all that? Certainly it moves better now. If you revisit Du Camp, I would be curious to know what you think of it." When Du Camp wanted further cuts, Flaubert told Bouilhet that any more enforced self-mutilations would be the death of him. Bouilhet called him hypochondriacal, and Flaubert turned this harsh reassurance to account with a metaphor likening the damage inflicted by publishers to the disease contracted from whores. "How can you expect me to keep calm and stay confident after all the internal bashings (those are worse than the physical) I've suffered, one after another. Hasn't every book I've written brought on another bout of syphilis? All I have to show for long, painful coitus is a lovely chancre on my pride." Doing the conventional thing — living in Paris and airing one's work — had been foolish, he lamented. Gone was his world of artistic serenity. "Now I'm full of doubts and vexation and experiencing something new: Writing palls on me! I feel for literature the hatred of impotence." Bouilhet, who was much taken up with preliminaries to the staging of a verse play in five acts, *Madame de Montarcy*, at the Odéon theater, treated Flaubert's threats of withdrawal as a histrionic tantrum. "You're wrong to regret the forthcoming publication," he wrote. "You couldn't remain forever solitary. Scornful dismissals of the public don't work. Stupid though it is, the public unwittingly keeps us on our toes, and I do believe that this confrontation enlarges us." *Madame de Montarcy* would in fact have a successful run.*

Whatever enlargement might come of a confrontation with the general

---

*The production was a source of municipal pride for Rouennais. *Le Figaro* reported that a delegation of forty compatriots offered him a banquet at the Trois Frères Provençaux. On public, Flaubert's struggle with *La Revue de Paris* promised only to diminish him, in every sense. Laurent-Pichat joined Maxime Du Camp in urging that Emma's country wedding — a vulgar, ribald feast — be cut and the scene at the agricultural fair abridged. Did they fear that government censors would find these passages objectionable, the one as political satire and the other on grounds of obscenity? Or were they exercising censorship to satisfy their own literary taste? Both, no doubt. On July 14, Bastille Day, Du Camp sent Flaubert an imperious proposal, with Laurent-Pichat's notes attached, that had much the same effect as a royal *lettre de cachet* condemning its recipient to imprisonment in the fortress. If Louise's ear had still been available, Flaubert might have filled it with the suspicions he had voiced years earlier: that he "weighed" upon Du Camp, that Du Camp, who had all but omitted him from the published photographs taken in Egypt and dropped him completely from his account of the voyage, wanted him gone. Du Camp wrote:

> A warm recommendation was the only comment I made when I gave Laurent your book. We independently reached for the same saw to shorten it. His advice is good and you should take no other. In the matter of publishing it with us, let us be the *masters* of that: we shall make the cuts we consider indispensable. You will then publish it as a volume in whatever form suits you: that will be your affair. My deep-seated conviction is that if you don't do as I say, you will compromise yourself seriously and launch your literary career with a tangled work whose style will not suffice to retain interest. Be brave, close your eyes during the operation, and trust us, not necessarily for our talent but for the experience we have acquired in such matters and our affection for you. You buried your novel beneath a heap of things, all handsome but all superfluous.

The furious author arranged to confront Laurent-Pichat and had three meetings with him, during which tempers flared over several dozen deletions, mostly of details that reflected the author's penchant for "ignoble reality." It would not do to show sauce drooling from an old duke's mouth, Emma's dance partner thrusting his knee between her legs, handkerchiefs mopping sweaty brows, a child suffering from colic, or (given the political situation) an asinine pharmacist striking Napoleonic poses and Charles's father dying of apoplexy after gorging himself at a "Bonapartist feast" with fellow veterans. But Laurent-Pichat gave no reason for the deletion of Charles's looking deeply into Emma's eyes, unless heads on pillows seemed excessively intimate. "Pichat has just said 'yes' to me. But there was friction

the evening of the premiere, they gave him a gilded crown with the enameled inscription: *Cornelio redivivo* (Corneille revived).

and I had to unsheath my sword, as they say. It is formally agreed that I will change *nothing*."* He celebrated his victory at the Théâtre du Cirque, where Frédérick Lemaître and Béatrix Person, the actress with whom he had begun an affair, were on the bill, making toasts backstage.

This was only the first episode of what proved to be a protracted struggle. *La Revue* did not commence serialization of *Madame Bovary* until October 1, a month late. Meanwhile, all summer long, Flaubert slaved over *La Tentation de Saint Antoine,* organizing it differently and lamenting the fact that Bouilhet was not at Croisset to hear him read it aloud. An invitation to attend the wedding of Élisa Schlesinger's daughter, Marie, in Baden-Baden excited fond memories, but financial problems kept him more or less housebound. He stayed put and wouldn't even visit Ernest Chevalier in Château-Gaillard, who had just been appointed imperial prosecutor for Metz after a stint as deputy prosecutor in Lyons. English lessons with Isabel Hutton's successor, Juliet Herbert, whose buttocks he could hardly resist grabbing, were his principal diversion. When the first part of *Madame Bovary* appeared at last, Laurent-Pichat received a conciliatory letter from Croisset. The vehemence of his self-defense, wrote Flaubert, should not be thought to indicate that he reveled in the squalor he described. "If you knew me better you'd know that I detest ordinary life and have always eschewed it as far as possible." He resolved, however, to visit it esthetically this once, "which is why I adopted a heroic method, meaning the fastidious observation of things and accepting everything, saying everything, painting everything." Laurent-Pichat's objections may have been judicious, but they went wrong by going too far. "You set yourself against the internal poetics that dictated its whole shape."

Their entente cordiale came unraveled several months later in an argument over the final installments, and the editor most responsible was Louis Ulbach, a priggish, high-minded journalist who will always be remembered for the dubious distinction of having hampered both Flaubert and Zola at the outset of their careers. (In 1867 he would prominently cite Zola's early novel *Thérèse Raquin* in an essay that characterized literary realism as *la littérature putride*.) Flaubert had grudgingly let him suppress that tour de force of curtained exhibitionism which is Emma's coach ride through Rouen with Léon, but now *La Revue* insisted that he sacrifice scenes in which Rodolphe and a notary both try to derive sexual advantage from her financial embarrassment. "In my opinion I have already given up a lot and the *Revue* would have me concede even more," he wrote to Laurent-Pichat on December 7. "Now understand, *I will do nothing*, I will

---

*"Nothing" was an exaggeration. He agreed to delete Emma's copulatory coach ride through Rouen with Léon.

make no corrections, I will delete nothing, not even a comma, nothing, nothing! . . . If the *Revue de Paris* feels that I am compromising it, if it's afraid, simply stop *Madame Bovary*. I couldn't care less." With greater composure, he went on to observe that the excision of such details would not whiten Emma's sepulchre. "By suppressing the hackney coach passage, you have removed nothing of what scandalizes . . . You're prosecuting details, but it's the whole of it that offends. The work's brutality lies at its heart, not at its surface. One doesn't bleach Negros and one doesn't alter the *blood* of a work. All one can do is impoverish it." Lest Flaubert make good a threat to sue, *La Revue* inserted a note of disavowal by the author, dated December 15. "Considerations that I need not examine have forced the *Revue de Paris* to suppress a passage in the December 1 issue," it read. "Its scruples having reconvened for the present issue, it has seen fit to remove several more passages. I am thus denying responsibility for the following lines and asking the reader to consider them fragments, not a whole."

The "considerations" Flaubert brushed aside refer to the fact that Napoleon III's government regarded *La Revue* as a hostile camp on account of its having published writers who, though not chiefly concerned with politics, had resigned university positions after the coup d'état. Any pretext to abolish the journal would have been seized upon, and "an affront to decent comportment and religious morality" (*outrage à la morale publique et religieuse et aux bonnes moeurs*) was the charge brought against Flaubert, the *Revue*, and the printer in January 1857. With two *avertissements*, or warnings, already in its police file, the review, were it convicted, would automatically lose its brevet, or license. Through influential friends, including Valentine Delessert, who petitioned Empress Eugénie on their behalf, Du Camp and Flaubert tried to have the charge vacated, but the Ministries of Interior and Justice held firm. Flaubert, Laurent-Pichat, and Auguste Pillet (the printer) were summoned to appear before the Sixth Correctional Chamber on January 24, 1857. When they did, their trial was postponed a week.

The brief presented against *Madame Bovary* may perhaps be better understood in the context not of fiction but of contemporary theater, and of the enormous success enjoyed during the 1850s and 1860s by France's preeminent playwright, Alexandre Dumas fils. Adultery was his obsessive theme. So strenuously did Dumas fils deplore irregular liaisons of the sort to which he owed his own illegitimate birth that he would, as the confrere charged with welcoming him into the French Academy declared, use any weapon at his disposal to punish unfaithful wives. "Let them beware, henceforth, of those pretty jade-handled knives that linger on tabletops, of those pistols their husbands have been toting in their pockets . . . Surely those women are stouthearted indeed who would not recoil before this formidable apparatus of moralization." With Dumas fils, the fomulaic, or so-called well-made, play did indeed become a vehicle devised to bring "the social law" home victorious while taking, en route, clever turns that gave the outlaw (courtesan, adulteress, rake, embezzler) a momentary but illusory advantage. Never was his audience allowed to leave the theater without the ruins of a foiled plot or the corpse of an illicit passion.

It could be said that Dumas wrote plays to purge theater, for his plays are typically "plots" against bourgeois order, his antagonists imposters who lead double lives or harbor reprehensible secrets, his denouements trial scenes in which the actor finds himself (or, more often, herself) unmasked, and his hero Society as represented by a stock character rather like the sleuth of modern detective novels, who unravels criminal schemes with remarkable lucidity. This sleuth, whom Dumas called the Reasoner, stood guard between stage and audience. However immoral a drama, the Reasoner was always there, orienting the public's moral perception from inside the play, assuring bourgeois spectators that they had the upper hand, distancing them from their own dark side with urbane analyses that reduced the underworld to something predictable, mechanistic, and ultimately weightless. Familiar with the deceptions of that world as only someone could be who had seen them played out often before, he did not censor what occurred onstage but filtered it through his cynical intelligence, or disarmed it in stylish speeches made to be taken home and quoted. "They quote his repartees and peddle his aphorisms. The number of people reputed for their wit who plagiarize him every day is countless," observed one critic.

If officialdom during the Second Empire had had its way, it might have required every published plot to include a Reasoner. When the government brought charges against *Madame Bovary*, Ernest Pinard, the imperial prosecutor pleading to have *Madame Bovary* banned from circulation, declared: "Who in this book can condemn this woman? No one. Such is our conclusion. In this book there is not one character who can condemn her. If you find a single judicious character, a single principle in virtue of which adultery is stigmatized, then I am wrong. But if there is not a single character who can make her bow her head, not an idea or line in virtue of which adultery is scourged, then it is I who am right and the book is immoral." It seems likely that he had in mind one or another of Dumas's affable custodians who upheld society's best interests, making sure that people not be left to their own devices, that imaginations not run amok, that virtue always win the day. What he voiced was a fear prevalent among bourgeois that without some such figure, anything might be possible. And, indeed, time proved him right, for time would see the formula Dumas deployed on behalf of a rational order turned to the account of Unreason by twentieth-century playwrights. In Pirandello's *Henry IV* and *Six Characters*, for instance, the Reasoner became the sleuth of an insoluble mystery, or the advocate of madness who indicts the criminal audience, proclaiming private delusions more real than the so-called real world.

Flaubert's prosecutor argued that *Madame Bovary* was "a painting admirable from the perspective of talent but execrable from that of morality . . . Monsieur Flaubert can embellish his paintings with all the resources of art but with none of its caution; there is in his work no gauze, no veils — it shows nature in the raw." Given that Flaubert invariably drew a curtain over Emma's erotic scenes, Pinard's accusation may seem odd, unless he meant that a discreet gesture at the penultimate moment of a striptease only whetted the reader's imagination, making nakedness even more lewd, or unless he concurred with Flaubert himself that the scandal of *Madame Bovary* had been bred into its bone. Realist literature was rightly stigmatized by Christian moralists, Pinard declared, not because it portrayed the passions — hatred, vengeance, love, are the stuff of life and art, he said — but because it portrayed them without that discipline of an inner preceptor. "Art that observes no rule is no longer art; it is like a woman who disrobes completely. To impose the one rule of public decency upon art is not to subjugate it but to honor it."

Ernest Pinard ended his indictment with the observation that adultery was always and everywhere to be decried for undermining the family upon which social order rested as a pillar upon its base. Maître Jules Sénard, in turn, began his response with a discourse on the family from which his client had issued. A Rouen notable who had risen to national prominence as president of the Constituent Assembly during the Second Republic, Sénard knew whereof he spoke in praising Achille-Cléophas and Gustave. Flaubert the father may very well have been his personal physician; Flaubert the son had been a friend since childhood of his son-in-law, Frédéric Baudry. "Gentlemen," he declared, "a great name and great memories carry obligations. M. Flaubert's children have not failed him. They were three, two sons and a daughter . . . The older son was deemed worthy of succeeding his father . . . The younger stands before you, at the bar. He who left them a considerable fortune and an illustrious name endowed them with the need to be men of heart and intelligence, useful men. The brother of my client threw himself into a career that exacts service to others every day. My client himself has devoted his life to study, to letters, and the work being prosecuted before you is his first." This work, he went on to say, was the fruit of deep study and long meditation. "M. Gustave Flaubert is a man of serious character, naturally drawn to grave matters, to sad things."

Flaubert agreed that these were not the circumstances in which to make a case for authorial impersonality. Guilt or innocence would hinge on conclusions about the novel's moral fitness, and Sénard, after extolling Flaubert's lineage, described *Madame Bovary* as a novel whose eloquence and power were employed only to dramatize illusions fatal to family life. Far from being licentious, the book was astringent. The sensual, edulcorated religion taught to young girls was, in Sénard's view, just one of the dangers Flaubert portrayed. "Ah! You will accuse me, in my portrait of modern society, of having confused sensualism and the religious element!" he exclaimed. "Rather, accuse the society in whose midst we find ourselves, not the man who, like [the seventeenth-century bishop] Bossuet, cries: 'Wake up and beware of the peril!' Saying to the paterfamilias, 'Take care, you are not giving your daughters good habits. In all those mixtures of mysticism there is something that sensualizes religion' — that is telling the truth. It is of this that you accuse Flaubert, it is for this that I praise his conduct. Yes, he has done well to warn families thus of the dangers of exaltation in young people who practice small devotions instead of embracing a strong, severe faith that would sustain them in their hour of weakness." Sénard deftly turned Pinard's shafts against the archer and fortified his plea by invoking the good opinion of a famous poet known for the "chasteness" of his writings: Lamartine. After the sixth and final installment of *Madame Bovary* in *La Revue*, Flaubert received an invitation to meet Lamartine. During their first exchange, Lamartine told him that it was the best book he had read in twenty years. Emma's suicide, an expiatory gesture incommensurate with her sins, had left him devastated. To make the book stand trial, he is alleged to have said, was utterly to misread its character. "The honor of our country and our era would be sullied were there a tribunal capable of condemning it."

Maître Sénard dwelt upon the moral rectitude of *Madame Bovary*, noting that it concluded not with a moribund Emma but with a Charles who is Charles to the end — simple, vulgar no doubt, yet touching in his dutifulness and unshakeable love. To prepare his lawyer, Flaubert had marshaled in his own defense literary works honored as fixtures of the classical canon. "All of classical literature authorized paintings and scenes that go far beyond those we allowed ourselves," declared Sénard (identifying with his client). "We could have justified much greater irreverence in the name of classical imitation. We didn't. We imposed upon ourselves a sobriety you will take into account. If, here and there, M. Flaubert may have overstepped the line he himself drew, let me remind you that this is a first work, that even if he is thought to have erred, his error will have no harmful effect upon public morals."

The tribunal deliberated for two weeks and had its verdict published in the *Gazette des Tribunaux* on February 9, 1857. After a litany of "givens," which included these:

Given that Gustave Flaubert protests his respect for propriety and everything connected with religious morality; given that his book has apparently not, like certain other works, been written for the sole purpose of pandering to sensual passions, to the spirit of license and debauchery, or to ridicule things that must be surrounded with universal respect; given that his only fault was to have lost sight on occasion of the rules that every self-respecting writer should not violate, and to have forgotten that literature, like art, will accomplish the good it is called upon to do only if it be chaste and pure in substance as well as in form; . . .

it ruled in Flaubert's favor. "Under these circumstances, since it has not been indisputably established that Pichat, Gustave Flaubert, and Pillet stand guilty of the violations imputed to them, the tribunal acquits them of charges brought against them and relieves them of court costs." The *Revue de Paris* would therefore survive to see another year (but only one more), and *Madame Bovary* to reach the public, in nearly unexpurgated form, as a book.

Whether Flaubert would let it appear between covers was the question. At first he seemed dead set against risking anything more on the work's behalf. His satisfaction with the favorable verdict didn't last long, to judge by letters written in its immediate aftermath. All who congratulated him were told that he would not publish the novel in any form if he had it to do over again, that a quarrel so alien to art left him thoroughly disgusted with himself, that he had come to regard the mutism of fish as an enviable state. And how could he record the fantasies of Saint Anthony for public consumption when officialdom had waxed wroth over a relatively inoffensive novel? How could one move one's pen with one's imagination fettered? "I wonder if it is possible to say anything nowadays, so ruthless is public hypocrisy," he wrote to Maurice Schlesinger, who kept abreast of Parisian talk of the town in Baden-Baden. "Even worldly people well disposed toward me find me immoral! Impious! It would be advisable in future that I not say this or that, that I watch my step, etc., etc.! Ah, how vexed I am, dear friend!" In a society allergic to unvarnished truth, where the daguerreotype gave offense (he claimed) and history found itself dismissed as satire, every idea conceived by his poor brain seemed reprehensible. "What I had planned to publish next, a book that cost me years of research and dry scholarship, would land me in jail." Schlesinger was presented with the portrait of a despondent victor stretched out on his couch, puffing smoke rings.

This portrait did not reflect the naked truth, however. In December, Louis Bouilhet's publisher, Michel Lévy, had proposed to bring out *Madame Bovary* in a collection that included works by Gautier, Stendhal, and George Sand. Flaubert agreed, and on December 24, 1856, they signed a contract the terms of which, though no better or worse than those a first novel normally commanded, would after *Madame Bovary*'s commercial success come to seem exploitative. There was no royalty arrangement. Flaubert received eight hundred francs net for a two-volume edition, with much restored of what had been cut by *La Revue de Paris* (though not before scenes had been rewritten half a dozen times, in a frenzy of perfectionism). It appeared in April, selling at one franc a volume.

The author broadcast complimentary copies far and wide. Champfleury, a vehement partisan of literary realism, wrote to say that nothing so remarkable had crossed his desk in ages: "You have struck the right chord on your first try. Stay with it [and] don't worry about the pipsqueaks and fashionmongers." Léon Gozlan, a chronicler once closely associated with Balzac, declared that the novel would put an end to the romantic pursuit of bluebirds: "The picture you paint of this poor woman's disorder has a dimension and finish seldom encountered in the same artist." From his home town of Grenoble, a young man of letters wrote that he felt well positioned to admire Flaubert for his finely observed descriptions of provincial life. Grenoblois women were an enthusiastic audience, he reported. "[They] bovarize a little on their own and have recognized themselves, not without pleasure, in your novel. My informant is a friend who teaches philosophy at the local lycée — a great bovarist himself, who read your novel before I did and brought me the first copy." From Guernsey (where Louise Colet had recently visited its most famous resident, running the risk of denunciation by Napoleonic spies), Victor Hugo sent high-flown, nebulous praise: "You have produced a beautiful book, sir, and I am pleased to tell you so. Between us there exists a kind of bond attaching me to your success. I recall your charming and noble letters of four years ago and see their shadow play on the beautiful pages you are giving me to read today. *Madame Bovary* is a real work." He dubbed Flaubert a "guiding spirit" of his generation and urged him to hold high the flaming torch of art. "I am in the shadows, but am enamored of light, which is to say that I love you."

As for public comment, France's most distinguished literary critic, Sainte-Beuve, devoted four long columns of *Le Moniteur Universel* to *Madame Bovary* in a review that expressed qualified admiration. He praised a book that left nothing to the improvisations of a facile pen. Truly "written" and "meditated," it was art, no doubt, but something less than high art, being imbued with the scientific spirit of an age distrustful of heights. "Apparently begun several years ago, it came to fruition at just the right moment. It is to be read after an evening in the theater listening to the clean, sharp-edged dialogue of Alexandre Dumas fils, or applauding *Les Faux Bonshommes*, or between two articles by Taine. For in many passages and guises I recognize a change of literary direction: toward science, a spirit of observation, maturity, strength, some harshness. They are traits affected by front-rank men of the new generation." Flaubert manifested all these traits in portraying characters, and vivid ones, from a clinical remove. To none of them, wrote Sainte-Beuve, did he betray a personal affinity. "Not one was groomed by him for any other purpose than precise and unvarnished portraiture, not one was spared as one might spare a friend. He has completely distanced himself from the scene, he is there only to see everything, show everything, and say everything, but in no nook or cranny does one glimpse his profile. The work is wholly impersonal. It is a great exhibition of strength." Was this strength not also the novelist's weakness? he asked. Was the deficiency of his virtue not the radical absence of virtue? Sainte-Beuve implicitly called upon Flaubert to imitate Dumas fils, with whom he otherwise shared an archness of perspective, and in future have at least one exemplar or Reasoner leaven his disreputable cast of characters. "The good is too absent. Not one character represents it . . . The story has a moral and a terrible one at that: its author hasn't articulated it in so many words, but it is certainly there for readers to draw."

Flaubert hastened to thank Sainte-Beuve for discussing the book at such length and in a largely favorable light. His only avowable point of contention was a personal one. "Don't judge me by this novel," he pleaded. "I am not of the generation to which you refer — not in my heart at least. I would rather belong to yours, I mean the good one, that of 1830. All my loves reside there. I am an old romantic mad dog, mad or crusty, as you wish. This book is for me a matter of pure art and set purpose. Nothing more. It will be a long time before I attempt anything like it again. It was *physically* painful to write. Henceforth I wish to live . . . in less nauseating milieus." He was told that in bourgeois Rouen, another milieu he regarded as nauseating, Sainte-Beuve's article had made a strong impression, if only by virtue of its length. For him, it thus served an intimately gratifying purpose. Like Émile Zola, who never ceased either to denigrate his hometown, Aix-en-Provence, or to want recognition there, Flaubert always insisted on knowing how tall he stood in the eyes of his spurned compatriots.*

A rejoinder to Sainte-Beuve's criticism came five months later, on October 18, 1857, in a review by Charles Baudelaire, who on August 27 had ap-

---

*One indication of his stature can be found in the memoirs of the photographer Nadar, published in 1864. He remembers meeting a young Rouennais of good family and assuming, in conversation, that the recent and greatly deserved success of *Madame Bovary* filled fellow Normans with pride. "'So you really find that beautiful?' [the Rouennais] replied, in a superior tone crushingly contemptuous of M. Flaubert. 'I myself don't find it so! Besides, the author is weird, and in Rouen we can't abide characters. Before 1848, *he set himself apart* by refusing to join the National Guard. And then suddenly, *without saying anything*, he left for Africa. *We don't like those types in Rouen!*'" Flaubert thought that the anecdote rang true.

peared before the same court as Flaubert and had faced the same charges, with different results. "Several critics have said: this work, which is truly beautiful in the detail and vividness of its descriptions, contains no character representing morality or speaking for the author's conscience," he wrote in *L'Artiste*, which had published excerpts from *La Tentation de Saint Antoine* (Flaubert's newly revised version) the previous January. "Where is he, that proverbial and legendary character whose obligation it is to explain the fable and guide the reader's intelligence? In other words, where is the indictment?" As one who would like to have seen internal preceptors beheaded, he called the question an "absurdity" based on a confusion of functions and genres. The true work of art needed no indictment. Nor did it need a lofty subject to achieve stature. The author of *Madame Bovary* meant to demonstrate that "all subjects are indifferently good or bad depending on the treatment they receive," and the most vulgar suited his purposes best. Baudelaire made himself Flaubert's ventriloquist. "Since our ears have been filled lately with the puerile nattering of various schools," he imagined Flaubert thinking, "since we have heard much talk of a literary program called 'realism' — an oath hurled nowadays at anything analytical, a vague and elastic word that signifies, for the philistine, not a new method of creation but the minute description of accessories — we will take advantage of this muddle . . . We shall stretch a nervous, picturesque, subtle, exact style over a banal canvas. We shall pour huge feelings into the most trivial adventure. Solemn, decisive words will escape from inane mouths." The heroine, he added, need not be a true heroine. Good looks, nerves, ambition, and fantasies of a superior world would suffice to make her interesting. "Our sinner will at least possess the virtue, a rather uncommon one, of bearing no resemblance to the ostentatious chatterboxes of the previous generation." Baudelaire also pointed out that Emma has a distinctly masculine temperament, and inferred that more of Flaubert than Sainte-Beuve allowed had seeped through the facade of authorial impersonality.

In a note sent from Croisset on October 21, Flaubert offered warm thanks. The review, he wrote, had given him enormous satisfaction. "You entered the arcana of the work as if our brains were mated. You've felt it and understood it thoroughly." What must have heightened his pleasure was the praise Baudelaire reserved for *La Tentation de Saint Antoine*, which abounded in qualities of lyricism and irony especially appealing to the poet. "There are dazzling passages," he wrote. "I do not refer only to Nebuchadnezzar's prodigious banquet or mad little Sheba, that miniature apparition of a queen dancing on the ascetic's retina . . . [but] to the undercurrent of rebellious suffering that traverses the work, the dark thread that guides one through this pandemoniacal glory-hole of solitude." It was everything Flaubert would have liked to hear from Bouilhet and Du Camp.

BY JUNE Flaubert was berating himself for having accepted the derisory fee of eight hundred francs, as if an author shrewder than he, or less disdainful of commerce, might have wrested better terms from Lévy, even for a first novel. With fifteen thousand copies sold and a second printing in the works, he calculated his loss at forty or fifty thousand francs, a sum that would have lightened Mme Flaubert's financial burden. (He may have equated income with masculinity, but he also did the opposite, priding himself in calculations of loss — sometimes greatly exaggerated — which, like his suffering, bespoke the purity and authenticity of his vocation.) The economics of Croisset were not what they had been, in part because Flaubert, to his mother's chagrin, spent more profligately than ever. Even as money was flowing through his fingers — ten thousand francs during the first part of 1857 alone, by his own account — none was being collected from a tenant farmer six thousand francs in arrears, despite the best efforts of Mme Flaubert's nephew, Louis Bonenfant, who now managed her estate. A fretful, cautious woman, she sold her carriage (one of the locals, le père Jean, would transport the Flauberts to Rouen whenever needed) and regretfully discharged Caroline's governess, Juliet Herbert.

Dedicating *Madame Bovary* to Jules Sénard as well as to Louis Bouilhet was a suitable gesture, for the attorney's excellent defense had freed it to profit from the furor of litigation. And fame, which came virtually overnight, seemed more desirable than it had been before he acquired it. "I am, it is true, showered with honors," he admitted to his cousin Olympe Bonenfant. "I am lambasted and vaunted, disparaged and extolled . . . What joy it would have given your poor father [François Parain], had he lived, to see celebrity conferred upon his nephew. . . . The newspaper articles would have made him swoon with pleasure or indignation."

Some years later, when the state consecrated Flaubert's fame by naming him to the Legion of Honor, a friend wondered whether official recognition had dispelled all bitter memories of the trial. It hadn't at all, he replied; he was clay for receiving impressions and bronze for preserving them.

XVI

An Island of His Own

PARIS IN 1857 was markedly different from the capital Flaubert had inhabited as a law student. Louis-Napoleon had not only crowned himself Emperor Napoleon III but had gone some way toward implementing an imperial dream that had begun to obsess him during his internment at the Ham prison fortress, when he declared, "I want to be a second Augustus, because Augustus . . . made Rome a city of marble." Such aspirations might have struck his jailer as megalomaniacal. By the late 1850s they were official policy. Road crews under the supervision of his indefatigable prefect, Georges Haussmann, had been hard at work prying open the Latin Quarter to let traffic flow unimpeded, and vehicles that formerly crept uphill in the narrow aisles of medieval streets now moved along a wide, graded thoroughfare known as the "boulevard de Sebastopol — rive gauche." It was soon to be renamed the boulevard Saint-Michel, after a statuary fountain installed near its intersection with the quay. At that intersection even more dramatic changes revealed themselves, for across the Pont Saint-Michel a huge gap opened to view on the Île de la Cité, where, shortly before, ten thousand members of Paris's lumpen proletariat had lived in unspeakable squalor. Gone were the dingy cabarets made famous by the popular novelist Eugène Sue in *Les Mystères de Paris,* the old morgue that Dickens found so oddly irresistible, the brothels along the rue Saint-Éloi, the maze of winding, cobbled alleys that got a thorough bath only when the Seine flooded them. Around the cathedral of Notre-Dame lay rubble-strewn earth, and from Quasimodo's vantage point one could clearly discern similar transformations on the Right Bank. There, cutting through the labyrinthine heart of revolutionary Paris, the boulevard de Sebastopol met the rue de Rivoli, which now ran east beyond its elegant sleeve of arcades. Neighborhoods sprawling between the Louvre and the place de la Bastille no longer formed a lower-class stronghold ideally suited to the barricades of guerrilla warfare and the propagation of cholera morbus. With those thrusts by Baron Haussmann's army they had lost their unbroken frontier, and before long they would be made to yield their inwardness as well.

People ruthlessly evicted from their homes were not alone in feeling lost. While Haussmann proudly saw his grand design unfold in the concentric rings, squares, circles, and radii that imposed theatrical logic on what had been higgledy-piggledy, nostalgia overcame writers and ideologues, who regarded this geometric scheme as fatal to a world fraught with memories. "I am a stranger to what beckons, to what is, as I am to these new, implacably straight boulevards . . . that no longer carry the scent of Balzac's world but announce some American Babylon," Jules de Goncourt noted in 1860. And three years later, with trouble brewing during legislative elections, Proudhon felt the spirit of 1848 gust through "Haussmann's new, monotonous, wearisome city with its rectilinear boulevards, its gigantic hotels, its magnificent but unvisited quays, its river sadly put to transporting sand and stone, . . . its squares, its theaters, its new barracks, its macadam, its legion of street sweepers and frightful dust: this cosmopolitan city where natives cannot be told from the Germans, Batavians, Americans, Russians, Arabs all about them." The socialist thus joined the royalist in opposing a self-crowned head whose capital embodied his stagecraft. Against *gai Paris* — which acquired that name at the 1855 Exposition, when foreigners did indeed invade the capital to admire it in the early stages of its metamorphosis — they kept alive the memory of *vieux Paris,* of a sacred place incubating itself without regard for the external world or the future.

It was Napoleon III's settled opinion that a government would be short-lived unless it made itself the impresario of "civilization's larger interests." In a state governed as much by technocrats bred on Claude Henri de Saint-Simon's philosophy as by Napoleon III himself, civilization's larger interests coincided with those of the entrepreneurial class furiously at work laying railroad track, stringing up telegraph lines, installing sewage systems, digging canals, building factories, launching steamships, founding department stores, and opening markets far beyond the confines of France. Although businessmen had received blessings from Louis-Philippe before 1848, not until Napoleon III's ascendancy did a ruler predicate his very raison d'être on the idea that capital must at all costs flow, and flow, wherever possible, into public works of a magnitude previously unimagined. "Government exists in order to help society overcome the obstacles to its progress . . . It is the beneficent mainspring of every social organism," declared the emperor. Recognizing that economic life could not expand unless it were freed from the shackles of traditional finance, he presided over a revolution that one historian describes as follows:

> The government loans of the old regime had been taken up, right down to 1847, by private banking firms, of which the Rothschilds were the most famous, and the use to which the money might be put was limited by their interests — those of an international plutocracy in close touch with the old dynasties of Europe . . . It was for this purpose that in 1852 the Brothers Péreire — a name not unknown in the financial affairs of the Revolution — founded the first Crédit mobilier, which did not limit itself to state loans, but laid itself out to finance industrial societies: and, in order to extend its influence beyond anything attainable by the old-fashioned family banks, offered its shares to the general public.

The danger was of overexpansion, which led to a crisis in 1867. When it occurred, with devastating results, the Rothschilds, among other old-line bankers, were quick to remind Europe that they had predicted it. But for fifteen crucial years, the Crédit mobilier and its partner, the Crédit foncier, together with the Comptoir d'escompte and numerous Sociétés de dépôt, all backed by the Bank of France, financed industry and agriculture, making Paris the financial center of the Continent.

What this revolution brought about was a state of affairs that inspired Dumas fils's oft-repeated quip in *La Question d'argent:* "Business? Why, it's simple: business is other people's money." With other people's money, the Péreires made millions financing the Austrian State Railroad, the Imperial Ottoman Bank, the Compagnie générale transatlantique, the Grand Hotel, public utilities and transportation companies in Paris, the Louvre department store. Money borrowed from the Péreires or raised by public subscription enabled zealots like Baron Haussmann and Ferdinand de Lesseps to reconstruct Paris and to dig a canal across the isthmus of Suez. Credit sponsored visionaries less grandiose than these. It thrived on dream: credit begot credit, disproving — or so it seemed in the heyday of Napoleon III — King Lear's arithmetic proclamation that "nothing will come of nothing."

To believe the Goncourts, Second Empire France was a nation remarkable for its venality, with everyone in it either defrauded or on the take. "France is like Molière's miser, closing its fist around dividends and property, ready to submit to any Praetorian or Caracalla, ready to endure knowingly any shame — so long as its profits are safe," they wrote. "Orders and castes have disappeared in a scramble where, like two fleeing armies, two kinds of men crush each other: those, the clever and the bold, who want money *per fas et nefas,* and the comfortable, who would keep their gain at any price." While these waspish observers often exaggerated the facts to portray a bourgeois society fully deserving of the opprobrium they heaped on it, it is undeniable that the industrial revolution bred speculators and peculators who swam in great schools toward the smell of instant profit.

Conspicuous among the latter was Napoleon III's half brother Charles, the duc de Morny, a bon vivant utterly without scruple about peddling the influence he enjoyed to satisfy his immoderate appetite for pleasure. Morny distinguished himself at court by the extent and flagrancy of his maneuvers. It was characteristic of the man that after representing France at Czar Alexander's coronation he should bring back from Moscow an eighteen-year-old bride, Princess Troubetzkoi, and along with her a paper, from which he would profit handsomely, granting Crédit mobilier the rights to construct a Russian railroad system. The emperor had built a Roman capital in Paris, so Morny built a Roman resort in Deauville, where courtiers laden with money might squander it at the huge, ornate casino. Incidental beneficiaries of this development, which transformed a coast once dear to them, were the Flauberts, who still owned sixty-five acres of farmland acquired in "Dosville" two decades earlier.

The enthusiasm for participation in capital markets was positively feverish. It raged in cafés and restaurants, where talk revolved around stocks, bonds, mortgages, debentures. It beset the clerks who queued up outside Parisian town halls on the eve of national loan subscriptions and stood there all night long. It shifted substantial fortunes from land to securities. It greeted de Lesseps in the person of a coachman who, after depositing him at the Compagnie universelle du canal maritime de Suez, proudly announced that he was one of his shareholders. It drove uniformed messengers between the Stock Exchange and the Central Post Office like yo-yos unreeled across Paris by an officer corps of brokers. Alexis de Tocqueville wrote that France had begun to look like an industrial company in which every operation was undertaken with the stockholder's profit in mind. The fever made itself felt everywhere, but nowhere more insistently, of course, than at its very seat, the Bourse, from which there rose a din loud enough to be heard until 10 p.m. by strollers blocks away on the boulevard des Italiens. Zola would describe the scene vividly in his novel *L'Argent,* insisting that speculation had become a substitute for religious exaltation, the Bourse a profane temple, the broker a shaman, financial jargon an incantatory language, and the mass of French a worshipful throng.

More conservative writers did not quarrel with Zola's metaphor, inclined though some might have been to qualify it or turn it against the godless doctrine on which he relied for the grand design of his fictional saga. Tradition had unquestionably been dealt a blow by circumstances beyond anybody's control. Where bourgeois wisdom held that the virtuous man planned, labored, saved; that he placed his faith in tangible things; that he found the reward for all he begrudged himself in his children's advancement; and that he set posterity a shining example of the golden rule, circumstances now urged men to believe that the magic attending stock market numbers augured a new dispensation. Paris swarmed with immigrants from provincial France who had come by railroad seeking fortune in the capital, only to end up in some squalid tenement outside the customs barrier eating dust all the days of their life. More Parisians than not went to bed hungry at night. But a gambler could always cite that other swarm on whom fortune had smiled, the golden dustmen who had struck it rich, the parvenus who justified Tocqueville's contention, "There is no longer a race of wealthy men, just as there is no longer a race of poor people; the former emerge every day from the bosom of the crowd and constantly return to it." Not since Revolutionary days, when the Convention made *sang,* or aristocratic blood, and *naissance*, or high birth, obsolete by decreeing 1792 Year 1, had Frenchmen with nothing to lose, but something to wager, greeted so warmly the prospect of losing their past.

The extent to which sudden wealth fostered conspicuous consumption was most apparent on the Boulevard, the district around the boulevard Saint Martin that encompassed the large theaters, operas, elegant cafés, and luxurious restaurants of Paris. Dignitaries came from every quarter to feast at the Café Anglais, the Café de Paris, the Café Riche, or La Maison d'Or, as the financial center of Europe became its gastronomic capital and chefs like Dugléré recaptured a position France had lost under Louis-Philippe. One nineteenth-century culinary historian declared that the Second Empire was for French cuisine what the reign of François I had been for the fine arts. "Weary of the superannuated, bourgeois cuisine of the previous regime, the new court spent heedlessly in its pursuit of luxury and its infatuation with appearances. Important households made themselves known by sumptuous receptions where the table had pride of place. The court, ministries, embassies, and many town houses became the schools at which great artists, exclusively French, received their training. All foreign courts were our tributaries." Like certain of the notable courtesans known as *lionnes* or demimondaines, restaurateurs became millionaires.

Appearances dictated that *Madame Bovary* be chastised and Baudelaire's *Fleurs du mal* expurgated, but Offenbach's *Gaieté parisienne* drove a thriving trade on the Boulevard, where impresarios exploited the public craze for spectacles of never-never land, feats of magic, displays of material wealth, glimpses of female crotch. There was still great theater to be had at the Comédie-Française between the waning of Rachel and the waxing of Sarah Bernhardt. And there was undoubted genius in Eugène Labiche's brilliant farces, which tumbled forth quickly enough, at the rate of eight or ten a year, to give many French actors full employment. Otherwise, dramatic art went into serious decline, as interest shifted from theater to conjury, with playwrights relying more and more on the technician who devised special effects. Victor Séjour's *The Madonna of the Roses,* for example, owed its entire success to a fire simulated with bengal lights, bellows, "spark," and lycopodium. When Dennery's *The Battle of Marengo* played at the Châtelet, the manager requisitioned several four-inch artillery pieces from the War Ministry and arranged to have their gun crews fire blank shells, without any assurance that the theater's glass roof could withstand the shock wave. A production of Meyerbeer's *The African Woman* at the Opéra took place on a stage transformed into an enormous ship that was made to rock fore and aft by hands working machinery underneath it. *King Carrot,* a *féerie,* or extravaganza, written by Victorien Sardou and Jacques Offenbach, in which an old magician who is dismembered and burned piecemeal emerges from the fire a young man, inspired devices of the utmost ingenuity. "The machinist's art uses all its resources in the construction of *trucs.* Some of them are veritable masterpieces," declared one technician. "The machinist is at once a carpenter, a cabinetmaker, and a mechanic. The study of design and of dynamics is indispensable to him. Physics and even chemistry furnish him many effects."

While the church was accrediting Bernadette's vision at Lourdes in hopes of recovering something of its authority from science, theater was discrediting occultism with gimmicks that enhanced the prestige of the engineer. Those who turned a deaf ear to Pius IX's *Syllabus of Errors* got all the magic they wanted on the Boulevard, where the supernatural, like everything else, became big business. Behind the backdrop and beneath the floorboards of several dozen stages, machinists and electricians, scene painters and upholsterers, locksmiths and blacksmiths, smoke-and-fire makers, fountain keepers, and lighting masters all did yeomen work in the service of yet another industry, the entertainment industry, which made fairy-tale scenes for the carriage trade, manufacturing them with the same fastidiousness that Viollet-le-Duc applied to his restoration of medieval fortresses and Napoleon III to the trappings of Napoleonic glory.

Just as Aristotle's precepts, after serving heroic drama during the seventeenth century, came to tyrannize its imitations, so Victor Hugo's defense of historically accurate decor came to justify virtuoso exercises in local color. Exploiting all the technology at their disposal for *féeries,* latter-day mechanics constructed Romantic environments from which the Romantic hero had disappeared. This disappearance was symptomatic. When Jules de Goncourt wrote, "Money is a very big thing that leaves men greatly diminished," he voiced the opinion held by many contemporaries that affluence had cost France her soul, that greatness had become the confection of newsmongers or paid auxiliaries, that the missing numeral between Napoleons I and III denoted a spiritual abyss in which the fallen soldiers of "la Grande Armée" had somehow fathered a nation of wee opportunists rising rank upon rank toward self-aggrandizement. Nothing was what it used to be, they lamented — not even opportunism. How could a writer create a character like Balzac's Rastignac when Rastignac's counterpart in modern France would succumb to the devil without making any overtures to some loftier principle? How could he create a Vautrin when the devil, far from exerting animal magnetism, had acquired a respectable paunch? "Ah, it is very difficult indeed nowadays to find a man whose thought has some space in it, who ventilates you like those great swells of air one breathes at the seashore," would sigh Norbert de Varenne, the poet in Maupassant's novel *Bel-Ami,* who sells his talent to a newspaper mogul. "I knew several such men. They're all dead."

Norbert de Varenne would mourn a golden age in 1885, the year Victor Hugo died. Flaubert similarly lamented France's spiritual impoverishment in 1857, when he regretted not belonging to the "good generation." That consummate swindler Robert Macaire was, he felt, as contemporary as ever.

WHEN FLAUBERT, accompanied by his pixilated valet, Narcisse Barette, left the rue de Londres in 1856 for a larger flat farther east, at 42, boulevard du Temple, he undoubtedly found irony and comfort in the knowledge that Robert Macaire had been born across the street, on one of the stages collectively devoted to the kind of blood and thunder that gave the boulevard du Temple its nickname, Boulevard du Crime. Haussmann's crews had yet to reach this neighborhood where stood theaters descended from the eighteenth-century fairground, side by side, still offering mime plays, vaudeville, and melodrama. From his perch, Flaubert could have looked out on the Petit-Lazari, the Délassements-Comiques, the Folies-Dramatiques, the Théâtre-Lyrique, the Cirque-Olympique, and the Funambules. If he leaned out the window, he could also talk to Mme Flaubert, who, with her granddaughter, occupied a flat on the third floor, immediately below his own. Each had four rooms, plus a kitchen. Their neighbors were a clock maker, a dyer, an itinerant vendor, a paper merchant, and Eugène Déjazet, the son of Louise Colet's good friend Virginie Déjazet, an actress famous in her day. Directly opposite number 42 was a hall for wedding banquets where the festivities were plainly visible through a large window. Watching men in black and women in white cavort ("like monkeys," as he put it) was one of the bachelor's chief amusements, except on warm days, when the music drove him to distraction.

Not everyone with whom Flaubert kept company in Paris dwelt in the realm of arts and letters. Prominent among the *hommes du monde* he befriended was Jules Duplan, a humorous, literate businessman trained in his youth to be a painter, whom he had met in 1851 through Maxime Du Camp. As slight as Flaubert was portly, Duplan imported silk goods and Oriental carpets for the firm of Marronnier et Duplan, regularly traveling around the eastern Mediterranean. He and his brother Ernest, a notary, did Flaubert practical favors whenever he needed one.

Another worldly presence was Ernest Feydeau, to whom Théophile Gautier introduced Flaubert. Feydeau, who had published a volume of verse in 1844 at age twenty-three, had given up dreams of a full-time literary career to become a stockbroker when he got married, but professional life in the financial world did not expunge his love of the arts. Growing up among painters and poets in Montmartre, he had, as an adolescent, mingled with the likes of Balzac, Jules Janin, Gautier, and Delacroix at Gavarni's studio near his parents' flat. What had marked him so profoundly was not to be forsworn, and so he shuttled between fellow brokers at the Bourse and his friends at *L'Artiste,* purchasing bourgeois comfort with handsome commissions while turning out novels — the first of which, *Fanny,* made him famous. His real passion was for ancient Egypt; between 1857 and 1861 he brought out a three-volume work entitled *Histoire générale des usages funèbres et des sépultures des peuples anciens.* This hectic, versatile existence would have been unmanageable if not for a schedule as idiosyncratic as Flaubert's, but in reverse. Feydeau sat down to write each day at 4 a.m., when Flaubert was finally surrendering the night, and ended his literary labors at 11 a.m., when Flaubert might still be sleeping or lingering over breakfast. He visited Croisset more than once, always mindful of admonitions by his host to entertain himself with long solitary walks in the morning. Although his extramarital exertions were thought to verge on erotomania (a reputation seemingly incompatible with his alleged habit of retiring at 8 p.m.), the death of his young wife in 1859 devastated him. He would remarry two years later and by his second wife father the Feydeau who made that name synonymous with bedroom farce.

After Louis Bouilhet, down-at-heel and lonely in Paris, which he had always found overwhelming, and thoroughly disheartened by theater politics, set up house with Léonie Le Parfait thirty miles downriver at Mantes in

May 1857, Feydeau, a man as self-congratulatory as Bouilhet was self-critical, became Flaubert's most constant companion during the Paris season. Their crowd assembled every week at Flaubert's own flat or at Feydeau's, or around Apollonie Sabatier's table, or in the salon of Jeanne de Tourbey, another kept woman of exceptional beauty with an aristocratic fiction for a name (whose successive lovers included the prince de Polignac and possibly Napoleon III's cousin Prince Napoleon, known as Plon-Plon). If the circle had one defining center, it was the magazine *L'Artiste,* over which Théophile Gautier came to preside in 1856 with his mind firmly set against contemporaries who made literature accountable to the political imperatives of statesmen, the utopian programs of ideologues, or the moral sensibilities of the church. This much-loved, consummately versatile man of letters had long since outgrown the pink doublet he wore as a Romantic provocation at the premiere of Hugo's *Hernani* in 1830, but he retained his allegiance to Art for Art. As relevant as ever was the pugnacious manifesto he had written two decades earlier to introduce *Mademoiselle de Maupin,* his novel about a young noblewoman's transvestite experiment. "What purpose does this book serve?" is the first question newspaper editors ask any new candidate for serialization, he had proclaimed.

> How can it be applied to the moralization and well-being of the most populous and indigent class? What? Not a word about society's needs, nothing civilizing and progressive? How can one write poetry and novels that lead nowhere and do nothing to advance our generation . . . ? Society suffers . . . The poet's mission should be to search for the cause of this malaise and cure it. He will do so by sympathizing heart and soul with humanity . . . We await this poet, we summon him with all our might. When he appears, he will receive the acclaim of the crowd, palm branches, wreaths, admittance to the Prytaneum.

Describing this rendition of "the utilitarian style" as an effective substitute for laudanum, he interrupts it "lest readers fall asleep over the preface" and attacks the enemy with gusto.

> No, you goitrous imbeciles, a book doesn't make gelatin soup. A novel is not a pair of seamless boots, nor is a sonnet a syringe expressing one continuous stream. A drama is not a railroad, or any of those other essentially civilizing things, and doesn't help humanity forward on the road to progress . . . Metonymy is not material for a cotton bonnet. One cannot shoe oneself with a simile or use an antithesis as an umbrella . . . and one would be no better clothed in a strophe, antistrophe and epode than the wife of that ancient cynic who, considering her virtue sufficient raiment, went in public naked as a hand.

Was there anything absolutely useful on this earth and in this life? he asked (apart from the absolutely useful act of spurning all French newspapers).

Gautier and his companions were as apt to delight in the ravings of Sade as in the stylistic qualities of a Horatian ode. Maniacal bawdry on the one hand and passionate formalism on the other were subversive alternatives in a society fearful of horns and contemptuous of wings. Flouting bourgeois canons of good taste while cultivating great refinement of language, they disdained the middle ground. In one sense at least *Madame Bovary* may be said to illustrate their extremism, for the published work, every line of which had been read aloud and polished to a fare-thee-well, belies the existence of preparatory notes that describe Emma in crude, pornographic detail. Gautier, a *beau parleur* who kept listeners spellbound with extemporized monologues that sounded like publishable prose, could, when it suited him, exhibit the world's foulest mouth.* Likewise the same Flaubert whose letters abound in references to Sade's *Malheurs de la vertu* and *Philosophie dans le boudoir* tortured himself over redundant prepositions, and all the more devotedly for knowing that a sensible bourgeois would have considered the exercise gratuitous. "We chat about the difficulty of writing a sentence and giving it rhythm," wrote Jules de Goncourt. "We take great care with rhythm, a quality we value [in prose]; but in Flaubert's case, it borders on idolatry. For him a book is to be judged by reading it aloud: 'It has no rhythm!' If its pauses don't accord with the natural play of human lungs, it's worthless. And with a sonorous magniloquence that produces echoes of bronze, he chants from memory a portion of Chateaubriand's *Martyrs:* 'Now that's rhythm, isn't it! It's like a flute and violin duo . . . And you may be certain that all the historical texts we read have survived because they're cadenced. It's true even of farce; look at Molière in *Monsieur de Pourceaugnac;* and Monsieur Purgon in *Le Malade imaginaire.*' Whereupon he recites the entire scene in his resonant bull's voice." The *homme plume,* or "pen man," as Flaubert styled himself, could draw upon an immense storehouse of prose and poetry without recourse to his library, and when he did reach for books he hadn't opened in years, he demonstrated an almost photo-

---

*A letter to Apollonie Sabatier from French-occupied Rome gives an idea of Gautier's style, at once lewd and mannered: "There is a splendid American pox here, as pure as at the time of Francis I. The entire French army has been laid up with it; boils are exploding in groins like bombshells, and purulent jets of clap vie with the fountains in the Piazza Navona; folds of peeled skin hang like coxcombs in crimson festoons from the multitude of sappers, sapped in their own foundations; tibias are exfoliating like ancient columns of greenery in a Roman ruin; the deltoids of the staff officers are spangled with constellations of pustules, lieutenants walking in the streets look like leopards, so dotted and spangled are they with roseola, freckles, coffee-colored marks, warty excrescences, horny and cryptogamic verrucae and other secondary and tertiary symptoms, which appear after a fortnight."

graphic memory of the exact page on which certain lines appear. These feats gave him great satisfaction, according to his niece Caroline.

In Flaubert's mind, making oneself a storehouse was an integral part of the literary enterprise. "Read voraciously . . . Reread *all* the classics," he told an aspiring young writer. The more one knew, the larger one bulked. *Madame Bovary,* which neither exploited his erudition nor increased the sum of it, had held him hostage to something oppressively mundane. But in 1857, ignoring the advice pressed on him by friends, who wanted yet another Norman novel, as well as his own doubts, he undertook a project that would require him — with scores of learned tomes at his side — to command a historical void. That void was Carthage in 241 BC, the great mercantile city to which Rome laid waste almost one century later at the behest of Cato the Elder. The novel that eventually emerged was *Salammbô.*

Explanations for this choice may not be far to seek. The African sun, the Mediterranean Sea, and the desert would encompass a savage drama — the *bellum inexpiabile,* or truceless war — that promised to set his imagination free, as Egypt had done during his sabbatical from European constraints. And the French judiciary could hardly insist upon a Reasoner dispensing nineteenth-century moral prescriptions in a city-state whose priesthood enforced human sacrifice. There was also the romance of arcane scholarship. Hooked on everything Greek, Roman, biblical, and Punic, Flaubert would play the historian he had wanted to be ever since his school days without relinquishing the privileges of a fabulist. Afterward he would be able to pitch into *La Tentation* more "authoritatively," with one book legitimizing the other. Where so little was known, how many readers would in the end know more than he? Like an island to which no one could dispute his claim, Carthage offered safety from judgment. He would master its government, conjure up its palaces, populate it as he pleased, clothe its people, invent its inner life, and spill its blood. He would write a self-referential book that "said nothing," that "proved nothing," that escaped all categories. "I'm tired of ugly things and nasty milieus!" he exclaimed in a letter. "The *Bovary* will have left me disgusted with bourgeois mores for a good long time. For a few years perhaps I shall live in a splendid subject, far from the modern world . . . What I am embarking upon is quite mad and will fail with the public. No matter! One must write for oneself first of all. It's the only way of making something beautiful." Did the prospect of unsuccess strike him as another, unavowed inducement? While rejoicing in *Madame Bovary*'s triumph, the author who likened the agony of writing to the rough embrace of a monk's hair shirt may have longed for the comfort and virtue of martyrdom. We love what tortures us, he repeatedly told correspondents.

The historical event that inspired Flaubert was the revolt of mercenaries hired by Carthage during the First Punic War, which began in 264 BC with Roman and Carthaginian armies clashing at Messana (Messina). The struggle lasted twenty-three years. In battles on land and sea for possession of Sicily, neither power gained more than a temporary advantage in battles until 241, when a decisive confrontation took place near the islands off Drapanum (Trapani) on Sicily's west coast. Carthage lost its fleet and withdrew from Punic strongholds in Sicily such as Agrigentum, agreeing to pay a large indemnity. But more strife ensued at home. The mercenaries, who had not been given their promised wages, attacked Carthage instead of dispersing to their countries of origin. Led by a Lybian named Matho and a Greek named Spendius, this polyglot horde — Lybians, Gauls, Spaniards, Greeks, Numidians — surrounded the great city-state, only to be slaughtered when a Carthaginian army under Hamilcar Barca (Hannibal's father) succeeded in raising the siege and waging successful campaigns through the hinterland. Mercy was neither expected nor shown. With its shifting alliances, seesawing movements, brilliant generalship on both sides, and bloodshed that laid a gigantic feast for North African carrion feeders, the war dragged on until 237 BC.

Toward the end of 1861, Flaubert informed Maurice Schlesinger that his days from 8 a.m. to dusk were spent in Paris libraries taking notes (though we know from another letter that he generally napped during the late afternoon), and his evenings on the boulevard du Temple doing the same. He had plowed through Procopius, Diodorus of Sicily, Polybius, Appius, Strabo, transactions of the Académie des inscriptions, articles in the *Revue Archéologique,* Dureau de la Malle's *Province de Constantine* and *Economie politique des Romains,* Littré's *Histoire naturelle.* He met with his former history professor at the collegiate school, Adolphe Chéruel, perhaps to secure paternal blessings. He spoke of beginning the novel in June, but another six months passed before he put pen to paper. His scholarly labors continued at Croisset, where he reestablished himself on May 2, and at the municipal library of Rouen. Amassing encyclopedic knowledge of the Mediterranean world in 250 BC required total immersion. What vegetation was there in North Africa, and what was the lie of the land? What could be learned or inferred about Punic deities? What might Moloch's temple have looked like? What were the weapons and tactics of land warfare? With what jewels and robes might he deck a Carthaginian woman? To answer these and other questions, he studied Pliny's *Historia naturalis,* Xenophon's *Anabasis,* Silius Italicus's *Punica,* Samuel Cahen's Hebrew Bible with Talmudic commentary, Isidore of Seville's *Origins,* Justus Lipsius's three-volume *De militia romana,* seventeenth-century Latin treatises (Johannes Selden's *De dis syris syntagmata II* and Johannes Braun's *Vestitus sacerdotum hebraerum*), and modern monographs recommended by Alfred Maury, a professor at the Collège de France.* The syllabus was daunting. Of the article on Carthage in the *Catholic Encyclopedia,* Flaubert wrote to Duplan that he knew it *"par peur"* — "I knew it by fear" — mistakenly substituting *peur* (fear) for *coeur* (heart). Fearful he was, as his letters consistently reveal. "I am lost in books and am frustrated because I can't find all that much in them"; "I'm suffering vertigo over the blank page, and my sharpened quills cluster like a bush of nasty thorns"; "I am full of doubts and terrors — the more I advance, the more timid I become"; "I'm afraid of getting bogged down in the topographical side of things"; "My Punic readings have drained me"; "I feel exhausted, old, withered"; "I believe I'm in a mess here . . . I daresay there are days when I feel I've set sail on a sea of shit, pardon the expression." But Flaubert's moods shifted from one end of his digestive tract to the other, and metaphors of ingurgitation often recur in boastful accounts of his elephantine "capacity" (to use a term favored by the professional, and banqueting, bourgeoisie). "Do you know how many volumes about Carthage I have now scarfed down?" he asked Duplan on July 29. "Around one hundred! And in the past fortnight I have swallowed all eighteen tomes of Cahen's *Bible.*" To Duplan again he wrote with Rabelaisian flair that he was "belching folios" and suffering "bookish indigestion." There were spells of black despair, when he would have bartered his notes for three seconds inside the skin of his characters: no literature told him how Carthaginians thought and dreamed and loved. At other times he despised the suggestion of sympathetic correspondents that he renounce the project, arguing — as much to brace himself as to convince them — that he was "in" Carthage and bent on digging deeper. The past of *Madame Bovary* and the future of *La Tentation,* he declared, felt equally remote.

In fact both works were still very much on his mind, especially the former. It could not have been otherwise in the summer of 1857, for Juliet Herbert, who had walked him through *Macbeth* the previous fall, devoted her last season at Croisset to translating *Madame Bovary* into English, and a portion of almost every evening was set aside for review. Smitten by the governess, whose good looks made this daily intermission from Carthage the more welcome, Flaubert called her work a masterpiece. At his behest, Michel Lévy contacted English publishers, but to no avail. None would risk the legal consequences in a land much less tolerant of allusions to carnal pleasure than France.† As Hamilton Aïdé, a cousin of the Collier sisters and

*Maury was closely associated with Napoleon III, who called upon his erudition in writing a life of Julius Caesar.

†The first English translation would not appear until 1886, a year before the translation of Zola's *La Terre,* which resulted in a prison sentence for Henry Vizetelly, the publisher vilified by the National Vigilance Association. Flaubert's publisher did not suffer a similar fate, but

a poet, predicted: "A translation would be most difficult to introduce, since you know full well that, *where novels are concerned,* English mores surpass the Roman in severity." And indeed, Gertrude Collier Tennant, to whom Flaubert had sent a copy, instantly proved his point. "Dear Gustave," she wrote from Russell Square on June 23,

> I have often imagined writing to you — in English (for I am losing my French), then in French, then I'd decide that it was useless to open my mind, then I saw the good letter you wrote to my dear cousin Hamilton, then I read *a little* of your *Madame de Bovary* [*sic*] — and finally that impelled me to tell you at least what I think of it, in memory of our Trouville days.
>
> To put it bluntly, I am amazed that you, with your rich imagination, with your admiration for everything beautiful, have written, could have set your pleasure in writing, something *so hideous* as this book! I find it all so bad! — And the *talent* invested in it makes it doubly detestable! Truth to tell, I didn't read every word, for when I plunged into it here and there I felt myself gasping for air, like the poor dog thrown into *"il grotto del cane."*

How he could have told a tale so utterly devoid of the good and the beautiful mystified her. One day he was sure to see the rightness of her argument that works whose sordid revelations make people feel "unhappy" and "bad" served no useful purpose. Meanwhile, Mme Flaubert, she supposed, must be mortified by her son's literary turpitude. "Now that we've done forever with *Madame de Bovary,* let's not speak of it again," she concluded. "My husband and dear children . . . sincerely hope that the career opening before you will be employed in the cause of something *good.*" Flaubert is not known to have answered the letter, which must have made him appreciate Juliet Herbert all the more, even as it augured ill for the fate of her translation. His answer would be the scenes of starvation, human sacrifice, and cannibalism in *Salammbô.*

Since the publication of *Madame Bovary,* the postman delivered far more mail than previously, some of it from theater people eager to adapt the novel or, if a stage adaptation had already been planned, to recommend themselves for a specific role. But much of it came from readers without professional motives. Notable among the latter was Marie-Sophie Leroyer de Chantepie, a fifty-six-year-old spinster who was to be Flaubert's most prolific correspondent during the late 1850s and early 1860s, unburdening

---

worse befell the translator of *Madame Bovary,* Karl Marx's daughter Eleanor Marx Aveling. Like Emma, she poisoned herself (after learning that her common-law husband, Edward Aveling, had secretly married another woman).

her troubled soul in long, anguished letters, which he answered with unfailing solicitude. Born to minor gentry rooted in the western Loire valley, Marie-Sophie lived near Angers on property that afforded her an independence and knew almost nothing of the world beyond Anjou except through books. Catholicism, socialism, and literature had variously guided her mind to the cul-de-sac in which she found herself when *Madame Bovary* entered her life. Educated at convent school, where live embers of joy had been efficiently stamped out, she devoted herself well past her twenties to a mother guilt-ridden for having divorced her first husband during the Revolution, when divorce briefly became legal and easily accomplished. Marie Catherine Leroyer de Chantepie exacerbated Marie-Sophie's religious scruples with her own obsessive fear of damnation. During the 1830s an alternative faith presented itself in the form of socialism, to which Marie-Sophie was led by her physician. George Sand, with whom she initiated a correspondence as prolific as the one with Flaubert, encouraged her social radicalism, and after the death of Marie Catherine, Marie-Sophie's estate, Tertre Saint-Laurent, became a ramshackle phalanstery housing fourteen dependents, among them her godson, an adopted orphan, and a Polish refugee. "They have no livelihood and count on me for everything they need," she told Flaubert. "My father left me ten thousand francs of income from farmland, which isn't enough to support a throng that consumes without earning. I must have recourse to expedients and deny myself everything." Everything included conjugal love. She had been in love with an opera singer named Eugène, and there had been one or two prospects of marriage, but her misgivings gained the upper hand when George Sand, whom she asked for advice, declared marriage to be an "odious" institution. Fourteen people did not fill the emotional void. Nor had socialism freed her from the influence of Catholic demonology. Haunted by guilt even for imaginary sins, she could neither confess them nor cease to want absolution.

Meanwhile she read novels, wrote and published several herself, contributed reviews to a local newspaper, and corresponded with great literary figures of the day, Michelet as well as Sand and Flaubert, whom she obviously regarded as surrogate confessors. Her first letter to Flaubert set the tone of all that followed. "You have written a masterpiece true to nature," she declared. "Yes, here are the mores of the province in which I was born and have spent my life; this will suffice to tell you, sir, that I have understood the sorrows, the troubles, the miseries of poor Madame Bovary. I recognized her straightaway, loved her as a friend I might have known. I identified with her completely! No, your story is not a fiction, it is a truth, this woman existed, you must have observed her life, her death, her suffering." Of all the novels written by France's best authors during the previous thirty years, none, not even *Eugénie Grandet,* in whose titular heroine she also recognized herself, had affected her so profoundly. "I myself have suffered too much in life not to be dry of tears . . . Well, since yesterday I haven't stopped weeping over poor dame Bovary. I couldn't sleep a wink, she was there before my eyes . . . and I am inconsolable . . . Ah, how, sir, did you come by your perfect knowledge of human nature! Yours is a scalpel applied to the heart, the soul! You have shown the world in all its hideousness." When Flaubert refuted her view of "dame Bovary," calling Emma "a woman of false poetry and false sentiments" inferior in every way to his correspondent, the refutation fell on deaf ears. Like Emma, she felt a swan in a duckpond, enduring the malicious gossip of bigoted neighbors and the monotony of village life. Like Emma, she could not find a clergyman's ear. And like Emma, she sought refuge in theater. "The external world is not mine. Only in a theater auditorium do I come alive, for I want, as Mme Bovary does, to sleep on and on or not exist at all. Angers' playhouse is very poor and yet I feel at home there. That is my universe, I have no other. I have never left my province. I don't know Paris."

Marie-Sophie sent Flaubert a lithograph based on a portrait, with armorial bearings in one corner, of a pretty, refined woman, goose quill in hand, painted thirty years earlier. Flaubert explained that he could not reciprocate, as he had not been painted or drawn since childhood. Eschewing portraits, for fear of being hostage to an external image (in much the same way that he vetoed illustrated editions of his work), suited him, and the difference in age, when his correspondent revealed hers, set his mind at rest. No demands would be made of him. Since leagues and decades separated them, he felt free to draw closer. "We shall chat together like *two* men," he wrote on March 30, 1857, three months after his thirty-fifth birthday. "I am honored by the trust you place in me. I don't believe myself unworthy of it." Her confidences were immediately repaid with his. The willful sacrifice she had made of love and happiness spoke to painful separations in his own life, he assured her. "Why [this shrinking back]? I have no idea. It may have been a matter of pride, or of fright. I, too, have loved in silence." The hallucinatory color with which unbidden pictures impressed themselves upon her mind's eye was familiar to him, he wrote, describing his nervous disorder boastfully, without identifying it.

At twenty-one I nearly died of a nervous illness brought on by a series of irritations and troubles, by late nights and anger. It lasted ten years. (I have felt, I have *seen* everything in Saint Theresa, in Hoffmann and Edgar Poe; people visited by hallucinations are not strangers to me.) But I've come out of it *steeled* and suddenly rich with experience of all sorts of things I had hardly brushed against.*

He regretted that their affinity did not make for a meeting of minds in religion and politics. Though drawn more to religion than to almost anything else, he was neither troubled by the idea of absolute extinction nor enchanted by any one sect. "Each dogma in particular is repulsive to me, but I consider the feeling that engendered them to be the most natural and poetic expression of humanity. I don't like those philosophers who have dismissed it as just foolishness and humbug. What I find in them is necessity and instinct. I therefore respect the Negro kissing his fetish as much as I do the Catholic kneeling before the Sacred Heart." Humbug, in his view, pertained to other realms, above all politics. "I have no sympathy for any political party or, to put it bluntly, I execrate all of them because they all seem parochial, false, puerile, attacking the ephemeral, lacking an ability to compass the whole and ever to rise above the *useful*. I hate despotisms." Despotic was any system that proposed to harness individual energies for the accomplishment of a common order. "I am a rabid liberal, which is why socialism seems to me a pedantic horror that will spell the death of all art and morality. I have witnessed almost all the uprisings of my time." Although it was Edmund Burke, not Flaubert, who wrote, "In a democracy, the majority of the citizens is capable of exercising the most cruel oppressions upon the minority, whenever strong divisions prevail in that kind of polity, as they often must; and that oppression of the minority will extend to far greater numbers, and will be carried on with much greater fury, than can almost ever be apprehended from the dominion of a single sceptre," one can easily see how Flaubert, under the banner of liberalism, might have marched in step with him.

Did he ever tire of hearing Mlle Leroyer de Chantepie, whom he truly admired, praise *Madame Bovary* as a masterpiece? Only when he thought he could never again equal himself. And when he protested that he was far from the "savant" she believed him to be, his blush expressed as much satisfaction as modesty. Nothing in this epistolary friendship proved more satisfying, however, than the role of healer-mentor-confessor-father conferred on him, at his invitation, by a much older woman (who suffered from frequent migraines). He assured her more than once that he would always gladly lend her an ear. "I am a great doctor of melancholy, trust me," the anatomist's son wrote on one occasion. "It seems to me that if I were living

---

*It is most likely that he had had at least partial seizures since 1854 and, as we shall see, was apparently to suffer a major one in January 1860.

with you, I would cure you." Marie-Sophie needed no further encourage-ment. Long letters written without paragraph breaks, as if the emotion in-forming them couldn't pause, arrived at regular intervals, all of them returning obsessively to her struggle with demons, her dysfunctional clan and phenomenal capacity for devotion, the paralysis of will that kept her from either entering the confessional booth or turning her back upon it once and for all. The worn garment of Catholic doctrine clung to her like the shirt of Nessus. "I do not lack the faculty of self-examination, my life is a continual analysis of my feelings and thoughts," she assured him. "But what I experience are internal hallucinations, moral illusions that hold sway in the intellectual world where everything escapes perception. How does one contradict doubts of conscience? I am certain that when I speak to you of confession, you think I belong to a different century, or rather to an ex-tinct world, but I was raised with these beliefs. Look at it from my perspec-tive; true or false I believe in confession, in the presence of God in Communion. And judge my terrors! No, by the world's lights, there is no real fault for which I need reproach myself, all my terrors arise from the ac-complishment of these two awesome duties: confession and Communion. For several years my soul has not been calm enough to commune. I haven't been able to confess for a year; I blame myself, but my ideas get muddled and I've gone half mad over this." A correspondence with the abbé Bessières, vicar of the Madeleine in Paris, did not assuage her. "[He] is as-tonished that I can be as unhappy as I am in the service of God. He then tells me that I exaggerate most of my faults and that the others never ex-isted except in my mind. He goes on to say that confiding has its limits, . . . which presumably means that I can refrain from explaining many things. Therein lies the illness, I know it, I feel it more keenly than anyone, but wherein lies the remedy? Put yourself in my place, suppose that one is guilty of a thousand imaginary faults, one more painfully unavowable than the next, nameless things, indefinable and repugnant to oneself, and that one feels obliged to voice what one refuses even to think . . . It's a martyr-dom, don't you see. If I had committed any of those specific transgressions or errors that everyone recognizes, I would not hurt as much as I do." Out of the blue, during peaceful remissions, a "wicked life" would envelop her own. "It's as if an evil genius had laid hold of my soul and begotten a dark double."

Had Flaubert at this point known anything of her mother's guilt, he might have wondered whether Marie-Sophie had been raised by Marie Catherine to view herself as the fruit of a poisoned tree, whether the un-nameable fault for which she craved absolution stemmed from the original sin of her mother's divorce. All he could do was rally her against her dark double. "Why are you talking about remorse, fault, vague apprehensions and confession?" he asked.

> Let go of all that, poor soul! for love of yourself. Since you feel you have a clean conscience, you can stand before the Eternal and say: "Here I am." What should one fear when one isn't guilty? And of what can men be guilty, incommensurate as we are with good and evil alike? All your woes derive from an excess of unfocused thought. With a voracious mind that lacks external nourishment, you've become your own predator and eaten yourself to the bone.

The therapies he urged upon her were those he practiced upon himself. Marie-Sophie having made it abundantly clear that she was as likely to travel abroad as an Angevin hawthorn hedge to set sail down the Loire, he tried to separate her from her estate and its inhabitants.

> In the name of heaven and above all of reason, swear off all the doctors and all the priests of the world and stop living so much *in your soul* and through it. Leave! Travel! Regale yourself with music, paintings and horizons. Inhale God's good air and leave all your worries behind you. I have been moved and uplifted, I assure you, by what you've told me about your life. This devotion to strangers fills me with admiration! There, I've said it. I won't take it back. I like you enormously, you are a noble heart. I wish I could squeeze your two hands and kiss your forehead! But allow me to offer, with brutal candor, some advice I know will not be taken . . . Make sure your many charges have what they will minimally need to survive, and *take off!* Leave your house. It's the only way.

None of the objections she was certain to raise could possibly stand up against her need for tranquillity, he insisted.

Should she never leave her house, there was peace of mind to be found in studious reclusion. When at first Marie-Sophie expressed a hunger for knowledge and sought Flaubert's professorial guidance, he demurred. But professing proved irresistible. Before long she received not only a syllabus but a prolegomenon on reading itself. "Read Montaigne, read him slowly, deliberately! *He will calm you,*" he wrote from Croisset in June 1857. "And don't listen to people who speak of his egoism. You'll love him, you'll see. But don't read him the way children read, to amuse yourself, or the way strivers read, to instruct yourself. No. Read *to live.* Provide your soul with an intellectual atmosphere composed of emanations from all the great minds. Cultivate Goethe and Shakespeare. Read translations of the Greek and Roman authors: Homer, Petronius, Plautus, Apuleius, etc. . . . It's a question of *working,* do you understand? I don't like to see a nature as beautiful as yours fall apart in grief and unemployment." Elsewhere he insisted that she commit herself to a regular, "exhausting" schedule of work. "Life is such a hideous business that the only way to tolerate it is to avoid it, and one avoids it by living in Art . . . Read the great masters, but while doing so try to understand what makes them great, to draw near their soul." In Flaubert's intellectual gastronomy, the more one absorbed of substantial matter, the less room there would be for dark doubles to poach on one's self-esteem. "You will love yourself more because you have stored more things in your mind." The soul is a "wild beast," he observed, always ravening and always ready to feed upon us unless we arrange to keep it gorged.

The truth of his image was borne home in a dozen letters that vacillate between the confident dictums of the guide and the lamentations of a disoriented wayfarer. Flaubert could hardly get the starstruck Marie-Sophie to imagine her correspondent at his wits' end, but not for lack of trying. *Salammbô* — or *Carthage,* as he originally entitled the novel — filled him with anguish, he informed her in his first allusion to it. A letter written several months later, on his thirty-sixth birthday, enlarges upon a thought that had been hounding him ever since his postgraduate voyage in 1840, when he had noted disconsolately that he felt outside the world around him, that his eyes did not absorb beauty but, on the contrary, distanced him from it. A voyeur despite himself, he told Marie-Sophie, he couldn't enter his characters, "palpitate" with them, lose himself in an empathetic leap. And being thus locked out, or in, made him reach for the language of seizures. "I've undertaken an accursed work in which all I see is fire and which leaves me despairing," he wrote.

> I *feel* that I'm engaged in imposture, do you understand? And that my characters must not have spoken as they do. It's no small ambition, wanting to enter the heart of men who lived more than two thousand years ago in a civilization with nothing analogous to our own. I glimpse the truth, but it doesn't penetrate me, emotion is lacking. Life and movement are what make one shout: "That's it!" though you may never have seen the models. And I yawn, I wait, I gather wool and bristle. I have endured other such sad periods in my life, when the wind goes out of my sails.

Marie-Sophie comforted him as best she could with assurances that his new book would turn out well, that she rejoiced in the prospect of reading it, that he lacked the repose to judge what he had already written, and that Paris, where he arrived midway through the third week of December for the winter season, would improve his outlook. She called him "my son." But her endless raptures over *Madame Bovary* only sharpened his fear that he was riding for a fall. Would he disappoint? Or make himself ridiculous? Or ever receive permission to grow beyond his province? In the eyes of Marie-

Sophie, whatever Flaubert wrote after 1857 would be supererogatory, though she might deny it, and when the idolized author was remembering his thirty-sixth birthday, his devotee was marking the first anniversary of her encounter with Emma. "I don't know if you'll ever do better than *Madame Bovary;* that seems impossible to me," she wrote. "I read the book a year ago and I feel as sad on this anniversary as on that of a beloved woman whose death I witnessed . . . I am glad to have been one of the first to understand and admire your novel. I await the one you're writing." She advised him not to trouble himself excessively over form.

Unlike Marie-Sophie, Flaubert had no dependents to hinder him from traveling abroad, and the thought of doing so matured during the winter of 1857–58, a difficult winter that began with a bang, quite literally. On January 14, three grenades exploded beside the emperor's carriage as it approached the old opera house, killing 8 horse guards, wounding 141 spectators, and wrecking the carriage, but leaving Louis-Napoleon and Eugénie unharmed. The would-be assassin was an Italian exile named Orsini, who held France responsible, because of its nonintervention, for Austria's continued stranglehold over Italy. Flaubert (whose flat at 42, boulevard du Temple was quite near the one from which another Italian nationalist, Fieschi, had rained fire on Louis-Philippe twenty-three years earlier) lay in bed with a heavy cold. His servant, Narcisse Barette, who slept in the kitchen, caught it, and the two took turns nursing each other. Meanwhile there was unpleasantness of another kind. Marc Fournier, director of the Saint-Martin theater, proposed to stage *Madame Bovary* in an adaptation by Dennery, the prolific hack known for his Boulevard extravaganzas. After desultory negotiations, Flaubert turned him down, bragging to one correspondent that he had thrown away thirty thousand francs. Negotiations also took place that winter with La Rounat, director of a state theater, the Odéon, but not over *Madame Bovary.* Louis Bouilhet had written a verse play entitled *Hélène Peyron,* the second of his five staged plays, and had already arranged to have it produced by La Rounat when problems arose. In the quarrel that ensued, each party regarded himself as blameless. La Rounat declared their arrangement null and void; Bouilhet went shopping for another theater, found none, and retired to Mantes. Flaubert volunteered to beard La Rounat on his behalf, which he did, and the ever-staunch, competent proxy ultimately won out. La Rounat agreed to stage *Hélène Peyron* (which would have a successful run), without improving Flaubert's settled opinion that theater people were a stoatlike subspecies of humanity.

By March 1858 he had decided that *Salammbô* urgently called for a tour of Tunisia. The month was spent on hectic preparations, which Mme Flaubert almost thwarted by falling ill with what was diagnosed as pleurisy.

He left on April 12 after satisfying himself that she would recover completely under Achille's care and bidding farewell to his "dear correspondent" in Angers.* The ache of separation tempered his excitement, he wrote. Still,

> one must ply one's trade, follow one's vocation, do one's duty in a word. Hitherto there has been no weakness for which I need reproach myself and I never take half measures. I must leave, I've even delayed it too long. The whole winter was frittered away on pedestrian foolishness of one kind or another, not to mention the illnesses all around me, my mother's being the most serious . . . How we suffer in our affections! Love is sometimes as difficult to bear as hatred!

The news of his intended voyage saddened Marie-Sophie, who felt bereft. Leaving for parts unknown seemed terribly enviable to her. She had never seen anyone depart, even for the next world, without wanting to follow them. "Here I am, stuck in the same place!" Work would be her salvation, she said, and, indeed, the hours she had recently devoted to an essay on the Thirty Years' War for a prize competition (following Flaubert's bibliographical pointers) had been enjoyable. But as soon as it was done her familiar ghosts visited her, returning in strength during the Lenten season of a Jubilee Year, marked by endless processions. How might she find the intelligent priest with a "broad, lofty" view of the world to help her fulfill her obligations?

SMOKING ALL the way, Flaubert had his own ghosts for company on the long voyage south. In Marseille a two-day layover gave him time to recover from the train ride by consuming pots of bouillabaisse, attending the theater, loitering through the brothel district, visiting the museum, and happily spending time with peacocks and lions at a zoo in the Saint-Loup hills. He sat among sailors in out-of-the-way cabarets. And he made two pil-

---

*Most of the letters Flaubert received from his mother (which undoubtedly contained despairing complaints about his financial improvidence), Achille, and Caroline were later destroyed by his two nieces. One that survived gives a good idea of what he faced when it came to separating. Dated May 3, it awaited him when he set foot in North Africa. "At last you've reached the goal of your voyage, poor old man, and are at last on terra firma," his mother wrote. "That's one less worry for me. If you are a man of your word, half the time your voyage is to last has elapsed and I hope that we shall be close to seeing each other again in three weeks. My dear little Caroline, who is still very affectionate and sweet to me, is very hurt that you had no word for her in your letter, she feels that you are forgetting her . . . I believe I told you that Flavie won't be coming until the end of the week. The result is that I was all alone with my memories of the past and anxieties about the present . . . I shall count on receiving a letter next Sunday. I congratulate you on the conquests you've made en route, but don't accept any invitations. I've endured enough separation."

grimages to the building that enshrined his memory of Eulalie Foucaud. What had been the Hôtel de Richelieu now housed a bazaar on the parlor floor and a barbershop where, in commemoration of his true erotic awakening, he had himself shaved. "I shall spare you commentary and Chateaubriandesque reflections on the flight of days, the fall of leaves and of hair," he wrote to Bouilhet. "Even so, I hadn't thought or felt so deeply in a long time. Philoxène would say: 'I reread the stones of the staircase and the walls of the house.'"*

On the sea leg of his voyage Flaubert was too sick to engage fellow passengers, most of whom appear to have been settlers and soldiers. His ship, the *Hermus,* rolled perilously in the violent current sweeping along the Algerian coast and crashing against headlands. It anchored in the Gulf of Sora. From his hotel high above Philippeville (now Skikda), originally a Phoenician port situated in the gap between coastal cliffs to the west and wide beachfront to the east, he could view roofs sloping down toward the sea and a road luxuriantly wooded with myrtle and arbutus. Letters of introduction had preceded him here and in Constantine, some miles inland, where several days later the son of the bey served as his guide. "He led me through the bazaars, which reminded me of those in Upper Egypt," he noted in his diary (which also mentions an eye inflammation). "All the men brown faced, in white dress. I got . . . an agreeable whiff of the Orient; it came to me in gusts of hot wind." With a French official named Vignard he descended one thousand feet into the gorge over which this ancient capital of Numidia perches and rode horseback along the Rhummel between sheer walls of red rock, joined two hundred feet above the stream by four natural limestone arches. The place was, in his words, wondrous and satanic. As he watched bearded vultures circling overhead, it pleased him to think that in Paris, at that very moment, people were queuing up for theater tickets on the boulevard du Temple. He had made good his escape.

A fortnight later Flaubert wrote to Bouilhet that he was enjoying himself without giving a thought to his novel. In fact, the novel shaped his whole itinerary, and what he saw during the six weeks in North Africa was almost all material for *Salammbô.* After calling at Bône, the *Hermus* made for Tunis's port at La Goulette, where boatmen ferried passengers across Lake Tunis. The yellowish water of that shallow, fetid expanse reminded Flaubert of the Nile. And flamingos in their thousands added pink and black to the palette. By nightfall of his first day ashore he had toured the souks of the Central Medina and climbed uphill to the belvedere for a broad view of the Medjerda River valley. Africa invigorated him. The normally unmatutinal Gustave made up his mind to rise early, to cover as much ground as pos-

*Philoxène Boyer, a poet and mutual friend.

sible, and to retire only after he had taken notes on everything observed during the day.

A letter dated May 8 informed Bouilhet that he had already spent eight to fourteen hours a day, for four straight days, surveying the ruins of Carthage, and had become thoroughly familiar with the city in various guises of both day and night ("Je connais Carthage à fond"). How did he occupy himself eight or fourteen hours a day? What did he mean by "thorough"? True, there was familiarity to be gained with the landscape, with sunbeams and moonlight playing over scattered debris, with the bay lapping on a fabled shore. But of physical Carthage little had yet been revealed, aside from crumbling walls and cisterns. Archeologists began to dig in earnest several decades later, whereupon vestiges of Byzantine, Vandal, Roman, and finally Punic habitation came to light layer by layer. Had Flaubert reconnoitered the site in 1900, he would have seen Roman Carthage in the skeleton of its fortifications, its aqueduct, Hadrian's theater, an odeum, a colosseum, baths, a temple to Asclepius, and, on Byrsa Hill, the portico of a Capitoline temple. This was not possible in 1858. As for Punic Carthage, it awaited Francis Kelsey, the American who in 1925 led an expedition that reached down twenty-five centuries on a plot sacred to Ba'al Hammon (or Moloch) and to the Punic goddess of love and fertility, Tanit (Astarte). In this precinct known as Salammbô, Kelsey unearthed no temples. His team did, however, discover a "Tophet," or burial ground, presenting evidence of the sacrificial rites mentioned by ancient historians and luridly evoked by Flaubert.* Dedicatory stelae aligned like tombstones bore the triangle associated with Tanit, and cinerary urns in their midst were found to contain the charred bones of young children, lambs, and goats.

His hours on horseback took Flaubert well beyond Carthage proper. Among other excursions whose purpose was to help him visualize battlefields and the movement of armies, something he would describe as brilliantly as any historian of warfare, one led north to Utica, where Hamilcar, in a famous maneuver anticipating Hannibal's at Cannae, surprised his enemy from the rear after marching across the silted mouth of the Bagradas (the modern Medjerda). En route, Flaubert, accompanied by a dragoman named Bogo and an armed escort, memorized every feature of the alluvial

---

*The term *Tophet* is of biblical origin and appears in *Jeremiah:* "Thus saith the Lord of hosts, the God of Israel, the which whosoever heareth, his ears shall tingle. Because they have forsaken me, and have estranged this place, and have burned incense in it unto other gods, whom neither they nor their fathers have known, nor the kings of Judah, and have filled this place with the blood of innocents; they have built also the high places of Baal, to burn their sons with fire for burnt offerings unto Baal, which I commanded not, nor spake it, neither came it into my mind: therefore, behold, the days come, saith the Lord, that this place shall no more be called Tophet, nor The valley of the son of Hinnom, but The valley of slaughter." It was associated with the worship of Moloch.

plain. "To the left, low mountains with great, bluish undulations; to the right, a stretch of terrain screens one's view," he wrote in his journal.

> At the end of this first plain a second one; the vegetation ceases after the olive groves (the first one is called Rastabiah and the second Menihelah; we halted at Sabel-Settaban, a fountain with three columns), and one enters an arid landscape. The mountains disappear. On our right, a deserted santon. Bedouins armed to the teeth pass nearby. The olive groves are where they murdered Bogo's father. The valley gives way to a small mountain, and suddenly yet another plain, this one immense, unfolds before us . . . The Medjerda is as wide as the Seine at Bapaume and yellowish . . . One hour later we arrive at Mezel-Goull (the Devil's Rest).
>
> The dowar, or encampment, lies at the bottom, or rather at the entrance, of a ravine. We dismount and hunt for scorpions; the mountain is bare and shagged with little thornbushes . . . We smoke our pipes outside, in an enclosure made of dried cowpats; we almost trip over small cows lying in the yard. The dowar dogs bark. They are used to barking incessantly, all night long, to chase away jackals. For human intruders, they alert the encampment with a different kind of bark.

Utica's outskirts, where so much carnage had been wrought by so many, abounded in indefinable ruins. The party puzzled over them and advanced to Cape Gammarth, which commanded a spectacular view of the Mediterranean coastline extending southeast beyond the beacon at Sidi-bou-Said.

Flaubert departed Tunis on May 22 with a spahi for protection. Eager to answer questions he had about his physical courage, but intent as well on leaving nothing unseen of what might enrich the novel, he returned to Constantine by land, venturing into regions where, as he proudly told Jules Duplan, Europeans seldom set foot. The route dipped into the Tell, the central province, and passed through two cities of great interest, Dougga and Le Kef. For Roman architecture, Dougga was quite the most remarkable site in North Africa, with magnificent temples clustered around the central square, columns of polychrome marble studding a forum behind the capitol, and the triumphal arch of Septimius Severus, among much else. Le Kef lay farther west, near Algeria, on a rocky spur of Jebel Dyr overlooking Jugurtha's Table, a huge mesa named for the Numidian king who held off Roman armies from 111 to 106 BC. It had acquired its Arabic name, meaning "the rock," in the seventeenth century; the Romans had called it Veneria and the Carthaginians Sicca. It was, indeed, to Sicca that Carthage tried to shuffle off disgruntled mercenaries before the great rebellion, a fact very much on Flaubert's mind during his brief sojourn — and then he visited the Sanctuary of Tanit, where Carthaginian girls of noble birth sacrificed their virginity to placate the goddess who ensured abundant harvests.

His journal entry, however, written at Croisset several weeks after the event, records only the hospitality lavished upon him in the city. "The caid's house, at the very top: a masonry bench to the left in front of the door, an interior court, an enormous straight staircase, large room," he noted. "An excellent Turkish bath; rais Ibrahim, undaunted by the heat, comes to visit me in the last sweat room. It is he again who gives me the eternal cup of dense coffee. A luxurious Arab dinner. Slept well." His departure was treated as a solemn event, with seven horsemen and a score of people on foot escorting him. He spent one night among friendly Bedouins near Souk-Ahras, another among vicious fleas in a mill house, and, having consumed a bottle of Bordeaux at lunch, entered Constantine half-drunk. Four days later the steamer left Stora bound for Marseille.

There were soon to be warm reunions in Paris, and possibly an intimate one with Jeanne de Tourbey. Though Louise Colet, who caught sight of him from afar on one occasion, thought he was altered much for the worse, and Jules de Goncourt described a conglomeration of ruined features — red mottled skin, puffy eyelids, bulging eyes, full cheeks, a rough, drooping mustache — many women still found him attractive. At Croisset he slept for three days and, when he felt wakeful enough, completed his journal, which had been neglected since Le Kef. His last entry was a prayer or supplication: "May I exhale in my book all the energies of nature that flowed through me [in Africa] . . . May the power to resurrect the past be mine. Mine! I must do it, reaching for the Beautiful, but hewing to the truth and bringing alive what was. Have pity on my will, God of souls! Give me the strength — and the Hope."

THE GOD of souls, a mercurial divinity, wasn't always helpful during the composition of *Salammbô,* which lasted longer than the *bellum inexpiabile* itself. Bouilhet, who came up from Mantes periodically for intense editorial sessions, should have known better than to predict that the book would progress "smartly." Smartly was seldom how Flaubert's books progressed, even when he didn't have a heavy load of erudition to truck or the cadenced sentences of prose poetry to measure or descriptive overgrowth to prune at Bouilhet's patient insistence. As soon as he had sharpened his quills, distress calls from Croisset went out to various correspondents, the majority to Ernest Feydeau. On August 28, 1858, Flaubert informed his friend that he had finished a whole chapter, after toiling "like fourteen oxen." Would there be gratitude, he wondered, for all he had put into it? "It's doubtful, since the book will not be entertaining; a reader will need real fortitude to suffer the four hundred pages (at least) of this construction." In November 1859, with the novel almost half-written, none of his doubts had yet retreated. They seem, on the contrary, to have grown more aggressive, and once again he complained about unappreciated labor, declaring to Feydeau that such projects made no sense. "In each line and every word of it I have to surmount difficulties that will go unrecognized, and perhaps this is as it should be . . . When *Salammbô* is read, I hope the author will not enter the reader's thoughts! Few people will guess what sadness provoked the attempt to resuscitate Carthage, how I've lost myself in it out of disgust with modern life!" The writing and the poring over dozens of scholarly tomes every night until 3 or 4 a.m. exhausted him. "I feel I've taken a wrong turn. There's no firm ground underfoot, I'm constantly missing the mark, and yet I persevere." In warm weather he took evening dips in the Seine. But his increasingly nocturnal life, the anguish and dark premonitions, the permanent miasma of pipe smoke and desiccating heat of log fires affected his health. Bronchitis kept him wheezing that fall. He suffered rheumatic pain in one shoulder. Carbuncles came and went.

More worrisome, however, were two incidents, both described elliptically. Driving his carriage home from an excursion to the countryside in September 1859, he was, he wrote without comment, almost crushed by a locomotive. Had he perhaps suffered one of his "absences," or worse, at a level crossing? Four months later, in Paris, he fell near his apartment building and smashed his face against the pavement, making it home severely bruised but with nothing broken. Dr Achille Flaubert wrote to Jules Cloquet that it was a recurrence of his former condition and wondered whether it was possible for "epileptiform accidents" to manifest themselves again after long remission. Whatever the clinical opinion may have been, his seizure surely lent deeper color to Flaubert's feeling that he stood on shaky ground as a man and an artist, that his work was always defective, that he would never master Greek, that he could never quite wrap his mind around a subject or achieve the ideal form, that his fire was low. In October 1861, six months before completing *Salammbô,* he wrote yet another despairing letter to Feydeau. "You can't imagine how weary and anguished I am . . . The more I advance, the graver my doubts about the book as a whole; I perceive its defects, irremediable defects that I shall not attempt to remove, a mole being preferable to a scar."

His anguish was poured into Matho. Flaubert made of Matho, the gigantic Libyan who had led the mercenaries' rebellion, a Romantic nomad moving from camp to camp outside Carthage, a barbarian in animal skins condemned to gaze religiously at the gleaming citadel and desire the inaccessible beauty behind its walls. For this warrior, victory will be not wealth but union with the woman he worships, Hamilcar's daughter Salammbô. Here is how Flaubert describes him besieging the city of Hippo-Zarytus while anticipating the future siege of its ally Carthage:

The town was protected by a lake that communicated with the sea. It had three lines of fortifications and a wall with towers on the heights overlooking it. Matho had never maneuvered against such defenses. Moreover, the thought of Salammbô obsessed him, and he would drift off into thoughts about the enjoyment of her beauty or the delights of prideful revenge. Bitter, furious, incessant, was his need to see her again. He thought at one point of entering Carthage as a mediator in the hope that once there he could seek her out. He often sounded the signal for assault and, without waiting for anything or anyone, darted onto the moleworks. Here he'd wreak havoc, tearing up stones and slashing right and left. The barbarians would imitate him. They dashed forward pell-mell to scale the rampart, but overloaded ladders regularly buckled, hurling numbers of men into the sea . . . At length the tumult would subside and the soldiers withdraw, before renewing the assault. Matho could then be seen outside the tents, wiping his blood-splattered face and turning his gaze toward Carthage, beyond the horizon.

Entering Carthage by main force or by subterfuge in order to possess Salammbô is the one thought that animates Matho, and the pitched battles, the long gory rounds fought by pugilists neither of whom will surrender, reflect his obsessiveness. Were it a struggle for finite rewards — as the historical conflict certainly was — it might admit of finite solutions, but this is Flaubert's *bellum inexpiabile,* a truceless war whose terms are All or Nothing. Matho will win Salammbô or he will die at her father's hands. The issue is Being, and geography conforms to this radical vision. As Emma Bovary believes that there is no salvation outside Paris, so for Matho there can be none outside the citadel. "He lay flat on his stomach, digging his nails into the earth and sobbing. He felt miserable, puny, abandoned. Never would he possess her, he couldn't even seize a town."

Toward the end, Flaubert writes that the men Matho commands are "riveted to the horizon of Carthage" and contemplate its high walls from afar "while dreaming of the infinite delights to be enjoyed therein." Their intense longing for something paradisiacal, for a "beyond," amplifies Matho's. Could they scale the wall they would escape the redundancy of battles won or lost in a haphazard war. Here each slaughter resembles the next, and this futile eventfulness works against the possibility of growth, of dramatic development, of wisdom. As in Beckettian theater, days will unfold in a progression of wear until they end in martyrdom or suicide. "I believe the novel moves smartly and concisely, but the general action goes nowhere," he fretted, only half committed to the "repeated effects" that he was sure would not sit well with readers; frustrated by the knowledge that those effects, which he himself viewed as an impediment, embodied his will to subvert dramatic movement of a conventional kind. (It would be subverted again in *L'Éducation sentimentale,* with Carthage prefiguring the village brothel evoked so fervently, after an aimless life, by the protagonist who could not bring himself to enter it at fifteen.) Matho finally enters Salammbô's city, a chained, mutilated captive walking a gauntlet of infuriated Carthaginians, and drops dead in his beloved's presence. "A man leaped upon the corpse. Though beardless, he wore on his shoulder the mantle of the priests of Moloch and in his belt the knife used to cut up sacred meat, its haft terminating in a golden spatula. With one thrust he split open Matho's chest, tore out his heart, and served it up to Schahabrim [the high priest], who made of it an offering to the Sun."

The temporal element is complemented by the space in which large events keep splintering into anticlimaxes. Where Carthage's enemy moves, nothing coheres. Recruited from all around the Mediterranean, the "barbarians" represent diverse nations, observe a multitude of religious practices, wield various weapons, sleep in tents of every description, trade in different currencies, and die according to cultural tradition, and their female camp followers do likewise. Flaubert dwells upon this heterogeneity with enumerations that portray a chaotic world, indulging his appetite for exotic nomenclature at the expense of his precept that writing is the art of sacrifice. Hamilcar commands and Carthage obeys, but Matho cannot orchestrate wild men who speak in mutually incomprehensible tongues. A ruse by the wily Carthaginian bargaining for peace is enough to sow division among them when victory is within reach. "The Barbarians were troubled: the proposition of immediate loot set them dreaming," writes Flaubert. After Hamilcar alludes to "informants," they worry about a traitor in their midst,

> never suspecting that [Hamilcar's] braggadocio concealed a trap, and they began to regard one another with distrust . . . They awoke at night panic-stricken. Several abandoned their companies. Fantasy dictated their choice of army, and the Gauls with Authoritus joined the men of the Cisalpine province, whose language they understood. The four chiefs conferred every night in Matho's tent, and, squatting around a shield, they attentively repositioned the little wooden dummies invented by Pyrrhus for representing military maneuvers . . . A vexed Matho walked about gesticulating. For him the war against Carthage was a personal affair, and he felt indignant that the others interfered without being willing to obey him. Authoritus divined his words from his face.

Marooned on blood-soaked fields in the land of Babel, expatriates yearning for the end of days also long for a harmonious center — one language, as it were — and watch Hamilcar among his entrenched soldiers like children bereft of the powerful father who once commanded them. (As children who rebelled against a father is indeed how Flaubert characterizes the mercenaries throughout *Salammbô*. Polyglot, they babble. Gullible, they are snared. Impulsive, they demand immediate gratification. Tactics and principles are constantly swamped by emotion: the fickle horde may cower after hacking the enemy to pieces, or recoil from shadows after hurling themselves fearlessly against a spiked barricade.) Matho stands apart. What he imagines is himself united with Salammbô in an ecstatic kingdom all his own, not unlike Henry and Émilie in *L'Éducation sentimentale* (first version) imagining themselves ecstatically united across the ocean. It is one of Flaubert's oldest themes. Beyond the sacred city lies the Edenic garden, and Matho speaks of an island twenty days' journey by sea covered with gold dust and verdure, where immense mountain flowers sway like thuribles, spraying incense. "In lemon trees taller than cedars, milk white serpents bring fruit down upon the lawns. The air is so soft you cannot die." They will live in a crystal grotto hewn out of the hillside. "No one inhabits this land; I shall become king."

Transcendent homes are desert mirages, however. The island does not exist outside Matho's mind. Nor does Carthage exist as Matho's men imagine it. Who indeed occupies that beatific "center"? No one. Exiled intermittently from the republic of which he has been appointed suffete, or supreme magistrate, is Hamilcar himself, commanding at the behest of an inconstant bourgeoisie who honor him in victory and vilify him in defeat. When the city-state turns against him, the indignant general is tempted to storm it at the head of the rebel army and must conceal his son Hannibal lest priests immolate the child to placate Moloch. As for Salammbô, even she feels barred from a numinous home. Denied initiation into the community of Tanit's virgin priestesses by her father, who envisages a politically expedient marriage for her, the heroine identifies with the moon goddess, seeing in her the mother she lost in childhood. Salammbô waxes and wanes. Finally, during festivities celebrating her arranged marriage to Narr'Havas, king of the Numidians, she suffers a mortal eclipse. "From her ankles to her hips she was enveloped in a network of tiny, nacreous links that shone like fish scales," writes Flaubert.

> A blue zone girdled her waist, allowing her breasts to be seen through two crescent-shaped slashes, where carbuncle pendants hid the nipples. Her headdress was made of peacocks' plumage, starred with jewels; a broad, flowing mantle, white as snow, fell behind her — her elbows were close against her body, her knees pressed together; circlets of diamonds were clasped on her arms; she sat perfectly upright in a hieratic position.

Her father and the bridegroom occupied lower seats. Narr'Havas was robed in a golden-colored simarre and wore his crown of rock salt, from beneath which fell two locks of hair, twisted like the horns of Ammon; Hamilcar was attired in a purple tunic, brocaded with golden vine leaves, and wore his battle sword girt to his side. In the space enclosed by the tables, the python of the temple of Eschmoun lay on the ground between puddles of rose oil; holding its tail in its mouth, it described a large black circle in whose center rose a copper column supporting a crystal egg, and as the sun shone upon it, prismatic rays flashed out.

Behind Salammbô were ranged the priests of Tanit in flaxen robes. At her right the Elders, bedecked with their tiaras, formed a great golden line. In a long green line on the left were the Rich, bearing emerald scepters; and in the far background stood the priests of Moloch, their mantles giving them the appearance of a violet wall. Other colleges occupied the lower terraces. The multitude filled the streets or crowded on rooftops, and reached in long rows to the summit of the Acropolis.

When a vainglorious Narr'Havas rises to toast the genius of Carthage, Salammbô drinks from another cup and instantly dies, falling backward with her hair unknotted, like Emma. In Flaubert's fictional universe, marriage kills.

FLAUBERT MAY have been a suave deputy when called upon to represent other people's interests, but he could not look after his own judiciously. Money — the scorning it and the possession of it as measures of personal worth — was too fraught with ambivalent meaning to allow rational negotiation, and demanding better terms from Michel Lévy made him feel like a supplicant dependent upon a stern father. Not that there had been much room for negotiation before *Salammbô*. The contract with Lévy for *Madame Bovary* was unfair only in retrospect. A first novel seldom sold out its first edition of one or two thousand copies straightaway, if at all; most never warranted a second edition. No one would have regarded as niggardly the eight hundred francs Lévy had paid up front, it being a common arrangement among publishers to pay a flat fee for permission to publish as many editions as the market bore over a stipulated period of time — five years in the case of *Madame Bovary*. What may be seen as ungenerous was the mere five-hundred-franc bonus Flaubert received later, in the aftermath of the trial, which had given *Madame Bovary* fortuitous wings. By 1862 more than thirty thousand copies had been sold. Flaubert felt cheated, and even persuaded himself, by the arithmetic of affluent destitution, that he had lost thousands on his masterpiece. But he preferred not to duel Lévy face-to-face in new contract negotiations. Ernest Duplan, his notary, acted for him, presenting terms that tested the publisher's faith in his author. Flaubert wanted thirty thousand francs, an exorbitant fee.* He insisted that Lévy buy *Salammbô* sight unseen, convinced as he was that the publisher would spurn his novel after reading it and that it would, thus stigmatized, suffer one humiliating rebuff after another. He also insisted that it be published without illustrations; what the text conjured in the reader's mind was illustration enough. Publisher and notary shuffled through August, whereupon Bouilhet intervened on Flaubert's behalf. Lévy, he subsequently wrote (on August 19, 1862), would buy *Salammbô* blind for ten thousand francs if Flaubert extended Lévy's lease on *Madame Bovary* and signed a second contract agreeing to begin work on a modern novel, for which Lévy would pay another ten thousand francs on delivery. Furthermore, Lévy offered to spread the rumor that *Salammbô* had been bought for thirty thousand francs and to publicize the book vigorously, setting aside his doubts that a "Carthaginian novel" stood any chance whatever of succeeding, even with fanfare. Bouilhet urged Flaubert, and his mother (whom Flaubert consulted in all matters financial), to accept. "Your pride is safe: you will not be read before the settlement. Your next work is securely placed. How many tribulations avoided! In one stroke you sign a treaty for twenty thousand francs, ten thousand of them payable immediately and the remainder whenever you deliver your new novel (it need not be more than one volume long and nothing compels you to devote five years to it)." Flaubert agreed to the arrangement. Bouilhet congratulated himself on having terminated an "interminable" affair in just one hour.

Salammbô appeared on November 24. Two weeks later Sainte-Beuve, with whom, as we shall see, Flaubert and others regularly gathered at a restaurant called Magny's, published the first installment of a long essay-review that made no concession to friendship. Though compliments were paid along the way, his judgment was, on the whole, decorously unfavorable. Everyone agreed, Sainte-Beuve declared in a preamble, that after *Madame Bovary* Flaubert should produce a sequel featuring a cast of characters involved in events of greater scope and consequence.[†] "One might

---

*In 1864, Lévy paid Balzac's widow eighty thousand francs for the right to publish a forty-five-volume edition of his complete works, which included ten early novels not found in previous editions of Balzac's collected works. According to Bouilhet, Jules Sandeau, a well-known member of the French Academy, received three thousand francs for his novels and Gautier half as much.

†This had originally been Bouilhet's advice and opinion. On July 18, 1857, he wrote to Flaubert: "I may be wrong, but I think the clever thing to do . . . would be to write another closely observed work, even if it should be your last such novel. It would redound to the advantage of your pocket and your reputation . . . Not that I'm afraid that the book you have in mind will be a flop, only that, however praiseworthy, it will, because of its subject, not make the same splash."

have wished that this vigorous brush, this skill at plumbing depths, this boldness of expression, had been applied to another equally contemporary subject, equally alive but less circumscribed," he wrote. "Human nature is perhaps not altogether insipid, base or perfidious; there is honesty, elevation, tenderness or charm in certain characters: why not put oneself in the way of encountering several such — indeed, just one — amid the stupidity, malice, and fatuousness that otherwise prevail?" A sequel without the excessive description found in *Madame Bovary* and the "perpetual tension" that sheds indiscriminately strong light on every object would show his art to advantage. But, Sainte-Beuve continued, the stubborn streak responsible for Flaubert's artistic swagger led him to disappoint such expectations. "As a proud, ironical artist who claims not to crave the public's approval or his own success, resisting advice and hints, obstinate and inflexible, he temporarily left the field of modern fiction in which he very nearly achieved excellence and betook himself elsewhere with his tastes, predilections, secret ambitions. A traveler in the Orient, he wanted to revisit some of the regions he once traversed and to do so studiously, the better to depict them. An antiquarian, he became fascinated with a lost, obliterated civilization, and set about bringing it back to life, recreating it out of whole cloth."

Suffice it to say that Sainte-Beuve's brief against *Salammbô* alleged brutality for its own sake, a lack of verisimilitude, a geographical muddle, a derivativeness of vision, a freewheeling use of history, a glut of furniture, apparel, and jewelry. The whole book, he sighed, is paved not only with good intentions but with precious stones. Thus, when Matho secretly enters Salammbô's house one night after wading into Carthage through its aqueduct and negotiating a labyrinth of corridors, the action cannot proceed until Flaubert has made an inventory of the rare baubles that fill her bedchamber. "It is exquisite chinoiserie." And what of Matho? he asked. No one would have been more astonished by this character than Polybius, our chief source of information about him. "We have long been mocking those novels or tragicomedies of bygone days, where Alexander, Porus, Cyrus and Genseric are all pictured as lovesick heroes. But Matho, the African Goliath, committing childish follies out of love seems to me no less false. It doesn't square with nature or history." Flaubert couldn't do right. Faulted for straying from nature and history, he is belittled for shadowing the mast of other French writers, notably Chateaubriand. Salammbô put Sainte-Beuve in mind of the Druid priestess Velléda in *Les Martyrs* — Chateaubriand's novel about a young Greek taken hostage by Rome under Diocletian who leads a dissolute life; reinvents himself as a Roman officer; rises to become governor of Armorica, where he is captivated by Velléda; embraces Christianity in the aftermath of her suicide; and ultimately dies a martyr to the faith. "In this laboriously wrought book M. Flaubert merely follows Chateaubriand's lead, imitating the epic sweep that his predecessor, forty years ago, brought to a portrait of Greco-Roman civilization tilting with Christianity." Sainte-Beuve praised Flaubert for poetic descriptions of Carthage seen from afar but spoiled the compliment by insinuating that they had been modeled after Chateaubriand's panorama of Athens in *L'Itinéraire*. Elsewhere he claimed to detect a parallel with scenes in *Atala*.

Then, too, Sainte-Beuve, who had buttoned himself against romantic grandiloquence, found Flaubert's penchant for it offensive. The writing was rich in "strong, male qualities," but it impressed him as overwrought. Equally extravagant was the violence, which he attributed to a chronic nineteenth-century settling of accounts with the pastoral sentimentality of an earlier age: wolves had been unleashed upon the shepherd and the flutist.

On this point I set aside French delicacy and all that has been said by galled critics rushing to judgment. I recognize that art does not concern itself above all with the reader's sensibilities, any more than it seeks above all to provide moral instruction. Neither does it necessarily seek to do the opposite. That most universal and hospitable of critics, Goethe, whom no one would accuse of parochialism, . . . nonetheless recoiled before protracted scenes of a hideous nature and thought that art should finally orient itself toward the beautiful, the dignified, the agreeable. If you adduce the example of Shakespeare, who embraced men with their passions and souls with their abysses, sparing himself no situation, however atrocious, I shall applaud the example and say to you: Do as he does, show us people and things as they are, neither gilding them nor making them uglier than they are.

In conclusion, he wrote that the egregious length of his review should be considered the measure of his esteem, that Flaubert's undertaking was bold and the accomplishment of it attested to his power. "A mania for the impossible characterizes the mighty. Certain proud, wild birds will alight only on crags so remote that, in Homer's expression, only the sun sets foot there." Though he didn't conquer or subdue Africa, Flaubert had come away from his adventure in no way diminished. "He enjoys the esteem of learned archeologists and semitic scholars, . . . and of eminent minds . . . eager to meet the author whose vigor has been so heroically deployed." Satisfied that the rage boiling out of *Salammbô* must have been spent on an African shore, Sainte-Beuve proclaimed that Flaubert would do his talent justice by taking up where he had left off five years earlier. "May he give us then — understanding that he is sufficiently a master of style to relax his vigilance and move faster — a powerful, well-observed, vivid work with the subtle, biting qualities of the first but with at least one consoling feature somewhere in it."

Flaubert wrote a long rejoinder that Sainte-Beuve appended to the review in the fourth volume of his collected essays *Nouveaux lundis*. He answered every cavil, deftly marshaling his sources. We learn that "carbuncles formed by the urine of lynxes," one among many bizarre details to which Sainte-Beuve had taken exception, came from Theophratus's *Treatise on Gemstones.** The temple of Tanit, which Sainte-Beuve found utterly fanciful, rested on a solid base. "I am sure I reconstructed it as it was, . . . with the medals of the duc de Luynes, with everything known about the temple of Solomon, with a passage from Saint Jerome cited by Selden (*De diis Syriis*), with a plan of the very Carthaginian temple of Gozzo, and best of all, with the ruins of the temple of Thugga [that is, Dougga], which I inspected myself, and about which, so far as I know, travelers and antiquarians have never written." He declared that there were no gratuitous descriptions. However elaborate, they were all intended to serve the characters and the action. As for verisimilitude, he insisted upon the plausibility of his Carthage. "I couldn't care less about archeology! If the color is not even, if certain details jar, if the mores do not derive from religion and the facts from passions, if the characters are not of a piece, if the dress is not appropriate to customs and architecture to climate, if, in a word, there is no harmony, I am in the wrong. Otherwise, I'm not." What he found more disheartening than the possibility that he had failed was the critic's unwillingness to pry open his own imagination. "The milieu irritates you, I know it, or rather, I feel it! Instead of clinging to your personal point of view, that of a man of letters, a Modern, a Parisian, why didn't you place yourself where I stand? . . . I believe I was less harsh toward humanity in *Salammbô* than in *Madame Bovary*. It seems to me that there is something inherently moral about the love that drew me toward extinct religions and peoples."

Flaubert heard from Jules Duplan, who inveighed against Sainte-Beuve, calling him a salacious old courtier. Other friends joined the chorus of support, just as lesser critics took their pitch from Sainte-Beuve and trumpeted derision. The most savage review was written by Wilhelm Froehner, an assistant curator of antiquities at the Louvre. It is thought, with good reason, that he acted as the creature of government officials hostile to Flaubert's circle. There was much pedantic brawling in the pages of *L'Opinion Nationale,* from which Froehner did not emerge unscathed, but the erudite pawn received his due for services rendered on this and other occasions with an ap-

---

*Flaubert, a lifelong admirer of Voltaire, delighted in the more outlandish superstitions of mankind, much as he did, conversely, in the pat phrases or clichés that constitute his *Dictionary of Received Ideas*. A real find for him was *Médecine et hygiène des Arabes* by Émile-Louis Bertherand. He wrote to Bouilhet about grasshopper poultices in use among Algerian Arabs, about infertile women inhaling the fumes of burning lion hair and swallowing the scum that accumulates in the ears of donkeys.

pointment to the Legion of Honor. While pretending to imitate the fakir indifferent to vermin crawling over his body as he fixedly contemplates the sun, Flaubert paid close attention to articles written about him. "Along with the *Journal pour Rire,*" he told Duplan on January 12, 1863, "I have *La Vie Parisienne,* which thrashed me, *L'Union, La Patrie* (yesterday's), *La Revue Française,* etc. It's going well. Try to procure the other reviews you mentioned, I don't remember which ones or know where to find them. I'm making a collection." How Mme Flaubert felt about *Salammbô* is nowhere recorded, but nasty reviews upset her, and a particularly acerbic one in *Le Figaro,* which Flaubert tried to hide, filled her with dread that her son might challenge the author to a duel.

There were also accolades. The Romantic generation praised him effusively. Hector Berlioz wrote: "My dear M. Flaubert, I wanted to run across town and pay you a visit, which proved to be impossible, but I can't delay a moment longer in telling you that your book filled me with admiration, with astonishment, with terror even . . . I'm frightened of it, I've dreamed about it the last few nights. What a style! What archeological knowledge! What imagination . . . Allow me to shake your powerful hand and call myself your devoted admirer." No reponse was more prized than an article by George Sand in which the great lady, who did not regard *Salammbô* as a brave fiasco or a cathartic or a parenthetical tour de force, declared his imagination to be as fecund and his power of description as awesome as Dante's. "What a sober and powerful style to contain such exuberance of invention!" she exclaimed. Flaubert had been introduced to Sand at the theater four years earlier. He had subsequently visited her once at her apartment on the rue Racine. Now he sent her a note of thanks and received in reply a letter assuring him that gratitude was unnecessary for what her conscience had required her to do. "My dear brother," she wrote.

> Whenever the critical fraternity does its duty I hold my tongue, preferring to produce than to judge. But everything I had read about *Salammbô* before reading the novel itself was unjust or inadequate. I would have considered silence remiss, if not craven, which may amount to the same thing. Adding your opponents to mine doesn't bother me — a few more, a few less . . .
>
> We hardly know each other. Come visit me when you have the time. It's not far away. I'm always here.

Flaubert answered without delay:

> I am not grateful to you for having performed what you call a duty. Your kindheartedness moved me and your sympathy makes me proud. That's all. The letter continues your article and even surpasses it, and I don't know what to say

except that I am exceedingly fond of you . . . As for your cordial invitation, I shall answer as a true Norman by saying maybe yes, maybe no. Perhaps I shall suddenly appear on your doorstep one day next summer. For I am very eager to see you and chat.

He did not surprise her at Nohant that summer, but the door had been opened to a friendship — an *amor amicitiae,* as Sand called it — that would, in due course, enrich both their lives. He asked her for a photographic portrait, which she gave him reluctantly, assuring him that her face did not represent her as well as her heart and mind.

Another woman of great prominence with whom the book found favor was Eugénie. The empress decided to attend a costume ball dressed as Salammbô and directed the formerly reprobate novelist to submit drawings of his heroine in full regalia. Happy to do her bidding (so long as the images did not appear between book covers), Flaubert contacted an artist named Alexandre Bida, who then pressed into service his friend Eugène Giraud, Princess Mathilde Bonaparte's protégé. This sartorial assignment came to nothing, however, when Eugénie, fearing perhaps that Salammbô's gown might be inappropriately risqué, plumped for a less exotic role.*

Salammbô's wardrobe never became the fashion at court, but the novel engendered popular entertainment in the form of a parody whose cast included Hortense Schneider, the actress-singer made famous by Offenbach. Entitled *Folammbô, Ou Les Cocasseries carthaginoises* (Mad-ammbô, or Carthaginian High Jinks) and advertised as a play "illustrating Carthaginian mores in verse of various feet, some a yard long," it opened at the Palais-Royal theater on May 1. By then Flaubert had returned to Croisset, where seizures, boils, rheumatism, and a stomach ailment laid him low.† Reports that *Salammbô* had been the subject of vituperative sermons at two of Paris's richer churches, the Trinité and Sainte-Clotilde, provided an agreeable distraction from his afflicted body. Parishioners there were warned that the author's despicable goal was to revive paganism, which qualified him for a place in hell alongside Voltaire and Sade. Execration may have helped sales. *Salammbô* went through four editions in six months, encouraging the optimistic forecast that Flaubert might suffer what Henry James, describing a

---

*Such concerns were soon to appear a bit dated. In the late 1870s, after the publication of *L'Assommoir*, Zola's best-selling work about life in the Paris slums, slumming became an act of inverted snobbery, and uppercrust Parisians attended "The Hooligan's Ball" dressed up as Zola's characters in an urban evocation of Marie-Antoinette's rustic make-believe at the Versailles dairy.

†In this instance he attributed the outbreak of boils to paint fumes from work being done on the ground floor. Cutaneous eruptions could have resulted from mercury rubs, but he seems to have taken mercury in a syrup.

prolific woman novelist who longs for the respect that attends commercial failure, called "the hard doom of popularity."

One last note. Another decade would pass before Flaubert could begin to appreciate the dimension of praise from his childhood friend Laure de Maupassant, née Le Poittevin. "My dear old mother and I love to evoke the past during our long autumnal evenings," she wrote from Fécamp. "As soon as the dinner table is cleared, we gather at the fireplace, I open [*Salammbô*] and read aloud. My son Guy is as attentive as anyone; upon hearing your descriptions, which are sometimes so elegant and sometimes hair-raising, his dark eyes flash, and I believe that the noise of battle and the trumpeting of elephants resound in his ears."

XVII

⌒

Entering Middle Age

CAROLINE HAMARD would no doubt have loved to join the Maupassant clan during their long autumn *veillées* instead of studying historical texts assigned by her uncle. Mme Flaubert sometimes visited Fécamp with her during the summer, and those excursions were welcome events, remembered not so much for the company of Guy, an imperious playmate four years her junior whose games featured boats and spiders, as for the warmth his grandmother imparted. In Victoire Le Poittevin, Guy's grandmother, Caroline found a woman as unlike Mme Flaubert as two lifelong friends could be. At sixty-five she was still wearing gaily colored clothes, still writing verse and reciting it, still appreciating her own jokes so heartily that her hair, still in ringlets, flapped against her wrinkled cheeks. Laughter seldom, if ever, came from Caroline Flaubert, a figure aloof in her bereavement and wont to evoke happier days. While at Fécamp an old lady behaved girlishly, at Croisset youth was anachronistic. Not to say that the rough edge of life had spared the Maupassant household. Like little Caroline, Guy had a father in name only. Émile Hamard was usually stupefied by alcohol and Gustave de Maupassant besotted with mistresses. After fifteen years of marriage, when Guy was eleven, Laure de Maupassant would induce her husband to sign a separation agreement, formalizing a fait accompli.

Starved for a more enveloping and demonstrative love than her grand-mother could provide, Caroline found emotional release in blind rages or in raptures of worship. Mme Flaubert was sufficiently a woman of her social mi-lieu to insist upon Catholic Communion, and Caroline, once they established themselves on the boulevard du Temple, took instruction nearby at the Saint-Martin parish church. A kind, handsome catechist filled the girl with reli-gious zeal. Thereafter, her Fridays were to be meatless. For nightly prayers she improvised a tiny chapel, complete with birthday candles. And back in Crois-set, where Flaubert began the history lesson every day as soon as the one o'clock ferry at La Bouille whistled its departure, she often wandered bare-foot up the wooded hillside on imaginary pilgrimages to the holy sites once visited by her uncle. Flaubert took an indulgent view of her religiosity. (He might have been less indulgent if she had sought consolation in music, as her mother had done, and murdered silence at the piano.) Her other uncle, the luxuriantly bearded and sharp-featured Achille, was far from benign. "When-ever he showed up for dinner on a Friday I was terrified," she wrote. "When my two eggs were served, he'd never fail to make one of those wisecracks that chilled me." Resentment born of the well-founded impression that Caroline enjoyed greater favor in Mme Flaubert's eyes than his own daughter, Juliette, undoubtedly whetted the doctor's anticlericalism.

With no society of close friends her own age, Caroline bonded with Flavie Vasse de Saint-Ouen, the sister of Flaubert's friend Emmanuel, a woman twelve years older than she, who offered her emotional nourishment. Flavie was a surrogate mother, a model of pious exaltation, a sister, a confidante, and in fact more of everything that defined Caroline's emptiness than Flavie could ultimately bear to be. Soon a rival for Caroline's affections emerged in the person of her drawing teacher, Johanny Maisiat. Having no other students, this painter of floral still lifes who preached art better than he practiced it devoted himself to Caroline, with consequences that her grand-mother deplored. "Our walks through the Louvre, where he explained the masterworks to me; those hour-long classes before a famous plaster cast, the Venus de Milo; the Parthenon bas-reliefs, which we examined in minute detail; then, at Croisset, our open-air sessions, the observation of light and shade, the magnificence of color: these studies delighted me. I bestowed all my tenderness upon the man who afforded me such pleasure, and when, on the eve of my eighteenth birthday, it was proposed that I should make a suitable, honorable, bourgeois (in a word) marriage, I felt as if I had been cast down from Parnassus." That *mariage de raison* would, as we shall see, spell disaster for her and her uncle Gustave alike.

Flaubert's own life comported with his image of himself as a sad, learned, balding forty-year-old whose many appetites had been cheated of satisfaction by literature.* Instead of serious affairs, there were epistolary flirtations and bitter epilogues to extinct romances. Grim news came from Baden-Baden, where Maurice Schlesinger lived modestly after suffering financial reverses. His daughter, Maria, the infant at Élisa's breast when Gustave first met them in Trouville, had become a pianist and married an architect. His son, Adolphe, on the other hand, played nothing but the tables at Baden-Baden's casino, gambling away whatever he could extract from his mother.† Maurice had every reason to believe that the ne'er-do-well would have stolen his Beethoven manuscripts to satisfy his addiction. Dismayed by their son's self-squander, her unhappy marriage, and their rootless life in a community of privileged transients, Élisa showed signs of mental derangement. Everything caused her pain: people's conversation, slight breezes, birdsong. Unable to cry, to read, to write, to wash herself, to assuage stinging pains in her arms or banish the idea that her veins had been emptied of blood, she was committed to a sanatorium near Achern in Württemberg. The staff diagnosed her as a hypersensitive melancholic whose recovery called for a period of complete separation from an incompatible husband. "I've learned about the publication of your book [*Salammbô*]," Schlesinger wrote to Flaubert on December 16, 1862. "Since I'd be extremely interested in reading it, I beg you to send me two copies, one for me and one for Maria. Throw in your first book and I will make sure that it reaches the author of an article on *Salammbô* in the *Gazette Universelle* . . . Kindly include as well some chocolate bonbons for Maria's children . . . My poor wife is still sick in a sanatorium. I haven't seen her for ten months. She cannot be visited lest any emotion, good or bad, unbalance her." Flaubert promptly complied and asked to be kept informed of Élisa's condition, which did not improve. "My poor Z, as I told you, has been in a mental hospital for ten months," Schlesinger answered several weeks later. "She hasn't written us a word, she says that writing hurts and stirs her up when she ought to stay calm. My boy, Adolphe, is in Paris against my wishes; the scamp has given me all kinds of trouble, has cost me a fortune and until now has been absolutely good for nothing." Having resolved to

---

*This despite the abundant evidence that literature made him alluring to women of every disposition. *Madame Bovary* dazzled Marie-Sophie Leroyer de Chantepie. *Salammbô* had a similar effect on an aging courtesan named Esther Guimont, whose former lovers included a prince and a prime minister. In a brief note Mlle Guimont assured him that if she were a little younger, she would pay him a visit and give him ultimate proof of her enthusiasm.

†The previous year, 1861, Flaubert had written to Jules Duplan from Trouville, where he spent a week with his mother calling in long-standing debts to his father: "There are chapters of my youth here behind every bush and house. I have so many memories ensconced in these parts that when I arrived the other day, my head was swimming with them . . . Ah! I had soul-stirring loves, many erections, dreams galore, many shots of eau-de-vie with people now dead."

see for himself how matters stood with Élisa and bring her home if she seemed no better, he naively proposed that Flaubert should elicit a diagnosis from Achille. This could not be done, Flaubert answered, without clinical information. "Send me a legible letter [Schlesinger had terrible handwriting] in which all the symptoms of her illness are set forth, the time, the origin, etc., and I promise you a categorical response." It is not known whether Schlesinger did as instructed or what impression Élisa made on Flaubert when he visited Baden-Baden in July 1865. Her story thenceforth was one of remissions and breakdowns.

Louise Colet's story, on the other hand, was one of belligerent visits to her romantic past, and in 1859, more than five years after Flaubert's rebuff, she hoisted another fictional petard against him, *Lui*. One year earlier, George Sand had published a novel about her affair with Alfred de Musset during the 1830s. Entitled *Elle et lui,* it prompted Musset's surviving brother, Paul, to publish a contrary version, *Lui et elle.* The exchange caused a stir, which Louise exploited in her book with a twofold purpose: making it known that Musset, alias Albert de Lincel, had passionately loved *her* as well, and having him pronounce an authoritative denunciation of Flaubert, here presented as "Léonce." Léonce is the elusive genius cherished by his forlorn mistress, a marquise named Stéphanie de Rostan. Urged by her young son to welcome Albert's advances, Stéphanie-Louise yields in an apparent act of maternal obedience and, having virtuously broken faith with Léonce, insists that Albert read his letters for whatever light he can shed on the enigmatic recluse. Albert likens Léonce's heart to Harlequin's hump; it is a pseudo-organ, infinitely expandable but utterly insensitive, into which everything enters and from which nothing emerges. "The battle is joined between this man and me," he declares.

> I find him odious not only because I love you but because I also feel him to be the antagonist of my mind and all of my instincts. See here (he said, picking up a letter and perusing it): a young man burning with love spends four pages extolling solitude. You are his life, he says, yet he willfully holds you off and sentences himself to hard labor. He squelches the affections of his heart in hopes of being inspired, which is like emptying a lamp of oil so that it may burn brighter. Bear this in mind about the life of truly great men, that they have all conquered their genius only with love fortifying them! What do they want, these little Origens of art for art's sake who imagine that they will fructify by emasculating themselves!

Albert goes on to deride Léonce's preoccupation with style as the hobgoblin of a wooden artist mistaking prose for marquetry. "If the idea doesn't make the word palpitate, I'm not interested in it!" he exclaims, avenging all the tough lessons drilled into his ventriloquist by a generous Flaubert. "If the folds of drapery rustle over a mannequin, will it excite me? (Whereupon Albert burst into laughter, like a fresh young thing mocking the factitious beauty of a painted coquette.)"* The fact that Louise found a home for *Lui* at Michel Lévy Frères, which published it on October 15, 1859, may have contributed to the shrillness of Flaubert's negotiations over *Salammbô* two and a half years later. It revived much more than he could easily brush off of the woman whom he had once called "the Muse" but now regarded as an implacable Fury. He urged Ernest Feydeau to buy the book for laughs. "She really lambastes your friend. Two other works by her will illuminate this story and its author, so read: (1) *La servante,* a poem in which our boy Musset is ripped apart as vigorously as he is extolled in *Lui,* and (2) *Une histoire de soldat,* a novel whose main character is yours truly. You can't imagine how swinish *Lui* is . . . Meaning to rehabilitate Musset, it does a better job of putting him in storage than *Elle et lui.* I myself come off as insensitive, miserly, altogether a somber dunderhead." This is what one gets, he wrote, for "copulating with Muses." Did the book upset him? A fatuous rant against womankind gives the lie to his assertion that Louise's barbs had barely pricked him. "This publication has convinced me once again of women's deep-seated immorality," he declared to Feydeau, sparing not even those women whom we know he held in high esteem. "You will object that that one [Louise Colet] is a monster, which I deny. There aren't any monsters, alas, and if there were, as many men could fill the role as women. But one thing no man would do is treat a former mistress as she has her ex-lover. Women have no notion of rectitude. The best among them have no compunctions about listening at doors, unsealing letters, counseling and practicing a thousand little deceits, etc. It all goes back to their organ. Where man has an Eminence, they have a Hole! That eminence is Reason, Order, Science, the Phallus-Sun, and the hole is night, humidity, confusion." Here the "bourgeoisophobe" propagated a myth as commonly received among bourgeois as any of those he liked to deride. What annoyed him most, he told a sympathetic woman friend, was the caricature fixed in many people's minds of Flaubert the lush, the jester, the rake, the bohemian pedant. "Much good it does that I don't consider myself either a hypocrite or a poseur; I am still misjudged. Whose fault is that? Mine no doubt? . . . I must do penance for being so tall and having a ruddy complexion." Would

---

*Flaubert could comfort himself with a letter from the great historian Jules Michelet, whose book *La Mer* he had praised in detail. "Your genius, dear sir, dear friend," Michelet responded, "is a glass that magnifies and embellishes . . . What a fine, singular phenomenon: a superior man who likes the production of others and is sympathetic to it. It's something I seldom encounter." Émile Zola, among others, would make the same observation.

his correspondent believe, he asked, that he was still as timid and elegiac as an adolescent preserving faded bouquets in a dresser drawer?

Louise's about-face with Musset might have led Flaubert to anticipate that praise would follow hard upon defamation in his case as well. After reading *Salammbô,* she wrote to Flaubert's friend Edma Roger des Genettes that it transported her and, because she was nothing if not fair-minded, hoped that her admiration for the masterwork would be communicated to its author (who by then was rereading it with a harshly critical eye). "Very beautiful, very great, impeccable firmness of style: the African horizons, the mercenaries' camp, Hamilcar, the child Hannibal, make exceptional pages. Now there's a work!" The vulgar would inevitably prefer *Madame Bovary,* which she called an "impure pastiche" of Balzac, but *Salammbô,* she insisted, was what gave the true measure of Flaubert's greatness as a writer and thinker. "Almost everything about it fills me with enthusiasm." In no way did personal feelings color her opinion, which came, she said, from beyond the grave of a relationship. "I tell you this as if he and I were both dead. He can no longer make my heart leap or my senses quiver. Never again will I squeeze the hand of that insidious Norman. But I recognize the very proud, very real, very great talent manifest in this book." Edma reported back that Flaubert had spoken tenderly of Louise (without feeling obliged to thank her directly for the indirectly proffered compliments), but this excited her indignation. "The spirit of justice, from which I never deviate," she huffed, "compels me to recognize the talent in *Salammbô.* But if you told the author as much, you should, to complete the picture, also let him know that I scorn his character utterly and am revolted by his premature decrepitude."

FLAUBERT WAS otherwise surrounded by friendly faces, many belonging to women whose affection mattered more than their allegedly generic habit of eavesdropping on conversations and steaming open letters. One even belonged to a militant feminist five years his senior from Rouen, Amélie Bosquet, the author of a compendious survey of Norman traditions, legends, and superstitions (*La Normandie romanesque et merveilleuse*), who had not yet written her novel about the plight of working women or launched her assaults on the misogynistic Civil Code. They met in 1858 at Rouen's municipal library, where she did research under the aegis of the librarian, André Pottier, and were soon meeting for regular conversation, often at Croisset or at her flat. Flaubert could not range as freely with Amélie as with Bouilhet, but he found in his brilliant compatriot a worthy interlocutor. "Our conversations were quite animated," she recalled, "and we'd often spend two or three intoxicating hours together. The intoxication was completely intellectual, mind you, and if I may judge of his experience from mine, I would say that all the heat of our beings was absorbed by our brains."* Amélie had been born out of wedlock; her mother, a weaver, resolved that, unlike most girls from the working-class district of Martainville, she should receive formal instruction, and put her through a school run by two elderly dames in which the daughters of bourgeois families concerned about such things learned the graces and pieties of another age. The school lost its best-furnished mind when Amélie graduated. Thereafter she came increasingly to spurn religion, though the manners bred into her tempered her anticlericalism. Living at home with her mother and stepfather, a man of means who eventually adopted her, she became a prolific writer of serial novels — some published between covers under the male pseudonym Émile Bosquet, and one the beneficiary of Flaubert's editorial ministrations. Flaubert, in turn, poured himself into her ear. "The other Sunday I stood crestfallen at your carriage entrance," he wrote in July 1860. "You had told me that you don't leave the house on Sunday, and I came at three o'clock hoping to chat with you until seven. I am bone weary from carrying two whole armies on my back, thirty thousand on one side, eleven thousand on the other, not to mention elephants and elephantarchs." Months later (on the anniversary of the Saint Bartholomew's Day Massacre, which, as he noted, Voltaire commemorated every year by developing a fever), she was invited to be his audience at Croisset. "So you like what you've heard of *Salammbô,* my dear confrere? Good. Would you like a second reading in the middle of next week, say Wednesday or Thursday? Drop me a line the evening before and come for lunch." When Amélie decided to deploy herself on a larger stage after her mother's death and left Rouen for Paris, her departure saddened Flaubert. More and more, companionship was crowding out of three seasons into only one.

During that one season in Paris, the winter, Flaubert was a frequent host and guest. No matter how one felt about him, wrote Maxime Du Camp, it was impossible not to be struck by his breadth, his zest, and the ingenuously direct way in which he voiced his opinions. "Eager to please and good at it, he flirted with women, who found his quirkiness intriguing, and made a show of gentle paternity with young, aspiring writers."† Invitations abounded. There were those from Jeanne de Tourbey and from Paule

---

*Amélie is not known to have had any lovers, and she never married. When Flaubert told her that she seemed perhaps excessively proud of her virtue, she replied: "No, I am not as proud of my virtuous conduct as you think, because I know very well that it's not virtue for its own sake . . . At my age [she was fifty-one at the time] there are a thousand reasons for a woman to be discreet and none to be otherwise. What can I do: I'm reasonable, it's my misfortune. I recognize that a woman governed by reason is a failed being."

†It was more than show; as with friends, he read their works conscientiously and commented upon them at length.

Sandeau, an admirer married to Jules Sandeau, the novelist and academician best known for inspiring his lover's nom de plume, George Sand. Others came from Hippolyte Taine, Frédéric Baudry in Versailles, Dr Jules Cloquet — soon to be made a hereditary baron by his most eminent patient, Napoleon III — and Edma Roger des Genettes, a stylish, highly cultivated woman (the daughter of Valazé, a prominent Girondin revolutionary whose report to the Convention in 1792 had laid the basis for Louis XVI's trial) with whom he traded sentiment and philosophy. He saw Du Camp, when the peripatetic Maxime wasn't in Calabria fighting under Garibaldi against the king of the Two Sicilies, in Baden-Baden convalescing from persistent bouts of arthritis, separating from his mistress Valentine Delessert, or establishing an intimate relationship with her successor, Adèle Husson. Duplan, who had gone bankrupt but through influential friends found cushy employment as an assistant to the banker and art collector Henri Cernuschi, often dined with him, while Bouilhet showed up intermittently, avoiding Paris unless rehearsals of his latest play required his presence (a short-lived comedy, *Oncle Million,* opened at the Odéon on December 6, 1860). Flaubert exchanged visits with Jules Michelet, whose wide-ranging meditations — on woman, the family, the sea, insects, witchcraft — he praised extravagantly. He continued to see Gautier, Feydeau, Du Camp, and Baudelaire at Apollonie Sabatier's on Sundays until 1862, when la Présidente, forsaken by Mosselman for a much younger mistress, auctioned everything she owned of value, vacated her famous apartment at 2, rue Frochot, rejected her ex-lover's guilt money, and took cramped quarters near the Bois de Boulogne. "When you have nothing better to do, write to me," Flaubert urged her. "When you want to cry and don't dare to, send me your tears. Everything that affects you is relevant to me. I was distressed the other day seeing you in your present condition, but unhappily there isn't much I can do about it . . . Men are swine, decidedly, and living is a filthy business . . . Don't despair . . . One must constantly repeat to oneself the imperishable words: 'Who knows?' It helps one fall asleep, and during the night the wind may shift." The inveterate pessimist was undoubtedly more astonished than anyone when his wisdom was borne out eight years later; in 1870 the immensely rich Marquis of Hertford, with whom Apollonie had had a brief affair after separating from Mosselman, bestowed upon her a lifetime annuity of twenty-five thousand francs, which allowed her to support various relatives, occupy a town house, and ride through the Bois in her own carriage.

The year 1860 marked the beginning of another important friendship. On January 10 Flaubert accepted a dinner invitation from two brothers he had met at *L'Artiste,* Edmond and Jules de Goncourt, who had just begun their *Art du dix-huitième siècle.* Edmond, eight years older than Jules, was

Flaubert's exact contemporary. Born into a family whose patents of nobility had been confirmed by Louis XVI two years before the Revolution, these dapper Parisians would always be the more jealous of their "de" for having it frequently questioned. There were aristocratic connections of a tenuous kind on the mother's side as well. Their father, like Louis Bouilhet's, had fought under Napoleon in the terrible Russian campaign. Promoted major, he had suffered grievous wounds, and Edmond remembered a frail man dandling him on his knees, describing the retreat from Moscow in deep snow, and letting him touch his scarred saber cuts. He passed away two years after the great cholera epidemic of 1832, which had claimed the second of two Goncourt daughters to die in childhood. Jules and Edmond had little ghosts shadowing them through life.

Their mother, Annette-Cécile de Goncourt, coped as best she could, with help from a rich woman friend, her brother (another Napoleonic officer), and a relative whose house outside Paris became the family's summer resort. Hers was the condition of the shabby genteel. Hoping to increase her revenue, which an incompetent land agent couldn't punctually collect from tenant farmers, she lost part of an already compromised fortune in speculative ventures. Thus did Edmond, who wanted to study paleography, find himself apprenticed at nineteen to a solicitor. He hated the law, and what followed, a government clerkship, may have been even more repugnant. Mme de Goncourt wrote to a friend that the position was "if not brilliant, at any rate a beginning," but in Edmond it prompted thoughts of suicide. Annette-Cécile died in 1848 without having yet resigned herself to the likelihood that Edmond and Jules, who showed greater promise of intellectual accomplishment than his older brother, might be unsuited to gainful employment of a conventional kind. Indeed, their inheritance freed them from bourgeois expectations, and his mother had been dead only three months when Jules, fresh out of lycée with high honors, informed a friend: "I have made a very firm resolution and nothing will deter me, neither sermons, nor good advice, even from yourself whose friendship I have fully enjoyed. *I shall do nothing,* to use an expression which is erroneous but commonly bandied about."

Traveling, with brushes if one could paint and across the Mediterranean if one could afford it, was the preferred way of doing nothing. Equipped with all the requisite paraphernalia, plus notebooks in which to make the first entries of what became their most voluminous and justly celebrated work, the *Journal,* Jules and Edmond wandered south, often on foot, to Marseille. In November 1849 the two disembarked at Algiers, where, as Flaubert and Du Camp would soon be doing in Cairo, they feasted their eyes on Africa. "Nothing in the Western world has given me this," wrote

Jules, an earnest watercolorist. "It is only over here that I have drunk the air of Paradise, this magic philtre of oblivion, this Lethe flowing so quietly from everything around me and drowning memories of my native Paris." Edmond must have been less ecstatic, having contracted an intestinal disease that permanently impaired his health, but nothing was betrayed of disparate feelings or cross purposes. It's as if, long before they produced their first book, the two had taken fraternal vows never to let the contingent world pry them apart. Edmond, who played father or mother or both to his mordant, volatile sibling, remarked upon their "phenomenal duality." Theirs would be a life lived in common, and consecrating this arrangement was a double desk made for them in 1850 by a carpenter from their ancestral village of Goncourt, near Nogent. They could sit at it together, writing face-to-face all that they cosigned.

Their first book, a novel entitled *En 18 . . . ,* consisted of acerbic harangues strung together in a nominal plot. Although one well-known critic paid it compliments, it was otherwise ignored and might still have been even if Louis-Napoleon's coup d'état had not taken place on the day of its publication. It sold sixty copies. Thereafter the brothers devoted themselves to the eighteenth century, first in *La Société française pendant la Révolution,* then in *La Société française pendant la Directoire,* culling from newspapers and rare pamphlets owned by a neighbor the farrago of anecdotes they served up as social history. Their research led to no chance encounters with Flaubert at the Bibliothèque Impériale, for they worked behind the scenes. It was the forgotten detail or private event that brought the past alive for them rather than political and economic chronicles of note. "What the public wants are solid, compact bodies of work where it can revisit old acquaintances and hear what it has already heard," Jules wrote. "It is cowed by things unknown, frightened by virgin documents. A ponderous tome in which . . . I'd flog page after page of familiar facts would earn me many times more than a history of the eighteenth century as I understand it — recounted in manuscript letters and unpublished documents that reveal every aspect of the century." Accordingly they collected autographs (among much else) and published *Les Portraits intimes du XVIIIe siècle* at their own expense. This was followed, in 1858, by an intimate "history" of Marie-Antoinette.

The brothers lived almost next door to Jules Duplan on the rue Saint Georges in the Bréda quarter of lower Montmartre, a neighborhood known for the harlots who congregated there as much as for its population of artists, and they mingled with both colonies. Jules, his mother's fair-haired child, may have been more vulnerable to women's charms than the brittle Edmond. We know that one brief affair left him momentarily heartbroken. But intimate portraits suited both of them better than physical intimacy. Jules, in a misogynistic rage, spoke of the "moral nausea" he felt after sexual intercourse, declaring that the woman he had enjoyed in her lacy, satiny bed looked, through postcoital eyes, like a torso recovering from surgery. For the younger Goncourt, who might have echoed Descartes' *larvatus prodeo* (I go forward masked), half the pleasure of carnal relations was a simulated nakedness. "There is deep down in me, waiting ready but not yet having found an outlet, one single ambition: to possess a woman worth the trouble, to remain impenetrable, and to break her on the wheel, as they said in the eighteenth century, while appearing to surrender myself," he wrote in the *Journal* (which he sedulously kept until his death of syphilitic dementia at forty). Not that inflicting pain gave him pleasure, he protested, only that it seemed to him an agreeable form of superiority to keep one's face hidden while making love and "to appear a mere child to a woman really under one's dominion." Being the master was indeed what he found to be "the greatest and most beautiful thing in love." Edmond alone had access to the closed book of Jules' psyche and his journal.

By the same token, discovering the secrets of women heightened the joy of penetrating them, and this was notably so with Maria Lepelletier, a young midwife of Rubensian proportions who became the brothers' shared mistress.* Maria, the daughter of a poor boat builder, divulged everything. She had been seduced at thirteen by a comte de Saint-Maurice, who kept her hostage on his estate, where other young women were to be seen romping around the grounds naked under muslin gowns. Freedom came when Saint-Maurice shot himself dead, but it may have seemed hardly preferable to imprisonment. Pregnant and penniless except for diamond earrings and a watch, she was delivered of her child and robbed of her jewels by a midwife, who sold her to an entrepreneur. She lost the child, bore another, learned midwifery, practiced at a maternity hospital ravaged by puerperal fever, then at a nursing home (where she successfully delivered the child of a dwarf by caesarean section), and somehow emerged from this maelstrom a buoyant, warmhearted spirit. The brothers took copious notes, which they put to good use in *La Fille Élisa, Soeur Philomène,* and *Germinie Lacerteux.*

The praise Flaubert lavished on their first consequential novel, *Charles Demailly: Les Hommes de lettres,* brought a rare blush of affection to the *Journal.* Flaubert's friendship, which displayed itself in a "robust familiarity" and "generous expansiveness," made the brothers proud, wrote Jules. A note from Flaubert reporting that Louis Bouilhet, whom they had met over din-

---

*The tables would be turned on them by their lifelong maidservant, Rose, whom they regarded as a domestic nun, only to learn after she died of her passionate involvement with a young layabout living off her wages and money stolen from them. The brothers turned their discovery to account in their best-known novel, *Germinie Lacerteux.*

ner at his flat, was enchanted by *Charles Demailly* made them prouder still. And the alacrity with which he helped them find medical informants for a novel in progress confirmed his bona fides. They, in turn, were soon made privy to the doubts that haunted him during the composition of *Salammbô* and sat through readings that began at four in the afternoon and lasted, with a break for dinner, until two in the morning. "The solemnity will take place next Monday," Flaubert warned them before one such exhibition of stamina.

Here's the program:
1. I shall begin to howl at precisely four, so come at around three;
2. at seven, an oriental dinner. You will be served human flesh, bourgeois brains and tigress clitorises sautéed in rhinoceros butter;
3. after coffee, a resumption of the Punic ranting [*gueulade*] until the audience collapses.
— Does that suit you?

It didn't suit them. Nor did the text, which left them gagging on a surfeit of description, like parched nomads being force-fed halvah. But this ordeal was the price of admission to Sunday afternoons on the boulevard du Temple, when Flaubert, often wearing a knitted red and white striped waistcoat, helped everyone banish the Sunday blues with conversation that skittered from Buddha to Goethe to Sade. "We'd plunge into the mysteries of sensual life, the abyss of weird tastes, and monstrous temperaments," wrote Jules. "We analyze fantasies, whims, the follies of carnal love. We philosophize over Sade, we theorize over Tardieu . . . It's as if the passions were being examined through a speculum." Flaubert was often invited to 43, rue Saint-Georges, where a valet in nut brown breeches, a green topcoat, a white tie, and a hat surmounted by a black cockade greeted guests. During the early 1860s he would also meet the Goncourts on the rue Taitbout at the apartment of their mutual friend Charles-Edmond Chojecki, a gregarious, learned émigré who had left Poland under duress years earlier, established himself in the cultural life of Paris, and gained political influence as Prince Jérôme Bonaparte's private secretary. Friends knew him to be not only a distinguished man of letters but a well-regarded Egyptologist, whom authorities would call upon in 1867 to organize the display of Near Eastern antiquities at the Paris Exposition.

Even before Jules and Edmond declared to Flaubert, in a letter sent from Bar-sur-Seine on July 10, 1861, "You are decidedly part of ourselves, and we, although two, feel ourselves somewhat incomplete when you are not around," the seamless garment had begun to fray. Few people ever entered the Goncourts' domain without getting mugged in their *Journal*. Flaubert was no exception, and he didn't realize it.* Early along, Jules criticized Flaubert the stylist for being insufficiently an observer of modern life. "Fine, art for art, art that proves nothing, the music of ideas, the harmony of the sentence, we share that creed," he wrote. "But there are days when dedicating oneself to so little seems a meager vocation. Is there not the danger of irrelevance in isolating oneself from the movement of one's time, in disencumbering oneself of humanity to polish a sentence, to avoid assonances, as Flaubert advises us to do?" Brewing underneath this summary manifesto was resentment of a confrere's greater talent and prestige. The brothers fumed over the attention paid to Flaubert, as if oxygen were being sucked out of the air they breathed, and esthetic qualms eventually turned into ad hominem attacks. What came to matter more than Flaubert's alleged isolation from the movement of his time was his "coarseness." Obsessed with the notion of an innate finesse that proved their own nobility, they insisted upon his lack of it. (Two decades later, Émile Zola, another friend who stood by the Goncourts loyally but like Flaubert occupied center stage, joined him in their gallery of bourgeois oafs.) After hearing Flaubert reminisce about Louise Colet, the brothers wrote: "No bitterness, no feelings of resentment on his part toward this woman who seems to have bewitched him with her furious and self-dramatizing passion . . . There is a coarseness of nature in Flaubert that draws him to these sensually formidable women . . . whose transports, whose tantrums, whose crude or spiritual raptures knock the stuffing out of love." That Flaubert was deaf to everything but brass and percussion in the concert of human affairs is a recurrent theme. "We recognize it today, there are barriers between us and Flaubert," Jules announced on March 16, 1860, months before declaring that he and Edmond felt incomplete without him.

At his core there is a provincial and a poseur. One vaguely senses that wanting to astonish fellow Rouennais played a part in launching him on those great voyages. His mind, like his body, is fleshy and bloated. Delicate things do not appear to touch him. He is sensitive above all to the bass drum of language. There are few ideas in his conversation, and they are presented with much fanfare and solemnity. His mind, like his voice, is declamatory. The stories, the faces he sketches, have the musty odor of subprefectural fossils. His white vests, which went out of fashion ten years ago, are those with which Macaire courts

*"What you say about the Goncourts pleases me," he wrote to a mutual friend, the princess Mathilde, in 1865. "Their niceness is angelic and their wit diabolical." In his letters, he always greeted them as *"mes bichons,"* or "my pets."

Eloa . . .* He is lumpish, excessive and heavy-handed in everything, in jesting, in jousting, in imitating Monnier's imitations.

Drawing verbal caricatures became therapeutic exercise for them. In one, which was inspired by Flaubert's pronouncements at a soiree, he is seen as a heavy-handed circus strongman fumbling with paradoxes that a nimble Théophile Gautier juggles blindfold. Spitefulness did not, however, prevent them from being courteous, or from accepting an invitation to Croisset during the fall of 1863.† If anything, they flew up hungrily, like vampire bats on the wing, and Flaubert did not disappoint. From a trunk full of Oriental paraphernalia, which included his beloved tarboosh, he produced enough garments to dress the male cast of *Abduction from the Seraglio*. Rummaging through manuscripts acquired mysteriously, he found, among much else, the detailed confession of a homosexual guillotined in Le Havre after murdering his unfaithful lover. They had him read aloud his travel notes from Egypt, which took one entire day, with pauses for a smoke. It left them exhausted. "About everything under the sun he has a thesis in which he can't possibly believe, or a delicately chic opinion formulated just for show; there are paradoxes of modesty, and excessively self-deprecating invocations of Byron's orientalism or Goethe's *Elective Affinities*."

WHEN THE Goncourts brought themselves to profess esteem for Flaubert, it was most often in the context of deeds that showed him being unworthy of it, or falling short of himself. During their sojourn at Croisset they were obliged to hear their host read a three-hour-long *féerie* recently concocted by himself, Bouilhet, and Charles d'Osmoy — "a work of which I thought him incapable, respecting him as I do," wrote Jules, who saw very little of the beautiful Norman countryside that weekend. They found *Le Château des coeurs* (The Castle of Hearts) exceptionally vulgar. What they may not have known was that it had a history as old as the billiard-table stage of the Hôtel-Dieu and that Flaubert had never outgrown his love of theatrical recreation. Years earlier he and Bouilhet had written a mock tragedy called *Jenner, or The Discovery of Vaccine*. It was not their only such entertainment. In 1846 they had brightened Sundays at Croisset by improvising a dozen scenarios for dramas, comedies, comic operas, pantomimes. After 1848, Flaubert sketched a farce called "Le Parvenu," another called "L'Indiges-

---

*Eloa is a character in a three-act comedy by Benjamin Antier and Frédérick Lemaître.

†Well-suited to them is George Eliot's comment about the acidulous Mr. Phipps in *Scenes of Clerical Life:* "Heaven knows what would become of our sociality if we never visited people we speak ill of: we should live like Egyptian hermits, in crowded solitude."

tion, ou Le Bonhomme," and "Pierrot au sérail" (Pierrot in the Seraglio), a six-act pantomime reminiscent of Piron's eighteenth-century fairground harlequinades. The imagination that brought forth Homais, the bombastic pharmacist in *Madame Bovary,* might have peopled the stage with memorable grotesques, if only some ampler dramatic faculty had helped it work fragments into a full-blown comedy of manners.

It did not surprise Bouilhet in 1863, then, that Flaubert, glumly marking time between novels, should challenge him to collaborate on that most popular of Second Empire spectacles, the *féerie* — or illusionist wonder play — and make a Trojan horse for social satire. Jules Duplan, his dutiful assistant (whose framed portrait sat for a time on the mantelpiece beside a yellow marble clock crowned with the head of Hippocrates), helped him assemble thirty-three specimens of the genre published during the previous three decades in *Le Magasin Théâtral, Le Monde Dramatique,* and elsewhere. "For two and a half months I've been engrossed in a project that I finished only yesterday," Flaubert wrote to Mlle Leroyer de Chantepie on October 23, one week before the Goncourts' ordeal. "It is a *féerie* that will never be staged, I fear. I shall write a preface [he never wrote one], more important to me than the play itself. I simply want to draw public attention to a splendid, capacious dramatic form that, until now, has framed very mediocre stuff. My work is far from having the requisite seriousness, and I tell you in confidence that I'm a bit ashamed of it." Nevertheless, such seriousness as there was might discourage theater directors, for whom frivolity meant packed houses, and might vex the government censor. "Certain scenes of social satire will be considered too blunt."

Blunt is understating the case. *Le Château des coeurs* begins conventionally enough with fairies from all around the world gathering to consider the fact that evil gnomes who rule mankind have stolen human hearts, stored them in a remote castle, and substituted mechanical contrivances. After a thousand years of servitude, the good fairies must try one last time to restore to men their humanity, but an invasion of the castle will succeed only if their ranks include true lovers. Jeannette, an illiterate farm girl who has adored Paul de Damvilliers since childhood, and Paul, a disinherited gentleman artist who doesn't yet have eyes to recognize the sublimity behind her rough exterior, enter, along with several prize specimens of the heartlessness from which fairies must protect them as they move toward requited love in a universe populated by churls, misers, cynics, embezzlers, lickspittles, and venal hussies. Off they go on separate paths to Paris, where the enemy never sleeps. Opposing the Queen of the Fairies is the King of the Gnomes, a cartoon copy of Goethe's Mephistopheles, who, seizing upon Jeannette's misguided notion that Paul would want her if she were not uncouth, transforms her into a fashionable lady, then into a prototypical bourgeoise, and finally into a spangled empress with dwarfs crouched at the foot of her golden throne. The first metamorphosis takes place on the Île de la Toilette, a land redolent of cologne in which wigs grow like cabbages, fields sparkle with silver paillettes, nature is anathema, and haute couture is royalty. Paul spurns her under her gorgeous trappings. For her next transformation the gnome flies her to the Realm of the Stewpot, where, on a holy day, the entire population has gathered at a town square around a gigantic cauldron to hear the "grand pontiff," ladle in hand, reconsecrate the central artifact of their culture. "Citizens, bourgeois, old crusts!" he exclaims. "On this solemn day, we have come together to worship the thrice-sainted stewpot, emblem of those material interests we hold so dear that the emblem itself may serve as our divinity." In the past year, he reminds them,

> you have stayed philosophically at home, thinking only about yourselves and business. And you have forborne from ever raising your eyes to the stars, knowing that to do so is to risk falling into wells. Just keep pottering along on the straight and narrow. It will lead to repose, wealth and consideration! Don't fail to hate all that is exorbitant or heroic. Above all, no enthusiasm! And don't alter any part of anything — ideas, overcoats — for individual happiness as well as public well-being are to be found only in temperance of spirit, immutability of customs, and the gurgle of the stew.

Momentarily lulled by the siren song of Jeannette disguised as an enveloping bourgeoise, Paul flees when scissors arrive to trim his beard and a top hat to give him respectability. Jeannette as empress has no more luck, but all comes right in the end. Paul's eyes open, hearts are restored to mankind, which instantly shows signs of moral color, and, in a final apotheosis, the lovers enter the fairies' heavenly palace. One character has refused a heart, but the fairy queen reassures Paul that the earth will always want a touch of evil.

Though one cannot say for certain who contributed what to *Le Château des cœurs,* or whether tasks were always distributed systematically, it appears that Bouilhet did much of the plotting and Flaubert almost all the writing. Flaubert would also do most of the footwork to find a director undaunted by the prospect of bourgeois audiences leaving the theater flustered and of a fortune being spent on illusionist effects.* "We have spent the whole day working, Monsignor [Bouilhet] and I," he informed his niece on November 19, "but frankly I'm disgusted with the thing . . . My doubts about its

---

*Flaubert wanted his aversion to received ideas and hackneyed images dramatized by having them converted, wherever possible, into material reality. The man called a pillar of strength, for example, would instantly become a pillar.

success have subsided, but there's nothing in it of what I love in literature. Meanwhile I'm postponing something else. Instead of spending part of my winter devising strategies for getting it accepted, I'd prefer to be working up enthusiasm for another novel and remaining in Croisset, denned like a bear. I've begun to share everyone's opinion that I'm going downhill." By December 4, when he finished *Le Château,* his opinion of it and of himself had improved. He took great pains to find the play a home on Paris's Boulevard, in the face of mounting evidence that directors considered it unproduceable. A group from the Châtelet theater visited his flat to hear him read it through, but nothing came of that trial, nor of subsequent talks with another theater. The three dispirited collaborators — Flaubert, Bouilhet, and d'Osmoy — then let the matter drop. Several years later, Offenbach refused *Le Château* on the grounds that it did not lend itself to lyrical development. Another decade would pass before Émile Bergerat, the editor of a new magazine, *La Vie Moderne,* would rescue it from Flaubert's bottom drawer.

What Flaubert the playwright did to arrange a happy marriage for his characters, Flaubert the uncle conspicuously failed to do for his eighteen-year-old niece, "Caro," with whom he now exchanged letters reminiscent of those once written to her mother. In 1863 a gentleman twelve years older than Caroline Hamard, Ernest Commanville, asked Mme Flaubert for her granddaughter's hand in marriage. He had seen her three years earlier at the wedding of Achille Flaubert's daughter, Juliette, and had waited to propose until the tall, beautiful blonde with periwinkle blue eyes came of age. Commanville, who imported timber from Scandinavia, was not only an established merchant but to all appearances a man of honor, having inherited his father's bankrupt sawmill near Dieppe, made it solvent, and satisfied creditors. He impressed Mme Flaubert more than Caroline. Determined that her granddaughter, whose father had squandered a fortune, should be well provided for, the old lady urged Commanville upon Caroline and no doubt felt free to demand Flaubert's help. How matters stood in December 1863 is revealed by a letter from Flaubert to his niece, and her reply. "Well, my poor Caro, you are still undecided, and perhaps no further along now after your third interview [with your suitor]?" he wrote from Paris on the twenty-third.

> It is so grave a decision that I would feel exactly as you do if I were in your lovely skin. Look, reflect, probe your entire person (heart and soul) to decide whether the gentleman holds within himself a promise of happiness. We cannot live by poetic ideas and exalted sentiments alone. On the other hand, if bourgeois existence bores you to death, what should you do? Your poor old grandmother wants to see you married, fearing that you will be left all alone after her death. And I, too, dear Caro, want you coupled with a responsible fellow who will make you as happy as possible! When I saw you weeping so copiously the

other evening, it broke my heart. We love you very much, dear Bibi, and the day of your marriage will not be a cheerful one for your two old companions. Though I am not inclined to jealousy, the fellow who becomes your spouse, whoever he may be, will displease me at first. But that's neither here nor there. I'll pardon him in due time and love him and cherish him if he makes you happy.

After stating that he couldn't advise her one way or another, he nudged her down the path of bourgeois prudence:

What argues in favor of Monsieur C. is the way he's gone about doing things. Furthermore one knows his character, his background, his relations, all of which would be unknowable in a Parisian milieu. Might you perhaps find more brilliant people here? Yes, but wit and *charm* are almost the exclusive appanage of bohemians! Well, the idea of my niece married to a poor man is so atrocious that I won't consider it for a second. Yes, dear one, I declare that I'd rather see you marry a rich grocer than an impecunious luminary. For you would have to contend not only with the great man's poverty but with demonstrations of brutality and tyranny that would drive you mad or leave you brain-dead. I realize that living in wretched Rouen is much on your mind, but it's better to live fortunate in Rouen than penniless in Paris. Then again, should the lumber business become even more prosperous, what would prevent you from establishing yourself here [in Paris]?

Since she was unlikely, in his view, to find anyone smarter and more cultivated than herself, why not settle for material comfort?*

Caroline wanted to escape Rouen, as her mother had done, but her mother's example was the strongest argument against it. She found herself running *sur place* in a squirrel cage of impossible alternatives, with no confidants apart from her uncle, to whom she wrote on Christmas Eve that her indecision, which had reached the ears of Rouen society, could not continue.

I dread the thought that in a few days I'll have to say yes or no. Certainly Monsieur C. (as you call him) has many things to recommend him. Yesterday we made music together; he's a good musician, much better than le père Robinet, and M. Engelman told me that he has talent. While chatting, he told me that he had been tutored at one point by Bouilhet. I would very much like to hear what Bouilhet has to say about him, whether he considers him an intelligent chap . . .

---

*In a letter to Caroline written several weeks earlier, Flaubert, inquiring about one of her new acquaintances, asked, "What is she like? What is her social position?"

M. Bidault's information is very good. It's ridiculous of me to be asking questions all around, but I'm afraid, so very afraid, of making a mistake. Then, too, poor old dear, the idea of leaving you causes me great pain. But you'll still come visit me, won't you? Even if you should find my husband too *bourgeois,* you'll come for your Liline's sake, won't you? You'd have your own room under my roof, with the kind of big armchairs you like.

In one last desperate ploy, Caroline told her grandmother to inform Commanville that she would never bear children. The vow of barrenness (influenced as well by the mortal consequences of her own birth) apparently did nothing to dampen his ardor or weaken his resolve; white bouquets arrived every week from Paris's most fashionable florist, and by February 1864, preparations for a spring wedding were in full swing. The fuss being made over her blunted the killing edge of thoughts about a life to be lived with someone she hardly knew and didn't love. And intermediaries spared her from conversation with her estranged father. Flaubert prevailed upon a notary named Frédéric Fovard, whom he knew through Maxime Du Camp, to inform Émile Hamard of the material security Commanville could offer Caroline before the fiancé solicited his blessings. Lest Hamard, who lived in bohemian unkemptness, scare away Commanville, he was given money to buy a decent suit of clothes and to find accommodation at a proper hotel. It was hoped that the allowance would also persuade him to absent himself from the ceremony.

The wedding took place on April 6. Afterward thirty guests gathered for lunch at Croisset. During a tête-à-tête with her husband in the garden pavilion, Caroline reasserted her prenuptial vow never to bear children and learned only then, from a flabbergasted Commanville, that Mme Flaubert had never informed him of it. "How could she not have understood better the child she had raised?" is the question Caroline was still asking decades later in *Heures d'autrefois.* "How could she not have shied away from the responsibility of marrying me off when she had proof that I was perfectly indifferent to my fiancé and without any understanding of conjugal duty? I suffer at having to reproach her memory, but the facts alone can indicate how egregiously I was sacrificed in the most important act of a woman's life . . . M. Commanville heard a harsh and cruel disclosure. Ours was therefore a dismal honeymoon."

Caroline revealed nothing of their unhappiness in letters from Italy, where the newlyweds made for Venice. On the contrary, she tried very hard, though the effort gave her splitting headaches, to convince her family that their coercion had been providential, and a guilty Flaubert, who wanted to believe it, was easy to persuade. "What interests me most about your voyage is your postscript," he wrote on April 14, "namely, that you are taking great pleasure in your companion and that the two of you get along famously. Continue like that for another fifty years and you will have done your duty." The humor undoubtedly escaped her. Or was humor intended? To help her learn the skills of managing a bourgeois household, but above all to have her company in Gustave's absence, Mme Flaubert, who needed constant reassurance that she was not superfluous, rented a flat on the quai du Havre in Rouen, next door to Caroline's future residence. Caroline would at times find the arrangement stifling.

As soon as the Commanvilles departed Croisset, Flaubert began to plot the outline of what he called his "Paris novel," or, in describing it to Mlle Leroyer de Chantepie, "a moral history of the men of my generation; 'sentimental' might be more accurate." There were many visitors to Croisset in April. While Flaubert did not complain about it, this postmatrimonial traffic, coming after months of prematrimonial drama, tired the ailing, seventy-year-old Caroline Flaubert, who now needed the assistance of a lady companion. Often present was Achille's family: his wife, Julie, their daughter, Juliette, their son-in-law, Adolphe Roquigny, their three-year-old grandson. It had been at the wedding of Juliette and Roquigny, a well-to-do landowner whom Flaubert quite liked, that Ernest Commanville met Caroline Hamard, and perhaps the memory saddened him when Juliette bore a second child, on New Year's Day 1865. Children did not make this corner of Normandy ring with laughter, however. In late July 1865 at Ouville, near Dieppe, Adolphe Roquigny locked himself in a water closet one day and, within earshot of his wife, blew his brains out. "I stayed up there overnight, among women in tears, their screams and despair," Flaubert wrote on August 2. "The sun shone brilliantly all the while, swans played on an ornamental lake, and pink clouds floated overhead."

Roquigny's shot reverberated through Croisset, where nights were often sleepless. Tormented by shingles, Mme Flaubert kept everyone up, screaming, crying, and stamping her feet. Flaubert avoided family grief by barricading himself in his study with old, familiar demons, who insisted, as he began *L'Éducation sentimentale,* that he was fundamentally unsuited to write about the modern world. Fantasies of flight across India and China also served to distance him from the household, although he could in fact have found asylum nearby if he had given himself permission to seek it among the hospitable friends made since 1862; George Sand in Berry, Ivan Turgenev in Baden-Baden, and Princess Mathilde Bonaparte Demidoff in Saint-Gratien issued open invitations. At that moment his inner leash wasn't slack enough.

Instead he corresponded. How the remarkable trio of Sand, Princess Mathilde, and Turgenev had come to enjoy his company is another matter, and the subject of a crowded chapter in Flaubert's social life.

XVIII

❦

Imperial Society

DEEPLY CONCERNED about his mother's uncertain health, Flaubert escorted her to Vichy in August 1862, the year a railroad line reached the spa. They spent a month there and would do the same in 1863, three or four weeks being the length of time routinely prescribed for *curistes*. Although he pictured himself a dutiful chaperon who joined the bathers out of boredom, there was more to it than that; he complained of joint pain, neuralgia, and chronic gastritis, which may have been caused by the potassium bromide commonly taken by epileptics in the 1860s.

Under Louis XIV the mineral springs had attracted an enthusiastic clientele of highborn ladies, notably Mme de Sévigné, who declared herself miraculously cured of her paralyzing rheumatism. It was the nineteenth century, however, that put this small town in central France on the thermal map of Europe, beginning with Napoleon I's decision to create an elegant pleasance called the Parc des Sources. By 1830 buildings and baths had been enlarged but, even so, soon proved inadequate for all the valetudinarians of Louis-Philippe's regime. Colicky, gouty, arthritic Frenchmen traveled across the Auvergne in ever-greater numbers. Hotels sprang up, and during the 1840s an orchestra conducted by Isaac Strauss came to mitigate the austere rituals of thermalism. Vichy grew apace after 1860. The fashionable resort

was indeed as much a child of Second Empire France as Deauville, Trouville, and Biarritz. Embankments were built along the Allier, which flows
through town, as part of a master plan that resulted in the draining of
marshland and its replacement with acres of formal gardens, new roads, and
villas. Not until 1903 would Vichy get an opera house, but in 1865 an ornate casino appeared for the delectation of patients inclined to gamble.
Those who wanted lustier entertainment had no difficulty finding the
brothel recommended to Flaubert by a doctor friend. Where wealth convened, wantons abounded, and the railroad made Vichy easy of access.

In the early 1860s, any pleasure seeker of means would have chosen
Baden-Baden over Vichy, which still catered to the kind of dedicated convalescent whose day dawned long before Flaubert awoke. "The hour at
which one takes one's bath may vary, but on the whole people are early risers," wrote two journalists of the time. At 6 a.m. *curistes* started filing into
thermal establishments for prescribed doses of the salutary water, like true
believers at early-morning Mass. "At nine o'clock letters and newspapers
are distributed," they went on.

> At ten o'clock one has one's lunch, which always includes carrots, a mandatory
> vegetable in the diet of the unwell. From eleven to two one plays whist or domi-
> nos; women embroider and young ladies duel one another at the piano. At two
> everyone dresses up. At three another excursion to the springs. From 3:30 to
> 4:30 music in the park. Immediately after the last polka a third excursion to the
> springs. Suddenly all the hotel bells begin to ring, inviting guests to dinner,
> which is served punctually at five, with carrots of course. From six to seven there
> are games: skittles or pitching ten-centime coins into wooden clogs . . . Hordes
> of Savoyard urchins are out begging . . . From seven to eight the bandbox offers
> military music, and from eight to ten one gathers in the salons of the thermal es-
> tablishment for balls, concerts or theatrical presentations. By eleven, all of Vichy
> is asleep.

One connoisseur of European spas, Ivan Turgenev, who sampled Vichy
in 1859, found it dreary, with too much inane provincial chitchat, too little
greenery, and a prosaic river. The hurdy-gurdy grinding beneath his window would never have been tolerated at Karlsbad or Ems, he declared.
Three years later, Flaubert complained of everything except organ grinders
and sparse foliage. Vichy had meanwhile spruced up, but grocer types
presided at hotel common tables, and during the heat of June 1863, when
he lay in a sweat reading Herzen's memoirs, Goethe, and Balzac, the bourgeoisophobe may have wondered whether spa life was a rehearsal for pur-
gatory. Vichy, he wrote, teemed with "ignoble bourgeois," including many
Rouennais, which made him wary of chance meetings. Nowhere to be

seen, on the other hand, were those itinerant trollops who frequented watering places. "They'll flock here when the emperor arrives; that's the rumor anyway. A very likeable bourgeois [Dr Willemin, assistant inspector of the springs, whom he had met in Egypt] informed me that a new house of prostitution has opened since last year, and further obliged me by giving me the address." Perhaps Willemin, like the physician who diagnosed Flaubert's problem as the malaise associated with "seminal engorgement," prescribed more frequent intercourse. If so, the prescription went unheeded. "I'm no longer carefree enough, or young enough, to worship street-corner Venuses," he told Amélie Bosquet. To Louis Bouilhet he explained in more picturesque language that the infernal heat drained him of all desire. "One's brain melts and one's animal spirits are perturbed. I feel as flaccid as a dog's dick after copulation and am constantly flushed, panting, moist, collapsing upon myself, and incapable . . . of any vehement projection." His principal companion at Vichy in June 1863 was his unhappy niece. They strolled through the leafy Parc des Sources at risk of meeting compatriots and sat together under poplars on the riverbank, she with her sketchpad, he with a book, thinking his thoughts out loud. In the evening he would stand by the Allier to watch the sun set. On Sundays, when Caroline attended Mass, he walked her to her devotions, as far as the church door.

Had Flaubert stayed in Vichy one more day, until July 7, 1863, he would have witnessed a more animated scene. Napoleon III arrived in the afternoon surrounded by one hundred horse guards and with a numerous entourage. This being his third visit (the Flauberts had missed him by one day the year before as well), expectations were strong that it would become an annual event. The emperor occupied a villa designed by his architect, Le Faure, in a compound of similar houses, outbuildings, and stables some distance from the Parc des Sources. In due course half the government — the influential half — settled nearby. The duc de Morny, who owned a château in the vicinity, was apt to join him at the springs, where Napoleon sometimes greeted well-wishers after daily treatment for bladder stones. The minister of foreign affairs, the minister of finance, the legislative party leader, titled diplomats, and marshals could assemble at a moment's notice to discuss affairs of state in an unfortunate foreshadowing of the 1940s Vichy regime. Couriers were now a common sight. So were petitioners. "One can safely assert that the Emperor's sojourn at Vichy begot a species of bather who hardly ever bathed and drinker who never drank," wrote Albéric Second, a seasoned Vichy watcher.

> Most prominent are the people ambitious of one thing or another. They naively hope that by greeting the Emperor they will obtain a tax collectorship, the Legion of Honor, a prefecture, a chamberlain's key . . . or merely a tobacco con-

cession. They can be recognized by the extremely worn brim of their hats, which they've tipped over and over again. Another camp includes those who let it be known that they have court connections and are invited to every party.

It was no secret that the official pander, Count Bacchiochi, recruited demireps and available Vichysoisses for trysts with the lecherous emperor. But Albéric Second didn't dare write about it. Nor could he signal the presence of Marguerite Bellanger, Napoleon's latest mistress — a tall, vigorous twenty-five-year-old blonde who threatened to wear him out in bed even before political opponents celebrating their gains in the elections of April 1863 stripped him of power. Though resigned to her husband's priapism, Eugénie considered this affair especially subversive. Late in July she descended upon Vichy, only to retreat in great distress after four days.

FLAUBERT HAD no need of Vichy to suggest or establish access to the imperial court, and several friends could have dropped his name at the Tuileries without raising eyebrows. Fame had washed away the sin imputed to him five or six years earlier by a state prosecutor. Dr Jules Cloquet was one such friend. Another was the eminent classicist Alfred Maury, who had guided him in his research for *Salammbô;* as keeper of the Tuileries archives, he was one of Napoleon III's erudite auxiliaries during the 1860s, when the inscrutable little man on his tottery throne seemed more interested in writing a life of Julius Caesar than in governing a contentious nation. Yet another was Hortense Cornu, wife of a painter whom Flaubert knew through Jules Duplan. Born Hortense Lacroix, this astute, plainspoken lady had been brought up as Napoleon III's foster sister, sharing his childhood in exile and remaining a lifelong confidante despite her republican sympathies. During his imprisonment at Ham, she supplied him with the books he requested as well as literature of her choosing about the condition of the working class.

Hortense Cornu admired Flaubert, even if she found his florid compliments cloying. Mathilde Bonaparte, on the other hand, embraced him wholeheartedly. The friendship that began on January 21, 1863, when Flaubert attended a reception at the princess's mansion, placed him well within the Bonaparte family circle.

Mathilde — the daughter of Catherine of Württemberg and Napoleon's youngest brother, Jérôme — was born five years after Waterloo into a strange life of privileged connections and illustrious pariahdom. Related through her mother to English, German, and Russian royalty, she belonged on her father's side to the clan of deposed princelings who had assembled in Rome around the family matriarch, Letizia Bonaparte. By consent of the European powers, Jérôme and his family joined them when Mathilde was three, and there she lived until age eleven among relatives breathing the air of remembered glory. During those eight years, Sundays began with Mass followed by ritual visits: first to Letizia, known as Mme Mère, a small woman always dressed in a black turban who held court at the Palazzo Rinuccini; then to her rotund, art-loving granduncle, Cardinal Fesch, at the Palazzo Falconieri; and finally to Aunt Hortense Beauharnais Bonaparte at the Palazzo Ruspoli. Her parents' residence, the Palazzo Nunez, was a repository of Napoleonic memorabilia, with military hats and gloves displayed beneath engravings of the battles in which Napoleon had worn them. Mathilde's aversion to Albion survived the instruction of an English governess.

If history had not already impressed her as a hostile bailiff, it must have done so in the aftermath of the July Revolution, when Bonapartist political intrigue convinced Pius IX to banish Jérôme from the papal territories. Tuscany offered him asylum, and the family (including Mathilde's younger brother, "Plon-Plon") found new quarters in a palace beside the Arno. Jérôme soon ingratiated himself with Florentine society, while Catherine made a good Swabian wife to her unfaithful spouse, nicknamed Fifi, whose prodigal habits were subsidized by the king of Württemberg and Catherine's first cousin, Czar Nicholas of Russia.

In time, a darkly beautiful, accomplished Mathilde became the object of matrimonial schemes. The first was a family affair betrothing her to her first cousin, Hortense's son, Louis-Napoleon. The prospect of a quasi-incestuous union may have terrified him or, more likely, aggravated his grandiosity. In any event he vanished one day, and by the time news reached Florence of his abortive putsch at Strasbourg, he was a prisoner awaiting transportation to America. Soon afterward, Adolphe Thiers, France's once and future prime minister, proposed to broker a match with Louis-Philippe's eldest son. Nothing came of this either. Ultimately the successful candidate proved to be an immensely rich Russian more often seen in Paris's Jockey Club and artists' studios than in Saint Petersburg society. Anatoly Demidoff, whose ancestor Nikita had built a mining and munitions empire under Peter the Great, wanted the stamp of Mathilde's Napoleonic name on his gold. Jérôme, who had lost credit when Catherine died in 1835, wanted a son-in-law with deep pockets. And Mathilde — unlike young French romantics yearning for the restoration of their souls outside France, in a Levantine cradle — yearned for a passport to the country from which she had been banished since birth. Demidoff's villa outside Florence, a palazzo housing forty thousand volumes and a magnificent art collection, may have been awesome, but the town house he owned near the Invalides was the existential real estate that argued his suit most persuasively. Demidoff would prevail upon Louis-Philippe to end the Bonapartes' exile.

Of their marriage, which took place in 1840, the same year Napoleon's remains were brought back from Saint Helena and interred at the Invalides, it may fairly be said that although romantic feelings had humanized its contractual stipulations, the bloom went off it very quickly. After whirls through the courts of France and Russia, the couple, already bitterly at odds, settled in Florence, where Demidoff, ever the playboy, betrayed Mathilde with more than one woman, his most flagrant indiscretion being a love affair with Marie-Valentine Talleyrand-Périgord, Duchess of Dino. Once apprised of Demidoff's misbehavior, Czar Nicholas ordered him home on pain of having his passport revoked and income from his iron mines confiscated. Mathilde, now twenty-five years old, made haste to Paris after petitioning the czar in the following terms:

> I come to beg Your Majesty's august protection on the gravest and most important occasion of my life. For six years of marriage, during which I have struggled to fulfill all my duties, I have been the object of every humiliation, every insult, every kind of ill-treatment a woman may experience. I have always hesitated to lay my complaint at Your Majesty's feet, because I felt that I must not complain until the cup was about to overflow . . . Today, Sire, I ask that you put an end to my suffering by separating me from a man who has no further right to my esteem or to my affection.

As Nicholas exercised patriarchal authority in such matters, he dictated terms of separation highly favorable to Mathilde, barring Demidoff from France and requiring him to provide his wife an annuity of two hundred thousand francs (tantamount to several million dollars). Her debt-ridden father went on her payroll with an allowance generous by most standards.

Mathilde had meanwhile acquired a lover in the person of Alfred-Émilien de Nieuwerkerke, another connoisseur, though nothing like as rich a one as Demidoff. Enamored of this tall, handsome, blond-bearded count (whose father, Charles O'Hara de Nieuwerkerke, had been a gentleman of the bedchamber to Charles X), she openly consorted with him and received the artist friends he introduced to her. Nieuwerkerke had studied sculpture, but sculpting was not the avocation for him that painting was for Mathilde. In Florence she had found solace from matrimonial anguish at her easel, and she stayed with art in Paris, profiting from the tutelage of Eugène Giraud, a former Prix de Rome laureate.

Because the otherwise straitlaced Orléans family — Louis-Philippe and Queen Adelaide — had made her welcome at the Tuileries despite her irregular life, she could only deplore their misfortune; nevertheless the king's downfall in February 1848 worked to her advantage by paving the way for Louis-Napoleon's rise. History took an ironical turn when, twelve years after the Strasbourg folly that had aborted their engagement, Mathilde and her cousin reunited platonically at the Élysée palace, which he came to occupy as president of the Second Republic. (The sale of Demidoff diamonds confiscated by Mathilde after her separation from Anatoly had financed Louis-Napoleon's campaign for the presidency.) Thenceforth she abounded in a sense of her Bonapartism, acting the hostess at state receptions until displaced, in 1853, by Louis-Napoleon's bride, Eugénie de Montijo. The whole clan fattened under this new dispensation. Mathilde's self-indulgent father was appointed governor of the Invalides with a splendid apartment and forty-five thousand francs a year, before he moved to even more desirable quarters at the Luxembourg as president of the Senate. Her brother, Prince Napoleon, became France's ambassador to Madrid, obtained the rank of general, laid claim to an entire wing of the Palais-Royal, then built himself a palazzo of Pompeian inspiration on the avenue Montaigne. Napoleon III bought Mathilde the elegant Louis XVI mansion on the rue de Courcelles in which she presided over a salon most of whose habitués were recommended sooner or later for appointment to the Legion of Honor. What Mathilde wanted from her cousin she generally got, and no wish was pressed upon him more insistently than that her lover should be made head of the Louvre, despite his philandering. In 1849, Louis-Napoleon appointed Nieuwerkerke director general of French museums and fourteen years later superintendent of Fine Arts.*

Her mansion did not come free of obligation. It served as a diplomatic annex to the Tuileries throughout the Second Empire, and during the Universal Exposition of 1867, Flaubert would sympathize with her for having to entertain the many dignitaries who had converged upon Paris. A glamorous presence at foreign embassies, Mathilde, upon whom Napoleon III had bestowed the title of Imperial Highness, staged as many balls and dinner parties as she attended elsewhere. Neighbors must have come to recognize the livery of every nation on earth. "She is one of the noble figures of our age," Marshal Canrobert later recalled, "and on her admirably regular countenance she wears the mask of the Caesars. Her mind is fashioned exactly like her uncle's, all of a piece; she has never understood abstractions which cannot be applied . . . But there are no intellectual efforts which she does not admire, no great and noble things in which she does not take an interest. She always acts according to her heart and her feelings, without worrying about what people will say or think of her." Hubner, the Austrian ambassador, claimed that Italians and Poles conspiring to throw off foreign yokes gath-

---

*With the advent of Empire, family pensions increased exponentially. Jérôme received an annuity of one million francs, Plon-Plon three hundred thousand, and Mathilde two hundred thousand, in addition to a like amount from Demidoff (who had enough left over to become one of Tuscany's foremost philanthropists).

ered in her salon. When Cavour dispatched the beautiful young Countess Castiglione to Paris in the cause of Italian independence, a welcome mat was indeed laid for her there. Any sympathy for conspiratorial Poles, on the other hand, would have been tempered by her loyalty to the czar.

The presence at 24, rue de Courcelles of Carpeaux, Saint-Saens, Dumas père, Musset, Maxime Du Camp, Gounod, Mérimée, Viollet-le-Duc, and others gave color to Canrobert's portrait of Mathilde as a woman who concerned herself with the life of the mind. Being partly eclipsed by Eugénie in affairs of state may have made her the more ambitious of sovereignty in Paris's cultural life. But her respect for intellectual distinction was genuine enough. She hired a historian chosen for her by Sainte-Beuve to guide her beyond the conventional bounds of a nineteenth-century woman's curriculum, and she considered her meeting with Sainte-Beuve himself, which took place at Plon-Plon's apartment in 1861, a providential conjunction. The great critic became her guru, her spiritual arbiter, and even — he was sixteen years older than she — a father more attentive to her sensibilities than Jérôme had ever been. Until shortly before his death in 1869, she was to enjoy with him a friendship that restored, week after week, the self-esteem relentlessly undermined by Nieuwerkerke.

Sainte-Beuve's visits on Saturday and Wednesday evenings were ritual highlights of Mathilde's social calendar throughout the 1860s. She anticipated them excitedly, and later in life (when a second generation of her salon included young Marcel Proust, who described her walking through the Bois de Boulogne in *Within a Budding Grove*) compared his conversation to the inexhaustible fortune of a prodigal man. To hear Sainte-Beuve descant upon literary subjects was to forget his tubby, slit-eyed appearance. It utterly transfigured him. "Here I am, settled on the shores of the world's most beautiful lake," she wrote to him in September 1862 from Lago Maggiore.

> The sunshine is brilliant, the warm air gives one a sense of well-being, one's body seems to disappear, to lose awareness of its existence.
>
> My thoughts nonetheless go out to Paris. At every moment I want news of the people I've left behind, especially of you. I can't tell you how much I value the proofs of sympathy you give me. The delightful habit of seeing you every week is one of the greatest pleasures of my life. And so on Wednesdays and Saturdays . . . I always look back towards a past which I hope to begin again on my return.

Grateful for her adulation, Sainte-Beuve took a proprietary view of Wednesday soirees. They were "his" Wednesdays, he reminded her in January 1866, as if she needed reminding. Not only on the rue de Courcelles but at Mathilde's commodious summer house in Saint-Gratien, where he enjoyed brief sojourns, his place was quite secure. He peopled her salon with his own cast of characters, these being, for the most part, the writers who regularly gathered around him at Magny's restaurant. Anyone Mathilde invited on her own would have had to pass muster.

At Mathilde's soiree of January 21, 1863, the Goncourts noted, they and Flaubert were apparently the only undecorated males. Crosses denoting high rank in the Legion of Honor were as ubiquitous as the diamonds dripping from the necks of bare-shouldered ladies. Old James de Rothschild was there, making his presence felt even more emphatically than Plon-Plon, whom Flaubert had met through Ernest Feydeau, or for that matter the emperor, a veiled figure whose demeanor seemed somnambulistic to Jules de Goncourt. But most eyes were fixed on Eugénie in a voluminous red gown that might have led one to mistake her for a high-spirited, stylish courtesan. Full of grace and pretty gestures, she looked — in Goncourt's view — more like the queen of Baden-Baden than the empress of France. It was on this occasion that she asked Flaubert to provide her with drawings of Salammbô's wardrobe for her costume ball.

Finding himself in such company pleased Flaubert — something that would not have been admissible in the intellectual circles he eschewed. His satisfaction is evident in a note sent from the château of Compiègne on November 12, 1864, when he was attending one of the week-long imperial house parties known as *séries* to which the social elite of Second Empire France craved invitations. Flaubert wanted Duplan to purchase a bouquet of white camellias at a fashionable flower shop near the Opéra. "I insist that they be superchic (for one must give a good account of oneself when one belongs to an inferior social class)," he told his friend. "The box should arrive here on Monday morning so that I may present them in the evening. The florist can send me the bill, or else you pay it yourself, *ad libitum*. For heaven's sake, don't forget, I'm counting on you." He relished the thought that his presence in room 85 on the third floor of the château would have confounded Rouennais who still regarded him as Achille's quirky brother. "Bourgeois would have been still more astonished to learn of my successes there," he wrote to his niece soon afterward. "I do not exaggerate. In short, far from being bored, I had a very good time. The only hard parts were the changes of dress required in the course of the day and the punctual agenda. I'll tell you all about it."* There were fireworks to celebrate Eugénie's name

---

*There is a vivid description of these *séries* in *Son Excellence Eugène Rougon,* the sixth volume of Zola's *Rougon-Macquart.* It is based in part on conversations with Flaubert. As for Flaubert's "successes," the memoirs of Countess Stéphanie de Tascher de la Pagerie, *Mon séjour aux Tuileries,* suggest that they were not entirely what he made them out to be. "Gustave Flaubert . . . was parading in our midst. He has deep, observant eyes, but his high color resembles that of an inebriate. In *Salammbô* he gave proof of immense talent and erudition,

day, and Flaubert watched in the company of the comtesse de Beaulaincourt, Princess Ghyka, the prince of Orange, the marquis and marquise de Cadore, the comtesse de Montebello, and Baron Haussmann. Not at all to his taste, presumably, was the afternoon hunt, for which Napoleon, flanked by gentlemen wearing three-cornered eighteenth-century hats, had donned a yellow and gold uniform.

Between galas there were dinners on the rue de Courcelles and sojourns at Saint-Gratien that brought Flaubert and Princess Mathilde together in a more intimate way. What they undoubtedly saw of themselves in each other, and liked, may be inferred from the Goncourts' *Journal*. "We decided that people are severe and exacting toward someone of her rank, and that few bourgeois would show such good nature and kindness," wrote Jules.

> We thought of the freedom of manner, the thoughtfulness, the charming brusqueness, the vivid, passionate talk, the artistic language that never minces matters, the slashing at everything, the mixture of virility and feminine touches, the conglomeration of faults and virtues, marked with the stamp of our time, all new and hitherto unknown in an Imperial Highness, which make this woman the prototypical nineteenth-century princess, a kind of Marguerite de Navarre in the skin of a Napoleon.

Mathilde thought nothing of sitting down on her staircase to converse with Flaubert (seated one step below her). Intensely proud of her Napoleonic plumage, she was yet quite capable of telling a sycophantic lady who had asked whether princesses have the same feelings as other women that she should address her question to a princess by divine right. High or low when one or the other suited her, not unlike Flaubert embracing a Platonic ideal of style or being flagrantly uncouth, she answered to the title "Son Altesse" but hankered after unbuttoned camaraderie with men friends. The latter also knew her as a childless woman who pampered them in every endearing way. Sainte-Beuve dubbed her "Notre Dame des Arts," and Flaubert became a prime beneficiary of her strong maternal instinct. Was it a mannish mother he sought? No one embodied the type more perfectly than Mathilde except George Sand, who would assume even greater importance than she in his life during that decade. To Sainte-Beuve, Mathilde's Wednesdays were "his" Wednesdays, but to Flaubert Mathilde was "his" princess. And so she often seemed to be. It disappointed her that he wouldn't interrupt the writing of *L'Éducation sentimentale* for more frequent holidays at Saint-Gratien. She wanted his photograph. She would

---

an incomparable richness of thought and expression, but the hero and heroine are rather too much creatures of flesh. Matter is excessive in his works and in his person."

have had him join her at Lago Maggiore. She plied him with gifts, which moved him to observe on one occasion that he could thank her more un-inhibitedly if she were a simple bourgeoise. "You know, though you may deny it, that I'm timid." While reading he cut pages with a little Indian knife she had given him, and when he lifted his eyes from the page, he be-held one of her watercolors on the wall of his study or a bust of her sculpted by Barre. In 1866 Mathilde prevailed upon the minister of public instruction, Victor Duruy, to tap Flaubert for membership in the Legion of Honor. "I don't question M. Duruy's goodwill, but I imagine that he was nudged, just a little?" he wrote to acknowledge her benefaction. "There-fore the red ribbon is something more meaningful to me than a favor, it is almost a memento. I didn't need it to think very often about Princess Mathilde."*

EVERY OTHER Monday, beginning in November 1862, Sainte-Beuve and friends met for dinner where the princess wished she could join them, at a restaurant called Magny's on the Left Bank near the Pont Neuf. Flaubert might have remembered it from his law-school days as one of those eater-ies favored by poor students and hungry travelers boarding coaches or dis-embarking in the courtyard of the Auberge du Cheval Blanc next door. Under the Second Empire, it rose above these humble origins, like many another parvenu. Born a vulgar pothouse, it became, behind its unremark-able facade, an elegant establishment with serious cuisine, private dining rooms, consecration by the Guide Joanne (the Michelin of the day), and bourgeois habitués, one of whom, Dr François-August Veyne, Sainte-Beuve's friend and physician, introduced the critic to M. Modeste Magny. It was Veyne's idea that they regularly assemble there with confreres as an informal dining club. Sainte-Beuve, the animating spirit of Princess Mathilde's salon, wanted a salon all his own, and thus did "dinner at Magny's" enter the annals of French literary life. "This had always been a dream of his," wrote Sainte-Beuve's secretary, "for he considered that such gatherings helped to break down prejudices and to foster mutual under-standing and esteem."

What his heterogeneous group would deliberately avoid being was a lit-erary brotherhood after the fashion of those pledged to some creed in an age prolific of "isms" — most notably "realism," whose apostles, led by Jules Husson (alias Champfleury), had met during the 1850s a few blocks

---

*Edmond de Goncourt would not be decorated until August 1867 (Jules died before his turn came), and Flaubert, knowing their capacity for umbrage, took pains to disarm them. "The joy is mixed, since I am not sharing it with you. In any event, I'm not exactly deliri-ous over it. My head hasn't swollen and I shall deign to greet you when we next meet."

away from Magny's at the Brasserie Andler on the rue Hautefeuille, just below Gustave Courbet's studio. *Realism* as the catchword for an esthetic program had been newly coined in 1850, when Champfleury said, apropos of an exhibition featuring *The Burial at Ornans,* that henceforth critics would obligatorily side with realism or against it. Always the zealous proselytizer, he shaped his manifestos around Courbet's work but wrote novels as well. The virtue of close observation, the portrayal of provincial life, a ban on historical subjects, artistic legitimacy conferred upon the ugly and the beautiful alike, the unembellished representation in art of the common man and the commonplace: these were the pieties guiding orthodox practitioners. In Champfleury's work, *reality,* like God, is capitalized. "The metier of those who investigate Reality is perhaps harder than that of the woodcutter," he wrote. "The latter must accumulate a pile of chips before reaching the core, but the cries heard by the solitary worker in his room are more strident and threatening than any to be heard in the forest. All the magpies and jays in the vicinity chatter away, all the serpents slither out of the brush hissing: 'The search for Reality is forbidden.' Nevertheless, there leaps from the merest iota of truth a live, bright flame that fills the patient seeker's heart with joy and repays him the effort demanded by his work." Young men over whom Champfleury exercised a transforming influence were not legion, but they made noise for many times their number against the sounding board of 1848. And like the "quarante-huitards," the forty-eighters who amalgamated Christ and revolution in civic ceremonies, they spoke the language of catechumens anticipating a new life. "My real life dates from him," asserted Jules Troubat, Champfleury's private secretary, who later became Sainte-Beuve's. "It was he who transformed it, who took the *nothing* I was and made something of me. He gave me a goal, he showed me the path to follow, he dissipated the vagueness in which I had floated until then . . . Literature was a serious enterprise for him. He said to me one day, 'It is a ministry.'"

To be sure, Flaubert, the Goncourts, and even Sainte-Beuve held some of the same beliefs as the realists. No one trumpeted the virtue of observation louder than Flaubert, who had independently chosen a provincial setting for *Madame Bovary,* suffocated his heroine (and himself) in the commonplace, given ugliness full play, and been brought to book for it. Flaubert did not issue public manifestos or approve of prefaces. The Goncourts did, and the preface to *Germinie Lacerteux* became, for many doctrinaire realists, a canonical argument. "Living in the nineteenth century, in a time of universal suffrage, democracy, and liberalism," they wrote, "we asked ourselves whether what are called 'the lower classes' did not have a right to the Novel, whether this world beneath a world, the common people, must remain under literary interdict and the disdain of authors, who have hitherto kept silent about whatever heart and soul the people might have."

But the Magny crowd lined up behind Flaubert's dictum that the artist who straps his imagination to an iron bed of dos and don'ts ends up, like Procrustes' victims, smaller for it, that Art falls to its knees when made to bear the burden of systematic doctrine. Otherwise, these diverse spirits stood together only in reminding newcomers that it was incumbent on everyone to hold nothing back. Etiquette departed before the main course arrived. Rare were Mondays on which opinions didn't collide in a free-for-all that moved from literature to French society to works in progress, to the boudoirs and closets of history, to God, to events of the day, and ultimately, when enough wine had flowed, to personal revelations. On March 28, 1863, for example, everyone spoke his piece about religion in honor of the new inductee, Ernest Renan, who would create widespread controversy three months later with *La Vie de Jésus,* which infuriated clergymen while offering lapsed Christians a dedivinized Christ worthy of adoration for his human qualities. As the Goncourts report it, Sainte-Beuve dilated upon paganism and Christianity (each virtuous at birth, both corrupt in old age), whereupon the discussion turned to Voltaire. The Goncourts contended that in his nonpolemical writings Voltaire embodied "the perfection of mediocrity," and held their ground against assaults that might have been even more irate if Flaubert had been present that evening. "He was a journalist, nothing more!" they exclaimed. "What is his *Siècle de Louis XIV* if not old-fashioned historical writing fraught with the untruths and conventions discredited by science and nineteenth-century scrupulousness? . . . And what remains? His theater? *Candide?* It's only La Fontaine in prose and emasculated Rabelais. Compare it to *Rameau's Nephew.*" Sainte-Beuve retorted that France could not consider itself free until a full-length statue of Voltaire had been erected in central Paris. The brawl continued over Rousseau, in similarly indelicate language. Hippolyte Taine, looking every bit the stiff, bespectacled, costive schoolmaster, stooped as far as he could bend with the assertion that Rousseau was a servile onanist. The slur earned him his bona fides at Magny's, to the obvious consternation of a well-mannered Renan, who hardly spoke (but attended future dinners). Amid the brouhaha, people managed to have private chats, in one of which Sainte-Beuve, remembering the grand spectacle of Napoleon's regiments marching through his hometown of Boulogne half a century earlier, told Jules de Goncourt — a dangerous confidant if ever there was one — that for him military glory eclipsed every other kind. "Great generals and great geometers are the only people I esteem." Goncourt thought that *"gloire"* signified the sexual conquests Sainte-Beuve imagined he could easily have made in a Hussard's uniform. At a previous meeting, Sainte-Beuve had described the lifelong agony of being caged in an ill-proportioned physique.

Sainte-Beuve might have looked more natural behind a pulpit than astride a warhorse, but in fact his distrust of the black surpassed his infatuation with the red, and in varying degrees his entourage shared that prejudice. Bred into their bones was the staunch anticlericalism of midcentury skeptics. At Magny's on July 6, 1863, Sainte-Beuve lamented Bishop Félix Dupanloup's successful campaign to bar the great lexicographer Émile Littré from the French Academy. In a pamphlet entitled "Avertissement aux pères de famille et à la jeunesse," Dupanloup, a powerful cleric, had denounced Littré as an exponent of the godless materialism propagated by Auguste Comte and Charles Darwin. Hopping mad over this flagrant injustice, Sainte-Beuve had resigned his position on the committee supervising the French Academy's dictionary and praised Littré in three long articles. Before long there would be more vituperation against the church, with echoes in the dining room at Magny's. To Flaubert, the political opposition seemed stupid for attacking the empire, or the emperor, instead of pitching into the religious question, which he regarded as the only one that mattered. In 1867, when a right-wing senator voiced indignation at Renan's being nominated for an official honor, Sainte-Beuve, who had been appointed a senator at Mathilde's behest (senators were not elected), defended him vigorously, inveighing against a regressive body of opinion that abhorred everything of the Enlightenment. "Thank you, my dear Master, for us, for everyone!" Flaubert exclaimed. The club had more ovations for its founder several months later when he expostulated in the Senate about a petition by Catholic citizens of Saint-Étienne to remove the works of Voltaire, Rousseau, Michelet, Renan, and others from public libraries. "All who are not submerged in the crassest stupidity, all who love art, all who think, all who write, owe you an enormous debt of gratitude, for you have pleaded their cause and defended their God," wrote Flaubert, who had read Sainte-Beuve's speech in the official government paper, *Le Moniteur.* "The *measure* and precision of your language only set in relief the extravagance . . . of their ineptitude . . . You politely spat Truth at them. They won't be able to wipe off the spittle."

Sainte-Beuve envisioned a "worldwide diocese" of minds intent on working humanity free from its blind submission to dogma. But if one may believe the Goncourts' *Journal,* there were times when his club less closely resembled an enlightened vanguard than a collection of brilliant crackpots released from their asylum for a night on the town. Jules de Goncourt recounts a December evening that began as a shouting match over seventeenth-century authors. Flaubert gave Bossuet's prose low marks and joined the chorus of dissent when Taine assigned La Bruyère a niche below La Rochefoucauld. Renan proclaimed Blaise Pascal the greatest writer in the French language, whereupon Gautier, his hackles rising, declared Pascal to be "a prize nincompoop." Paul de Saint-Victor and Taine were heard at either end of the table, the one reciting Hugo's verse and the other formulating neat paradoxes about Goethe and Schiller. A knock–down, drag–out fight broke out over rhetorical questions and then over nothing in particular, with everyone talking at once. Sainte-Beuve witnessed the melee with a pained expression on his face, wrote Goncourt. "Out of this pandemonium came atheistic professions of faith, bits and pieces of utopia, shreds of conventional discourse, systems for nationalizing religion." To cap it all was the unedifying spectacle of Taine — a man whose "calm and reason" Flaubert envied — puking out the window, returning with streaks of vomit in his beard, and for the better part of an hour professing the superiority of his Protestant God. Gautier and Saint-Victor, superstitious men, made sure that they weren't thirteen sitting at table. If need be, a fourteenth diner was recruited from outside.

In shouting matches among fellow writers, Flaubert proved more than equal to the occasion. Several of the Magny crowd had heard his *gueulades* at Princess Mathilde's on Wednesday evenings and at his own flat when, after the publication of *Salammbô,* he began to receive friends regularly on Sunday afternoons during his Paris season. But the opportunity for conversation with new acquaintances was the best thing about gatherings at Magny's. One such conversation would ultimately enlarge his world. On February 28, 1863, Charles-Edmond Chojecki brought along Ivan Turgenev, who (as we shall see) visited Paris between long residences at Baden-Baden and his estate in Russia. He and Flaubert took an immediate liking to each other. The next day, Turgenev, who didn't ordinarily feel so much at ease with men, especially Frenchmen, sent Flaubert his *Rudin, Diary of a Superfluous Man,* and *A Sportsman's Sketches.* Two weeks later, Flaubert responded from Rouen.

> I've just read the volumes and I cannot resist the urge to tell you that I am delighted. You have long been a master for me. The more I study you, the more astonished I am by your talent. I admire your manner, which is at once vehement and restrained, and your sympathy, which extends to the lowliest beings . . . Just as I want to be riding horseback on a road white with dust . . . when I read *Don Quixote,* so your *Sportsman's Sketches* makes me want to be jolting in a troika over fields blanketed with snow and hearing wolves howl . . . What a mixture of tenderness, irony, observation, and color! How artfully they blend! How beautifully you bring off your effects! What sure-handedness!

The letter, Turgenev declared, made him blush with pride and embarrassment. "I would like to have deserved the praise, but in any case I am very glad that my books pleased you, and I thank you for telling me so." His hope was that Flaubert would return before he himself had left Paris for Baden-Baden. "I would be happy indeed to cultivate a relationship that has begun under such favorable auspices and which, if things work out as I wish, may grow into an entirely frank and open friendship." This overture earned him another shower of bouquets from Rouen. "What I admire above all in your talent is *distinction* — a sovereign quality," Flaubert wrote on March 24. "You somehow find a way of portraying the truth without banality, of being sentimental without mawkishness, and comical with no hint of the gutter. You don't resort to theatrical gimmicks but achieve tragic effects through sheer brilliance of composition." In return Flaubert was sent two more works, one of them being *Fathers and Sons,* which he read during the spring of 1863. Turgenev moved on that May to Baden-Baden and invited Flaubert, who could not bring himself just then to set aside *L'Éducation sentimentale.* Eventually Flaubert did visit Baden-Baden, but not until mid-July 1865, when Turgenev was away on one of his periodic trips to the family estate at Spasskoe in Orel province. It would be 1868 before their paths crossed again.

The invitation that lured Flaubert to Baden-Baden came from Maxime Du Camp, whose path during the previous two summers had crossed Turgenev's almost every day on the terrace of the casino (decorously called the Maison de Conversation). By 1865 Du Camp was a changed man. The Garibaldi campaign had ended his manic pursuit of adventure and had compromised his health. Afflicted with rheumatism, he was urged to take the waters. In 1862, at Baden-Baden, which attracted an extraordinary conglomeration of Europeans each summer — royalty, radicals, diplomats, gamblers — he met an affluent French couple his own age, Adèle and Émile Husson, who occupied the most prominent villa on Baden-Baden's Lichtentaler Allee. After twenty years of marriage, the childless Hussons were happy to enlarge their household. With Du Camp as Adèle's lover and Émile's friend, they formed a ménage à trois rather like Turgenev's with Pauline and Louis Viardot. Du Camp thus found a contentment he had never known. Adèle may not have inflamed him, but he had had enough of fire. "La mère Husson is well [her health was fragile; she had a weak heart] and sends you her fond wishes," he wrote to Flaubert in May 1863. "She likes you very much, often speaks of you, and would be delighted to have you become a familiar presence at her fireside. She is a good woman, calm, not at all tormenting, and is all one can expect of her impossible sex." This emotional anchorage influenced the nature and scope of Du Camp's creative life. He lost interest in fiction (after publishing two novels about his stormy affair with Valentine Delessert, to one of which Turgenev contributed a preface) but also turned away from the nomadic self who had written *Souvenirs et paysages d'Orient, Le Nil, L'Éxpédition des deux Siciles,* and every second chapter of *Par les champs et par les grèves.* What began to focus his haphazard energies in the late 1860s was a book about Paris. Long a zealous admirer of engineers and technocrats schooled in Saint-Simonian thought, many of whom were employed by the great city builder Baron Haussmann, Du Camp decided one day while crossing the Pont Neuf to embark upon an encyclopedic tour of Paris's inner workings. He would open up the metropolis, travel from system to system, analyze the functioning of each, describe the interdependence of all, and thus enable Parisians to understand what made their urban entity tick. While the Romantic generation often portrayed Paris as a place of mysterious depths (Eugène Sue in his vastly popular *Mystères de Paris,* for example, and Balzac in the *Comédie humaine*), Du Camp set out to elucidate a rational organism. The project would occupy him for almost ten years and would result in six thick volumes, with long, immensely detailed chapters on public and private transport, hospitals, the post, the fire brigade and police, prisons, religious establishments, cemeteries and funerals, educational institutions and academies, sanitation, the wholesale market. The documentation for each chapter puts one in mind of the immense files that Émile Zola was soon to compile for *Germinal* and *Au Bonheur des Dames.* Between 1867 and 1875 Du Camp's adventures were all intramural. For *Paris, ses organes, ses fonctions et sa vie* he accompanied detectives on their rounds, followed doomed men to the guillotine, had himself locked up with inmates of a lunatic asylum, stood with customs agents at the barrier, splashed through Haussmann's sewers, and waded through the gore of abattoirs.

Adèle may have given him a hearth at which to gather himself together each day, but the angel of death spurred him on. It had brushed past him shortly after he began his magnum opus and claimed his oldest and dearest friend, Louis de Cormenin, who succumbed to colon cancer in November 1866. While Flaubert kept warning Du Camp against the slippery slope of a project that would corrupt his sensibility and induce him to find beauty in "administrative literature" as Titania had found it in Bottom's donkey ears, Cormenin had been unfailingly supportive. "My heart is heavy and bruised," Du Camp wrote to Flaubert on November 28, 1866. "What I felt was limitless friendship, and for forty-four years I was so accustomed to loving him that half of me has been lost since his death. You're right, let us draw close together; he is the first of our crowd to go. It's a warning that we must love one another more and better, if that were possible." Du Camp wrote to him again three weeks later: "You have no idea the extent to which I have *let go of the world*. All I ask is that life leave me be and not separate me from those I love. I care so little about the rest that if I told people how little I care they wouldn't believe me. I work because my labor earns me six or seven thousand francs, and with that supplement I can afford many more nice things. If I had an independent income of twenty-five thousand francs, I'd spend my time reading and hunting and wouldn't write a line. Is that wisdom, laziness, experience or disdain? I'm not sure, maybe all four, but that's the way it is."

Time restored his appetite for recognition and eventually persuaded him that it might be worthwhile courting the men who could elect him to a vacant seat in the French Academy.

Although Louis de Cormenin's death clearly affected Flaubert, far more distressing was his mother's gradual decline. In 1864 Caroline Flaubert had turned seventy. Tormented by ailments for which old people commonly sought relief at spas, she had also grown rather deaf. The shrieks that pierced the quiet of Croisset night after night when she lay bedridden with shingles awakened her son's worst fears. Then, two years later, she suffered a slight stroke. How much longer would she live? And how could he endure Croisset without her? The ground was shifting underfoot, and Flaubert, who hated change, began in that perilous decade to reach for hands capable of saving him from the abyss, or breaking his fall. Mathilde Bonaparte extended hers, and others did likewise.

There was Juliet Herbert. Before traveling to Baden-Baden in July 1865, Flaubert spent seventeen days in London visiting his niece Caroline Commanville's former governess and touring the city (for material to furnish a scene in *L'Éducation sentimentale,* he told Caroline). Like Jane Farmer, Juliet had become a family friend, but with even closer ties. Unlike Jane, Juliet, who was thirty-six in 1865, had not married, and she returned to Croisset for visits of a fortnight or more every summer. At year's end they regularly exchanged gifts. On one occasion Flaubert sent her Girault-Duvivier's *Grammaire des grammaires,* in which she may have wished to see a cover for tender feelings as well as a frank tribute to her linguistic attainments. What we know for certain is that the prospect of joining her in June 1865 excited him.

Juliet's mother, Catherine, whose husband had died bankrupt sometime before 1840, ran a girls' school in an eighteenth-century terraced row house in Chelsea between the King's Road and Cheyne Walk and had raised four undowered daughters there, all of whom received enough instruction to earn their livelihood in genteel drudgery as governesses. Flaubert found lodgings nearby, one or two blocks from the Thames at Battersea Bridge, where James Whistler, a neighbor, painted the lights of Cremorne. No doubt much time was spent with Juliet, though Flaubert's scribbled notes tiptoe around their relationship, seldom indicating whether he saw the sights alone or in her company. On July 2 the Herberts had him join them for a Sunday dinner *en famille* that lasted until eight o'clock, when he strolled over to Cremorne Gardens and followed the crowd milling around a huge pagoda lit by colored lamps. Several days later, under a satin blue sky, he visited Hampton Court, whose picture gallery and gardens had been opened to the public early in Queen Victoria's reign (with the proviso, it seems, that no one smoke indoors or out, for a punctilious guard made him extinguish his pipe). A bevy of little girls, whom he took to be orphans on a picnic, captured his attention:

> Children playing under enormous chestnut trees. The "orphans" in red skirts and white capes fill three omnibuses; they're crammed right onto the open deck. A little food wagon follows. The children fall upon it, they sit in a circle on the lawn. In the middle, lunch baskets, pewter cans brimming with milk. Before the provisions are distributed, a hymn. The women (assistant schoolmistresses) serve them. Nothing prettier and more affecting. The girls all board the omnibuses together, singing *God Save the Queen* and Scottish airs. There are long trails of sunlight on the lawn.

Would Flaubert, who couldn't understand any foreign language, have recognized the airs as Scottish if Juliet hadn't been there to tell him so? On another clear day he sailed upriver to London Bridge and watched boaters water-jousting on the Thames. There were excursions to the Crystal Palace and Kew Gardens interspersed with comprehensive tours of the National Gallery, the Bridgewater Collection, the British Museum, and Grosvenor House, where Rubens's painting of Ixion on Olympus embracing the phantom of Hera dazzled him. He adored Rubens. There were several explicitly mentioned dinners with Juliet at home and in hotel restaurants. The two walked across Battersea Bridge on the afternoon of July 12, several hours before he bade her farewell. His diary says nothing more. Was it a tearful parting? Did he express love or desire, or intimate that he might be freer after the completion of *L'Éducation sentimentale,* or rail against Juliet's uncle William Herbert, an immensely rich builder, who offered his nieces no help? And how did they explain themselves to a very proper Mrs. Herbert?

Even less is known about the fortnight he spent in London one year later. But the fact that he returned, and would have crossed the Channel yet again in 1867 if not for severe attacks of colic, is itself revealing. When Juliet visited Paris after the Franco–Prussian War of 1870–71, she and Flaubert were intimate: that much seems clear. They may have become lovers earlier, but any circumstantial idea of how the relationship evolved cannot be learned from correspondence. The secrecy that cloaked their affair in life extended beyond the grave, and letters, such as there must have been, no longer exist.

On the other hand, letters Flaubert exchanged with George Sand have survived in abundance. Only three or four of them predate 1866, which is to say that the seeds of friendship sown by Sand in her laudatory review of *Salammbô* lay dormant for three years, awaiting a propitious season. It came after the death of Alexandre Manceau, her longtime companion, in August 1865. Flaubert had seen Sand three times during the interim: twice at her Paris flat before the premiere of her *Marquis de Villemer* in late February 1863; then at the Odéon theater for the premiere itself, an enthusiastically applauded performance, where they sat together in Prince Napoleon's box; and once again in May 1865.

They may have met on other, unrecorded occasions, but the friendship appears to have crystallized on February 12, 1866, when Sand, feeling somewhat less bereft of Manceau since the birth of a granddaughter, attended her first Monday dinner at Magny's. Present were Gautier, Flaubert, Sainte-Beuve, the distinguished chemist Marcellin Berthelot, Bouilhet, and the Goncourt brothers. "I was welcomed with open arms," she noted. "They've been inviting me for three years. Today I decided to go there *alone,* which solves the problem. I didn't want to be brought by anyone. They all sparkle, but with vanity and a fondness for paradox, the exceptions being Berthelot and Flaubert, who don't talk about themselves." Flaubert appealed to her more than anyone else in the group, though why this was she couldn't yet say. The Goncourts, whom she found excessively sure of themselves, were struck by her apparent lack of self-assurance. "She is there, beside me," wrote Jules, "with her beautiful, charming head, which has come to look more and more mulatto. She seems intimidated by the company and whispers in Flaubert's ear: 'You're the only one here who doesn't make me feel uncomfortable' . . . Her small, marvelously delicate hands all but disappear inside lace cuffs." The description is more flattering, if less subtle, than a portrait Alexis de Tocqueville had sketched in his *Recollections.* He, too, was charmed.

> I found her features rather massive, but her expression wonderful; all her intelligence seemed to have retreated into her eyes, abandoning the rest of her face to raw matter. I was most struck at finding her with something of that naturalness of manner characteristic of great spirits. She really did have a genuine simplicity of manner and language, which was perhaps mingled with a certain affectation of simplicity in her clothes. I confess that with more adornment she would have struck me as still more simple. We spoke for a whole hour about public affairs, for at that time one could not talk about anything else.

The literary luncheon that had occasioned these comments had taken place in 1848, between the two insurrections. Under Napoleon III Sand found it prudent to hold her tongue; indeed, talk at Magny's rarely dwelt on politics. In any event, the congregation of stout egos, each vying for center stage, didn't encourage long, quiet tête-à-têtes. Louis Bouilhet's modesty was exceptional enough to be noted. Everyone, she wrote, sat enveloped in pipe smoke and spoke at the top of his voice.

A week after the Magny dinner Sand was pleased to have Flaubert fetch her at her son's apartment in the former Feuillantines convent near Val de Grâce and escort her to a dinner party given by Sainte-Beuve, whom she had known since the early 1830s. At another of these Sainte-Beuve dinners, on May 2, she and Flaubert joined Princess Mathilde and Hippolyte Taine. During Flaubert's Paris season they met four more times at Magny's. By May 21, when sixty-two-year-old Sand appeared in a peach-colored dress, prompting Jules de Goncourt to surmise that she was intent on "raping" Flaubert, the buffoonery in their correspondence had come to reflect a playfulness not unlike the kind Flaubert enjoyed with close men friends.* Just before finishing her latest novel, *Le Dernier Amour,* she asked Flaubert whether she might dedicate it to him. "I've grown accustomed to placing my novels under the patronage of a beloved name."

Late in that unusually peripatetic summer, events strengthened the bond. Flaubert had no sooner reestablished himself at Croisset after a fortnight in London than he returned to Paris, dividing himself there between Mathilde, who fed him dinner most evenings at Saint-Gratien, and Sand, who was anxious about the reception of a play she had written with her son, Maurice Sand, *Les Don Juan de village*. "A play by me and my son opens [at the Vaudeville] on August 11," she had written to him on July 31 from Nohant, her home in Berry. "Can I possibly do without you that day? This time I shall feel some *emotion,* because of my dear collaborator. Be a good friend, and try to make it!" He did as bidden and obliquely reported his impression to the Goncourts. "I attended the soft flop of *Les Don Juan de village*. Theatrical matters are incomprehensible to me. Why so much ballyhoo over *Le marquis de Villemer* and so little over *Les Don Juan*?" Flaubert's reservations about Sand the writer hardly dulled his admiration of Sand the woman. Behind her back she was "la mère Sand." To her face, in letters, she

---

*In response to a facetious letter from Sand, Flaubert invented a character named R. P. Cruchard — a Jesuit confessor popular with beautiful women — and wrote a Voltairean spoof entitled *Vie et travaux du R. P. C.* by R. P. Cerpet de la S. de J. (dedicated to the baronne Dudevant, that is, George Sand). Thereafter, Flaubert signed many of his letters to Sand "Cruchard." There is an implicit play on words here. Flaubert certainly derived the name from *cruche,* meaning both "ass" or "dolt" and "pitcher." Cruchard is, as it were, a cracked jughead.

was "mon chère Maître." Her fame, her astonishing fecundity, her intellect, her androgyny, her spaciousness of character, her wealth of experience, all made her a master. Indeed, they made her, in his view, something more like a force of nature to be embraced, albeit cautiously, for the strength she infused. "Mon chère Maître" expressed many things. It was respectful. It may also have had facetious overtones, like his nickname for Bouilhet, "Monseigneur." But the salutation served above all to maintain an affectionate distance, to qualify what she called a camaraderie, to neutralize the powerful woman whose last lover, Alexandre Manceau, had been only four years older than Flaubert, now forty-five. How could he entirely believe her when, early in their correspondence, she declared: "If the Good Lord were fair, I would become a man now that I am no longer a woman. I would have physical strength and say to you: 'Come, let's tour Carthage, or some other place.' But there's nothing for it. One marches toward childhood, which has neither energy nor gender." Still, it helped to settle an unspoken issue.

In August 1866, Sand informed Flaubert, who had just returned to Paris from Caroline Commanville's house at Dieppe, that she was hoping to visit him after a weekend on the Channel coast. She would, she said, spend a day at Croisset and another in Rouen: she wanted him to show her the sights but otherwise would not impose upon his hospitality. The prospect thrilled everyone. Caroline was invited down from Dieppe for the occasion, and Flaubert sent Sand precise directions in a note to which his mother appended a postscript assuring her that she came as an honored guest. "I arrive at Rouen at one o'clock," Sand wrote in her diary. "I find Flaubert at the station with a carriage. He leads me around the city, the beautiful monuments, the cathedral, the city hall, Saint-Maclou, Saint-Patrice; it's marvelous. An old charnel house and old streets, very curious." Two or three hours later they proceeded to Croisset, where the female party, which included Mme Vasse de Saint-Ouen, could not have been more incredulous had an elderly mermaid risen from the Seine and glided into their parlor on her fishtail, trailing water weeds. Did the celebrated writer make everyone comfortable with that simplicity noted by Tocqueville? It seems so, but not right away, according to Caroline, who found her recherché hairdo, held together by velvet fillets with daisies pinned to them, remarkably tasteless. Conversation was stilted. Shy among strangers, Sand gave her hosts few words to hang on, and some of those quite unladylike, as she sat near Flaubert chain-smoking thin, pink cigarettes until the dinner bell rang. A copious meal washed down with fine wines may have loosened her tongue. It certainly loosened Flaubert's, for after dinner came the recitation of his work to which literary guests were always subjected. Jules de Goncourt would have complained bitterly. Sand, who had as much stamina for listening as for writing, heard 150 pages of *La Tentation de Saint Antoine* (in the 1856 version) with pleasure. "Superb" was the compliment she paid it in her diary. That evening and the following one they chatted past 2 a.m. Awake earlier than usual, Flaubert accompanied his indefatigable guest on a ferry ride to La Bouille in windswept rain. "Frightful weather," Sand noted, "but I stand outside, on the deck, watching the water, which is superb. And the river banks *idem* . . . We return at one, build a fire, dry out, drink tea." Touring the Flaubert property, she climbed uphill to view the river valley before returning for dinner. "I get dressed; we dine very well. I play cards with the two old ladies [Mme Flaubert and her friend Mme Vasse de Saint-Ouen]."

On her arrival in Paris, Sand sent Flaubert a note thanking him for the warm welcome she had received in his lovely, well-regulated milieu, where a "nomadic animal" as foreign as she might have been found to disturb the canonical order of things. The family treated her like one of their own, she wrote, "and I could see that this great *savoir-vivre* came from the heart." Her own heart rose to meet it. "There is a good, gallant boy in the great man you are, and I love you with all my heart." Images of Croisset stayed with her. "Your house, your garden, your *citadel* — it's like a dream . . . Yesterday, crossing the bridges, I found Paris very small. I want to go back. I didn't see enough of you and your environment." The lace shawl she had forgotten was perhaps an earnest of her desire to return. In the meantime she established her presence amid the Flauberts with surrogate objects. On September 29 an engraving based on Thomas Couture's portrait of her arrived at Croisset. It had been preceded by her collected works, which filled seventy-seven volumes in the Michel Lévy edition. She suggested, coyly, that Flaubert put them on shelves out of sight and read one or another when his "heart" urged him to do so.

Flaubert, who told her (not altogether truthfully) that the whole family had yielded to the "irresistible and involuntary seduction" of her person, was as keen on having her return as she on paying him a second visit.* "Here's what I propose," he wrote. "My house will be encumbered [with painter-plasterers] and incommodious for a month. But toward the end of

*Caroline would always dislike George Sand. In conversation with the American novelist Willa Cather many years later, she explained why (without owning up to the jealousy she always felt toward competitors for her uncle's affection). "George Sand she did not like," wrote Cather. "Yes, she readily admitted, her men friends were very loyal to her, had a great regard for her; *mon oncle* valued her comradeship; but [she] found the lady's personality distasteful. I gather that, for [her], George Sand did not really fill any of the great rôles she assigned herself: the devoted mistress, the staunch comrade and 'good fellow,' the self-sacrificing mother. George Sand's men friends believed her to be all these things; and certainly, she herself believed that she was. But [Caroline] seemed to feel that in these various relations [Sand] was self-satisfied rather than self-forgetful; always self-admiring and a trifle unctuous."

October or the beginning of November . . . nothing should prevent you, I hope, from staying here, this time for a week at least! You will have a room furnished with 'a pedestal table and everything needed for writing,' as requested. Is that all right? There will be only three of us, my mother included." Sand's second visit would last ten days. Flaubert later reported to Edma Roger des Genettes that the author of seventy-seven volumes spent afternoons writing her seventy-eighth and hours more chatting with him until 3 a.m., much as she had done with Honoré de Balzac three decades earlier, at Nohant. "There is no better woman, no one more good-natured and less conceited . . . Except when she's on her socialist hobbyhorse being a little too benevolent, her perceptive, commonsensical mind goes to the core of things." To Sand herself he confided on November 12 that he had felt completely unhinged since her departure two days earlier. "It seems like ten years since I've seen you! My mother and I can talk of nothing else. Everyone here cherishes you. Under what constellation were you born that you combine such diverse qualities, so many and so rare! I don't know quite how to define the feeling I have for you, but it's a *special* tenderness I've felt for no one else until now. We got on very well, didn't we? It was charming . . . We parted just when many unspoken things were gathering on our lips, isn't that so? There are doors yet to be opened between us." His only request was that she disguise Croisset if she wrote about it, since he wanted no one peering into his citadel.

For her, the carefree visit had been equally agreeable. "Age does not affect your handsome, open face, which has something paternal about it," she replied. "One senses in you a spirit of infinitely protective kindness, and your calling your mother 'my girl' [*ma fille*] one evening brought tears to my eyes."* She would have remained longer but for her reluctance to keep him from his work and a restlessness more pronounced in her sixties than ever before. "I am afraid of becoming too attached and of wearying others. The elderly should be extremely discreet. I can tell you from afar how much I love you without harping on it. You are one of the *rare* beings who have remained impressionable, sincere, in love with art, uncorrupted by ambition, unintoxicated by success."

Sand, whose life revolved around children and grandchildren, gave Flaubert room to feel whatever he felt for her. She also nurtured him, in person and in what soon became a prolific correspondence. Most of her letters demonstrate it, but none more affectingly than those that try to help him take the measure of his genius, to dispute the voice of self-doubt, to set him straight when he misrepresented others in anger or feigned indif-

*Sarah Bernhardt paid him similar compliments some years later. She, too, found him handsome.

ference to the opinion of all but twelve readers or damned himself as wrongheaded. "Each of us," she declared, "is free to embark on a fishing smack or a three-masted vessel. The artist is an explorer whom nothing may halt and who is neither right nor wrong in charting his course one way or another: his destination sanctifies everything. It is for him to know, after gaining some experience, under what conditions his soul functions best." Her own experience of people, she wrote, enabled her to understand and love him as quickly as she did. *Vous* was soon supplanted by *tu* and her earlier salutations by "my cherished old troubadour."

IN APRIL 1867, Napoleon III, who had been reinventing Paris ever since the coup d'état of 1851, inaugurated a Universal Exposition that would, before it closed in October, attract more than six million people to the splendid new capital. Among his most important guests were the czar and the czarina, the king of Prussia, the khedive of Egypt, the mikado's brother, the sultan of Turkey, the Habsburg emperor, and — no stranger to Paris — the Prince of Wales. During seven months hardly a week passed that the emperor did not have occasion to greet some potentate alighting at a railroad station and lead him in military pomp to the Palais des Tuileries, where gala after gala preempted other, more banal affairs of state. The grandest ball of all took place on June 10, honoring Czar Alexander II, and present at it, along with Europe's crowned heads, was Gustave Flaubert, who had been invited by Eugénie for no other reason, he surmised, than that the sovereigns insisted upon seeing one of France's "most splendid oddities." From a balcony he surveyed the gardens, where porcelain lanterns illuminated the walks like "big, brilliant pearls." Alive with beautiful women in long gowns that barely covered their bosoms, it was, he thought, a stage set for passion. "The flowerbeds seem outlined in light, the trees look painted, the lawns made of emerald. There are white globes in the foliage . . . The fountains change color every minute and from time to time a ray of electric light races across the grounds."

Theaters, restaurants, and shops all along the boulevards drove a thriving trade as Paris mobilized its vast pleasure industry for visitors, who arrived by the trainload or boatload from every quarter. French was the language least heard on Paris streets, according to one reporter. The polyglot horde filled the Théâtre des Variétés when Offenbach's *The Grand Duchess of Gérolstein* opened on April 12. It fed its eyes on women doing the cancan with total abandon at dance halls like Bal Mabille, to which it found its way by following an erotic Baedeker published under the title *Parisian Cytheras*. It stood still on June 6, when a Polish exile fired at Czar Alexander II sitting in Napoleon III's carriage — but not for long. There were fireworks of a more artful kind to be seen in the Tuileries gardens and gorgeous carriages in the Bois de Boulogne. Gravitating to light, to movement, to fanfare, to novelty, it beheld Paris's cultural treasures in the spirit of that innocent abroad Mark Twain, who wrote: "We visited the Louvre at a time when we had no silk purchases in view, and looked at its miles of paintings by the old masters." Could old masters hold their own against Blondin waltzing on a tightrope with blazing Catherine wheels fastened to his body? When the great aerialist performed in a suburban pleasure garden, the horde flowed away from Paris like the sea at ebb tide. And when, in October, this horde left Paris for good, laden with silk from Lyons' looms, the image graven on its mind was more likely to have been of machines displayed in the Palace of Industry than of paintings in the Louvre.

The Palace of Industry occupied the Champ-de-Mars, where the Eiffel Tower was to rise on the occasion of another exposition twenty-two years later. Standing amid gardens and grottoes laid out by Adolphe Alphand, architect of the Bois de Boulogne, this bourgeois coliseum, as the Goncourt brothers dubbed it, was an immense iron-and-glass oval whose bulk dwarfed the minarets, pagodas, domes, cottages, and kiosks built to represent national states for half a year. Unlike the Eiffel Tower, the Palace of Industry would not survive the abuse heaped on it by those who, with the French penchant for giving native diseases foreign names, lamented France's "Americanization"; but while it stood it embodied more ostentatiously than any American structure the materialist worldview to which Pius IX had addressed himself in the encyclical *Syllabus of Errors*. "Paris is getting colossal," Flaubert wrote to George Sand after the Tuileries ball. "It's becoming disproportionate and crazy. Are we perhaps returning to the ancient Orient? One has the impression that idols will soon be springing from the earth. We are threatened by a Babylon."

Had Pius ever seen the bourgeois coliseum, its six concentric galleries might have put him in mind not so much of Babylon as of Dante's Hell, especially by day, when a roar of machinery drowned the hubbub of the crowd and vapor from stationary steam engines billowed toward the glass roof. To tour these mile-long galleries was, if one believed in progress, to rejoice in man's victory over nature, or, if one did not, to witness the spectacle of pride running before a fall. Here industrial Europe displayed itself at its most vainglorious. There were machines of every order and dimension: compressed-air machines, coal-extracting machinery, railway equipment, spinning machines, sewing machines, electric dynamos, hydraulic lifts. There were locomotives and large-scale models of those railroad stations that epitomized the nineteenth century's architectural syncretism. There was a show on the history of labor, where proletarian visitors who could pay the price of admission were given to understand that they had prospered well enough since 1848 to afford the clothes, utensils, and gadgets laid before them in grotesque profusion. Beneath this glass roof nothing could contradict Louis-Napoleon's optimism, not even a fifty-eight-ton steel cannon manufactured by Krupp of Essen for King Wilhelm of Prussia. "A writer for the official bulletin wondered what earthly use it could have beyond frightening everyone to death. More offensive to Parisian sensibilities was the fact that it was remarkably ugly, though in the end [the jury] did give the cannon a prize," notes one historian. With political reality suspended for the moment, inklings of doom were no less unwelcome on the Champ-de-Mars than the paintings of Manet, who exhibited his work in a shack outside its perimeter, charging fifty centimes' admission. Only tiresome Cassandras dared to suggest aloud that the cannon, when primed, might one day point at France, that a prize would not muzzle it, that its jury could become its fodder. Flaubert dismissed them contemptuously. "'The political horizon is darkening.' Can anyone say why? Still, it's darkening . . . Bourgeois are fearful of everything! Fearful of war; fearful of strikes; more than half convinced, out of fear, that Eugénie's little boy, the Imperial Prince, is going to die . . . To find another example of such stupidity, one might go back to 1848." In this spirit of denial, sightseers pressed on heedlessly, orbiting around and around until their journey led them to the outermost ring, where they restored themselves in cafés and restaurants, one more exotic than the next. At night the palace's wall shimmered with gaslight and women in native costumes from all over the world brought forth native dishes, and scarlet-clad gypsy bands played czardas, and French flower girls selling Parma violets mingled with the crowd.

To the correspondent of *Punch,* "Epicurus Rotundus," nothing about the Palace of Industry was so revealing of its ethos as the garden around which it had been built. "The heart of this garden, the center of all these monster rings, which made you feel as if you had got into Saturn, was a little money-changing office," he wrote. "I liked this cynicism." There were those who reaped fortunes of irony from the knowledge that in Robespierre's day Parisians gathered two hundred thousand strong to worship the Supreme Being on this very spot. Where civic devotions had taken place at a Revolutionary altar known as "the Sublime Mountain," now, like the hub of an immense carousel, there stood a money pavilion. The arrangement was no more cynical, however, than Napoleon III's proposition that a government could get away with violating legality or even liberty but would be short-lived unless it placed itself at the head of civilization's "larger interests." Iconoclasts and believers alike — bourgeois bashers and the Goncourt cousin who prayed every night that his urine might clear up, his hemorrhoids shrink, and Anzin coal continue to rise on the stock market — found it altogether suitable that Mammon should occupy dead center, like an omphalos.

Flaubert visited the exhibition three times, first with Princess Mathilde shortly before the official opening, a second time in April, and four months later, at the end of July, with his mother. Would he have portrayed this panorama of epic clutter in a novel about Second Empire France provisionally entitled *Sous Napoléon III* if he had ever gotten around to writing it? For the moment his energies were taken up by the tumult of 1848 and the novel he had been preparing since 1864, although his correspondence with a family notary leaves no doubt that money was nearer dead center of his mind than he wished it to be. "I find nothing more *painful* than continually leaning on my mother," he wrote to Frédéric Fovard, who had at Mme Flaubert's request exacted from him a tally of his considerable debts to a tailor, an upholsterer, and a fashionable haberdasher. "Try to persuade her that I am not surrendering myself to wild orgies! Alas, I wish I were, I'd be a little more cheerful! And since she has decided to pay my debts, let her do it right, *right,* without too much recrimination . . . I entrust you with my sorry nerves, which are frayed by all this." His mother assured him that she was not angry but insisted upon a more rational disposition of her resources. He would receive 700 francs a month during his four months in Paris and 1,200 francs for the remainder of the year ("when all your needs are taken care of"), plus 1,050 francs to cover eight months' rent for the Boulevard du Temple flat: a grand total of 5,050 francs. "That way, my poor old dear," she proposed, "I could repair things that are falling apart here and giving what your poor father left me the appearance of dereliction." Of the 16,337 francs that constituted her annual income, 9,000 had gone to Flaubert the previous year, leaving her with 7,377 francs for household expenses, which included the salaries of old Julie (who was going blind), a cook, and a gardener and his wife. "You understand that this can't continue, and I hope that you love your poor mother enough to restrict yourself to what she can reasonably give you and spare her from being an old lady financially strapped for the first time in her life. About my silverware, you have more settings than I, which also doesn't make much sense." Her son clearly liked to cut an elegant figure.

Although Mme Flaubert never ceased to fret, it was not she who ended up in straitened circumstances.

XIX

⁓⁓⁓

L'Éducation sentimentale

EVEN AT his most sociable, Flaubert never strayed too far from the manuscript on his table. Throughout the 1860s, when demolition crews were leveling the Paris of his youth, he was reconstructing it in a novel about a generation adrift in time. The title he eventually chose, *L'Éducation sentimentale,* was itself a memento, having served for a novel written twenty years earlier. He didn't feel altogether happy with it, but a man haunted by loss and change may have found it as difficult to discard old titles as old pipes. After decades in limbo, this one had acquired a yellow complexion that suited his new text peculiarly well.

Nothing came easily, least of all the choice of material. With *Salammbô* behind him, an anguished perplexity filled the void. He wondered whether to revise *La Tentation de Saint Antoine* once more, to develop the themes later embodied in *Bouvard et Pécuchet,* or to do something entirely different. "I back and fill among a thousand projects," he told the Goncourts. "Writing a book is a long voyage for me, in rough water, and the mere thought of it makes me queasy. There you have it, a blue funk on top of a barren imagination. I'm stymied." By April 1863 he had embarked, but with forebodings that his voyage would lead him across a dull expanse to an arid shore. In metaphors of sexual impotence and spiritual dryness, he protested that by its very nature his idea for the novel allowed of no ripening, no climax, no epiphany. "I don't have 'Grace,' as the pious say, or, as pigs would put it, I can't 'get it up.' That's where *L'Éducation sentimentale* stands at the moment. I lack facts. I don't see any principal scenes. It doesn't form a pyramid. In short, it disgusts me." Thoughts of turning back nagged him, but, with Louis Bouilhet's constant encouragement, he persevered, and in September 1864 pen was finally put to paper for the brilliant opening scene of his work. "Here I am, hitched since last month to a novel of modern mores that will take place in Paris," he told Mlle Leroyer de Chantepie on October 6, 1864, shortly before the imperial *séries* at Compiègne. "I want to do a moral history of my generation; 'sentimental' would be more accurate. It's about love, passion, but passion of a specifically modern kind, which is to say, inactive. The subject, as I have conceived it, rings true, I believe, but for that very reason is probably not very entertaining. It's thin in facts, in drama, and the action spans too much time. I have my hands full and am sorely vexed."

Flaubert's correspondence seldom sounded a confident note about *L'Éducation sentimentale* during the entire four and a half years of its composition. While creating a modern antihero in Frédéric Moreau, he kept berating him for his modernity. How could so ineffectual a character captivate readers? And furthermore, how could he, Flaubert, reconcile a "bourgeois" subject and the scientific stringency of his age with the exaltation to which art aspires? There was no making a silk purse out of a sow's ear. "Modern life is not compatible with beauty, so I won't mess with it again. I've had enough." Later the self-criticism became more focused. To Alfred Maury, for example, he declared that conceptual flaws might result in a mediocre book. "Though I mean to portray a psychological state hitherto ignored — it's quite genuine — the milieu in which my characters disport themselves is so teeming and copious that on every page they risk being swallowed by it. I must therefore make background material of the very things I find most interesting. I skim subjects I would like to treat at length. It's not simple."

His anxiety about aimless characters flitting like shadows through a tumultuous city reflected a fear that the novelist in him might be subjugated by a historian bent on learning "everything" (so he told Sainte-Beuve) about France of the 1840s. He traveled around Paris for hours, notebook in hand, to chronicle Frédéric's hectic movements, and visited as much of the Île-de-France as necessary. To furnish a chapter on the pottery business of an entrepreneurial blusterer named Jacques Arnoux, he spent hours in an outlying neighborhood with artisans glazing earthenware. Newspaper archives yielded abundant detail. When he wasn't consulting major dailies at public libraries (the discomfort of which exasperated him), he was tracking down ephemera born on the eve of revolution. "Can you tell me where I might find the collected *Tintamarre* of 1847?" he asked one acquaintance. "They're not in any public library . . . If Commerson [the publisher] has them, can you borrow them for me? I'd return them after twenty-four hours." His most provocative research was the study of works that had shaped revolutionary discourse in the 1840s. Convinced that any social order championed by ideologues, be they secular or religious, would stifle individuality with collective precepts, he reviled utopian thinking. Fourier, Lamennais, Lacordaire, Proudhon, Saint-Simon, Louis Blanc, and their patron saint Jean-Jacques Rousseau were all, in his view, pledged to systems based upon the individual's fatal subservience to a group, a guild, a church, or a caste. Under their assortment of canonical robes, there was little to distinguish them from one another. "As for [me, I continue my] socialist readings — Fourier, Saint-Simon, etc.," he wrote to Amélie Bosquet in July 1864. "How those people oppress me! What despots. What churls! Modern socialism reeks of the schoolmaster. Those folks are stuck in the Middle Ages and a caste mentality. Their common rallying point is hatred of freedom and of the French Revolution." He repeated himself to George Sand two years later. "Don't you think, deep down, that we've been rambling since '89? Instead of taking the highway, that broad, handsome avenue designed for triumphal processions, we fled into byways and are mucking about in a quagmire. Might it not be wise to return momentarily to Holbach? Before admiring Proudhon, should we not be acquainting ourselves with Turgot?"* It did not escape him that Sand in greener days had associated herself closely with one of those ideologues straddling radical economics and Christian revelation. *Consuela* had been written under the influence of Pierre Leroux, who drew upon Scripture, Eastern religion, and Saint-Simon for his egalitarian creed. Sand had collaborated with him when he founded *La Revue Indépendante*. By 1848 they had parted ways, but each made his voice heard during the Revolution, Leroux as an elected deputy, Sand as the author of "Lettre au peuple" and "Lettre aux riches."

Although his "chère maître" urged Flaubert to take a more charitable view of the idealism that motivated zealous forty-eighters, she had no problem setting politics aside to inform, encourage, and console. All three ministries were regularly asked of her. "You," he wrote in November 1866, "you don't know what it's like to sit for a whole day with your head in your hands trying to wring out the right words. Ideas flow from you in a broad, constant stream. With me they're a thin rivulet, it takes great labors of art to effect a cascade. Ah! I will have experienced everything there is to know

---

*Baron d'Holbach, an encyclopedist and friend of Diderot, propagated materialism in his philosophical writings and opposed all positive forms of religion. Turgot, an economist belonging to the physiocratic school, espoused the doctrine of free trade.

of those torments of style! In short, I spent life gnawing my heart and brain. That is what your friend is essentially all about!" It seemed profligate to her that anything created at such cost should remain in his bottom drawer. Why, she wondered, didn't he publish the account of his trek through Brittany with Maxime Du Camp? Why be afraid to show one's wens and warts? "You're coy; you don't find everything you've done worth exposing. In that you're wrong. Everything that comes out of a master is instructive and one mustn't be afraid of revealing one's drafts and sketches. Even those are well above the average reader, who is offered so much at his own vulgar level that he can't elevate himself, poor devil." She counseled Flaubert as well against masking his richly furnished self behind an impersonal facade. "Be stouthearted for the novel," she wrote. "It's exquisite, but the odd thing is that a whole side of you doesn't disclose or betray itself in what you do." The absence of Balzacian harangues did not reflect a dearth of ideas, he had protested several weeks earlier. "Do you doubt, because I spend my life trying to construct harmonious sentences . . . that I, too, have my little opinions about things of this world? Alas, yes! and I'll even croak of frustration for not uttering them." Sand harbored no such doubts, of course, and, like Louis Bouilhet, who reestablished himself in Rouen in 1867 as director of the municipal library, willingly sat through marathon readings at Croisset. On May 25, 1868, for example, she noted in her diary that Flaubert led her up to his study at 9 p.m. after some atrocious singing by a family friend. "He reads me three hundred excellent pages; I'm entranced."

There may have been no truth to a local legend propagated by Flaubert that the abbé Prévost, when still a Benedictine monk attached in the 1720s to the Saint-Ouen chapter, wrote *Manon Lescaut* at Croisset, but the case can be made that Frédéric Moreau was born under Prévost's roof, as a neurasthenic descendant of his protagonist, the chevalier des Grieux. Both heroes are young men who have just graduated from provincial collegiate schools when their stories begin. They are both set to undertake further study, Frédéric in law and des Grieux in theology. Each at that pivotal moment encounters a woman who dazzles him and, eyes riveted to the femme fatale, loses his social compass. Feeling fully alive thenceforth only in the magnetic field of her presence, they abandon the professional course dictated by parents and custom.

It is on a steamboat paddling upriver toward his hometown of Nogent-sur-Seine in September 1840 that Frédéric first appears. After graduation, the fatherless eighteen-year-old has visited a rich bachelor uncle in Le Havre, ingratiated himself at his mother's behest, and now, on his return from Normandy, he unhappily contemplates the prospect of a long, tedious summer in his provincial backwater, to be followed by law studies. Like

Flaubert's portrait of Charles Bovary as the inarticulate bumpkin mocked at the Collège royal, his description of Frédéric among passengers boarding the *Ville-de-Montereau* in Paris will become a defining image.

> People arrived out of breath. Barrels, cables, hampers full of linen impeded circulation. The crew couldn't be bothered with questions. There was much jostling. Packages were hoisted between the two drums, and a hiss of steam escaping through sheets of metal and blanketing everything in a white cloud absorbed the racket. The forward bell tolled incessantly . . . At last the vessel departed.
>
> A young man of eighteen, with long hair and holding a sketchbook under his arm, stood near the tiller, motionless. Through the early-morning fog, he was contemplating steeples, edifices he couldn't identify. In a farewell glance he embraced the Île Saint-Louis, the Cité, Notre-Dame; and soon, with Paris receding from view, he heaved a big sigh. . . .
>
> The tumult abated. Everyone had taken his place. Some passengers continued to stand as they warmed themselves around the engine, and the stack emitted a plume of black smoke in slow, rhythmic belches. Droplets streamed down the brass fittings. A slight vibration coming from inside made the deck tremble, and the two wheels slapped the water rapidly.

Everything is energy and bustle on a boat that clearly epitomizes the industrial age, everything except Frédéric, standing by himself, motionless. While the vessel puffs, sweats, and trembles from the exertion of moving its cargo forward, against the current, Frédéric, who is destined to accumulate missed opportunities, looks backward amorously at Paris and its unidentifiable landmarks as at a beautiful passerby he couldn't bring himself to approach. Distance goes hand in hand with immobility. His fellow travelers, ordinary people living in the moment, contemplate riverine cottages and wreathe domestic fantasies around them. Some, writes Flaubert, would have liked to own one and make it their permanent home, "with a good billiard table, a rowboat, a wife, or some other dreamed-of possession." Not Frédéric, whose mind is elsewhere. Flaubert's dreamer sees nothing of the passing scene, or sees it through an inner fog. His sketchbook remains blank. "He mused on the room he would occupy [in Nogent], on the plot for a drama, on subjects for painting, on future passions." And when he does move, the impulse to do so is a private twinge rather than an urge to mingle. "He felt that the happiness that his excellence of soul had earned him was slow in coming. He recited melancholy verse to himself; he crossed the deck in rapid steps; he walked right up to the bow, on the bell side." It's as if this jerky sequence, punctuated by semicolons, were keeping the beat of inner turmoil. Frédéric can be either motionless or rapid.

His walk across the deck proves to be fateful. Regaling people at the bow end is Jacques Arnoux — a demonstrative character, part bon vivant and part mountebank, modeled after Macaire (Daumier's, if not Frédérick Lemaître's) as well as Maurice Schlesinger. Frédéric meets Arnoux, then spies his little daughter and his wife, Marie, who instantly becomes an object of rapturous scrutiny. "Her whole person was silhouetted against a background of blue air" is how Flaubert, using the same image that had served fifteen years earlier to describe his first glimpse of Kuchiuk-Hanem at Esna,* introduces the woman Frédéric will woo in vain.

> Never had he seen anything like the splendor of her dusky complexion, the seductiveness of her figure, fingers so delicate that light passed through them. He regarded her workbasket with astonishment, as no common object. What was her name? Where did she live? What had her life been, her past? He wanted to acquaint himself with the furniture in her room, all the dresses she had ever worn, the people she habitually saw. Subdued by some deeper longing, the desire for physical possession gave rise to a painful and unlimited curiosity.

Just as young Gustave saved Élisa Schlesinger's shawl from the sea, so here Frédéric saves Mme Arnoux's from the Seine, in a gesture that prefigures his fantasy of rescuing the beloved herself from a vulgar, unfaithful husband. Her laconic acknowledgment of his gallantry only reinforces his conviction that he is a superfluous man. To contemplate his idol is to feel all the more irrelevant. "The more he regarded her, the more he felt abysses opening between them," writes Flaubert. "He thought that it would soon be necessary to part, before extracting a word from her, even before leaving any memory of himself." When at length they reach Nogent, he sees her lost in thought at the spot he had occupied earlier. "On the quay, Frédéric turned around. She was standing near the tiller. He packed a glance with his entire soul and sent it toward her. She remained motionless, as if he hadn't done anything whatever."

It makes perfect sense that a young man who runs before himself or lags behind should experience the voyage most vividly when it's over, in his mind's eye. The entire episode is relived, as by a novelist seeing more at an imaginative remove than close up, during Frédéric's ride home in the family carriage. "Little by little, his memory brought back every stage of the journey — Villeneuve-Saint-Georges, Ablon, Chatillon, Corbeil, other places — and in such sharp focus that he now observed new particularities, more intimate details. Her foot protruded beyond the outermost

---

*"A woman standing at the top of an outside staircase opposite us, bathed in light, silhouetted against the blue background of the sky."

flounce of her dress, shod in a slender ankle boot of brown silk. The duck-cloth canopy on deck formed a wide platform over her head, and little red tassels along its border trembled continually in the breeze." She had the perfection of a literary heroine, Flaubert continues. "There was nothing about her he would have wanted to change. The universe had just grown larger. She was the luminous point at which the totality of things converged. And, rocked by the movement of the carriage, his eyes half-closed, his gaze in the clouds, he surrendered to a dreamy, boundless joy." Then the supine passenger suddenly takes the driver's seat and sets a demonic pace. "Blood coursed into his face, his temples buzzed, he cracked his whip and shook the reins so vigorously that the old family retainer cautioned him: 'Gently! Gently! You'll ruin the horses' wind.'"

Frédéric belongs to the illustrious literary family of nineteenth-century adolescents from provincial France whose mettle is corroded by submersion in Parisian society. Like Balzac's Edmond de Rastignac, he studies law but soon abandons the study of it, his exclusive preoccupation being to draw nearer the Arnoux, which he does through a character named Hussonnet. The premises of Arnoux's gallery and magazine, *L'Art Industriel* (obviously patterned on Maurice Schlesinger's *Gazette Musicale*), become a second home for the spellbound Frédéric. He spends his days there hoping to glimpse Marie, wondering whether to reinvent himself as a painter, and meeting other habitués among whom he busily loiters. The novel leads everywhere and nowhere, like a maze of paths all running into culs-de-sac. No sooner does Frédéric receive an invitation to dinner from the Arnoux, where Mme Arnoux's hospitality is construed as a warrant for hope of future bliss, than she absents herself. Several years later, when after a tortuous courtship they are about to make love, the Arnoux boy falls grievously ill, thwarting their rendezvous and disposing Marie to blame herself for the child's sickness. "Incapable of action," Flaubert writes of Frédéric, "cursing God and accusing himself of cowardice, he turned around and around in his state of desire, like a prisoner in his cell. Suffocated by anguish, he remained motionless for hours on end, or had crying jags." Good fortune and bad alike conspire to hold him hostage to his chimera. At one point his mother, who has suffered financial reverses, calls him home. He has all but resigned himself to the prospect of an obscure, conventional life in Nogent when news arrives that his rich uncle has died and left him an inheritance sufficient to free him from Champagne. The career of this feckless dreamer drifting in a world that spoils his dreams and pretentions at every turn can then resume.

However different in other respects, Flaubert's protagonists are alike in their sentimental ineducability. Feeling at one with the world or falling out of it, they swell or deflate but never really grow. Where everything is boundlessly one thing or another — an oceanic fullness or a Sahara of deprivation — there is hardly room for development. Adventures are redundant, experience does not beget maturity or knowledge, and, indeed, the Flaubertian novel tends to come full round, like horses on a carousel. The white dress Emma wore as a virgin at convent school is the white dress in which she has herself buried. *Salammbô* begins with a feast in Carthage for the victorious mercenaries at which Matho is transfixed by Salammbô; it ends with another feast at which a chained, flayed Matho remains transfixed, his battles having been waged for naught. The last chapters of *L'Éducation sentimentale* find Frédéric Moreau adrift in middle age and revisiting his adolescent transports, first in a reunion with Mme Arnoux, then in conversation with Charles Deslauriers, his bosom friend since childhood, who has also run a futile course through life. They agree that their lackluster existence is to be blamed on chance, on circumstances, on France, on the nineteenth century. Then they evoke naive school days and delightedly recall their visit to a whorehouse just outside Nogent on a Sunday during vespers when townspeople wouldn't see them, all dressed up, carrying bouquets for the bawd. It came to nothing. "The summer heat, fear of the unknown, a kind of remorse and even the pleasure of seeing at a glance so many women at his disposal made such an impression on him that he turned pale and stood there motionless, dumbstruck." Charmed by his embarrassment, the women had burst into laughter, which to him sounded like mockery. He turned tail and fled, with Charles following, and their misadventure became an article of local lore. "That's when we had it best!" Frédéric exclaims. "Yes, maybe so, that's when we had it best!" Charles concurs in a closing whimper. Nogent, seen at the outset as Frédéric's oppressive destination, thus reappears at the end as the prelapsarian homeland from which he fell into his pursuit of an unachievable consummation. He had fallen into history, into the quotidian, and into Paris. "He moved in society, and he had other loves," writes Flaubert, "but his persistent memory of the first one rendered all that followed insipid. And when the vehemence of desire abated, the bloom went off it. His intellectual ambition had likewise failed. Years passed, and he came to tolerate the unemployment of his mind and the inertia of his heart."

Irony gives *L'Éducation sentimentale* its coherence as well as its general air of hurry-scurry. Not for nothing did Flaubert have Frédéric graduate from the collegiate school at Sens (Achille-Cléophas's alma mater — itself an ironical association). Embedded in the name Sens, which also means "sense," is a double entendre that reflects Flaubert's view of his character as a man generally baffled by events.* A mystifying agency governs men, women, human affairs. Nothing can be situated where there is no center or circum-

---

*Hussonnet calls Frédéric "un jeune homme du collège de Sens et qui *en* manque" (a young man from the college of Sens, who has none).

ference, in a world of fluid identities, convenient allegiances, bravado, puffery, betrayal. Novelists may give a palpable shape or direction to the lives they portray, but to Flaubert all is randomness, and the randomness subverting dramatic structure denies Flaubert's characters a release from their endless improvisation. They don't experience closure, for the novel has no proper denouement. Lives go on and on, wearing out or wearing thin, but never making sense. Is it any wonder that Franz Kafka read and reread *L'Éducation sentimentale* and compared it to the biblical wandering in the wilderness? "[Moses'] dying vision of [Canaan] can only be intended to illustrate how incomplete a moment is human life," Kafka observed in his diaries, "incomplete because a life like this could last forever and still be nothing but a moment. Moses fails to enter Canaan not because his life is too short but because it is a human life. This ending of the Pentateuch bears a resemblance to the final scene of *L'Éducation sentimentale.*" In a letter to Mlle Leroyer de Chantepie written some years before *L'Éducation,* Flaubert warned against the vaingloriousness of humans embracing ideologies, religions, creeds that offer a solution. "A solution!" he exclaimed. "The goal! The cause! We'd be God if we grasped the cause. And as we advance it will recede indefinitely, for our horizon will broaden." Spinoza's *Ethics* was his uncited authority here.

The language of these personae echoes the mutually incomprehensible babble of mercenaries in *Salammbô*. Love and political will become mere verbiage in Frédéric's self-deluding avowals to a courtesan, in the ideological jargon of bourgeois republicans, in the rodomontade of all political aspirants. People utter repetitive drivel. They talk past one another as, for example, at a meeting of one of the political clubs spawned by the February Revolution. Not least among the argumentative fools present there is a retired teacher who proposes that "European democracy" adopt a common language. When Frédéric, who has, despite himself, agreed to run for office in the elections of April 1848, tries to wrest the podium from a Spaniard speaking Spanish, his protestations go unheard. The 1848 insurgency, toward which Flaubert's narrative sweeps the flotsam with whom it has acquainted us, is in fact a logorrheic nightmare. Every citizen has his tirade. "[Frédéric] visited all [the clubs], or almost all of them," we are told.*

> The red and the blue, the furious and the calm, the puritanical, the unbuttoned, the mystical and the boozy, those at which people decreed the death of kings, those at which one denounced petty-bourgeois frauds; and everywhere tenants were heaping opprobrium on landlords, the smocked crowd joined battle with

---

*Historically, this would not have been possible. Clubs pullulated. By one count, there were 276 of them in Paris.

the frocked, rich conspiring against poor. Some, who portrayed themselves as martyrs of police brutality, called for indemnities, others begged to have their inventions financed. Or else there were plans for phalansteries, for cantonal bazaars, for systems of public felicity. Now and again real intelligence flashed through the clouds of fatuous vaporizing. A just cause would be adequately summarized in a curse and real eloquence rolled off the tongue of an oaf wearing the crossbelt of a saber over his bare chest. Aristocrats with hands left unwashed so that they'd look calloused took the floor to eat humble pie. A patriot would recognize them, the most virtuous would abuse them, and they would stalk out enraged. Denigrating lawyers was an earnest of one's good sense, and it behooved one, whenever possible, to use these phrases: "to bring one's stone to the construction site," "social problem," "workshop."

It suited Flaubert's purpose to have Frédéric tour political clubs during his halfhearted venture into public life with a posturing ham actor as his impresario.

On May 16, 1869, shortly before 5 a.m., Flaubert, in Paris, wrote to Jules Duplan that he has just finished *L'Éducation,* after toiling since eight o'clock the previous morning. Another such communiqué elicited congratulations from Louis Bouilhet, who was troubled by poor health. Having a fair copy made of the manuscript took nine or ten days, in the course of which Flaubert read several chapters at Princess Mathilde's salon. Greatly impressed by what she had heard, Mathilde without too much arm-twisting prevailed upon him to read the entire novel in four afternoon sessions of four hours each. One guest, the poet François Coppée, remembered him as a giant whose formidable mustache didn't accord with the frills of his fine linen shirt, the shiny wide-brimmed hat tilted over one ear, or the patent leather half boots, in which he strode to a squeaking of new leather. "He carried his head loftily. His whole bearing was that of the romantics . . . One could still make out fine features in his florid, swollen face . . . And a truly Merovingian mess of hair hung in graying, tousled locks from his half-denuded pate. This older Gustave Flaubert was no longer handsome, but he was still superb."

If Michel Lévy assumed that dealings with Flaubert would be less Merovingian than in the past because the contract for *Salammbô* had included contractual terms for "a modern novel," he was soon disabused of the notion. The author was to receive ten thousand francs plus a proportion of that sum based upon the number of pages by which *L'Éducation* exceeded *Salammbô*. Flaubert, who foresaw that the novel would appear in two volumes, wanted ten thousand francs for each and asked George Sand, who was on excellent terms with Lévy, to play go-between, as if to distance himself from his own avidity. "Attached is my contract with the child of Israel (reading it one might cry out: 'God of the Jews, you win the day!')," he wrote to her.* "Look it over, act on my behalf, dear master." Her mediation was seemingly effective. "I saw Lévy today," she replied five days later, on May 18. "I began cautiously and saw that he would not repeal the contract for anything. I then spoke highly of the book and remarked that he had gotten it cheap. 'But,' he said, 'if it comes out in two volumes, twenty thousand is what I'll pay, that's understood.' It seems to me that you will have two volumes, no? I insisted and he said: 'If the book is successful, I'm not going to quibble over an additional two or three thousand francs.' I said that you would not ask anything of him, that that was not your way, but that I myself would pursue the matter on your behalf, unbeknownst to you, and he said to me when we parted, 'Rest assured that I am not saying no. If the book does well, the author will profit.'" Flaubert was instructed to let her manage everything and broach the matter with Lévy again at a time of her choosing.[†]

Flaubert delivered the manuscript on August 11. Lévy, whom he called Michel when he wasn't calling him names, sent it to his printer straightaway, with no qualms except about the title. Although Flaubert, as we have seen, shared those qualms, he asserted that friends — Sand, Turgenev, Maxime Du Camp — had not helped him come up with something better. In any event, the title most accurately conveyed his idea. September and October were devoted to reading proof. Letters traveled ceaselessly between the publisher at 2bis rue Vivienne and the author at 4, rue Murillo, where Flaubert took up residence that fall in a quiet, elegant flat on the fifth floor of a new building facing the Parc Monceau. Lest the legislative session scheduled to open in mid-November and expected to be highly contentious distract the public from cultural news, he urged the printer to hurry with proof. *L'Éducation sentimentale* appeared on November 17. Reviews followed soon thereafter.

In 1869, when, by law, illustrated periodicals needed permission to publish images of an author, Flaubert withheld his consent from the famous caricaturist Gill, explaining that he reserved his face for himself. Alas, he had no such control over reviews, most of which were vehemently hostile, including one in *Le Droit des femmes* by Amélie Bosquet, who took exception to Flaubert's unkind portrait of a feminist touting her cause during the Revolution; she saw herself in it, lampooned. Barbey d'Aurevilly, a Catholic royalist, attacked him on every conceivable ground in *Le Constitutionnel:* the novel lacked originality; its hero lacked heroism; its other char-

---

*The quotation is from Racine's play *Athalie*.

[†]By "two or three thousand francs," Lévy was referring to the difference between the sum he owed Flaubert, according to the terms of their contract (that is, the page count), and the twenty thousand francs Flaubert was asking. It amounted to four thousand francs.

acters lacked character; its plot — to the extent that it had one — was woolly; its title was ambiguous. Was it a novel? asked a critic in *Le Figaro*. No, thought Duranty in *Paris-Journal*. Better describe it as a "compendium of descriptions" or assign it to the shelf of memoirs and chronicles. But a memoir or chronicle that strove for impartial contempt in its chapters on the Revolution, sparing neither bourgeois nor insurgent, neither utopian socialist nor Catholic reactionary, angered every partisan. The *Journal des Débats* found it reprehensible that he had not given "heroic bourgeois" at war with "Parisian demagogy" their due. A left-wing paper, *L'Opinion Nationale*, wanted recognition of the country's "elements of generosity and renewal." There was no trial this time, but there was no need for official litigation when ten or twelve critics played the part of public prosecutor, arguing morality against an author enchanted with the gutter, a vulgarian criminally insensitive to the sublime in human affairs. Vulgar was almost every reviewer's watchword. Francisque Sarcey, a well-known columnist, declared that the book had nauseated him. Like his colleagues, he found the last scene particularly offensive. Had they known of the letter in which Flaubert once told Louise Colet that he wanted to write a book about nothing, most would have agreed that in *L'Éducation sentimentale* he had accomplished his goal.

Although this panning did not have the same visceral effect on him that his book had had on Sarcey, the tone of negative reviews surprised him. "Your old troubadour is being energetically disparaged by the papers," he wrote to George Sand.

> Read last Monday's *Le Constitutionnel* and this morning's *Le Gaulois;* it's cut-and-dried. I'm pictured as a scoundrel and a cretin. Barbey d'Aurevilly's article is a model of its kind and good old Sarcey's is scarcely less violent. These gentlemen protest in the name of morality and the ideal! I've also been savaged in *Le Figaro* and in *Paris* by Cesena and Duranty. I don't give a damn, mind you, but I am nonetheless astonished by so much hatred — and bad faith.

All the reviewers, he went on to say, cited the last scene — Frédéric's account of visiting Zoraide Turc's brothel at Nogent — as proof of his turpitude. "It's skewed, of course, and Sarcey compares me to the Marquis de Sade, whom he declares he has never read!" Equally vexatious was the behavior of certain friends who had received complimentary copies. They spoke to him about everything except *L'Éducation sentimentale* for fear of compromising themselves, he thought. "Brave souls are rare. The book is nonetheless selling very well, despite the politics, and Lévy seems content."

If unfavorable notice really mattered so little, he would not have pretended that his novel was doing quite well (two years after publication, the first edition of three thousand copies had not yet sold out). Nor would he have urged George Sand to join the battle against detractors with a review of her own. She did as bidden, and afterward gave Flaubert a brief lecture. His astonishment at the malevolence of confreres was itself astonishing, she thought. "You are excessively naive. You don't know how original your book is, how the strength of it must ruffle certain personalities. You think that what you write will simply pass unimpeded, like a letter in the post. Come, come!" The novel's strongest point, in her view, and the virtue least likely to be appreciated, was its design. "I insisted upon this [in my piece] . . . I tried to make the unsophisticated understand how they should read it, for success or failure hinges upon their response. I didn't bother with the nasties, as they don't want others to succeed; it would have been doing them too much honor." Critics addled by theory were as bad as those stewing in malice. "Don't trouble yourself with all that," she wrote. "March straight forward. Have no system, and obey your inspiration."

Flaubert, who diligently summarized every review for his files, found solace in several of them, the most important being one by a writer not yet thirty who had just begun the fictional saga that was to make him a towering presence on the literary scene. "When I hear the critical fraternity convict Gustave Flaubert of showing nothing new, of glancing off surfaces, I'm tempted to shout, 'So much the worse for you if you miss his meaning,'" wrote Émile Zola, whose *Thérèse Raquin* had appeared two years earlier and impressed Flaubert. "What the author adduces are the obscure depths of being, our muted desires, our violent impulses, our failures of nerve, all the impotence and energy that inform the absurdities of everyday life. And he is by no means a simple scribe.* He is a gifted poet whose music is written for sympathetic ears. If you don't hear it, you're clogged with blood or bile. Be of a nervous disposition and it will penetrate you." The musical image recurs. "With immense skill, he remains earthbound yet gives his words such vibrancy that they seem blown down on us by a heavenly trumpet." As for the plethora of description imputed to Flaubert, Zola agreed that *L'Éducation sentimentale* was dense with it.

> I would venture to say that description is the basic material of his works. But let me be clear. His method is essentially descriptive; he admits only facts, dialogue, gestures. His characters make themselves known to us by speech and action. Rather than analytic expositions as in Balzac, there are short scenes giving play to personalities and temperaments. We thus necessarily have description, for it is through the external that he acquaints us with what's inside . . . As soon as he

*"Scribe" — *greffier* — may be a reference to Balzac's celebrated formulation of the idea behind *La comédie humaine*: "French society was to be the historian, I merely its secretary."

has pushed a character onto the stage, the latter must introduce himself to the public and live out in the open, naturally, never showing the strings attached.

L'Éducation, in this argument, illustrated the congruence of people and their environment, the intimacy between psyches and objects that became the linchpin of Zola's own esthetic creed. "Milieus make beings, things add to human life," he affirmed.

> [In Flaubert] the most trivial objects acquire voices; they are alive, they speak and all but move. A very curious example of this may be found in *Madame Bovary*. Léon, the love-struck clerk, is mutely courting the doctor's wife one evening at M. Homais' place. He notices Emma's dress trailing on the floor around her chair. And the author adds: "When Léon felt cloth under the sole of his boot, he'd recoil as if he had stepped on someone." There we have human nerves being observed by an author whose eye for such detail is the most remarkable feature of his talent.

L'Éducation astonished Zola. After he had done reading it, he wrote, its fifty or sixty characters kept dancing before his eyes in a confusion of episodes.

Ten days before the year ran out, a letter arrived from Hauteville House on Guernsey. Victor Hugo thanked Flaubert for sending him his books. "They are profound and powerful," he wrote. "Those that portray present-day life leave a bittersweet taste." *L'Éducation sentimentale* both charmed and saddened him. "I shall reread it the way I reread books, by opening them randomly, at any page. Only writers who are also thinkers can stand the test. You belong to that strong race. You have Balzac's penetration, and style in the bargain. When will I see you?"

Flaubert once told his niece Caroline that he always, incorrigibly, believed in the judgment of others, distrusting his own. *L'Éducation sentimentale* presents a case in point. With the passage of time he showed a disposition to side against the most clearly modern aspects of the work. In 1879, when *L'Éducation* came out under a different imprint, he wrote to Edma Roger des Genettes that it lacked the "falsity of perspective" indispensable to all works of art. His friend Dr Charles Robin said as much, and he agreed. "The sphere must have a point off which light glints, there must be a summit, the work must form a pyramid." To J. K. Huysmans he observed that there is no "progression of effect" in the novel. "At the end, readers have the same impression they had from the outset. Art is not reality. Whatever one does, one is compelled to select from among the elements that reality furnishes." His unsympathetic appraisal, which could have been signed by any one of the "nasties," did not prevent him, however, from ascribing *L'Éducation*'s unsuccess to a mass murderer named

Troppmann, whose trial and execution in 1869 had enthralled all of France: people had flocked to kiosks rather than bookstores. And he defended his work on moral grounds. "I don't believe anyone has gone further than I in upholding a standard of probity. As for the conclusion, I admit that all the stupidities it inspired still weigh on my heart."

FLAUBERT APPRECIATED George Sand's mothering. In 1869 the extended Sand family made much of him over the Christmas holidays, which he spent at Nohant, where half a dozen children had the run of the house and Mme Sand's son, Maurice, mounted puppet shows on a stage constructed for the purpose. No one laughed louder than Flaubert or provoked more laughter, especially when he dressed up as a woman to dance the cachucha.

But he laughed and clowned with a heavy heart, and not only because the panning of *L'Éducation* continued to hurt. His disappointment had been sharpened by personal loss in that last year of the decade. Sainte-Beuve, who had been gravely ill for quite some time, unable to write except standing or lying, died on October 13, half an hour before Flaubert dropped by his flat on the rue Montparnasse. "Another one gone!" Flaubert informed Maxime Du Camp in Baden-Baden. "Our little band is diminished! The few of us left on the raft of the *Medusa* are disappearing." With whom could he talk about literature now? he asked. "That man loved it. And although we were not exactly friends, his death upsets me deeply. Everyone in France who holds a pen has experienced an irreparable loss." Princess Mathilde was grief-stricken, the more so as she had broken with Sainte-Beuve in a fit of temper when he published an article implicitly criticizing the regime's church policy in an opposition newspaper, *Le Temps*.

At that moment Flaubert might have suspected that he would not have many more literary conversations with another friend, Jules de Goncourt, who was following Baudelaire into the last, hellish phase of syphilitic dementia. During much of 1869 the Goncourt brothers traveled hither and yon in a desperate attempt to restore Jules' health: from the spa at Royat to the seashore at Trouville to a small country house near Saint-Gratien owned by Princess Mathilde. The least noise, not all originating outside his head, distracted Jules. Unable to sleep, he worked as best he could on a study of his dear friend Gavarni, and finished it with Edmond's help. Several months later, the passionate connoisseur of eighteenth-century French painting couldn't recognize the name Watteau. "Minute by minute, I see the haggard mask of imbecility slipping over this beloved face, which was once the very image of intelligence and irony," Edmond wrote in April 1870. "It is being gradually stripped of affection. It is being dehumanized." Aphasia became more pronounced. Memory went, then words, though ancient words returned at the very end, when he cried out: "Mother, Mother, to me, Mother." He died on June 20, 1870. Edmond pictured him a martyr to art rather than a victim of the pox, attributing his death to the endless toil imposed by devotion to a lapidary ideal.

The most grievous loss had come before these others. Louis Bouilhet died on July 8, 1869, at the age of forty-eight, after a brief illness. He began to complain in March of extreme exhaustion and various disorders, including edema, for which he had recourse to a fashionable nostrum called Wlinsi paper. Doctors prescribed one thing and another. There were occasional reprieves, but ultimately nothing helped. "Weird things are happening in my body; I've resolved to pay it no more heed," he wrote to Flaubert on April 24. As he grew sicker, the need to talk about it overcame his fear of being tiresome. "I'm dyspeptic and defiant, I admit it," he wrote on June 2. "There's physical cause, really there is. I assurè you that I am very sick, at times, and annoyances I would formerly have brushed off now enrage me." If he suspected that Flaubert wasn't taking him seriously enough, he had reason to think so, for on June 24 Flaubert wrote to George Sand: "My poor Bouilhet worries me. His nerves are so bad that doctors have advised him to take the waters at Vichy. He's in the grip of hypochondria. How strange, he who was once so cheerful!" A chilly, tight-fisted, provincial Bouilhet had infiltrated his old friend during the previous three years, he observed in a brief memoir. Did Flaubert feel that "hypochondria" was another symptom of this unhappy alteration? His misjudgment may have been encouraged by the presence in Bouilhet's life of a famous psychiatrist, Augustin Morel, medical director of the Saint-Yon asylum in Rouen and author of *Traité des dégénerescences physiques, intellectuelles et morales de l'espèce humaine*. At any rate, Flaubert learned the plain truth from his friend in Vichy, Dr Willemin, who wrote to him that Bouilhet, afflicted with kidney disease, was doomed. Achille Flaubert examined him and confirmed the death sentence. In July, Flaubert shuttled between Croisset and Bouilhet's house on the rue de Bihorel in Rouen. There he was faithfully cared for by Léonie Le Parfait, who refrained from suggesting that their common-law marriage be officialized lest Bouilhet realize the hopelessness of his situation. The truth was revealed, however, by Bouilhet's two sisters, pious old maids who came down from Cany vehemently insisting that he receive last rites. Their enraged brother would not allow a priest near him and, according to Flaubert, spent his dying days with a work by La Mettrie, the most godless of eighteenth-century philosophes. His final delirium was a collaborative gesture of sorts. Imagining the scenario of a drama about the Inquisition, he wanted Flaubert to hear it and called for him. He then shuddered, repeated the word *adieu*, tucked his head under Léonie's chin, and passed away.

Flaubert couldn't heed Bouilhet's call. The novelist who had created a paragon of bad timing in Frédéric Moreau had gone to Paris after convincing himself that Bouilhet looked stronger; as at Sainte-Beuve's bedside, he showed up too late for farewells. His concierge on the boulevard du Temple woke him at 9:00 a.m. with a telegram announcing Bouilhet's death. "I was alone," he wrote to Maxime Du Camp in Baden-Baden.

> I packed a bag . . . Then I paced the streets [near Saint-Lazare] until 1:00. It was hot outside, around the train station.* From Paris to Rouen I sat in a crowded carriage, opposite a tart who was smoking cigarettes and singing, with her feet propped on the banquette. When I saw the steeples of Mantes I thought I would go mad . . . I turned so pale that the woman offered me eau de Cologne, which helped. I was thirstier than I had ever been, even in the desert at Quseir.

In Rouen, on the rue de Bihorel, Flaubert couldn't bring himself to look inside the coffin, as he had done at the funerals of his sister, his father, and Alfred Le Poittevin. "I no longer have inner fortitude. I feel *worn*." One witness claimed to have seen him suffer an epileptic seizure, but there's no mention of it in his notes. He spent that first night out of doors on a mat in the garden, lying awake, looking at the moon, and thinking about his voyage through Egypt with Maxime. The tears he hadn't shed began to flow the next day, when he saw Bouilhet's coffin nailed shut for burial. Flanked by Charles d'Osmoy and his brother Achille, Flaubert followed the hearse along streets reminiscent of other such mortal processions to the Cimetière Monumental, where Bouilhet was interred near Flaubert's father in a ceremony that attracted several hundred mourners, including the prefect. "Would you believe that en route, behind the casket, I was able to relish the grotesqueness of the ceremony?" he exclaimed, furnishing another example of the distance that armed him against loss but also gave him an eye for the strangeness of the customary and an ear for the clink of received ideas. "I could hear the remarks that [Louis] was making to me about it. He was speaking in me. I had the impression that he was there, at my side, and that the two of us were following someone else's cortege. It was beastly hot, a storm was brewing. I was damp with sweat, and the climb to the Cimetière Monumental did me in." Achille and another mourner helped him away before the eulogies began.

"Poor old Monsignor," Flaubert wrote several days later, using one of his affectionate nicknames for Bouilhet. "My poor Bouilhet, how I loved you! I would have liked to see you rich and acclaimed! Triumphant! . . . What a loss! What an irreparable loss! What sure taste! What ingenuity! How he helped me clarify my ideas! What a critic! What a master! With him dead, I've lost my literary compass. Come, take heart. — Farewell."

---

*In a private memoir, he noted that he spent most of his time inside the Gare Saint-Lazare, dining on a veal cutlet and stuffed tomatoes, and having his hair trimmed in Félix's salon.

As he had denied the gravity of Bouilhet's illness by alleging hypochondria, so now Flaubert denied the finality of Bouilhet's death by struggling to keep his friend's name and image alive. There was the matter of a play Bouilhet had completed early in June, *Mademoiselle Aissé*. Plans to stage it at the Odéon theater would quite possibly have lapsed if not for Flaubert, who nagged the Odéon directors month after month. When they finally scheduled a production late in 1871, with Sarah Bernhardt as the titular heroine, he insisted on participating in every aspect of it. Bouilhet had never been so diligent on his own behalf. Flaubert played Bouilhet's impeccable steward, recommending actors, attending rehearsals, doing research for costumes in the Cabinet des Estampes of the Bibliothèque Nationale, and working on the stage set. Earlier, Michel Lévy had brought out Bouilhet's unpublished poems, *Dernières chansons,* with a preface by Flaubert. Another valiant attempt was made to resuscitate the long-buried *Château des cœurs*.

There was also the matter of a commemorative monument. "Being born Norman in literature has great advantages," Jules de Goncourt observed in July 1869, when still lucid enough to be splenetic. "Flaubert alive and Bouilhet dead are both proof of it. There is already talk of raising a monument to him — a monument to poor Bouilhet, who never had his own stamp or instrument and may never have written one original hemistich, Bouilhet the dramatist who spent his whole life making Hugo-like sublimity the way one makes a silk neckerchief!" He didn't live to gloat over the disappointments subsequently experienced by Flaubert on the committee charged with designing Bouilhet's monument and raising money for it. Not until 1877 did Rouen approve the construction of the fountain surmounted by a bust that now stands beside the municipal library. City councilmen had rejected this proposal earlier, provoking Flaubert's most famous diatribe against his compatriots. But that eloquent outburst awaits another chapter. Let us simply note here that Bouilhet was more alive for him in the heat of battle with ungrateful philistines than in the bust that commemorates his hollow victory, and note as well that it was Flaubert's second painful melee with Rouen over an image, the first having been over Pradier's head of Achille-Cléophas.

Jules Duplan died seven months after Bouilhet, in March 1870. Flaubert felt this loss all the more keenly for having visited Duplan twice a day in February at his deathbed. When the end came he reached out to Ivan Turgenev, with whom he had knit closer during the Russian writer's brief sojourns in Paris. "The great sorrow of this past winter was the death of my most intimate friend after Bouilhet," he wrote. "Those two blows, dealt in swift succession, have wrecked me. If that weren't enough, there is the lamentable state of two other friends, not so close to be sure, but nonetheless part of my immediate entourage. I have in mind Feydeau's paralysis and

Jules de Goncourt's imbecility. Sainte-Beuve's disappearance, pecuniary vexations, the nonsuccess of my novel, etc., etc., and, to top it all off, the rheumatism of my servant [Émile Colange, Narcisse Barette's successor, who had to be hospitalized]." A disfiguring outbreak of eczema completed his misery. Why, he asked, did Turgenev live so far away? "You are the only man with whom I like to converse. I no longer see anyone who concerns himself with art and poetry. The plebiscite, socialism, the 'International' and other such rubbish encumber everybody's brain."

Certainly Flaubert did not lack friends. He could call upon Du Camp when Du Camp wasn't in Baden-Baden, but Du Camp's close reading of *L'Éducation sentimentale* produced notes to Flaubert that betray a fundamental antipathy to Flaubert's esthetic purpose, and by then Du Camp was otherwise taken up with research for *Paris, ses organes*. George Sand, whose keen literary judgment he valued, gave him all the wealth of an informed heart, but Sand's world was her family. A fraternal soul mate, to whom he could speak *solus ad solum,* had always kept him seated in a sense of his own worth, and now he was bereft of one. What Montaigne, another melancholic, wrote about Étienne La Boëtie chimed with Flaubert's sentiments: "I was already so used and accustomed to being, in everything, one of two, that I now feel I am no more than half of one . . . There is no deed or thought in which I do not miss him — as he would have missed me; for just as he infinitely surpassed me in ability and virtue, so did he do so in the offices of friendship."

IN 1868 Louis-Napoleon jotted down notes for a novel he intended to publish as a serial in one of the official newspapers. It may have been inspired by Montesquieu's *Lettres persanes,* the Persian being a French shopkeeper named Benoit who immigrates to the United States in 1847, returns in April 1868, and, with eyes innocent of everything that had happened in France during the twenty-one-year interval, discovers a land utterly transformed for the better. The black ironclads at anchor in Brest, where he disembarks, have ended the naval supremacy of England. The railroad that speeds him to Paris, the electric telegraph that announces his arrival, the modern capital he doesn't recognize, all speak of France's rise from rags to riches. A crowd milling around the Hôtel de Ville has gathered not in protest, as he imagines at first, but to exercise its right to vote under a law of universal suffrage. M. Benoit notes that debtors are no longer imprisoned, that workers have been granted the right to strike, that measures have been taken to help the old and destitute, that public health boasts an impressive new Hôtel-Dieu on the Île de la Cité. "There are no riots, no political prisoners, no exiles!" he exclaims while observing that the lower cost of living brought about by free trade is a boon to all and all alike.

The emperor's desire to be seen as Saint George slaying the dragon of pauperdom was not baseless. The aggregate income of French industry rose by double that of the English during his regime, and agriculture, despite the deep-seated conservatism dramatized by Zola in *La Terre,* thrived. But most industrial workers did not benefit from liberal economics. Conditions for them were generally deplorable, and in newspapers that enjoyed far more freedom than M. Benoit remembered, urban discontent often spoke louder than rural prosperity. The reforms Napoleon sponsored in defiance of hard-line Bonapartists (Eugénie among them) only exasperated liberal opposition to his rule. Every concession made the remnants of despotism less tolerable. Deputies could no longer be easily intimidated. The financial sleight of hand by which Haussmann circumvented legislative authority to subsidize his epic reconstruction was exposed in a series of articles wittily entitled "Les Comptes fantastiques d'Haussmann."* The rabidly antigovernment paper *La Lanterne* set an example of scurrilous journalism. A law granting limited freedom of assembly begot 1848-style debating societies that transgressed those limits with impunity. Under the liberal Émile Ollivier, whom Louis-Napoleon appointed prime minister in January 1870, social and administrative reform progressed apace, and several months later a constitution formalizing parliamentary government was ratified by plebiscite. But opposition persisted, from both right and left. The emperor tired of it, tired even of governing. Tormented by sciatica, rheumatism, and bladder stones, which caused him to hemorrhage from the bladder, he appeared increasingly listless. Lord Malmesbury, who had been England's foreign secretary in the 1850s, found him "much altered in appearance and looking very ill" during an informal visit.

The enemy abroad proved to be as intractable as the opposition at home. Since Austria's defeat at Sadowa in 1866, every turn of events had brought Prussia nearer the brink of war with France. Louis-Napoleon found himself caught between Bismarck, who held that "the general organization of Germany" required a collective bloodbath, and a French populace incensed by Prussian self-aggrandizement but solidly arrayed against measures that might have given France a daunting response to it, notably universal military service. Private life offered no escape from his dilemmas. While he grew more indecisive, Eugénie grew more bellicose. Would her son ever rule if her husband did not campaign? Charles Oman, the English historian, makes clear how matters stood in his description of a ceremony he witnessed as a child on holiday in France. "The Prince Imperial, then a boy of twelve, was a cadet, and was to drill a company of other cadets of his own age on the gravel in front of the Palace," he wrote.

---

*Literally, "The Fantastic Accounts of Haussmann," a play on *Les Contes fantastiques d'Hoffmann* (The Tales of Hoffmann), *contes* and *comptes* being homonyms.

On a bench overlooking the gravel sat a very tired old gentleman, rather hunched together, and looking decidedly ill. I do not think I should have recognized him but for his spiky moustache. He was anything but terrifying in a tall hat and a rather loosely fitting frock coat . . . Behind him stood the Empress Eugénie, a splendid figure, straight as a dart, and to my young eyes the most beautiful thing that I had ever seen . . . She was wearing a zebra-striped black-and-white silk dress, with very full skirts, [and] a black-and-white bonnet. But it was the way she wore her clothes, and not the silks themselves, that impressed the beholder, young or old . . . The Empress was a commanding figure, and dominated the whole group on the terrace — the Emperor, huddled in his seat, was a very minor show. She appeared extremely satisfied and self-confident as she watched the little manoeuvres below. Her son, the Prince Imperial, . . . drilled his little flock with complete success and not a single hitch or hesitation. His mother beamed down upon him. The boys marched off, and the spectators broke up after indulging in a little Vive l'Empereur.

Louis-Napoleon may well have been thinking that compared with King Wilhelm's huge, well-oiled machine, his army loomed no larger than this diminutive band. An attempt at reform had produced a reserve manifestly unfit for battle. The general staff lacked cohesion. The legislature had cut the defense budget. But among patriots, a mystical belief in the Napoleonic legend, brave rhetoric, and exorbitant faith in the new chassepot rifle outweighed evidence that counseled against force of arms. As such evidence mounted, war fever spread, until it seemed to young Charles Oman, at least, that France was one large parade ground. "In France there seemed to be bands and banners or military display almost every day, . . . congresses of orphéonistes with gorgeous lyres on their standards, or of pompiers with magnificent brass helmets," he recalled. "The soldier was everywhere, very conspicuous because of his various multicoloured and sometimes fantastic uniform: . . . the trooper of the Cent Gardes — the hundred horsemen — in the brightest sky-blue, with cuirass and steel helmet; the bearskins of the grenadiers of the Imperial Guard; the white breeches and black gaiters of the original grognards of Napoleon I; the Zouaves of the Guard with their floppy tasselled headgear and immense baggy breeches, with yellow lace upon their absurdly small cut-away jackets."

Émile Zola regularly interrupted the extravaganza with a memento mori in *La Tribune*, predicting that unless France sobered up, the parti-colored cast of actors would soon be indistinguishable skeletons. On All Souls' Day 1868 he mourned Frenchmen who had fallen in battle throughout Europe and pictured an old lady bereft of her son scanning the horizon for Sebastopol. The fallen were evoked again in July 1869, when workers began sprucing up the Champs-Élysées with oriflammes to celebrate the hundredth anniversary of Napoleon I's birth. "The administration should assemble not the quick but the dead," Zola proclaimed. "It should sound the call to arms all over Europe, in Italy, in Spain, in Austria, in Russia. And from all these battlefields, hordes would rise. Ah, what a festive gathering it would make, a gathering of the butchered. Paris would be too small." Flaubert envisioned a regressive movement to racial warfare. The imminent slaughter, he wrote to George Sand in July 1870, wouldn't even have a pretext. "It's the desire to fight for its own sake."

Had Zola and Flaubert read the foreign minister's diary, they would have found the opposite of warmongering. "I want peace, and so does France," Count Napoleon Daru wrote upon taking office. "Our policy is to maintain the status quo; to achieve this, let us avoid upsetting Europe. We must prevent ourselves from raising 'questions,' and if they do crop up, let us snuff them out immediately." But his observation that Prussia, too, wanted peace betrays singular ignorance of the pains Bismarck was taking to fabricate a casus belli. Events soon disabused him. Bismarck laid a trap in July 1870 when he prevailed upon King Wilhelm's relative Leopold to present his candidacy for the vacant throne of Spain, knowing full well that France could not allow itself to be sandwiched between Hohenzollerns. What followed might have been staged by Giraudoux in a nineteenth-century version of *La Guerre de Troie n'aura pas lieu*. Leopold withdrew his candidacy at Wilhelm's urging, but Daru's successor, the duc de Gramont, a militant Catholic animated by hatred of Protestant Prussia, thought that Louis-Napoleon should elicit from Wilhelm a promise never again to put Leopold forward. Wilhelm agreed. Bismarck then went to work and, with some mischievous editing of a telegram sent from the spa at Ems, made the agreement sound like an outright refusal. Even so, Louis-Napoleon and Ollivier would have given diplomacy another chance. They could not. Inflamed by the press, which generally denounced Prussia's "slap in the face," Parisians mobbed the streets demanding satisfaction. Eugénie made it known that there was no avoiding war "if one cared for the honor of France." On Bastille Day the cabinet assembled and, after five hours, authorized Leboeuf, minister of war, to order mobilization. The army, Leboeuf declared with a rhetorical flourish that swept aside inconvenient facts, was prepared "down to the last gaiter button." (The Prussian army outnumbered the French by several hundred thousand and had superior artillery.) Two days later, legislators voted funds for war. When Adolphe Thiers, the former prime minister, attempted to argue against the jingoistic hysteria, he was heckled by colleagues of every political stripe; he then joined the majority. Only 10 of 255 in parliament demurred. It took courage to do so. The huge crowd that had gathered outside the Palais Bourbon, spilling across the bridge and draping itself over statuary, went wild when news spread of the legislature's vote. One spectator was re-minded of the frenzied populace in ancient Rome climbing the Vestals' tribune at the Coliseum to demand the execution of a gladiator.

In a letter to George Sand, Flaubert unhappily endorsed the truth of Plautus's maxim, quoted by Hobbes, that "man is a wolf to man" — *homo homini lupus* — and began the third and final version of *La Tentation de Saint Antoine*. No sooner had war against Prussia been declared, on July 19, than news arrived from Rome that a Vatican Council had voted to recognize the doctrinal infallibility of the pope. Votes were cast during a violent thunder-storm, which some took to be a divine expression of protest against the new idolatry.

XX

<em>~~~~~~~~</em>

War Years

CABDRIVERS IN the neighborhood of the Parc Monceau, the Bibliothèque Impériale, and the Bibliothèque de l'Institut came to recognize Gustave Flaubert during the frigid winter of 1869–70. He commuted regularly between his flat on the rue Murillo and those two great repositories, with an occasional sortie farther afield to the Bibliothèque de l'Arsenal. When not lying incapacitated by recurrent bouts of flu, organizing a benefit to raise money for Louis Bouilhet's monument, or sleeping, which he did a great deal of, he spent his time reading esoterica. *La Tentation de Saint Antoine* sent him back to fourth-century Egypt and theological creeds comparable in their profusion to the utopias spawned during the 1840s. His bibliography was stupendous. It included Jacques Matter's history of Gnosticism, the abbé Pluquet's dictionary of heresies (*Mémoires pour servir à l'histoire des égarements de l'esprit humain par rapport à la religion chrétienne*), Saint Augustine's *De haeresibus*, Adolphe Franck's work on the Kabbalah, Saint Epiphanius's *Contra octoginta haereses opium eximium*, Philostratus's narrative of Apollonius of Tyana's travels and miracles, Isaac de Beausobre's history of Manichaeanism, Le Nain de Tillemont's encyclopedic monograph on the ecclesiastical history of the first six centuries, Gibbon's *Decline and Fall*, Eugène Haag's history of Christian dogmas, Kant's *Critique of Pure Reason*. To

George Sand he complained about the ordeal of plowing through Plotinus's rebarbative *Enneads*, all six sections of it. In March, Alfred Maury was asked to help him find material on Saint Pacoma's *Revelations* and a Coptic manuscript entitled *Pistis-Sophia*. Sand thought that he might be overdoing it. He thought otherwise. "No, my dear, good-hearted Master!" he rejoined. "What I need now is not country air but work."

A bleakness worse than anything he could remember made him vulnerable to illness and exhaustion. It may not have been until the noise over *L'Éducation sentimentale* subsided that Bouilhet's absence began to sink in. Bouilhet had been the audience for whom he wrote his books and the midwife who delivered them, he told George Sand. "He understood my thought more clearly than I did. His death has left a void of which I become more sensible every day." Flaubert soldiered on, reading one recondite text after another, as if to stuff the empty place with erudition or to hermetically seal it off from life, but it yawned ever wider. In the figurative sense, all of his letters, especially those to Sand, had a black border of bereavement. They dwelt on his intellectual solitude, his "black melancholy," his peevishness, his misanthropy. He would turn fifty in 1871, but old age was upon him even before he had rounded out his half century, he lamented. "I won't have it," Sand protested. "You are not entering old age. There is no old age here in the sense of 'peevish' and 'misanthropic.' On the contrary, when one is good, one becomes better, and since you are already better than most, you are bound to become exquisite. Moreover, you boast when you represent yourself as angry with 'everything and everyone.' You're incapable of it. In the face of sorrow you are vulnerable, like all tender souls. The tough-minded are those who don't love. You will never be tough, much to your credit. Neither should one live alone. When you've recovered, you must embrace life and not husband your strength for yourself alone." Her message didn't chime with his devotion to the struggles of a desert anchorite.

George Sand hoped that spring would change things for the better. It had the opposite effect. Croisset, where Flaubert reestablished himself in May, might have helped him mend physically, but the emotional toll taken by his work spoiled the good of walks in the woods, swims in the Seine, and copious meals. He set aside *La Tentation* to write a preface for Bouilhet's posthumous poems and found himself thinking incessantly about the poet himself. Croisset was fraught with memories of his indispensable friend. "Here I encounter his ghost behind every bush, on the couch in my study, even in my clothes, in the dressing gowns he'd borrow," Flaubert confided to Edmond de Goncourt on June 26, 1870, four days after attending Jules' funeral at the Montmartre cemetery. A similar lament reached Caroline Commanville in Luchon, the Pyreneen spa where spectacular scenery failed to distract her from her loveless marriage. "My life has been completely upset by Bouilhet's death. I no longer have *anyone* to talk to! It's hard!" Not much of what he said each day made an impression on Mme Flaubert, who had become quite deaf. Altogether unwell, the old lady spoke about little but her ailments and the family fortune, which was less robust than ever, though hardly wasted. She complained that vendors were taking advantage of their extreme negligence to rob them blind. Bills were raining on her "like roof tiles." Could she afford to replace the unmarried servant who had been dismissed after getting pregnant, unapologetically, for the second time in three years?

Flaubert hoped to improve his own finances by asking Michel Lévy for the few thousand francs the publisher had said he wouldn't quibble over if *L'Éducation sentimentale* made money. Their conversation only added hurt pride to loneliness. That *L'Éducation* had lost money was irrelevant, Flaubert felt. Didn't the profits from *Madame Bovary* justify his request? And in any case what were four thousand francs to Lévy, who was building handsome new offices for the firm on rue Auber, near the Opéra? "Can you imagine, he proposed to *lend* me three or four thousand francs, interest free, *provided* my next novel belong to him on the same terms, that is, eight thousand francs a volume," he fumed in a letter to George Sand, who had told Lévy that Flaubert was strapped for cash.

> If he didn't say it once, he said it thirty times: "I am doing this to oblige you, my word of honor"! So, his generosity, his tender feelings for me all come down to this, an advance on my next book, with a fee fixed in advance . . . He must think me a real numbskull, since I didn't betray my astonishment. I said I would consider it, but there's no consideration to be given. I don't lack friends, beginning with you, who would lend me money *interest free*. Thank God it hasn't come to that . . . I am content to repeat, with Athalie, "God of the Jews, you've won the day!"

Her reply was more levelheaded than his complaint. "What do you expect? The Jew will always be a Jew," she began, placating him with a slur that reflected the anti-Semitic bias commonly shared by nineteenth-century socialists without infringing on her affection for Lévy.*

---

*An article by Sand's former mentor Pierre Leroux illustrates the point. Entitled "Jews as Kings of the Age," it invokes nostalgically the age of Napoleonic glory. "Am I then as ancient as Methusaleh? I'm only fifty! Only fifty years separate the victories of our fathers and the notable deeds of M. de Rothschild! Are such reversals conceivable? Napoleon's true successor is the Jew, who, dry-eyed and with a soul moved only by the passion for gain, foresaw the future when the present hung in the balance at Waterloo, and who interpreted Holy Scripture in his own way, saying to himself: the fruits of victory will be gathered not by those who fight here but by those who will fight tomorrow at the London Stock Exchange."

It could have been worse. He bought one volume from you, the contract didn't spell things out clearly. Had he been so disposed, he might have given you only ten thousand francs and said that the rest of the manuscript was also his. He honestly didn't expect two volumes, for he was surprised when I mentioned it, and at first, in an unguarded moment, he blurted out: "But in that case it's twenty thousand francs." He must have realized, on second thought, that the contract leaves much to his discretion; I've never heard him repeat that figure in subsequent talks . . . So there it is, he's paid you sixteen thousand and intends to pay no more. I still hope to bring him around, but it will take some doing.

When Sand offered him as much as he needed, he gratefully declined, for Dr Cloquet had meanwhile lent him three or four thousand francs, and his nephew Ernest Commanville, who now handled his financial affairs, had somehow winkled several thousand more out of his own account. He was determined to break with Lévy. "I won't even answer him. These quarrels are screamingly disruptive . . . I'd rather live less well and give money no thought whatever."

He would indeed find another publisher, but, as we shall see, the future did nothing to resolve an inner conflict between the "bourgeoisophobe" who measures his force by the negations in him and the bourgeois for whom money argued manhood, between Flaubert suffering the humiliation of dependence and Flaubert exploiting the generosity of a parent. He could more easily separate himself from Lévy than from his native demons. "Oh! How I would love to stop thinking about my poor *self!*" he protested to George Sand on July 2. "I feel lost in the desert."

FIVE MONTHS later, a sinister force swept him out of his study and distracted him from Bouilhet, Lévy, and Saint Anthony. It spoke German.

When Louis-Napoleon, suffering terribly from stones, arrived at Metz on July 28 to take command of the army, it was assumed on both sides that France would march first. "Whatever the road beyond our frontiers," he told the troops in his Order of the Day, "we shall come across the glorious tracks of our fathers. We shall prove worthy of them. All France follows you with its fervent prayers, and the eyes of the world are upon you. Hinging on our success is the fate of liberty and civilization." His rhetoric rang hollow, not least because the invalid could barely sit on a horse much less develop a capacity for generalship. Neither he nor his commanders — Bazaine, MacMahon — had anything like the military intelligence and dominant will of Count Helmuth von Moltke, who turned France's confusion into early victories, first at Wissembourg, then at Fröschwiller, where, by one account, fallen soldiers in their light blue jackets lay so densely packed that the battleground looked like a field of flax. After several more ferocious engagements in which artillery won the day, German troops had gained an open road through the Vosges Mountains into Lorraine. Meanwhile another German army had advanced on Metz and its immense fortifications from Saarbrücken, forcing a bewildered French general staff to improvise defensive strategies. One week after his invocation of Great Shades, the emperor — a defeated man who, as one witness wrote, looked "much aged, much weakened, and possessing nothing of the bearing of the leader of an army" — would have retreated to Paris, had Eugénie not discouraged it. "Have you considered all the consequences that would follow from your return to Paris under the shadow of two reverses?" she objected. Instead, he left General Bazaine in command and pitched camp at Chalons-sur-Marne in Champagne, where a new Rhine army was to be assembled from raw recruits, battalions of the Garde Mobile, and remnants of Mac-Mahon's demoralized corps, which had narrowly escaped the German pincer movement. Bazaine never made it west with his 154,000 men. Moltke fought him at Gravelotte, drove him back into Metz, and detached several corps to keep him bottled up there while wheeling en masse toward a decisive confrontation on the Meuse.

Flaubert's letters make only one thing clear, that the fog of war obscured any understanding on the home front of these calamitous events. "No news of the army!" he wrote to his niece from Paris during the second week of August, when he and Michel Lévy were discussing a posthumous edition of Bouilhet's verse. "I've just come from the place de la Concorde. Everything is calm. But the lily-livered attitude of Parisians is unspeakable! I'm indignant. The most contradictory rumors are circulating. All one can say for sure is that everyone is reeling. And what a frightful mess we're in . . . As for advice, I have only one piece of it to give you: *Prudence!*" A week later, on August 17, he informed George Sand that waiting for news had made writing and reading impossible. By then the Hobbesian pessimist had become a swaggering patriot frustrated that he could not bear arms, who decided instead to serve as a volunteer nurse at the Hôtel-Dieu under Achille. "If Paris is besieged, I'll go down there and shoot. My rifle is primed," he wrote to Sand. "But until then I'm in Croisset where I *must* remain." He predicted, accurately, that a "social" war would follow the conflict with Germany. "That's where universal suffrage, a new God I find quite as stupid as the old one, will have led us."

The day before Flaubert wrote to Sand, Louis-Napoleon arrived at Chalons, where he and his general staff lost precious time balancing political exigency against military logic. The great question was whether to march east again and somehow unite with forces commanded by Bazaine, or to give up Alsace-Lorraine and fall back on Paris. More irresolute than ever, Louis-Napolcon ordered a retreat on the advice of staff, who thought that Bazaine might not escape his besieged position, then reversed himself at the urging of Eugénie, who made it known through the minister of war,

Palikao, that Paris would rise against the Empire unless he emerged victorious from battle. German cavalry sighted near Chalons forced the army to decamp for Reims, thirty miles away, but there 130,000 men stood paralyzed, like an ancient horde awaiting divine omens. Mac-Mahon finally took matters in hand and reissued the order to retreat, whereupon chance played him dirty. No sooner had the order been drafted than a message arrived informing him that Bazaine expected to break free. This optimistic announcement altered everything. If Bazaine could free himself from Metz, the matter would no longer be one of marching to his relief but of joining him in battle. Mac-Mahon immediately made an about-face and gave orders for the westward retreat to be canceled. Ill-trained and ill-supplied columns then wound east across the stubbled chalk plateau of Champagne toward phantom comrades. After three days their situation became desperate. While reports of an enemy presence abounded, nothing was seen of Bazaine, who had in fact never ventured outside his fortified position. Harried by Saxon troops erupting from the Argonne forest, Mac-Mahon found himself cut off on three sides, and when he decided to flee north toward Belgium, the government forbade it. Palikao did not think that prudence was the better part of valor. "Should you abandon Bazaine," he warned, "revolution will break out in Paris and you yourself be attacked by the entire enemy force . . . You have at least thirty-six hours' march over the crown prince [Frederick William of Prussia], perhaps forty-eight; you have nothing in front of you but a feeble part of the contingents blockading Metz . . . Everyone here has felt the necessity of freeing Bazaine, and the anxiety with which we follow your movements is intense."

Where politics dictated military strategy, the result was self-immolation. German cavalry watched from afar as Mac-Mahon's soldiers marched forward, not knowing whither or why. A first disastrous engagement occurred on August 30 at Beaumont, near the river Meuse. The next day other units crossed the Meuse five miles downstream, within sight of a fortified town called Sedan, which lay cradled between marshlands and wooded slopes. There, in what he viewed as an eminently defensible position, Mac-Mahon declared that his men should rest. And there, in what Moltke knew to be a gigantic snare, they died by the thousands when German artillery rained shells upon them from hilltop batteries. On September 1, 1870, after twelve pulverizing hours of bombardment, Napoleon III hoisted the white flag. In a message to the king of Prussia, he surrendered his sword and complied with a request that he invest an officer with full power to negotiate the army's capitulation. Moltke then ordered his own troops to march on Paris. One day earlier, on August 31, Flaubert had assured an unidentified correspondent that the tide was apparently turning in France's favor. "A prisoner who escaped from the hands of the Prussians gave one of my friends *excel-*

lent news this morning," he wrote. "Mac-Mahon and Bazaine have gained the upper hand. The latter has worked wonders during the past fortnight."

Louis-Napoleon had fallen, but not yet France. In Paris, a reenactment of 1848 took place on September 4. Once again the populace invaded the Palais Bourbon. Once again deputies of the left (who were opposed to a council of regency, under Eugénie) departed for the Hôtel de Ville, waded through an immense crowd, and declared France a republic. Like the Orléans family, Eugénie fled to England, where Louis-Napoleon, after six months of imprisonment, would join her in the three-story Georgian mansion she occupied at Chislehurst, not far from Greenwich. His cousin, Prince Napoleon-Jérôme had preceded him and set up house in London as the consort of a well-traveled harlot named Cora Pearl. On September 3, one day before the Government of National Defense seized power, Princess Mathilde, accompanied by two servants, left her house on the rue de Courcelles. At Dieppe, Dumas fils, who spent summers nearby, advised her against boarding the Channel steamer, as inspectors were reportedly on the lookout after seizing baggage believed to be hers. Did it contain certain precious objects and silver plate formerly hidden for her at Croisset? Rumor had it that customs found a huge fortune, forty or fifty million francs, and the *Journal de Rouen*, among other newspapers, published this canard. All Mathilde remembered was a dash for the Belgian frontier, which she crossed at Mons with a single trunk of linen. Apart from her pictures and jewels, most everything of value had been left at her town house and at Saint-Gratien, where German officers made themselves comfortable.

On September 7, when Mathilde was resident at Mons, Flaubert sent her a message through Claudius Popelin, her most recent lover. Days were spent waiting for word from the front, he reported. What news they had seemed to indicate that the wind was shifting in France's favor, and Flaubert, always at war with the epileptic who couldn't sally forth, roared his loudest.

> What reassures me is that no one is thinking about peace. If the Prussians reach Paris, it will be formidable. All of France will hurry to the capital. Better that this country should suffer extinction than be humiliated! But we'll conquer them, we'll drive them back beyond the Rhine, to the beat of drums. The most peaceable bourgeois, men like myself, are perfectly resolute in our determination to die rather than surrender. Who would have said that six months ago! Whatever comes of all this, another world will begin. And I feel too old to learn new ways.

Deploring the fragility of mankind's civilized order while proudly expounding a genealogical myth that justified his claim to savage bloodlines, he spoke for and against war without fear of contradiction. A letter to

George Sand written on the same day as the one to Mathilde is typical. "One must accustom oneself to what is man's natural state, that is, to evil," it begins.

> Greeks of the Periclean age created art without knowing whether they'd have anything to eat the following day. Let us be Greeks! However, I must admit to you, dear master, that I feel myself to be rather more savage than Greek. The blood of my forebears, the Natchez or the Hurons,* boils in the literary man's veins, and I have a serious, senseless, animal *desire to fight*. Try to explain it! The idea of making peace now exasperates me. And I'd rather Paris were set ablaze (like Moscow) than see Prussians entering it. But it hasn't yet come to that. I've read several *exemplary* letters from the front. A country in which soldiers write such things cannot simply be swallowed up. France is a feisty old nag, and its spirit will show . . . My nephew Commanville has been commissioned to make *a thousand* biscuit cases a day for the army, in addition to huts. You can see that we're not asleep up here.

After September 4 he was no longer a volunteer nurse preparing for the arrival of casualties but a National Guardsman taking lessons in what he called "military art" to defend his township. Neighbors elected him lieutenant, and he played the part enthusiastically. At riverside drills, his big, sonorous voice barked commands that must have traveled clear across the Seine. A drawing of Flaubert in baggy, blue dress with an ill-fitting kepi perched on his large head suggests that the would-be warrior cut a Falstaffian figure marching his men back and forth, or, toward the end of September when German troops surrounded Paris, leading them on night patrols through the Canteleu woods. "Just now," he wrote to Caroline, "I gave 'my men' a paternal lecture, in which they were told that anyone who retreated would find my saber thrust through his belly and that I should be dealt with likewise. Your old duffer of an uncle rose to epic heights! What a strange thing the brain is, especially mine! Would you believe it that now I feel almost cheerful! Yesterday I resumed work on my book and have my appetite back! Everything wears away, even anguish!"† Along with a junior lieutenant and the captain, he informed Canteleu's mayor that he would re-

---

*The "Huron" is based upon the life of an ancestor in his maternal line. One branch of the family settled in Canada in the seventeenth century, the Lepoutrelles. A Jean-François Le Poutrel de Bellecourt entered the fur trade.

†One scholar, who found no record of Flaubert's service in departmental archives, concluded that he had never been a member of the National Guard but had improvised a squad consisting of a doctor friend named Fortin, a farmhand, a shoemaker, and a ferryman. It is most unlikely, however, that Flaubert would have perpetrated a hoax on Caroline.

sign unless a court was established to punish indiscipline. "We have no authority over our pitiful militia." By then the situation did not warrant bravado. In correspondence, "we're waiting for the Prussians" became a doomsday refrain. Only a month later he was to lament that the upshot of it all would be a world of abject militarism.

The Germans subdued and garrisoned the belt of country between Alsace-Lorraine and the Île-de-France so quickly that Moltke began to entertain the possibility of hunting game back home in Prussia during the fall. He thought his men could sit tight at a safe distance from Paris's perimeter forts until the besieged city surrendered to hunger. With Bazaine's army sequestered and Mac-Mahon's disbanded, was not France, outside the encirclement, defenseless? Neither he nor Bismarck anticipated one of the more remarkable second efforts in the history of warfare. On October 7, Léon Gambetta, a famously dynamic orator serving as minister of the interior, escaped from Paris in a balloon, joined fellow ministers at Tours, and, with General de Freycinet, improvised a whole new army, the Army of the Loire, which proceeded to drive Bavarian troops out of Orléans. Alarm spread all along the line of German positions. The Loire valley became a war theater, forcing this provisional government to relocate farther south, in Bordeaux.

This accomplishment was a candle flickering in the gloom. On October 23, Flaubert, who was certainly not alone in laboring under the misapprehension that the war had claimed few lives until then, wrote to Princess Mathilde that if Bazaine should break out of Metz and the Loire Army march on Paris, defeat might yet be averted. "Parisians will collectively hurl themselves upon the enemy, I don't doubt it." The French had enough cannon and men, he breezily asserted. All they lacked was Napoleon. "What we need are leaders, a staff in full command. Ah, for a man! A man! Just one! A good brain to save us! As for the provinces, I consider them lost. The Prussians can fan out indefinitely, but so long as Paris is not taken, France still breathes." Did he believe it? Perhaps not, and in any event the outer ripples of war disturbed his optimism. With factories closed and farmsteads torched, the unemployed and dispossessed wandered in bands through the Norman countryside. There were days when three or four hundred showed up at Croisset. To make matters worse, the Bonenfant relatives, eleven adults and three children, descended upon him and stayed for some weeks, first at Croisset, then at Rouen. Besieged from without by beggars who occasionally turned nasty and from within by distressed kinfolk, Flaubert couldn't concentrate on anything. "What a sad sheik is Bonenfant," he grumbled to Caroline, who had left Dieppe for London at Commanville's insistence. "The man can't even carry a package! [He has gone to Rouen and] I'm feeling better now that I can't hear him coughing, spitting, and blowing his nose. He'd wake me up in the morning, through the walls. His noises reached my study from the back of the garden."* Still, he conceded that being guests in these circumstances was as painful as being a host.

For many, the candle flickered out on October 27, when Bazaine's surrender freed thousands of crack German troops to serve elsewhere. The ill-trained French often acquitted themselves well on the Loire front and around Amiens, but these were, at best, campaigns of heroic futility. The siege had reduced Parisians to starvation, Krupp cannons kept lofting shells into the capital from miles away, and German forces marched inexorably down the Seine valley and west from Gisors across the alluvial plain.

They arrived on December 5. Twenty-five thousand famished, bone-weary French troops had spent the previous night massed in front of the Hôtel de Ville, expecting to defend the city. At 5 a.m. their general pulled them back toward Honfleur and left the municipal council, which included Achille Flaubert, to tell furious Rouennais that he considered resistance with a ragtag division unthinkable. In midafternoon, fifes and drums led the German Eighth Army Corps down the rue de Beauvoisine to the Hôtel de Ville, where its commandant showed the mayor a street map of the city indicating the location of billets for eight thousand troops. Infantry were assigned to houses along the quay, cavalry to the Faubourg Cauchoise. Natives and invaders would stew together, in one infamy.

By then, Flaubert and his mother, who could hardly walk, had moved out of Croisset to occupy the Commanvilles' flat on the quai du Havre. They now shared it with two enemy soldiers, which wasn't as bad as sharing the house at Croisset with ten dragoons who, in their absence, ended up occupying every room. "What a night, the one preceding our departure from Croisset," he wrote to Caroline on December 18, not knowing whether the letter would travel across the Channel but needing to believe that conversation with the outside world was still possible in a virtual state of siege. The billeted soldiers behaved tolerably well. Intolerable were the scabbards of German officers scraping the sidewalk, the neighing of German horses, the compulsory labor of fetching hay. "Time not spent in running errands for our German masters . . . is spent in whispering questions among ourselves or weeping in a corner. I wasn't born yesterday, and I've suffered major losses in life. Well, they were nothing compared with what I'm enduring now . . . What shame! What shame!" Complaints of frequent nausea may have referred to the prodrome of epileptic seizures or to the ef-

---

*Since his voyage in Egypt, Flaubert used the term *sheik* to signify, as he defined it himself, "an inept old man of independent means, well-considered, well-established." Flaubert's correspondence with Caroline became aleatory in November and December, when German troops occupied the Caux region and the Vexin normand, interrupting postal routes.

fects of potassium bromide. His "sore brain" made writing anything, even letters, difficult, he told Caroline. With all that, he had under his care a mother who moved about the flat leaning on furniture, when she moved at all. His niece's return had become imperative. It was her duty to rejoin them as soon as she could do so safely, he asserted, and he drummed home the message a month later, in more recriminatory terms. "Your poor grand-mother goes from bad to worse. There are days when she no longer speaks at all (her head causes her so much pain, she says). She complains that no one pays her visits, and when people do so, she doesn't utter a word! If the war drags on and your absence as well, what will come of it! Ah, how dis-astrous was your decision to go away! We wouldn't have suffered half as much if you had remained." Giving the knife another twist, he added that the old lady often woke up in the dead of night tearfully calling for her granddaughter.

Fearful that damage might have been done at Croisset, where his valet, Émile Colange, kept watch, he went to see and ascertained that the Huns, so-called, had not invaded his study except to borrow books, which he found littered about in other rooms. Quantities of wood — three or four hundred francs' worth, he estimated — had been burned. With work on *La Tentation* suspended, Flaubert felt lost, sleeping even later than usual and reading vagrantly. His circle of friends, when they drifted back from abroad or from the front, included Charles Lapierre, a journalist whose wife, Valérie, and widowed sister-in-law, Léonie Brainne, had inherited Rouen's second daily, *Le Nouvelliste de Rouen*, from their father. It also included Ed-mond Laporte, who would stand by Flaubert loyally in the coming years. A self-made man far more cultivated than most men of that description, La-porte ran a lace factory at Grand-Couronne, near Rouen, which he had re-stored to prosperity after becoming its director in 1859 at age twenty-seven. Eleven years younger than Flaubert, he was an appreciative ear for brilliant prose and a sober mind for finances. Then there was Achille Flaubert, to whom Gustave drew closer during that difficult juncture. Much put upon, his older brother wore two hats, being both chief surgeon at the Hôtel-Dieu and a member of the municipal council, which mediated painfully between a foreign overlord and a hostile, exploited population. At one point it was rumored (falsely) that he had been killed by local hooligans shooting up City Hall.

On January 24 the Duke of Mecklenburg replaced Manteuffel in Rouen, and Flaubert's fears that the occupation might get worse under a new master proved to be well-founded. Hundreds of families in the work-ing-class district of Saint-Sever found themselves squeezed into alcoves when billeted troops arrived at night. The German quartermaster de-manded that the city, which normally consumed sixteen thousand head of cattle a year, provide him nine thousand a week. More horses needed more fodder. "What rage! What desolation!" Flaubert cried. "This frightful war never ends! Will it end when Paris capitulates? But how can Paris surrender? With whom will Prussia wish to treat? How does one establish a government? When I contemplate the future, . . . I see only a great black hole and feel dizzy."

All of his questions were answered in due course. On January 17, 1871, the last French army corps patched together under Gambetta's provincial administration was defeated by General von Werder's troops near Belfort, in the east. After several weeks of clandestine shuttling between Paris and Versailles, where Bismarck had established German headquarters, Jules Favre, minister of foreign affairs, negotiated an armistice on January 28. Its central provision was that France would, in free elections, form a government with which Germany could treat. When word of the armistice reached Bordeaux, Gambetta took umbrage. Instructed to announce elections for February 8, he obeyed, but in a spirit of defiance. "In place of the reactionary and cowardly Assembly of which the enemy dreams," ran one decree placarded on streets throughout Bordeaux, "let us install an Assembly that is truly national and republican, desiring peace, if peace assures our honor . . . but capable of willing war also, ready for anything rather than to assist in the murder of France." Implacable resistance to the Germans, or *la guerre à outrance*, was by then the position of only a small minority, except among working-class Parisians and in Alsace-Lorraine. Frenchmen wanted peace, and Gambetta, honoring what he acknowledged to be the general will, resigned his ministries. Up north wagons laden with food entered Paris, which surrendered its perimeter forts.

Flaubert, who fulminated against the surrender ("France is so low, so dishonored, so disgraced that I wish it to disappear completely"), may not have understood just how fortunate he had been until, during this lull, stories about the siege reached him from Paris. After Moltke had encircled the capital on September 19, many writers and artists had rallied to its defense by joining the National Guard (no longer a bourgeois preserve). Manet was commissioned lieutenant and served in the artillery under the painter Ernest Meissonier, famous for his battle scenes. Degas commuted between Montmartre and a gun emplacement in the outer fortifications ten miles away. Trapped by an enemy they couldn't engage, men played at war but starved in earnest, along with several million other prisoners whose dreams of rescue became a martyrdom of hunger. "I spent all my time queuing up at the door of butchers, bakers, coal men, marching, standing at the fortifications," recounted one survivor. "What an existence! It's unbelievable, the suffering we endured and the things we ate. There was nothing left in

Paris but black pudding and stringy horsemeat, expensive and dry, oh so dry. A potato was a miracle . . . I almost ate a dog's head, which the butcher sold as veal." Once the quarter-million sheep grazing in the Bois de Boulogne had been consumed, Parisians dined on rat pie, or if they had Victor Hugo's means, on bear slaughtered at the zoo. One of Paris's gastronomic palaces, Voisin, served Edmond de Goncourt elephant sausage. People tried to fool hunger by spending long hours in bed.

Early in February, Paris invaded Bordeaux, or so it seemed when journalists, power brokers, actresses, and boulevardiers flocked south, some to observe the newly elected Assembly, which met at the Grand-Théâtre, others to convalesce. Second Empire high life resumed after a morose intermission. "The streets swarmed with officers of every rank and branch," wrote one witness in that city, "with wheeler-dealers alert to opportunity . . . with vendors hawking an illustrated newspaper whose title, *La Victoire*, stung us in those days of defeat. Hotels were taken by storm, theaters were booked solid every night. Bordeaux's population grew hourly, and almost all the deputies arrived before the inaugural meeting." One deputy who came late was Victor Hugo. Hailed en route from Paris by crowds shouting, "Vive Victor Hugo! Vive la République!" Hugo met even larger crowds in Bordeaux, where he, Louis Blanc, Gambetta, and Clemenceau joined against rural conservatives eager to buy peace at any price. A minority within parliament, these republican stalwarts found support outside it among Bordelais whose demonstrations became so boisterous that light infantry and horse guards ended up patrolling the streets. Horse guards were present in force on February 28, when Adolphe Thiers, elected chief executive ten days earlier with a mandate to negotiate a peace treaty at Versailles, set forth Bismarck's draconian terms. By evening it was common knowledge that Germany wanted Alsace and Lorraine, in addition to five billion francs — a huge indemnity. On March 1, after hearing eloquent protests, the legislature yielded. "Today a tragic session," Hugo wrote in his diary. "First the Empire was executed, then, alas, France herself! They voted the Shylock-Bismarck treaty."

At its penultimate meeting in the Grand-Théâtre, the Assembly, led by a conservative majority who feared Paris — where three revolutions had taken place since 1789 — voted to reconvene on March 20 in yet another theater, the Palais de Versailles. Preoccupied more with the enemy still camped in Rouen than with the Assembly, Flaubert, as usual, wished a pox on everybody's house, cursing the Prussians, the French, and the spirit of militarism that would, he felt certain, imbue postwar society. To George Sand he wrote that any illusions he had had about progress and humanitarianism were now extinct.

What barbarism! What a step backward! I resent my contemporaries' having filled me with the feelings of a twelfth-century brute! *I'm choking on bile!* These white-gloved [German] officers who smash mirrors, who know Sanskrit and throw themselves on the champagne, who steal your watch and then send you their calling card, this war for money, these savage sophisticates, are more horri-fying to me than cannibals. And everyone is going to imitate them, is going to be a soldier! Russia now has four million of them. All of Europe will be in uni-form. If we take our vengeance, it will be supremely ferocious, and note that that is all people will think about, avenging themselves on Germany, nothing else! No government will stand unless it exploits this passion. Murder on the grand scale will be the goal of all our efforts, France's ideal!

The fire of *revanchisme* (revengism) that was to burn for fifty years and in-cinerate millions in the trenches of World War I made his letter sadly pre-scient. What Flaubert didn't anticipate, however, was a holocaust ignited by the *revanchisme* that set French against French. This internecine conflict lay much nearer at hand.

Making Versailles the seat of government conveyed a political message distasteful to republicans, but of greater immediate consequence was the Assembly's decision to end two moratoria that had alleviated the suffering of trapped and unemployed Parisians since September 1870: one suspend-ing payment due on promissory notes, the other deferring house rent. This move could hardly have been more callous. When Paris, impoverished by siege, most needed a helping hand, rural France showed her a mailed fist, and survivors of Prussian artillery now found themselves condemned to bankruptcy, eviction, or both. "Very bravely but not with impunity had the Parisians suffered . . . the privations and emotions of the siege," wrote the vicomte de Meaux, a prominent royalist. "At first we provincials couldn't reason with them. It seemed as if we did not even speak the same language and that they were prey to a kind of sickness, what we called 'fortress fever.'" Like M. de Meaux, who saw patriarchal order threatened by wild-eyed savages, many otherwise humane legislators did not let their humanity hinder them from abolishing the small stipend that fed National Guardsmen or authorizing the state pawnshop to sell material deposited during the siege. These measures, which promised further misery to several hundred thousand inhabitants of an economic wasteland, alienated the capital en masse. Debt-encumbered shopkeepers, idle workers, and artisans with tools in hock made common cause against an enemy all the more vengeful for being French. Indeed, German soldiers camped outside Paris became mere spectators as hatred of the foreigner turned inward.

To be sure, the legislature might not have been so stiff-necked had Paris not challenged its authority. After the elections of February 8, republicans in Paris had presumed that the Assembly's provincial deputies would restore monarchical government, and their indignation voiced itself through the National Guard, which emerged as a quasi-political organism. On February 24 delegates from two hundred guard battalions ratified a proposal to replace France as a centralized state with autonomous, confederated "collectivities." Swearing never to surrender arms or to recognize any commander-in-chief chosen by Thiers, this counter-Assembly of "federals" held a rally at the place de la Bastille, where beneath the monument lay Parisians killed exactly twenty-three years earlier, on February 24, 1848. Orators harangued large crowds, and for three days National Guard bands played martial music, lowering their banners as they trooped past a Liberty draped in red cloth. Army regulars joined them, along with several thousand "mobiles," who then sought to enlist sailors at the naval barracks across town.

The authorities felt helpless in the whirlwind of what soon became a full-scale revolt. Policemen now avoided working-class districts, where some had been set upon violently. A mob forced the warden of Sainte-Pélagie prison to free demonstrators interned since January, and another raided the Gobelins police barracks for its stock of chassepot rifles. Pillaging took place throughout as the city armed itself against invasion. Until Bismarck agreed not to occupy Paris, National Guardsmen kept close watch at batteries situated on Montmartre and Belleville, ready to fire away, and rumors of a Prussian entry were announced by drummers beating *rappels*. Drums beat everywhere. But less ominous sounds also rent the air in late February and March, during this interregnum. Vendors appeared in their thousands as Paris came to resemble a huge kermis, half festive and half bellicose. "At one end of the square in front of City Hall, on the river side, besotted National Guardsmen wearing immortelles in their buttonholes march to a tambour and salute the old monument with the cry of 'Vive la République,'" noted Edmond de Goncourt. "Along the rue de Rivoli, every imaginable product may be found displayed on the sidewalk, while vehicles transport death and replenishment in the street: hearses cross wagons laden with dried codfish."

A week or so before the Assembly established itself at Versailles, Adolphe Thiers rode up from Bordeaux in high dudgeon, and his reappearance was a spark to tinder. Although this eloquent Provençal had fought hard against Napoleon III, working-class Frenchmen hated him for sins older than the Second Empire: he still bore the nickname "Père Transnonain" almost forty years after the "massacre of the rue Transnonain," when as Louis-Philippe's interior minister he had ordered General Bugeaud to crush striking Lyonnais silk workers. People had also not forgotten his denunciation of the "vile multitude" in June 1848, when yet another massacre took place, nor his advocacy of an electoral law with residence requirements calculated to disenfranchise two hundred thousand Parisians. Thiers may have shrunk since then, but the diminutive author of several books about Napoleon I had yielded nothing of his belief in the sacredness of private property. All five feet of him argued a political vision that impeached the nomad, the immigrant, the socialist, the crowd. Freedom was what he desired, he had once proclaimed, but a freedom that sheltered affairs of state from the twofold influence of imperial courts and proletarian crowds rather than the freedom of factions.

Far from seeking to assuage the new de facto government of Paris — a Central Committee elected by the two hundred National Guard battalions midway through March — Thiers resolved to sweep aside this mutinous group with a coup de main and subjugate Paris. His chief objective was the gun park atop Montmartre, where 171 cannon made a formidable battery. Early on the morning of March 18, General Paturel cordoned off lower Montmartre between Clichy and Pigalle, as troops led by General Lecomte marched south from Clignancourt. The operation ran smoothly until they seized the guns. It then became clear that, since Lecomte's regulars were without equipment to transport heavy artillery downhill, nothing had been accomplished, and the delay in summoning horse teams proved fatal. At dawn Montmartre was still asleep, but two hours later the army found itself marooned in a sea of villagers, among whom women greatly outnumbered men. Four times Lecomte ordered his men to fire, but they wouldn't. Neither the National Guard nor Montmartre's mayor, Georges Clemenceau, could control the mob, which vented its rage on Lecomte and on a retired general named Clément Thomas whom curiosity had drawn to the boulevard de Clichy. "Everyone was shrieking like wild beasts, without realizing what they were doing," Clemenceau recounted. "I observed then that pathological phenomenon which might be called bloodlust." The bodies of both generals were found at nightfall riddled with bullets.

For Thiers, reports of troops breaking ranks all over town brought back memories of February 1848, when he had urged Louis-Philippe to leave Paris and recapture it from without. The king had rejected his advice, but now God alone stood above Thiers. As soon as he had beaten a retreat, he issued general evacuation orders, spurning colleagues who felt that the army should entrench itself at the École Militaire or in the Bois de Boulogne. Forty thousand men were thus marched out of Paris, never to serve again. Up from the provinces came fresh recruits "uncontaminated" by the capital, and before long one hundred thousand men occupied camps around Versailles. The day of reckoning was imminent, Thiers proclaimed on March 20, reassuring not only antirevolutionary Parisians stranded in a hostile environment but Bismarck as well, whose patience with quarrelsome Frenchmen had worn thin. Forty-eight hours later, Versailles took over where Germany had left off several months earlier, after the armistice. It declared Paris under siege once again.

In Paris, forsaken ministries were staffed by tyros who somehow improvised essential services. The National Guard's Central Committee became, perforce, an alternative government, though its avowed program was to organize elections for a Communal Council and then dissolve itself. "The existing powers are basically provisional," it announced on March 20. "We have only one hope, one goal: the safety of the country and the final triumph of the democratic republic, one and indivisible." It sought approval of its mandate from beleaguered district mayors like Clemenceau in the naive belief that this would square Paris with Versailles, but councilmen elected on March 26 had no such scruples or illusions. Moderate republicans were few, and most resigned straightaway, leaving the high ground to militants whose hatred of a government that they believed had traded honor for peace exacerbated visions of a new political and social order. "I am voting for the reddest of the reds, but in God's name, if I knew of something more radical than the red flag I would choose that instead," declared one resident of Belleville, a working-class neighborhood. Paris turned very red indeed on March 28, the day it proclaimed itself a commune in front of the Hôtel de Ville. Newly elected members all wore red sashes. They stood under a canopy surmounted by a bust of the republic, draped in red. And overhead flew a red flag. Forming up to music first heard during the 1789 Revolution, National Guard battalions played the "Marseillaise" as people sang and cannon fired salvos. It was, wrote Jules Vallès in *Le Cri du Peuple*, "a revolutionary and patriotic festival, peaceful and joyous, a day of intoxication and solemnity, . . . and one that compensated for twenty years of empire, six months of defeats and betrayals."

By then it was clear that in Versailles a policy of conciliation with the Communards would find few friends right of center. Georges Clemenceau implored the government to hold municipal elections under its own auspices and blunt the Central Committee, but his plea went unheard. Given a choice between force and pragmatism, legislators chose inaction. "Meeting follows meeting, and emptiness yawns ever wider," Émile Zola despaired. "The majority will brook no mention of Paris . . . This is a firm resolve: Paris doesn't exist for them, and its nonexistence sums up their political agenda." In Versailles, Zola regretfully informed readers of *La Cloche*, Paris seemed very far away. "People there imagine our poor metropolis swarming with bandits, all indiscriminately fit to gun down."

Paris needed no instruction from Versailles in the art of gross political caricature, and neutral parties had reason to observe that Communards were spoiling for Armageddon as fervently as right-wing deputies. A movement whose initial goal had been municipal independence soon consecrated the rift between the ancien régime and the new order. "The communal revolution . . . inaugurates a new era of scientific, positive, experimental politics," the Commune proclaimed on April 19 in a manifesto fraught with terms used elsewhere by writers seeking to legitimize "naturalist" fiction.

> It is doomsday for the old governmental and clerical world, for militarism, bureaucracy, exploitation, speculation, monopolies, privileges to which the proletariat owes its servitude and the nation its disasters. May this great, beloved fatherland deceived by lies and calumnies reassure itself! The struggle between Paris and Versailles is of a kind that cannot end in illusory compromises.

Throughout April, decrees rained thick and fast in Paris. Rent unpaid since October 1870 was canceled. The grace period on overdue bills was extended three years. Night work for bakery workers was made illegal. Newspapers voicing opposition were suppressed. A Labor and Exchange Commission authorized producers' cooperatives. Mortmain property was nationalized when church was separated from state. And anticlericalism demanded measures secularizing education. "Religious or dogmatic instruction should . . . immediately and radically be suppressed, for both sexes, in all schools and establishments supported by the taxpayer," demanded Éducation nouvelle, a group whose leader subsequently helped individual school districts reform their curricula. "Further, liturgical objects and religious images should be removed from public view. Neither prayers, nor dogma, nor anything that pertains to the individual conscience should be taught or practiced in common. Only one method should hold sway, the experimental or scientific, which is based upon the observation of facts, whatever their nature — physical, moral, intellectual." As priests and nuns were religious images incarnate, most removed themselves from the classroom.

February and March were nomadic months for Flaubert. In mid-February, following Caroline's return from England, he accepted an invitation to keep her and Ernest Commanville company in Neuville near Dieppe. He stayed until mid-March, when the occupation of Croisset by as many as forty soldiers called him home for a brief inspection. On the seventeenth, he and Alexandre Dumas fils visited Brussels to see Princess Mathilde, who had recently had a tearful reunion with Louis-Napoleon at a Belgian border town after the latter's release from Hohenlohe prison. Less than one week later Flaubert crossed the Channel, took a room at Hatchett's Hotel on Dover Street in London, and spent several days with Juliet Herbert. By the thirtieth he was back at Neuville. What he had learned

here and there of events in Paris elicited from him no sympathy for the insurgents. Flaubert the landlord felt threatened; Flaubert the apostle of high
culture declared that the end of the "Latin world" lay at hand; Flaubert the
native son accused Communards of deflecting the hatred of compatriots
from France's true enemy; and Flaubert the epileptic, always fearful of losing his mind, declared that Paris had suffered a seizure after months of congestion induced by the siege. Which Flaubert spoke loudest depended on
his relationship with his correspondent, but generally all four joined in
reciting an irate litany. On March 31, three days after the proclamation of
the Paris Commune, he unburdened himself at length to George Sand.
How could France have believed that the word *republic* would vanquish a
million well-disciplined men? The magic of revolutionary rhetoric had
fogged people's brains. "Always the same old refrains! Always the same
bunkum!" he exclaimed.

> And now there is the Paris Commune reverting to the Middle Ages, plain and
> simple! . . . It's really showing its colors in the matter of rent legislation. The
> government has seen fit to meddle with Natural Law and rescind contracts
> drawn between individuals. It affirms that we don't owe what we owe and that
> one service is not repaid by another. The enormity of such ineptitude and in-
> justice!

His prediction was that conservatives who wished to preserve the republic, if for no other reason than to preserve order, would regret the fall of
Napoleon III and privately welcome Prussian intervention. Like Maxime
Du Camp, a friend from whom he sometimes took his cues, Flaubert foresaw the rational middle ground in public life being overrun by zealots of
one persuasion or another. Were evangelical socialists all that different from
retrograde Catholics? For him the answer was obvious. "I hate democracy
(as it is understood in France) because the 'morality of Scripture' upon
which it rests is immorality itself; it is the exaltation of grace at the expense
of justice, it is the negation of Law," he wrote to Sand in late April. "The
Commune rehabilitates assassins, just as Jesus pardoned the thieves, and men
taught to curse Lazarus, who was not a bad man, just a wealthy one, virtuously pillage the mansions of the rich. That dictum 'The republic is beyond
dispute' in no way differs from 'The pope is infallible.' Formulas and gods,
they are forever with us!" The only government he could advocate, he declared, would be a mandarinate of learned men. If France was salvageable,
its salvation lay in the empowerment of a "legitimate aristocracy." Prussia,
Gambetta, and the Commune would never have gained the upper hand had
Paris been well supplied with citizens grounded in a knowledge of history.
"What have Catholics always done to ward off imminent danger? They

make the sign of the cross while recommending themselves to God and the saints. We are far more sophisticated. [During the war] we went around shouting, 'Long live the republic!' evoking the memory of 1792, *never doubting* that it would bring success."

Versailles marshaled its legions against Paris. The day of reckoning announced by Thiers on March 20 was to be a week of slaughter and arson commemorated in historical accounts as *la semaine sanglante.* It began on Monday, May 22, when government troops poured through five gates and swept across western Paris in pincer columns. Had General Mac-Mahon, who set up headquarters that day at the Trocadéro, known that the Commune's only preparation for urban warfare was an immense barricade on the place de la Concorde, his army might have taken City Hall by dusk. Instead it regrouped after its headlong advance, giving the populous quarters time to fortify themselves. Montmartre, with cannons unmanned, fell almost immediately, but elsewhere resistance stiffened. Some two hundred barricades rose overnight, and the Versaillais fought their way eastward street by street, as fires set to impede them or to destroy obnoxious monuments raged out of control. The Tuileries Palace was soon ablaze, then the entire rue de Rivoli, the Ministry of Finance, the Palais de Justice, the Prefecture of Police, the three-hundred-year-old Hôtel de Ville. Paul Verlaine, who lived on the quai de la Tournelle, across the Seine from City Hall, witnessed this conflagration.

> [I saw] a thin column of black smoke come out of the campanile of the Hôtel de Ville, and after two or three minutes at most, all the windows of the monument exploded, releasing enormous flames, and the roof fell in with an immense fountain of sparks. This fire lasted until the evening, and then assumed the form of a colossal brazier; this in turn became, for days after, a gigantic smoldering ember. And the spectacle, horribly beautiful, was continued at night by the cannonade from the hills of Montmartre, which from nine that night to three in the morning provided a fireworks display such as had never been seen.

In due course spectators saw the July Column burning like a torch over the doomed Faubourg Saint-Antoine. By Saturday, May 27, all that remained unconquered of Paris was its northeastern corner. Caught between implacable Versaillais and German troops bivouacked just beyond the ramparts, many National Guardsmen drew their last breath in Père-Lachaise cemetery. Those who didn't fall among the mausoleums were lined up against a wall known ever since as "the wall of federals" (*le mur des fédérés*), shot, and thrown into a common pit.

Fifty-six hostages, including Archbishop Georges Darboy, died between May 22 and May 28, but the vengeance thus exacted by the Commune pales beside the carnage wrought by Versailles, whose army entered Paris intent on making it a killing field. When Montmartre fell, its residents paid dearly for the murder of Generals Lecomte and Thomas. "The massacres that were to grow more fearsome as the week advanced now began," writes one historian. "Forty-two men, three women, and four children were shot in front of the wall where Lecomte and Clément Thomas had been killed . . . A court-martial was improvised in the fatal house on the rue des Rosiers [a street in Montmartre, since renamed], and for the rest of the week batches of prisoners were brought there to be executed. Bare-headed, they were made to kneel down before the wall until their turn came." At least twenty thousand Parisians suffered the same fate, far more than had died during the Terror of 1793–94. Corpses lay strewn behind ruined barricades, on the riverbanks, against walls throughout the city, and their number grew even after May 28, as people taken prisoner in battle or denounced by neighbors (the government received some four hundred thousand anonymous letters) were brought before execution squads. A shallow grave dug in the square Saint-Jacques overflowed with them. Blood ran down gutters there and elsewhere, coloring the Seine red. After a walk through the city, Émile Zola recorded his impressions for readers of *Le Sémaphore de Marseille*. "Never will I forget . . . that frightful mound of bleeding human flesh, thrown haphazardly on the towpaths," he wrote. "Heads and limbs mingle in horrible dislocation. From the pile emerged convulsed faces . . . There are dead who appear cut in two while others seem to have four legs and four arms. What a lugubrious charnel house!" Twenty thousand bodies, he estimated, lay unburied throughout the capital.

> With warm days upon us, they will breed disease. I don't know if the troubled imagination plays a part here, but while loitering among ruins I smelled the heavy, noxious air that hangs over cemeteries in stormy weather. It all looks like a grim necropolis where fire hasn't purified death. Stale odors redolent of the morgue cling to sidewalks. Paris, which was called the boudoir or the hostel of Europe under the Empire, no longer gives off an aroma of truffles and rice powder, and one enters it holding one's nose, as in some foul sewer.

For Zola as for Flaubert, everything spoke to the reality of a *bête humaine* trampling civilization underfoot, and evidence just as gruesome abounded in Versailles, where the Orangerie, the riding school, and the stables became hell on earth for forty thousand prisoners. Crushed together, starved, and taunted by the locals, many ended up dashing out their brains or dying of disease before they could be court-martialed. "Measures taken against fugitive insurgents are more and more severe," Zola noted.

Appalled though he was by Versailles' bloodlust, the search for those who had perpetrated heinous crimes justified, in Zola's view, the inconvenience of needing a permit to enter and leave Paris. When he and Flaubert became good friends during the 1870s, neither sought to persuade the other that Communards had been pardonably misguided idealists, more sinned against than sinning. Nor, indeed, did George Sand disagree with her beloved "troubadour" on this score. "What will be the backlash of the infamous Commune?" she asked two weeks after the army reconquered Paris. "I who have so much patience with my species and for a long time viewed things through rose-colored glasses now see only shadows. In judging others my model used to be myself. I had largely gained mastery of my own character, I had quelled useless and dangerous eruptions, I had seeded the volcano with grass and flowers, which blossomed, and I imagined that everyone could correct or contain himself . . . And here I awaken from a dream to find a generation divided between cretinism and delirium tremens. Henceforth anything can happen."

On August 11, 1871, Flaubert attended a court-martial of Communards at Versailles, thinking perhaps that it might provide material for a future novel about Second Empire France. "The spectacle nauseated me!" he exclaimed to Agénor Bardoux, a friend from law-school days who was now an elected deputy. "What beings! What paltry monsters! But the simplemindedness of the soldier-boys judging them. There are no words to describe the fatuousness and cynicism of your confreres, the attorneys for the defense." While the spectacle made him sick, did it also fascinate him? No doubt. *La Tentation de Saint Antoine* in its third version, which Flaubert had been writing since 1869, may serve as an ironical commentary on *la semaine sanglante*, on the trial, and, above all, on his own fantasies of murder and rapine. When, in the first scene, a gust of wind riffles through Saint Anthony's Bible, arresting itself at Esther, it opens a trapdoor to the hermit's lower depths. Described in chapter 9 of that book is the carnage Jews wreaked upon their enemies during Ahasuerus's reign. "Then comes the number of people slain by them — seventy-five thousand," Anthony muses. "They had suffered so much! Moreover, their enemies were the enemies of the true God. And how they must have delighted in avenging themselves thus by the massacre of idolaters! Doubtless the city must have been crammed with the dead! There must have been corpses at the thresholds of the garden gates, upon the stairways, in all the chambers, and piled up so high that the doors could no longer move upon their hinges! . . . But lo! here I am permitting my mind to dwell upon ideas of murder and of blood!"

XXI

Orphanhood

FLAUBERT SADLY reported to Mathilde that the upheavals of 1870–71 had aged his mother by ten years. Caroline Commanville's impression upon returning from England was that her uncle had grown older even more noticeably than her grandmother; and had she told him so, he would not have been surprised. In a letter to George Sand written shortly before the war, he had described himself as a fossil unrelated to the world around him. One year later that feeling was a shade more somber. He liked to quote a line from Goethe's conversations with Eckermann, "Forward, beyond the tombs!" but nostalgia for the lost and the absent often washed over him, especially on Sundays, when Louis Bouilhet's ghost reappeared at the front door of Croisset carrying a sheaf of verse under his arm. To Princess Mathilde, Flaubert reminisced about evenings at 24, rue de Courcelles and bright days at Saint-Gratien. It was as if a great chasm had opened between the present and the Paris of yesteryear, as if during the Commune, Paris had become another ghost. "It sounds cynical, but it's true that one grows accustomed to doing without Paris and almost believing that it no longer exists," he told Mathilde.

By April 1871 Germans had evacuated the house, if not yet Canteleu. They would withdraw from the region entirely in June. Flaubert moved back to Croisset and with unprecedented alacrity took up *La Tentation de Saint Antoine* where he had left off months earlier. Friends were treated to none of the lamentations that normally accompanied progress reports. Like a repatriated exile kissing the soil of his homeland, he blessed his study and the work done therein. For one brief moment, the martyrdom of letters yielded to the consolation of letters. "This extravagant opus distracts me from the horrors of Paris. When we find the world too awful, we must seek refuge in another." If George Sand, who undoubtedly seconded his observation, had visited Croisset, she would have heard sixty pages read aloud, including a chapter, or most of one, on fourth-century heresies. His spirits boosted him high enough to see himself completing the manuscript by the middle of 1872, which would indeed prove to be the case. As soon as Paris opened again, he began the search for material not available in Rouen. Having decided to drive poor Anthony madder than in the two previous versions with a disquisition on Eastern religion, he borrowed Frédéric Baudry's *Études sur les Védas* from its author and a French translation of *The Lotus of the Good Law* from Ernest Renan. When Caroline stayed in Paris, she acted as his factotum, succeeding Jules Duplan in that role, though his valet might also be sent down for an urgently needed item. The bibliography of *La Tentation* is formidable. Early in June, Flaubert himself visited the capital. Thanks to Renan, the curator of Oriental manuscripts at the Bibliothèque Impériale, which was still closed to the general public, he spent hours in the library or sent researchers there in his place. Renan, Baudry at the Arsenal, and Maury at the Archives had their brains picked for information on Oriental religions. Otherwise, he found time to view the great buildings burned out by Communard firebrands and the neighborhoods wrecked in fighting at barricades. "The odor of corpses disgusts me less than the fetid egoism exhaled by all mouths," he wrote to George Sand on June 10. "The spectacle of immense ruins is nothing compared with that of Parisian brainlessness . . . Half the population wants to strangle the other half, . . . and Prussians no longer exist! They are excused. *People admire them!!!* 'Reasonable' men want to become naturalized Germans."

A full-blown tirade against Germany was reserved for a letter to Ernest Feydeau several weeks later. What could be more hateful than Teutons with doctoral diplomas tucked under their spiked helmets shooting up mirrors and carting away grandfather clocks? He swore that he would never be seen in the company of a German, as if he had ever known or enjoyed the company of Germans, apart from Maurice Schlesinger, whom he couldn't see again for another reason. Schlesinger had died four months earlier, on February 25. That made one less survivor with him on the raft of the *Medusa*.

In Flaubert's case, normalcy, or a semblance of it, returned when the French bourgeoisie came once again to bear the brunt of his rage, and an occasion for vituperation arose in December 1871. The committee concerned with honoring Louis Bouilhet, which Flaubert chaired, raised money to build a small fountain surmounted by a bust of the poet and submitted plans to the Rouen city council. The latter decided that it could not award Bouilhet's memory four square meters of public space. Various reasons were adduced, the crucial one being that the proposed honoree had insufficient stature. Flaubert, who could hardly separate his own literary accomplishment from his friend's and regarded Bouilhet's editorial ministrations as an essential act of midwifery, organized an aggressive response. He urged men whom Bouilhet had tutored to petition the council collectively. He prodded literary friends, some of whom had contributed money as subscribers, to raise a hue and cry. Hopeful that Rouen would be shamed by critical acclaim for Bouilhet's *Mademoiselle Aissé*, which was to open at the Odéon theater in Paris with Sarah Bernhardt, he worked tirelessly on the production. And finally, he lambasted the municipal council, in an open letter published first by *Le Temps* in Paris, then as a pamphlet by *Le Nouvelliste de Rouen*. His peroration was a broad impeachment of a class that never hesitated, he said, to plant city squares with statues of generals and merchant princes.

This affair, which may be trivial in itself, assumes greater meaning when understood as a sign of the times — as a characteristic trait of your class — and it is not you alone whom I address, gentlemen, but all bourgeois. So I say to them:

Conservatives who conserve nothing,

The time has come to follow a new path, and since there is so much talk nowadays of regeneration, I exhort you to change your frame of mind. Show some initiative for once! The French nobility lost its soul when, over a span of two centuries, it acquired the sentimental disposition of its valets. The bourgeoisie has approached the beginning of the end by similarly abasing itself. I don't see that the newspapers it reads differ from those of common folk, that the music with which it regales itself is any different from that of the dance hall, that its pleasures are any loftier than those of the populace. In one group as in the other one finds the same love of money, the same respect for faits accomplis, the same need of idols to be destroyed, the same hatred of superiority in every form, the same spirit of denigration, the same crass ignorance!

There are seven hundred deputies in the Assembly. Among them, how many could name the principal treaties marking our national history, or give the dates of six French kings? How many are familiar with the basics of political economy . . . ? The municipality of Rouen, which unanimously denied the merit of a poet, is perhaps totally ignorant of the rules of versification, and doesn't need to know them so long as it doesn't concern itself with poetry.

To be respected by what is beneath you, respect what is above you! Before sending the multitude to school, educate yourselves! Enlightened classes, seek enlightenment.

Because of this contempt for intelligence, you fancy yourselves practical, positive, imbued with common sense! But one is not truly practical unless one is something more than that. You would not enjoy all the benefits of industry if your eighteenth-century forebears had rallied to no other ideal than material utility. Germany has been the butt of endless jokes about its ideologues, its dreamers, its nebulous poets, but you have seen where its nebulousness has led it, alas! Your billions have paid it for all the time it didn't waste building neat systems. I seem to think that that dreamer, Fichte, reorganized the Prussian army after Jena.

You, practical? Come now! You can hold neither a pen nor a rifle! You allow yourselves to be despoiled, imprisoned, and butchered by thugs! You don't even have the instincts of the brute, which is to defend oneself.

If this salvo was unlikely to extract a water fountain from his antagonists, it gave him at least the inestimable satisfaction of drawing blood. In any event, nothing he said changed their minds about Bouilhet, especially after the premiere of *Mademoiselle Aïssé* on January 6. Francisque Sarcey, whose judgment made plays or broke them, dismissed Bouilhet's as a vapid melodrama tricked up in hexameters. It didn't run much past February.

When *Mademoiselle Aïssé* was in rehearsal, Flaubert commuted between his flat and the Odéon theater every day, often on foot and accompanied by Pierre Berton, the male lead, who vividly recalled his "talking literature" throughout the three-mile walk in a self-intoxicated state. He knew much of Victor Hugo's poetry by heart, according to Berton. "I can still see him on the place du Carrousel in front of the still burned-out Tuileries, and stupefied passersby contemplating this giant with a thick, drooping mustache and flushed face . . . standing on tiptoe, stretching one arm toward the sky, and declaiming [*Bivar*] in a thunderous voice." There was much talk about Bouilhet, which invariably reduced Flaubert to tears.

Flaubert paid for his exertions on Bouilhet's behalf with an attack of pharyngitis. It did not take him long, however, to resume *La Tentation*. He was once again spending hours bent over monographs at the ex–Imperial Library and hours more writing at home, where an audience for his work intermittently appeared in the person of Ivan Turgenev. George Sand begged him not to live so much in his head. "Move around, shake yourself, acquire mistresses or wives, whichever you prefer," she wrote. He objected that sentences did not in fact matter more than people to him, and there was, indeed, much society during that winter season. He dined with Victor Hugo. He saw as much of Théophile Gautier as Gautier's declining health allowed. His acquaintance with the buxom young widow Léonie Brainne blossomed into a romantic friendship, almost certainly an intimate one (to judge by the compliment he paid her legs, a reference to passionate kisses, and an "anniversary"). Frédéric Baudry, Edmond de Goncourt, and Jeanne de Tourbey, who would presently marry a count, all hosted dinner parties.* He attended two masked balls. Once the government granted Princess Mathilde permission to return from exile, habitués of her salon gathered around her again, though no longer on the rue de Courcelles. After 1871 she occupied a smaller town house on the rue de Berri. On Sunday after-noons Flaubert himself played host to his circle of men friends, which in-cluded not only Goncourt and Turgenev but the younger faces of Alphonse Daudet, Guy de Maupassant, and Zola, who earned his living as a parlia-mentary reporter for *La Cloche.* "Journalism weighs upon me so that I no longer have an hour to myself," Zola apologized on February 2, 1872, in a note that accompanied a copy of his *La Curée.* "I want very much to drop by some Sunday afternoon and shake your hand. In the meantime, let my novel serve as a calling card."

Flaubert might have thoroughly enjoyed this bustle if not for Mme Flaubert's failing health. While the family sought proper help, Caroline acted as her grandmother's *dame de compagnie,* and the old lady, living with her at her house on the rue de Clichy in Paris, was more than she could handle. Flaubert had planned to accompany his mother to Croisset at Easter, when every scent and sign of German occupation would have dis-appeared beneath a fresh coat of paint. But she insisted on moving back be-fore the workers had left, as if knowing that death might claim her at any moment and wanting to die nowhere else. On March 31 Flaubert reported to George Sand that his mother, camped amid the debris of renovation, was worse off than ever.

One week later, on April 6, Caroline Flaubert breathed her last at age seventy-nine, after thirty-three hours of death throes. Flaubert informed friends in brief communiqués, such as this one to Maxime Du Camp: "*My mother just died!* I've gotten no sleep in nearly a week! I'm shattered. I em-brace you, my dear Maxime, my old companion!" Several days later he walked uphill to the Cimetière Monumental in yet another funeral proces-sion and buried his lifelong companion beside Achille-Cléophas. Letters of condolence abounded. Victor Hugo assured him that he was "one of those high summits buffeted by every wind but equal to their assaults." Sand's

---

*Jeanne de Tourbey, who is thought to have served as a model — one among others — for Proust's Odette, married the comte de Loynes in the early 1870s. For two decades, during the period of the Dreyfus affair, when her lover was the literary critic Jules Lemaître, lumi-naries of the French right would regularly convene at her salon.

sympathies were down closer to earth. "I am with you all day and all evening, at every moment, my poor dear friend," she wrote. "I would like to be near you and I suffer the more for being stuck here. I want you to tell me that you have the courage you'll need. That worthy, cherished existence drew to a close slowly and painfully; from the moment she became infirm, she surrendered, and there was nothing you could do to distract and console her. Your incessant and cruel preoccupation is over. It ended the way things of this world do, with a sundering more painful than the clinging itself! Repose is a bitter conquest! You will miss being worried about her. I know it. I know that consternation which is the aftermath of one's struggle against death. Well, my poor child, all I can do is open a maternal heart to you. It's no substitute for the one you lost, but it joins yours in your bereavement."

Flaubert feared that in losing his mother he might also have lost house and home. What he learned when the family gathered to hear their notary read Mme Flaubert's will was that she had indeed bequeathed Croisset not to him but to Caroline Commanville, with the proviso that he retain the right to occupy his rooms there for the rest of his life, or until such time as he got married. "I've just had a difficult week, old man!" he wrote to Goncourt on April 19. "The week of the *inventory!* It's grim. I had the feeling my mother was dying all over again and we were robbing her." It was a substantial estate. In the division of property that took place during the following months, his share, which consisted for the most part of income-bearing farmland, notably the acreage at Deauville (which yielded almost 6,000 francs a year), was estimated to be worth 260,000 francs. By 1875 its value had increased substantially. In addition, there were the 105,000 francs he had inherited from Achille-Cléophas, or what remained of that bequest. This would have been more than enough to support a comfortable life if the inheritance had included financial prudence, and if family affairs hadn't subsequently taken a wicked turn.

Caroline, who, like her grandmother, often suffered migraines when under stress, stayed at Croisset three weeks. Only after she left did the wisdom of George Sand's remarks become fully apparent to him. Although friends made sure that he had conversation — Léonie Brainne and her sister Valérie Lapierre paid him visits; Edmond Laporte, whose company he enjoyed, came whenever work allowed — the house felt like a mausoleum, especially at the dinner table, where his was often the only place setting. Many tears were shed, and there is reason to believe that there were several epileptic seizures. We know that *La Tentation* emerged from limbo on May 30, for Flaubert wrote to Caroline on the twenty-ninth that he would immediately begin "making sentences" again. It bespoke the transitoriness of everything, he told Mathilde, that just three weeks after being torn apart he could resume his familiar routine. But grief was not quite so lenient, and he resumed work fitfully. "I am reasonable. I force myself to do something if only to numb myself. My heart isn't in it. I lose myself in memories like a dreamy old man." His memory peopled the empty house with beloved ghosts, summoning sister Caroline and Uncle Parain, Alfred Le Poittevin and Bouilhet and that femme fatale of his adolescence, Élisa Schlesinger, who had in fact rematerialized one year earlier, after Maurice's death, in a letter from Baden-Baden. A meeting had taken place at Croisset in the autumn of 1871, when Élisa was visiting Normandy with her two children, who had inherited the Hôtel Bellevue in Trouville. The occasion for their next reunion was her son Adolphe's marriage in Paris on June 12. Flaubert attended the wedding Mass and sobbed all through it. Several months later he wrote a letter to *"ma vieille Amie, ma vieille Tendresse,"* replying to one of hers. "I can't see your handwriting without my pulse quickening! So this morning, I avidly tore open your letter, hoping that it would announce a visit. Alas, no! When will you come? Next year? I would so much like to receive you *in my home*, to have you sleep in my mother's room." Élisa then became a true ghost. He never saw her again.

On July 7 Flaubert joined Caroline at Luchon (the Pyreneen spa he had visited with Dr Cloquet twenty-two years earlier), in the hope that mountain air would calm his nerves. Being advised by the resident physician not to smoke irritated him. So did his noisy hotel, the amorphous plot of a Dickens novel he had brought along, the bourgeois *curistes* whose conversation exemplified "modern Banality," and almost everything else except a local zoo and the company of his niece, to whom he felt closer than ever since the death of Mme Flaubert. Caroline's mourning was laced with resentment, the measure of which Flaubert could not have taken until she confided in him at Luchon. As she later described it, "I opened myself to him completely, and he understood then the misery of my union with M. Commanville, how little my husband cared about my heart and my head." She told him that her heart and her head had long been occupied by Baron Ernest Leroy, a gentleman thirty-six years older than she, who governed all of upper Normandy as the imperial prefect. They had met at a ball soon after her marriage and almost immediately fallen in love. Though middle-aged, with grown daughters, Leroy proved to be a swain still capable of romantic follies. He intercepted her on the street; he hid violets in her pew; he gazed at her windows from a skiff half-hidden among reeds fringing an island opposite her apartment on the quai du Havre. Wherever she went — Paris, Rouen, Neuville — Leroy turned up. His gallantry thrilled the isolated, lovelorn woman. "Tall, slender, elegant, not handsome but with passionate eyes, a pale complexion, a fatal countenance, as they say in novels" is how she remembered him. "His manners were exquisite, his intelligence rather ordinary, but I realized that only much later, after his death, upon acquiring a critical sense. He pleased me just as he was, and thenceforth I was no longer alone." Did they consummate their liaison? Caroline declared that her "imprudences" led her as far as the bedroom door but not past it, that she could not have given herself to Leroy without leaving Commanville and thus devastating her family. Did her imprudences alert Commanville? A long voyage through Scandinavia may have been undertaken in 1869 not only for business reasons but to remove her from Rouen. And Caroline's niece, Lucie Chevalley-Sabatier, believed that Commanville bought a town house on the rue de Clichy in Paris for the same reason. Neither stratagem worked as well as the Franco–Prussian War. Caroline met with Leroy once after her return from England. At age sixty he obtained a captaincy in the militia, joined the Loire campaign, and was decorated for bravery on the battlefield, but he never saw her again. Exhausted and sick, he died on July 9, 1872, two days after she and her uncle arrived at Luchon.

Flaubert's correspondence leaves little doubt that he had been aware of a relationship at the time. He occasionally alluded to it, or to her hobnobbing in high social circles, with a mixture of avuncular pride and paternal jealousy. He may have convinced himself that the attachment didn't run deep, for to imagine it otherwise would have been to give her her emotional due, to acknowledge his complicity in burying her under the dead weight of an arranged marriage, and then perhaps to be consumed by guilt. Now he could no longer ignore the true state of affairs. Nor, however, could he rescue her from prison. He could only be the mentor he had always been and keep her mind alive inside it. "It was at my uncle's side that I continued to find the intellectual sustenance I needed. Thanks to him I went on developing. Days spent at Croisset were always good days." In a first exchange of letters after Luchon, Caroline did not disparage Commanville or weep over Leroy. She had read all of Herodotus and asked Flaubert to suggest works for a course of study. He recommended Thucydides, Demosthenes, Plutarch, Leconte de Lisle's translations of Aeschylus, and Thirwell's history of Greece in eight volumes, which she would find at Croisset.

For consolation of another kind, Caroline had recourse to a charismatic Dominican priest named Henri-Martin Didon, who served as prior of a monastic community in Paris when not delivering sermons to mass audiences all over France. Known for modernist views that anticipated Leo XIII's encyclical Rerum Novarum, Didon — a friend to other cultivated, unfulfilled ladies as well — became Caroline's confidant and spiritual adviser. Her parlor in Paris was to be his second home.*

---

*Flaubert seems to have liked Didon but may have surreptitiously poked fun at him in the

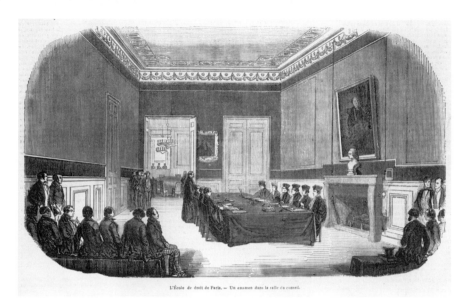

L'École de droit de Paris. — Un examen dans la salle du conseil.

An examination in progress at the Paris Law School. It was with great trepidation that Gustave appeared before a panel such as this in August 1843. (Bibliothèque Historique de la Ville de Paris)

Gustave Flaubert at twenty-one, as imagined after his death by the Rouen artist Edouard de Bergevin. There are no images of Flaubert between childhood and middle age. To a publisher who wanted a photograph of him, Flaubert wrote: "You will see my photograph nowhere. I have refused to have my portrait painted by artist friends of great talent. Nothing will make me yield." (Bibliothèque Municipale de Rouen. Photograph Thierry Ascensio-Parvy)

Maxime Du Camp at twenty-two, the year after he met Flaubert. (Musée Flaubert)

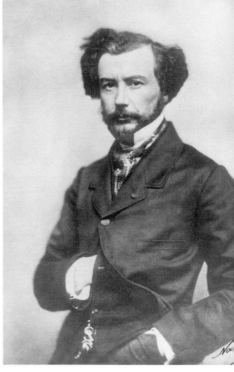

Maxime Du Camp in an official pose, rehearsing his election to the Académie française years before the event. Photograph by Nadar. (Bibliothèque Nationale de France)

Louis Bouilhet. A rare portrait of the friend whom Gustave called his literary midwife and to whom he dedicated *Madame Bovary*. (Archives départementales de la Seine-Maritime)

Ernest Chevalier as attorney general of Angers. (Musée Flaubert. Photograph by C.H.U. Rouen)

Dr. Jules Cloquet, the Flauberts' lifelong friend, who accompanied Gustave on his grand tour after graduation from the collegiate school. At the time of this portrait he was a professor at the Medical School and Napoleon III's private physician. (Bibliothèque Municipale de Rouen)

"The Propylaea of the Temple of Thutmose." A photograph taken by Maxime Du Camp at Thebes during his voyage with Flaubert. (The Metropolitan Museum of Art, The Robert O. Dougan Collection, Gift of Warner Communications, Inc.)

Louise Colet in her fifties. (Bibliothèque Nationale de France)

Louise Colet, the young beauty, portrayed by Franz Winterhalter. (Bibliothèque Nationale de France)

The sculptor James Pradier's drawing of his family. Louise Pradier, who may have gone into the making of Emma Bovary, is at the center. (Bibliothèque Nationale de France)

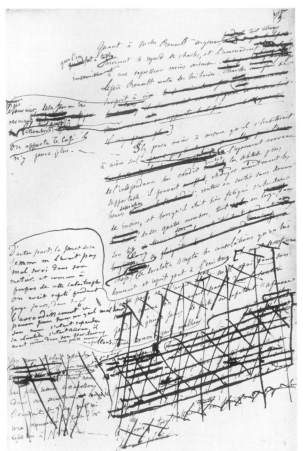

A page of the manuscript of *Madame Bovary*. "Happy are they who don't doubt themselves and whose pens fly across the page," Flaubert wrote to Louise Colet. (Bibliothèque Municipale de Rouen)

Flaubert's study at Croisset, with windows looking out on the Seine. His gilded Buddha can be seen on the left. Watercolor by Rochegrosse. (Bibliothèque Municipale de Rouen)

The gilded Buddha that was a
fixture in Flaubert's study.
(Bibliothèque Municipale de
Rouen)

Jules Sénard, the attorney who
successfully defended Gustave
Flaubert against a charge of
obscenity brought by the state after
the publication of *Madame Bovary*.
(Bibliothèque Municipale de
Rouen)

Portrait of Marie-Sophie Leroyer de
Chantepie in her twenties. Although
Flaubert never met her in person, she
became his haunted and indefatigable
correspondent after the publication of
Madame Bovary. Artist unknown.
(Courtesy of Dr. Daniel Anger)

Charles Sainte-Beuve, Frances's preeminent literary critic during Gustave's lifetime and founder of the Magny literary circle. (Bibliothèque Municipale de Rouen. Photograph by Thierry Ascensio-Parvy)

LES DEMOLITIONS DE LA PLACE SAINT-GERMAIN-DES-PRÉS, POUR LE PERCEMENT DE LA RUE DE RENNES; dessin de MM. Delanu[...], Voir page 750.

Buildings being leveled at the place Saint-Germain in 1867, during the reconstruction of Paris under Napoleon III. (Bibliothèque Nationale de France)

Their month together at Luchon, which nurtured Flaubert's fantasy of restoring with Caroline something of the ménage he had had with his mother, caused a brief estrangement from another woman, Juliet Herbert. Having made plans to see her annual lover early in August, Juliet resented the fact that she had to cancel them because, Flaubert informed her, he would not yet be back from Luchon. Juliet was indignant. As a governess in the household of Lord and Lady Conant, she could not easily arrange and rearrange holidays. On this occasion, her employers apparently made some allowances. She visited Paris a month later than planned, and all was set straight in assignations that took place, at Flaubert's insistence, under a cloak of secrecy; Caroline knew about them, but no one else heard Juliet Herbert mentioned by name. "I think that a week from now my dear companion . . . will visit you in your 'delicious villa,' whereupon the ordinary routine of my solitary life will resume," he wrote to his niece on September 14. There would be more reunions, one of them described to friends as a fortnight of sexual exuberance. How Juliet viewed them is a matter of conjecture, for her correspondence was destroyed, but they are unlikely to have been tied in her mind to matrimonial aspirations. If she imagined at any point that Mme Flaubert's death had made Flaubert more marriageable, a wiser thought must have told her that intimacy with him required the interposition of an English Channel. Or perhaps Flaubert himself made this known to her, as he did in a letter to George Sand. "I don't believe that I'm an egotistical monster," he wrote on October 28, 1872. "My *self* gets so scattered in books that I spend entire days without feeling it . . . As for living with a woman, marrying, which you advise me to do, I find the notion preposterous. Why that is *I have no idea;* that's just how things are. Figure it out for me. The feminine being and my existence don't make a proper fit. Then too, I'm not rich enough. And then . . . and then I'm too old and, what is more, too honorable to sentence anyone to a life term with yours truly. Deep down in me there is a cleric people don't know about." Not that he hadn't had passionate love affairs, he declared in a subsequent letter. "But chance and circumstances made me increasingly solitary. Now I'm alone, absolutely alone." Once more he blamed his bachelorhood on his modest wealth, as if the lack of a golden stepstool were all that prevented him from reaching the altar. "I don't have enough income to take a wife, nor even enough to reside in Paris six months of the year, so I can't change my way of life."

His did enjoy companionship of a kind. That fall Edmond Laporte gave him a beautiful greyhound. He accepted it, overcoming his fear of rabies

---

person of Cruchard, the reverend father invented for George Sand's delectation, whom Flaubert describes as a veritable Isaiah in the pulpit and the spiritual darling of society women.

(which may have been epidemic at that moment), and named it Julio. Juliet Herbert contributed a dog collar.

THE *Tentation de Saint Antoine* that Flaubert completed ten days before his departure for Luchon differed markedly from previous versions. Mostly gone were Anthony's dialogues with allegorical figures. The mystics whose followers mingled in the great stew of fourth-century Alexandria are made to proselytize succinctly. What Baudelaire had read in 1846 and called a "pandemoniacal glory-hole of solitude" remained just that, but now the chaos was more artfully deployed.

Seven well-articulated chapters replaced the shaggy tripartite scheme of 1849 and 1856. As in those versions, Flaubert's dream play unfolds between nightfall and sunrise. Assailed one evening by visions of gluttony, wealth, and power, Anthony flagellates himself. He succeeds only in exciting more fantasies. Desire breaches his mind in the person of the Queen of Sheba and prepares the way for religious doubt, with heresiarchs (Tertullian, Valentinus, Manes, Montanus, Arius, *inter alios*) queuing up to torment him. When they exit, pagan deities file through. Anthony has meanwhile been joined by the devil, who conceals his horns and cloven foot in the trappings of piety. Laying hold of him, Satan transports Anthony high above the earth, through empty space, where the spellbound saint hears his captor proclaim the universe to have neither limits nor purpose. Close upon this hallucination follows another in which Death and Lust — the former a haggard crone, the latter a beauty — tug him this way and that. When lust triumphs, everything is seen as deliriously fertile. Monsters breed before Anthony's very eyes, plants sprout, insects swarm, metals crystallize, frosts effloresce, monads vibrate, and the dreaming hermit beholds this extravaganza of propagation with rapture. Soon afterward day dawns.

Among the many letters in Flaubert's correspondence that describe writing as a monkish pursuit, none argues his identification with Anthony more clearly than one answering questions about the creative process posed by Hippolyte Taine. "Yes," Flaubert wrote in November 1866, "the internal image is *always* as true for me as the objective reality of things, and after very little time the embellishments or modifications I have introduced can no longer be distinguished from what reality furnished me in the first place." Imaginary characters getting under his skin could drive him crazy, he continued.

> Or rather, it is I who am in their skin. When I described Madame Bovary's poisoning, there was such a strong taste of arsenic in my mouth, I was myself so thoroughly poisoned, that I had two successive bouts of indigestion — very real

bouts, for I vomited my entire dinner. Not every detail gets recorded. Thus, for me M. Homais has faint scars of smallpox. Whatever the passage I'm writing, I *see* the scene fully furnished (including stains in the wood), but I don't elaborate.

The images conjured by artistic intuition pass before his eyes, he wrote, with the fuguelike rapidity of "hypnogogic hallucinations."

Like the phantoms that besiege the writer, those that torment Anthony gain weight and volume from the carefully portrayed desert into which Flaubert marches them. The scene set in his first chapter, based upon notes made while sailing in a cangia two decades earlier, is as specific as the prologue of a Balzac novel.

It is in Thebaid, at the summit of a mountain, on a platform rounded off into the form of a half-moon, and enclosed by large rocks. The Hermit's cabin appears in the background. Built of mud and reeds, it is flat-roofed and doorless. A pitcher and a loaf of black bread can be distinguished within; also, in the middle of the room, a large book resting on a wooden stand; while here and there, scattered reeds, two or three mats, a basket, and a knife lie upon the ground.

Some ten paces from the hut, there is a long cross planted in the soil; and, at the other end of the platform, an old palm tree twists over the abyss, for the sides of the mountain are perpendicular; and the Nile appears to form a lake at its base.

The view to right and left is broken by a line of boulders. But on the desert side, like a vast sequence of sandy beaches, immense undulations of an ashen-blond color extend behind one another, rising higher as they recede; and far in the distance, beyond the sands, the Libyan chain forms a chalk-colored wall, lightly shaded by violet mists. On the opposite side is the setting sun. To the north, the sky is tinged pearl gray, while at the zenith purple clouds sweep across the blue vault like ragged tufts of a gigantic mane. These rays of flame grow darker; the azure spots acquire a nacreous pallor; the shrubs, the pebbles, and the earth all now seem as hard as bronze; and throughout space there floats a golden dust so fine as to become one with the vibrations of light.

Saint Anthony, who has a long beard, long hair, and wears a goatskin tunic, is seated on the ground cross-legged, weaving mats. As soon as the sun disappears, he utters a deep sigh, gazes upon the horizon, and exclaims: "Another day! Another day gone!"

Here, as in *L'Éducation sentimentale*, the drama begins when some inner crisis rouses a quiescent soul. Like Frédéric suddenly leaving the stern rail where he had stood motionless to explore his vessel, Anthony suddenly feels impelled to climb the rocks around the hut. This restlessness signals a mutiny that will give free rein to his imagination. With desire ascendant,

Frédéric encounters Marie Arnoux but cannot tell at first whether she is real or an apparition. Neither does Anthony know whether the images that flood his mind come from within or without. Either way, they mark the end of a pious day. Cross-legged at the outset of chapter 1, he falls into a trance at its conclusion, with Sheba waiting to make her languorous entrance. It is a fall in both senses, and the artist haunted by his characters merges with the epileptic caught in a hallucinatory vortex, unable to speak.

> And suddenly in the air above there appear and disappear successively — first, a stretch of water, then the figure of a prostitute, the corner of a temple, a soldier, a chariot with two white horses prancing. These images appear suddenly, as in flashes — outlined against the background of the night, like scarlet on ebony. Their motion accelerates. They file past with vertiginous rapidity. Sometimes again, they pause and gradually pale and melt away, or else float off out of sight, to be immediately succeeded by others. Anthony closes his eyes.

As the images multiply around him menacingly, he feels no sensation save a burning contraction in the abdomen. "Despite the tumult in his brain, he is aware of an enormous silence that separates him from the world. He tries to speak — impossible! He feels as though all the bands of his life were breaking and dissolving." Finally unable to resist, he falls prostrate upon his mat.

What comes of this event is not a plot but a dream sequence that once again invites comparison with *L'Éducation sentimentale*. As Frédéric, the hero whose adult life is a saga of free association, wanders from one encounter to another, so Anthony, stripped of dogmatic security, is visited by one creed after another. Descendants of Flaubert's earliest literary passion, *Don Quixote*, both works can be read as chronicles of futile vagabondage. More deliberately than *L'Éducation*, *La Tentation* makes a point upon which Flaubert insisted in his correspondence with Mlle Leroyer de Chantepie. "The horizon perceived by human eyes is never the shore, for beyond that horizon lies another, and another!" he wrote on May 18, 1857, anticipating the "vast sequence of sandy beaches" Anthony surveys from his desert eyrie. "So the quest for the best religion or the best form of government strikes me as foolishness. In my view the best one is the one that's moribund, because in dying it makes way for another . . . It is because I believe in the perpetual evolution of humanity and its incessant forms that I hate all the frames into which people want to stuff it." Contemptuous of gospel truth, he assembles the fictions devised by men to satisfy their craving for knowledge of first causes, for a redemptive pathway, a "solution," a teleological beacon, and parades them past Anthony like tasseled jesters. Toward the end of *La Tentation*, it is the devil who expresses Flaubert's aversion to infallibilism, denying Anthony the comfort of orthodoxy and limits.

> Behold the sun! From its surface leap vast jets of flame, casting forth sparks that scatter beyond to become worlds hereafter — and further than the last, far beyond those deeps where you see only night, whirl other suns — and behind them others again, and beyond those yet others . . . without end! . . . Nothingness is not — there is no void! Everywhere and forever bodies move upon the immutable background of Expanse — and if it were bounded, it would not be expanse, but a body only. It is limitless!

His lesson in humility continues with a caveat that clearly echoes the appendix to part 1 of Spinoza's *Ethics*. "Yet the knowledge of things comes to you only through the medium of your mind. Like a concave mirror, it deforms the objects it reflects; and you have no means whatever of verifying their exactitude. Never can you know the universe in all its vastness; consequently it will never be possible for you to obtain an idea of its cause, to have a just notion of God, nor even to say that the universe is infinite — for you must first be able to know what the Infinite is!"

The fallen angel is a perverse agent who abets the saint's desire for knowledge while humbling him with the formidable prospect of worlds beyond worlds. Under his influence, Anthony shrinks with doubt and swells with pleasure, his pleasure being a rapturous response to the aura of fertility goddesses. Between visitations from Diana of Ephesus and Cybele, he delights in movement, odor, light, color. "I feel the desire to lie flat upon the earth that I might feel her against my heart; and my life would be imbued with her eternal youth!" Overwhelming him is the vision of a blond, heavy-lidded, dimple-kneed Venus primping before a celestial mirror. To be sure, Flaubert has Anthony make amends for succumbing to the allurements of Nature by reciting the Nicene Creed, but *La Tentation* leaves no doubt that the argument between Mother Earth and God the Father will continue within its vexed hero as surely as night follows day. Anthony's last words, spoken after he has seen Nature throw up forms that attest to her boundless ingenuity, are a pantheistic Gloria.

> Bliss! Sheer bliss! I have beheld the birth of life! I have seen the beginning of motion. My pulse throbs even to the point of bursting! I long to fly, to swim, to bark, to bellow, to howl! Would that I had wings, a carapace, a shell — that I could breathe out smoke, wield a trunk — make my body writhe — divide myself everywhere — be in everything — emanate with odors — burgeon like plants — flow like water — vibrate like sound — shine like light, squatting

upon all forms — penetrate each atom — descend to the very bottom of matter — be matter itself!

No sooner has he uttered the wish to be matter (much as Atys, in an earlier passage, longs to be his mother, Cybele) than day breaks, with the face of Christ beaming down from inside the disk of the sun.

That Flaubert wrote Anthony's farewell to night soon after his mother's death gives the passage a special poignancy. One is again put in mind of Freud's comments about the "oceanic" feeling at the beginning of *Civilization and Its Discontents*. When Flaubert felt most fearful of falling out of the world is when his hero imagined himself merging with it. Bereft of the woman to whom he owed his life, he has Anthony yearn for plenitude inside an all-encompassing womb.

The manuscript of *La Tentation* lay on Flaubert's desk for eighteen months. It was not published until April 1874, and by someone other than Michel Lévy. The author broke with his publisher in March 1872, after a heated quarrel over Louis Bouilhet's posthumous verse, *Dernières chansons*, which Flaubert had persuaded Lévy to bring out under his imprint. Lévy agreed to pay the printer, on condition that he be reimbursed. Flaubert spared no expense in the design and production of a luxurious volume, bulked up by blank pages between each of the fifty-two poems, without ever consulting Lévy. The matter came to a head on March 20, 1872, when Lévy warned that he would forgive no debt incurred on behalf of a work whose literary merit he considered doubtful. Flaubert exploded, shouting accusations that apparently had no basis in fact. "He went back on his word, which I experienced as a slap in the face," he reported to George Sand. "I went pale, then turned red . . . Never has la maison Lévy seen anything quite like that scuffle . . . It left me unstrung, the way I feel after being heavily bled. How humiliating to fail at something after one has given it one's heart, one's mind, one's nerves, one's muscles, one's time." Despite her own fondness for Lévy, Sand might have understood why Flaubert wished to divorce himself from the publisher, but Flaubert went much further than she found reasonable in declaring that he had made a firm decision "not to make the presses groan for many long years" because he wanted nothing more to do with printers, publishers, newspapers, "and above all because I want to hear no talk of money!" He confessed that his aversion to the subject was pathological. "Why does the mere sight of a *bill* infuriate me? It borders on dementia. I'm quite serious. Note that I've bungled everything this winter. *Aïssé* didn't turn a profit. *Dernières chansons* almost resulted in a lawsuit . . . Heaven help me from bungling *Saint Antoine* as well."

Disheartened though he was by his failure to enhance his friend's posthumous reputation and to make some money for Louis's common-law widow,

Léonie Le Parfait, would Flaubert have reacted so belligerently had he not identified so strongly with Bouilhet? In vilifying Lévy for his indifference to *Les Dernières Chansons*, did he not fear that Lévy would form the same poor opinion of *La Tentation*? And would that verdict not humiliate him all the more for being rendered by a man who, in his eyes, wielded paternal authority? He had wanted Lévy to buy *Salammbô* sight unseen. Now he found a way of avoiding the world's judgment altogether: he would reject the rejector and snub not only Lévy but every other publisher. By 1873 there were several suitors. "I treat them impudently," he wrote to Edma Roger des Genettes on January 22, boasting that he had them climb the stairs on rue Murillo again and again only to send them away empty-handed, rather like the garret dweller in Baudelaire's *Mauvais Vitrier* who has a glazier walk up seven flights with his wares on his back for the pleasure of shouting: "What? You have no colored glass?" In short, he demonstrated his virility without exposing his member.

The complaints aired on March 20 cannot explain the intensity of Flaubert's animus against Lévy. That fire was fed by the kindling of his youth, and earlier disappointments made his failure to advance Bouilhet's cause excessively painful. Why, he wondered some weeks after the quarrel, did the indignation that Lévy had provoked still oppress him? "How is it I even think about him?" A year later he had not yet put the matter to rest. "I've begun not to think continually about Michel Lévy anymore," he wrote to George Sand. "That hatred was becoming manic and hindering me. I'm not completely rid of it, but the thought of that wretch doesn't give me palpitations now . . . On the other hand, I'll print nothing whatever in the future rather than traffic with Merchants." The vow of silence has a childish ring to it. He would spite the bourgeois world by disappearing from it, like Anthony. He would not only write hermetic works, he would write them for himself alone (and a few invited guests).

Sand, who took this threat seriously, urged him to let her find him another publisher, but her good offices proved unnecessary, for in 1873 a dapper, charming young man named Georges Charpentier, who had just inherited his father's publishing house, sought him out. It impressed Flaubert greatly that Charpentier visited Croisset, shared two meals, petted the hound throughout their conversation, listened to his host read an unproduced play of Bouilhet's, and when he left thanked him for his hospitality. All very un-Lévy-like. With Zola under contract, the willful Charpentier was bent on capturing Flaubert before pursuing Goncourt and Daudet, and on that day, June 20, he succeeded. He proposed to republish *Madame Bovary* in an edition that included speeches delivered by the prosecution and defense at the trial of 1857. A new edition of *Salammbô* would have an appendix containing, among other documents, Flaubert's detailed letter of rebuttal to Froehner. Charpentier couldn't yet lay claim to *L'Éducation sentimentale*, but he acquired *La Tentation de Saint Antoine*, which Flaubert had been tinkering with since June 1873.

When Flaubert finally delivered the manuscript of *La Tentation*, he did so with the solemnity and reluctance of an author surrendering the child that had, in its three mutations, spanned his creative life. Twenty years later, Charpentier's partner, Maurice Dreyfous, clearly recalled the scene, which took place at their bookstore on the rue de Grenelle.

> He entered with an uncharacteristically calm, heavy step. His face was much less ruddy than usual, and his gestures more sober. In his hand he held a small package, a notebook wrapped in very luxurious white paper and with a blue-gray silk ribbon around it. After a cordial greeting, he handed me the notebook and in a shaky voice attempting to sound brave, he uttered these few words: "That, my dear fellow, is *Saint Antoine*."

As Dreyfous reached out to accept the manuscript, Flaubert withdrew it in a slow, involuntary movement, undid the bow himself to reveal a white folder with knotted loops of white silk on one side. Flaubert opened it.

> The manuscript . . . was written on wide sheets of fine paper called ministerial paper. It wasn't the original manuscript but a copy, a masterpiece of calligraphy, flowing, limpid, flawless. Here and there one saw a few punctuation marks added by the author in different ink.

Flaubert turned the pages tenderly, commending their appearance and thinking perhaps about the poor copyist who, to his secret satisfaction, had been driven half-mad by the multitude of unfamiliar names. Charpentier broke the spell with practical questions, but Flaubert shilly-shallied, as if postponing further a separation that had already been postponed almost two years. When the time came to give *La Tentation* an independent existence, he caressed it once more and backed away.

Publication was delayed some months so that the book would not appear at the same time as Victor Hugo's novel *Quatrevingt-treize*. As Flaubert feared, critics treated his enigmatic work roughly. There were several exceptions, one being a review in *Le Bien Public* by Edouard Drumont, who proclaimed Anthony's survey of pagan deities with the devil superior to Faust's adventures with Mephistopheles.* Turgenev wrote from Germany

---

*Drumont, a minor figure on the literary scene, acquired notoriety as the author in 1886 of *La France juive*, a ranting compendium of anti-Semitic fables that became one of the great best sellers of the century.

that *La Tentation* had received favorable notice in a Berlin newspaper. But the reception was overwhelmingly hostile. In *Le Constitutionnel,* Barbey d'Aurevilly, a fervent Catholic royalist, who had already savaged Flaubert's other works, noted the contrast "between the hero of the book and its author, between a pious, ardent saint of grand proportions" and "the coldest man of our times, the most materialist in talent, the most indifferent to moral things." Saint-René Taillandier, who found *La Tentation* unreadable, held Flaubert up to ridicule in *La Revue des Deux Mondes* for supposedly declaring, "I want to seize a moment of the ancient world at which all the religions of East and West mingled in the bosom of the Roman Empire. What contrast! What strange shapes! What unheard-of apparitions. Now *there* is something to test my strength!" Even friends were reported to have made unkind remarks. The only compliments, he complained to George Sand, came from professors at the Strasbourg School of Theology, from Father Didon, and from his butcher's cashier. "What astonishes me about several of these critical reviews is the barely concealed *hatred* of me, me as an individual, a campaign of denigration I'm hard-pressed to explain. I don't feel wounded, but this avalanche of inanities makes me sad. One would rather inspire good feelings than bad. Aside from that, *Saint Antoine* is no longer on my mind. This summer I shall begin work on another book, wine from the same cask." Though he could not have convinced himself (as he had previously done with *L'Éducation sentimentale*) that *La Tentation* would be well received, the chorus of execration did continue to prey on his mind. Two and a half months after telling Sand that he had put the work behind him, he asked Charpentier to keep track of articles written about it. "I value that pile of rubbish." Renan had promised him a review; Flaubert dunned him for it almost until the end of the year. He might have done the same with Théophile Gautier, who appreciated learned grotesquerie, but Gautier had been in his grave since October 1872.

In the usual way, George Sand did her best to comfort him. "Be valiant and *satisfied*, since *Saint Antoine* is selling well," she wrote from Nohant on April 10. "What difference does it make if someone bashes you in this paper or that one? Once upon a time it meant something — now it means nothing. The public is no longer what it used to be, and journalism no longer exerts the least literary influence. Everyone is a critic and arrives at his own opinion." In her opinion, *La Tentation* was "a masterpiece, a magnificent book."

It is noteworthy, from a broader perspective, that Sand's opinion was echoed nine years later by young Sigmund Freud, who read most of *La Tentation* on a train trip to Gmunden with Josef Breuer. "I was already deeply moved by the splendid panorama, and now on top of it all came this book which in the most condensed fashion and with unsurpassable vividness throws at one's head the whole trashy world," he wrote to his future wife in July 1883, several months before arriving in Paris to study with Jean Charcot. "It calls up not only the great problems of knowledge," he continued, "but the real riddles of life, all the conflicts of feelings and impulses; and it confirms the awareness of our perplexity in the mysteriousness that reigns everywhere. These questions, it is true, are always there, and one should always be thinking of them. What one does, however, is to confine oneself to a narrow aim every hour and every day and get used to the idea that to concern oneself with these enigmas is the task of a special hour, in the belief that they exist only in those special hours. Then they suddenly assail one in the morning and rob one of one's composure and one's spirits." What impressed him above everything else, he concluded, after elegantly summarizing what he called a Walpurgisnacht, was "the vividness of the hallucinations, the way in which the sense impressions surge up, transform themselves, and suddenly disappear."

The other literary work Freud described enthusiastically to Martha Bernays that year was *Don Quixote*.

XXII

❧

"We are all of us émigrés, left over from another age."

AFTER 1871, Flaubert's letters harp on the idea that the war had created a historical rift separating him from his spiritual environment. Everything dear and familiar to him lay on the nether side of the divide, in an ancien régime of literary sensibilities. No matter that Magny still served dinner every night: "dinner at Magny's" was now an extinct ritual. "If we scrounged around, might we not assemble a little group of émigrés?" he proposed to Edma Roger des Genettes. "For we are all of us émigrés, left over from another age." To George Sand he declared, only half-facetiously, that he might end up like the old cleric who according to Montaigne never left his room in thirty years because of the "inconvenience caused by his melancholy." He claimed to see very few people. "Anyway, with *whom* can I associate? The war has hollowed out abysses." At that juncture, no Russian exemplified better than Flaubert the observation that Chekhov was to make about his fellow Slavs, that they love recalling life but do not love living.

With whom could he associate? Only Turgenev came to mind. Turgenev alone gave him complete satisfaction, he declared. "What a man! What conversation! What taste!" Sand knew full well that Flaubert did not lack literary company of a high order during the winter season in Paris. Several evenings were spent with Victor Hugo, for example, whose impromptu recitations of Tacitus's *Annals* and Bossuet's funerary sermons were music to his ears. But Hugo the amiable host (in his home on the rue de Clichy, quite near that of Caroline Commanville) couldn't ever quite domesticate Hugo the Immortal. One didn't cozy up to a legend. In Turgenev, on the other hand, Flaubert recognized a kindred soul who shared his sense of being nowhere, of drifting anachronistically among bourgeois, unmarriageable women, and confreres pledged to esthetic programs or political ideologies that struck them both as crude, if not worse. They shared as well the knowledge that fame had not cured them of childhood. By 1868, when they became intimate, these were not young men imagining themselves shaping the future but two saddened giants entering their fifties convinced that they had no posterity — that they had washed up on a barren island.

For Turgenev, life began on an island, of sorts, in 1818. The family estate, which he later called "my Patmos," encompassed twenty villages spread over more than thirty thousand acres in Orel province. The manor, Spasskoe, was itself a populous community equipped with barns, mills, stables, ateliers, an infirmary, and even a theater where serfs trained in music and dance gave performances whenever so bidden by Turgenev's mother, Varvara Petrovna. Until he entered Moscow University, Ivan had known no schoolmates other than his brother, Nikolai. Like young princes they received instruction from private tutors, who organized a curriculum that bespoke their parents' ambition to raise them as European gentlemen. Although profoundly Russian in other respects, Sergei and Varvara Turgenev spurned Slavophile doctrine. At age four Ivan was taken abroad on a grand tour through Germany, Austria, Switzerland, and France, which ended with a long sojourn in Paris. Sergei, who had won citations for bravery during the war against Napoleon, hewed to aristocratic tradition in speaking French at home, and Varvara, the rich commoner he married for her five thousand serfs, imitated him. It was her habit to call Ivan "Jean."

Being Varvara Petrovna's favorite son entitled Ivan to bear responsibility for the pain that unfaithful men, including her husband (who died young), had inflicted on her, and everything we know suggests that in the matter of sadistic strategies her imagination was as prompt as her will. "She herself, in inventiveness and in far-sighted and calculated malevolence, was far more dangerous than her hated favorites who carried out her commands," wrote Turgenev's friend Annenkov. "No one could equal her in the art of insulting, of humiliating, or of causing unhappiness, while at the same time preserving decency, calm, and her own dignity." At Spasskoe, midway between the Black Sea and the Caspian, where no civil or religious authority dared to overrule her, she administered a despotic queendom, giving her domestic staff ministerial titles as well as foreign patronymics. Her whim was law, law was enforced by her private constabulary, and for any number of petty trans-gressions a serf would be flogged or find himself exiled to some village far from his kinfolk. Addressing the mistress without having been granted that privilege was one such offense. But most peasants never saw their owner ex-cept during her summer inspection tour, when, like *la Maison du Roi,* Spasskoe became a caravan progressing in state through one terror-stricken hamlet after another. Otherwise she governed from an office that the few who could enter were invited to regard as a throne room. It contained a dais, and behind the dais hung a portrait of Varvara Petrovna herself.

That image may have been what Turgenev envisioned years later, before leaving France on a homeward journey the prospect of which filled him with dread. "Russia can wait — that immense and somber figure motion-less and masked like the Sphinx of Oedipus," he told a friend. "Set your mind at ease, Sphinx. I shall return to you and you can devour me at your leisure, if I do not solve your riddle for yet a little while." Varvara's rule had nurtured in him a hatred of violence (which did not, as with Flaubert, pre-clude fascination), a strong tendency to identify with victims of it, and a belief that succumbing to passion must inevitably prove fatal. What made him the bachelor who engaged throughout his life in inconclusive ro-mances and an ironist who mocked even the objects of his deepest sympa-thy also made him an expatriate who preferred to contemplate his beloved mother country from afar.

In any event, to write or talk honestly about Russia involved great risk after the Decembrist plot of 1825, when the regime had stifled all discus-sion. Turgenev's critical intelligence did not awaken until the years 1839–41, which he spent as a student in Berlin reading Hegel with Karl Werder, rooming with Michael Bakunin, and staying up late with other members of the Russian intelligentsia whose passports had not yet been confiscated by Czar Nicholas's secret police. Even more critical for his development, per-haps, was a trip through Italy, where art offered relief from the political-philosophical systems furiously colliding in boardinghouses up north.

Already the marvelous raconteur whose conversation would enliven drawing rooms all over Europe, Turgenev did not seem cut out for solitary work. Brilliant but weak willed, he impressed the historian T. N. Granovsky as hopelessly dilettantish, and Turgenev, who had a high-pitched voice oddly unbefitting his majestic frame, concurred in that opinion. Without financial hardship to spur him on, he no sooner set himself goals than he lost sight of them and drifted off course. An academic career evaporated when, after passing the examination for a professorship in philosophy, he chose not to write his thesis. Then, on the strength of a paper titled "Some Remarks on the Russian Economy and the Russian Peasant," he was ap-pointed to a post at the Interior Ministry. Before long, government service bored him, and a leave of absence for medical reasons turned out to be a final farewell.

That this waffling signaled not infirmity of purpose but a growing sense of his literary vocation became apparent the closer he drew to men connected with the review Pushkin had founded several years earlier. Turgenev wrote verse before he attempted fiction, and *Parasha,* a long narrative poem styled after *Eugene Onegin,* made Saint Petersburg sit up and take notice. Lauded by Belinsky — the critic who stood foremost in defending Pushkin, Lermontov, and Gogol against Russia's establishment — *Parasha* won Turgenev support even in Spasskoe; Varvara Petrovna was pleased to learn that his writing of poetry, which she deemed unworthy of gentlemen, had not been an altogether frivolous enterprise.

Varvara Petrovna could forgive her son literature. Far more troublesome was a passion strong enough to pry him loose from her, which declared itself in 1843 when Turgenev met the world-renowned Spanish soprano Pauline Garcia Viardot, who had come to sing Rossini at the Imperial Opera. Twenty-one years old, or half the age of her husband and impresario, Louis Viardot, this extraordinary woman cast spells on men with a narcissistic allure that more than compensated for her homeliness. "She is ugly but with a kind of ugliness which is noble, I should almost like to say beautiful," exclaimed Heine. "Indeed, the Garcia recalls less the civilized beauty and tame gracefulness of our European homelands than she does the terrifying magnificence of some exotic and wild country." Maternal but wrapped up in her career, sensual and yet aloof, Pauline Viardot intimated pleasures quite irresistible to a man like Turgenev, who according to one friend said the physical side of relationships with women had always mattered less to him than the spiritual side, consummation less than the emotions preceding it. This was another trait he and Flaubert shared in common.

For the rest of his life, Turgenev's movements were dictated as often by the desire to be near Pauline as by the need to wander alone, ambivalent feelings about his motherland, or force of circumstance. Perching on the edge of another man's nest sometimes induced vertigo, but it suited him better than having no nest at all. Ultimately the awkward ménage à trois he made with Pauline and Louis Viardot became a stable family in which he found contentment.

In 1845 he visited the Viardots at Courtavenel, their country estate outside Paris, and reluctantly went home after several months spent exploring France. His next visit began in 1847 and lasted three years, or long enough to let him familiarize himself with the cultural world that had nurtured Pauline. Courtavenel, where Turgenev stayed when not at the Viardots' town house on the rue de Douai, was a gathering place for such luminaries as George Sand, Ary Scheffer, and Giacomo Meyerbeer. He found himself taken up by *tout Paris,* which meant that invitations abounded, and the letters he sent to Pauline during her extensive concert tours provide a chronicle of events in music, theater, and society. But her absences also afforded him the opportunity to withdraw from the world. Courtavenel, which he called "the cradle of my fame," was where he wrote, among much else, the stories brought together as *Sketches from a Sportsman's Notebooks.*

Why he left France in 1850 — when fear of being infected by the revolutionary epidemic that had swept through Europe made Russia less hospitable than ever to liberal minds — is a question Turgenev himself couldn't answer simply. Reasons of the heart tugged both ways. Although he blessed Pauline Viardot for the amorous tyranny she exercised over him, another quite different view of love emerges from his play *A Month in the Country,* which he wrote at Courtavenel. "Love, whether happy or unhappy, is a real calamity if you give yourself up wholly to it," proclaims Turgenev's mouthpiece. "You will find out what it means to belong to a petticoat, what it means to be enslaved, to be infected, and how shameful and wearisome such slavery is." It hardly mattered that France had recently become a republic; he lived in a despotic state.

Furthermore, to linger abroad and befriend political exiles such as Alexander Herzen, over whom Czar Nicholas's secret service kept close watch, was to run the risk of suffering their fate. Bigamous in his loyalties, Turgenev did not want to find himself either in Russia without an escape route westward or in Europe permanently cut off from the language in which he dreamed, the land that peopled his imagination and afforded him his leisure, the literati who knew how well he wrote, the government that took his words seriously enough to consider him dangerous.

A grim fascination with danger would reveal itself years later in his remarkable essay about the execution of the mass murderer Troppmann at Roquette prison in Paris. Seeing a doomed man hustled through grim ceremonies must have evoked for Turgenev the punishment dealt him soon after his return to Petersburg. In 1852 Nicolai Gogol died. Russian officialdom, which viewed Gogol as a mortal enemy for having satirized the regime, forbade public notice to be taken of his death, but Turgenev managed to elude censorship and published a eulogistic obituary. He was arrested, jailed, and exiled to Spasskoe, where he languished for eighteen months. Not until the Crimean War ended did authorities grant him permission to travel outside Russia. By then, 1856, he had written *Rudin,* which shows the novelist fully in possession of his style and themes.

When Turgenev visited Courtavenel again, it became abundantly clear that he could not take up where he had left off six years earlier with Pauline, who had meanwhile borne Louis several more children. "My health is good, but my spirit is sad. Around me there is a regular family life . . . What am I here for, and why . . . should I be turning my gaze back-wards?" More submissive than ever, he told his friend Nekrasov that he would "dance on the roof, stark naked and painted yellow all over" if asked to do so by Pauline. Even the jester's role was refused him, however, and for some years Turgenev led a restless existence, stopping at Courtavenel en route to London, Paris, Vienna, Berlin, Petersburg, and Spasskoe. In Rus-sia, snubs from belligerent young radicals like Dobrolyubov, who had no use for Turgenev's gradualist view of social change, aggravated his sense that he was a peripheral figure. And yet the periphery was the environment that suited him best in many respects. Between 1859 and 1863 he brought out three major novels, including *Fathers and Sons.*

Heeding signs of wear in her voice, Pauline Viardot retired from the op-eratic stage to establish a school at Baden-Baden, and Turgenev, who finally had his devotion rewarded with the intimacy (platonic perhaps) for which he yearned, lost no time joining her there. Her retirement marked the end of his incessant wandering. Baden-Baden would be home for him from 1863 until war broke out between France and Prussia. During those seven years life revolved around the Viardots' villa, where musical soirees brought together artists, statesmen, and a Gotha Almanac of aristocrats who regu-larly gathered at the spa. On one occasion or another, Turgenev met the king and queen of Prussia, Bismarck, the empress Eugénie, Wagner, Brahms, and Clara Schumann. "There is no necessity for a writer to live in his own country, at least there is no need to do this continually," he argued in a let-ter to his Russian confidante, the countess Lambert. "I see no reason why I should not settle in Baden-Baden. I do this not out of any desire for mate-rial delights . . . but simply so as to weave a little nest in which to await the onslaught of the inevitable end." At first his nest was a rented flat, but even-tually he built a villa complete with a theater in which Pauline's school per-formed little operas dreamed up by Turgenev himself. The writer did not consider it beneath him to appear onstage as a comic pasha or, when Pauline gave organ recitals, to work the pump for her.

It was unquestionably his own predicament he described in observing that the Don Quixotes of his age kept running after Dulcinea even though they knew her to be an ugly hag. The ambivalence of his relationships with women and of his feelings about nests extended to the realm of ideas, where a deep-seated skepticism denied him the comfort that others found in crypto-religious systems. "He who has faith has everything and can never suffer any loss, but he who doesn't have it has nothing, and I feel this all the more deeply since I belong to the company of those who have no faith," he wrote to the countess. "Still, I do not lose hope." Always at odds with him-self, he would have liked to believe but instead wrote novels that expose the sham in fanatical creeds. His urbane demeanor concealed anguish from which he could not escape by embracing some god, and this *dégagement* mystified extremists, who, because they recognized no middle ground, invariably imputed to him sympathy for the enemy camp. How well psychological pithiness fared in Russia may be seen from the reception given *Fathers and Sons*. Turgenev was damned as loudly by the right as by the left for having created, in Bazarov, its nihilist hero, a character who on the one hand enhanced the prestige of revolution and on the other furthered the cause of reaction.

Turgenev loathed Bazarov's philistinism, but the clinical distance from self for which his character strives was an ideal he endorsed to the extent of remaining awake during stomach surgery and watching it progress much the way Bazarov observes himself die. "During the operation I was thinking about our dinners," he later told Edmond de Goncourt, "and I sought those words with which I could convey to you the exact impression of steel breaking my skin and entering my flesh . . . like a knife slicing a banana." Haunted by death from an early age, when thoughts of death quite possibly masked a fear of castration, he arranged to starve his sexual being, to regard his body as yet another provisional abode, and it is revealing that at thirty-five he, like Flaubert, already called himself an old man. This same strategy helped him create novels whose most obvious characteristic is their pervasive irony — an irony that throws a kind of distant light on human turmoil. His search for the mot juste while on an operating table with his guts laid open was what had made him the writer partisans couldn't tolerate. It exemplified his whole literary vocation.

And it promoted the spiritual kinship he felt with Flaubert, to whom he wrote on one occasion: "Oh, we have hard times to live through, those of us who are *born spectators* [emphasis Turgenev's]." Flaubert as well expected art to rise above "personal inclinations and nervous susceptibilities."

Equally erudite, hypersensitive, romantic, and allergic to the language of received opinion, the two very large men (who together weighed just under five hundred pounds, as George Sand impishly observed*) exchanged several letters after their first meeting in 1863, as we have seen, but their mutual admiration did not become something more than that until 1868. "From the first I have felt a great liking for you — there are few men, particularly Frenchmen, with whom I feel so relaxed and yet so stimulated," Turgenev wrote from Baden-Baden in May of that year. "It seems to me that I could talk to you for weeks on end, but then we are a pair of moles

---

*Sand was so intrigued by their combined weight that she had the statistic (222 kilograms) posted on a door. It has thus been determined that in 1873 Turgenev, who stood three inches taller than Flaubert at six feet three inches, weighed 110 kilograms (242 pounds) and Flaubert, who protruded farther than his Russian friend, 112 kilograms (246 pounds).

burrowing away in the same direction." *L'Éducation sentimentale* appeared one year later, and Flaubert's novel about a character drifting in the manner of Turgenev's own "superfluous man" consecrated their affinity.

Events conspired, however, to deny them the nourishment of each other's mind. As soon as war broke out, the Viardots, like Caroline Commanville, sought refuge across the English Channel. Turgenev joined them in London, where the literary world offered him hospitality. Even as Flaubert was vituperating against the barbarians who had evicted him from Croisset, Turgenev was practicing his English on Ford Madox Brown, Swinburne, George Henry Lewes, and George Eliot. The two might have crossed paths when Flaubert visited Juliet Herbert in March, but most of 1871 had slipped away before they met again.

Peacetime saw Turgenev move into rooms on an upper floor of the Viardots' Paris town house. Even then, a meeting was often thwarted. Turgenev regularly suffered violent attacks of gout, which kept him housebound. "When I wrote to you that it was difficult to undertake anything at all, I never said a truer word," he wrote on November 27. "This last night, the ankle of my bad foot swelled up quite suddenly, and now I can neither put on a boot nor put my foot to the ground. So 'Anthony' will have to be put off — it's really awful luck — unless you would like to come here yourself with the manuscript. Or shall we wait a couple of days? . . . Here I am, and I sheepishly shake your hand in disappointment." The next day, in yet another note of apology, he explained that he had agreed to furnish a Saint Petersburg paper with an obituary of his uncle Nicholas Turgenev. "It must be sent off by tomorrow evening, so here I am shackled to the task. Dear old Anthony must wait until the day after tomorrow." But Flaubert was no slouch when it came to postponements, and at times it was he rather than Turgenev who begged off. "Well then! Here we are in the middle of December — and no Flaubert?" Turgenev queried on December 11, 1872. "Unfortunately I am not like Muhammad — I cannot go to the mountain. I cannot go at all — for I have not been out of my bedroom these last two weeks — and God knows how long this state of affairs will continue! My gout is at least as obstinate as the Versailles Assembly . . . Now then, make an effort and come to Paris." Flaubert replied on his fifty-first birthday that he could not yet face the prospect of shuttling around in railroad carriages.

So you won't see me before January 15. When I've embraced you, I shall go see Mme Sand, who seems not to want to come to Paris this winter because her play isn't going to be produced. The censor has banned it . . . Poor dear friend, how upset I am to hear that you are still suffering! You seem to be pretty fed up. A quarter of an hour of my company wouldn't be likely to cheer you up. I'm in a sepulchral frame of mind. I really feel like a good long talk with you, especially about the book I'm brooding over. It's going to involve me in a lot of reading. But when I've vomited my gall, perhaps I shall feel more settled. The *Nouvelliste de Rouen* printed your "King Lear of the Steppe" at the beginning of November. It was a tribute to you on the part of the editor, who knew you were supposed to be visiting me then.

Between their attacks of gout or spleen, migrations to spas, and seasons of reclusion in Spasskoe or Croisset, the men formed a strong bond. Although Flaubert affectionately called his friend "a large, soft pear," Turgenev found himself cast almost from the first in the dominant role, with Flaubert relying upon him as he did upon George Sand. It was for Flaubert to voice fears that he had lost his creative power, bungled his life, or embarked upon a lunatic enterprise, and for Turgenev to succor him, praise him, hurry him along. "Don't tarry too long over *Saint Antoine,* that's my refrain," he advised in February 1870. "Don't forget that people judge you according to the standards you yourself have established, and you're bearing the weight of your past." Four years later, writing from Russia, he helped him cope with disappointment. "*Antoine* is decidedly not something for a mass audience: ordinary readers shy away from it in horror — even in Russia. I didn't think that my compatriots were as delicate as that. No matter. It is a book that will endure, in spite of everything." Flaubert's plans for *Bouvard et Pécuchet* elicited a cautionary letter warning him against Cyclopean erudition. "The more I think about it, the more I see it as a subject to deal with *presto* in the manner of Swift or Voltaire. You know that has always been my opinion. The plan you told me about seemed charming and funny. If you make it heavy, if you are too learned . . . Anyway, you're at work kneading dough." This correspondence, which chronicles many broken appointments, also speaks of Turgenev's loyal effort to disseminate Flaubert's work in Germany and Russia. No literary agent could have been so assiduous. He dunned magazine editors, arranged reviews by influential critics, found translators, and translated into Russian two stories from *Trois Contes* (Three Stories) himself, taking great pains over them.

While Flaubert assured George Sand that she and Turgenev were the only mortals to whom he could unburden himself, there is no way of knowing if he told Turgenev about his seizures, or if Turgenev, for his part, answered questions Flaubert may have posed about Pauline Viardot. Did they ever sort out the contents of Turgenev's observation that the two were "born spectators" or talk about fetishes, marriage, their secret ambitions, their fear of death? All one knows for certain is that their closeness was bound up with a staunch belief in each other's art. However wrongheaded Turgenev found the plan for *Bouvard et Pécuchet,* he treated Flaubert the artist as a luminous exception to the rule that French writers, including

many with whom he often associated, were deficient in taste and seriousness of purpose.

Flaubert repaid the compliments in kind. When *Spring Torrents* came out,
he declared that he would have liked to be a professor of rhetoric for the
sole purpose of explicating Turgenev's works. "I believe I could make even
an idiot understand certain brilliant artifices." The novel (about a lonely,
middle-aged man grasping for the love he mislaid in young manhood) was
everybody's story, he exclaimed. "Alas! It makes one blush on one's own account. What a man is my friend Turgenev! What a man!"

In October 1872 Turgenev spent three days at Croisset, during which
Flaubert read him *La Tentation*. He wanted to reciprocate, but Flaubert
wouldn't embrace his suggestion that they tour Russia together. It was difficult enough to arrange a sojourn *à trois* at Nohant with George Sand, who
observed in the course of it that Flaubert, though he danced an exuberant
fandango, was less disposed than Turgenev to set literature aside and participate in the antic life of the household. Most meetings took place in Paris,
at Pauline Viardot's Thursday evening musicales or on Sunday afternoons at
Flaubert's flat on the rue Murillo.

Almost always the first to arrive on those Sunday afternoons, Turgenev
would fill a large armchair and await Edmond de Goncourt, Alphonse
Daudet, and Émile Zola. These five honored their sabbatical solidarity by
calling themselves *les Cinq*. The low-ceilinged flat, with walls covered in
cretonne but conspicuously bare of pictures, seemed too small for its tenant. An architect's table that served as a writing desk stood near the middle
of the main room, away from distracting views of the Parc Monceau. In
winter, Flaubert wore a skullcap and a loose brown robe. For warm
weather, Zola wrote some years later, he had designed a voluminous red
and white striped culotte, together with a tunic that made him look the
picture of a lounging Turk. "He claimed that it was for comfort, but I'm
inclined to believe that this attire derived from romantic fashions, for I also
saw him in checkered pants, frock coats pleated at the waist, and wide-
brimmed fedoras cocked over one ear." Sunday being his servant's day off,
Flaubert opened the door himself, embraced guests winded by the steep ascent, and led them into his smoke-filled flat. "We'd cover many subjects at
a gallop," wrote Zola, "always doubling back to literature, the latest book or
play, general questions, radical theories, but pressing on and analyzing indi-
viduals. Flaubert thundered, Turgenev told delightfully pungent tales,
Goncourt formulated sharp judgments in an idiom all his own, Daudet imbued his anecdotes with incomparable charm." Afternoons lasted from one
to seven o'clock.

Extending their collective range beyond the limits of Flaubert's flat and
the confines of Sunday afternoon, they arranged to dine in style at monthly

intervals. The number five may have been sufficiently defining high above the Parc Monceau, but at street level a title more expressive of their fraternity was needed. What did all five have in common? By April 1874, each had a tale of blighted theatrical ambition to tell. Goncourt still railed against a cabal that had driven his play *Henriette Maréchal* off the stage of the Comédie-Française nine years earlier. Daudet's *Arlésienne,* for which Bizet composed incidental music, had earned him nothing during its brief run at the Vaudeville. Turgenev's *A Month in the Country,* written in 1849, had reached the stage twenty-three years later only to die of exposure. Zola's *Les Héritiers Rabourdin* was dismissed as a feeble imitation of *Volpone.* And, as we shall see, a play by Flaubert, *Le Candidat,* flopped at the Odéon in March 1874, sharpening his previous disappointment over *Le Château des coeurs.* Among these gifted novelists, producing unsuccessful plays became a kind of initiatory ordeal, and so it was that they decided in April to celebrate their brotherhood at a *Dîner des Auteurs sifflés,* or Dinner of Jeered Authors, the first of a series, which Daudet remembered in *Trente ans de Paris* as grand occasions for gluttony.

> Flaubert wanted Rouen duck à l'étouffade; Edmond de Goncourt, with his exotic appetite, relished sweetmeats flavored with ginger; Zola, shellfish; Turgenev, caviar. We were not easily fed, and the Parisian restaurants must remember us. We moved around a lot. At one point we dined at Adolphe and Pelé's, behind the Opéra; at another on the place de l'Opéra-Comique; then at Voisin's, where the cellar satisfied all our demands and reconciled our different palates. We'd sit down at seven o'clock, and at two in the morning we had not yet finished. Flaubert and Zola dined in their shirtsleeves, Turgenev reclined on the couch. The better to talk in private, we'd turn the waiters out of the room — an entirely useless precaution, as Flaubert's voice carried from top to bottom of the house.

The moveable feast begot another ritual. Because Flaubert felt lonely when his colleagues scattered, Zola, who lived in a modest neighborhood not far from the Parc Monceau, would walk him home through the gaslit streets, pausing for leisurely chats at every intersection. *La Conquête de Plassans,* the fourth volume of his *Rougon-Macquart,* had greatly impressed Flaubert.

However unproductive one or another of the group may have been at his writing desk on the day of a feast, language always gushed forth at the banquet table. Zola remembered himself delivering a six-hour brief against Chateaubriand. More than one argument flared over various "isms" in vogue. And Flaubert gladly lectured about the criteria that distinguished good prose from bad. "Once I witnessed this very typical scene," wrote

Zola. "Turgenev, who retained his friendship with, and admiration for, Prosper Mérimée, wanted Flaubert . . . to explain why he thought that the author of *Columba* wrote badly. Flaubert read a page from it, and he stopped after every clause, prosecuting the 'whiches' and the 'thats' [*les 'qui' et les 'que'*], fuming over hackneyed expressions such as 'to take arms' or 'to lavish kisses.' The cacophony of certain syllabic sequences, the dryness of sentence endings, the illogical punctuation — everything received bad marks." Meanwhile Turgenev, obviously amazed at this autopsy, sat wide-eyed. "He explained that he knew of no other writer who scrupled in quite that way." Expressing the same amazement, Turgenev described to his compatriot Kovalevsky the fastidiousness with which Flaubert had revised his French translation of a Pushkin story from *Belkin's Tales.* He made spun gold from plain yarn. "I did not recognize my translation. What language! No one writes that well in France!"

Literary talk sometimes led to bouts of collective self-revelation, and in the *Journal* Goncourt describes his colleagues trading confidences with the zeal of adolescents eager to win approval, to entertain, or simply to talk dirty. One free-for-all took place over bouillabaisse at a tavern behind the Opéra-Comique, when the normally decorous Turgenev related a sexual escapade he had had during his *Wanderjahren.* "I was summoned back to Russia from Naples. I had only five hundred francs," Goncourt quotes him as saying.

> There were no railroads then. The voyage involved many difficulties and left me no allowance for love. I found myself on a bridge at Lucerne watching ducks with almond-shaped spots on their heads. Next to me a woman stood against the parapet. It was a magnificent evening. We began to chat, then to stroll, and we strolled into the cemetery . . . I can't remember ever having felt more desirous, more excited, more aggressive. The woman lay down on a large tomb and lifted her dress and petticoats so that her buttocks touched the stone. Beside myself with excitement, I swooped on her and in my haste and awkwardness caught my rod in gravelly tufts of grass, from which I had to extricate it. Never has coitus given me such keen pleasure.

Zola lacked Turgenev's anecdotal flair and store of exotic props. Unlike Flaubert, he knew little or nothing about Parisian brothels. For sheer lasciviousness he couldn't match Daudet, who claimed to have explored countless pudenda, often two at a time. But if Goncourt's *Journal* is the measure, he spoke about himself more ingenuously than they.

> Zola tells us that in his student days he would sometimes spend a whole week in bed with a woman, or anyway never get out of his nightshirt. The room *reeked*

of sperm, as he put it. He declares that after these orgies his feet felt like cotton and in the street he'd grab shutter latches for support. Now he's very sensible, he says, and has intercourse with his wife every ten days. He confesses several curious idiosyncrasies of nervous origin having to do with coitus. Two or three years ago, when he began *Les Rougon-Macquart,* he couldn't sit at his desk after a night of conjugal effusion, knowing beforehand that he couldn't construct a sentence, write a line. Now it's the opposite.

It remained for Flaubert, this once, to elevate their banter from the crotch to the heart. He remembered himself as a boy of eleven in love with a girl whom he had met at a wedding. The expression *donner son coeur* (to give one's heart away) was much on his mind. He had just learned it and, interpreting it literally, wondered whether his father could be induced to operate upon him. If so, he would have a coachman wearing a plumed cap deliver his heart to his inamorata in a hamper of the kind that grateful patients often sent to the Hôtel-Dieu filled with fish or game. "I saw my heart placed, bloodlessly, on the buffet in my little wife's dining room."

Turgenev, Zola, and Goncourt had all been present on March 11, 1874, at the flop that gave Flaubert his credentials for membership in the Club of Jeered Authors. It came seven months after he first told his friends about a scathing political comedy that might never get past the censor if he succeeded in doing what he intended to do. A theatrical entrepreneur named Carvalho, director of the Vaudeville — where *La Dame aux camélias* had had its famous run in the 1850s — was given the scenario of *Le Candidat* and waxed enthusiastic over it. His enthusiasm did not wane when Flaubert read the finished work to actors at the Vaudeville in December (fortifying himself beforehand with a dozen oysters, a steak, half a bottle of Chambertin, and brandy). The cast made an optimistic prediction that audiences would be rolling in the aisles. "However (there is always a however)," he wrote to Caroline, "there may be revisions. I realized today that Carvalho definitely knows his business. His comments chime with those of . . . Turgenev, who spent an entire day at my place. He returned in the evening after dinner and didn't leave until one in the morning. Only people of genius behave so obligingly."

His cast should have been his claque. In *Le Candidat* Flaubert showed no sign of having attempted to create a sympathetic character. Worse yet, he gave no indication of having learned how to write for the stage, although *Le Candidat* might have succeeded brilliantly as a puppet play. Its main character, Rousselin, a rich, retired bourgeois, is eager to consecrate his newly minted fortune and escape the boredom of provincial life with a seat in the National Assembly. His dream comes true after a series of intrigues involving patronage, blackmail, adultery, the lure of his daughter's dowry, empty words, and swift betrayals. Expediency reigns supreme. Rousselin turns every color of the political spectrum while promising workers one thing, artisans another, and an influential landowner named Bouvigny yet another. At the outset he is a red radical; at the end he is lily-white. Judged only by intricacy of plot, *Le Candidat* rivals Labiche's comedies, but that is all they have in common. While strenuously aiming for the funny bone, Flaubert hits it only once, when, in a scene reminiscent of the prefectural counselor's oration at the Yonville fair, Rousselin is shown in an empty village café rehearsing his imminent appearance before local electors.

Zola, whose *Héritiers Rabourdin* had been applauded by Flaubert, loved the play. "Into *Le Candidat* you put more powerful and truly comical observation than one of our hacks would draw on to churn out theater for ten years." But Zola was a minority of one. In *Le Moniteur Universel,* a former friend, Paul de Saint-Victor, dismissed the work as "false and common, boring and cold, without movement and without invention, poor in observation and heavy of spirit." It presented marionettes rather than people, he declared. The same criticism recurs in *Le Journal des Débats,* where Auguste Vitu likened Flaubert's characters to the flat, coarsely colored Épinal images sold for a penny at fairgrounds. It was incumbent upon the critic, wrote Vitu, to remind Flaubert that a play devoid of characters on whom the audience can drape its sympathies was foredoomed. *Le Candidat* made it clear to everyone who saw it, he concluded, that "M. G. Flaubert does not know theater and lacks the natural gift that, in some few prodigies, compensates for inexperience."

Not surprisingly, Edmond de Goncourt found these reviews excessively kind. Why was it, he wondered, that the papers did not eviscerate *Le Candidat* as they would have done if he, Goncourt, had been its author? But even George Sand, who seldom found fault with Flaubert's work, couldn't pay *Le Candidat* any compliments. "We have read *Le Candidat* and we are about to reread *Antoine,*" she wrote from Nohant on April 3 (the "we" including herself, her son, and her daughter-in-law). Sand's view that *La Tentation* was an indubitable masterpiece hadn't changed, but in *Le Candidat* Flaubert had fallen far short of himself.

> You, my friend, don't see it, *you* as spectator witnessing an action and wanting to interest yourself in it. The subject is sickening, too real for the stage and treated with too much love of reality. Theatrical illusionism has the perverse effect of making a real rosebush seem less real than a painted one. And even then the rosebush painted by a master is less persuasive than something crudely painted on sized cloth. It's the same with plays. Yours isn't fun to read; quite the contrary, it's sad. It doesn't provoke laughter, and since none of the characters holds one's interest, one is not interested in what happens. This doesn't mean

that you cannot and should not write for the theater, [only that] writing for the theater is more difficult, a hundred times more difficult, than writing literature to be read. Unless one is Molière and portrays a very particular milieu, eighteen tries out of twenty fail.

She urged him to remember that her negative remarks only validated the sincerity of her praise when she offered it. Newspaper reviews didn't interest her. "Individual judgments, where theater is concerned, prove nothing. Proof lies in the effect a play has on the collective being, and I read it from that perspective. If *Le Candidat* had been a success, I would have been happy with your success but not with the play. There's talent in the workmanship, of course. How could there not be? But you've used bricks and mortar to build a house that doesn't sit well on its plot. The architect chose the wrong terrain . . . You made it *exact,* and the art of theater disappears."

Flaubert resorted to lenient self-criticism as a defense against public disparagement, consoling himself by telling Sand that no reviewer had identified the faults that spoiled *Le Candidat*. In other words, he may have sired a cripple, but since he alone knew why the child limped, his was the only negative review worth anything. Sand's reflections appear not to have impressed him. "All the talk about theatrical arcana is highly comical!" he sneered. "One might think that the theater surpassed the limits of human intelligence, that it is a mystery reserved for those who write like cabdrivers. *The question of immediate success* trumps every other. It is the school of demoralization!"

The failure of *Le Candidat* heckled him throughout the fall and winter of 1874–75. Why write at all, he wondered, when the public has been spurning his work for years? A black cloud hung over Croisset. It followed him to Paris, where he resided from mid-November 1874 to May 1875. Sleeping ten or twelve hours every night, he could hardly bring himself to continue *Bouvard et Pécuchet*. It was, he told George Sand, a "dog of a book." To Edma Roger des Genettes he declared that only an accursed soul could conceive the idea of embarking on something like it. "At last I've finished the first chapter and have outlined the second, which will encompass medicine, chemistry, geology — all within the space of thirty pages! — and secondary characters to boot, for there must be a semblance of action, some kind of story line so that the thing doesn't read like a philosophical dissertation," he wrote to her in mid-April. "What throws me into despair is the fact that I no longer believe in my book. The difficulties yet to be encountered crush me in advance." It is quite possible, moreover, that Flaubert suffered multiple seizures during this period. A word he used repeatedly, *fêlé,* meaning flawed or cracked, suggests as much. The postscript to one letter, signed "Cruchard, de plus en plus fêlé," states that "cracked" was no exaggeration, since he felt the contents of his brain "leaking out." Had he not confided to Taine on a previous occasion that epileptic seizures produced the sensation of images escaping his memory "like torrents of blood"? And had seizures not always left him drained? His torpor was no doubt intensified by regular doses of potassium bromide. He felt irremediably worn, old, and lonely — as lonely as a voyager lost in the wilderness, he told George Sand. "I am at once the desert, the nomad, and the camel."*

His physician, Dr Hardy, knew from experience that this was one camel unlikely to seek refreshment at a watering hole. In July 1874, Flaubert had visited Kaltbad, a spa near Lucerne, at Hardy's urging, and had taken exception to almost everything he found there: the Swiss Alps, the dauntless middle-European hikers who carved the sites they visited into their alpenstocks, the impeccably dressed waiters who looked like guests at a funeral. He couldn't see anything beyond the unlovely faces of Germans crowding the spa. "What toilettes [these ladies have]! What heads! Not a bright eye among them, not a decent bit of ribbon, not a well-shaped boot or nose, not a shoulder worth dreaming about." Boredom had kept his pipe lit, and pipe smoke had vitiated the mountain air. Countries without a history were devoid of interest, he wrote to George Sand. "I wouldn't trade the Vatican museum for all the glaciers in Switzerland." His spirits had risen only toward the end of his *cure,* when Laporte joined him in Kaltbad after doing business in Neufchâtel. Laporte gladly played the straight man to Flaubert's jackanapes. On their trip home, he obsequiously called him "Your Excellency" in the presence of customs agents, Flaubert having decided to identify himself as a "plenipotentiary minister."

IN THE early 1870s, when the National Assembly couldn't bring itself to leave Versailles and monarchists held out against the official proclamation of a republic, France was obsessed with parliamentary debate about this fundamental issue. The fact that politics could bother him, Flaubert wrote to a friend in January 1873, was a sure sign of decadence. "I am exasperated with the Right, to the point of understanding why the communards wanted to burn down Paris." Raving madmen were preferable to idiots in his opinion, if only because their reign did not generally last as long.

What had parliamentary debate accomplished since the fall of the Commune? Observers who thought that the entire left had been fatally compromised were soon proven wrong. By-elections held on July 2, 1871, saw republicans emerge victorious, the most prominent among them being

---

*He may have had in mind literal experiences of wandering lost. On at least one occasion, he couldn't find his way from one street to another in a familiar neighborhood of Rouen. He wandered for half an hour, like those patients described by the neurologist Dr John Hughlings Jackson as being in a "dreamy state."

Léon Gambetta. After five mute months he had found his voice again, though civil war had meanwhile persuaded him that only a republic built along conservative lines stood any chance of surviving opposition from monarchist ranks. It soon became obvious that the fallen demagogue was determined to find his account in making common cause with the adroit strategist of conservative republicanism, Adolphe Thiers. These two formed a tenuous marriage of convenience. Gambetta minded himself during parliamentary debate but felt freer outside the Assembly, and on campaigns through provincial France he made speeches that could not fail to rattle Thiers in Versailles. "Haven't we seen laborers in the cities and fields win the vote?" he asked a sympathetic crowd at Grenoble. "Don't the omens suggest that our land, which has tried every other alternative, intends at last to risk a republic and call upon the new social reserves [*nouvelles souches sociales*]? Yes, I descry, I feel, I proclaim the emergence of new social reserves." Thiers was later to complain that Gambetta never had the clear-cut ideas of a real statesman, that he always retreated into the role of tribune, which he played most naturally.

Lest the "new social reserves" emerge right away, the heterogeneous right, which still greatly outnumbered the left, sought to act in concert. At daggers drawn since 1830, Legitimists (supporting the Bourbon pretender, Charles X's childless heir Henri, comte de Chambord) and Orleanists (supporting Louis-Philippe's grandson, the comte de Paris) now agreed that Chambord should reign as a constitutional monarch and be succeeded by the comte de Paris. What this arrangement, called fusion, did not consider was the obstinacy of Chambord, who lived in a castle near Vienna, as cut off from the world as a Pirandellian solipsist. Chambord wanted all or nothing. Either restoration would be a faithful restoration of the kingdom France had abolished in 1830 along with Charles X, or it would enthrone someone other than himself. His absolute proviso was that the country raise the white lily-spangled flag, and rational heads tried in vain to make him compromise when he came home after four decades abroad. "[That flag] has always been for me inseparable from the absent fatherland; it flew over my cradle, I want it to shade my tomb," he declared in a statement published on July 6 by the royalist paper *Union*. "[Under that flag] the unification of the nation was achieved; with it your fathers, led by mine, conquered Alsace-Lorraine, whose loyalty will be the consolation of our misfortunes . . . I have received it as a sacred trust from the old king, my grandfather, dying in exile . . . In the glorious folds of this unblemished standard I shall bring you order and liberty! Frenchmen! Henri V cannot abandon the flag of Henri IV!" Eighty die-hard Legitimists in the parliament stood firm behind Chambord, but a majority of conservative deputies dissociated themselves from his manifesto. As patriotic gentlemen repelled by anachronism on the one hand and revolution on the other, they pledged allegiance to the tricolor flag and campaigned for a state that would be neither lily-white nor republican blue. In an age of dumb ideas, Flaubert wrote to Sand in 1873, that of fusion was the crowning stupidity, an assertion upon which he enlarged two months later in a letter to his niece. "How ignorant of history can one be to believe still in the efficaciousness of one man, to await a Messiah, a Savior! Long live the good Lord and down with Gods! Can one brush against the nap of a whole nation? Deny eighty years of democratic development? Return to the age of charters granted by the high and mighty? Chambord's partisans being angry with their liege lord is a comic spectacle . . . No matter! Saint-Louis's descendant . . . spared us some major disasters." The restoration of monarchy and the Commune were both historical inanities, he asserted. So, he thought, was a Napoleon IV.

The schism in conservative ranks involved not only monarchical absolutism but Catholic orthodoxy, and here the manifesto that divided the parties was a papal bull. Seven years earlier, in his *Syllabus of Errors*, Pius IX had declared war against secular Europe by denouncing the separation of church and state; claiming for his church control of all culture and science; rejecting freedom of faith, conscience, and worship; enumerating eighty "errors" altogether; and insisting that the pontiff neither could nor should make any concession whatever to progress, liberalism, and modern civilization. The *Syllabus* marked France profoundly. Cultivated prelates resisted Rome, but the lower clergy embraced popish obscurantism with fervor, and in rural parishes, where miraculous visitations were regularly reported, it was the lower clergy who made themselves heard. "Of all the mysteries that fill Church history, I don't know any that equals or surpasses this swift and complete transformation of Catholic France into a farmyard annex of the Vatican's *anticamera*," one liberal Catholic wrote shortly before the Vatican Council proclaimed the pope to be infallible and his episcopate universal. "I won't immolate justice and truth, reason and history in a sacrificial offering to the idol whom lay theologians have enthroned at the Vatican." While accumulating multifarious religious creeds for *La Tentation de Saint Antoine*, Flaubert inveighed against Lamennais's *Essai sur l'indifférence*, in which the church is represented as the repository of all truth.

War did not halt the ultramontane movement. On the contrary, it gave it further impetus, as Catholic clergy used France's defeat to advance the view that God had thus punished a wayward child. The imperial saturnalia was over, repentance was in order, and devout souls, many of whom wore the insignia of the Sacred Heart, flocked to holy sites throughout France. Flaubert thought that Catholicism, with its worship of sacred entrails, had come to resemble the cult of Isis. In 1873 a national pilgrimage sponsored by the Assumptionists saw thousands descend upon Lourdes, La Salette,

Pontmain, Mont-Saint-Michel, Chartres, and Paray-le-Monial for expiatory demonstrations that became political rallies. "Suspended in midair,
equally incapable of adopting the republican format that promises terror
and the monarchical format that demands obedience and respect," declared
Monsignor Pie at Chartres, "the French are a people [who] await a leader,
who invoke a master." One hundred fifty deputies heard Pie preach this
message and soon afterward went farther afield to hear Monsignor de Lese-
leuc bless them at Paray-le-Monial. "Since assembling in Versailles, you
have often asked forgiveness of God for France's crimes," said the bishop.
"You have often made honorable amends to the Sacred Heart of Jesus for
the ingratitude shown him, especially during the last eighty years." It did
not escape those present that eighty years earlier, in Year 1 according to the
Revolutionary calendar, Louis XVI had been guillotined.

Liberal Catholics as well believed that France would fall apart if she did
not harness herself to religious principles, and the quasi-official term for
the government they exercised, l'Ordre Moral, bespoke their staunchly patriarchal agenda. Men like Albert de Broglie, who was eventually to replace
Thiers as prime minister, regarded the church as society's frontline defense
against havoc wrought in the name of liberty, fraternity, and equality —
above all, equality. Universal suffrage exasperated them. (But it also exasperated anticlerical elitists like Flaubert, who insisted that when the masses,
being collectively devoid of intelligence, ceased to believe in the Immaculate Conception, they would, none the wiser, vest their belief in the hocus-
pocus of spiritualist seances.) Opposing universal suffrage was one thing;
disavowing the secular state or imagining the ancien régime to be a Holy
Land that promised redemption from modern turmoil was something else
again, and over this issue moderates often clashed with zealots. When, for
example, construction began on the Basilique du Sacré-Coeur in Montmartre, the Assembly, which authorized its founders to break ground, rebuffed a monarchist deputy who would have had legislators join priests in
consecrating the cornerstone. Such behavior infuriated the Holy See. "I
must tell France the truth," Pope Pius told French visitors in June 1871.
"There is in your country an evil worse than the Revolution, worse than
the Commune with its escapees from hell spreading fire through Paris.
What I fear is the wretched politics of Catholic liberalism. That's the real
scourge." He declared that he could suffer overt enemies more easily than
coreligionists who "propagate and sow revolution even as they pretend to
reconcile Catholicism with freedom."

The right-wing majority in parliament did not easily abandon all hope
that the Bourbon pretender could be brought around. Meanwhile, it improvised government under the redoubtable Adolphe Thiers, who, having
caught his second wind at the age of seventy-four, energetically tackled the

many problems that beset France. Repairing war damage, inventing an economy, negotiating new frontiers, building up the army, and calming restive cities, this plump, high-strung little man, who looked more like a ninepin than a pillar of state, manipulated the contentious legislature by flattering all hopes with bland courtesy. After three decades of writing history, he enjoyed making it, and some observers wondered whether he did not, indeed, fancy himself the First Consul reborn. Certainly he had a Napoleonic zest for administration. But what kept him in power was a general belief that he alone could manage Bismarck, whose Kulturkampf against Catholics in Germany reinforced the Prussian disapproval of religio-monarchical stirrings in France. So long as German troops occupied French soil, which they would do until France paid Germany the five billion francs in full, Thiers was on safe ground. Taking advantage of domestic turbulence, he pled the case for a conservative republic and exploited foreign relations to demand a title less nebulous than "chief executive."

Thiers triumphed nominally on August 31, 1871, when fellow deputies, in a masterpiece of ambiguous legislation called the Rivet Law, named him president of the French Republic while implying that France might yet become a monarchy:

> Until the country's definitive institutions are established, our provisional institutions must, for the sake of labor, of commerce, of industry, assume in everyone's eyes, if not such stability as only time can vouchsafe them, stability enough to harmonize conflicting wills and end party strife. [Furthermore], a new title, a more precise appellation may, without working fundamental change, have the effect of demonstrating the Assembly's intention to abide by the pact concluded at Bordeaux. May an extension of the chief executive's period in office . . . stabilize the office without its being inferred that this compromises the sovereign rights of the Assembly.

Now deputy, prime minister, and president all three, Thiers would have liked a free hand, but the majority, who feared his elusiveness even more than his tongue, controlled him through ministerial accountability.

Month after month, parliamentary adversaries wrestled over everything from reform and trade policy to military law and administrative organization. When Thiers tried to make prefects his satraps and mayors his appointees, the conservative bloc, which held sway in rural France, championed decentralization. When he sought to impose tariff barriers, the Assembly rose in defense of free trade. When he insisted upon a small professional army — small enough to quiet Germany's fear that France might march east at the earliest opportunity — squires who had only recently had him sue for peace advocated universal conscription. These skirmishes postponed the main battle, and on November 13, 1872, Thiers joined it. In a report to the nation, he declared: "[This] is the government of the country; to resolve anything else would mean a new revolution, and the one most to be feared. Let us not waste time in proclaiming it, but instead let us use time to stamp it with the character we desire and require. A committee selected by you, the Assembly, . . . gave it the title of Conservative Republic . . . The Republic will be conservative or will not be." In by-elections held during this period, republicans won thirty-one of thirty-eight seats nationwide.

It was in fact one such contest that led to Thiers's fall. On April 28, 1873, Charles Remusat, a moderate who held the post of foreign minister under Thiers, ran against a left-wing republican, Barodet, and lost decisively. Among conservatives, this event sharpened regrets of the kind Edmond de Goncourt had voiced in his journal almost two years earlier: "Society is dying of universal suffrage. Everyone admits that it is the fatal instrument of society's imminent ruin. Through it, the ignorance of the vile multitude governs. Through it, the army is robbed of obedience, discipline, duty . . . Monsieur Thiers is . . . a very short-term savior. He fancies that he can save present-day France with dilatory tactics, finagling, political legerdemain: small means cut to the measure of his small frame."

Having raised five billion francs in short order and thus liberated French territory, Thiers had outlived his position as the indispensable negotiator. He could no longer rely on Bismarck to save him from the consequences of Remusat's defeat, for which conservative legislators blamed him. They excoriated a government hospitable to "new barbarians [who] threaten society's very foundations" and, flouting national sentiment, demanded that the cabinet be reconstituted without republican ministers. Thiers stood firm, but Duc Albert de Broglie, the conservative leader, drafted a resolution to the effect that recent ministerial modifications had not given conservative interests their due. It carried by a narrow margin, whereupon Thiers, vowing revenge, stepped down. "Barodetan foolishness is in full flower," Flaubert wrote to Sand. "My God! My God! How vexatious it is to live in such times! You can't image the torrent of inanities that swirls around one. How wise you are to live far from Paris!" On May 21 the Assembly named Marshal Mac-Mahon president, and Mac-Mahon, almost exactly two years after he had led Versailles' troops against the Commune, sounded the call for moral order. "With God's help and the devotion of our army, which will always be an army of the law, with the support of all loyal men, we shall together continue the work of liberating the country and reestablishing moral order in our land," he declared in his first presidential message. Albert de Broglie, the grandson of Mme de Stael and Benjamin Constant and the son of a Broglie who had sided with Louis-Philippe in 1830, became prime minister of what would soon be dubbed "the Republic of Dukes." George Sand wondered whether she was witnessing an opera or an operetta.

The speed with which France paid Germany the indemnity was more a measure of her determination to have foreign troops evacuate occupied territory than of financial robustness. An agricultural crisis associated with falling prices throughout Europe had hurt every economic sector in the country, half of whose population, even with the exodus of young people from rural France, continued to live off the land. Industry stagnated. But many entrepreneurs had already been dealt a severe blow by the war itself, and one such blow made itself felt at Croisset. Intellectually roiled by the politics of his age, Flaubert would suffer from them materially when Ernest Commanville, who acted as his banker, shocked him with the news that he, Commanville, was, and had been for several years, teetering on the verge of bankruptcy.

Flaubert had been aware of trouble earlier on, but he indulged his aversion — his "pathological" aversion, as he described it — to all talk of money. Not until October 1874, when Commanville couldn't immediately honor his request for one thousand francs, did he entertain serious questions about his nephew's affairs. These had begun to go awry just before the war and had got much worse in the 1870s as a consequence of the economic recession. Commanville had bought raw timber from Scandinavia on credit, expecting to mill it at Dieppe and sell the finished board at a great profit. Unfortunately, prices for foodstuffs and industrial goods plummeted, whereupon his risky operation backfired. Encumbered on the one hand with debts that far exceeded a million francs and, on the other, with promissory notes he couldn't collect, he tried by devious maneuvers to satisfy his creditors and at length called upon the family for support. Flaubert's correspondence with Caroline reflects his mounting anxiety during the spring and summer of 1875, when somnolence gave way to insomnia. "Should your husband right his boat, should I see him earning money again and being as confident of the future as he once was, should I squeeze an annual income of ten thousand francs out of Deauville so as never again to fear poverty for us two, and should *Bouvard et Pécuchet* satisfy me, I believe I would have no more complaints in life," he wrote to Caroline on May 10. A letter from Flaubert to Caroline dated July 9 implies that the latter had aired the idea of saving Commanville from his improvidence by selling Croisset, or that Flaubert understood this to be her intention. "It is sweet of you to send me tender greetings," he wrote, "but I rebel when you say: 'Let us harden our hearts to the sight of a tree, to familiar rooms, to a cherished bauble the separation from which might seem to rob us of our spiritual substance.' I've spent my life depriving my heart of its rightful nourishment.

I've led an austere, laborious existence. I can't take any more. All the tears
I've choked back are now spilling out . . . And then the idea of no longer
having my own roof, a *home,* is intolerable. I now view Croisset with the
eye of a mother contemplating her consumptive child and thinking: 'How
much longer will he last?' And I cannot accustom myself to the thought of
a definitive separation. But the prospect of your ruin is what distresses me
most!" Three days later he implored her to keep him informed of all de-
velopments. "How much longer can Ernest hold out? It's my impression
that the final catastrophe is near. I'm expecting the other shoe to drop any
minute now. What a situation!" Frantic negotiations were taking place to
obtain a grace period, an arrangement for repayment in installments, or
partial forgiveness of the debt. Caroline and Ernest Commanville had
meanwhile left their town house on the rue de Clichy for a small apartment
on the rue du Faubourg Saint-Honoré, near the Étoile, where Flaubert,
wanting more spacious quarters and perhaps fearing his isolation on the rue
Murillo with the recurrence of seizures, would, before the year was out,
become their next-door neighbor.

To stave off a creditor named Faucon, Caroline decided to sell some government bonds, but a court hearing was required for authorization to revise
the terms of her marriage contract, which made the dowry inviolate.
When such authorization was not granted, as one gathers it was not, she
arranged to pay Faucon an annual sum of five thousand francs over ten
years, drawn upon income from her portfolio and secured by two of
Flaubert's friends, Raoul Duval and Edmond Laporte. Even so, bankruptcy
would not have been averted in the summer of 1875 without the enormous
sacrifice made by Flaubert himself. He sold the farm at Deauville and
bought Commanville's most pressing debt, without requiring guarantees, a
suicidal act of avuncular devotion. Had the imperious, embittered Caroline, who was undergoing hydrotherapy for acute anemia and migraines,
prodded her uncle's sore conscience? Had he been inspired by the sense of
family honor that saw him mount a white horse on other occasions? Was
the gift an expression of aristocratic contempt for bourgeois prudence? Was
he fearful of losing Caroline's love and determined to create a bond of financial dependence? All the above were no doubt at play. "Even if there is
a favorable outcome, we will be left with just about enough to scrape by,"
he wrote to George Sand.

> All my life I've sacrificed everything to peace of mind. Now it's lost forever. You
> know that I'm no poseur, so believe me when I say that I'd like to croak as
> quickly as possible, because I'm sunk, emptied, and a hundred years old. I would
> need to work up enthusiasm for an idea, for a book. But *faith* is now lacking.
> And all work has become impossible for me. I'm worried about my material fu-

ture, but my literary future seems even more dismal. There's nothing left of it. The wise thing would be to seek employment straightaway, a lucrative position. But what am I good for? And at fifty-four one doesn't change one's habits, one doesn't remake one's life. I've braced myself against misfortune. I've striven to be stoical. Every day I make great efforts to work. Impossible, impossible! My poor brain is mush.

The fear that material concerns had invaded his brain like Prussian dragoons (or a "child of Israel") and evicted the artist surfaces in many of his letters. To Léonie Brainne, for example, he insisted that one couldn't "make art" unless one were free of material cares. "From now on I'll no longer be free of them! My brain is overloaded with base preoccupations. I've been brought low! Your friend is a fallen man!" To Edma Roger des Genettes he complained of having lost the best part of his mind. "I believe that I shall never be able to write two consecutive lines. I've braced myself against misfortune. Every day I swear oaths to myself and *want* to work. Impossible!" Bound up with the feeling that he had "fallen" was his fantasy of a world innocent of money, guarded by Achille-Cléophas. "My poor good-natured father couldn't even do sums," he assured Caroline, "and up to the moment of his death I had never seen a court summons. We lived in complete disdain of commerce and money matters! And what security, what well-being!"

So alarmed was George Sand that she immediately inquired of a mutual friend, Agénor Bardoux, who had just been appointed undersecretary of justice, whether remunerative employment could be found for Flaubert. She herself proposed to buy the house at Croisset, in the event of its being put up for sale, and let him live out his life there. Had she not written, in her autobiography, that the attachment to old dwellings in which the history of one's life was inscribed indelibly on every wall made perfect sense to her? Her offer brought tears to Flaubert's eyes. By October, the situation seemed less desperate, or so he led Sand to believe. With what remained of his two hundred thousand francs, he purchased the debt held by Commanville's most intransigent creditor and arranged to have his nephew give him money when needed. Caroline had apparently been authorized to pledge a portion of her personal income, and a liquidator was expected to settle accounts. "Since there is no pressing issue right now, I prefer not to think about the situation," he told Sand on October 11. "I am cravenly divorcing my mind from thoughts of the future, or would like to. Enough of business! My God, my God! I've had more of it than I can bear during the past five months." In fact, the situation remained desperate. Four days earlier he had written to Ernest Commanville: "Our income (that is, your wife's and mine) is pledged, and for the present we don't have a sou coming in. Far from it! What we must pay annually (according to my small calculations) exceeds by four thousand francs what we can expect to receive. Bankruptcy had to be avoided above all. Very good! But we promised more than we can afford."*

Flaubert sent these letters from Brittany, where he had arrived on September 16, hoping to put things right in the company of an old Rouen friend, Georges Pouchet, who directed the marine research center at a fishing port called Concarneau. His residence for six weeks was an inn from which the view encompassed a forest of masts and the town's medieval fortifications. He swam every afternoon, weather permitting, and took long walks. In all weather he ate quantities of seafood prepared by the innkeeper, Mme Sargent, who didn't stint. Diversions were few. Pouchet gave him lessons in natural history on their rambles along the coast. He watched religious processions, observed events in the experimental fish pond, and contemplated sunsets that transformed Concarneau into a luminous wonderland. Sleeping became easy again. The otherwise nocturnal Flaubert blew out his candle at ten and rose at eight or nine. Apart from the duc de Saint-Simon's memoirs, a selection of which someone had lent him, he read only newspapers, but encountered no one interested in discussing politics, least of all Pouchet, whose powerful simplicity of purpose seemed unattainable. "How I envy G. Pouchet! There's someone who works and is happy! While he spends his days bent over a microscope in the laboratory, [I] sadly daydream beside the fireplace in an inn. At the moment children are playing marbles beneath my windows and there's a clacking of wooden clogs. The sky is grayish; night is descending little by little. Mlle Charlotte has brought me two candles." Searching for an image of discomposure more appropriate to his circumstances than that of the nomad on his camel, he told Caroline that he felt as rootless as kelp washed ashore by the surf.

His excursion was helpful, even if an autumnal melancholy followed the anguish of late summer. Concarneau put him happily in mind of Trouville as it once was, before the proliferation of villas gave it an air of gimcrack splendor. Above all it distanced him from Ernest Commanville and from *Bouvard et Pécuchet,* the research yet to be accomplished for that compen-

---

*Family finances are unclear. Valued at 129,000 francs in the notarial record of 1872, Deauville represented by far Flaubert's most substantial property. He sold it for 200,000 francs, which — if these calculations are correct — would have brought his total inheritance, including money inherited after his father's death, to something between 300,000 and 400,000 francs. It isn't known how much of his father's inheritance had been spent during the intervening years. What is certain is that the value of property in Deauville increased by magnitudes in the late nineteenth and early twentieth centuries. As Herbert Lottman notes, the Flaubert farm was later sold to Baron Henri de Rothschild, who built a large villa on it. In the 1920s, before the crash, a wealthy American named Ralph Beaver Strassburger (president of the Huguenot Society of Pennsylvania) bought it for 8 million francs, an enormous sum at the time.

dious novel weighing upon his mind as heavily as his nephew's financial embarrassment. During his first week at Concarneau, he began to plot a short story based upon the medieval legend of Saint Julian the Hospitaller, which he knew from the stained glass of Rouen Cathedral. In late September, friends were told about this new project. "I want to get started writing a little story, to see if I'm still capable of constructing a sentence," he wrote to Laporte. "I seriously doubt it. I believe I spoke to you about Saint Julian the Hospitaller . . . It's nothing at all and I attach no importance to it." It was a means of keeping himself limber for the big effort, whatever that might be. "I no longer believe in myself, I find myself empty, not a consoling discovery," he wrote to Edma Roger des Genettes. "*Bouvard et Pécuchet* was too difficult, I'm giving it up; I'm looking for another subject, unsuccessfully so far. Meanwhile there is 'Saint Julien l'Hospitalier' . . . It will be very short, thirty pages or so. If I find nothing and feel better, I'll resume *Bouvard et Pécuchet*." Short in length but richly textured, "Saint Julien" recounts the legend of a young nobleman whose maniacal stag hunts transcend mere sport, much as the carnage wrought by Matho in *Salammbô* surpasses ordinary warfare, preparing the way for a life of saintly self-abnegation commensurate with his bloody exploits. That this story would join two others in a work more familiar to subsequent generations than any of his others except *Madame Bovary,* Flaubert could not have imagined.

When Flaubert returned to Paris early in November, it was to his new flat five flights up at 240, rue du Faubourg Saint-Honoré, at the corner of avenue Hoche, near the Arc de Triomphe. He brought with him ten pages of his story and set about learning all he could about medieval venery. Financial imbroglios and *Bouvard et Pécuchet* had been temporarily put behind him. Like so many revenants in his life, they would catch up with him.

Two friends who welcomed the news that he had abandoned *Bouvard et Pécuchet* were Turgenev and George Sand. It has already been mentioned that Turgenev, after hearing Flaubert summarize his plan for it, had advised him to treat the subject in the manner of Swift or Voltaire. A year later it was obvious that Flaubert's ambitions did not make for ironical succinctness, and Turgenev, who eventually translated "Saint Julien l'Hospitalier," blessed the new project. "I am very happy indeed with the idea of *thirty* pages!"

As for George Sand, when a shaken Flaubert reached out to her inviting guidance, his most devoted friend spoke her mind freely in an exchange of philosophical letters. "I don't need to believe in the certain salvation of the planet and its inhabitants to believe in the necessity of the good and the beautiful," she wrote on January 12, 1876, only months before her death. "But I myself must keep climbing to my last breath, not out of some imperative need to find a 'good place,' and with no assurance of finding one, but because my only joy lies in traveling the high road with those who are near and dear." The literary school that concerned itself almost exclusively with social and individual squalor was repugnant to her.

> I flee the sewer, I seek what is dry and clean because I know that that is the law of my existence. Being human doesn't amount to all that much. We're still very near the ape from which it is said we descend. Well, all the more reason to distance ourselves from monkeys and reach for those relative truths our race is permitted to understand. Poor, limited, humble though they are, let us grasp them as best we can and not allow them to be taken from us.

At bottom she believed that she and Flaubert thought alike:

> But I practice this simple religion and you don't, since you allow yourself to lose heart; you aren't thoroughly imbued with it, since you curse life and desire death, not unlike a Catholic hoping to be rewarded, if only in the form of eternal repose. You have no guarantee that you will receive compensation. Life is perhaps eternal, and consequently work is as well. If such be the case, let us bravely soldier on. If it be otherwise, if the *self* should perish entirely, let us seek the honor of having accomplished our task. We have no categorical duties except to ourselves and our brethren. What we destroy in ourselves, we destroy in them. Our degradations degrade them, our falls pull them down.

She who had declared in her memoirs that the condition of self-understanding is self-forgetfulness, that one does not truly grasp oneself until losing oneself in a sweeping consciousness of mankind, reprimanded Flaubert for depriving others of his wealth by clinging to an ideal of impersonality.

> You read, you dig, you work more than I and a host of others. You have acquired more erudition than I shall ever possess. Thus, you are a hundred times richer than all of us. You are rich and you cry poverty. Should alms be given to a beggar whose pallet is stuffed with gold but wants to subsist on well-turned sentences and perfect words? Dummy, rummage through your pallet and eat your gold. Nourish yourself on the ideas and feelings you've squirreled away in your head and your heart. Words and sentences, the *form* you make so much of, will naturally flow from your digestion. You consider it an end in itself, it is only an effect. Happy effects only come out of an emotion, and an emotion only comes out of a conviction. One is not moved by the thing in which one doesn't ardently believe.
>
> I'm not saying that you don't believe. On the contrary, the affection, the protectiveness, the charming, simple goodness that mark your life all speak of a man

with strong beliefs. But for some reason you want to be another man when it comes to literature — one who must disappear, one who annihilates himself, one who exists not! What an odd compulsion! . . . No, I don't say that you should personally take the stage. There is, indeed, nothing to be gained by that . . . But hiding one's opinion about one's characters and thus leaving the reader uncertain as to what he or she should think is to bargain for incomprehension. At that point the reader leaves you.

A believer in didactic fiction, Sand blamed Flaubert's moral neutrality for the unsuccess of *L'Éducation sentimentale.*

The book was misunderstood; I told you so more than once, but you didn't listen. It needed a brief preface or, wherever the opportunity presented itself, a moral clue, if only a felicitously placed epithet condemning evil, characterizing moral weakness, recognizing effort. All the characters in that book are weak. All come up short, except those with bad instincts. Your intention was precisely to portray a deplorable society that encourages bad instincts and subverts noble efforts. When we are not understood it is always our fault. What the reader wants above all else is to penetrate our mind, and you disdainfully cloak yours. He believes that you scorn him, that you wish to mock him. I understood you because I know you. But what if the book had been given to me unsigned? I would have found it beautiful yet baffling, and would have wondered whether the author was immoral, skeptical, indifferent or aggrieved.

I have already taken issue with your favorite heresy, which is that one writes for twenty intelligent people and doesn't give a fig for the rest. It's patently untrue, since the lack of success galls you. Anyway, there weren't even twenty favorable reviews of this very considerable, well-made book. No, one mustn't write for twenty people or for one hundred thousand. One must write for all who are hungry to read and can profit from good books. One must occupy the highest point in one's nature and make the moral meaning of one's work perfectly transparent.

Flaubert did not take offense. Nor did he apologize in his reply for being unable to square his view of the literary vocation with hers. "Here is what I believe essentially separates us, dear master," he wrote on February 6, 1876.

In all things you first leap to heaven before returning to earth. Your starting point is the ideal . . . , which accounts for your gentleness, your serenity, and, not to mince words, your greatness. Whereas I, poor bugger, am weighed down by soles of lead. Everything moves me, tears me, ravages me, and I struggle to ascend . . . Were I to adopt your worldview, I would make myself a laughing stock, that's all. You preach in vain, I can have no temperament but my own, nor any esthetic but that which derives from it. You accuse me of not following "nature's course." Well, where does that leave the virtue of discipline? What are we to do about that? I admire Monsieur de Buffon's putting on elegant cuffs to write. That luxury is a symbol. Anyway, I innocently strive to be as *comprehensible* as possible. What more can be expected of me?

As for revealing my personal opinion of the people I put onstage — no, no! a thousand times no! I don't recognize myself as *having the right* to do it. If my reader does not get the moral drift of a work, then the reader is an imbecile, or else the work is *false,* in the sense of being inexact. For a thing is good if it is True. Obscene books are immoral because untruthful. When reading them, one says: "That's not the way things are."

Mind you, I detest what is conventionally called "realism," although I have come to be regarded as one of its pontiffs.

The public's taste mystified him more than ever, he complained. A few days earlier he was the only spectator laughing at a Labiche comedy called *Le Prix Martin,* which folded. "I defy anyone to tell me how one pleases people. Success is a consequence and must not be a goal. I've never sought it (though I desire it) and seek it less and less."

What he did seek, however, was Sand's approval, which meant a great deal to him. In May 1876 he told her that she would recognize her influence in a story he had begun, entitled "L'Histoire d'un coeur simple." He felt that its heroine would please her. She would realize that he wasn't as "stubborn" as she thought after all.

SAND WAS weakening rapidly and, as we shall see, would not live to read "Un coeur simple."

Nor, indeed, would Louise Colet, who had followed Flaubert's career from afar. Louise's last years were lonely and errant. Unlike Princess Mathilde, she could not reconstitute a salon after the war. Her coterie had dispersed, and some who remained kept their distance for fear of being associated with her inflammatory writings. A book sympathetic to the Commune, *La Vérité sur l'anarchie des esprits en France,* did not win her many friends among the literati. More invidious was an article in which she trampled on Sainte-Beuve's grave, debunking the critic who hadn't taken her seriously enough by revealing what she knew of his sex life. Paris became a hostile place, and then her health deserted her. To recover it, she went south, fetching up at San Remo, where she lived from hand to mouth for two years within view of Genoa's prison fortress — a tall, stout, black-gowned figure taunted by urchins in the neighborhood of her cheap boardinghouse. By the summer of 1875 she had returned to Paris, still ailing, and taken up residence at the Hôtel d'Angleterre on the rue Jacob, with plans for a book about the Orient and for a three-volume collection of her verse. The former, *Les Pays lumineux: Voyage en Orient,* was published posthumously.

Louise died at her daughter's flat on the rue des Écoles on March 8, 1876. News of her passing reached Flaubert immediately and gave him pause, though not for long. "You're quite right about the welter of feelings stirred up in me by the death of my poor Muse," he wrote to Edma Roger des Genettes. "Her reawakened memory launched me back over the course of my life. But [I] have become more stoic in the past year. I've trampled over so many things, just to be able to go on living! In short, after one afternoon spent with days long gone, I willed myself not to think about them any longer and returned to my task. Yet another end!"

XXIII

~~~~~

A Fruitful Intermission

GEORGE SAND died three months after Louise Colet. She had been experiencing abdominal pain for quite some time. On March 25, 1876, Flaubert received a letter in which she spoke of cramps severe enough to double her over. "Physical suffering is a good lesson when it leaves your mind free: one learns to tolerate and conquer it. There are moments of discouragement when one throws oneself on one's bed, but I always think of what my old curate said during attacks of gout: 'It will pass or I will pass, one or the other.'" True to her stoical creed, she worked every day, kept abreast of what friends were publishing, put on a brave face for her family, and inconvenienced herself for people in need. With one foot in the grave, she gave Flaubert's predicament her undivided attention, contacting a financier who might be able to bail out Commanville. Not until late May, when matters took a dramatic turn for the worse, did her physician conclude that the pain was caused by an occlusion. Still able to eat but unable to eliminate, she had become grotesquely bloated. The last words in her journal were entered on May 29. "Delicious weather. I'm not suffering much. I walk all around the garden. I give Lolo a lesson [Lolo being Aurore, her granddaughter]. I reread a play by Maurice. After dinner Lina [her daughter-in-law] goes to the show at La Châtre. I play bezique with Sagnier. I draw, Lina returns at midnight." She hardly rose from her bed again. The pain, alleviated momentarily by an esophageal irrigation with seltzer water, grew so intense that her moaning filled the house. On June 7 she bade farewell to her granddaughters, and in the early-morning hours of June 8 she lost consciousness. Death came quickly. Unopposed by the grief-stricken Maurice, Sand's estranged daughter Solange made arrangements for a religious burial after securing authorization from the archbishop of Bourges. That decision, which may have been partly vindictive, served at least to fortify Sand's reputation among Berrichon peasants as a sainted neighbor.

The funeral was held on June 10. Some fifteen people came down from Paris, including Flaubert, who took the overnight train with Ernest Renan and Prince Napoleon. Country folk crowded around the chapel at Nohant telling their beads and muttering prayers in a scene that could have been posed for one of Sand's novels. Afterward, in torrential rain, a priest and choir boy led mourners through ankle-high mud to the graveyard, where Paul Meurice read Victor Hugo's potted eulogy. "The throng of peasant women wrapped in their dark cloth mantles and kneeling on the wet grass, the gray sky, the cold drizzle which kept pelting our faces, the wind whining through the cypresses and mingling with the sexton's litanies, touch me far more than this conventional eloquence," wrote an American friend. Even less to Flaubert's taste than the oratory were the Catholic litanies. When he wasn't weeping copious tears, he was privately vituperating against the daughter who had allegedly betrayed her mother's convictions, and he made a special point of informing Marie-Sophie Leroyer de Chantepie, with whom he had seldom corresponded since the war, that Sand hadn't found God *in articulo mortis,* whatever the newspapers might report. "You want to know the truth about Mme Sand's last moments. Here it is: *she received no priest.* But as soon as she died, her daughter, Mme Clésinger,* requested authorization of the bishop of Bourges to hold a religious burial service, and no one in the house (except perhaps her daughter-in-law, Mme Maurice) defended the ideas of our poor friend. Maurice was so utterly stricken that he had no energy left, and then there were foreign influences, wretched considerations inspired by bourgeois." Still, grief had its way with him, overriding his indignation. "The death of poor mother Sand caused me infinite pain," he wrote to Turgenev. "I broke down twice at her burial: first while embracing her granddaughter Aurore (whose eyes, that day, resembled hers so closely that it seemed a resurrection), and then when her coffin was being carried past me." On the same

---

*Solange was married to the sculptor Auguste Clésinger.

day he told Maurice Sand that he felt he had buried his own mother once again. The woman whom Renan described as the aeolian harp of her age wouldn't be vibrating anymore to his thoughts and feelings.

The three companions who had arrived on the night train returned by the same means, wet and exhausted. At Croisset, after traveling from Paris in a compartment with Englishmen who, much to his annoyance, played cards throughout, he tidied up his desk, downed a jugful of cider, and ate dinner in what he described as sweet, beneficent silence, thinking of his mother. The next morning, he resumed work on "Un coeur simple." Edma Roger des Genettes may have been surprised to learn that in the wake of these sad events her good friend was less gloomy than usual. "To tell the truth," he confided, "I'm delighted to be back home, like a stodgy petit bourgeois, among *my* armchairs and *my* books, in *my* study, with a view of *my* garden. The sun is shining, the birds are lovers serenading one another, the boats are gliding noiselessly on the glassy smooth river, and my story progresses! I shall probably have finished it in two months."

Had death made him more alert to nature blooming all around him? It's as if Flaubert's sanguine double had been let out of the closet for a brief exhibition. Propriety kept him from displaying himself to everyone in this nakedly contented state. Princess Mathilde, for one, was not allowed to see him except in mourning clothes. His heart, he told her, had become a necropolis, with the "void" growing ever wider and the earth ever emptier. But writing to Turgenev a fortnight after Sand's funeral, he rejoiced in a newfound vigor. "I feel *astonishingly good!* I take pleasure in the greenery, the trees, the silence as never before! I'm back swimming in the cold river (a ferocious hydrotherapy) and work like a demon." Early risers walking on the towpath were liable to see him standing by his window at daybreak after toiling through the night. Earlier risers might have overheard snatches of "Un coeur simple," for in the absence of friends, he recited what he had written to the tulip tree, the moon, and the river. Oppressive heat enveloped the valley that summer, protecting Croisset from visitors like a second wall around the house, and draining everyone — everyone but Flaubert, who regularly took vigorous late-afternoon swims. Edmond Laporte came whenever the Regional Council of Upper Normandy, to which he had been elected, was not in session. So did Georges Pouchet and Frédéric Baudry. These were the exceptions, however. Caroline spent weeks at her spa in the Pyrenees. Defeated by the weather, Mathilde cut short a vacation in Normandy and withdrew to Saint-Gratien. Turgenev stayed put in a chalet at Bougival, near Paris. For company Flaubert had the family retainer, blind old Julie, and the gardener. There was also "Loulou," a stuffed parrot destined to gain immortality as the Holy Ghost in "Un coeur simple." He had acquired this newest totem through Dr Pennetier, director of the Rouen Museum of Natural History, which possessed various specimens.

The thought that in writing "Un coeur simple" he was keeping faith with George Sand beyond the grave may have given the task a certain urgency. He may also have felt rejuvenated by a tale that owed so much to Julie, who did little else now but reminisce with Flaubert, after dinner, about "the old days." And perhaps the sight of Loulou, or the rightness of a final chapter he could expect to reach in months rather than years, made his petty pace less frustrating. How long had Emma Bovary's journey taken from convent school through the episodes of a brief, tortured womanhood to the kiss she plants on a crucifix thrust at her on her deathbed? In just one summer, Félicité, the simple heart, would accomplish a life of virtuous servitude and, with her dying eyes, see the surrogate dove hovering overhead.

Flaubert gave her the name of Emma's maid and undoubtedly pictured her from the first as Emma's foil. " 'L'Histoire d'un coeur simple' [its original title] is nothing more or less than the account of an obscure life, that of a poor country girl, devout but not mystical, matter-of-factly devoted, tender with a tenderness redolent of freshly baked bread," he wrote to Edma Roger des Genettes on June 19. "She loves successively a man, the children of her mistress, a nephew, a graybeard whom she cares for, and at last her parrot; when the parrot dies, she has it stuffed and, dying in turn, confuses the parrot with the Holy Spirit. This is not at all ironical, as you suppose it to be, but, on the contrary, serious and very sad. I want to arouse pity, to make sensitive souls weep, being one such soul myself." Where Emma the actress is an alien consciousness in her native milieu, forever yearning for romantic homelands, Félicité the faithful shepherdess is embedded in rural Normandy. Where Emma's imaginative life revolves around fantasies of social promotion, Félicité is a servant whose unquestioning self-sacrifice argues the nobility of service. Emma fills her emotional void with material goods; Félicité, who owns nothing, polishes her mistress's copper pots to a fare-thee-well, as a writer might polish sentences for art's sake. Something very like the hallucinatory play of art ultimately brings Félicité the bliss that eludes Emma, whose spirit has no heaven to fly to. At the conclusion of *Madame Bovary,* Flaubert dwells upon physical corruption — the decay of Emma's corpse, the black liquid that drools from her mouth, the pale, viscous film that veils her eyes, the powdery white of her lashes, the stench only half-disguised by burning incense. The farm country she had scorned gathers her into its spongy heart. Félicité, on the other hand, when she leaves the world she had served without expectation of reward, transcends it in a last, redemptive vision. Still occupying the room in which she had lived before her mistress's death, she learns that the parish will build an altar in her courtyard for the procession of Corpus Christi. Custom dictates that the person thus honored should make an offering to be placed next to the monstrance, and Félicité, who has only one precious possession, offers Loulou. The ceremony unfolds as she lies at death's door. "The factory guild, the cantors, the children, lined up around three sides of the courtyards," writes Flaubert. "The priest slowly ascended the steps and placed his great gold sunburst of a monstrance on the lace coverlet. Everyone knelt in profound silence, and the censers swinging in wide arcs slipped on their chains. A bluish vapor entered Félicité's room, her nostrils flared with a mystical sensuality. She then closed her eyelids. Her lips were smiling. The movements of her heart slowed one by one, each beat weaker than the one before, softer, like a fountain playing lower and lower, like a fading echo. And when she exhaled her last breath, she thought she saw a gigantic parrot hovering in the blue gape of heaven." Flaubert harks back even here to Emma Bovary, whose life and death were also associated with a bird. The coach called "The Swallow" (*"Hirondelle"*) on which she rode to Rouen for trysts with Léon is, at the end, heard clattering back from the city, but not heard by Emma herself. Rigor mortis has already set in.

Having always conveyed his imagination to the Mediterranean for an orgy after working it on native grounds, Flaubert did so again after "Un coeur simple" with "Hérodias." Félicité had no sooner been buried than the table was set for the savage feast at which Salome dances her dance and John the Baptist's head arrives on a platter. Thus in September the simple maid gave way to the hard-hearted dominatrix with imperial ambitions who took her name from her second husband, Herod Antipas. Once again, thick tomes piled up around Flaubert, the most important being Josephus's *The Jewish War* and *Antiquities of the Jews,* F. de Saulcy's *Histoire d'Hérode,* Renan's *Vie de Jésus,* and the Bible itself. Like *Salammbô,* "Hérodias," which runs to fewer pages than "Un coeur simple" though it may not seem so, was distilled from hundreds of pages of notes on Roman administration, biblical toponymy, numismatics, Hebraic astrology. Flaubert delved into the contentious, inbred posterity of Herod the Great. After the king's death in 4 BC, Palestine was divided among three sons, the middle one being Antipas, tetrarch of Galilee, who acquired the dynastic title Herod when Emperor Augustus deposed his older brother. Central to Flaubert's plot as well as to the biblical account is Antipas's matrimonial history. Married first to the daughter of a Nabataean emir, he discarded her for Herodias — the wife of his half brother Philip and the daughter of another half brother — thus flouting the Mosaic law, which countenanced union with a brother's wife only for levirate marriage. John the Baptist vehemently denounced Antipas, who would have silenced him straightaway had he not feared a popular uprising. The story upon which Flaubert enlarged is told in Matthew 14:

> And when he would have put him to death, he feared the multitude, because they counted him as a prophet. But when Herod's birthday was kept, the daughter of Herodias danced before them, and pleased Herod. Whereupon he promised with an oath to give whatsoever she would ask. And she, being before instructed of her mother, said, Give me here John the Baptist's head in a charger. And the king was sorry: nevertheless for the oath's sake, and them which sat with him at meat, he commanded it to be given her. And he sent, and beheaded John in the prison. And his head was brought in a charger, and given to the damsel and she brought it to her mother.

In Josephus's *Jewish War,* Herodias appears briefly as a virago jealous of her brother Agrippa, who has succeeded to the tetrarchy east of Antipas's after ingratiating himself with young Caligula. Determined that a more elevated title than tetrarch should be conferred upon her weak-willed husband, Herodias nags him to petition the emperor in person.[*]

Machaerus, the great redoubt perched on a ridge between the Dead Sea and the Moabian hills, is where Flaubert has Antipas's birthday celebration take place, but the feast turns out to be a free-for-all not unlike the barbarian saturnalia in *Salammbô*. Threatened with invasion (this was historical fact), Antipas has summoned military officers, civil servants, and representatives of the sects that agitate his realm. Pharisees, Sadducees, Samaritans, Essenes, mingle querulously, and into this potpourri Flaubert introduces a Roman proconsul, Vitellius, accompanied by his gluttonous son, Aulus, the future emperor. When it begins at last, the feast is a contest of voices, creeds, and tongues. Pandemonium reigns until Herodias enters. Salome then performs her dance, casting a spell upon the tetrarch. John's fate is sealed and his head promptly brought up from the dungeon below.

What Flaubert found irresistible in the story was the struggle between militant holiness and a ruthless eroticism, mirroring his own conflict. Had he not jocularly assigned people nicknames borrowed from the Marquis de Sade's novels, which he knew well, yet taken to signing his letters "Polycarp," after the embattled second-century saint famous for his diatribes against corruption and heresy?[†] While elsewhere — in *La Tentation,* in "Saint Julien" — godliness and blind instinct fight it out in an individual

[*]According to Josephus, the couple were rewarded for their temerity with permanent exile in Spain.

[†]Constantly on Polycarp's lips in his last years were the words: "Oh good God, to what times hast thou spared me, that I must suffer such things!" Flaubert liked to quote them, on his own account.

psyche, here they are separate characters at daggers drawn, Herodias and John, with the regal vamp using her seductive daughter Salome to silence the voice of moral authority. That voice comes thundering out of the deep in a magnificent clap of biblical imprecation when someone lifts the hatch over John's cell. The prison *is* a voice, a disembodied voice soon to be matched against a young woman's beautiful body. The sinuous lines of the dance Salome performs ultimately prove more persuasive than the movement of John's rhetoric. It is around these contrasting tours de force, the *almah*'s murderous gyrations and the prophet's language, that Flaubert clearly meant to organize "Hérodias."*

Had everything gone as planned, both "Hérodias" and "Saint Julien l'Hospitalier" would have appeared in Turgenev's Russian translation before *Trois Contes* (the third story being "Un coeur simple") appeared in France, priority being a condition stipulated by Mikhail Stasiulevich, the publisher of *Vestnik Evropy* (the European Herald), who paid French contributors handsome fees. Flaubert wanted Turgenev to have the last of his stories in hand when he left Paris for Russia in March 1877 and accordingly worked around the clock. By mid-February "Hérodias" was complete. "Stasiulevich writes to me," Turgenev informed Flaubert, "that on further reflection he prefers to couple the two legends in the April 13 issue. That's his business and maybe he's right. I've written a little preface. This should affect its publication here in France. Stasiulevich states that since I told him 'Hérodias' is as long as 'Saint Julien,' he will use my estimate to calculate the fee — and pay up straightaway."†

Two newspapers, *Le Moniteur* and *Le Bien Public,* published Flaubert's stories in serial form between April 12 and 22, 1877. The book came out on April 24 and received enthusiastic reviews. There were exceptions, to be sure. Francisque Sarcey, in a lecture published by his newspaper, made it known that he found "Hérodias" incomprehensible (though he admired the other stories), and Ferdinand Brunetière, a champion of literary convention who was destined to occupy a seat in the French Academy, condemned Flaubert's pessimism, his show of erudition, his swipes at "bourgeois virtue," his "comic brutality." But most critics saw in *Trois Contes* the work of an author who, mellowing at last, had made his peace with society. What may have encouraged this view was the publication several months earlier of *L'Assommoir,* Émile Zola's powerful novel about the working poor of Paris.

---

*This conflict also informs "Saint Julien," where the two meanings of venery — debauchery and hunting — suited Flaubert's purpose.

†There were no copyright laws to prohibit anyone from translating a French work into Russian. As it turned out, "Hérodias" was uncoupled from "Saint Julien" and published in the May issue — early enough to foil prospective rivals.

The slang spoken by Zola's characters, even more than the depiction of urban squalor, offended critics of every stripe, with conservative and leftist outshouting each other in a contest of impeachment. "The crude and relentless obscenity of detail and language aggravates the immorality of situations and characters," wrote a government reporter, who recommended that the book be barred from sale at railroad station kiosks. *Trois Contes* could only profit by comparison. It might have been hailed as a born classic out of sheer gratitude to Flaubert for not fouling himself alongside Zola in the wallow of naturalism.

Praise also came from the many to whom Flaubert sent complimentary copies. Louise Colet's former protégé Leconte de Lisle declared that he had read *Trois Contes* twice. "Your first story, 'Un coeur simple,' is a marvel of limpid prose, of flawless observation and language perfectly matched to thought . . . You are a great and powerful talent; no one is more convinced of it and more pleased than your old friend." Another poet, Théodore de Banville, went so far as to say that he had never read anything as "completely beautiful" as *Trois Contes.* "What a feast for a poet! There is grace and joy in every word!" Achille Flaubert was not a man to enthuse, least of all over his brother, but even he thought that Gustave had done himself proud. "Yes, my dear friend, I received *Trois Contes* a fortnight ago and devoured it. Since then I haven't had time to reread it, but my intention is to offer myself that pleasure in due course and savor the stories slowly, for I was very taken with them and believe that you have never written anything better, and I know that you usually write rather well."

IF *Trois Contes* experienced any misfortune, it came in the form of political events that monopolized the public's attention all summer long and hindered sales. The latest convulsion began on May 16, 1877, but this famous day, known simply as *"seize mai,"* marked the denouement of a drama that had begun four years earlier, with Thiers's fall from power and Mac-Mahon's accession to the presidency.

In August 1873, when parliamentary royalists renewed their overtures to the pretender, Henri, comte de Chambord, Marshal Mac-Mahon happily anticipated the prospect of being replaced by a king, despite the fact that almost no one outside parliament wanted Chambord enthroned, least of all the right wing's own peasant constituents, who, though deeply Catholic, wondered whether a Bourbon monarch might not bring back the ancien régime under which their forefathers had groaned. "The return of Henri V is the greatest chimera that could possibly have entered the heads of intriguing politicians," Marcellin Berthelot wrote to Ernest Renan from a rural lookout. "Anything is possible except that. Mark my words, the peasant will rise in thirty or forty districts, because he really fears . . . that the common lands he got in 1793 will be taken away from him . . . One must distinguish pilgrimages and popular superstitions — which represent art and ideality for all poor people — from acquiescence in the clergy's will to dominate . . . People throng to pilgrimage sites, but not one in ten would countenance Henri V."

Blind to reality, Chambord's suitors returned from visiting him in Austria with hopes that a new dispensation lay at hand. The pretender did not disabuse them until October 29. On that day he published an open letter stating that any a priori restraints upon his will — which would be imperative in a constitutional monarchy — were unacceptable. He would never become the legitimate king of the Revolution and "inaugurate a salutary regime with an act of weakness," he vowed. "My person is nothing, my principle is everything . . . When God has resolved to save a people, he takes care that the scepter of justice be placed in hands strong enough to grasp it." On this sanctimonious note Chambord exited from French history, leaving royalist ranks broken. "Our rulers can't bring themselves to give us a definitive, more or less definitive, government," Flaubert wrote to Princess Mathilde, "but the important thing is that we are, thank God, delivered from the nightmare of monarchy. Hosannah!"

The moderate right regrouped immediately. Its design was to prop up Mac-Mahon for the long haul and to invest his office with such power that a republic, if formally instituted, would be a constitutional monarchy in disguise. Broglie, the prime minister, achieved one goal by getting Mac-Mahon's term extended. A law promulgated on November 20, 1873, stated that the executive power would be entrusted for seven years to Marshal Mac-Mahon. "His power will continue to be exercised with the title of president of the Republic . . . unless modified through some constitutional process." But this so-called Septennate did not console Legitimists, who had meanwhile agreed to blame the collapse of plans for a Bourbon restoration on the Orleanist Broglie. Thenceforth Broglie found himself regularly attacked by his erstwhile allies.

Bent upon queering relations with Germany, hard-core monarchists implemented a *politique du pire,* and encouraged the Catholic newspaper *L'Univers* to publish a pastoral denunciation of Bismarck's Kulturkampf, his "culture war" against the Catholic Church in Germany. When France officially recognized the Kingdom of Italy, which did not honor the pope's temporal power, rallies were held to protest this impious diplomacy. Before long the extreme right joined the extreme left to expel Broglie from office with a vote of no confidence. Another Orleanist (whom Broglie would in fact control) replaced him.

The law that promulgated the Septennate called upon the National Assembly to organize a constitutional commission, which was duly elected, and throughout 1874 thirty truculent Frenchmen did nothing but argue. Even as *Le Siècle* declared that the French could not continue to live in a tent, the deputies wrangled over nomenclature, with those on the right vetoing all formulas that incorporated the word *republic* or overtly legitimized republicanism. They might have wrangled another year had not an ex-royalist lawyer named Henri-Alexandre Wallon introduced some common sense. "All interest was concentrated on the affirmation or rejection of the word 'republic'; France had the thing, should she still be denied the name?" is how the historian D. W. Brogan put it. On January 30, 1875, when the commission was debating the law for the election of the president, Wallon proposed an amendment that said: "The president of the Republic will be elected by the plurality of votes cast by the Senate and Chamber of Deputies united in a National Assembly." This simple statement effectively ratified the republic. "By providing for a regular succession to the Marshal," Brogan observed, "it ended the personal and temporary character given to the executive. It did not 'definitively' establish the Republic. What was definitive? But it ended the rule of the provisional."

Wallon's amendment passed by only one vote among 704 cast. By liberating men who were frozen in mutual suspicion, it sparked a common purpose, and with every subsequent item the majority grew larger. After several months, France's Third Republic was crudely knocked together. Monarchical in design, it featured many of the safeguards against popular rule for which Broglie had lobbied, above all a bicameral legislature whose upper house, or Senate, could, at the president's request, dissolve the lower one, or Chamber of Deputies. Although universal suffrage applied to the latter, election to the former was based on a system that gave disproportionate influence to rural, traditionally Catholic, sparsely populated counties; further, seventy-five of three hundred senators would be elected for life by the Chamber, where in 1875 the right still outnumbered the left.

The left had good reason to swallow its gorge and take up residence in this jerry-built structure, which violated almost every republican canon. Certainly leftists recognized that if ever they should gain control of the entire legislature, they could disarm a hostile executive or anyway fight at equal odds. But they also saw how chronic improvisation had been serving those who argued that another Napoleon was needed to restore order. With Bismarck forging a European alliance against France while France lay paralyzed by internecine conflict, Bonapartists were able to exploit the public's thirst for revenge. Several had become deputies, and, to the chagrin of monarchists and republicans alike, Napoleon III's former equerry, the baron de Bourgoing, won a by-election in March 1874. "Fear! That is their great political tool. They engender it, they inoculate it, and, once they've frightened a certain class of citizens, they present themselves as saviors, the better to strip people of their freedoms, of their civil dignity, of their public rights," Gambetta declared at a public rally, inveighing against what he called "Caesarian democracy, this order obtained by force, this brutal power, this clerical connivance, this patronage accorded to representatives of old aristocratic clans." More than any other factor, the knowledge that "Caesarian democracy" had not lost ground in the countryside, in the army, in the administration, and in the magistrature impelled Gambetta to make his peace with the sober Orleanists. However hastily contrived, a body of law offered some protection against despotism, he thought. And so it did. It saved France then, and it would save her again thirteen years later, when General Georges Boulanger astride his black stallion very nearly became Napoleon IV.

Mac-Mahon, the soldier famous for his exploits during the Crimean War, occupied the Élysée Palace as if it were the Malakhov fortress, from whose mined rampart he had declared twenty years earlier, "Here I am; here I stay." By law he could remain there until 1880, but legislators were obliged to go home when the National Assembly that had governed France since 1871 dissolved itself on December 31, 1875, and in elections held soon afterward, conservatism suffered a heavy blow. Ignoring Mac-Mahon's advice to reject all who might disturb the security of lawful interests or threaten France with the propagation of antisocial doctrines, voters returned republican candidates en masse. For every deputy seated right of center, three sat left of it, and in the Chamber of Deputies Léon Gambetta's voice rang triumphant. Frenchmen had just given proof of their aversion to the clerical politics that informed every move of those formerly controlling the Assembly, he exulted. It behooved France to break with ultramontanism (subservience to the pope), lest that attitude distort her foreign policy. But in no way would republicans "weaken," "diminish," or "modify" the powers of the president of the republic.

The mental powers of the president were already diminished, or so a highly placed personage informed Goncourt. Unable to focus on objects left of left center (especially voluminous ones like Gambetta) without turning livid, Mac-Mahon appointed as prime minister Jules Dufaure, a seventy-eight-year-old whose republicanism, like his frock coat and rhetorical style, evoked the fashion of 1830. Age did not shield him. Damned by the right for having dismissed conservative functionaries, Dufaure found himself damned by the left for not having made the purge complete. Caught between Catholics, who insisted that his government deplore the omission of religious ceremony from state funerals, and anticlericals, who held that the state must remain neutral, he proposed a compromise obnoxious to both. The Chamber of Deputies and the Senate, ignoring Dufaure, clashed time and time again over religious matters. When the Chamber sought to disqualify priests from the juries that granted university degrees, the Senate, where conservatives enjoyed a bare majority, stood firm. It stood firm again when the Chamber questioned the raison d'être of France's Vatican embassy. And when Gambetta persuaded the lower house to cut several items from the budget for public worship, the upper house hastened to restore them.

Dufaure's diplomatic skill availed him even less in clashes provoked by left-wing deputies demanding exoneration for convicted insurgents. As minister of justice under Thiers, Dufaure had organized the machinery of prosecution that tried Communards, and this deed left him stranded between hostile allies and kindred foes. The leftist Chamber passed an amnesty bill over his protests; the rightist Senate then rejected it with a complicitous wink in his direction. Frustrated by the ambiguity of his position, he resigned on December 3, 1876, after nine months in office. Flaubert was crestfallen to see his friend Agénor Bardoux, a ministerial undersecretary on whom he might have counted for favors, go down with the premier.

To succeed Dufaure, Mac-Mahon appointed Jules Simon, a gifted intellectual whose occasional departures from leftist orthodoxy had earned him the reputation among conservatives of being the *merle blanc,* or "white blackbird," they could deal with. "You know full well that I am both deeply republican and deeply conservative" is how he characterized himself in his inaugural address to parliament, and proofs were furnished immediately. He might have stayed the course by tacking both right and left if waves from abroad hadn't capsized him. In January 1877, Pope Pius IX — he of the *Syllabus of Errors* — summoned good Catholics everywhere to condemn Italy's leftist regime, specifically the Clerical Abuses Law with which that regime had armed itself for use against recalcitrant priests. The pope was echoed by the bishop of Nevers, and crowds marched throughout France in sympathy. Simon, while noting the restraint of the French episcopate, vowed to maintain order. But republicans wanted something more than order. They wanted ultramontane politics suppressed, brutally if need be, and most of them backed a resolution to that effect after hearing Gambetta echo Voltaire's *"Ecrasons l'infâme!"* with "Clericalism! There is the enemy!" A leader devoid of followers, Simon the white blackbird now found himself shunned as a mutant by every political species. Mac-Mahon accepted his resignation.

It would take supreme arrogance or desperation or both for Mac-Mahon to challenge the republican majority at this juncture, but challenge it he did on May 16, 1877. Proclaiming himself responsible to France rather than to parliament, he named Albert de Broglie prime minister and had an envoy inform the Chamber that he would not suffer "radical modifications of all of our great administrative, judicial, financial, and military institutions."

Three hundred sixty-three republican deputies thereupon let it be known that France was not a mere figment of Mac-Mahon's sovereign will, stating on May 17:

> The chamber, which deems it important, in light of the present crisis and the mandate it received from the nation, to recall that a preponderance of parliamentary power as exercised by ministers whom elected representatives may call to account is the basic condition of government by the people for the people . . . declares that the confidence of the majority will be bestowed only upon a cabinet free to act as it sees fit and resolved to govern in accordance with republican principles that alone guarantee order and prosperity at home and peace abroad.

This challenge was no sooner made public than Mac-Mahon adjourned parliament. When it reconvened a month later (republican prefects and sub-prefects having meanwhile been sacked) the so-called 363 inveighed against Broglie's right-wing cabinet. Had custom prevailed, a vote of no-confidence would have brought down the government, but Mac-Mahon, faced with yet another Hobson's choice, decided, shockingly, to dissolve the Chamber of Deputies.

Elections were not scheduled until September, which meant that candidates had more than three months for campaigning, and slogans flew thick all summer long. "Paris is insufferable," complained Théodore Duret, the art critic. "Thought is completely absorbed by the forthcoming elections and the crisis that will follow. All signs favor us [the republicans], but after the return of the 363, what will happen?" Flaubert was equally exasperated, on several counts. "That idiot Mac-Mahon is seriously harming the sale of *Trois Contes,* but I console myself, for after all I didn't expect anything like the commercial success of *L'Assommoir,*" he wrote to Edma Roger des Genettes. A letter to Princess Mathilde, sent from Croisset one month later, on June 30, suggested that Mac-Mahon's high-handedness might tilt even conservatives to the left. "In my retreat, I don't hear people discoursing on politics, thank God. All the same, I fear Mac-Mahon's secret ideas for the election! Does the man have any ideas? What does he want? Conservatives I know are turning red. That's the upshot of all this." By late August the summer heat had become more intense, and Flaubert boiled over, especially in correspondence with Léonie Brainne, who never inspired as much restraint as Mathilde. "Two things sustain me: love of Literature and hatred of the Bourgeois, the latter being resumed, condensed, nowadays, in what is called the Great Party of Order. Alone in the silence of my study, I can work myself up just thinking about Mac-Mahon, Fourtou [minister of the interior], and our prefect Lizot. After five minutes I have a paroxysm of rage, and that relieves me. I'm calmer afterward. Don't think I'm joking. Why such indignation? I wonder. No doubt about it, the older I get, the more easily I'm offended by fatuousness, and in all of history I know nothing as *inept* as the men of May 16. Their stupidity makes my head spin."

Adolphe Thiers's dream of one day recovering executive power came to nothing when he died on September 3, but his vengeance survived him. From beyond the grave he posed an even more serious threat to Mac-Mahon, for left-wing republicans who had shunned the live politician rallied around the dead statesman. Posthumously absolved of sins committed against the proletariat, Thiers, whose widow would not authorize a state funeral, received tribute from multitudes of workers as his flower-laden hearse clattered across eastern Paris to the cemetery where Communards had made their last stand during *la semaine sanglante*. This demonstration was viewed by the monarchist Goncourt as proof of France's desire for a strong hand, and by Flaubert the elitist republican as reason to expect reprisals. "For me," Goncourt noted in his journal, "the idolatry that attended Thiers's funeral bears striking witness to France's monarchical temperament. In its president it will always want a monarch, a dominator, and not a servant of elected assemblies." Flaubert, who had witnessed the funeral, wrote to Edma Roger des Genettes that it was splendid. "This truly *national* demonstration thrilled me. No matter that I never much liked the king of sententious bourgeois. Compared with those around him, he was a giant. And furthermore he had a rare virtue: patriotism. No one resumed France as he did, whence the huge effect of his death." But he feared that the Moral Order would answer with harsh measures of the kind recently taken at Dieppe, where Lizot, the prefect, had banned a public lecture on Rabelais, and at Le Havre, where, in an attempt to quarantine France from the plague of Darwinism, the same Lizot had silenced a lecturer engaged to discuss the recent revelations of geology. Flaubert called this censorship a delirium of stupidity. "If I could, I would condemn my prefect to spend twenty-five years in New Caledonia studying the formation of the earth and reading French literature." It delighted him to learn during the campaign that in one Norman town, Laigle, electoral bills posted by Mac-Mahon's candidate had been smeared with excrement. "Merde pour l'Ordre Moral" was how he greeted Zola, and others. But nothing gave him greater pleasure in that politically fraught year than a scandal involving the comte de Germiny, one of France's highest-ranking magistrates, who was caught in a public urinal on the Champs-Élysées, sodomizing a young male clerk. For the bourgeoisophobe, this nicely sabotaged the whole Moral Order. "It's the kind of anecdote that consoles us and helps one put up with existence."

After they won the national elections in October, republicans hastened to neuter the presidency. Dissolution was Mac-Mahon's chief weapon against a recalcitrant Chamber, and this prerogative they made him surrender. "We must, in our national interest, resolve the present crisis once and for all," he wrote in a dictated and grudgingly signed message that was to shape France's political course until 1939. "The exercise of the right of dissolution is nothing more than recourse to a court from whose judgment there is no appeal: it cannot serve as a system of government." With Mac-Mahon stripped of effective power, the republican majority went about unseating seventy-two deputies in whose electoral campaigns priests and notabilities were alleged to have exerted undue influence. What became axiomatic thereafter was the principle that corrupt behavior manifested itself only in conservative ranks. No republican legislator would ever face expulsion because a Masonic lodge, an anticlerical schoolmaster, or a like-minded prefect had endorsed his candidacy.

WITH *Trois Contes* completed in February 1877, Flaubert could apply himself earnestly to the task of commemorating dead friends, above all Louis Bouilhet. Revived after years of quiescence was the proposal for an ornamental fountain. Unfortunately, Bouilhet had not meanwhile grown in stature, quite the contrary. Once again Rouen's municipal council questioned his literary credentials, and once again Flaubert objected. Bouilhet's credentials were irrelevant, he declared, since his bust would be subordinate to the fountain. "It's a matter of urban administration, not a literary matter. If we were asking to adorn our fountain with the face of a gorilla, we should be chartered to do so, since we wish to bestow a publicly useful monument upon the city." This casuistic argument unexpectedly carried the day, and in September Flaubert communicated the good news to Agénor Bardoux, who sat on his committee.

Flaubert also pulled strings on behalf of George Sand, as a member of the committee organized to honor her with a monument in Paris. Presuming upon the friendship of Gertrude Collier Tennant, by then a well-connected socialite, he begged her to ask Lord Houghton, Richard Monckton Milnes, whether that distinguished man of letters might consent to form a committee in London for promoting the Sand monument and include among its members George Eliot, who had already expressed support. The fact that Victor Hugo would be his counterpart in Paris was mentioned as an inducement.

During the spring of 1877, which fell between his deliverance from *Trois Contes* and his confinement in *Bouvard et Pécuchet,* Flaubert enjoyed a busy social life. There were teas with the Renans, Wednesday dinners at Princess Mathilde's, evenings in the company of Léonie Brainne. A very rich woman with loose purse strings named Marguerite Pelouze (who, Flaubert claimed, knew his works by heart) gave him one more elegant Parisian apartment to dine in and, better yet, King François I's bedroom at Chenonceaux, her Renaissance castle on the Cher river, to sleep in.* Increasingly important to him was the company of Georges and Marguerite Charpentier. During the Paris season, his Friday evenings were often spent mingling with men of power and influence at the Charpentiers' establishment on the rue de Grenelle.

A book could be written about that remarkable couple. Until France collapsed during the Prussian juggernaut, Georges Charpentier had given no indication that he would someday acquire the capacity or desire to run the famous publishing house founded by his father. Handsome and raffish, he lounged at Tortoni's on the boulevard des Italiens, where fellow playboys addressed him familiarly as "Zizi." His wit, his wardrobe, his nonchalance, and his eye for art promised a life of rich bohemianism. But in fact there was more gilt than gold to this haut bourgeois. At war with Charpentier senior — who during the 1860s allowed himself to be persuaded by a malevolent woman under whose sway he had fallen that his son was the issue of an adulterous liaison — Georges became a vagabond, visiting his abandoned mother in Bougival every weekend and camping during the week with hospitable friends. Father and son made some sort of peace before the former's death, but in important ways the warfare continued beyond the grave. The elder Charpentier's shrew had prevailed upon him to deny his family the lion's share of his estate and nearly cheated Georges of the Bibliothèque Charpentier.

After his father's death in 1871, Zizi reformed. No sooner had he taken command of the firm than he married a woman well suited to him. Like Georges, Marguerite Lemonnier knew how it felt to surrender upper-class expectations. Under Napoleon III, her father, Gabriel, had been *joaillier de la couronne,* or jeweler to the crown. The title carried social weight, which meant that for Marguerite there were English and German nannies, holidays at a family château near Bretigny-sur-Orge, gowns from the House of Worth, birthday gifts from Isabella of Spain, musical soirees, teas with the titled, crinolined ladies billowing through her parents' salon all year-round. That salon looked out upon the place Vendôme, where Napoleon I stood overhead, protectively. Marguerite saw him every day. But she did not see

*Flaubert visited Mme Pelouze at Chenonceaux in May 1877, when he might have liked to chat up her brother, Daniel Wilson. Wilson, a deputy who signed the manifesto of the "363," would acquire great notoriety in 1887, the year Mme Pelouze herself went bankrupt. Serving as undersecretary of finance during the presidency of his father-in-law, he was arraigned for selling appointments to the Legion of Honor. It brought down the Grévy administration. How Flaubert met Mme Pelouze is not known. It is known that her fortune was immense.

him crash in May 1871, when Communards supervised by Gustave Courbet tore down the column glorifying his victorious campaigns. By then, Lemonnier had gone bankrupt.

As a hostess without a salon could no more happily resign herself to a life of obscure motherhood than an actress without a stage, Marguerite made the Bibliothèque Charpentier the vehicle for her boundless social energy. "In some considerable degree, our success was her doing," affirmed Charpentier's partner, Maurice Dreyfous. "As early as 1872 she organized a series of receptions that showed to great advantage the charm of her person and the agreeableness of her intellectual culture, which she wore lightly. Delighted to find a meeting place where they could resume relations interrupted by the tragic events that had befallen France, the literary elite came in force. Little by little the salon . . . filled with an elegant crowd, and the gatherings became fashionable. Unpublished plays by house authors were performed by famous actors, who found their reward in the sense of intellectual community they enjoyed with Charpentier's intimates." Assembling people unlikely to meet under any other roof, Mme Charpentier, in whose own character the wry patrician mingled with the affectionate mother, displayed a genius for conciliation. Her Friday-evening soirees, which introduced writers, painters, actors, music-hall celebrities, industrialists, and political potentates to one another, were her serial novel. Auguste Renoir evoked them charmingly for his son. "[My father] had come to know the family well, as he had painted Charpentier's mother in 1868," Jean Renoir wrote in *Renoir, My Father.* "He met him again as a result of an exhibition which he and Berthe Morisot and Sisley organized. Berthe Morisot was the sister-in-law of Manet, a great friend of M. Charpentier. The distinguished publisher came to the exhibition and bought Renoir's *Fishermen on a Riverbank* for 180 francs. As he was leaving with his picture, he invited my father to come to some of Mme Charpentier's receptions. Her salon was celebrated, and deservedly so, for she was indeed a great lady . . . 'Madame Charpentier reminded me of my early loves, the women Fragonard painted,' he'd say." This small, plump, frizzy-haired Egeria, whom Renoir immortalized in *Madame Charpentier and Her Children,* held court in a town house that had space enough for her guests as well as her husband's business. Groomed by Napoleonic society, Marguerite created a republican salon where fuglemen of the left found themselves enveloped in an atmosphere of Parisian chic. At 11, rue de Grenelle, boundaries disappeared, and on any given Friday evening Léon Gambetta might have been seen greeting Sarah Bernhardt, Yvette Guilbert entertaining Georges Clemenceau, Aristide Bruant or the duchesse d'Uzès chatting up Edouard Lockroy, minister of commerce and industry.

Charpentier, in turn, became a regular at Flaubert's Sunday afternoons on the rue du Faubourg Saint-Honoré, where he found himself surrounded by the best of his stable and others soon to enter it, such as Guy de Maupassant, who vividly described a typical gathering. When the doorbell rang, he wrote, Flaubert would throw a veil of thin red silk over his escritoire, hiding the paper mess and his hallowed paraphernalia. Often present was a timid, bespectacled Hippolyte Taine, who would have recognized in Frédéric Baudry and Georges Pouchet, if they showed up, the pallor of fellow savants. Those three, outnumbered by the literati, did more listening than talking.

> In due course, [Flaubert] would greet Alphonse Daudet, who embodied the animation and gaiety of Parisian life. With a few words he'd draw hilarious profiles, beaming his lovely southern wit on everyone and everything . . . Émile Zola then made his appearance, out of breath for having climbed six flights and always followed by Paul Alexis. He'd ensconce himself in an armchair and quickly glance around to read on people's faces their state of mind and the tenor of conversation. Seated at a slight angle, with one leg slung underneath him, holding his ankle and speaking little, he'd listen attentively. Others arrived in turn. I see the publisher Charpentier, who could have passed himself off as an adolescent if not for the white strands in his long black hair . . . He'd laugh easily, with a young, skeptical laugh, and promised everything asked of him by the writers who had him cornered. Almost always the last to arrive was a tall, slender man . . . whose lineaments expressed nobility and haughtiness. He had the look of a gentleman, the refined and nervous air characteristic of the highly bred. This was Edmond de Goncourt.

As Paul Alexis tagged after Zola, so young Henry James arrived on the coattails of Turgenev, whom he revered (even after seeing the Russian put on old shawls and crawl on all fours for a charade at Pauline Viardot's). The spirited talk at 240, rue du Faubourg Saint-Honoré did not encourage him to open his mouth. "What was discussed in that little smoke-clouded room was chiefly questions of taste, questions of art and form; and the speakers, for the most part, were, in esthetic matters, radicals of the deepest dye. It would have been late in the day to propose among them any discussion of the relation of art to morality, any question as to the degree in which a novel might or might not concern itself with the teaching of a lesson. They had settled these preliminaries long ago, and it would have been primitive and incongruous to recur to them." George Sand had had no compunctions about broaching this subject with Flaubert, but for James it was a matter of not appearing hopelessly conventional to pugnacious Frenchmen all of one mind about the relationship between morality and literature. As he remembered it, the conversation, in its intensity and variety, made up for the bareness of the room. "Flaubert was huge and diffident, but florid too and resonant, and my main remembrance is of a conception of courtesy in him, an accessibility to the human relation, that only wanted to be sure of the way taken or to take."

Their common aversion to pulpits, their well-established rituals, and the convivial atmosphere disguised rifts that James could not have suspected. One such was exposed by the publication of *L'Assommoir*, which disturbed Zola's allies almost as much as it did his antagonists. The fame Zola suddenly acquired made Edmond de Goncourt insanely jealous. Eclipsed by his young confrere, he tried to console himself with the thought that Zola had robbed him blind. "[From my manuscript of *La Fille Élisa*] I read Zola the description of Élisa tramping the pavement and, what do you know, I encounter it [in *L'Assommoir*], not plagiarized wholesale but most assuredly inspired by my reading," he noted. "The same chiaroscuro, the same pitiable shadow trailing her. It's all there, right down to 'Monsieur, écoutez-moi donc' — a phrase used in the Quartier Saint-Honoré but not on the Chaussée Clignancourt [the setting of Zola's novel]." *L'Assommoir* was nonetheless an artistic fiasco in his estimation. While the best of Zola came from him, Edmond de Goncourt, the worst bespoke a vulgarian whom he professed to hold in contempt. "Zola triumphant resembles a parvenu who has unexpectedly struck it rich . . . In his enormous, gigantic, unprecedented success I see a reflection of the public's aversion to style. For now that he has quite obviously renounced good writing, the book he's published is declared a masterpiece."

L'Assommoir affected Flaubert in various ways, proceeding from dislike to admiration. At first the lapidist for whom prose writing was a fundamentally aristocratic enterprise spoke louder than the scatological Garçon who had admonished Ernest Feydeau some years earlier to bear in mind that no subject or word, however crude, should be banned from the thesaurus of novelists. He found Zola's use of argot repugnant. It did not help that *Les Rougon-Macquart* was growing apace while *Bouvard et Pécuchet* lay stunted. "Like you, I've read bits of *L'Assommoir*," he told Turgenev (who had complained about "too much stirring of chamber pots" in it). "I didn't like it. Zola is falling victim to inverted preciosity . . . He is being carried away by his *system*. He has principles that cramp his brain." But letters written several months later are more evenhanded. His opinion shied away from the huffing of female correspondents scandalized by the novel. "My niece's revulsion surpasses yours," he wrote to Edma Roger des Genettes in February 1877. "Her disgust rises to fever pitch and renders her absolutely unjust. Too many books like this one would not be desirable, but there are superb chapters, a narrative that goes full tilt, and incontrovertible truths. It stays too long in the same gamut, but Zola is a powerful bloke and you'll see what success he'll have." When his prediction was borne out, he exclaimed (to Léonie Brainne): "Zola's *L'Assommoir* is a huge success! It has sold *sixteen* thousand copies in one month! I'm tired of having people rant about this book, and of hearing my own chatter, for I defend it whenever it's attacked . . . What's certain is that the work is significant." By April, *L'Assommoir* had become "a masterpiece," far superior to Goncourt's novel about prostitution, *La Fille Élisa,* which he found comparatively slender and anemic. "In these long, unsavory pages there is real power and an incontestable temperament." After this, would his own work, he wondered, not seem to qualify for assigned reading in girls' boarding schools?

Flaubert's strongest bond to writers of the next literary generation was with Guy de Maupassant, whom he called his student or disciple. Although Guy had met Flaubert before the war, it appears that the young man acquired color and weight for him only later, in 1872 or 1873. The older of Laure Le Poittevin's two sons by her husband, Gustave de Maupassant, a gentleman-painter of modest attainments, had been raised in an unquiet household, shifting between Paris and country houses rented first at Miromesnil, near Dieppe, then up the coast from Le Havre, near the fishing village of Étretat. The couple finally built "les Verguies" in Étretat itself, but being propertied did nothing to arrest Gustave de Maupassant's roving eye. Laure tired of his infidelities, and in 1862 he agreed to separate from the family. Two years later, at thirteen, Guy, who had been taught mostly by his mother and the local curate, was bound over to an institution run by priests. There, at Yvetot, he remained through the second form. When sacrilegious pranks led to his being dismissed, he entered the Collège de Rouen for one last year of secondary school and at that point may have compared notes with Flaubert, who knew something about expulsion. The two saw each other from time to time during his year-long residence, often in the company of Louis Bouilhet, on whom Guy called almost every week at the little house he then occupied. One encounter occurred in November 1868. All three ended up visiting the Saint-Romain fair. "I walked up the rue de Bihorel to show my poems to my illustrious and exacting friend, Bouilhet," Maupassant later remembered.

When I entered the poet's study, I made out two tall, portly men through a cloud of smoke, both slumped in armchairs, puffing away and chatting . . . I kept my verse hidden in my pocket, sat demurely on a chair in the corner, and listened. Toward 4 p.m., Flaubert rose. "Let's go," he said, "accompany me to the end of the street. I'll walk to the ferry." When we reached the Boulevard, where the Saint-Romain fair is held, Bouilhet suddenly asked, "What do you say we tour the booths?" And they began to loiter, side by side, head and shoulders above everyone else, amusing themselves like children and making pointed remarks about the crowd. From people's faces they deduced their characters and improvised conversations between husbands and wives, replete with Norman-isms, the Norman drawl, and the perpetually astonished air of locals. Bouilhet played the man and Flaubert his spouse.

Bouilhet's reflections on the literary craft stayed with Guy, who turned out to be his last and most distinguished pupil. Bouilhet died a few weeks before the young man passed his baccalaureate exam.

Unlike those other laureates for whom the Seine was a vale of tears winding south to the École de Droit, Maupassant might have enjoyed the practice of law. He joined them in Paris, but fate sidetracked him. When he returned one year later, he came as a soldier in the Quartermaster Corps of a division detailed to Rouen and served in that theater until the Prussians occupied Normandy: Bismarck had, in effect, expelled him from law school. After the war, unable to afford tuition, he became a government functionary in the Naval Ministry, earning the meager income of a low-level civil servant but living where he wished to live. It was toward the end of the year that his acquaintance with Flaubert, whom he still called "Mon-sieur Flaubert," evolved into friendship.

It would be a special friendship, avuncular or even filial. Alfred Le Poit-tevin's preeminence in family lore encouraged Guy to regard Flaubert as his uncle incarnate. Flaubert gave him access to that golden age when Caroline, Gustave, and Laure had gathered adoringly around Alfred. Letters are fraught with evocations of it. In January 1872, Laure told Flaubert that Guy was thrilled to have been consulted by him about the choice of poems for Bouilhet's posthumous collection. "I thank you for helping this boy as you have, and for being what you are to him," she wrote. "I feel I'm not alone in recalling times past, those good times when our two families were only one . . . My eyes see things in strange perspective when I look backward. What is distant moves to the foreground palpably, while the present recedes and pales. Nothing will ever consign those happy years of childhood and youth to oblivion." By February 1873, Guy was attending Flaubert's Sun-days, which Laure thought of as an atavistic ritual. "I can't tell you . . . how pleased I am . . . to see my son thus welcomed by the best of my old friends . . . Doesn't the young man bring back a thousand memories of that dear past when our poor Alfred held forth so well? The nephew resembles the uncle, you said so yourself, and I see, with maternal pride, that on closer examination the resemblance has not proved illusory." Flaubert assured Laure that in Guy she had reproduced her brother rather than her husband. "Despite the difference in our ages I consider him 'a friend'; and then, he reminds me so strongly of my poor Alfred! It sometimes frightens me, es-pecially in the way he bows his head while reciting verse. What a man he was, that one! He has remained, in my memory, beyond compare. Not a day passes that I don't think of him." Guy, in turn, confused the uncle he apparently resembled with Flaubert, whose idealization of Alfred attained mythic proportions. "Our weekly talks have become such a habit and necessity that I cannot refrain from chatting a little by letter," he wrote in June 1873 to Flaubert in Croisset. "In conversation with you, I often think I am hearing my uncle, whom I never knew but whom you and Mother have spoken of so often and whom I love as if we had been comrades or father and son . . . I can picture your meetings in Rouen. Would that I had been there among all of you instead of here with friends my own age." Alfred was thus a portmanteau for everybody's regrets. Flaubert would have liked to be younger and Maupassant older. The Alfred whom Maupassant saw in Flaubert would have made a congenial father; the Alfred Flaubert saw in Maupassant was his incomparable chum. Flaubert yearned for what he had lost, Maupassant for what he had never enjoyed.

In July 1876, when his valet, Émile, was crowing over the birth of a son, Flaubert wrote to Caroline that such joy as he would have found ludicrous in former days now seemed enviable. Age, he told her, had softened him to the consistency of "an overripe Edomite pear." But Guy de Maupassant certainly did more than anything to foster this upwelling of paternal sentiment. By 1876 Flaubert had dubbed Guy his adopted son and, indeed, behaved like a concerned parent. He bolstered the young man in any way he could. It was with letters of recommendation from Flaubert that Guy gained access to Catulle Mendès at the *République des Lettres,* where he published several articles (one on Flaubert himself), and to Edgar Raoul-Duval at his short-lived paper, *La Nation.* Two years later, with another letter, this one addressed to Agénor Bardoux, who had been appointed minister of instruction and fine arts by Dufaure during his second premiership, Flaubert helped Guy escape from his odious desk at the Naval Ministry. Moral precepts occasionally trooped after these practical maneuvers. When a despondent Maupassant voiced terminal ennui — complaining that he found "women's asses" as monotonous as "men's minds," that events offered no variety, that vices were paltry and good turns of phrase in short supply — Flaubert urged an ascetic regimen upon him. "You lament the monotony of ass; there's a simple remedy for that — don't avail yourself of it," he wrote on Assumption Day 1878.

> Vices are paltry, you say. Well, what isn't? As for turns of phrase, search and you will find. My dear friend, you seem thoroughly out of sorts, and your glumness pains me, since you could be putting your time to more agreeable use. You *must* — listen to me, young man — you *must* work more than you do. I've come to suspect you of being rather indolent. Too many whores! Too much canoeing!

Too much exercise! Yes, sir! The civilized man doesn't need as much locomotion as physicians pretend. You were born to write verse, so do it! "All the rest is vanity," beginning with your pleasures and your health.*

On the other hand (one hand was always wrestling the other to a draw in that paradoxical nature), Flaubert looked upon Guy's sexual athleticism with a mixture of paternal pride, adolescent glee, and voyeurism. "Your letter delighted me, young man!" he wrote in July 1876. "But I urge you to moderate your activity, for the sake of literature . . . Beware! Everything depends on the goal you have in view. A man who has plumped for art doesn't have the right to live like others." To Edmond Laporte he reported waggishly that during a brief cure at the Swiss spa of Loèche, the irrepressible Maupassant had cuckolded a pharmacist and on his way back home romped through the town brothel in Vesoul. A letter dated April 18, 1878, teased Laporte with veiled references to another of Maupassant's priapic exploits. "As for young Guy, he is such a fine specimen that I'll tell you nothing about him, but prepare yourself for some whoppers. He offered us a *performance* at which you were sorely missed." We know from J. K. Huysmans that this performance had taken place ten days earlier, after the monthly gathering of Zola's circle at the *Dîner du Boeuf nature*. Spirits may have been higher than usual when someone proposed that all fourteen diners repair to a neighborhood brothel. There, for their collective delectation, Maupassant demonstrated his stamina with an overtasked whore, ejaculating five times. Several weeks later he told a friend that the feat had enhanced his image in Flaubert's eyes.

FLAUBERT HAD dined with that crowd the previous year, on April 16, 1877, at a restaurant called Trapp's near the Saint-Lazare railroad station. Much hullabaloo had surrounded the meal, which was touted by the young associates of Émile Zola who organized it — Paul Alexis, Octave Mirbeau, Henri Céard, Huysmans, Léon Hennique, Maupassant — as the inaugural event of the naturalist movement. Newspapers had been alerted, and those that took notice published parodic articles. *La République des Lettres* claimed that the menu would include a purée of Bovary soup, salmon-trout à la Fille Élisa, truffled chicken à la Saint Antoine, artichokes au Coeur Simple, naturalist parfait, and liqueur de l'Assommoir. Lampoonists followed suit in cabaret acts, and naturalism inspired a multitude of cartoons, the most famous showing a porcine Zola astride a sow with grimy piglets advancing single-file behind him, their little tails intertwined.

Although Flaubert, who was emphatically un-French in his rooted dis-

*Maupassant was an expert sailor and powerful oarsman.

like of schools, may not have wanted to lend his name to a literary program about which he had serious qualms, or to give it legitimacy by being present at Trapp's, he found the occasion enjoyable. In any event, he could hardly turn his back on young writers, several of whom rated *L'Éducation sentimentale* above *Madame Bovary.* Adulation was adulation (even if Flaubert, in most other circumstances, might have comforted himself with Goethe's maxim: "A time comes when every man [put on earth to accomplish a mission] must be ruined"). He needed as much of it as he could get during the slow, painful gestation of *Bouvard et Pécuchet,* a book unlikely to ingratiate him with the public.

XXIV

~~~~~~~~~~

The Unraveling

FAR FROM hoping to ingratiate himself, Flaubert embarked upon *Bouvard et Pécuchet* with one purpose in mind, he told Léonie Brainne in October 1872, and that was to "exhale my resentment, vomit my hatred, expectorate my gall, ejaculate my anger, purge my indignation." By then he had written an outline and begun research, in the course of which he would, by his own estimate, read fifteen hundred volumes. Turgenev's advice that he imitate Voltaire or Swift fell on deaf ears. The rapier thrust wasn't good enough. Only cannon fire would do, and once again Flaubert proved himself a nineteenth-century man for girth and ambition. In an age that produced any number of three-decker novels and ten-volume histories, he could only conceive a work of massive, ponderous derision. Modern ideas were to don those fools' caps worn by the fourth-century creeds that drove Saint Anthony half-mad and this time march encyclopedically through the dim retreat of two studious ex-clerks. Indeed, Flaubert, who saw *La Tentation de Saint Antoine* and *Bouvard et Pécuchet* as kindred works, thought that he should delay publication of the former until he had written the latter.

The seed from which *Bouvard et Pécuchet* grew had already been planted when he completed his first version of *La Tentation*. On September 4, 1850, in Damascus, he dashed off a letter to Louis Bouilhet urging him not to forget a project they had discussed before their separation. "You do well to think about the *Dictionary of Received Ideas,*" he wrote. "It would need a good preface stating that the work intends to connect the public with tradition, order, general convention, but phrased ambiguously, so readers wonder whether or not it's a joke on them. It would be a strange work, yet liable to succeed because of its topicality." Two years later, the idea was still very much alive and inspiring misanthropic reveries during the composition of *Madame Bovary.* "I'm becoming a moralist," he informed Louise Colet. "Perhaps it's a sign of old age. Whatever the case, I've certainly shifted toward high comedy. The itch to tongue-lash human beings is sometimes unbearable and I'll do it someday, ten years hence, in a long novel with great scope. Meanwhile, an old idea has returned, my *Dictionary of Received Ideas.*" One exemplary candidate for ridicule was Auguste Comte, whose *Essai de philosophie positive* had been given to him by Paul-Émile Botta in Jerusalem. He found its conglomeration of Catholicism and socialism doubly abhorrent and vowed to savage the "deplorable utopias" agitating French society. This he would do in chapter six of *Bouvard et Pécuchet* (as he had already done in *L'Éducation sentimentale*).

His project then went underground. When it resurfaced after a decade of quiet gestation, it more closely resembled the future *Bouvard et Pécuchet,* for now it featured two characters whom Flaubert described as *cloportes* (which may be translated in this context as "stooges").* He was attracted to the story of his *cloportes,* he wrote to Jules Duplan in 1863. "The plan is good, of that I'm sure, despite the frightful difficulties I'll have avoiding monotony in the narrative. If it materializes, it will get me kicked out of France and Europe." As the novel he had just begun, *L'Éducation sentimentale,* presented difficulties no less formidable, he debated with himself whether to abandon it in favor of what he now called *Les Deux Cloportes,* "The Two Stooges." It was an embarrassment of quagmires, a contest of losers, and in the end these two zealous autodidacts, who would illustrate his dictum that mankind is a mere "thread" foolishly bent upon seeing the entire weave of creation, were made to wait their turn behind Frédéric Moreau. They would wait nine long years, but by 1863 they had already been given names, faces, and a rudimentary curriculum. It had become clear, moreover, that the *Dictionary of Received Ideas* would occupy a subordinate position, within the text itself or appended to it, once there was a text.

---

*No one English word adequately conveys the meanings and connotations of *cloporte*. In the twentieth century it was used in a highly derogatory sense by writers such as Louis Guilloux and Jean-Paul Sartre. English-French dictionaries often translate it as "creep." (At its most literal, it denotes a "woodlouse.") Punning with its constituent syllables (*clos,* or "closed," and *porte,* or "door"), it is slang for a concierge or doorkeeper. Ideas of foolishness and burying oneself or living behind closed doors have accreted to the word.

While Flaubert tried out various surnames before committing himself to "Bouvard" and "Pécuchet" (Bumolard, Dubolard, Bolard, Bécuchet, Manichet), the two clerks who meet on a city bench never had features other than those they were born with.* From conception, Pécuchet was seen as a sexually repressed virgin — gaunt, dark, morose, pointy-nosed — and Bouvard as a rotund, curly-blond, sociable widower. Their intrinsic difference shouldn't be forgotten, Flaubert noted when friends were first being told about the new project. It was now 1872, and an early announcement of the work in progress went to Edma Roger des Genettes. "I'm beginning a book that will occupy me for several years," he wrote on August 19. "It's the story of two simple blokes who copy out the farcical entries of what purports to be a critical encyclopedia. Does this sound familiar? I'll need to study many things I'm quite ignorant of: chemistry, medicine, agriculture." Soon afterward he informed Caroline that he was delving into "medical philosophy," the first of his major assignments. "I must confess that the plan, which I reviewed yesterday evening after dinner, seems to me first-rate, though the whole enterprise is crushing, frightful." At that point he could explain in broad outline, if not yet in the detail of every realm his characters ultimately visit, how the story would unfold. By August 1874, when he began writing it, notes and scenarios had multiplied.

How indeed was his story to unfold after the two lonely, middle-aged men resting on a bench near the place de la Bastille in the sweltering heat of a summer day make each other's acquaintance? Bouvard and Pécuchet learn that they are both copyists frustrated by their mindless employment. The friendship they strike up soon becomes a vital liaison that opens them to the world. Torn from lives of dull routine, they tour Paris's cultural palaces with a growing hunger for knowledge of all that lies beyond their ken. But the unattainable "beyond" creates another prison. "Having more ideas, they suffered more pain. Every time a mail coach crossed their path, they wanted to board it. The quai aux Fleurs made them sigh for the countryside." Providence intervenes when Bouvard's putative uncle, who turns out to have been his father, dies, leaving him a fortune. The clerks resign their clerkships and purchase one hundred acres of flat farmland outside a village called Chavignolles, somewhere between Caen and Falaise, where Flaubert had decided to situate them while reconnoitering Normandy with Edmond Laporte in June 1874. It was, he remarked, a "stupid plateau."

---

*Flaubert invested names, once he settled on them, with the essence of his characters and was loath to change any. In the 1860s, when told by a relative in Nogent-sur-Seine that there were a number of Moreaus living in the region, he declared that it was too late for him to find another surname, though *L'Éducation sentimentale* was still a work in progress. "A proper noun is *something very important* in a novel. It is *capital*. One can no more change a character's name than his skin."

There, the credulous students will have serial misadventures in an obstinate groping for certainty and knowledge. Their quest begins outside their front door. After dismissing a tenant farmer dead set against innovation, they buy tools, attire themselves suitably, read the *Catechism of Agriculture* (among much else), delight in technical jargon, fancy themselves progressive squires whose efforts will earn them recognition, and proceed to treat the soil with all the obtuseness of Charles Bovary operating on a clubfoot. Everything that can go wrong does. Flaubert's text is fraught with calamity, thanks not only to the pitfalls described in books he read but to those suggested by Maurice Sand and the husband of Edma Roger des Genettes. Methane gas from sheaves drying in accordance with the Clap-Mayer system makes a bonfire of the wheat harvest. Bouvard's compost, which he prepared exuberantly, yields foul-smelling crops. Different varieties of melon seeds crowded together in a forcing bed produce hybrids that taste like pumpkins. When the odd couple don't misconstrue what they read, what they read confounds them with contradictory prescriptions. One manual recommends that marl be used to alkalize the soil, while another calls it harmful. Following Gasparin's *Cours d'agriculture,* Bouvard declares the practice of leaving fields fallow a "Gothic prejudice," only to find it cogently defended by Leclerc in *Cours de culture et d'acclimatation des végétaux.* Their modern equipment, scorned by the peasant help, rusts away. Scarecrows become perches for undeceived birds that devour their fruit. Their espaliers refuse to be trained. Their stomachs rebel against beer brewed from germander leaves. Their preserves rot. "Could it be that arboriculture is a joke?" asks Pécuchet. "Like agronomy!" Bouvard replies. A failed experiment is the last straw. Hoping to make amends for their disastrous flirtation with nature by inventing something sweet, a cordial dubbed "bouvarine," they combine coriander, kirsch, hyssop, ambrette seed, and calamus in a secondhand still, which promptly explodes. When they recover their wits, or enough of them to contemplate another brave venture, Pécuchet says: "Maybe the problem is that we don't know chemistry!"

Thus will they persevere for twenty years, through fourteen disciplines ranging from chemistry to anatomy, physiology, medicine, geology, archeology, history, literature, politics, gymnastics, spiritualism, metaphysics, religion, and education. The pattern established in the chapter on agriculture holds good for most that follow. Bouvard and Pécuchet read voraciously, apply what they learn from books to the material world, note the discrepancy between the two, encounter a melee of self-intoxicated theorists where they had once expected to find a court of sober, scientific law; they despair and, like shipwrecked sailors jumping onto another leaky vessel, look for truth in another realm.

Of special importance to Flaubert was the chapter on medicine, for which he studied life-size anatomical mannequins procured by Laporte. No sooner does the postman deliver a mannequin rented from its manufacturer in Paris than Bouvard and Pécuchet begin disassembling it, muscle by muscle, with Lauth's *Manuel de l'anatomie* near to hand. More generally, the *Dictionnaire des sciences médicales* serves as their bible.

> They noted . . . extraordinary examples of childbirth, of longevity, of obesity and constipation. If only they had known the famous Canadian de Beaumont (who had a fistula opening into the stomach, which allowed doctors to perform unusual physiological experiments), the polyphagians Tarare and Bijoux, the dropsical woman from the Eure district, the Piedmontese who visited the water closet every twenty days, Simorre de Mirepoix, who died ossified, and that former mayor of Angoulême whose nose (exhibiting five lobes, descending over his mouth and covering his chin) weighed three pounds! The brain moved them to philosophical reflection. They clearly discerned the *septum lucidum* with its two lamellae, and the pineal gland, which resembled a little red pea. But there were peduncles, ventricles, arcs, pillars, floors, ganglia, fibers of every kind, Pacchioni's depressions and Pacini's bodies; one might lose oneself in the massive tangle and wear out one's existence.

Eschewing the brain (where their author as well had reason to fear fatal entanglements), they study simpler organs and experiment on a poor stray dog. Bouvard and Pécuchet aspire to "suffer for science," but it's the dog that bleeds. Their mentor is the local physician, Vaucorbeil. Confounded once again by contradictory systems without ceasing to revere the systematizers, they plump for François Raspail's theory that worms are the cause of all dysfunction and camphor a universal remedy.* Armed with this panacea, they give their medical advice to gullible villagers, brazenly confronting Vaucorbeil in a scene somewhat reminiscent of the confrontation between Dr Canivet and Charles Bovary. When their farmer's wife, Mme Gouy, contracts typhoid, and Pécuchet, not knowing that the disease ulcerates the intestines, has her eat meat, Vaucorbeil exclaims, "This is a veritable murder!" Undeterred, Pécuchet invokes the authority of Raspail and Van Helmont, who endorsed the precept that "dieting compromises the vital principle." They tug their helpless patient this way and that. Clinical practice is what makes a good physician, says Vaucorbeil, to which Pécuchet responds: "Those who revolutionized medicine did not practice it! Van Helmont, Boerhaave, Broussais himself." Later he will tremble at the prospect of being arraigned for murder if Mme Gouy should die. She doesn't, and a dauntless Pécuchet proposes that he and his partner learn ob-

---

*Flaubert would have had in mind Raspail's futile intervention when his sister was dying.

stetrics with a mannequin used to train midwives. But Bouvard, who has meanwhile been cured of his belief in the immunological benefit of hemorrhoids, refuses. "The mainsprings of life are hidden from us, and afflictions are too numerous, our remedies problematical," he concludes, paraphrasing the great physiologist Claude Bernard, "and in no author does one find a reasonable definition of health, of sickness, diathesis, or even of pus."

Flaubert's animus against Rouennais who regarded him as the leafless branch of his family tree was an inexhaustible source of fuel for *Bouvard et Pécuchet*. The erudite rampage through medical theory and practice splashed a little mud on Achille's shingle and generally impugned the liberal professions, or *capacités,* in which his hated bourgeois brethren vested such prestige.* It may well be, furthermore, that the spectacle of risible ideas parading through society under the banner of science served to make his epileptic hallucinations seem relatively innocuous. Better yet, it invited readers to view the narrator as an omniscient figure, "everywhere felt and nowhere seen," looking down on poor, self-deluded humanity from the devil's gallery. Had this "last testament," which bespeaks the unwavering line of Flaubert's thought, not already been foreshadowed in the first version of *L'Éducation sentimentale*?

His plan was to circle back to his characters' original occupation in a second volume, with Bouvard and Pécuchet drawing on all they had read for an anthology of hollow assertions about scientific and moral progress, about salvation through technology, about the future fraternity of all mankind. Seated opposite each other at a double desk, they would become copyists again, producing a voluminous *sottisier* (a collection of foolish quotations). But in what guise? When all is said and done, have they not seen the light of unknowability? Have these obstinate seekers who antagonize the village notables — the priest, the doctor, the mayor, the notary, the count — blundered their way beyond the reach of received ideas? Is the double desk at which they copy entries into their *sottisier* an analogue of the garden Candide cultivates after his many misadventures? "No reflection! Let's copy!" Flaubert has them exclaim in a scenario. "The page must get filled, the 'monument' must be completed. — Equality of everything, of good and evil, the beautiful and the ugly, the insignificant and the characteristic. Only phenomena are true." His reborn copyists are neither the perfect embodiment of Murphy's Law nor the Laurel-and-Hardy-like simpletons he pictured when he still thought of them as *cloportes* and concerned himself

---

*He told Léonie Brainne that he held the medical tribe in even lower esteem than the literary. And to George Sand he wrote: "What self-assurance doctors have! What nerve! What asses they are, for the most part."

more with the inanity of their diet than the nobility of their hunger. As the book unfolds, they become increasingly Flaubertian. "Bouvard and Pécuchet . . . formulated abominable paradoxes . . . They cast doubt on the probity of men, the chastity of women, the intelligence of government, the people's common sense . . . The evidence of their superiority rankled. Since they defended immoral theses, they themselves were thought to be necessarily immoral, and this assumption made the case for slanderous rumors. A pitiable faculty then began to develop in them, that of perceiving stupidity and finding it intolerable." The future anthologists of the *sottisier*, who will demonstrate their love of mind even in the act of recording its futile errands, are here, toward the end, fully fleshed. "Insignificant things made them sad: newspaper advertisements, a bourgeois profile, a fatuous remark overheard in passing . . . They felt the weight of the whole earth on them."

During the long suspension of work on *Bouvard et Pécuchet,* Flaubert had confided to George Sand that it would be his definitive testament. The Kid would make humanity choke on its own indigestible mass of pseudo-erudition. "B. and P.," he nicknamed it. When he took "B. and P." up again after *Trois Contes* in June 1877, his spirits were high. High spirits did not dispel the fear that he might end up writing a merely comic work, but for the moment that mood held sway, and emblematic of it was a gorgeous Bokharan robe Turgenev had sent from Russia. Flaubert liked to wrap himself in it, despite the summer heat, claiming that it stimulated his brain. "During the past two days I've done excellent work," he informed Caroline on June 6. "At times, the immense scope of this book stuns me. What will come of it? I only hope I'm not deceiving myself into writing something goofy rather than sublime. No, I think not! Something tells me I'm on the right path! But it will be one or the other." Anyone who could help was put under an obligation to acquire books or elucidate detail, and no one more than Edmond Laporte, who answered every call, even when burdened with anxiety over the closing of his lace factory. In September 1877 he accompanied Flaubert on a jaunt through the countryside around Falaise, where Bouvard and Pécuchet were destined to ponder inscrutable megaliths. For one week at least, Laporte, who had been given the nickname "El Bab" (an Arabic translation of Laporte, "the door"), converted his friend to a matutinal way of life. "We rise at six in the morning (yes!) and retire at nine in the evening," Flaubert reported. "We spend the whole day traveling hither and yon, mostly in small open carriages, with the cold air nipping our snouts. Yesterday, at the seaside, it was unbearable . . . We're feeling great . . . Laporte is 'full of attentions' for me. What a good fellow!"

His sense of well-being lasted only as long as Nemesis was looking the other way, or so it must have seemed in 1877 when Ernest Commanville's financial embarrassments threatened once again to wreak havoc. Almost two years had passed since the first crisis. Order had apparently been restored. Courts had authorized the liquidation of Commanville's assets at Dieppe, and Caroline would repay a large debt in annual installments of five thousand francs, to be guaranteed by Laporte and Raoul-Duval. The two hundred thousand francs Flaubert had given his nephew would satisfy other needs, including his own for a regular allowance. But the assets were not liquidated after all. Instead, Commanville decided to save his mill if possible by creating a joint-stock company and selling shares. Flaubert, whom Caroline had already admonished to live more frugally, was urged to find rich investors. He embraced the challenge with a combination of panic and alacrity, recognizing that his own economic survival depended upon Commanville's and wanting, as in the past, to demonstrate his competence in the practical world, to rescue from disaster a "bourgeois" incapable of helping himself. Letters were sent, strings were pulled, interviews were arranged. Madame Pelouze, who came up specially from Chenonceaux for a meeting, pledged fifty thousand francs. Her name was a lure, and Raoul-Duval cast it into his pool of rich associates. Through Charles Lapierre, Flaubert secured Commanville an introduction to at least one tycoon, who may or may not have invested after visiting the sawmill at Dieppe. Whenever elegant hostesses were needed, Valérie Lapierre and her sister Léonie Brainne made themselves available. And Flaubert reached out to other women friends. "You know that I'm completely ruined," he wrote to Edma Roger des Genettes on June 18, 1877. "We must get out of this mess somehow, by selling Croisset perhaps, even giving up a pied-à-terre in Paris and living elsewhere, I have no idea where, or on what. During the two years Commanville spent trying to get his factory started again, he hadn't had any luck. Well, it was I who found the first investors in a joint-stock company he would like to form. Here's how things stand. He needs a capital base of one million francs. His factory, his materiel and land are valued at 600,000 francs, which leaves 400,000. Of that amount 120,000 have been raised in a fortnight. There you have it in a nutshell. We've negotiated the first, most difficult obstacle." If only Commanville could set himself up in time, the Universal Exposition scheduled for 1878, a whole village of wooden pavilions to be built between the Champ-de-Mars and the Trocadéro, would profit him, Flaubert told Adèle Husson. "No one wants to travel from Paris to Dieppe to see his plant . . . but those who do immediately open their purses . . . I've heard that your friend Archdeacon [*sic*] could help a lot. Needed is a 200,000 franc loan, which would be guaranteed. Are you on close enough terms to ask him to give the matter his consideration?"

In October 1877, Flaubert assured Turgenev that his nephew's prospects had improved. (His habitual underlining of *"les affaires,"* the term for business, was analogous to putting it between quotes: it distanced him from it as from the thing it signified.) Not that he always trusted Commanville's accountancy. One letter shows him politely questioning it. If there were other such letters, more explicit and irate, Caroline, who was tempted after her uncle's death to expunge whatever reflected badly upon her in the correspondence, mislaid them. Of his anger there is no doubt, but he may have preferred to maintain civil relations and suspend disbelief, so long as he received an allowance. Under the circumstances, what better outlet for rage than the *sottisier?*

Another lull followed. Flaubert continued to run the gauntlet of merciless tutorials, along with B. and P., taking pride in his endurance when he wasn't complaining that it would be the death of him. "This bloody book has me quaking," he confided to Zola on October 5, 1877. "It won't make any sense except as a whole. There aren't any brilliant bits; the situation is always the same; for variety I must catch different facets. I'm afraid it will be deadly dull. Patience is needed, let me tell you, since there are another three years of work left, though I should be over the hump in five or six months." In warm weather he seldom missed his afternoon swim and casually attended to the minutiae of domestic life — hanging pictures, having his bathtub replumbed, fitting the garden banister with an ornamental knob. Nothing in his demeanor suggested that soon an estate agent might, for all he knew, be showing Croisset to potential buyers. The lord of the manor took proprietary walks with his greyhound, Julio, or lounged among the untended flower beds, aware no doubt of children spying on him through the entrance gate. "For me, he was a being like no other, exotic and fantastic, a mysterious personality whom I regarded in a confusion of wonder and respect," one neighbor recalled. "I never believed he was Norman. He was Persian or Turkish, Chinese or Hindu, I couldn't decide which, but for sure he came from some distant place and had a distinctive nature. The fabulous accoutrements made me think he might well be a prince . . . When my nanny wanted to treat me, she'd walk me past his front gate, where I'd gaze at him smoking his pipe, slouched in a large armchair. I'll always remember with tender emotion his pink and white striped culottes and his house robes, the floral designs of which were pure poetry." This spectator had company on Sundays, when families from Rouen made Flaubert a side show on their dominical excursions into the countryside.

When he traveled at all, it was to the flat he retained on the rue du Faubourg Saint-Honoré or, occasionally, to Chenonceaux. He spent several weeks in Paris that September, enjoying his annual reunion with Juliet Herbert while leading Caroline and others to believe, as he had done the previous year, that he was consorting with Mathilde at Saint-Gratien.* On September 12, Turgenev received this message from him: "Don't be astonished by my long sojourn in the capital. I'm here (*inter nos*), detained *veneris causa!!!*"

Flaubert came to Paris in late December for the winter season. He holed up with dozens of books and read two a day on average, thanks to his concierge, who effectively guarded against unexpected callers. Paris didn't tempt him, least of all with the insipid fare at Boulevard theaters. But neither did he shut himself away completely. Caroline lived on the same landing. Every Sunday his literary friends dropped by. On Wednesday evenings he was often to be found at Princess Mathilde's dinner table, among eight or ten other guests, most of whom had come down in the world since Napoleon III's abdication. And on Fridays he often rubbed shoulders with the republican elite at Marguerite Charpentier's salon. For all his fulminating against politicians, Flaubert loved to chat up the powerful ones. He felt comfortable in their presence, unlike, say, Edmond de Goncourt, who couldn't forgive him any success, social or literary. "After dinner, Flaubert sweeps Gambetta into another room and closes the door behind him," the diarist noted on January 18, 1878, when Gambetta was presiding over the Chamber of Deputies. "Tomorrow he will be able to say: 'Gambetta is my intimate friend.' It's truly remarkable, the attraction that notoriety of every kind exercises upon this man, his need to approach it, to rub against it, to crash its private space! It wouldn't matter whether the notable was a famous wax merchant or a cosmopolitan dentist." Unmentioned in the *Journal* is the pleasure Flaubert took in exploiting the influence he thus acquired for friends needing government support. Flaubert failed to wangle Zola an appointment to the Legion of Honor, but not for lack of trying. Without his mediation, Maupassant might have languished at the Naval Ministry. The prospect of no longer being used by Flaubert may have consoled Agénor Bardoux for his fall from power in February 1879. Flaubert had also hectored him to secure employment for Edmond Laporte when his business failed.

Soon enough, the benefactor found himself, to his immense chagrin, in need of benefaction. Three years earlier, Bardoux had given serious thought to arranging a state pension for Flaubert and been discouraged by his friend as follows:

I can't tell you how deeply moved I was by the plan you and Raoul-Duval devised . . . But my dear friend, judge the situation for yourself. In my place, you would surely not approve it. The disaster that has befallen me in no way con-

---

*Flaubert let Laporte in on the secret; after Flaubert's death Caroline replaced the woman's name with dots in his correspondence, but everything points to Juliet, of whom she was, no doubt, jealous. Jealousy was exacerbated by snobbery.

cerns the public. It was my responsibility to manage my affairs better, and I don't think the state budget should feed me. News of this pension would be announced, published, and perhaps assailed in the press and in the Chamber! How could we respond? Yes, others enjoy the same favor, but what others are allowed I am forbidden. Then again, I haven't *yet* reached that point, thank God.

However, since things will be very tight, if you can find me a post in some library paying three or four thousand francs with a place to live (as at the Mazarine or the Arsenal), that would suit me just fine. I assume it's out of the question, though.

This letter, written on August 31, 1875, a day after he sold his Deauville farm, suggests that Flaubert may still have believed in the reliability of a providential father. By September 1878, God had obviously forsaken him, joining the capitalists who wouldn't salvage what remained of his nephew's business. At that point, few people cared to pretend that Commanville might still reestablish himself, or that he hadn't criminally mismanaged everyone's finances. What, indeed, remained of the family fortune? Apparently little if anything, apart from Croisset, Caroline's portion (the income from which should have been shared with Commanville's principal creditor), and the dregs of Flaubert's inheritance. Unable to afford their pied-à-terre at 240, rue du Faubourg Saint-Honoré, the Commanvilles moved into Flaubert's larger flat next door. Croisset could not be sold unless Flaubert relinquished his right to occupy it for the rest of his unmarried life. Would he refuse Caroline, whom he refused nothing else? "God only knows what will become of us!" he wrote to Léonie Brainne on December 10, 1878. "Commanville will earn money one way or another! No matter, whatever follows will not be pleasant. I swear, my heart is sinking! And the worst is not the lack of money, the privations that result, the complete absence of freedom. No, that's not what enrages me. I feel my mind *soiled* by these base preoccupations, by these commercial dialogues. I sense that I'm becoming a grocer." How could he defend his vulnerable self against a foreigner more alienating than Prussia? As for attempts to find Flaubert employment in some bookish institution, he declared that he wouldn't hear of it. "Never! Never! Never! I refused what my friend Bardoux offered me . . . In the worst possible case scenario, I could live in a country inn on fifteen hundred francs a year. I would do that sooner than accept a penny of public funds . . . Anyway, what position am I qualified to fill?" Gossip about Flaubert's home life painted an even darker picture. "His ruin is supposedly complete," Goncourt reported, "and the very people for whom he ruined himself out of affection are said to begrudge him the cigars he smokes. His niece is quoted as exclaiming: 'My uncle is a singular man, he doesn't know how to tolerate adversity!'"

Staunch friends tried to rescue him, *malgré lui*. During the fall and winter of 1878, when they lobbied politicians on his behalf, he acted like a tormented bachelor wondering whether to preserve his independence or to make an advantageous marriage. Goncourt, who found Flaubert rather more sympathetic in these desperate circumstances, recommended him for a librarianship at Compiègne, which went in the end to Sainte-Beuve's former secretary Jules Troubat. Lobbying became hectic after New Year's, when other friends learned that Samuel de Sacy, chief librarian of the Mazarine collection at the French Institute, would not live much longer. They wanted this plum for Flaubert, aware though they must have been that de Sacy's obvious successor was his deputy, and Flaubert's old friend, Frédéric Baudry. Hippolyte Taine broached the idea in a letter to which Flaubert responded on January 10, 1879. "I can't tell you how moved I am by your friendly attentions," he wrote.

> Poor old de Sacy's office wouldn't suit me, and here's why. It would force me to live in Paris. With the three thousand francs I'd earn, I would be poorer than I am at present, since life is cheaper in the countryside. True, the apartment tempts me. But it would be folly, I'd starve to death there. I'm better off staying in my hut as long as possible, and visiting Paris occasionally. Moreover, occupying a government post, whatever it may be, fills me with a stupid but *invincible* repugnance. That's your friend for you.

By no means certain was it that he would have been poorer with three thousand francs and free lodging at the institute. Until Commanville found a buyer for his property in Dieppe, or shareholders, Flaubert had very little income. "We can't say anything or make any plans, even short-term, so long as the sale hasn't gone through," he complained to Caroline. "It can't happen soon enough for me! When it's accomplished I'll have a few thousand francs to live on while finishing *Bouvard et Pécuchet*. I'm more and more irritated by this meager existence, and the state of permanent uncertainty gets me down. Much as I try to fight it, I feel that I'm succumbing to despair. It's high time something happened."

Troubles don't come single spy, and to prove the point, Flaubert, wobbly with exhaustion from sleepless nights, or quite possibly overcome by an epileptic seizure, fell on the ice at Croisset that January, breaking a leg.* The accident, he said, occurred five minutes after he read a note from Turgenev urging him to get more exercise. Friends and acquaintances who read about

---

*The fall had been preceded by a peculiar sensation in his epigastrium, or upper abdomen — a common harbinger of seizures and the symptom that announces Saint Anthony's hallucination in *La Tentation*.

it in *Le Figaro* sent letters of commiseration by the dozen. Achille, in Nice with Julie, couldn't help, but his personal physician, Fortin, set the bone competently. Laporte shuttled between Grand-Couronne and Croisset to nurse his friend, braving the intense cold and fording flooded roads. The injury confined Flaubert for weeks to the second floor of his house but banished at least the terrible loneliness about which he had often complained earlier in the winter.

His benefactors in Paris would not have been far wrong if they thought that a bedridden Flaubert might condone their efforts more readily than an ambulatory one. On February 3 Turgenev arrived at Croisset and stayed two days, in the course of which he persuaded his host to give the Mazarine post serious consideration. Zola, who had declared that a Paris winter without Flaubert was a dismal prospect, lost no time informing Marguerite Charpentier. "[Turgenev] swayed Flaubert. He won't say yes definitely, however, before finding out what his salary will be. Turgenev has just telegraphed him he thinks it's six thousand francs and expects an affirmative reply." Zola urged her to set in motion the machinery of influence. She did as bidden, according to Turgenev, whose main concern was the political favor Baudry enjoyed through his father-in-law, Sénard. Flaubert became a passive office seeker avowedly eager to have the position but wanting assurances that he wouldn't be rebuffed. "I've put aside my foolish pride and accept," he wrote to Turgenev on the fifth, "for dying of hunger would be an idiotic way to croak." After three more days, his scruples had been completely routed. "More than ever am I of a mind not to sacrifice myself for the excellent M. Baudry. So, let my friends act! You know that I am on very good terms with Mme [Juliette] Adam, Gambetta's friend, and with Mme Pelouze, a friend of Grévy [president of the republic]." What clouded his enthusiasm, however, was a deep-seated feeling that desire could only result in humiliation.

Setting himself against Baudry — a scholar far better qualified than he to administer the great library, a childhood friend whose erudition had at various times served him well, and the son-in-law of the lawyer who had successfully defended him in the *Madame Bovary* trial — did not do Flaubert credit. But in any event, the idea that de Sacy's job was ripe for the picking turned out to be as illusory as the hope of restoring Commanville's fortunes. On February 13 he received this telegram from Turgenev: "Don't give it any further thought. Flat refusal. Details to follow." The letter that followed makes reference to Juliette Adam, a woman of great intellectual verve whose salon had become Gambetta's private court. "On my return [from Croisset], we decided that I would try and speak to Gambetta, then to Ferry [minister of education], and if necessary to Baudry," Turgenev wrote.

Thursday evening — first letter from Zola (enclosed) — and then a lull. I requested an interview with Mme Ed. [Edmond] Adam; no answer. Monday morning — a letter from Zola accompanying a note from Mme Charpentier (I enclosed them as well). You can imagine my amazement. I took a carriage and went straight to the presidential palace to see Gambetta . . . I was not received, but . . . the next day I received a letter from Mme Edmond Adam, who they had told me was in Cannes. I put on my suit, white tie — and was soon shoulder to shoulder with a host of political notables in that drawing room where France is effectively governed and administered . . . I explained the matter [to my hostess] . . . "But Gambetta is right here — he's having an after-dinner smoke — he shall be informed of the matter straightaway." She came back two minutes later: "Impossible, my dear sir! Gambetta already has other people in mind!" The dictator arrived with measured step: ministers and senators surrounded him like trained dogs dancing around their master. He started to talk to one of them. Mme Ed. Adam took me by the hand and led me to him; but the great man declined the honor of making my acquaintance — and said, loud enough for me to hear: "I don't want it — I've said so — it's impossible." I made myself scarce and then came home, *plunged,* as they say, in thoughts upon which I needn't elaborate. And that's how much one can trust fine words and promises.

Worse yet, this account appeared two days later on the front page of a conservative paper, *Le Figaro,* with parodic exaggerations calculated to show Gambetta in the most unflattering light. "Thus," it read, "one of the foremost writers of his age will not succeed M. de Sacy because M. Gambetta doesn't want it. The argument that M. Flaubert lacks the requisite administrative titles doesn't hold water. Did M. Ulbach, who has been named to the Arsenal, have them? That's the way we are governed." From Berlin, en route to Russia, Turgenev wrote that the reporter's source could not have been any of the only three people to whom he had spoken of the incident — Pauline Viardot, her husband, and Zola.

Flaubert had expected humiliation, and humiliated is how he felt upon finding himself portrayed in *Le Figaro* as a spurned candidate. The article enraged him. Here was another bitter pill to swallow, he lamented to Maupassant. He cursed the day he had first had the idea of signing his name to a book. "There's no undoing it, alas! But I am exasperated by the attention paid to my person . . . People inveigh against the Inquisition, but reporters are Dominicans in another guise, that's all. To get at Gambetta they're prepared to queer my relations with Mme Adam and advertise my *destitution.* Punishment!" It was punishment for not conforming to his lifelong motto, "Hide your life," and perhaps as well for trying to outmaneuver an old friend who, he now acknowledged with bureaucratic punctilio, had a "hierarchical" claim upon the Mazarine directorship.

Attempts to help Flaubert did not stop there. Indeed, Baudry himself made one such attempt, proposing that a sinecure — an honorary librarianship providing a stipend and quarters at the institute — be created for him at the Mazarine. Flaubert declared that he could not accept "alms," that he didn't deserve it, that it would invite public scrutiny, that the family who had ruined him rather than the government ought to bear the burden of feeding him. His family could only feed him wormwood, and he knew it, having just been told (in late February 1879) that the sale of Commanville's assets would fetch two hundred thousand francs, not six hundred thousand, and that none of the proceeds would be available to reimburse him.* How should he pay the chambermaid's wages when he could now barely afford the train fare to Paris? He was in fact dead broke, but pride and fear continued to defend against patronage. On March 6 Maupassant warned him that the minister of education, Ferry, seemed intent on offering him an honorific title with emoluments. "The offer would be presented as official homage and not as the conferring of a pension upon a man of letters," he wrote. "You would be obliged neither to live in Paris nor to perform any active service. Drawn from funds assigned under chapter 25 . . . this measure is in no way anomolous. Their assumption is that the arrangement will overcome your resistance." Flaubert's resistance was not to be underestimated. He had nothing left but pride, he answered, and felt that he could no longer write if pride were forfeited.

> A pension disguised as "homage" would be an intolerably heavy burden for me. The "honorific title" accompanying it would reek of pity. Note that this nomination must be inserted in the official *Gazette*! I would then fall back into the hands of the reportorial crowd. The measure would be criticized, discussed, and your friend scoffed at.

There were, on the other hand, certain conditions under which it might be possible to enjoy both the honor of virtue and the advantages of dishonor.

> Should title and pension be kept secret, I would accept them, but temporarily, with every intention of giving them up if fortune were to favor me (I would even promise to do so) — a hypothesis that could become reality whenever Caro's elderly aunt dies.

---

*This provoked a rare outburst. "I, his biggest creditor, am to receive nothing?" he scolded Caroline. "Must one conclude that Ernest has duped himself once again? What does he spend his days doing? I understand why he's not cheerful, why he has fits of despair, but whose fault is that? . . . I promised myself not to speak to you about all that, but I do anyway, despite myself."

He reiterated his argument, more emphatically, in a second letter. "If I am *sure,* absolutely sure, that the transaction will take place between the minister and me, no one else, I accept with gratitude and on condition (in my own mind) that it be a loan, a temporary measure of help." Rather than wait upon fortune, he would ask his brother for an annual stipend the equivalent of what Ferry was offering. Achille's family raked in one hundred thousand francs a year, he claimed. "They can easily afford to spare five thousand of that." Soon afterward, Maupassant informed Caroline, in a self-congratulatory note, that he had prevailed upon her uncle to accept the pension.

He spoke too soon, or prevailed to no effect, for after weeks of equivocation the ministry withdrew its offer, leaving Maupassant to explain that it lacked funds for a substantial pension but could award him a sinecure at the Mazarine under Baudry. Flaubert later learned that Victor Hugo had vigorously intervened on his behalf. This tortuous drama thus came full circle and Flaubert was now, in May, disposed to accept what he had rejected in February. "I prefer it that way, it's no longer alms," he told Caroline. "To be sure, three thousand doesn't equal five, but there may be a means of increasing the amount later. In any event, my conscience will rest easier." His conscience was still quarreling with him when the appointment at the Mazarine became a fait accompli in late May.

As for his brother, Flaubert had no sooner broached the issue of financial support than Achille offered him three thousand francs a year. The gesture was so spontaneous that he thought it must have been a portent of senility (doctors had in fact diagnosed a "softening of the brain" in Achille) or, at best, an evasive maneuver. "I'll bring it up again and won't be at all surprised if he has completely forgotten our talk. It was one of those situations in which rogues get everything they ask for."

The meetings with Ferry at the Ministry of Education and with Achille took place in June, most of which he spent in Paris. Another event that made his sojourn unusually salutary was the annual Salon, which — thanks to strings he pulled — had accepted a portrait of Dr Jules Cloquet by Caroline. Flaubert (whose taste in art was decidedly more for Carolus Duran than Edouard Manet) limped dutifully through the vast hall and afterward did everything to tout his niece's custom, thinking that she might, *à la rigueur,* earn her livelihood as a painter. Cloquet paid a handsome fee for his own portrait.

FLAUBERT MAY have been saved from total ruin, but the Commanvilles' crisis dragged on month after month, taking a physical and emotional toll on everyone involved in it. While Ernest Commanville struggled yet again to raise money for yet another sawmill, Caroline spent more time at her easel, unburdened herself to Father Didon, wove romantic fantasies around her uncle's friend the poet Hérédia, corresponded with Flaubert when they weren't together at Croisset, and described the incapacitating afflictions for which she could no longer afford a spa: neuralgia, anemia, migraines, chronic fatigue. Nerves were terribly frayed, as one gathers from the letter Flaubert sent to her on May 16:

> My Loulou,
> I left your place yesterday *tormented by remorse.* For some time my person and my correspondence have been very disagreeable! But consider the extenuating circumstance that I am distraught, that I hold back a hundred times more than I let out, having no one to pour myself into. I who was born so expansive! The needs of my heart go unfulfilled, and my solitude is complete.

His own catalogue of complaints was impressive. The broken bone, which had healed quite well, apparently aggravated his rheumatism. After train rides between Rouen and Paris, his feet were generally swollen. The drug he took for epilepsy may have contributed to his exhaustion. It often caused an outbreak of eczema. At year's end he reported a gouty inflammation of joints in his right hand. He had lumbago, eye trouble, tonsillitis, excruciating toothache. All but one of his upper teeth had been extracted. "The life I lead isn't very hygienic," he told Léonie Brainne, understating the case. The trencherman so ill equipped to chew couldn't eat meat, but what he ate, he ate to excess. Walks became rare events. In any event he moved around gingerly, limping.

The anger Flaubert didn't dare vent on Caroline warped his judgment. Subjugated by his moody, willful niece, he showed a brazen face to anyone who crossed her. Ranks were closed against a hostile world, and relegated to that world with shocking arbitrariness was his most devoted friend, Edmond Laporte. In 1878 Commanville's creditor Faucon had agreed to extend the deadline for repayment of his loan on condition that the guarantors, Laporte and Raoul-Duval, renew their commitment. At Flaubert's behest, Laporte, who distrusted Commanville, reluctantly agreed. What he wouldn't do was sign the agreement in person, knowing that Faucon wanted to meet a regional counselor with political influence, and Flaubert took Laporte's side. "Ernest has some nerve being indignant because Laporte didn't want to visit Faucon!" he complained to Caroline in January 1879. "And he accused him of 'turning against him,' a sly remark intended to drive a wedge between us. I'd better stop . . . Funny how someone can think that he alone has rights while everyone else is duty bound to serve him." Ten months later, when Commanville wanted yet another extension and Faucon a second renewal of the guarantors' commitment (presumably with interest), Laporte refused. Things had not gone well for him. His factory had closed, his savings had dwindled even as he was planning to get married, and necessity had forced him to accept the post of Inspector of Labor for the Nevers region in central France. He could not risk mortgaging his property. Goaded by Caroline and Commanville, Flaubert begged him to reconsider. "*It is urgent* that Faucon be discouraged from initiating a legal protest, to avoid useless fees, and you alone have the credentials. Isn't that the term, credentials?" he wrote on September 27. "So, write to him immediately . . . Since you are averse to seeing Faucon, tell him that your fortune consists entirely in immovable assets and that to fulfill your obligations you would have to borrow . . . Have him give us another five or six months . . . (We will have extricated ourselves from this mess by then, somehow or other.) Your signature is good, bankers respect it . . . *There is no other way out of it right now,* dear boy. *Do it, I beg you.* I'm sick and tired of all these stories, that's the truth." Laporte thought it inexcusable of Commanville to have put Flaubert in the position of siding with one party or the other and urged his friend to recuse himself. Under duress, Flaubert begged him once again.

> I am astonished by a letter from you, which Commanville has just showed me. It seems to me that you don't understand the situation. Is that possible? Faucon could require you to pay him fourteen thousand francs before the end of the year. He agrees to delay the due date a year and for this slight service wants *twenty-five thousand francs!* Now, Commanville has found a capitalist who will reimburse Faucon straightaway and won't demand repayment for two years, half in December 1880, half at the end of 1881. Raoul-Duval has accepted this transfer . . . What prevents you from doing the same? What are you afraid of?

That Commanville was arrogant and deceitful couldn't have been more obvious, and in February 1880 Laporte served him papers demanding immediate repayment of a thirteen-thousand-franc debt (presumably the balance of the twenty-five-thousand-franc bank loan, unpaid and past due, for which Laporte had stood surety). When Caroline bewailed his "falsity," Flaubert, who not long before had called Laporte "without question my best friend," echoed her. Overnight, like suddenly devalued currency, Laporte's many proofs of devotion counted for nothing. To Edma Roger des Genettes, Flaubert lamented the fact that a man he rightly considered his *fidus Achates* had betrayed him with a demonstration of "base egoism." It made matters worse that Laporte, far from imagining their friendship compromised, expected it to continue as before. When it was borne in on him that a break had well and truly taken place, he grieved over the loss and would apparently never quite recover from it. But neither, perhaps, would Flaubert. "The intellectual state into which your deplorable complication has plunged me makes work *impossible,*" he wrote to Caroline. "I think about it incessantly. I am more worn out by it than tormented. I dare not even show my face in Rouen (where I must consult the oculist) for fear of meeting Laporte. I wouldn't know what expression to wear or what to say." The whole business stuck in his throat, he told her.

The two never saw each other again. In December, Laporte had sent Flaubert a New Year's greeting addressed to "my old friend." It read in part: "Whatever feelings about me may have been instilled in you by others, I wouldn't want the year to end without sending you all my affectionate wishes. Accept them as given. They come from a man who may be your best friend. I embrace you." Flaubert couldn't reply.

TO ALL outward appearances, life continued as before. The year 1879 closed with gifts of smoked salmon and caviar from Turgenev, who also sent his friend a French translation of *War and Peace.* Tolstoy's novel, which Flaubert would have loved unreservedly but for the author's philosophical digressions, was scarfed down as quickly as it took to write three pages about religion in the penultimate chapter of *Bouvard et Pécuchet.*

The previous September Flaubert had spent several weeks at 240, rue du Faubourg Saint-Honoré, at least one of them with Juliet Herbert. There had been many dinners, other reunions, and a visit of condolence to Saint-Gratien, where Mathilde was mourning the death of Napoleon III's son, Eugène — killed fighting Zulus with the British in South Africa, only nine years after Charles Oman had seen him as a child drilling his little troops at the Tuileries. Thereafter, from early December, Flaubert lived at Croisset in a fastness of ice and snow, slogging through the theological treatises, catechisms, and seminarists' manuals that Bouvard and Pécuchet must consult toward the end of their futile quest, and finding some consolation in the anticlerical politics of his patron, Jules Ferry, now prime minister. Even as Catholicism was taking its lumps at Croisset, the republican government was preparing to banish Jesuits from France. But neither this blow to the Moral Order nor Charpentier's republication of *L'Éducation sentimentale* (which would, he hoped, be more favorably received under a different imprint) cheered him. If anything, the jeremiad grew louder. To Edma Roger des Genettes, he groused about the "stupid or rather stupidifying [*stupidifiantes*]" works on his syllabus. "The religious pamphlets of Monsignor de Ségur, the lucubrations of Father Huguet, S.J., of Baguenault de Puchesse,

etc., of that excellent man M. Nicolas who thinks *Wolfenbüttel* is a man . . .
and as a result fulminates against Wolfenbüttel!* Modern religion is decidedly beyond belief, and Parfait, in his *Arsenal de la dévotion,* has only
scratched the surface. What do you think about this chapter title, in a manual called *Domestiques pieux:* 'On Modesty in Hot Weather'? And the advice
to maids not to accept service with actors, innkeepers and *dealers in obscene
engravings!* . . . And the imbeciles declaim against Voltaire, who was a truly
spiritual man!" Flaubert's own infernal book would leave him brain-dead,
he predicted to Léonie Brainne. He had had enough of it. If he knew anyone contemplating such a task as he had undertaken, he would have him
committed to the Charenton insane asylum. "What could be crazier than
pouring the ocean into a bottle, as your humble servant is doing." Still, he
reflected, would we do anything in this world if we didn't follow the lead
of false ideas? And by then he saw an end to *Bouvard et Pécuchet.* Ahead lay
the last chapter. His notes contained most of the egregious quotations
needed for the second volume, the *sottisier.*

Anticipating the final page, he began as early as December 1879 to plan
a celebration with friends at Croisset. "When January has passed," he wrote
to Zola on December 3, "you must come see me. Arrange it well in advance with our friends. It will be a little 'family revel' and will do me good.
At that point let's hope I'm into my last chapter." By mid–March of 1880
the fete had been scheduled to take place sometime during Easter week.
Flaubert informed Zola, who made all practical arrangements, that he
could provide four beds, and that absence for any reason, including death,
would be unacceptable. Coming from Paris were Zola himself, Charpentier, Daudet, and Goncourt. (Turgenev was still in Russia.) Guy de Maupassant had agreed to meet them at the Rouen railroad station with
coaches. On the eve of their arrival, Saturday, March 27, Flaubert wrote to
Caroline that the event would be "gigantic."

It may not have been gigantic, but it was a joyful reunion of friends who
had seldom seen one another since 1877. Looking picturesquely rustic in a
Calabrian peasant hat, an ample jacket, and pleated trousers that, in Goncourt's
description, accommodated his large behind, Flaubert welcomed them effusively as their coaches rolled up. Goncourt soon decided that the property
was lovelier than he remembered, with a fringe of beautiful, storm-twisted
trees, and the masts of schooners gliding past the parlor windows like huge,
stately kites. "The dinner was very good, and a turbot in cream sauce quite
marvelous," he wrote. "We drank many different wines and told bawdy stories all evening long, which had Flaubert shaking with laughter, the laugh-

*Wolfenbüttel, a town in Saxony, was known (among cognoscenti, if not necessarily by
Edma) for a library rich in incunabula. Gotthold Lessing, the great eighteenth-century German literary critic, was for many years its director.

ter of a child's pure mirth." Invited to read *Bouvard et Pécuchet,* he declined for once, fearful perhaps that it would have brickbats hurled at it, or would echo off a wall of polite civility. His friends therefore retired earlier than guests at Croisset usually could, to cold rooms peopled by family busts. "The next day," Goncourt continued, "we got up late and stayed indoors conversing because Flaubert declared that walking around would be a useless exertion. We departed after lunch." In Rouen, Goncourt, an avid collector, persuaded his companions to join him in touring antique stores. It turned out that most were closed on Easter Monday, so they repaired to a café, played billiards for two and a half hours, and caught the early-evening train to Paris.

Flaubert planned to follow in May and asked Caroline to clear out as much as possible of the furniture she had moved from her former flat at 240, rue du Faubourg Saint-Honoré into his. It annoyed him that he would not yet have completed his work by then. Moreover, the trip itself would be an ordeal, he thought, with the prospect of asinine conversation to be endured en route and the din of current events in Paris. But a respite from Croisset was desperately needed. He wanted time with Princess Mathilde, Edma Roger des Genettes, Léonie Brainne, and Maxime Du Camp.

Flaubert never reached Paris. He spent the evening of May 7 in the company of his physician, Charles Fortin, eating copiously and reciting Corneille. The next day he rose late as usual, bathed, performed his toilette, and read the morning mail while waiting for breakfast. Things then went terribly wrong. Overcome by an apparent heart attack, he summoned the maid, who, when she finally came upstairs, found him slumped on the couch, barely alive, clenching a bottle of smelling salts. Later, a rumor spread that he had suffered an epileptic seizure, but this was not the opinion of the physician, Achille's intern, who arrived from the Hôtel-Dieu an hour later. By then he was dead.

It was for Maupassant, the "disciple," whose literary star Flaubert had seen rising with the publication in April of "Boule de Suif," to dress Flaubert's corpse and communicate news of his death to those who had happily gathered at Croisset only six weeks earlier. They were informed that the funeral would take place on May 11. This time they made separate arrangements. Starting out from his country house at Médan, Zola caught a fast train at Mantes and on it encountered Daudet, along with a modest delegation of reporters. Goncourt had arrived in Rouen the previous evening.

Their hackney coach intercepted the funeral procession between Croisset and Canteleu. "We got out, we took off our hats," wrote Zola. "Our good and grand Flaubert seemed to be coming toward us, bedded in his coffin. I could still see him at Croisset, emerging from his house and planting big, sonorous kisses on both of my cheeks. And now, we met again, for the last time. He was approaching, as if to welcome us. When I saw the hearse with its drawn curtains, its horses at a foot pace, its gentle, funereal swaying, . . . I felt chilled through and through and began to tremble." There may have been as many as two hundred mourners. Maupassant had been instructed by the Commanvilles to bar Laporte from the mortuary chamber.

Bells tolled as the cortege, unraveling and dusty, wended its way uphill on a road that skirted fields of wheat. Canteleu did all it could for Flaubert at its decrepit little church. Five rustic cantors wearing soiled surplices struggled through the Latin liturgy. They were so inept that the crowd looked forward to what followed — a seven-kilometer walk to the Cimetière Monumental in Rouen, where Flaubert would join his parents and Louis Bouilhet. Those who expected their number to swell once they entered Rouen were disappointed. "At the city gates we found only a squad of soldiers, the minimum assigned to all deceased members of the Legion of Honor: negligible pomp for one so great," wrote Zola, whose description of the event evokes Emma Bovary's blind coach ride through the city with Léon. "Along the quays, then along the main avenue, clusters of bourgeois observed us curiously, not knowing who the dead man was, or associating the name Flaubert with his father and brother." The better informed among them, he claimed, had come to see Parisian journalists. "Not the least sign of bereavement on the faces of these onlookers. A city immersed in lucre . . . The fact is that on the eve of his death Flaubert was unknown to four-fifths of Rouen and detested by the other fifth." Zola exaggerated a truth, as was his wont, but remained perfectly true to Flaubert's dictum that hatred of Rouennais was the beginning of true discernment.

Charles Lapierre, director of the newspaper *Le Nouvelliste de Rouen*, spoke a few words at the cemetery. Mindful of her uncle's aversion to graveside rhetoric, Caroline had discouraged eulogies. Flaubert was not to be spared one last embarrassment, however. The pit had been dug for a smaller coffin. His got wedged halfway down, and when attempts to right it proved futile, the diggers were persuaded to wait until everyone had departed. Thus, Flaubert's burial, like *Bouvard et Pécuchet,* couldn't quite end. Goncourt, Zola, and Daudet left their friend suspended at an angle, his feet higher than his head, not yet in the earth nor any longer above it.

TEN YEARS after Flaubert's death, Guy de Maupassant remembered him as he might have wished to be remembered at the Cimetière Monumental. In 1879 Flaubert, needing moral support for a chore he would find excessively painful, had asked his young friend to spend two days at Croisset. There a kind of symbolic cremation had taken place, with Flaubert both corpse and officiant. Maupassant was shown a large trunk containing letters that spanned half a century. Flaubert had decided to sort through them and burn those that said more than he wanted known or too little to justify their survival. Exactly ten years earlier, Louis Bouilhet had done the same, much to Flaubert's annoyance. "Why?" he asked at that time. "Can it be that he sensed the approach of death? (Alfred also had this mania for autos-da-fé). I was vexed and felt a little duped on discovering that he hadn't saved a greater number of my letters." But the sensation caused by the publication in 1874 of Prosper Mérimée's love letters, *Lettres à une inconnue,* had taught him a lesson. Moving backward in time, from middle age to adolescence, the autobiographical triage lasted until daybreak. He read some letters aloud and others in silence; he cried over his mother's; he savored George Sand's; he threw handfuls into the fire, including one packet tied with a red ribbon, presumably Louise Colet's, which contained a ballroom slipper and a dried rose in a lacy, yellowing handkerchief. When it was over, Maupassant, unable to sleep, reflected upon all that had gone up in flames: memories of intimacy, expressions of family tenderness, traces of people briefly known and long forgotten, the chaff of everyday life. "All he had possessed, experienced, tasted was there," wrote Maupassant.

But the entire universe had passed through that strong, blue-eyed head, from the beginning of the world to the present day . . . He had been the dreamer who half lived in the Bible, the Greek poet, the barbarian soldier, the Renaissance artist, the yokel and the prince, the mercenary Matho and the doctor Bovary. He had also been the flirty petite bourgeoise of modern times and Hamilcar's daughter. He had been all of that in reality, not just in dream, for the writer who thinks as he did becomes what he feels . . . Happy are they who have received the "je ne sais quoi" of which they are at once the offspring and the victims, that faculty of multiplying oneself through the evocative and generative power of the Idea. During the exalted hours of work, they escape the congestion of real life in its banality, its mediocrity and monotony. But afterward, when they wake up . . .

Flaubert would no doubt have judged himself differently. A summing up more in the spirit of that incendiary night was the greeting he had sent to George Sand on New Year's Day 1869, several months before the publication of *L'Éducation sentimentale.* "I don't do anything that I'd like to do!" he lamented. "Because one doesn't choose one's subjects: they impose themselves. Will I ever find my own? Will the one that suits me perfectly ever fall from heaven? There are times, in my vainer moments, when I catch a glimpse of *what the novel must be!* [But it's like thinking] that the most beautiful church would combine the steeple of Strasbourg, the facade of Saint Peter's, the portico of the Parthenon. I am pledged to contradictory ideals! . . . *Living* is a metier for which I am not cut out! And yet, and yet."

Epilogue

THREE MONTHS after Flaubert's death, Croisset was bought by industrialists who lost no time making plans to build a distillery. By October the farmhouse had been torn down, the tulip tree leveled, and the yew hedges uprooted. Of the villa nothing remained but a skeleton of beams, which, as any passerby could plainly see, had been rotting away behind the white plastered facade. Two red-brick structures rose in its place, a warehouse for corn and a plant for mashing it. "The gabled warehouse is the last word in industrial design," wrote the gentleman who in childhood had often peeked at Flaubert through the entrance gate. "The distillery also has gables, with glass panes revealing a tangle of alembics and copper tubes." One huge pipe carried grain to fermentation vats, while another spewed foaming white detritus into the Seine. Where Flaubert had once moored his dinghy, vessels unloaded coal. Where he wrote *Madame Bovary*, stacks belched up smoke around the clock. Where, for more than thirty years, his had been the only lamp burning through the night, gas lanterns now illuminated the factory's bleak facade and cast an eerie light on the river.

AS FOR those who had drifted with him at various stages of his mortal journey, Flaubert would have called them companions on the raft of the shipwrecked *Medusa*. About some — Juliet Herbert, for example, who apparently inherited enough from her rich uncle's unmarried daughter to enjoy material security in old age — little is known. About others there is an ampler record.

About Ernest Chevalier, for example. In 1848, three months after the February Revolution, Flaubert had received a distraught letter from his oldest friend, who occupied the post of deputy public prosecutor in Ajaccio, Corsica, and was awaiting his fate under the new government. "I don't know what will become of me," Chevalier wrote. "I shall probably be replaced by some striver . . . Banditti have ganged up and are attacking gendarmes . . . The situation cannot last and I believe that I shall soon be near you." His forecast proved to be excessively pessimistic. The republic posted him to Grenoble. Then, under Napoleon III, he became a prominent magistrate in the imperial judiciary, serving with distinction as *procureur impérial,* or attorney general, in various provinces, including Anjou. He had been made a chevalier of the Légion d'Honneur in 1861. This did not work to his advantage after September 4, 1870. Dismissed from office, he retired to Chalonnes, a small town on the Loire, whose citizens elected him mayor. Five years after Flaubert's death, Chevalier won election to the Chamber of Deputies and sat on the right.

Edmond Laporte, who tilted in the opposite direction politically, married Marie Le Marquant in September 1882 and in time had two children by her. Appointed inspector of labor for the Paris region, he rigorously implemented laws protecting minors and women and in 1890 joined the French delegation at an international conference that concerned itself with formulating a common policy to improve the lot of factory workers. He was admitted to the Legion of Honor and became a fixture on the Regional Council of Lower Normandy, where his years of lascivious merrymaking with Flaubert and Maupassant did not inhibit him from campaigning against the spread of pornography. Except in that regard, Laporte's loyalty to Flaubert never flagged. That anything of Croisset survives today is due in part to him, for in 1905 he helped raise money to save its pavilion. His daughter Louise married René Dumesnil, a physician remembered for his copious writings about Flaubert.

Among other memorabilia Flaubert had burned that night in 1879 was an eight-year-old letter from Élisa Schlesinger announcing the death of Maurice. Flaubert had hoped then that Élisa might repatriate herself so that "the end of my life," as he put it, "will not be spent far from you." Instead she remained in Baden-Baden, under the same roof as her daughter and son-in-law. Her son, Adolphe Schlesinger, an inveterate gambler, who had fought in the French army during the Franco-Prussian War, recouped some of his losses by marrying an heiress to the Ruggieri fireworks fortune, in the ceremony witnessed by a tearful Flaubert. Élisa then suffered another nervous breakdown and was recommitted to the sanatorium at Illenau, this time for good. She died after thirteen years of internment, in 1888.

Marie-Sophie Leroyer de Chantepie, who also died that year, ended her days far more happily than Élisa. In 1877, when Angers reconstructed its municipal theater, Marie-Sophie became a charter member of the Association artistique des concerts populaires and donated funds to help poor schoolchildren attend performances of classical music. With her eyes failing, music became her salvation. Between symphonic concerts at the theater, she hosted musical soirees at home, to the dismay of Angers's bourgeoisie, who found it unseemly that an octogenarian should be organizing such entertainments and worse yet inviting Protestants and free-thinkers. No longer guilt ridden, the eccentric old lady, who on jaunts through town in her cabriolet wore clothes that had gone out of fashion half a century earlier, was known beyond Anjou. When she died, an English journal called *The Woman's Penny Paper*, noting her devotion to French artists, declared her worthy of posthumous membership in Angers's Académie des Sciences et des Belles-Lettres. It is not impossible that at some point she and Ernest Chevalier made each other's acquaintance.

The Académie française found Maxime Du Camp worthy of membership in February 1880, despite protests by the left, whose opposition derived principally from his hostile reflections on the Commune. He was elected just in time to earn a tart acknowledgment of the honor from Flaubert. "Your pleasure is mine, but I am nonetheless astonished, amazed, stupefied, and I wonder why you bothered [to solicit it], what purpose it served. Don't you remember the skits you, Bouilhet, and I improvised at Croisset, with farcical speeches of induction into the Académie française?" Du Camp missed Flaubert's funeral, pleading sickness. His absence did not exactly endear him to Caroline, but two years later, with the publication of *Souvenirs littéraires*, he made himself her sworn enemy by divulging Flaubert's secret — suggesting, with invidious compassion, that epilepsy had stunted him and was the reason he wrote as laboriously as he did. At his own desk, on which he kept a portrait of Flaubert, Du Camp wrote fluently, producing, among much else, addenda to his *Paris, ses organes*. What came to interest him most particularly were Paris's unfortunates and the private charities of every faith engaged in saving them from oblivion or crime. As a spry sixty-five-year-old, he visited night shelters for the homeless, accompanied nuns collecting goods on their rounds of the city's public markets, interviewed orphans at the abbé Roussel's remarkable Orphelinat d'Auteuil and paralytics in Catholic dormitories, examined accounts, inspected prisons, and visited the Oeuvres des libérées de Saint-Lazare, an organization created to help female convicts released from jail reintegrate themselves into society. The notes amassed in

Paris became the books he wrote in Baden-Baden, where he and the Hussons spent half the year: *La Charité privée à Paris* and *Paris bienfaisant*. Of a piece with his descriptions of the down-and-out were his admiring portraits of the virtuous who ministered to them, and underlying this tribute was a critique of the republican government's campaign against religious orders. A nonbeliever sympathetic to the clergy, Du Camp argued that the church deserved full recognition from the secular republic for its eleemosynary work. Flaubert would have taken issue with him, as well as with his lenient view of France's recent conqueror. In four anonymous articles subsequently published between covers under the title *L'Allemagne actuelle,* he supported a policy of reconciliation. More books followed, including one that he wished not to appear until after his death, *Souvenirs d'un demi-siècle*. Age transformed the gaunt, dapper Du Camp into a roundish figure with a fringe of white beard. At length his friends passed away and his spirit sagged. "I am no longer a sick nurse," he wrote in 1890. "Émile Husson (thirty-five years of life together) was buried last Monday. Frédéric Fovard, my old brother, my companion since 1843, will be buried tomorrow. Aglaé Sabatier, the Présidente, the memory of our youth, was buried last Saturday. I am devastated." Death claimed him in February 1894 in Baden-Baden. Present when his coffin was removed from the Husson villa to the Stifskirche for a solemn Mass were representatives of the German emperor and the czar. It arrived in Paris and at the Montmartre cemetery on February 12. Bereft of her husband, her lover, and finally her reason, Adèle Husson died six months later at the sanatorium in Illenau where Élisa Schlesinger had languished.

Word of Flaubert's death, which reached Turgenev in Russia at Spasskoe, came as a terrible blow to him. It had left him grief stricken, he wrote to Pauline Viardot's daughter Marianne (the wife of Gabriel Fauré). "After your family and Annenkov, he was, I believe, the man I loved most in the world . . . The last time I saw him [at Croisset] he had no premonition of what was soon to overtake him. Nor did I, and yet he spoke freely about death. He was preparing to finish his novel, he was thinking about future works* . . . Sometimes, in his letters, he said that this novel, which caused him so much pain, would kill him. If only he had completed it!" To Zola, Turgenev wrote: "It is not just that a remarkable talent has left us, but also a most wonderful man; he was the center of all our lives."

Although gout caused Turgenev enormous distress, it seldom kept him housebound for long. Indeed, he spent more time in Saint Petersburg than

---

*The future works about which he spoke included a book about Thermopylae as well as a novel about Paris during the Second Empire.

in Paris during the years 1880–81. Disposed — until Czar Alexander II's assassination — to underestimate or even justify terrorism, Turgenev found himself hailed by Russian university students as a great man, a would-be savior, a progressive mind capable of uniting left-wing elements, and he reveled in their adulation. But he also loved high society, which did not ostracize him for his flirtation with radical politics. Princess Worontzoff invited him to a grand, aristocratic dinner at her palace; the Grand Duchess Catherine and Princess Paskevich did likewise. After Saint Petersburg he returned to Orel province, where pleasures of a different kind awaited him. In his own private domain, he dreamed, wrote stories about the supernatural, went hunting, and, with a snuffbox at his fingertips, dilated on the state of Russia. Friends came from afar to stay with him. They included Leo Tolstoy, whose genius he proclaimed but whose evangelism made him squirm.

However much he craved the homage of young intellectuals, the glitter of Saint Petersburg society, the comfort of his native language, and the ambiance of childhood haunts, what Turgenev found irresistible in Russia was the prospect of rejuvenation. At sixty-one the white-maned literary lion fell in love with a twenty-five-year-old actress named Maria Gavrilovna Savina, who reigned over Saint Petersburg's Alexandrine Theater. Having chosen *A Month in the Country* for the fall 1879 season, Savina won universal acclaim as Vera and, offstage, exercised her charms upon a grateful dramatist. Not that she gave herself to Turgenev. It seems, indeed, that she did not. But then Turgenev, who by his own admission thrived more on platonic than on carnal love, did not importune her. Unconsummated trysts proved dolefully satisfying, and many such trysts took place. They met in Saint Petersburg, in Moscow, in Paris. Turgenev had Savina visit Spasskoe, and on one occasion, when she was traveling south, boarded her train at Mtsensk for the thirty-mile run to Orel. "Suddenly I notice that my lips whisper, 'What a night we could have spent together!' " he wrote to her after that fugitive assignation. "And immediately I realize that this will never happen, and that I will in the end depart this world without the memory of it . . . You are wrong to reproach yourself, to call me your 'sin.' Alas! I will never be that . . . My life is behind me, and that hour spent in the railway compartment, when I felt like a twenty-year-old youth, was the last burst of flame." Almost liberated from one disastrous marriage but already committed to what would be another, Savina found in this courtship an escape from her matrimonial entanglements. Meanwhile, Turgenev, who had never wed Pauline Viardot but remained bound to her, was enacting a mock version of adulterous love, tormenting his lifelong companion (when she confronted him) with denials that sounded like avowals.

On returning to France in September 1881, Turgenev seemed none the worse for his illusory dawn. That was the impression of English friends, who saw him that fall shooting partridge and entertaining fellow literati at a London dinner party organized by his translator. To judge by Goncourt's journal, which describes "les Cinq" — the original five — reunited around Flaubert's empty chair, this confident mood buoyed him through several seasons. "What with some of us having emotional problems and others enduring physical pain, death occupies the center of conversation all evening long, despite efforts to push it aside," Goncourt wrote on March 6, 1882. "Daudet declares that it harrows him, poisons his life, that whenever he takes a new flat he automatically wonders where his coffin will stand. Zola, in turn, speaks about his mother, who died at Médan. As the staircase was too narrow, she had to be lowered from the window, and since then he cannot contemplate that window without wondering who will emerge from it first, he or his wife." Turgenev took a superior view of their anguish. "Death is a familiar thought," Goncourt quotes him as saying, "but when it visits me, I give it the back of my hand . . . For us Russians, the Slavic fog has its therapeutic uses. It helps us escape the logic of our ideas and the hot pursuit of deduction . . . If you should ever be caught in a Russian blizzard, you would be told 'Forget the cold or you'll die!' Well, thanks to that fog, a snowbound Slav forgets the cold — and so, by the same strategy, does the idea of death soon efface itself and disappear."

In due course, however, his stoic resolve faltered, for by mid-April 1882 he found himself afflicted with a "neuralgia" that made it painful in the extreme to walk any distance or climb stairs. Gout-induced angina was Charcot's diagnosis, and the eminent physician, observing that medical science could be of little help, prescribed absolute immobility. Another renowned doctor put him on a milk diet, which may have done more to comfort him than a German contraption for treating rheumatism called Baunscheidts Lebenswecker. Turgenev's ordeal was the stuff of *Bouvard et Pécuchet*. Doted upon at Bougival by the Viardot family, he regarded himself as the victim of a medical paradox. "Imagine a man who is perfectly well . . . but who can neither stand nor walk nor ride without a sharp pain, rather like toothache, attacking his left shoulder," he wrote to a woman friend in Russia.

> What would you have me do in these circumstances? To sit, to lie down, then to sit again and know that in such conditions it is impossible to move to Paris, let alone to Russia . . . However, my state of mind is very peaceful. I have accepted the thought [that my condition will not get any better] and even find that it is not so bad . . . it is not too bad to be an oyster. After all, I could have gone blind . . . Now I can even work. Of course, my *personal* life is at an end. But still — I will be sixty-four in a few days' time.

After six months he felt stronger, and in November, accompanied by Henry James, he left Bougival for Paris, where he proceeded to lead a reasonable semblance of his former life, attending the opera, receiving innumerable Russians (among them the Grand Duke Constantine), having his portrait painted, enjoying Pauline Viardot's musical soirees, ringing in the Russian New Year at the Russian Artists' Club, watching Parisians in their hundreds of thousands throng around Léon Gambetta's funeral cortege on January 3, 1883. This schedule required great courage, as the slightest movement often caused him agony. But his "Slavic fog," along with morphine, helped him endure. Only one of the distinguished physicians brought in to examine him suspected that he had cancer of the spinal marrow.

Except for delirious spells, when he demanded poison or imagined himself surrounded by poisoners, Turgenev bore his cross nobly until the end, which occurred on September 3, 1883. "The religious ceremony flushed out a small horde of men with gigantic frames, squashed features, patriarchal beards — a microcosmic Russia whose presence here in the capital one had not suspected," Goncourt observed four days later. "There were also many Russian women, German women, English women, pious and faithful readers paying homage to the great and delicate novelist." Hundreds mourned him at the Russian church on the rue Daru, including a band of nihilists who laid a wreath from "the Russian Refugees," hoping to embarrass Czar Nicholas. Hundreds more mourned him at the Gare du Nord, where a chapel was rigged up to accommodate his casket until authorization for the homeward voyage came from Saint Petersburg. And mourners filled railroad stations in Russia, awaiting the funeral train as it made its way through an obstacle course created by the imperial government, which feared that Turgenev might posthumously incite rebellion. "One would have thought," wrote Stasiulevich, "that the corpse belonged to Solovei the Robber rather than to a great writer." Still, Turgenev finally made it home and was laid to rest beside his old friend Belinsky in the Volkova cemetery at Saint Petersburg.

THE PRINCIPAL events of Caroline Commanville's life after 1880 are recounted in Lucie Chevalley-Sabatier's *Gustave Flaubert et sa nièce Caroline*. From the financial whirlwind that had ripped through Croisset, spewing wreckage in every direction, Caroline preserved the manuscripts of Flaubert's major works but sold others, a portion of his library, and the house in which most of his writing had been accomplished. All that remains of it today is the little pavilion where everyone gathered after dinner on summer evenings. Commanville's creditors were apparently satisfied. Caroline's dowry, which had remained intact, was more than sufficient to pay for a new town house on the rue Lauriston in a fashionable quarter of Paris, near the Trocadéro. Here she stored her Flaubertiana and, according to Chevalley-Sabatier, defrayed expenses by boarding upper-class English girls recommended by Gertrude Tennant.

Of Caroline's editorial career, one may fairly say that she honored her trust as best she could, but that her preoccupation with appearances on the one hand and her high-mindedness on the other conspired to produce chastened versions of Flaubert's correspondence, notebooks, and travel writings. Much was published piecemeal. A first, very incomplete *Oeuvres complètes* appeared in 1885 under the imprint Quantin. Conard published another in 1909–12 for the compilation of which Caroline relied heavily on a writer named Louis Bertrand, who had unrestricted access to her archives.

Flaubert also bequeathed the possibility of new relationships. Caroline's small circle of friends came to include George Sand's beloved granddaughter Aurore, who turned twenty in 1886. If not for sentimental complications, it might also have included Don José Maria de Hérédia, a married man. "He admitted that he found me beautiful and was suddenly smitten when he saw me in mourning clothes, beside the grave," she wrote, preferring not to remember, perhaps, how seductively she had displayed her grief at the cemetery. "He made this passionate confession three or four months after my uncle's burial . . . I couldn't respond as he would have wished." In this matter as in most others, Caroline sought counsel from Father Didon, whose death in 1900 would affect her deeply. By then few of her family were still alive. Achille Flaubert, who retired from the practice of surgery in the late 1870s, died of stomach cancer two years after Gustave, in Nice. His widow, Julie, died one year later, at nearly the same time as Julie the family retainer, who had played such an important role in the rearing of Gustave and his sister. It was Caroline who cradled her head at the end.

Ernest Commanville contracted tuberculosis. Four years after his death in 1890, when there was nothing more to anchor her up north, Caroline moved to the Midi. With the bequest of her aunt, her dowry, royalties from Flaubert's works, and proceeds from the auction of his drafts and sketches and from the sale of her town house on the rue Lauriston, she could live well in a hillside villa overlooking Antibes. Flaubert's furniture had been translated to his promised land of lemon trees and olive groves. The gilded Buddha sat on a console in the entrance hall. His oak bookcases covered an entire wall of the salon. His large round worktable wasn't there, however, nor his porcelain frog inkwell: one had gone to Edma Roger des Genettes and the other to Guy de Maupassant. The Villa Tanit, as Caroline named her house, became a lure for literary scholars. Bertrand built his own villa next door, on a parcel of land Caroline had given him. Her year was divided thenceforth between the Côte d'Azur and Paris, where she spent most of every spring in a pied-à-terre on a private street near the boulevard Raspail.

It may have been that the pleasures of independence, after a loveless marriage, eventually began to pall, or that the loneliness she felt after Father Didon's death sparked a need for companionship, but in 1900 Caroline took it upon herself to propose marriage, and the man she chose was Dr Franklin Grout, a childhood friend (whose father, Dr Parfait Grout, had named both of his children for Benjamin Franklin). Franklin's sister, Frankline, served as go-between. "Do you think that your brother would be disposed to marry me?" asked Caroline, according to Frankline's daughter and her future niece, Lucie Chevalley-Sabatier. "I know he once loved me. It is my understanding that that has been one of the reasons why he never wed. I appreciate his palpable kindness. I admire his life of service to others. I know that he is a deeply cultivated man and wears his culture lightly. We share the same artistic tastes. Why should we not end our days together living in agreeable harmony?" Given a choice, she chose well. The embers of young love must have been banked for forty years in Franklin Grout; they glowed anew as soon as the proposal was received, and that fall, Caroline, a tall woman still more blond than gray at age fifty-four, who carried the weight of middle age gracefully, became a bride again. When in due course Grout retired, they greatly enlarged the Villa Tanit, adding bedrooms for guests and a salon large enough to accommodate two grand pianos. Much music was made there during the next twenty years, at soirees that enlivened the artistic world of the Côte d'Azur. Caroline's migraines were apparently a thing of the past. Until Franklin's death in 1921 she enjoyed the "agreeable harmony" she had bargained for.

After World War I, Caroline spent some time each summer at Aix-les-Bains, not so much for her infirmities as for the rich offering of concerts and operas. Her customary residence was the Grand Hôtel D'Aix, and there, in 1930, she met the American novelist Willa Cather, who describes her in a memoir entitled "A Chance Meeting." At a table near her own, Cather often noticed an old French lady dining alone.

> She seemed very old indeed, well over eighty, and somewhat infirm, though not at all withered or shrunken. She was not stout, but her body had that rather shapeless heaviness which for some detestable reason often settles upon people in old age. The thing one especially noticed was her fine head, so well set upon her shoulders and beautiful in shape, recalling some of the portrait busts of Roman ladies. Her forehead was low and straight, her nose made just the right angle with it, and there was something quite lovely about her temples, something one very rarely sees. As I watched her entering and leaving the dining-room I

observed that she was slightly lame, and that she utterly disregarded it — walked with a quick, short step and great impatience, holding her shoulders well back. One saw that she was contemptuously intolerant of the limitations of old age. As she passed my table she often gave me a keen look and a half-smile (her eyes were extremely bright and clear), as if she were about to speak. But I remained blank. I am a poor linguist, and there would be no point in uttering common-places to this old lady; one knew that much about her, at a glance.

Her inadequate French proved to be no obstacle, for the woman spoke excellent English and engaged her in conversation one evening. Several more conversations took place before Caroline, who now smoked ciga-rettes, revealed her literary antecedents. "The old lady made some com-ment on the Soviet experiment in Russia," wrote Cather.

My friend remarked that it was fortunate for the great group of Russian writers that none of them had lived to see the Revolution; Gogol, Tolstoi, Turgenev.

"Ah, yes," said the old lady with a sigh, "for Turgenev, especially, all this would have been very terrible. I knew him well at one time."

I looked at her in astonishment. Yes, of course, it was possible. She was very old. I told her I had never met anyone who had known Turgenev.

She smiled. "No? I saw him very often when I was a young girl. I was much interested in German, in the great works. I was making a translation of *Faust,* for my own pleasure, merely, and Turgenev used to go over my translation and cor-rect it from time to time. He was a great friend of my uncle. I was brought up in my uncle's house." She was becoming excited as she spoke, her face grew more animated, her voice warmed, something flashed in her eyes, some strong feeling awoke in her. As she went on, her voice shook a little. "My mother died at my birth, and I was brought up in my uncle's house. He was more than father to me. My uncle also was a man of letters, Gustave Flaubert, you may perhaps know . . ." She murmured the last phrase in a curious tone, as if she had said something indiscreet and were evasively dismissing it.

The meaning of her words came through to me slowly; so this must be the "Caro" of the *Lettres à sa nièce Caroline.* There was nothing to say, certainly. The room was absolutely quiet, but there was nothing to say to this disclosure. It was like being suddenly brought up against a mountain of memories. One could not see around it; one could only stupidly realize that in this mountain which the old lady had conjured up by a phrase and a name or two lay most of one's men-tal past. Some moments went by. There was no word with which one could greet such a revelation. I took one of her lovely hands and kissed it, in homage to a great period, to the names that made her voice tremble.

She laughed an embarrassed laugh, and spoke hurriedly. "Ah, that is not nec-essary! That is not at all necessary." But the tone of distrust, the faint challenge in that "you may perhaps know . . ." had disappeared. *"Vous connaissez bien les oeuvres de mon oncle?"*

Who did not know them? I asked her.

It must have immediately become apparent to Caroline that she had encountered a most unusual American and, where Flaubert's work was concerned, an interlocutor who met her on equal terms. They discussed *L'Éducation sentimentale* at length.

The old lady told me that she had at home the corrected manuscript of *L'Éducation sentimentale.* "Of course I have many others. But this he gave me long before his death. You shall see it when you come to my place at Antibes. I call my place the Villa Tanit, *pour la déesse,*" she added with a smile. The name of the goddess took us back to *Salammbô,* which is the book of Flaubert I like best. I like him in those great reconstructions of the remote and cruel past. When I happened to speak of the splendid final sentence of *Hérodias,* where the fall of the syllables is so suggestive of the hurrying footsteps of John's disciples, carrying away with them their prophet's severed head, she repeated that sentence softly: *"Comme elle était très lourde, ils la portaient al-ter-na-tiv-e-ment."*

They had lunch several days later and bade each other farewell. There were tears streaking Caroline's face powder, but she stood erect. "And the last words I heard from her," wrote Cather, "expressed a hope that I would always remember the pleasure we had had together in talking unreservedly about *'les oeuvres de mon oncle.'* Standing there, she seemed holding to that name as to a staff. A great memory and a great devotion were the things she lived upon, certainly; they were her armour against a world concerned with insignificant matters."

Caroline died the following year, 1931, weeks before her eighty-fifth birthday.

Acknowledgments

⁓

I WISH to thank the Florence Gould Foundation for a generous grant, and to recognize the generosity of another foundation, which wishes to remain anonymous.

For their indulgence and unstinting efforts on my behalf, I am deeply grateful to Donna Sammis and David Weiner at the Melville Library of the State University of New York, Stony Brook; and as well to their former colleague, Kathleen Horan. Marie Sweatt and Joan Vogelle of the Department of European Languages and Literatures at Stony Brook provided invaluable assistance. I am also indebted to staff at the Bibliothèque Municipale de Rouen (with special thanks to Françoise Legendre, its director, and to Thierry Ascencio-Parvy, its resident photographer); at Butler Library, Columbia University; and at the New York Public Library; the library of the French Institute in Paris; the Bibliothèque Nationale; the Archives départementales de la Seine-Maritime; the French National Archives; the Bibliothèque de l'Arsenal; and the Metropolitan Museum of Art.

I cannot adequately express my gratitude to Odile de Guidis, who, until her retirement several years ago, served as administrator of the Flaubert Program of the Institut des textes et manuscrits modernes (ITEM).

Madame de Guidis was a ministering angel to hundreds of scholars, myself included. No one walked into her office without benefiting from her guidance and enthusiasm.

At various stages along the way I received help from Daniel Anger, Paul Bénichou, Pierre-Marc de Biasi, the late Jean Bruneau, Alexandre Tissot Demidoff, Matthieu Desportes, Paul Dolan, Rachel Donadio, Daniel Fauvel, Almuth Grésillon, Jacqueline Hecht, Pierre Juresco, Elisabeth Kashey, Alan Miegel, Halina and Anatol Morell, the late Pierre Morell, Serge Pétillot, Nicholas Rzhevsky, Leon Sokoloff, Frances Taliaferro, Jacqueline Thébault, Paulette Trout, and Serge Wassersztrum. My heartfelt thanks to them all. I am pleased to acknowledge an especially large debt of gratitude to Yvan Leclerc, professor at the University of Rouen and Jean Bruneau's successor as editor of Flaubert's correspondence in the Pléiade Library. He extended a helping hand at our first encounter and has made my work easier with many extraordinary kindnesses.

This book owes much to Marlo Johnston, who shared not only her insights into Flaubert's character but facts about his life incidentally dredged up from the Bibliothèque Nationale during research for a biography of Guy de Maupassant. Odile de Guidis introduced us at ITEM one day ten years ago, and I have often had occasion to remember that chance meeting with gratitude.

In the matter of Flaubert's epilepsy I have been enlightened by the distinguished neurologist Dr. John M. C. Brust of Columbia Presbyterian Hospital, and by Farley Anne Brown. Their patience and generosity are greatly appreciated.

Constant friendship has helped me carry on during the years of writing. For that I am grateful to Christian Beels, Carol Blum, Michael Droller, Benita Eisler, Andrea Fedi, Joseph Frank, B. Bernie Herron, Phyllis Johnson, Roger Shattuck, and Brenda Wineapple.

I am indebted to Leon Wieseltier, literary editor of the *New Republic,* for his strong and effective support.

Adaptations of two chapters appeared in the *New England Review* and the *Hudson Review.* My thanks go once again to Stephen Donadio and Paula Deitz.

I have a primary professional debt to my agent, Georges Borchardt, whose wisdom and humor have served me well. At Little, Brown, Patricia Strachan has been a marvelous editor, and Helen Atsma, who shepherded the manuscript to production, an impeccable assistant. DeAnna Satre did an admirable job of copyediting the manuscript.

There isn't a page of this book that hasn't profited from the fine ear and keen mind of Ruth Lurie Kozodoy, dearest of friends and best of readers.

Notes

CORR.   *Correspondance,* the four volumes (to date) of Flaubert's correspondence in the Pléiade edition, edited by Jean Bruneau.

CHH.   *Oeuvres complètes,* the complete works of Flaubert in the Bardèche edition, published by the Club de l'Honnête Homme.

Prologue: Rouen
4. "I have seen Rouen": Chaline, *Les bourgeois de Rouen,* p. 392.
   "It completely overwhelmed my imagination": Henry Wadsworth Longfellow, *Outre-Mer: A Pilgrimage beyond the Sea,* pp. 22–24, quoted in Bertier de Sauvigny, *La France.*
5. "almost too intense for a mortal being": Willard, *Journal and Letters,* p. 27.
   "a labyrinth of delight . . . misty in their magnificence": Links, *Ruskins in Normandy,* p. 26.
   "fustians, vermillions": *Encyclopedia Britannica,* 11th ed., s.vv. "cotton manufacture."

I. The Surgeon at the Hôtel-Dieu
11. "form the basis of a solid education": "L'Ascendance champenoise de Gustave Flaubert," *Bulletin des Ecrivains de Champagne,* 16 (1958–59): 22.
12. "I needed your hand": Gelfand, *Professionalizing Modern Medicine,* p. 42.
    "knowledge of the Latin tongue": ibid., p. 67.
13. "The [surgeon] demonstrators will have": ibid., p. 86.
14. "The crude multitude": Jules La Mesnardière, *La Poétique* (Paris, 1640).
    "what surgeons paint": Xavier Bichat, *Notice historique sur la vie de Pierre-Joseph Desault* (Paris, 1795), pp. 11–12.
    "The old method did not give": Ackerknecht, *Medicine,* p. 32.
15. "Seizing the facts": Deloume, *Dupuytren,* pp. 50–51.
16. "Such, sir, is the assistant I am sending you": André Dubuc, "La nomination du père de Flaubert, en 1806, à l'Hôtel-Dieu de Rouen," *Bulletin de la Société des Amis de Flaubert,* no. 24 (May 1964): 44.
20. "On approaching Lisieux": Tulard, *Napoléon,* p. 291.
21. "wherein the cold remains of men": André Dubuc, "La nomination du père de Flaubert comme chirurgien-chef de l'Hôtel-Dieu de Rouen," *Bulletin de la Société des Amis de Flaubert,* no. 30 (May 1967): 39.

II. The Cynosure of All Eyes
23. "The political opinions of this physician": Dubosc, *Trois Normands,* pp. 102–3.
24. "He whose misfortune it is to live without religion": Dansette, *Histoire religieuse,* p. 204.
25. "The execution shall be preceded": Stewart, *Restoration Era in France,* p. 155.
    "One would think that the genius of France": Bertier de Sauvigny, *La Restauration,* p. 385.

26. "When at last the hour for mass arrives": Noiret, *Mémoires,* pp. 43–44.
28. "So long as you have only money": Chaline, *Les Bourgeois de Rouen,* p. 147.
29. "on the left": *CORR.,* vol. 1, p. 574 (January 15, 1850, to Louis Bouilhet).
30. "go see whether I'm in the back of the garden": Caroline Commanville, *"Souvenirs intimes,"* in Flaubert, *Oeuvres complètes,* vol. II, ed. (Paris: Conard, 1926), p. xi.
31. "Unconsciously one carries in one's heart": *CORR.,* vol. 2, p. 111 (June 13, 1852).
33. "What do you expect, my son": Baldick, *Life and Times,* p. 39.
   "The people . . . have so lost faith": quoted in ibid., p. 142.
34. "the greatest symbol of the age": *CORR.,* vol. 1, p. 227 (May 1, 1845, to Alfred Le Poittevin).
35. "Allons, prenons le patron": Amédée Fraigneau, *Rouen bizarre* (Rouen: Editions du Petit Normand, 1983), p. 101.
   "Friend, I'll forward": *CORR.,* vol. 1, p. 4 (January 1, 1831).
36. "The bills, the theater": ibid., p. 8 (March 31, 1832).
37. "Oh! father of French Tragedy": Bruneau, *Les Débuts littéraires,* pp. 40–41.
   "Had I been well directed": *CORR.,* vol. 1, p. 49 (January 23, 1839).
38. "Whatever people say": ibid., p. 278 (August 6 or 7, 1846).
   "It is not the thought": Lucas-Dubreton, *Louis-Philippe,* p. 258.
39. "I remember 1832": *CORR.,* vol. 2, p. 173 (June 6, 1843).
   "I lay flat on my stomach": Flaubert, *Mémoires d'un fou,* ed. Leclerc, pp. 277ff.
40. "an inexhaustible spring": *CORR.,* vol. 1, p. 284 (August 8 or 9, 1846).
   "When I love": ibid., p. 296 (August 12, 1846).

III. School Days
45. "To write an oration": Prost, *L'Enseignement en France,* p. 52.
46. "Our bourgeoisie, even the most humble": ibid., p. 267.
   "Children think, imagine, feel": ibid., p. 65.
47. "The ruling classes": ibid., p. 332.
   "Le beau est la splendeur": Bouquet, *Souvenirs,* p. 65.
   "It is widely believed at present": Archives Nationales, F17 20864.
49. "We are united": *CORR.,* vol. 1, p. 8 (April 22, 1832).
   "Man proposes": ibid., p. 12 (September 11, 1833).
   "Here I've written you two letters": ibid.
50. "As soon as he placed": ibid., p. 7 (March 31, 1832).
   "Louis-Philippe and family": ibid., p. 12 (September 11, 1833).
51. "as you would have done": ibid., p. 9 (August 23, 1833).
   "Return, return": ibid. (August 6, 1834).
52. "The dazzling brightness from without": *Trois Contes,* ed. P. U. Wetherill, p. 167.

IV. Stories and Histories
54. "lively, clear, precise": Archives Nationales, F17 20864.
56. "Ah, you tremble": "La Peste à Florence," in Flaubert, *Oeuvres complètes,* vol. 1, ed. Jean Bruneau, p. 77.
   "Philippe feared the renown": "Un secret de Philippe le Prudent," in ibid., p. 72.
57. "like a sharp sword": ibid., p. 73.
   "In every man's life": ibid., p. 78.
   "Here is a letter": ibid., p. 72.
58. "Of his own free will": Flaubert, *La première Éducation sentimentale,* ed. F.-R. Bastide, p. 159.
59. "Now that I'm no longer writing": *CORR.,* vol. 1, p. 24 (June 24, 1837).
   "I note with indignation": ibid., p. 20 (August 14, 1835).
60. "Unfortunately he has always wanted": Archives Nationales, F17 8011, and *CORR.,* vol. 1, p. 847.

61. "Oh! In there are men full of life": "Un secret de Philippe le Prudent," in Flaubert, *Oeuvres complètes,* ed. Bruneau, p. 47.
62. "The Orient with its fairies": ibid., p. 85.
    "Do you think I'll pray to you": ibid., p. 86.
63. "[Baptisto], whose fame he hated": ibid., p. 81.
    "People didn't know": ibid., p. 82.
64. "You lied": ibid., p. 83.
    "The bow leaped off the strings": ibid., p. 108.
    "'It's horrible'": ibid., p. 113.
66. "I trudged along laboriously": *CORR.,* vol. 1, p. 607 (March 13, 1850).
67. "vomiting five or six times": ibid., p. 22 (March 24, 1837).
68. "She was a very literary woman": Franklin Grout, *Heures d'autrefois,* p. 58.
69. "I know now what are generally called": *CORR.,* vol. 3, p. 269 (December 8, 1862).
    "Never have I made such voyages": ibid., vol. 2, p. 41 (January 31, 1852).
    "I have never known": ibid., p. 774 (November 4, 1857).
70. "[Dandyism] is a kind of cult": Baudelaire, "Le Dandy," in *Oeuvres complètes,* p. 899.
    "Mais, vers aucun désir": René Descharmes, *Alfred Le Poittevin,* p. 55.
71. "It's beautiful, this Gothic architecture": Bruneau, *Les Débuts littéraires,* p. 152.
72. "I would like to visit": *CORR.,* vol. 1, p. 460 (July 13, 1847).
    "I have in my ears": ibid., p. 169 (June 2, 1843).

V. First Love

74. "I am dying for freedom": from *Paris sous la monarchie de Juillet,* quoted in Simond, *Paris,* vol. 2, p. 119.
    "In fact, many of the people": Didier, *Letters from Paris,* p. 15.
75. "mercenary glory": Custine, *Souvenirs et portraits,* p. 154.
77. "I am resolved": Thompson, *Louis Napoleon,* p. 41.
78. "She might have been faulted": Flaubert, *Mémoires d'un fou,* in *Oeuvres de jeunesse,* ed. Claudine Gothot-Mersch, p. 485.
79. "Up to then": ibid., p. 488.
81. "I comforted him": Steinhart-Leins, *Flauberts Grosse Liebe,* pp. 36–37.
82. "She was near me": Flaubert, *Mémoires d'un fou,* in *Oeuvres de jeunesse,* p. 490.
    "To him belonged": ibid., p. 492.
    "Farewell for good": ibid., p. 493.
83. "a wild and wooly head": Chaline, *Deux bourgeois,* p. 170.
    "Ce sont de bonnes impressions": *CORR.,* vol. 2, p. 376 (July 7, 1853).
    "My father always used to say": ibid., p. 367 (June 28, 1853).
    "crazies and cretins": ibid., p. 341 (June 1, 1853).
84. "who would be useless": Flaubert, *Mémoires d'un fou,* in *Oeuvres de jeunesse,* p. 474.
    "So when will this society": ibid., p. 478.
85. "In everything I've told you": ibid., p. 512.
    "I'd lie down": ibid.
86. "Master Abailard": *CORR.,* vol. 1, p. 26 (September 22 or 23, 1837).
    "solitary onanism": ibid., p. 29 (September 13, 1838).
    "It does me good all over": ibid., p. 23 (March 24, 1837).
    "a fragile idea": Flaubert, *Mémoires d'un fou,* in *Oeuvres de jeunesse,* p. 471.
    "Around man": ibid., p. 509.
    "genuine, strong": "Rabelais" in ibid., p. 534.
87. "His otter-skin cap": "Une leçon d'histoire naturelle," in ibid., p. 197.
    "He sings what he writes": ibid., p. 199.
    "He hisses the curtain raiser": ibid., p. 201.
88. "peaceful and virtuous": ibid., p. 198.
    "He is a warm partisan": ibid., p. 199.

"Yesterday I visited": *CORR.*, vol. 1, p. 22 (March 24, 1837).

"our farm, which is called": Gérard-Gailly, "Gustave Flaubert et la Ferme du Côteau," *Le Pays d'Auge*, p. 24.

89. "the ruination of well-born young men": Rival, *Tabac*, p. 167.

"I've spent two days": *CORR.*, vol. 1, p. 27 (August 24, 1838).

"Ah! What vices I'd have": ibid., vol. 2, p. 387 (July 15, 1853).

90. "[My brother] is going to settle down": ibid., vol. 1, p. 42 (April 5, 1839).

"Tomorrow they marry": ibid., p. 44 (May 31, 1839).

91. "frank and loyal": Archives départementales de la Seine-Maritime, IT 1666–1667.

"a cog like everybody else": *CORR.*, vol. 1, p. 49 (July 31, 1839).

"I'll go study law, which, instead of opening": ibid.

"Absolutely not, I'll take the ignoble": ibid., p. 39 (March 18, 1839).

92. "Are you not the king": Flaubert, *Smar*, in *Oeuvres de jeunesse*, p. 551.

"All this seems to have been made": ibid., p. 555.

"Yes, nothingness far surpasses": ibid., p. 556.

"I know nothing": ibid., p. 559.

"How beautiful [the church] must have been": ibid., p. 586.

93. "a crown, a belief": ibid., p. 575.

"I am first in philosophy": *CORR.*, vol. 1, p. 56 (November 19, 1839).

94. "There was a shuffling of feet": ibid., p. 874.

"It would have been advisable": ibid., p. 57 (between December 11 and 14, 1839).

"We who signed": ibid.

"By refusing the *pensum*": ibid., p. 873.

95. "It's a terrible ordeal": ibid., p. 65 (July 7, 1840).

"Those delicious mornings": ibid., p. 60 (January 19, 1840).

96. "Finding you [their sons]": *Journal de Rouen*, August 18, 1840.

VI. The Grand Tour

99. "It's neither large, nor beautiful": Flaubert, "Pyrénées-Corse," in *Oeuvres de jeunesse*, p. 649.

"I can testify": ibid., p. 654.

100. "I heard loud lamentations": ibid., p. 659.

"Certainly being alone and staying": ibid., p. 666.

101. "To the left lay Roland's gap": ibid., p. 668.

"Letters! Letters!": *CORR.*, vol. 1, p. 66 (August 24, 1840).

"Never, my good Gustave": ibid., p. 69 (September 7, 1840).

"May your spirits": ibid., p. 68 (August 29, 1840).

102. "We speak of you": ibid., p. 70 (September 23, 1840).

"I have begun": ibid., p. 69 (September 7, 1840).

"*petit talent d'artiste*": ibid., p. 112 (July 9, 1842).

103. "Our vessel glides": Flaubert, "Pyrénées-Corse," in *Oeuvres de jeunesse*, p. 677.

104. "He is fortunate": Lear, *Journal*, p. 2.

"One is penetrated": Flaubert, "Pyrénées-Corse," in *Oeuvres de jeunesse*, p. 695.

105. "We could see one mountain range": ibid., p. 710.

106. "It's difficult to tear yourself away": ibid., p. 714.

"He checked into a small hotel": Goncourt and Goncourt, *Journal*, vol. 1, p. 709.

107. "You've become for me": Maurice Monda, "L'Eulalie de Flaubert," *Le Figaro*, November 14, 1931.

108. "At my age": ibid.

109. "diamonds up a pig's ass": *CORR.*, vol. 1, p. 75 (November 14, 1840).

110. "My brother was kicked by a horse": ibid., p. 83 (July 7, 1841).

"Hide your life": ibid., p. 89 (December 31, 1841). Flaubert's quotations *Cache ta vie et abstiens-toi* and *Cache ta vie et meurs* are elaborations of the Epicurean maxim.

"The mangiest ass": ibid., p. 77 (January 10, 1841).

111. "I still work at Greek and Latin": ibid., p. 94 (January 22, 1842).
"What am I doing": Flaubert, "Cahier intime de 1840–41," in *Oeuvres de jeunesse*, p. 747.
"sentimental ratatouille": *CORR.*, vol. 1, p. 94 (January 22, 1842).
"I saw nothing to cling to": Flaubert, *Novembre*, in *Oeuvres de jeunesse*, p. 776.
112. "I found myself on a plateau": ibid., p. 780.
"Just as I had experienced": ibid., p. 782.
113. "I would run my eyes": ibid., p. 808.
"Unknown to each other": ibid., p. 810.
"How empty is the world": ibid., p. 817.
114. "I was born with the desire": ibid., p. 774.
"He died, but slowly": ibid., p. 831.
"As spring approached": ibid., p. 783.
115. "Her pupil seemed to dilate": ibid., p. 793.

VII. A Fortunate Fall
117. "The students of medicine are mostly poor": Sanderson, *Sketches of Paris*, p. 137.
"He was too eloquent": ibid., pp. 156–57.
119. "The majority never step foot": E. de Labédollière, in "L'étudiant en droit," in Balzac, *Les Français peints*, vol. 1, p. 5.
120. "all things the French": *CORR.*, vol. 1, p. 92 (January 22, 1842).
"If it comes to that": ibid., p. 94 (January 22, 1842).
"Society high and low": ibid., p. 96 (February 24, 1842).
121. "Railroads furrow": ibid., p. 97 (March 15, 1842).
"my ferocious life": ibid., p. 108 (July 3, 1842).
122. "Your mother insisted": ibid., p. 109 (July 3, 1842).
"moral castration": ibid., p. 120 (August 1, 1842).
"Barbarous books": ibid., p. 115 (July 21, 1842).
"rabid Louis-Philippards": ibid., p. 119 (July 25, 1842).
123. "Do I desire": ibid., p. 117 (July 22, 1842).
"certificate of regular attendance": ibid., p. 116 (July 21, 1842).
124. "We boldly scrambled up": Philip Spencer, "New Light on Flaubert's Youth," *French Studies* (April 1954): 100.
"What a superb young fellow": ibid., p. 101.
"nature, though she has rather stinted": Thackeray, *The Students' Quarter*, p. 164.
125. "My coquetry": Spencer, "New Light," p. 101.
"From the heights of their false grandeur": Balzac, "L'épicier," in *Les Français peints*, p. 2.
126. "The shadows, the silence": Honoré de Balzac, *La Cousine Bette* (Paris: Gallimard [Folio], 1972), p. 78.
127. "Given the present state of minds": quoted in Thureau-Dangin, *Histoire de la monarchie*, p. 60.
128. "unrivaled sultans": E. de Labédollièrre, in Balzac, *Les Français peints*, p. 19.
"Here's what my life is like": *CORR.*, vol. 1, p. 128 (November 16, 1842).
129. "Think of it": ibid., p. 134 (December 10, 1842).
"what for": ibid., p. 138 (December 21, 1842).
130. "I'm alone now": ibid., p. 141 (February 9, 1843).
"Over there they go to the Opéra": ibid., p. 143 (February 10, 1843).
131. "I thank you for thinking of me": Collection Lovenjoul, Bibliothèque de l'Institut, H1366bis.
"I had ample opportunity": Heine, *Lutèce*, p. 306.
"juvenile blunder": ibid.
134. "my friend Du Camp": *CORR.*, vol. 1, p. 146 (March 11, 1843).
"sinuous like a woman": Du Camp, *Souvenirs littéraires*, p. 193.
135. "From now until August": *CORR.*, vol. 1, p. 160 (May 12, 1843).
"Here are two great lines": *Journal de Rouen*, May 5, 1843.

136. "provincial simpleton": *CORR.*, vol. 1, p. 184 (July 1843).
   "Such shenanigans": ibid., p. 185 (between August 3 and 6, 1843).
137. "likable humanitarian": ibid., p. 189 (September 2, 1843).
   "You're waiting for details": ibid., p. 195 (December 3, 1843).
138. "a mistress perhaps": *Correspondances* (Flaubert, Le Poittevin, Du Camp), ed. Yvan Leclerc, p. 81.
   "Theirs is a house": *CORR.*, vol. 1, p. 196 (December 3, 1843).
   "far from all bourgeois": ibid., p. 201 (December 20, 1843).
   "torrent of flames": ibid., vol. 2, p. 423 (September 2, 1853).
139. "There is scarcely a substance": Scott, *History of Epileptic Therapy*, pp. 37–38.
   "Too great a quantity": quoted in Temkin, *Falling Sickness*, p. 231.
140. "Madness and lust": *CORR.*, vol. 2, p. 377 (July 7, 1853).
   "Papa read your letter": ibid., vol. 1, p. 202 (January 17, 1844).
141. "congestion of the brain": ibid., p. 203 (February 1, 1844).
   "I almost came before Pluto": ibid.
   "You will understand": ibid., p. 204 (February 9, 1844).
   "First there is an indeterminate anguish": ibid., vol. 3, p. 572 (December 1, 1866).
142. "My illness will have had": *CORR.*, vol. 1, p. 214 (January 1845).

VIII. Deaths in the Family
144. "My bedside authors": *CORR.*, vol. 1, p. 210 (June 7, 1844).
145. "consented . . . practical life": ibid., p. 229 (May 13, 1845).
   "The most banal remark": ibid., p. 252 (September 16, 1845).
   "Break with the external world": ibid.
   "upheld by its own internal force": ibid., vol. 2, p. 31 (January 16, 1852).
   "Fornication no longer teaches me": ibid., vol. 1, p. 230 (May 13, 1845).
146. "on whom love had been lavished": ibid., p. 235 (May 26, 1845).
   "Normal, regular, sustained intercourse": ibid., p. 241 (June 17, 1845).
   "You and I are made": ibid., p. 227 (May 1, 1845).
   "It's raining marriages": ibid., p. 249 (August 13, 1845).
   "How his cock": ibid., p. 248 (July 1845).
   "How about his constancy!": ibid., p. 250 (August 15, 1845).
   "It will happen to you": ibid., p. 239 (June 15, 1845).
147. "There you are now": ibid.
   "Dès que je me connus": Descharmes, *Alfred Le Poittevin*, p. 106.
148. "Even in its higher stage": ibid., p. 150.
   "dear and great man": *CORR.*, vol. 1, p. 225 (April 15, 1845).
   "After our last separation": ibid., p. 220 (April 2, 1845).
149. "Find out what your nature is": ibid., p. 252 (September 16, 1845).
   "chisel away": ibid., p. 229 (May 13, 1845).
   "C'est dans une lente souffrance": Flaubert, *L'Éducation sentimentale*, in *Oeuvres de jeunesse*, p. 275.
150. "She had long, upturned lashes": ibid., p. 853.
   "Yesterday she visited me": ibid., pp. 921–22.
   "The whole earth disappeared": ibid., p. 922.
   "The monotony of their existence": ibid., p. 970.
151. "Monstrous desires": ibid., p. 1005.
   "He is a man": ibid., p. 1070.
   "He was a gullible": ibid., pp. 912–13.
   "A theater is as sacred": Flaubert, "Voyage en Italie," in *Oeuvres de jeunesse*, p. 1109.
152. "I no longer have hope": Flaubert, *L'Éducation sentimentale*, in *Oeuvres de jeunesse*, p. 928.
   "He who would heal": Flaubert, "Voyage en Italie," in *Oeuvres de jeunesse*, pp. 1023–24.
   "Theories, dissertations": ibid., p. 1035.

153. "If my brain": *CORR.*, vol. 2, p. 127 (July 6, 1852).

"What seemed at first glance": Flaubert, first version of *L'Éducation sentimentale*, ed. Bastide, p. 238.

"If what are called freaks": Flaubert and Du Camp, *Par les champs*, in *Oeuvres complètes* (CHH), vol. 10, p. 68.

154. "Poetry at its greatest": Flaubert, first version of *L'Éducation sentimentale*, ed. Bastide, pp. 244–45.

155. "Why need one write?": Du Camp, *Souvenirs littéraires*, p. 226.

156. "He often read us": ibid., p. 227.

"Unbeknownst to me": *CORR.*, vol. 2, p. 30 (January 16, 1852).

"You knew and loved": ibid., vol. 1, p. 254 (January 1846).

157. "I'm quite convinced": ibid., p. 70 (September 23, 1840).

"What you told me": ibid., p. 162 (May 20, 1843).

"In less than two years": ibid., p. 202 (January 17, 1844).

158. "You've heard about our big news": *CORR.*, vol. 1, p. 212 (November 11, 1844).

"If I had been your sister's father": *Correspondances* (Flaubert, Le Poittevin, Du Camp), p. 187 (November 26, 1844).

"because like all young newlyweds": ms. in the Collection Lovenjoul, Bibliothèque de l'Institut, H1366bis.

159. "Tell Gustave that yesterday": *CORR.*, vol. 1, pp. 215–16 (January 20, 1845).

160. "It's the Midi": Flaubert, "Voyage en Italie," in *Oeuvres de jeunesse*, p. 1086.

161. "The place was squat": ibid., p. 1087.

"an excellent lady": *CORR.*, vol. 1, p. 224 (April 15, 1845).

"After a while light and shadows": Flaubert, "Voyage en Italie," in *Oeuvres de jeunesse*, p. 1090.

162. "By all that you hold sacred": *CORR.*, vol. 1, p. 223 (April 15, 1845).

"One feels enraged": Flaubert, "Voyage en Italie," in *Oeuvres de jeunesse*, p. 1091.

"The exquisite sensations": *CORR.*, p. 226 (May 1, 1845).

"I reserve my face": in *Journal de Rouen*, December 5, 1869.

163. "The night! I inhaled it": Flaubert, "Voyage en Italie," in *Oeuvres de jeunesse*, p. 1092.

"it was really like passing": Nathaniel Hawthorne, *Passages from the French and Italian Notebooks* (Boston: Osgood and Co., 1873), pp. 249–50 (June 1, 1859).

"Something cheerful about her face": Flaubert, "Voyage en Italie," in ibid., p. 1102.

164. "Jutting mouth and chin": ibid., p. 1103.

"Small, very plump": ibid.

"to see one last time": *CORR.*, vol. 1, p. 228 (May 13, 1845).

"[I thought about] the unknown hair": Flaubert, "Voyage en Italie," in *Oeuvres de jeunesse*, p. 1107.

165. "[It] filled me with an exquisite joy": ibid., p. 1115.

"The program lasted": *CORR.*, vol. 1, p. 233 (May 26, 1845).

"Providence has us think": ibid., p. 235 (May 26, 1845).

"I used to believe": *Correspondances* (Flaubert, Le Poittevin, Du Camp), p. 114.

166. "Having collected a streetwalker": ibid., p. 122.

"rich in the bosom": *CORR.*, vol. 1, p. 240 (June 17, 1845).

167. "In truth, and perhaps as a result": Louis Delasiauve, *Traité de l'épilepsie* (Paris, 1854).

"I spent part of the summer": Du Camp, *Souvenirs littéraires*, p. 225.

168. "I could say to you": *CORR.*, vol. 1, p. 246 (July 10, 1845).

"As for our flat": Collection Lovenjoul, Bibliothèque de l'Institut, H1366bis.

169. "As I promised, my good mother": ibid.

170. "Seldom has our city": *Journal de Rouen*, January 18, 1846.

171. "As for myself, my eyes": *CORR.*, vol. 1, p. 257 (March 15, 1846).

"Straight as can be": ibid., p. 258 (March 25, 1846).

172. "Will I never resume": ibid., p. 259.

IX. Louis, Louise, and Max

174. "an unbridled audacity": Bruce Seymour, *Lola Montez* (New Haven, Conn.: Yale University Press, 1995), p. 78.

"I am leaving to fight": ibid., p. 81.

175. "His father had won the scepter": Louis Levasseur, "M. Flaubert," in *Les Notables de Normandie* (Rouen, 1872), p. 36.

"Sir Leudet was behind it": *CORR.,* vol. 1, p. 255 (late January 1846).

176. "setback": *Correspondance* (Flaubert, Du Camp), ed. Yvan Leclerc, p. 195.

"It will have to be settled": *CORR.,* vol. 1, p. 259 (March 25, 1846).

"When I confided to you": ibid., p. 411 (December 5, 1846).

177. "My mother and I . . . are very worried": ibid., p. 361 (September 24, 1846).

"There's no doubt": *Correspondance* (Flaubert, Du Camp), p. 203 (May 1846).

178. "We'd go over the edge": Du Camp, *Souvenirs littéraires,* p. 239.

"What are you doing with your carcass": *Correspondance* (Flaubert, Le Poittevin), ed. Yvan Leclerc, p. 69.

179. "I dreamed of love there": ibid., p. 106 (May 18, 1845).

"I fear that you are deluding yourself": ibid., p. 135 (May 31, 1846).

180. "Another one lost to me": *CORR.,* vol. 1, p. 270 (June 4, 1846).

"Every morning Pradier leaves": Du Camp, *Souvenirs littéraires,* p. 242.

181. "He is an excellent man": *CORR.,* vol. 1, pp. 320–21 (August 30, 1846).

"Alone in the desert": Joseph Jackson, *Louise Colet,* p. 18.

182. "When, after the Revolution": quoted in Joseph Jackson, *Louise Colet,* p. 20.

183. "Her verse has a rather lovely front": ibid., p. 110.

"The violent games": ibid., p. 63.

184. "He was looked upon": quoted in J. H. Randall, *The Career of Philosophy,* vol. 2 (New York: Columbia University Press, 1965), p. 445.

185. "I certainly would have been": quoted in Gray, *Rage and Fire,* p. 83.

"Soyez unis dans le danger": Joseph Jackson, *Louise Colet,* p. 96.

186. "Oh sad personality!": ibid., p. 114.

187. "I'm a poor excuse": *CORR.,* vol. 1, p. 299 (August 13, 1846).

"The gentle lilt": ibid., p. 316 (August 26, 1846).

"What irresistible force": ibid., p. 285 (August 9, 1846).

188. "I should like to bring you": ibid., p. 273 (August 4–5, 1846).

"What a memory!": ibid.

"joyous fire": ibid., p. 282 (August 8, 1846).

"You have made a wide breach": ibid., p. 286 (August 9, 1846).

"[The prospect] makes my head spin": ibid., p. 306 (August 21–22, 1846).

189. "You can see that I no longer have heart": ibid., p. 292 (August 11, 1846).

"I'm not doing anything": ibid., p. 311 (August 24, 1846).

"It's impossible": ibid., p. 285 (August 9, 1846).

"The two women": ibid., p. 309 (August 23, 1846).

190. "I'll leave it there like that": ibid., p. 302 (August 14, 1846).

"With this letter I christen": ibid., p. 367 (September 28, 1846).

"How can you possibly": ibid., p. 371 (September 30, 1846).

"I want to gorge you": ibid., p. 301 (August 14, 1846).

191. "My figure is no longer svelte": ibid., p. 807.

"You found me strong": ibid., p. 336 (September 12, 1846).

"Contre une heure d'amour": Joseph Jackson, *Louise Colet,* p. 18.

192. "paler, duller": *CORR.,* vol. 1, p. 338 (September 13, 1846).

"An emotional crisis": ibid., p. 337 (September 13, 1846).

"I wail a lot": ibid., p. 342 (September 15, 1846).

"I came, you accepted me": ibid.

193. "It is I who am alone": ibid., p. 338 (September 13, 1846).

"She's an old acquaintance": ibid., p. 366 (September 28, 1846).

194. "So you found my letter": ibid., p. 380 (October 8, 1846).
"For me a subject to be treated": ibid., p. 390 (October 14, 1846).
195. "I no longer write": ibid., p. 433 (January 30, 1847).
"What [*sic*] is Flaubert screwing": *Correspondance* (Flaubert, Du Camp), p. 213 (August 13, 1846).
"three-quarters of whose day": *CORR.*, vol. 1, p. 446 (March 7, 1846).
197. "our inevitable omelette": Flaubert and Du Camp, *Par les champs*, p. 482.
"This trivia constitutes": ibid., p. 265.
198. "The shape of seaweed": ibid., p. 300.
199. "Perhaps that's why they seem": ibid., p. 368.
"[People] don't dance, they turn": ibid., p. 409.
200. "We'd follow beaten paths": ibid., p. 540.
"bitter loneliness": ibid., p. 624.
"At the twilight of one society": ibid., p. 626.
"The difficulty of this book": *CORR.*, vol. 2, p. 62 (April 3, 1852).
201. "Happy are they": ibid., vol. 1, p. 477 (October 1847).
"The more I study style": ibid., p. 478 (October 1847).
"like two people who had married late": ibid., p. 481 (November 7, 1847).
202. "I smoked, I read": Flaubert, *Vie et travaux du R. P. Cruchard*, p. 30.
"I myself was muffled": *CORR.*, vol. 1, p. 494 (April 7, 1848).
"I couldn't prevent": Flaubert, *Vie et travaux du R. P. Cruchard*, p. 32.
203. "You who knew us in our youth": *CORR.*, vol. 1, p. 496 (April 10, 1848).

X. 1848
204. "dans la misère": *CORR.*, vol. 1, p. 221 (April 2, 1845).
206. "What taste!": ibid., p. 491 (late December 1847).
207. "from an artist's perspective": Du Camp, *Souvenirs de l'année 1848*, p. 51.
208. "His long brown beard": ibid., p. 54.
209. "Vengeance! Vengeance!": Agulhon, *Les Quarante-huitards*, p. 43.
210. "We saw the first mob rush": Du Camp, *Souvenirs de l'année 1848*, p. 95.
"Great landlords": Tocqueville, *Recollections*, p. 78.
"I explained that there were valuable paintings": Du Camp, *Souvenirs de l'année 1848*, p. 101.
211. "There is no longer authority": Stern, *Histoire de la Révolution*, p. 222.
212. "the magnetism of zealous crowds": Flaubert, *L'Éducation sentimentale*, ed. Wetherill, p. 296.
"a great nation like this": Normanby, *A Year of Revolution*, vol. 1, p. 96.
"A retrograde and oligarchical government": Agulhon, *Les Quarante-huitards*, p. 48.
213. "selfish, short-sighted": Price, *1848 in France*, p. 63.
"The people alone bore arms": Tocqueville, *Recollections*, p. 72.
214. "Enlightenment must reach": Price, *1848 in France*, p. 77.
"The population of kings": ibid.
215. "I'm gnawed by anger": *CORR.*, vol. 1, p. 497 (late May 1848).
216. "If you knew the effect": ibid., p. 499 (June 25, 1848).
217. "When I grew up enough": Franklin Grout, *Heures d'autrefois*, p. 42.
"Along their route shopkeepers": Du Camp, *Souvenirs de l'année 1848*, p. 239.
"In conversations": Tocqueville, *Recollections*, p. 162.
218. "without a battle cry": ibid., p. 136.
"I sat down, I examined my wound": Du Camp, *Souvenirs de l'année 1848*, p. 271.
"French civilization survived": ibid., p. 295.
219. "to the aid of society": Price, *1848 in France*, p. 113.
"The struggle these last few days": quoted in ibid., p. 117.
"He blames our social system": ibid., p. 120.
"the necessities of their condition": Tocqueville, *Recollections*, p. 136.

220. "You see that I'm not proud": *CORR.,* vol. 1, p. 502 (July 1848).

"I cherish the idea that one day": Frère, *Louis Bouilhet,* p. 104.

221. "I don't know what the dreams": CHH, vol. 12, p. 38.

222. "In evil as in good": Letellier, *Louis Bouilhet,* p. 119.

"Bouilhet, who blushed": Du Camp, *Souvenirs littéraires,* p. 236.

223. "There wasn't a Greek or Latin poet": ibid., p. 236.

"Be careful!": ibid., p. 240.

224. "I felt desperately unable": *La Tentation de Saint Antoine* (first version), in CHH, vol. 9, p. 29.

"Let it throw open its dormer": ibid., p. 59.

"which glisten like the steel of swords": ibid., p. 36.

"Have pensive adolescents": ibid., p. 180.

225. "Here [the knife] is what destroys": ibid., p. 97.

"A magistrate caresses thoughts": ibid., p. 243.

226. "Come here! I am repose": ibid., p. 244.

"But what if you were both lying?": ibid.

"[After the Sphinx]": Du Camp, *Souvenirs littéraires,* p. 290.

227. "You proceed by expansion": ibid.

"You must choose": ibid., p. 291.

228. "I need fresh air": *CORR.,* vol. 1, p. 506 (May 6, 1849).

"Furthermore, . . . he will ride horseback": ibid., p. 508 (May 12, 1849).

229. "Yesterday Gautier voiced an opinion": ibid., p. 518 (October 29, 1849).

"The idea of 'rescue'": Sigmund Freud, *Sexuality and the Psychology of Love* (New York: Collier Books, 1963), p. 56.

XI. Voyage en Orient: Egypt

231. "Why is it": Chateaubriand, *Itinéraire de Paris,* p. 220.

232. "land of prodigies": from Chateaubriand, *Itinéraire de Paris à Jérusalem,* in Berchet, *Le Voyage en Orient,* p. 591.

"All of those mountains have a name": from Lamartine, *Le Voyage en Orient,* in ibid., p. 635.

233. "human nature preserves": from Chateaubriand, *Itinéraire,* in ibid., p.133.

"Mademoiselle Malagamba": from Lamartine, *Le Voyage,* in ibid., p. 626.

234. "living, civility": Wilkinson, *Handbook for Travellers,* p. x.

"There are strolls on deck": *CORR.,* vol. 1, p. 524 (November 7–8, 1849).

"I feel a mariner's instincts": Flaubert, *Voyage en Egypte,* p. 165.

"An apprehensive and solemn impression": ibid., p. 168.

235. "There is crimson melting": ibid., pp. 179–80.

236. "I tasted Arab bread": ibid., p. 182.

"One already has presentiments": ibid.

"The streets of the bazaars": Wilkinson, *Handbook for Travellers,* p. 134.

237. "the most powerful man": *CORR.,* vol. 1, p. 529 (November 17, 1849).

238. "He couldn't have been more cordial": ibid.

"In vehemence of gesticulation": Macleod, *Eastward,* p. 13.

239. "the most intelligent": Du Camp, *Souvenirs littéraires,* p. 309.

240. "At first glance, these astonishing hulks": *CORR.,* vol. 1, p. 554 (December 15, 1849).

"I adore the desert": ibid., p. 550 (December 14, 1849).

241. "When I think . . . about my future": ibid., p. 561 (January 5, 1850).

242. "The sharif in a green turban": Flaubert, *Voyage en Egypte,* pp. 248–49.

243. "Traveling for our instruction": *CORR.,* vol. 1, p. 572 (January 15, 1850).

"in a nasty little cabaret": ibid., p. 729 (December 19, 1850).

"One day, to amuse the crowd": *CORR.,* vol. 1, p. 542 (December 4, 1849).

244. "They sleep in holes": Flaubert, *Voyage en Egypte,* p. 241.

"the firm, vehement will": Warburton, *Crescent and Cross,* p. 134.

245. "The first contains": *CORR.*, vol. 1, p. 582 (February 3, 1850).
"We're living": ibid., p. 588 (February 14, 1850).
246. "I stood a long time": Warburton, *Crescent and Cross*, p. 189.
247. "Feline gestures sorting": Flaubert, *Voyage en Egypte*, p. 268.
"unconscious fascinations": Warburton, *Crescent and Cross*, p. 276.
"She wore a tarboosh": Flaubert, *Voyage en Egypte*, p. 282.
248. "I covered her with my fur pelisse": *CORR.*, vol. 1, p. 607 (March 13, 1850).
"How sweet it would be": Flaubert, *Voyage en Egypte*, p. 287.
249. "You think up all kinds of ways": ibid., p. 592 (February 23, 1850).
250. "Shall I publish? Shall I not publish?": ibid., p. 601 (March 13, 1850).
"Do you know that we are": ibid., p. 610 (March 24, 1850).
"No, no, when I think about": ibid., p. 720 (December 15, 1850).
"At Thebes, [Alfred] was constantly": ibid., pp. 622–23 (May 17, 1850).
251. "We stop at every ruin": ibid., p. 614 (April 22, 1850).
252. "In whichever direction" : Du Camp, *Le Nil*, pp. 193–94.
253. "The paintings are as fresh": *CORR.*, vol. 1, p. 621 (May 17, 1850).
254. "To the right thirty or so": Du Camp, *Le Nil*, p. 219.
"a thousand tits": *CORR.*, vol. 1, p. 636 (June 2, 1850).
"a vulgar, upstart temple": Nightingale, *Letters from Egypt*, p. 157.
255. "Neither of us is either established": *CORR.*, vol. 1, p. 627 (June 2, 1850).
"We take notes": ibid., p. 628 (June 2, 1850).

XII. Voyage en Orient: After Egypt

258. "Syria is a beautiful land": *CORR.*, vol. 1, p. 662 (August 9, 1850).
"On the slope leading to": CHH, vol. 10, p. 557.
"His angular gestures": Du Camp, *Souvenirs littéraires*, p. 323.
259. "After my first visit": *CORR.*, vol. 1, pp. 666–67 (August 20, 1850).
"I am becoming a pig": ibid., p. 680 (September 4, 1850).
260. "I screwed three women": ibid., p. 668 (August 20, 1850).
"a theater exhibiting out-of-the-way life": Macleod, *Eastward,* p. 290.
261. "We enter a kind of small farm": CHH, vol. 10, p. 592.
"Great excess of men": ibid., p. 594.
"At the moment, Maxime": *CORR.*, vol. 1, p. 688 (September 9, 1850).
262. "Ah, how beautiful it is!": CHH, vol. 11, p. 29.
263. "There's nothing like travel": *CORR.*, vol. 1, p. 707 (November 14, 1850).
"Imagine a city": ibid., p. 704 (November 14, 1850).
"The feeling you had": ibid., p. 705 (November 14, 1850).
264. "No wall, no moat": ibid., p. 706 (November 14, 1850).
"the prodigality of ruins": CHH, vol. 10, p. 46.
"One of these days": ibid., p. 49.
265. "Never, I hope": *CORR.,* vol. 1 pp. 719–20 (December 15, 1850).
266. "Ah! If at least I knew Greek!": ibid., p. 709 (November 14, 1850).
"And the ruins!": ibid., p. 733 (December 26, 1850).
267. "Every time I've found myself ": Du Camp, *Souvenirs littéraires,* p. 341.
268. "Whenever someone arrived": CHH, vol. 11, p. 77.
"Dinner at the village": ibid., p. 102.
269. "The contemplation of these vagabond existences": ibid., p. 110.
"As far as the real voyage goes": *CORR.*, vol. 1, p. 743 (February 9, 1851).
"It's truly inexhaustible": ibid., p. 758 (March 9, 1851).
"Here in soft Parthenope": ibid., p. 760 (March 11, 1851).
270. "Things are closed": ibid., p. 759 (March 9, 1851).
"Well, yes, I have seen": ibid., p. 775 (April 9, 1851).
271. "It would be sacrificing": ibid., p. 703 (November 14, 1850).
"As far as my emotional state": ibid., p. 774 (April 9, 1851).

XIII. The Perfect Hostages

273. "Turning my head to the left": CHH, vol. 11, p. 156.
"Oh! Dreary are": *CORR.*, vol. 1, p. 809 (October 28, 1849).
"How I'm suffering": ibid., p. 804 (December 6, 1849).

274. "Poor Madame Colet": Joseph Jackson, *Louise Colet*, p. 158.

275. "Do I love Auguste?": from the unpublished diary of Louise Colet, Fonds Colet in Le Musée Calvet, Avignon, p. 46 (May 31, 1851).
"Will Gustave come see me?": *CORR.*, vol. 1, p. 810.
"I would have you": ibid., p. 782 (May 14, 1851).
"I in turn shall . . . give": ibid., p. 785 (June 18, 1851).

276. "I waited for her": ibid., p. 812.
"I would have liked at least": ibid., p. 813.
"Do you believe that my visit": ibid.

277. "I kissed him passionately": ibid., p. 815.
"You must have found": *CORR.*, vol. 2, p. 3.

278. "Poor child!": ibid., vol. 2, pp. 12–13 (October 23, 1851).
"I look forward to keeping": ibid., vol. 1, p. 906 (October 1, 1851).
"Is *all of China*": ibid., vol. 2, p. 419 (August 26, 1853).

279. "These people seem to have died": ibid., p. 6 (September 28, 1851).
"as if by magic": Corley, *Democratic Despot*, p. 54.

280. "The people . . . are intoxicated": ibid., p. 56.

281. "The great events of history": ibid., p. 81.
"It won't be tomorrow, then": Cate, *George Sand*, p. 624.
"Frenchmen! . . . With every passing day": ibid., pp. 104–5.

282. "Soldiers! . . . Be proud": Arnaud, *Le 2 décembre*, p. 59.
"frightful country": *CORR.*, vol. 2, p. 20 (December 8, 1851).
"The ennui that corrodes us": ibid.

283. "My heart is beating fast": *Correspondances* (Flaubert, Le Poittevin, Du Camp), p. 268.
"If I should publish": ibid., pp. 274–76.

284. "like a hedgehog": *CORR.*, vol. 2, p. 377 (July 7, 1853).
"My youth, of which you saw": *Correspondances* (Flaubert, Le Poittevin, Du Camp), p. 274 (October 21, 1851).
"You always push things": *CORR.*, vol. 2, pp. 279–80 (October 29, 1851).

285. "It's high time": *CORR.*, vol. 2, p. 51 (January 16, 1852).

XIV. *Madame Bovary*

286. "I've found it!": in Du Camp, *Souvenirs littéraires*, p. 314.

287. "When her lover's arms": Flaubert, "Passion and Virtue," in *Oeuvres de jeunesse*, p. 282.
"Still, I feel I would like to live": ibid., p. 300.
"There is a sweetness about it": Flaubert, *Mémoires d'un fou*, ed. Leclerc, p. 432.
"more woman": ibid., p. 408.
"With creditors hounding her": Du Camp, *Souvenirs littéraires*, p. 293.

288. "What are you doing?": *Correspondances* (Flaubert, Le Poittevin, Du Camp), p. 260.
"Ah, what a great study": ibid., p. 93 (April 2, 1845).

289. "I have sketched, botched": *CORR.*, vol. 2, p. 40 (January 31, 1852).
"What strikes me as beautiful": ibid., p. 31 (January 16, 1852).

290. "She wished she could have lived": Flaubert, *Madame Bovary*, ed. Gothot-Mersch, p. 38.
"Its floor was of marble": ibid., p. 48.

291. "Great and glorious before the days": Marcel Proust, *A la recherche du temps perdu*, vol. 1 (Paris: Gallimard [Pléiade], 1954), p. 177.

292. "with the fastidiousness": Flaubert, *Madame Bovary*, ed. Gothot-Mersch, p. 51.
"From the ballroom": ibid., p. 53.
"The first light of dawn": ibid., p. 55.

294. "I'd leap": Commanville, *"Souvenirs intimes,"* in Flaubert, *Oeuvres complètes,* vol. 2, ed. M. Bardèche, p. xxviii.
"He thus taught me": ibid.
"think like a demigod": *CORR.,* vol. 2, p. 402 (August 21, 1853).
295. "Mother Lormier is said": ibid., p. 226 (January 1, 1853).
"In every possible way": ibid., p. 374 (July 2, 1853).
"I have downed many glasses": ibid., p. 398 (August 16, 1853).
296. "A model of business prose": ibid.
"Stupidity and Mind": ibid., pp. 585–86 (August 1, 1855).
"One must know": ibid., p. 163 (September 25, 1852).
297. "What a poet!": ibid., p. 45 (February 16, 1852).
"Bad; one uses": ibid., p. 183 (November 28, 1852).
298. "wordless tendernesses": ibid., vol. 3, p. 96 (July 4, 1860).
"I've worked on them": ibid., vol. 2, p. 198 (November 28, 1852).
"Learn to be self-critical": ibid., p. 210 (December 16, 1852).
"Ah! Musette": ibid., p. 210 (December 19, 1852).
299. "Since we last saw each other": ibid., p. 75 (April 24, 1852).
"I'm setting it aside": ibid., pp. 88–89 (May 15, 1852).
"I reread them": ibid., p. 243 (January 29, 1853).
"I have continually seen": ibid., p. 110 (June 19, 1852).
300. "There was, in his attire": Flaubert, *Madame Bovary,* ed. Gothot-Mersch, pp. 141–42.
"Gentlemen, may I take the liberty": ibid., pp. 145–49.
302. "like the mountain": ibid., p. 58.
303. "Dear friend, . . . trains": *CORR.,* vol. 2, p. 323 (May 7, 1853).
"You won't soon forget": ibid., p. 102 (June 9, 1852).
"I hardly have the energy": ibid., p. 247 (February 17, 1853).
304. "Since [my thought]": ibid., p. 456 (October 25, 1853).
"It's been a fortnight": ibid., p. 893 (Colet's "Mementos" are included in this volume as appendix 2).
305. "How downcast": ibid., p. 900.
"The only way to enjoy peace": ibid., p. 313 (April 22, 1853).
"Your love penetrates me": ibid., p. 331 (May 21, 1853).
"I love you as I have never loved": ibid., p. 403 (August 21, 1853).
306. "You have been in my life": ibid., p. 383 (July 15, 1853).
"I want correspondence": Flaubert, *Lettres à Flaubert,* ed. Palermo di Stefano, vol. 1, p. 91.
307. "I bruised my knees": *CORR.,* vol. 2, p. 888.
"Musset has never separated": ibid., p. 126 (July 6, 1852).
"It's a shame": ibid., p. 66 (April 3, 1852).
"Thoroughbred horses": ibid., p. 385 (July 15, 1853).
"Genius, like a powerful horse": ibid., p. 251 (February 27, 1853).
308. "Today I rode my pen": ibid., p. 448 (October 12, 1853).
"She was charming": Flaubert, *Madame Bovary,* ed. Gothot-Mersch, p. 166.
"It was Larivière": ibid., p. 326.
"In order to know": ibid., p. 180.
309. "His paternal heritage": Levasseur, *Les Notables,* p. 30.
310. "I spoke eloquently": Bouilhet, *Lettres à Louise Colet,* p. 158.
"something intricate and profound": *CORR.,* vol. 2, p. 403 (August 21, 1853).
311. "You go at life tooth and nail": ibid., pp. 478–79 (December 14, 1853).
"For the moment I am in a state": Bouilhet, *Lettres à Gustave Flaubert,* p. 43.
"masturbating": *CORR.,* vol. 2, p. 459 (October 28, 1853).
312. "Who appointed us": ibid., p. 502 (January 9–10, 1854).
"I tried to love": ibid., p. 549 (April 12, 1854).
313. "I have learned": ibid., p. 572 (March 6, 1855).

"I thought, in good conscience": Bouilhet, *Lettres à Gustave Flaubert*, pp. 171–72.

"Bouilhet just couldn't": Louise Colet, "Mementos" in *CORR.*, vol. 2, p. 902 (December 4, 1853).

XV. On Trial

315. "Since I've struck out": *Correspondances* (Flaubert, Le Poittevin, Du Camp), p. 278.

317. "rich and sonorous": Charles Baudelaire, "Confession," in *Oeuvres* (Paris: Gallimard, 1951), *Fleurs du mal*, p. 117.

318. "hurry up": *CORR.*, vol. 2, p. 113 (June 26, 1852).

"Why do you keep harping": ibid., p. 120 (early July 1852).

"Do you think I'd be worthy": ibid., p. 52 (March 20, 1852).

"People are leaving me": ibid., p. 39 (February 1, 1852).

"pitiful": ibid., p. 200 (December 9, 1852).

"For him, for good old": ibid., p. 256 (March 5, 1853).

319. "diagnose": ibid., p. 253 (February 27–28, 1853).

"Action has always revolted me": ibid., p. 257 (March 5, 1853).

"It is easier": ibid., p. 772 (November 4, 1857).

320. "[She] seized the blue jar": Flaubert, *Madame Bovary*, ed. Gothot-Mersch, p. 321.

"The priest got up": ibid., p. 330.

321. "Imaginary characters drive me mad": *CORR.*, vol. 3, p. 562 (November 20, 1866).

"Mornings, lying face-to-face": Flaubert, *Madame Bovary*, ed. Gothot-Mersch, p. 34.

"To please her": ibid., p. 349.

322. "Yesterday, at last": *CORR.*, vol. 2, p. 613 (June 1, 1856).

"How can you expect me": ibid., p. 616 (June 16, 1856).

"You're wrong to regret": Bouilhet, *Lettres à Gustave Flaubert*, p. 71.

323. "A warm recommendation": *Correspondances* (Flaubert, Le Poittevin, Du Camp), p. 291.

"Pichat has just said 'yes'": *CORR.*, vol. 2, p. 620 (July 22, 1856).

324. "If you knew me better": ibid., p. 635 (October 2, 1856).

"You set yourself against": ibid., p. 636.

"In my opinion": ibid., p. 650 (December 7, 1856).

325. "Considerations that I need not examine": ibid., p. 633 (December 15, 1856).

"an affront to decent": ibid., p. 1344.

"Let them beware": quoted in Descôtes, *Le Public de théâtre*, p. 329.

326. "They quote his repartees": Parigot, *Théâtre d'hier*, p. 239.

"Who in this book": CHH, vol. 1, p. 380.

327. "a painting admirable": ibid., p. 375.

"Art that observes no rule": ibid., p. 381.

"Gentlemen, . . . a great name": ibid., p. 382.

328. "Ah! You will accuse me": ibid., p. 397.

"The honor of our country": ibid., p. 390.

"All of classical literature": ibid., p. 426.

"Given that Gustave Flaubert": ibid., p. 428.

329. "I wonder if it is possible": *CORR.*, vol. 2, p. 681 (February 11, 1857).

330. "You have struck the right chord": ibid., vol. 2, p. 1365.

"The picture you paint": ibid.

"[They] bovarize a little": Flaubert, *Lettres à Flaubert*, vol. 1, p. 149 (from Edmond About).

"You have produced a beautiful book": *CORR.*, vol. 2, p. 1367.

"Apparently begun several years ago": ibid., p. 1369.

331. "Don't judge me by this novel": ibid., p. 710 (May 5, 1857).

"'So you really find that beautiful?'": Nadar, *Mémoires du géant*, pp. 104–5.

332. "Several critics have said": Baudelaire, in *Oeuvres*, "*Madame Bovary*," p. 1000.

"Since our ears have been filled": ibid., p. 999.

"You entered the arcana": *CORR.*, vol. 2, p. 772 (October 21, 1857).

"There are dazzling passages": Baudelaire, *Oeuvres,* p. 1004.
333. "I am, it is true": *CORR.,* vol. 2, p. 773 (June 14, 1857).

XVI. An Island of His Own

334. "I want to be a second Augustus": quoted in Jean des Cars, *Haussmann* (Paris: Librairie Académique Perrin, 1978), p. 204.
335. "I am a stranger": Goncourt and Goncourt, *Journal,* vol. 1, p. 835.
336. "Government exists": Bonaparte, *Des idées napoléoniennes,* pp. 16–17.
    "The government loans of the old regime": Thompson, *Louis Napoleon,* p. 233.
337. "France is like Molière's miser": Goncourt and Goncourt, *Journal,* vol. 1, p. 371.
338. "There is no longer a race of wealthy men": quoted in Adeline Daumard, *Les Bourgeois de Paris au XIXe siècle,* p. 120.
    "Weary of the superannuated": Aron, *Le Mangeur,* p. 81.
339. "The machinist's art": Moynet, *French Theatrical Production,* p. 66.
340. "Money is a very big thing": Goncourt and Goncourt, *Journal,* vol. 1, p. 1157.
    "Ah, it is very difficult": Maupassant, *Bel-Ami,* p. 167.
342. "What purpose does this book serve": Théophile Gautier, *Mademoiselle de Maupin* (Paris: Garnier-Flammarion, 1966), p. 42.
    "No, you goitrous imbeciles": ibid.
343. "There is a splendid American pox": quoted in Quétel, *History of Syphilis,* pp. 123–24.
    "We chat about the difficulty": Goncourt and Goncourt, *Journal,* vol. 1, p. 685.
344. "Read voraciously": *CORR.,* vol. 2, p. 806 (April 1858).
    "said nothing": ibid., vol. 3, p. 95 (July 3, 1860).
    "I'm tired of ugly things": ibid., vol. 2, p. 822 (July 11, 1858).
346. *"par peur"*: ibid., p. 747 (July 26, 1857).
    "I am lost in books": ibid., p. 712 (May 9, 1857).
    "I'm suffering vertigo": ibid., p. 714 (May 14, 1857).
    "I am full of doubts and terrors": ibid.
    "I'm afraid of getting bogged down": ibid., p. 735 (June 24, 1857).
    "My Punic readings": ibid., p. 715 (May 16, 1857).
    "I feel exhausted": ibid., p. 750 (July 26, 1857).
    "I believe I'm in a mess": ibid., p. 735 (June 24, 1857).
    "Do you know how many": ibid., p. 747 (July 26, 1857).
    "belching folios": ibid., p. 726 (May 28, 1857).
347. "A translation would be most difficult": Flaubert, *Lettres à Flaubert,* vol. 1, p. 156.
    "I have often imagined writing to you": *CORR.,* vol. 2, pp. 1383–84.
348. "They have no livelihood": ibid., p. 755 (August 11, 1857).
    "You have written a masterpiece": ibid., pp. 654–55 (December 18, 1856).
349. "We shall chat together": ibid., pp. 696–700 (March 30, 1857).
350. "In a democracy": Edmund Burke, *Reflections on the French Revolution* (London: Dent, 1953), pp. 121–22.
    "I am a great doctor of melancholy": ibid., p. 821 (July 11, 1858).
351. "I do not lack the faculty": ibid., p. 722 (May 23, 1857).
    "[He] is astonished": ibid., p. 738 (June 30, 1857).
    "It's as if an evil genius": ibid., p. 704 (April 10, 1857).
352. "Why are you talking": ibid., p. 717 (May 18, 1857).
    "In the name of heaven": ibid., p. 760 (August 23, 1857).
    "Read Montaigne": ibid., p. 731 (June 6, 1857).
353. "Life is such a hideous business": ibid., p. 717 (May 18, 1857).
    "I've undertaken an accursed work": ibid., p. 783 (December 12, 1857).
354. "I don't know if you'll ever do better": ibid., p. 777 (November 10, 1857).
355. "At last you've reached the goal": Bibliothèque de l'Institut, ms., Collection Jouvenal H1366bis.
    "one must ply one's trade": *CORR.,* vol. 2, p. 803 (April 6, 1858).

"Here I am, stuck": ibid., p. 800 (March 13, 1858).

356. "I shall spare you": *CORR.*, vol. 2, pp. 807–8 (April 23–24, 1858).

"He led me": Flaubert, "Voyage à Carthage," in *Oeuvres complètes* (CHH), vol. 11, p. 181.

357. "Je connais Carthage": *CORR.*, vol. 3, p. 810 (May 8, 1858).

358. "To the left, low mountains": CHH, vol. 11, pp. 186–87.

359. "The caïd's house": ibid., p. 204.

"May I exhale": ibid., p. 208.

"It's doubtful": *CORR.*, vol. 2, p. 830 (August 28, 1858).

360. "In each line": ibid., vol. 3, p. 59 (November 29, 1859).

"You can't imagine": ibid., p. 179 (October 7, 1861).

361. "The town was protected": Flaubert, *Salammbô,* ed. Thomas, p. 169.

"He lay flat on his stomach": ibid., p. 170.

"riveted to the horizon": ibid., p. 436.

"I believe the novel": *CORR.*, vol. 3, p. 116 (October 1, 1860).

362. "A man leaped": Flaubert, *Salammbô,* ed. Thomas, p. 468.

"The Barbarians were troubled": ibid., p. 274.

363. "In lemon trees": ibid., p. 316.

"From her ankles": ibid., p. 461.

365. "Your pride is safe": Bouilhet, *Lettres à Gustave Flaubert,* p. 403 (August 19, 1862).

"I may be wrong": ibid., p. 97 (July 18, 1857).

"One might have wished": Sainte-Beuve, *Nouveaux Lundis,* vol. 4, pp. 31ff.

367. "On this point I set aside": Sainte-Beuve, *Nouveaux Lundis,* vol. 4, pp. 131–32.

368. "I am sure I reconstructed it": *CORR.*, vol. 3, p. 278 (December 23–24, 1862).

"I couldn't care less": ibid., pp. 282–83 (December 23–24, 1862).

369. "Along with the *Journal pour Rire*": ibid., p. 289 (January 12, 1863).

"My dear M. Flaubert, I wanted to run across town": *CORR.*, vol. 3, pp. 1207–8.

"What a sober and powerful style": Sand, *Questions d'art,* pp. 305–12.

"My dear brother": Flaubert, *Correspondance* (Flaubert, George Sand), p. 53.

"I am not grateful to you": ibid., pp. 53–54.

370. "illustrating Carthaginian mores": *CORR.*, vol. 3, p. 1273.

371. "the hard doom of popularity": Henry James, in *Collected Stories,* vol. 2, "The Next Time" (New York: Knopf, 1999), p. 225.

"My dear old mother": *CORR.*, vol. 3, p. 1217.

XVII. Entering Middle Age

373. "Whenever he showed up for dinner": Franklin Grout, *Heures d'autrefois,* p. 60.

"Our walks through the Louvre": ibid., p. 61.

374. "There are chapters": *CORR.*, vol. 3, p. 157 (June 8, 1861).

"I've learned about the publication": ibid., p. 1220 (December 16, 1862).

"My poor Z": ibid., p. 1233.

375. "Send me a legible letter": ibid., p. 291 (January 19, 1863).

"The battle is joined": Colet, *Lui,* p. 336.

"If the idea": ibid., p. 337.

376. "Your genius, dear sir": *CORR.*, vol. 3, p. 1119.

"She really lambastes your friend": ibid., p. 54 (November 12, 1859).

"This publication has convinced me": ibid., p. 57 (November 15, 1859).

377. "Very beautiful, very great": Gérard-Gailly, *Les Véhémences,* p. 191.

"The spirit of justice": ibid.

"Our conversations were quite animated": quoted in André Dubuc, "Flaubert et la Rouennaise Amélie Bosquet," *Bulletin de la Société des Amis de Flaubert,* no. 27 (December 1965).

378. "No, I am not as proud": Flaubert, *Lettres à Flaubert,* vol. 1, p. 557.

"The other Sunday I stood": *CORR.*, vol. 3, p. 97 (July 11, 1860).

"So you like what you've heard": ibid., p. 172 (August 24, 1861).

"Eager to please and good at it": Du Camp, *Souvenirs littéraires,* p. 533.

379. "When you have nothing better to do": *CORR.*, vol. 3, p. 218 (May 26, 1862).
380. "if not brilliant": Billy, *Goncourt Brothers,* p. 26.
　"I have made a very firm resolution": ibid., p. 29.
　"Nothing in the Western world": ibid., p. 34.
381. "phenomenal duality": Goncourt and Goncourt, *Journal,* vol. 1, p. 552 (October 28, 1858).
　"What the public wants": ibid., p. 325 (March 15, 1857).
382. "There is deep down in me": ibid., p. 1096 (July 1862).
　"robust familiarity": ibid., p. 691 (January 25, 1860).
383. "The solemnity will take place": *CORR.*, vol. 3, p. 152 (April 30, 1861).
　"We'd plunge into the mysteries": Goncourt and Goncourt, *Journal,* vol. 1, p. 1070 (May 4, 1862).
　"You are decidedly": Albalat, *Gustave Flaubert,* p. 185.
384. "What you say about the Goncourts": *CORR.*, vol. 3, p. 460 (October 1, 1865).
　"Fine, art for art": Goncourt and Goncourt, *Journal,* vol. 1, p. 763 (June 26, 1860).
　"No bitterness, no feelings": ibid., p. 1022 (February 21, 1862).
　"We recognize it today": ibid., p. 722 (March 16, 1860).
385. "About everything under the sun": ibid., p. 1350 (November 2, 1863).
　"a work of which I thought him incapable": ibid., p. 1347 (October 30, 1863).
386. "For two and a half months": *CORR.*, vol. 3, p. 352 (October 23, 1863).
387. "Citizens, bourgeois, old crusts!": CHH, vol. 7, p. 115.
　"We have spent the whole day working": *CORR.*, vol. 3, p. 359 (November 19, 1863).
388. "Well, my poor Caro": ibid., p. 365 (December 23, 1863).
389. "What is she like?": ibid., p. 189 (December 15, 1861).
　"I dread the thought": ibid., p. 367 (December 24, 1863).
390. "How could she not have understood": Franklin Grout, *Heures d'autrefois,* p. 63.
　"What interests me most": *CORR.*, vol. 3, p. 387 (April 14, 1864).
391. "a moral history": ibid., p. 409 (October 6, 1864).
　"I stayed up there overnight": ibid., p. 452 (August 2, 1865).

XVIII. Imperial Society
393. "The hour at which one takes": Second, *Vichy-Sévigné.*
　"ignoble bourgeois": *CORR.*, vol. 3, p. 332 (June 24, 1863).
394. "I'm no longer carefree enough": ibid.
　"One's brain melts": ibid., p. 334 (June 26, 1863).
　"One can safely assert": Second, *Vichy-Sévigné.*
397. "I come to beg": Richardson, *Princess Mathilde,* p. 51.
398. "She is one of the noble figures": quoted in ibid., p. 60.
399. "Here I am, settled": ibid., pp. 99–100.
400. "I insist": *CORR.*, vol. 3, p. 411 (November 12, 1864).
　"Bourgeois would have been": ibid., p. 412 (November 17, 1864).
　"Gustave Flaubert . . . was parading": ibid., p. 1331.
401. "We decided that people are severe": Goncourt and Goncourt, *Journal,* vol. 2, pp. 190–91 (August 16, 1865).
402. "You know, though you may deny it": ibid., p. 683 (August 29, 1867).
　"I don't question": ibid., p. 515 (August 16, 1866).
　"This had always been a dream of his": Baldick, *Dinner at Magny's,* p. 22.
403. "The metier of those": Creuzet, *Duranty,* p. 43.
　"My real life dates from him": ibid., p. 46.
　"Living in the nineteenth century": Goncourt and Goncourt, *Germinie Lacerteux,* pp. 23–24.
404. "the perfection of mediocrity": Goncourt and Goncourt, *Journal,* vol. 1, p. 1254 (March 28, 1863).
　"Great generals": ibid.
405. "Thank you, my dear Master": *CORR.*, p. 623 (March 30, 1867).
　"All who are not submerged": ibid., p. 659 (June 27, 1867).

406. "a prize nincompoop": Goncourt and Goncourt, *Journal,* vol. 1, pp. 1167–68 (December 21, 1863).

"Out of this pandemonium": ibid.

"I've just read": *CORR.,* vol. 3, p. 309 (March 16, 1863).

407. "I would like": ibid., p. 310 (March 19, 1863).

"What I admire above all": ibid., p. 312 (March 24, 1863).

"La mère Husson is well": *Correspondances* (Flaubert, Le Poittevin, Du Camp), p. 324 (May 8, 1863).

408. "administrative literature": Du Camp, *Souvenirs littéraires,* p. 555.

"My heart is heavy": *Correspondances* (Flaubert, Le Poittevin, Du Camp), p. 358 (November 28, 1866).

"You have no idea": ibid., p. 361 (December 20, 1866).

410. "Children playing": Flaubert, *Carnets de travail,* pp. 355–56.

411. "I was welcomed": *Correspondance* (Flaubert, George Sand), p. 59.

"She is there, beside me": Goncourt and Goncourt, *Journal,* vol. 2, p. 245.

"I found her features": Tocqueville, *Recollections,* pp. 134–35.

412. "I've grown accustomed": *Correspondance* (Flaubert, George Sand), p. 63 (May 14, 1866).

"A play by me": *CORR.,* vol. 3, p. 511 (July 31, 1866).

"I attended the soft flop": ibid., p. 514 (August 16, 1866).

413. "If the Good Lord were fair": ibid., p. 540 (October 1, 1866).

"I arrive at Rouen": *Correspondance* (Flaubert, George Sand), p. 72.

414. "and I could see": *CORR.,* vol. 3, p. 524 (August 31, 1866).

"irresistible and involuntary seduction": ibid., p. 525 (September 1, 1866).

"George Sand she did not like": Willa Cather, "A Chance Meeting," in *Stories, Poems, and Other Writings,* p. 827.

"Here's what I propose": *CORR.,* vol. 3, p. 531 (September 22, 1866).

415. "There is no better woman": ibid., p. 554 (November 13, 1866).

"It seems like ten years": ibid., p. 553 (November 12, 1866).

"Age does not affect": ibid., p. 555 (November 13–14, 1866).

416. "Each of us": *CORR.,* vol. 3, p. 530 (September 21, 1866).

"most splendid oddities": ibid., p. 649 (June 7, 1867).

"big, brilliant pearls": Flaubert, *Vie et travaux du R. P. Cruchard,* p. 55.

417. "We visited the Louvre": Mark Twain, *Innocents Abroad* (New York: Signet, 1966), p. 100.

"Paris is getting colossal": *CORR.,* vol. 3, p. 653 (June 12, 1867).

418. "A writer for the official bulletin": Burchell, *Imperial Masquerade,* p. 128.

"'The political horizon'": *CORR.,* vol. 3, p. 629 (April 8, 1867).

"The heart of this garden": Burchell, *Imperial Masquerade,* p. 126.

419. "I find nothing more *painful*": *CORR.,* vol. 3, p. 431 (April 12, 1865).

"That way, my poor old dear": autograph in the Collection Lovenjoul, Bibliothèque de l'Institut, H1366bis.

XIX. *L'Éducation sentimentale*

420. "I back and fill": *CORR.,* vol. 3, p. 230 (July 12, 1862).

421. "I don't have 'Grace,'": ibid., p. 319 (April 15, 1863).

"Here I am, hitched": ibid., p. 409 (October 6, 1864).

"Modern life": ibid., p. 416 (late November 1864).

"Though I mean to portray": ibid., p. 518 (August 20, 1866).

"Can you tell me": ibid., p. 498 (May 14, 1866).

422. "As for [me, I continue]": ibid., p. 400 (July 19, 1864).

"Don't you think": ibid., p. 537 (September 29, 1866).

"You, . . . you don't know": ibid., p. 566 (November 27, 1866).

423. "You're coy": ibid., p. 539 (October 1, 1866).

"Be stout-hearted": ibid., p. 555 (November 13–14, 1866).

"Do you doubt": ibid., p. 537 (September 29, 1866).

"He reads me": *Correspondance* (Flaubert, George Sand), p. 181.

424. "People arrived": Flaubert, *L'Éducation sentimentale,* ed. Wetherill, p. 3.
"With a good billiard table": ibid., p. 4.
"He mused": ibid.

425. "Her whole person": ibid., p. 6.
"The more he regarded her": ibid., p. 9.
"On the quay": ibid., p. 10.
"Little by little": ibid.
"A woman standing": Flaubert, *Voyage en Egypte,* p. 280.

426. "Incapable of action": Flaubert, *L'Éducation sentimentale,* ed. Wetherill, p. 69.

427. "The summer heat": ibid., p. 428.
"That's when we had it best!": ibid.
"He moved in society": ibid., p. 420.

428. "[Moses'] dying vision": *The Diaries of Franz Kafka: 1914–1923,* edited by Max Brod (New York: Schocken Books, 1976), pp. 195–96.
"A solution!": *CORR.,* vol. 2, p. 751 (June 6, 1857).
"[Frédéric] visited": Flaubert, *L'Éducation sentimentale,* ed. Wetherill, p. 304.

429. "He carried his head": Coppée, *Souvenirs d'un parisien,* pp. 111–13.
"Attached is my contract": *CORR.,* vol. 4, p. 44 (May 13, 1869).

430. "I saw Lévy today": ibid., p. 45 (May 18, 1869).

431. "compendium of descriptions": Lerclerc, *Gustave Flaubert,* p. 112.
"heroic bourgeois": ibid.
"elements of generosity": ibid.

432. "You are excessively naive": *CORR.,* vol. 4, p. 139 (December 10–11, 1869).
"Don't trouble yourself": ibid., p. 141 (December 14, 1869).
"When I hear the critical fraternity": "Livres d'aujourd'hui et de demain," in Zola, *Oeuvres complètes,* vol. 10, p. 918.
"I would venture to say": ibid., p. 919.

433. "They are profound and powerful": *CORR.,* vol. 4, p. 1119.
"falsity of perspective": CHH, vol. 16, p. 258 (October 8, 1879).
"progression of effect": ibid., p. 160 (February–March, 1879).

434. "I don't believe": ibid., p. 258 (October 29, 1870).
"Another one gone!": *CORR.,* vol. 4, p. 111 (October 1869).
"Minute by minute": Goncourt and Goncourt, *Journal,* vol. 2, p. 554 (April 8, 1870).

435. "Mother, Mother": ibid., p. 566 (June 18, 1870).
"Weird things are happening": Bouilhet, *Lettres à Gustave Flaubert,* p. 699.
"I'm dyspeptic": ibid., p. 707.
"My poor Bouilhet": *CORR.,* vol. 4, p. 60 (June 24, 1869).

436. "I was alone": ibid., p. 72 (July 23, 1869).
"I no longer have": Flaubert, *Vie et travaux du R. P. Cruchard,* p. 84.
"Would you believe": *CORR.,* vol. 4, p. 73.
"Poor old Monsignor": Flaubert, *Vie et travaux du R. P. Cruchard,* p. 86.

437. "Being born Norman": Goncourt and Goncourt, *Journal,* vol. 2, p. 533 (July 17, 1869).
"The great sorrow": *CORR.,* vol. 4, p. 185 (April 30, 1870).

438. "I was already so used": Michel de Montaigne, *The Complete Essays* (London: Penguin Books, 1991), p. 217.
"There are no riots": Corley, *Democratic Despot,* p. 296.

439. "much altered": ibid., p. 318.
"the general organization": Garrigues, *La France,* p. 174.
"The Prince Imperial, then a boy": Oman, *Things I Have Seen,* pp. 11–12.

440. "In France there seemed to be": ibid., p. 8.

441. "The administration should assemble": CHH, vol. 13, p. 234.
"It's the desire to fight": *CORR.,* vol. 4, p. 211 (July 22, 1870).
"I want peace": Corley, *Democratic Despot,* p. 313.

"if one cared for the honor of France": Garrigues, *La France,* p. 175.

"down to the last gaiter button": Corley, *Democratic Despot,* p. 333.

442. "man is a wolf": *CORR.,* vol. 4, p. 211 (July 22, 1870).

XX. War Years

444. "No, my dear, good-hearted": *CORR.,* vol. 4, p. 167 (March 3, 1870).

"He understood my thought": ibid., p. 153 (January 12, 1870).

"I won't have it": ibid., p. 173 (March 17, 1870).

"Here I encounter his ghost": ibid., p. 197 (June 26, 1870).

445. "My life has been completely upset": ibid., p. 201 (July 1, 1870).

"Can you imagine": ibid., p. 183 (April 29, 1870).

"What do you expect?": ibid., p. 186 (May 1, 1870).

"Am I then as ancient": quoted in Béatrice Philippe, *Etre juif dans la société française* (Paris: Editions Montalba, 1979), pp. 205–6.

446. "I won't even answer him": *CORR.,* vol. 4, p. 188 (May 4, 1870).

"Oh! How I would love to stop": ibid., p. 202 (July 2, 1870).

"Whatever the road": Howard, *Franco-Prussian War,* p. 78.

447. "much aged, much weakened": ibid., p. 133.

"Have you considered all the consequences": ibid.

"No news of the army!": *CORR.,* vol. 4, p. 220 (August 9, 1870).

"If Paris is besieged": ibid., p. 222 (August 17, 1870).

448. "Should you abandon Bazaine": Howard, *Franco-Prussian War,* p. 196.

"A prisoner who escaped": autograph to be published in a supplement to the Pléiade edition of Flaubert's correspondence.

449. "What reassures me": *CORR.,* vol. 4, p. 230 (September 7, 1870).

450. "One must accustom oneself": ibid., p. 231.

"Just now . . . I gave 'my men'": ibid., p. 240 (September 27, 1870).

451. "We have no authority": ibid., p. 253 (October 24, 1870).

"Parisians will collectively": ibid., p. 251 (October 23, 1870).

"What a sad sheik": ibid., p. 245 (October 5, 1870).

452. "What a night": ibid., p. 265 (December 18, 1870).

"Time not spent": ibid., p. 266.

454. "What rage! What desolation!": ibid., pp. 271–72 (January 23, 1871).

"In place of the reactionary": Howard, *Franco-Prussian War,* p. 444.

"France is so low": *CORR.,* vol. 4, p. 275 (February 1, 1871).

"I spent all my time": *Correspondance d'Émile Zola,* vol. 2, p. 278.

455. "The streets swarmed with officers": Olivier Got, "Bordeaux vu par Zola 1870–71," *Revue Historique de Bordeaux et du Département de la Gironde* 22 (1973): 110.

"Today a tragic session": Hugo, *Carnets intimes,* p. 108.

456. "What barbarism!": *CORR.,* vol. 4, p. 288 (March 11, 1871).

"Very bravely": Meaux, *Souvenirs politiques,* p. 46.

457. "At one end of the square": Goncourt and Goncourt, *Journal,* vol. 2, p. 739 (February 27, 1871).

458. "Everyone was shrieking": Edwards, *Paris Commune,* p. 142.

459. "The existing powers are basically": ibid., p. 155.

"I am voting for the reddest": ibid., p. 185.

"a revolutionary and patriotic": quoted in ibid., p. 186.

"Meeting follows meeting": Zola, "Chroniques et polémiques," in *Oeuvres complètes,* vol. 13, p. 445.

460. "The communal revolution": *La Commune de 1871,* p. 159.

"Religious or dogmatic instruction": ibid., p. 78.

461. "Always the same old refrains!": *CORR.,* vol. 4, p. 300 (March 31, 1871).

"I hate democracy": ibid., p. 314 (April 30, 1871).

462. "[I saw] a thin column": Paul Verlaine, *Oeuvres en prose complètes* (Paris: Gallimard [Pléiade], 1972), p. 547.

463. "The massacres that were to grow": Edwards, *Paris Commune,* p. 322.

"Never will I forget": quoted in Henri Mitterand, *Zola Journaliste* (Paris: Armand Colin, 1962), p. 147.

"With warm days upon us": *Le Sémaphore de Marseille,* June 3, 1871.

464. "What will be the backlash": *CORR.,* vol. 4, p. 335 (June 14, 1871).

"The spectacle nauseated me!": ibid., p. 330 (August 11, 1871; corrected date).

"Then comes the number": Flaubert, *La Tentation,* ed. Gothot-Mersch, p. 58.

XXI. Orphanhood

465. "It sounds cynical": *CORR.,* vol. 4, p. 309 (April 24, 1871).

466. "This extravagant opus": ibid., p. 318 (May 3, 1871).

"The odor of corpses": ibid., p. 331 (June 10, 1871).

467. "This affair, which may be trivial": CHH, vol. 12, pp. 60–61.

468. "I can still see him": quoted in *L'Art du Théâtre* 12 (December 1901).

"Move around, shake yourself": *CORR.,* vol. 4, p. 473 (January 28, 1872).

469. "Journalism weighs upon me": Zola, *Correspondance,* vol. 2, p. 312.

"My mother just died!": CORR., vol. 4, p. 508 (April 6, 1872).

"one of those high summits": Flaubert, *Lettres à Flaubert,* vol. 2, p. 97.

470. "I am with you all day": *CORR.,* vol. 4, p. 509 (April 9, 1872).

"I've just had a difficult week": ibid., p. 510 (revised date, April 19, 1872).

471. "I am reasonable. I force myself": ibid., p. 525 (May 15, 1872).

"ma vieille Amie": ibid., p. 585 (October 5, 1872).

"I opened myself": Franklin Grout, *Heures d'autrefois,* p. 75.

"Tall, slender": ibid., p. 77.

472. "It was at my uncle's side": ibid., p. 76.

473. "I think that a week from now": *CORR.,* vol. 4, p. 573 (September 14, 1873).

"I don't believe that I'm an egotistical monster": ibid., p. 599 (October 28, 1872).

"But chance and circumstances": ibid., p. 611 (November 25, 1872).

474. "Yes . . . the internal image": ibid., vol. 3, p. 562 (November 20, 1866).

475. "It is in Thebaid": Flaubert, *La Tentation,* ed. Gothot-Mersch, p. 51.

476. "And suddenly in the air": ibid., p. 64.

"The horizon perceived by human": *CORR.,* vol. 2, p. 719 (May 18, 1857).

477. "Behold the sun!": Flaubert, *La Tentation,* ed. Gothot-Mersch, p. 211–14.

"I feel the desire": ibid., p. 177.

"Bliss! Sheer bliss!": ibid., p. 237.

478. "He went back on his word": *CORR.,* vol. 4, p. 504 (March 31, 1872).

"not to make the presses groan": ibid.

479. "I treat them impudently": ibid., p. 646 (January 22, 1873).

"How is it I even think": ibid., p. 521 (April 29, 1872).

"I've begun not to think": ibid., p. 650 (March 12, 1873).

480. "He entered with an uncharacteristically": Dreyfous, *Ce qu'il me reste,* pp. 272–73.

481. "between the hero of the book": *CORR.,* vol. 4, p. 1368.

"I want to seize a moment": ibid.

"What astonishes me": ibid., p. 794 (May 1, 1874).

"I value": ibid., p. 829 (July 10, 1874).

"Be valiant": ibid., p. 790 (April 10, 1874).

"I was already deeply moved": Ernest Jones, *The Life and Works of Sigmund Freud,* vol. 1 (New York: Basic Books, 1963), p. 175.

XXII. "We are all of us émigrés, left over from another age."

483. "If we scrounged around": *CORR.,* vol. 4, p. 647 (February 22, 1873).

"inconvenience caused by his melancholy": ibid., p. 641 (February 3, 1873).

"Anyway, with *whom* can I associate?": ibid., p. 642.

"What a man!": ibid.

484. "She herself, in inventiveness": Schapiro, *Turgenev,* p. 16.

485. "Russia can wait": Turgenev, *Ivan Tourguéniev,* p. 21.

486. "She is ugly": Schapiro, *Turgenev,* p. 42.

487. "Love, whether happy": ibid., p. 75.

"My health is good": ibid., p. 164.

488. "dance on the roof": ibid., p. 129.

"There is no necessity": ibid., p. 205.

"He who has faith": ibid., p. 146.

489. "During the operation": Goncourt, *Journal,* vol. 3, p. 252 (April 25, 1883).

"Oh, we have hard times": *CORR.,* vol. 4, p. 320 (May 6, 1871).

"personal inclinations": *CORR.,* vol. 2, p. 691 (March 1857).

"From the first I have felt": ibid., vol. 3, p. 753 (May 26, 1868).

490. "When I wrote to you": ibid., vol. 4, p. 417 (November 27, 1871).

"It must be sent off": ibid., p. 418 (November 28, 1871).

"Well then! Here we are": ibid., p. 623 (December 11, 1872).

"So you won't see me": ibid., p. 625 (December 12, 1872).

491. "Don't tarry too long": ibid., p. 163 (February 20, 1870).

"*Antoine* is decidedly": ibid., p. 815 (June 5, 1874).

"The more I think about it": ibid., p. 833 (July 12, 1874).

492. "I believe I could make": ibid., p. 693 (August 2, 1873).

"He claimed that it was": "Les Romanciers naturalistes," in Zola, *Oeuvres complètes,* vol. 11, pp. 129–31.

493. "Flaubert wanted Rouen duck": Alphonse Daudet, *Trente ans de Paris,* pp. 335–36.

"Once I witnessed": "Les Romanciers naturalistes," in Zola, *Oeuvres complètes,* vol. 11, p. 150.

494. "I did not recognize": M. M. Kovalevsky, "Vospominaniia ob I. S. Turgeneve," in *Turgenev v vospominanie,* vol. 2, pp.139–154. (Moscow, 1969), p. 150.

"I was summoned back to Russia": Goncourt and Goncourt, *Journal,* vol. 2, pp. 1134–35 (May 5, 1876).

"Zola tells us": ibid., p. 1059 (April 4, 1875).

495. "I saw my heart placed": ibid., pp. 1133–34 (May 5, 1876).

"However (there is always a however)": *CORR.,* vol. 4, p. 752 (December 11, 1873).

496. "Into *Le Candidat* you put more powerful": Zola, *Correspondance,* vol. 2, p. 352.

"false and common": quoted in CHH, vol. 7, p. 34.

"M. G. Flaubert does not know": ibid.

"We have read *Le Candidat* and we are about": *CORR.,* vol. 4, pp. 784–85 (April 3, 1874).

497. "All the talk": ibid., p. 788 (April 8, 1874).

"dog of a book": ibid., p. 978 (October 11, 1875).

"At last I've finished": ibid., p. 920 (April 15?, 1875).

498. "I am at once": ibid., p. 917 (March 27, 1875).

"What toilettes [these ladies have]!": ibid., p. 836 (July 14, 1874).

"I wouldn't trade": ibid., p. 824 (July 3, 1874).

"I am exasperated with the Right": ibid., p. 632 (January 4, 1873).

499. "Haven't we seen": quoted in Rémond, *La Vie politique,* vol. 2, p. 309.

"[That flag] has always been for me": quoted in Brogan, *France under the Republic,* p. 83.

500. "How ignorant of history": *CORR.,* vol. 4, p. 732 (November 4, 1873).

"Of all the mysteries": quoted in Dansette, *Histoire religieuse,* p. 322.

501. "Suspended in midair": ibid., p. 349.

"I must tell France the truth": ibid., p. 342.

502. "Until the country's definitive institutions": quoted in Rémond, *La Vie politique,* p. 306.

503. "[This] is the government of the country": quoted in Chapman, *Third Republic of France*, p. 37.
"Society is dying of universal suffrage": Goncourt and Goncourt, *Journal*, vol. 2, pp. 827–28 (July 11, 1871).
"new barbarians [who] threaten": Mayeur, *Les Débuts*, p. 26.
"Barodetan foolishness": *CORR.*, vol. 2, p. 657 (April 24, 1873).
"With God's help": quoted in Mayeur, *Les Débuts*, p. 27.
504. "Should your husband right his boat": *CORR.*, vol. 4, p. 926 (May 10, 1875).
"It is sweet of you": ibid., pp. 931–32 (July 9, 1875).
505. "How much longer": ibid., p. 934 (July 12, 1875).
"Even if there is a favorable outcome": ibid., p. 946 (August 18, 1875).
506. "From now on I'll no longer be": ibid., p. 965 (October 2, 1875).
"I believe that I shall never be able": ibid., pp. 945–46 (August 18, 1875).
"My poor good-natured father": quoted in Francis Abrière, "Les Ennuis d'Argent de Gustave Flaubert," *Mercure de France*, November 1, 1934, p. 522.
"Since there is no pressing issue": *CORR.*, vol. 4, p. 978 (October 11, 1875).
"Our income": ibid., p. 975 (October 7, 1875).
507. "How I envy G. Pouchet": ibid., p. 983 (October 17, 1875).
508. "I want to get started": ibid., p. 967 (October 2, 1875).
"I no longer believe in myself": ibid., pp. 969–70 (October 3, 1875).
"I am very happy indeed": ibid., p. 979 (October 15, 1875).
"I don't need to believe": *Correspondance* (Flaubert, George Sand), pp. 516–18.
510. "Here is what I believe": ibid., p. 521.
512. "You're quite right": Flaubert, *Oeuvres complètes* (CHH), vol. 15, p. 444 (after March 13, 1876).

XXIII. A Fruitful Intermission

513. "Physical suffering is a good lesson": *Correspondance* (Flaubert, George Sand), p. 528.
"Delicious weather": Sand, *Agendas*, vol. 5, p. 354.
514. "The throng of peasant women": Cate, *George Sand*, p. 731.
"You want to know the truth": CHH, vol. 15, p. 455 (June 17, 1876).
"The death of poor mother Sand": ibid., p. 460 (June 25, 1876).
515. "To tell the truth": ibid., p. 457 (June 19, 1876).
"I feel *astonishingly good!*": ibid., p. 460 (June 25, 1876).
516. "'L'Histoire d'un coeur simple'": ibid., p. 457 (June 19, 1876).
517. "The factory guild, the cantors": ibid., vol. 4, p. 225.
519. "Stasiulevich writes to me": *Correspondance* (Flaubert, Tourguéniev), p. 202.
"bourgeois virtue": quoted in Flaubert, *Les Trois Contes*, ed. de Biasi, p. 45.
520. "The crude and relentless obscenity": quoted in Zola, *Les Rougon-Macquart*, vol. 2, p. 1561.
"Your first story": Flaubert, *Lettres à Flaubert*, vol. 2, p. 279.
"What a feast": ibid., p. 280.
"Yes, my dear friend": ibid., p. 281.
"The return of Henri V": Renan, *Correspondance* (Renan, Berthelot), pp. 435–36.
521. "inaugurate a salutary regime": quoted in Mayeur, *Les Débuts*, p. 30.
"Our rulers can't bring themselves": *CORR.*, vol. 3, p. 733 (November 12, 1873).
"His power will continue": Rémond, *La Vie politique*, vol. 2, p. 308.
522. "All interest was concentrated": Brogan, *France under the Republic*, p. 109.
"Fear! That is their great political tool": quoted in Rémond, *La Vie politique*, pp. 311–12.
524. "Clericalism! There is the enemy!": Rémond, *L'Anticléricalisme*, p. 185.
"radical modifications": quoted in Rémond, *La Vie politique*, p. 354.
525. "The chamber, which deems it important": ibid., p. 353.
"Paris is insufferable": Zola, *Correspondance*, vol. 3, pp. 112–13.
"That idiot Mac-Mahon": CHH, vol. 15, p. 567 (May 30, 1877).

"In my retreat": ibid., p. 577 (June 30, 1877).

"Two things sustain me": ibid., p. 591 (August 23, 1877).

526. "For me . . . the idolatry": Goncourt and Goncourt, *Journal,* vol. 2, p. 1199 (September 3, 1877).

"This truly *national* demonstration": CHH, vol. 15, p. 602 (September 17, 1877).

"If I could, I would condemn": ibid., p. 603 (September 17, 1877).

"Merde": ibid., p. 614 (October 1877).

"It's the kind of anecdote": CHH, vol. 15, p. 511 (December 14, 1876).

527. "We must, in our national interest": quoted in Rémond, *La Vie politique,* p. 358.

"It's a matter": CHH, vol. 15, p. 350 (April 30, 1877).

529. "In some considerable degree": Dreyfous, *Ce qu'il me reste,* p. 177.

"[My father] had come to know": Jean Renoir, *Renoir, My Father* (Boston: Little, Brown, 1962), pp. 140–41.

530. "In due course, [Flaubert]": Maupassant, *Pour Gustave Flaubert,* pp. 105–6.

"What was discussed": Leon Edel, *Henry James: The Conquest of London, 1870–1881* (New York: Avon, 1978), p. 221.

531. "Flaubert was huge": James, *Notes on Novelists,* p. 72.

"[From my manuscript]": Goncourt and Goncourt, *Journal,* vol. 2, pp. 1160–61 (December 17, 1876).

"Like you, I've read": CHH, vol. 15, p. 510 (December 14, 1876).

"My niece's revulsion": ibid., p. 540 (February 1877).

532. "Zola's *L'Assommoir* is a huge success!": ibid., p. 544 (March 3, 1877).

"In these long, unsavory pages": ibid., p. 551 (April 2, 1877, to Edma Roger des Genettes).

"I walked up the rue de Bihorel": Maupassant, *Chroniques,* pp. 142ff.

533. "I thank you for helping": Flaubert, *Lettres à Flaubert,* vol. 2, p. 72.

"I can't tell you": ibid., p. 133 (February 19, 1873).

"Despite the difference": *CORR.,* vol. 4, p. 647 (February 23, 1873).

534. "Our weekly talks have become": *Correspondance* (Flaubert, Maupassant), p. 86 (June 24, 1873).

"women's asses": ibid., p. 141 (August 3, 1878).

"You lament the monotony": CHH, vol. 16, p. 71.

535. "Your letter delighted me": ibid., vol. 15, p. 473 (July 23, 1876).

"As for young Guy": ibid., vol. 16, p. 41.

XXIV. The Unraveling

537. "exhale my resentment": *CORR.,* vol. 4, p. 583 (October 5, 1872).

538. "You do well to think about": ibid., vol. 1, p. 678 (September 4, 1850).

"I'm becoming a moralist": ibid., vol. 2, p. 208 (December 17, 1852).

"deplorable utopias": ibid., vol. 1, p. 679 (September 4, 1850).

"The plan is good": ibid., vol. 3, p. 315 (April 2, 1863).

539. "A proper noun is *something*": autograph (July? 6, 1868). To be published by Gallimard in the supplement of Flaubert's correspondence.

"I'm beginning a book": *CORR.,* vol. 4, pp. 558–59 (August 19, 1872).

"I must confess that the plan": ibid., p. 561 (August 22, 1872).

"Having more ideas": Flaubert, *Bouvard et Pécuchet,* ed. de Biasi, p. 39.

"stupid plateau": *CORR.,* vol. 4, p. 816 (June 24, 1874).

540. "Could it be that arboriculture": Flaubert, *Bouvard et Pécuchet,* ed. de Biasi, p. 79.

541. "They noted . . . extraordinary examples": ibid., pp. 101–3.

"suffer for science": ibid., p. 101.

"This is a veritable murder!": ibid., p. 115.

"dieting compromises": ibid., p. 116.

"Those who revolutionized medicine": ibid.

542. "The mainsprings of life": ibid., p. 118.

"What self-assurance": *CORR.,* vol. 4, p. 774 (February 28, 1874).

"No reflection!": Flaubert, *Bouvard et Pécuchet,* ed. de Biasi, p. 456.

543. "Bouvard and Pécuchet . . . formulated": ibid., pp. 319–20.

"During the past two days": CHH, vol. 15, p. 569 (June 6, 1877).

"We rise at six": ibid., p. 604 (September 26, 1877).

544. "You know that I'm completely ruined": ibid., p. 573 (June 18, 1877).

"No one wants to travel": ibid., p. 588 (August 16, 1877).

545. "This bloody book": ibid., p. 609 (October 5, 1877).

"For me, he was a being": "Notes et souvenirs: La Maison de Flaubert," *La Vie populaire,* December 7, 1890.

546. "Don't be astonished": *Correspondance* (Flaubert, Tourguéniev), p. 216.

"After dinner, Flaubert sweeps": Goncourt and Goncourt, *Journal,* vol. 2, p. 1219.

"I can't tell you": *CORR.,* vol. 4, p. 949 (August 28, 1875).

547. "God only knows": CHH, vol. 16, p. 107 (December 10, 1878).

"His ruin is supposedly complete": Goncourt and Goncourt, *Journal,* vol. 2, p. 1275 (December 10, 1878).

548. "I can't tell you how moved": CHH, vol. 16, p. 121 (January 10, 1879).

"We can't say anything": ibid., p. 130 (January 1879).

549. "[Turgenev] swayed Flaubert": Zola, *Correspondance,* vol. 3, p. 289.

"I've put aside my foolish pride": *Correspondance* (Flaubert, Tourguéniev), p. 250.

"More than ever": ibid., p. 252 (February 8, 1879).

"Don't give it any further thought": ibid., p. 255.

"On my return": ibid., pp. 255–56.

550. "Thus . . . one of the foremost writers": CHH, vol. 16, p. 149.

"There's no undoing it": ibid., p. 148 (February 16, 1879).

551. "I, his biggest creditor": CHH, vol. 16, p. 162 (March 1, 1879).

"The offer would be presented": *Correspondance* (Flaubert, Maupassant), p. 179 (March 6, 1879).

"A pension disguised": ibid., p. 180 (March 7, 1879).

552. "If I am *sure*": ibid., p. 182 (March 9, 1879).

"I prefer it that way": CHH, vol. 16, p. 207 (May 10, 1879).

"I'll bring it up again": ibid., p. 210 (May 16, 1879).

553. "My Loulou": ibid., p. 209.

"The life I lead": ibid., p. 278 (December 3, 1879).

"Ernest has some nerve": CHH, vol. 16, p. 125 (January 18, 1879).

554. "*It is urgent*": ibid., p. 253 (September 27, 1879).

"I am astonished": ibid., p. 254 (September 28, 1879).

"without question": ibid., p. 228 (July 3, 1879).

555. "The intellectual state": ibid., p. 256 (October 8, 1879).

"Whatever feelings about me": ibid., p. 290 (December 1879).

"stupid or rather stupidifying": ibid., p. 258 (October 8, 1879).

556. "What could be crazier": ibid., p. 241 (August 21, 1879).

"When January has passed": ibid., p. 277 (December 3, 1879).

"The dinner was very good": Goncourt, *Journal,* vol. 3, pp. 68–69 (March 28, 1880).

557. "We got out, we took off our hats": "Le Romanciers naturalistes," in Zola, *Oeuvres complètes,* vol. 11, p. 122.

558. "At the city gates": ibid., pp. 124–25.

559. "Why?": Flaubert, *Inédits.*

"All he had possessed": Maupassant, *Pour Gustave Flaubert,* pp. 126–27.

"I don't do anything": *CORR.,* vol. 4, p. 3 (Jamuary 1, 1869).

Epilogue

560. "The gabled warehouse": *La Vie populaire,* December 7, 1890.

561. "I don't know what will become of me": ms., Bibliothèque de l'Institut (H1366bis).

"the end of my life": *CORR.,* vol. 4, p. 322 (May 22, 1871).

562. "Your pleasure is mine": *Correspondance* (Flaubert, Du Camp), pp. 430–31.
563. "I am no longer a sick nurse": Senneville, *Maxime Du Camp*, pp. 394–95.
   "After your family": Schapiro, *Turgenev*, p. 289.
   "It is not just that": Turgenev, *Turgenev's Letters*, p. 261.
564. "Suddenly I notice": Schapiro, *Turgenev*, p. 299.
565. "What with some of us having emotional": Goncourt, *Journal*, vol. 3, p. 156.
   "Death is a familiar thought": ibid.
   "Imagine a man who is perfectly well": Schapiro, *Turgenev*, p. 321.
566. "The religious ceremony": Goncourt, *Journal*, vol. 3, p. 273.
   "One would have thought": Schapiro, *Turgenev*, p. 331.
567. "He made this passionate confession": Franklin Grout, *Heures d'autrefois*, p. 96.
568. "Do you think that your brother": Chevalley-Sabatier, *Gustave Flaubert*, p. 194.
   "She seemed very old indeed": Cather, "A Chance Meeting," in *Willa Cather*, p. 815.

Selected Bibliography

A full bibliography of the biographical literature up to 1988 is available in D. J. Colwell's *Bibliographie des études sur G. Flaubert.* 4 vols. Egham, UK: Runnymede Books, 1988–1990.

Flaubert's Works

Editions and Correspondence

Bibliothèque de Flaubert: Inventaires et critiques. Edited by Yvan Leclerc. Rouen, France: Publications de l'Université de Rouen, 2001.

Carnets de travail. Edited by Pierre-Marc de Biasi. Paris: Balland, 1988.

Correspondance. Edited by Jean Bruneau. 4 vols. Paris: Gallimard (Pléiade), 1973–97. Vol. 5, in ms., edited by Yvan Leclerc.

Correspondance (Flaubert, George Sand). Edited by Alphonse Jacobs. Paris: Flammarion, 1992.

Correspondance (Flaubert, Goncourt). Edited by Pierre-Jean Dufief. Paris: Flammarion, 1998.

Correspondance (Flaubert, Maupassant). Edited by Yvan Leclerc. Paris: Flammarion, 1993.

Correspondance (Flaubert, Tourguéniev). Edited by Alexandre Zviguilsky. Paris: Flammarion, 1989.

Correspondances (Flaubert, Le Poittevin, Du Camp). Edited by Yvan Leclerc. Paris: Flammarion, 2000.

Les lettres d'Egypte de Gustave Flaubert. Edited by Antoine Youssef Naaman. Paris: Nizet, 1965.

Lettres à Flaubert. Edited by Rosa M. Palermo di Stefano. 2 vols. Naples: Edizioni Scientifiche Italiane, 1997–98.

Lettres inédites de Flaubert à son éditeur Michel Lévy. Edited by Jacques Suffel. Paris: Calmann Lévy, 1965.

Oeuvres complètes. Edited by Jean Bruneau. Paris: Seuil (l'Intégrale), 1964.

Oeuvres complètes. Edited by Maurice Bardèche. Club de l'Honnête Homme, 1971–75.

Oeuvres de jeunesse. Edited by Claudine Gothot-Mersch. Paris: Gallimard (Pléiade), 2001.

Individual Works

Bouvard et Pécuchet. Eds.: P.-M. de Biasi (Livre de Poche); S. Dord-Crouslé (Garnier-Flammarion); C. Gothot-Mersch (Gallimard, "Folio").

Carnet de voyage à Carthage. Edited by C. M. Delavoye. Rouen, France: Publications de l'Université de Rouen, 1999.

Vie et travaux du R. P. Cruchard et autres inédits. Edited by Matthieu Desportes and Yvan Leclerc. Rouen: Publications des Universités de Rouen et du Havre (PURH), 2005.

La première "Éducation sentimentale." Edited by F.-R. Bastide. Paris: Seuil, 1993.

La Tentation de Saint Antoine. Eds.: C. Gothot-Mersch (Gallimard, "Folio"); J. Suffel (Garnier-Flammarion).

L'Éducation sentimentale. Eds.: P.-M. de Biasi (Livre de Poche); S. Dord-Crouslé (Garnier-Flammarion); P. M. Wetherill (Classiques Garnier).

L'Éducation sentimentale: Les Scénarios. Edited by T. Williams. Paris: Corti, 1992.

Les Mémoires d'un fou, Novembre, Pyrénées-Corse, Voyage en Italie. Edited by Claudine Gothot-Mersch. Paris: Gallimard (Folio), 2001.

Les Trois Contes. Eds.: P.-M. de Biasi (Livre de Poche); S. de Sacy (Gallimard, "Folio"); P. M. Wetherill (Classiques Garnier).

Madame Bovary. Eds.: P.-M. de Biasi (Imprimerie Nationale); C. Gothot-Mersch (Classiques Garnier); J. Neefs (Livre de Poche).

Mémoires d'un fou, Novembre, et autres textes de jeunesse. Edited by Yvan Leclerc. Paris: Garnier-Flammarion, 1991.

Par les champs et par les grèves (with Maxime Du Camp). Edited by Adrianne Tooke. Geneva: Droz, 1987.

Salammbô. Edited by E. Maynial (Classiques Garnier); J. Suffel (Garnier Flammarion); H. Thomas Gallimard (Folio).

Voyage en Egypte. Edited by Pierre-Marc de Biasi. Paris: Grasset, 1991.

Other Resources

Nineteenth-century newspapers consulted include *Le Journal de Rouen, Le Nouvelliste de Rouen,* and *Le Figaro.*

The Bibliothèque de l'Institut possesses an important collection of Flaubert family letters (H1366bis) and unpublished correspondence of Maxime Du Camp in the Lovenjoul Collection. The Musée Calvet in Avignon possesses the manuscript diary of Louise Colet. Fonds Colet, cote 6416.

The *Bulletin de la Société des Amis de Flaubert* and its successor, the *Bulletin Flaubert-Maupassant,* contain numerous articles of biographical interest. They are not listed individually; those from which I quote are cited in the notes.

The Heineman Collection of the Piermont Morgan Library includes Flaubert's notes on ancient history, the Bible, Manicheanism, Greek grammar, Greek mythology, *The Iliad,* and so forth (MS89).

Important sources are the Flaubert dossiers, 92N series, at Rouen's Bibliothèque Municipale (which possesses the manuscript of *Madame Bovary*) and notarial records (wills and marriage contracts recorded by two firms, Boulen and Bidault) at the Archives départementales de la Seine-Maritime. The Archives also has a dossier (2 OP/516/17) containing detailed information about the German occupation of Canteleu and Croisset in 1870. The archive of the Lycée Corneille and dossier F11/20864 at the Archives Nationales contain documents bearing upon the Collège royal.

Ackerknecht, Erwin. *Medicine at the Paris Hospital, 1794–1848.* Baltimore: Johns Hopkins University Press, 1967.

Adam, Juliette. *Nos idées avant 1870.* Paris: Lemerre, 1905.

Agulhon, Maurice. *1848, ou L'apprentissage de la République: 1848–1852.* Paris: Seuil, 1973.

————. *Les Quarante-huitards.* Paris: Gallimard (Folio), 1992.

Albalat, Antoine. *Gustave Flaubert et ses amis.* Paris: Plon, 1927.

Almanach de Rouen. Rouen: Nicétas Periaux, 1832–.

Arnaud, René. *Le 2 Décembre.* Paris: Hachette, 1967.

Aron, Jean-Paul. *Le Mangeur du dix-neuvième siècle.* Paris: Laffont, 1973.

Arrigon, L. J., ed. *Cent ans de vie française à la "Revue des Deux Mondes."* Paris: Hachette, 1929.

Asselain, Jean-Charles. *Histoire économique de la France: De l'ancien régime à la Première Guerre Mondiale.* Paris: Seuil, 1984.

Auerbach, Erich. *Mimesis.* Princeton, N.J.: Princeton University Press, 1968.

Auriant, C. *Koutchouk-Hanem: L'Almée de Flaubert.* Paris: Mercure de France, 1943.

Bailbé, Joseph-Marc, and Jean Pierrot, eds. *Flaubert et Maupassant: Écrivains normands.* Paris: Presses Universitaires de France, 1981.

Baldick, Robert. *Dinner at Magny's.* London: Gollancz, 1971.

————. *The Life and Times of Frédérick Lemaître*. London: Hamish Hamilton, 1959.

Balzac, Nodier, et al. *Les Français peints par eux-mêmes: Encyclopédie morale du dix-neuvième siècle*. Paris: L. Curmer, 1840.

Bardèche, Maurice. *Flaubert*. Paris: La Table Ronde, 1988.

Barnes, Julian. *Flaubert's Parrot*. New York: Vintage Books, 1990.

Bart, Benjamin. *Flaubert*. Syracuse, N.Y.: Syracuse University Press, 1967.

Baudelaire, Charles. *Oeuvres*. Paris: Gallimard (Pléiade), 1951.

Bellanger, Godechot, et al. *Histoire générale de la presse française*. Vol. 2, 1815–1871. Paris: Presses Universitaires de France, 1969.

Bem, Jeanne. *Clefs pour "L'Éducation sentimentale."* Paris: J.-M. Place, 1981.

————. *Désir et savoir dans l'oeuvre de Flaubert*. Neuchâtel: À la Baconnière, 1979.

Bénichou, Paul. *Le Sacre de l'écrivain*. Paris: Gallimard, 1996.

Berchet, Jean-Claude. *Le Voyage en Orient*. Paris: Laffont, 1997.

Bergerat, Émile. *Les Années de bohème*. Vol. 1 of *Souvenirs d'un enfant de Paris*. Paris: Fasquelle, 1911.

Bertier de Sauvigny, G. de. *La France et les français vus par les voyageurs américains, 1814–1848*. Paris: Flammarion, 1982.

————. *La Restauration*. Paris: Flammarion, 1955.

Biasi, Pierre-Marc de. *Flaubert: Les Secrets de l'homme-plume*. Paris: Hachette, 1995.

Billy, André. *The Goncourt Brothers*. London: André Deutsch, 1960.

————. *La Présidente et ses amis*. Paris: Flammarion, 1945.

Blumer, Dietrich, ed. *Psychiatric Aspects of Epilepsy*. Washington, D.C.: American Psychiatric Press, 1984.

Bonaccorso, Giovanni. "Encore du nouveau sur Flaubert." *Stanford French Review*, 3 (Winter 1978).

Bonaparte, Louis Napoleon. *Des idées napoléoniennes*. Paris: Plon, 1860.

Borie, Jean. *Frédéric et les amis des hommes*. Paris: Grasset, 1995.

Borsa, S., and C. R. Michel. *La Vie quotidienne dans les hôpitaux en France au XIXe siècle*. Paris: Hachette, 1985.

Bouilhet, Louis. *Lettres à Gustave Flaubert*. Edited by Maria Luisa Cappello. Paris: CNRS Éditions, 1996.

————. *Lettres à Louise Colet*. Edited by Marie-Claire Bancquart. Rouen: Publications de l'Université de Rouen, 1973.

————. *Oeuvres de Louis Bouilhet*. Paris: Lemerre, 1891.

Bouquet, François-Valentin. *Souvenirs du Collège de Rouen par un élève de pension (1829–1835)*. Rouen: Cagniard, 1895.

Brogan, D. W. *France under the Republic, 1870–1939*. New York: Harper and Brothers, 1940.

Brombert, Victor. *Flaubert par lui-même*. Paris: Seuil, 1971.

————. *The Hidden Reader*. Cambridge: Harvard University Press, 1988.

————. *The Novels of Flaubert*. Princeton: Princeton University Press, 1966.

————. "Usure et rupture chez Flaubert: L'exemple de *Novembre*." *Contrepoint*, no. 28 (1979).

Brown, Frederick. *Zola: A Life*. New York: Farrar, Strauss and Giroux, 1994.

Bruneau, Jean. *Les Débuts littéraires de Gustave Flaubert, 1831–1845*. Paris: Armand Colin, 1962.

Bruneau, Jean, with Jean Ducourneau. *Album Flaubert*. Paris: Gallimard, 1972.

Burchell, S. C. *Imperial Masquerade: The Paris of Napoleon III*. New York: Atheneum, 1971.

Butor, Michel. *Improvisations sur Flaubert*. Paris: Éditions de la Différence, 1984.

Caron, Jean-Claude. *Générations romantiques: Les étudiants de Paris et le Quartier Latin, 1814–1851*. Paris: Armand Colin, 1991.

Cassagne, Albert. *La Théorie de l'art pour l'art*. Seyssel, France: Champ Vallon, 1997.

Cate, Curtis. *George Sand: A Biography*. Boston: Houghton Mifflin, 1975.

Cather, Willa. "A Chance Meeting." In *Willa Cather: Stories, Poems, and Other Writings*. New York: Library of America, 1992.

Chaline, Jean-Pierre. *Deux bourgeois en leur temps: Documents sur la société rouennaise du XIXe siècle.* Rouen: Société de l'histoire de Normandie, 1977.

——. *Les Bourgeois de Rouen.* Paris: Presses de la Fondation nationale des sciences politiques, 1982.

——. "Les contrats de mariage à Rouen." *Revue d'Histoire Économique et Sociale.*

——. *Rouen sous la monarchie de Juillet.* Rouen: Centre régional de documentation, 1971.

Chapman, Guy. *The Third Republic of France.* London: MacMillan, 1962.

Charle, Christophe. *Les Intellectuels en Europe au XIXe siècle.* Paris: Seuil, 1996.

Chartier, Roger, and Martin, Henri-Jean. Editors. *Histoire de l'édition française.* Vol. 3, Paris: Fayard, 1990.

Chateaubriand, Francois-René. *Itinéraire de Paris à Jérusalem.* Paris: Éditions Julliard, 1964.

Chennebenoist, Jean and Michel Davy. *Trouville depuis les origines connues jusqu'à 1830.* Tourgéville, France: 1986.

Chevalley-Sabatier, Lucie. *Gustave Flaubert et sa nièce Caroline.* Paris: La pensée universelle, 1971.

Chevron, J. "A propos des ancêtres champenois de Gustave Flaubert au XVIIIe siècle." *La Revue Historique de la Révolution Française* (October–December 1923).

Claudin, Gustave. *Mes souvenirs: Les boulevards de 1840–1870.* Paris: Calmann Lévy, 1884.

Colet, Louise. *Autour de Louise Colet.* Lyon: Presses Universitaires de Lyon, 1982.

——. *Lettres à Louise Colet.* Edited by Marie-Claire Bancquart. Rouen: Publications de l'Université de Rouen.

—— *Lettres inédites de Louise Colet à Honoré Clair.* Clermont-Ferrand: Presses Universitaires Blaise Pascal, 1999.

——. *Lui.* Paris: Michel Lévy, 1864.

——. Manuscript diary in the Avignon Municipal Library (Fr. Nouv. Acq. 23838). Published as appendix 2 in vol. 2 of Flaubert's *Correspondance,* edited by Jean Bruneau.

——. *Une histoire de soldats.* Paris: A. Cadot, 1856.

La Commune de 1871: Le Journal officiel avec ses décrets, affiches, et proclamations. Paris: Éditions de Delphes, 1965.

Coppée, François. *Souvenirs d'un parisien.* Paris: Lemerre, 1910.

Corbin, Alain. *Les Filles de noce.* Paris: Flammarion, 1982.

Corley, T. A. B. *Democratic Despot: A Life of Napoleon III.* New York: Clarkson Potter, 1961.

Creuzet, Marcel. *Duranty.* Paris: Nizet, 1964.

Custine, Astolphe de. *Souvenirs et portraits.* Monaco: Rocher, 1956.

Dansette, Adrien. *L'Histoire religieuse de la France contemporaine.* Paris: Flammarion, 1965.

Daudet, Alphonse. *Trente ans de Paris.* Paris: Marpon-Flammarion, 1888.

Daudet, Ernest. *Souvenirs de mon temps: Début d'un homme de lettres 1857–1861.* Paris: Plon-Nourrit, 1921.

——, ed. *Vingt-cinq ans à Paris (1826–1850): Journal du Comte Rodolphe Apponyi.* Paris: Plon, 1913.

Daumard, Adeline. *La Bourgeoisie parisienne de 1815 à 1848.* Paris: École Pratique des Hautes Études, 1963.

——. *Les Bourgeois et la bourgeoisie en France.* Paris: Aubier, 1987.

Debray Genette, Raymonde, ed. *Flaubert à l'oeuvre.* Paris: Flammarion, 1980.

——. *Métamorphoses du récit: Autour de Flaubert.* Paris: Seuil, 1988.

Deloume, Léon. *Dupuytren.* Limoges: 1935.

Demidoff, Alexandre Tissot. "Bonaparte and Demidoff: A Tale of Two Family Dynasties." *European Royal History Journal,* 32 (April 2003).

Des Cars, Jean. *La Princesse Mathilde.* Paris: Librairie Académique Perrin, 1988.

Descharmes, René. *Flaubert: Sa vie, son caractère, ses idées avant 1857.* Geneva: Slatkine, 1969.

——. *Alfred Le Poittevin.* Paris: Librairie des Amateurs, 1909.

Descôtes, Maurice. *Le Public de théâtre et son histoire.* Paris: PUF, 1964.

Désert, Gabriel. *La Vie quotidienne sur les plages normandes du Second Empire.* Paris: Hachette, 1983.

Didier, Franklin. *Letters from Paris.* New York: Seaman, 1821.

Didon, R. P. *Lettres à Madame Caroline Commanville.* Paris: Plon, 1930.

Douchin, Jacques-Louis. *La Vie érotique de Flaubert.* Paris: J. J. Pauvert, 1984.

Dreyfous, Maurice. *Ce qu'il me reste à dire: Un demi-siècle de choses vues et entendues, 1848–1900.* Paris: Ollendorff, 1912.

Dubosc, Georges. *Trois Normands.* Rouen: Henri Defontaine, 1917.

Dubuc, André, ed. *Les Rouennais et la famille Flaubert.* Rouen: Édition des amis de Flaubert, 1980.

Du Camp, Maxime. *Le Nil: Un Voyageur en Egypte vers 1850.* Paris: Sand/Conti, 1987.

———. *Souvenirs de l'année 1848.* Paris: Ressources, 1979.

———. *Souvenirs d'un demi-siècle.* Paris: Hachette, 1949.

———. *Souvenirs littéraires.* Paris: Aubier, 1994.

Dumesnil, René. *Flaubert: Son hérédité, son milieu, sa méthode.* Geneva: Slatkine, 1969.

———. *Gustave Flaubert: L'Homme et l'oeuvre.* Paris: Desclée de Brouwer, 1947.

———. *Guy de Maupassant.* Paris: Éditions Tallandier, 1947.

———, with René Descharmes. *Autour de Flaubert.* 2 vols. Paris: Mercure de France, 1912.

Dunham, Arthur Louis. *The Industrial Revolution in France, 1815–1848.* New York: Exposition Press, 1955.

Durry, Marie-Jeanne, presenter. *Europe: Colloque Flaubert* (Paris), nos. 485–87 (September–November 1969).

———. *Flaubert et ses projets inédits.* Paris: Nizet, 1950.

Duval, Vincent. *Traité pratique du pied bot.* Paris: J.-B. Baillière et fils, 1839.

Edel, Leon. *Henry James: The Conquest of London, 1870–1881.* New York: Avon, 1978.

Edwards, Stewart. *The Paris Commune, 1871.* New York: Quadrangle Books, 1971.

Fauvel, Henri. "Souvenirs sur Gustave Flaubert." *La Chronique Médicale,* nos. 14–15 (July–August 1908).

Fierro, Alfred. *Histoire et dictionnaire de Paris.* Paris: Robert Laffont, 1996.

Franklin Grout, Caroline. *Heures d'autrefois: Mémoires inédits.* Edited by Matthieu Desportes. Rouen: Publications de l'Université de Rouen, 1999.

Frère, Étienne. *Louis Bouilhet.* Paris: Société française d'imprimerie, 1908.

Galerant, Germain. *Flaubert et le secret de Madame Schlesinger: La vérité.* Luneray: Éditions Bertout, 1997.

———. "La nomination mouvementée du docteur Flaubert." *Histoire des Sciences Médicales,* no. 2 (1992).

Garrigues, Jean. *La France de 1848 à 1870.* Paris: Armand Colin, 2002.

Gastaut, H., and Y. Gastaut. "La maladie de Gustave Flaubert." *La Revue Neurologique* (Paris), nos. 6–7 (1982).

Gautier, Théophile. *Correspondance générale.* Vols. 4–12. Edited by Claudine Lacoste-Veysseyre. Geneva: Droz, 1985–2000.

Geispitz, Henri. *Histoire du Théâtre des Arts de Rouen 1817–1833.* Rouen: A. Lestringant.

Gelfand, Toby. *Professionalizing Modern Medicine.* Westport, Conn.: Greenwood Press, 1980.

Gérard-Gailly, Émile. *Flaubert et "les fantômes de Trouville."* Paris: La Renaissance du Livre, 1930.

———. *Le Grand Amour de Flaubert.* Paris: Aubier, 1944.

——— *Le Véhémences de Louise Colet.* Paris: Mercure de France, 1934.

Gerbod, Paul. *La Vie quotidienne dans les lycées et collèges au XlXe siècle.* Paris: Hachette, 1968.

Girardin, Madame Émile de. *Lettres parisiennes.* Paris: Charpentier, 1843.

Goncourt, Jules de, and Edmond de Goncourt. *Edmond de Goncourt et Alphonse Daudet: Correspondance.* Edited by A.-S. Dufief and P. Dufief.

———. *Germinie Lacerteux.* Paris: Éditions 10/18, 1979.

———. *Journal: Mémoires de la vie littéraire.* 4 vols. Paris: Fasquelle and Flammarion, 1956.

Gordon, Lady Duff. *Letters from Egypt, 1862–1869.* Edited by Gordon Waterfield. New York: Praeger, 1969.

Gothot-Mersch, Claudine. *La Genèse de Madame Bovary.* Geneva: Slatkine, 1980.

Goulemot, Jean, Paul Lidsky, and Masseau Didier. *Le Voyage en France*. Paris: Laffont, 1997.

Gray, Francine du Plessix. *Rage and Fire: A Life of Louise Colet*. New York: Simon and Schuster, 1994.

Grossir, Claudine. *L'Islam des Romantiques*. 2 vols. Paris: Éditions Maisonneuve et Larose, 1984.

Guérin, André. *La Vie quotidienne en Normandie au temps de Madame Bovary*. Paris: Hachette, 1991.

Guillaume, Pierre. *Médecins, église et foi: XIXe–XXe siècles*. Paris: Aubier, 1990.

Guiral, Pierre. *La Vie quotidienne en France à l'âge d'or du capitalisme, 1852–1879*. Paris: Hachette, 1976.

Heine, Henri. *Lutèce*. Geneva: Slatkine, 1979.

Henry, Gilles. *L'Histoire du monde est une farce, ou La Vie de Gustave Flaubert*. Condé-sur-Noireau, France: Charles Corlet, 1980.

Herval, René. *Histoire de Rouen*. 2 vols. Rouen: Maugard, 1947–49.

Houssaye, Arsène. *Confessions: Souvenirs d'un demi-siècle, 1830–1880*. 6 vols. Paris: E. Dentu, 1885–1891.

Howard, Michael. *The Franco-Prussian War*. New York: Collier Books, 1969.

Hugo, Victor. *Carnets intimes*. Paris: Gallimard, 1953.

———. *Choses vues: Souvenirs, journaux, cahiers*. Edited by Hubert Juin. 4 vols. Paris: Gallimard (Folio), 1972.

Jackson, J. H. "Lectures on the Diagnosis of Epilepsy." *British Medical Journal* (1879).

———. *Selected Writings of John Hughlings Jackson*. Edited by James Taylor. London: Hodder and Stoughton, 1931.

Jackson, Joseph F. *Louise Colet et ses amis littéraires*. New Haven: Yale University Press, 1937.

James, Helen, and Jane Cook. *The Story of Rouen*. London: Dent, 1911.

James, Henry. *Notes on Novelists*. New York: Scribner's, 1914.

Kurtz, Harold. *The Empress Eugénie*. Boston: Houghton Mifflin, 1964.

La Berge, Ann, and Mordechai Feingold, eds. *French Medical Culture in the Nineteenth Century*. Amsterdam: Rodopi, 1994.

Lapierre, Charles. *Esquisse sur Flaubert intime*. Évreux, France: Charles Hérissey, 1898.

Lapp, John C. "Art and Hallucination in Flaubert." *French Studies* 9, no. 4 (October 1956).

Lear, Edward. *Journal of a Landscape Painter in Corsica*. London: Robert John Bush, 1870.

Lebrun, Myriam. "La Vie de l'etudiant au Quartier Latin." In *L'Année balzacienne 1978*. Paris: Garnier.

Le Calvez, Eric, ed. *Gustave Flaubert: A Documentary Volume*. Farmington Hills, Miss.: Thomson Gale, 2004.

Leclerc, Yvan, ed. *La Bibliothèque de Flaubert*. Rouen: Publications de l'Université de Rouen, 2001.

———. *Crimes écrits*. Paris: Plon, 1981.

———. "Flaubert à Croisset là et hors là." In *Monuments historiques*, no. 156 (April–May 1988).

———. *Gustave Flaubert: "L'Éducation sentimentale."* Paris: PUF, 1997.

———. *La Spirale et le monument: Essai sur "Bouvard et Pécuchet."* Paris: Sedes, 1988.

Léonard, Jacques. *La Vie quotidienne du médecin de province au XIXe siècle*. Paris: Hachette, 1977.

Le Poittevin, Alfred. *Une promenade de Bélial et oeuvres inédites*. Edited by René Descharmes. Paris: Les Presses Françaises, 1924.

Les Cent-et-Un. *Paris, ou Le Livre des Cent-et-Un*. Paris: Ladvocat, 1831–34.

Letellier, Léon. *Louis Bouilhet*. Paris: Hachette, 1919.

Levasseur, Louis. *Les Notables de la Normandie*. Rouen: Imprimerie L. Deshays, 1872.

Links, J. G. *The Ruskins in Normandy*. London: Murray, 1968.

Lottman, Herbert. *Flaubert: A Biography*. Boston: Little, Brown, 1989.

Lough, John. *Writer and Public in France: From the Middle Ages to the Present Day*. Oxford: Clarendon Press, 1978.

Lucas–Dubreton, Jean. *Louis-Philippe*. Paris: Fayard, 1938.

Macleod, Norman. *Eastward*. New York: A. Strahan, 1866.

Martin-Fugier, Anne. *La Vie élégante, ou La formation du Tout-Paris 1815–1848*. Paris: Fayard, 1990.

Matoré, Georges. *Le Vocabulaire et la société sous Louis-Philippe*. Geneva: Slatkine, 1967.

Maupassant, Guy de. *Bel-Ami*. Paris: Gallimard, 1976.

———. *Chroniques, études, correspondance de Guy de Maupassant*. Edited by René Dumesnil. Paris: Librairie Grund, 1938.

———. *Pour Gustave Flaubert*. Brussels/Éditions Complexe, 1986.

Mayeur, Jean-Marie. *Les Débuts de la Troisième République, 1871–1898*. Paris: Seuil, 1973.

Maynial, Edouard. *Flaubert*. Paris: Nouvelle Revue Critique, 1947.

———. *La Jeunesse de Flaubert*. Paris: Mercure de France, 1913.

Meaux, Vicomte de. *Souvenirs politiques*. Paris: Plon, 1905.

Merlier, Georges, ed. *La Guerre de 1870–71 en Haute-Normandie*. Rouen: CRDP, 1972.

Mignot, Albert. *Ernest Chevalier et Gustave Flaubert*. Paris: E. Dentu, 1888.

Mitterand, Henri. *Zola*. Vols. 1–2. Paris: Fayard, 1999.

Mollat, Michel, ed. *Histoire de Rouen*. Toulouse: Privat, 1979.

Mollier, Jean-Yves. *L'Argent et les lettres*. Paris: Fayard, 1988.

———. *Michel et Calmann Lévy, ou la naissance de l'édition moderne*. Paris: Calmann-Lévy, 1984.

Morris, Edward Joy. *Corsica: Picturesque, Historical and Social*. Philadelphia: Parry and MacMillan, 1855.

Moynet, Jean-Pierre. *French Theatrical Production in the Nineteenth Century*. Binghamton, N.Y.: Max Reinhardt Foundation, with the American Theater Association, 1976.

Murray, John, ed. *Handbook for Travellers in France: Being a Guide to Normandy, Brittany, Etc.* London: John Murray, 1844.

Naaman, Antoine. *Les Débuts de Gustave Flaubert et sa technique de la description*. Paris: Nizet, 1985.

Nabokov, Vladimir. "On *Madame Bovary*." In *Lectures on Literature*. New York: Harcourt Brace, 1980.

Nadar [Félix Tournachon]. *Mémoires du géant*. Paris: Dentu, 1864.

Neefs, Jacques, and Claude Mouchard. *Flaubert*. Paris: Balland, 1986.

Newman, Ernest. *The Life of Richard Wagner*. 4 vols. New York: A. A. Knopf, 1933–1946.

Nightingale, Florence. *Letters from Egypt: A Journey on the Nile, 1849–1850*. London: Weidenfeld and Nicolson, 1987.

Noel, Eugène. *Rouen, rouennais, rouenneries*. Rouen: Editions de la Grande Fontaine, 1894.

Noiret, Charles. *Mémoires d'un ouvrier rouennais*. Paris: EDHIS, 1979.

Normanby, Constantine Henry Phipps. *A Year of Revolution*. 2 vols. London: Longman, 1857.

Oliver, Hermia. *Flaubert and an English Governess*. Oxford: Clarendon Press, 1980.

Oman, Charles. *Things I Have Seen*. London: Methuen, 1933.

Parent-Duchâtelet, Alexandre. *La Prostitution à Paris au XIXe siècle*. Paris: Seuil, 1981.

Parigot, Hippolyte. *Théâtre d'hier*. Paris Lecène and Oudin, 1893.

Periaux, Pierre. *Dictionnaire indicateur des rues et places de Rouen, 1819*. Brionne, France: Le Portulan, 1972.

Perrot, Philippe. *Les Dessus et les dessous de la bourgeoisie: Une histoire du vêtement au dix-neuvième siècle*. Paris: Fayard, 1981.

Plessis, Alain. *De la fête impériale au mur des fédérés, 1852–1871*. Paris: Seuil, 1973.

Pommier, Jean. "Les Maladies de Gustave Flaubert," "Sensations et images chez Flaubert: Essai de critique psycho-physiologique," and "Flaubert et la naissance de l'acteur." In *Dialogues avec le passé*. Paris: Nizet, 1967.

Ponteil, Félix. *Les Institutions de la France de 1814–1870*. Paris: Presses Universitaires de France, 1966.

Porter, Laurence, ed. *A Gustave Flaubert Encyclopedia.* Westport, Conn: Greenwood Press, 2001.

Porter, Roy. *The Greatest Benefit to Mankind: A Medical History of Humanity.* New York: Norton, 1997.

Poulet, Georges. "Flaubert." In *Études sur le temps humain.* Paris: Plon, 1949.

———. "La pensée circulaire de Flaubert." In *Les Métamorphoses du cercle.* Paris: Plon, 1961.

Pradier, James. *Correspondance.* Vol. 3. Edited by Douglas Siler. Geneva: Droz, 1988.

Price, Roger, ed. *1848 in France.* Ithaca, N.Y.: Cornell University Press, 1975.

Primoli, Joseph. "Gustave Flaubert à Saint-Gratien." *La Revue de Paris.* November 15, 1921.

Prost, Antoine. *L'Enseignement en France, 1800–1967.* Paris: Armand Colin, 1968.

Proust, Marcel. "A propos du 'style' de Flaubert." In *Contre Sainte-Beuve.* Paris: Gallimard (Pléiade), 1971.

Pyat, Félix, et al. *Nouveau Tableau de Paris au XIXe siècle.* Vols. 4–6. Paris: Madame Charles-Béchet, 1834–1835.

Quétel, Claude. *History of Syphilis.* Baltimore: Johns Hopkins University Press, 1990.

Raczymow, Henri. *Pauvre Bouilhet.* Paris: Gallimard, 1998.

Reibel, M. G. *Les Flaubert, vétérinaires champenois.* Troyes, France: Frémont, 1913.

Reid, Martine. *Flaubert correspondant.* Paris: Sedes, 1995.

Rémond, René. *L'Anticléricalisme en France de 1815 à nos jours.* Paris: Fayard, 1976.

———. *La Vie politique en France depuis 1789.* Vol. 2 (1848–1879). Paris: Armand Colin, 1969.

Renan, Ernest. *Correspondance* (Renan/Berthelot). Paris: Calmann-Lévy, 1929.

Richard, Charles. *Chenonceaux et Gustave Flaubert.* Paris: Librairie Sauvaitre, 1887.

Richardson, Joanna. *Portrait of a Bonaparte: The Life and Times of Joseph-Napoleon Primoli.* London: Quartat Books, 1987.

———. *Princess Mathilde.* London: Weidenfeld and Nicolson, 1969.

Ricord, Philippe. *Traité pratique des maladies vénériennes.* Paris: J. Rouvier and J. Le Bouvier, 1838.

Rival, Ned. *Tabac: Miroir du temps.* Paris: Librairie académique Perrin, 1981.

Robert, Marthe. *En haine du roman: Étude sur Flaubert.* Paris: Balland, 1982.

Rosanvallon, Pierre. *Le Moment Guizot.* Paris: Gallimard, 1985.

Rowley, Anthony. *Évolution économique de la France du milieu du XIXe siècle à 1914.* Paris: Sedes, 1982.

Sagnes, Guy. *L'Ennui dans la littérature française de Flaubert à Laforgue.* Paris: Armand Colin, 1969.

Sainte-Beuve, Charles. *Causeries du lundi.* Vol. 11. Paris: Garnier Frères, 1852–62.

———. *Correspondance générale.* Vols. 10ff. Edited by Jean Bonnerot. Paris: Didier, 1961–83.

———. *Nouveaux lundis.* Vol. 4. Paris: Michel Lévy, 1864.

Sand, George. *Agendas 1862–1876.* Vols. 3–5. Edited by Anne Chevereau. Paris: Jean Touzot, 1992.

———. *Correspondance.* Vols. 18–24. Paris: Classiques Garnier, 1990.

———. *Questions d'art et de littérature.* Paris: Calmann Lévy, 1878.

Sanderson, John. *Sketches of Paris: Familiar Letters to His Friends.* Philadelphia: E. L. Carey and A. Hart, 1838.

Sarcey, Francisque. *Souvenirs de jeunesse.* Paris: Ollendorff, 1885.

Sartre, Jean-Paul. *L'Idiot de la famille: Gustave Flaubert 1821–1857.* 3 vols. Paris: Gallimard, 1971–72.

Satiat, Nadine. *Maupassant.* Paris: Flammarion, 2003.

Schapiro, Leonard. *Turgenev: His Life and Times.* Oxford: Oxford University Press, 1978.

Scott, Donald. *The History of Epileptic Therapy.* Carnforth: Parthenon, 1993.

Second, Albéric. *Vichy-Sévigné, Vichy-Napoléon.* Paris: Plon, 1862.

Senneville, Gérard de. *La Présidente: Une égérie au XIXe siècle.* Paris: Stock, 1998.

————. *Maxime Du Camp.* Paris: Stock, 1996.

Seznec, Jean. *Flaubert à l'Exposition de 1851.* Oxford: Clarendon Press, 1951.

Siler, Douglas, ed. *Flaubert et Louise Pradier: Le texte intégral des "Mémoires de Madame Ludovica." Archives des lettres modernes,* 145 (1973).

————. "Les Années d'apprentissage," in *Statues de chair: sculptures de James Pradier.* Catalogue. Paris: Éditions de la Réunion des musées nationaux, 1985.

Simon, Jules. *L'École.* Paris: A. Lacroix, 1865.

————. *Premières années.* Paris: Flammarion, 1901.

Simond, Charles. *Paris de 1800 à 1900.* 3 vols. Paris: Plon, 1900.

Spalikowski, Edmond. *Âme et aspects de Rouen.* Rouen: Éditions Maugard, 1934.

Spencer, Philip. *Flaubert: A Biography.* London: Faber and Faber, 1952.

————. "New Light on Flaubert's Youth." *French Studies* (April 8, 1954).

Starkie, Enid. *Flaubert: The Making of the Master.* New York: Atheneum, 1967.

————. *Flaubert the Master.* New York: Atheneum, 1971.

Steegmuller, Francis. *Flaubert and "Madame Bovary."* New York: Viking Press, 1939.

————. *Maupassant.* New York: Grosset and Dunlap, 1949.

Steinhart-Leins, Helmut. *Flauberts Grosse Liebe.* Baden-Baden, Germany: Kairos Verlag, 1951.

Stern, Daniel. *Histoire de la Révolution de 1848.* Paris: Calmann Lévy, 1878.

Stewart, John Hall. *The Restoration Era in France.* Princeton, N.J.: Van Nostrand, 1968.

Suffel, Jacques. *Gustave Flaubert.* Paris: Nizet, 1979.

Taine, Hippolyte. *Hippolyte Taine: Sa vie et sa correspondance.* Paris: Hachette, 1902–7.

————. *Voyage aux Pyrénées.* Paris: Hachette, 1907.

Tastu, Amable. *Voyage en France.* Tours: Mame et Cie., 1855.

Temkin, Oswei. *The Falling Sickness.* Baltimore: Johns Hopkins University Press, 1994.

Thackeray, William. *The Students' Quarter, or Paris Five-and-Thirty Years Since.* London: John Camden Hotten, 1876.

Thibaudet, Albert. *Gustave Flaubert.* Paris: Gallimard, 1935.

Thompson, J. M. *Louis Napoleon and the Second Empire.* Oxford: Basil Blackwell, 1954.

Thureau-Dangin, Paul. *Histoire de la monarchie de Juillet.* Vol. 5. Paris: Plon, 1911.

Tocqueville, Alexis de. *Recollections.* New York: Doubleday, 1970.

Toutain, Jacques. *La Révolution de 1848 à Rouen.* Paris: Éditions René Debresse, 1948.

Trilling, Lionel. "Flaubert's Last Testament." In *The Opposing Self.* New York: Harcourt Brace, 1978.

Troyat, Henri. *Flaubert.* Paris: Flammarion, 1988.

Tulard, Jean. *Napoleon.* London: Weidenfeld and Nicolson, 1977.

Turgenev, Ivan. *Ivan Tourguéniev d'après sa correspondance avec ses amis français.* Edited by Ely Halpérine-Kaminsky. Paris: Fasquelle, 1901.

————. *Lettres inédites de Tourguenev à Pauline Viardot et à sa famille.* Edited by Granjard and Zviguilsky. Lausanne, Switzerland: Éditions L'Âge d'Homme, 1972.

————. *Turgenev's Letters.* Edited by A. V. Knowles. New York: Scribner's, 1983.

Unwin, Timothy, ed. *The Cambridge Companion to Flaubert.* Cambridge: Cambridge University Press, 2004.

————. "Louis Bouilhet, Friend of Flaubert: A Case of Literary Conscience." *Australian Journal of French Studies* 30, no. 2 (1993).

Villemessant, Hippolyte de. *Mémoires d'un journaliste.* Vols. 3–4. Paris: Dentu, 1873–75.

Vincenot, Henri. *La Vie quotidienne dans les chemins de fer au XIXe siècle.* Paris: Hachette, 1975.

Wagner, Richard. *My Life.* New York: Cambridge University Press, 1983.

Wall, Geoffrey. *Flaubert.* New York: Farrar, Straus and Giroux, 2001.

Wallon, Armand. *La Vie quotidienne dans les villes d'eaux, 1850–1914.* Paris: Hachette, 1981.

Warburton, Eliot. *The Crescent and the Cross.* 2 vols. London: Henry Colburn, 1845.

Wilkinson, Gardner. *A Handbook for Travellers in Egypt.* London: John Murray, 1858.

Willard, Emma. *Journal and Letters from France and Great Britain*. Troy, N.Y.: Tuttle (printer), 1833.

Young, Arthur. *Travels in France*. New York: Doubleday, 1968.

Zola, Émile. *Correspondance*. Vols. 2–3. Montréal: Presses de l'Université de Montréal, 1980–82.

———. *Les Rougon-Macquart*. 5 vols. Paris: Gallimard (Pléiade), 1960–67.

———. *Oeuvres complètes*. Paris: Cercle du Livre Précieux (Tchou), 1962–69.

Index

200, 231; of Flaubert family, 19, 373; in
France, influence of, 522, 523–24; in
Germany, 502, 521; at Hôtel-Dieu,
26–27; of Marie-Sophie Leroyer, 348,
351; papal infallibility, 500–501; pope
driven from Rome, 280; and Sand's
funeral, 514; Vatican Council, 442, 500;
works proscribed or criticized by, 405,
430–31, 481 (*see also* Jesuits, *below*)
dedivinized Christ, 404
Father Lacordaire's discourses on Christianity,
117
Flaubert's view of, 223, 259, 350, 461–62,
501, 514, 555–56
Jesuits (Society of Jesus), 43, 44, 412n;
unpopularity of, 25, 42; banished from
France, 555
Oriental, Flaubert's investigation of, 466
and sense of hierarchy among workers, 219
taught in high school, 44
Remusat, Charles de, 316, 502
Renan, Ernest, 404–6, 466, 481, 514–15, 517,
520, 527
Renoir, Auguste and Jean, 529
republicanism, 455, 456–57, 459, 498–99,
520–27
anticlericalism of, 460, 555, 563
in 1850 election, 281
Flaubert's, 59, 461–62, 521, 526
republican insurrections (1830s), 74, 209
republican press, 60
republican salon, 529, 546
La République des Lettres (periodical), 534, 535
Restoration, the. *See* Bourbon Restoration
Révoil, Antoine, and Révoil family, 181–82
Revolutionary Tribunal, 11
revolutions. *See* French revolutions; Russian
Revolution
Revue Archéologique (periodical), 345
Revue de Deux Mondes (newspaper), 481
La Revue de Paris (periodical), 283, 296,
315–20 *passim*, 321–25, 328, 330
La Revue Française (periodical), 369
La Revue Indépendante (periodical), 422
Rhetoric, as educational tool, 45–46, 60,
69, 91
Robert Macaire (play and character), 33–34
Roberts, Lewes, 5
Robespierre, Maximilien, 7, 418
Robin, Charles, 433
Rogier, Camille, 257, 259, 262, 269
Rohan, Abbé de, 25
Roland, Jeanne, 185
Romanticism, 33, 35, 91, 132, 165, 342, 408
disappearance of, 340
Gustave writes in idiom of, 55–57, 63, 65,
83, 87, 221
and the macabre, 99
Ronsard, Pierre de, 123, 190, 297
Roquigny, Adolphe, 391

Rossini, Gioacchino, 33
Rothschild, Baron Henri, 507n
Rothschild, James de, 98, 400
Rothschild, Mayer, 81, 128, 445n
Rothschild family, 336
Rouen, 3–8, 19, 32–36, 42, 50, 67
and monument to Bouilhet, 437, 527
revolt in, 215
Rousseau, Jean-Jacques, 25, 85, 165, 180, 312,
404–5, 422
Rowe, Nicolas, 32
royalists. *See* Bourbon Restoration
Ruskin, John, 5, 124
Russia, czarist, 25, 95
Decembrist plot (1825), 485; fears of revolu-
tion, 487
Napoleon plans to invade, 20; campaign,
197, 220, 380
Russian Revolution, 569

Sabatier, Aglaé, 563
Sabatier, Apollonie, 316–18, 320, 342, 343n,
379
Sade, Marquis de, 71, 73, 95, 140, 166n, 243,
370
Flaubert fascinated with, 70, 87, 88, 90, 343,
383, 518; compared to, 431
Saint Bartholomew's Day Massacre, 25, 71n, 99,
378
Sainte-Beuve, Charles, 114, 186, 274, 403,
404–6, 411, 412, 421, 438, 548
death of, 434, 436
Louise Colet and, 183, 511
Princess Mathilde and, 399–400, 401–2
reviews: *Madame Bovary,* 330–32; *Salammbô,*
365–68
Saint-Maurice, comte de, 382
Saint-Romain fair, 19, 34–35, 532
Saint-Saëns, Charles Camille, 399
Saint-Sever circus, 65
Saint-Simon, Claude Henri de, 239, 250, 335,
422, 507
Saint-Victor, Paul de, 406, 496
Salammbô. See Flaubert, Gustave: works
Sand, George, 89, 165, 281, 282, 486, 489
controversy over, 182
death of, 513–15; monument to, 527
as Flaubert's friend, 391, 401; and his finances, 445–46, 506, 513; relationship
with, 370, 411–16, 434, 438, 491, 492,
516, 530
Flaubert's letters to, 369–70, 414–15, 417,
422–23, 429–31, 435, 441–50 *passim,*
455–56, 461–66 *passim,* 473, 478–79,
498, 500, 505–6, 510–11, 542n, 543
granddaughter Aurore, 513, 514, 567
letters to Flaubert, 414–16, 430, 469–70,
508–10, 559; criticism by, 369, 411,
423, 432, 468, 481, 496–97
inspiration of name, 379

About the Author

Frederick Brown is also the author of *An Impersonation of Angels: A Biography of Jean Cocteau; Père-Lachaise; Theater and Revolution;* and *Zola.* A resident of New York City, he has twice been the recipient of both Guggenheim and National Endowment for the Humanities fellowships.